❧ THE ❧ WINDSOR STORY

Charles J. V. Murphy & J. Bryan III

A DELL BOOK

Published by
Dell Publishing Co., Inc.
1 Dag Hammarskjold Plaza
New York, New York 10017

Copyright © 1979 by J. Bryan III and Charles J. V.
Murphy

Dell ® TM 681510, Dell Publishing Co., Inc.

ISBN: 0-440-19346-X

Reprinted by arrangement with William Morrow and
Company, Inc.

Printed in the United States of America

First Dell printing—March 1981

To their in-laws

PREFACE

Charles J. V. Murphy

Since my collaborator and friend, J. Bryan III, has done the larger share of this book, it has fallen to me to relate how our collaboration began and why we have told the story of the Windsors as we have.

We came to know them rather well in the years after World War Two. Both of us were then officers in the U.S. Air Force Reserve, and we usually did our tours of duty in Paris at SHAPE—Supreme Headquarters Allied Powers Europe—first under Gen. Alfred M. Gruenther, U.S.A., then under Gen. Lauris Norstad, U.S.A.F. The hospitable Windsors would have us over for dinner at their mansion in Neuilly from time to time, and for weekends at their famous "Mill"—the Moulin de la Tuilerie—near Gif-sur-Yvette, half an hour from town.

The Windsor table, after the clatter and rush of the SHAPE mess, unfailingly offered an experience in sustained elegance and ornamental luxury hardly to be matched elsewhere. We liked our hosts. Neither of us considered himself an intimate; indeed, none of their other friends seemed to achieve that status, either. Prudence suggested that such intimacy could be a slippery, even a hazardous relationship. Being in their company, whether at cocktails beside the pool at The Mill, or at their gleaming table, or over coffee in the library walled with unread books, was like watching a brisk comedy of manners, with a famous actor and actress playing the roles in which their fateful love affair had cast them.

The longer we looked on, the more revealing and—on that account—the more unreal and pathetic it came to seem. The century's most celebrated romance was fraying out before our eyes. The Windsors' "court" was changing with the years; though the favorites were richer than ever, their ranks were increasingly made up of pushers, climbers, trimmers, tag-end aristocrats, and mere celebrities. There was an element of *determination* in the gaiety. The folktale had gone awry. In such company the Duke lost his former kingliness, bit by bitter bit, and his intended Queen was hardly to be recognized as a modern sister of the shepherdess who, in the timeless tale of enchantment, having succored the leader defeated in battle and bound up his wounds, sent him forth to regain his kingdom in duty and honor. The Duke's kingdom had now shrunk to the Duchess herself; for him and for her, there was nothing beyond; each had ended by defeating the other. The position she craved, he had forfeited irretrievably in order to have her. The love he craved, she could not give; perhaps she did not know the emotion at its deepest and purest.

That we might recount the rise and fall of King Edward VIII, and trace his singular devotion to Mrs. Simpson of Baltimore, occurred to Joe Bryan and me a year after the Duke's death in 1972. We started work immediately. Research took one or the other of us back to Europe a dozen times or more. The people we interviewed numbered in the scores; our correspondence fills a dozen cartons. Writing about royalty is a peculiar art form—one which comes easily to Europeans and to none so easily as to the British, doubtless because their enduring and respectable monarchy invites untiring practice. Though neither Bryan nor I, in our equally long and roughly paralleled careers as writers and editors, had ever been attracted to this esoteric field, we had each had passing professional encounters with royalty and its retinues.

Bryan, a former associate editor of the *Saturday Evening Post*, had written "profiles" of the Duke of Edinburgh and of Princess Margaret, and had spent three months in France working with the late Aga Khan on his memoirs. The Aga, who had been President of the League of Nations, fancied himself a world statesman; and his autobiography, as he visualized it, would commemorate his accomplishments as an adroit international negotiator and astute political prophet—this despite his confident reiteration in the late 1930's of the same unfortunate prediction which he had voiced in 1914: The great powers would not fight each other. The Aga's activities in diplomacy proving insufficient to fill out a book, Bryan ventured to suggest that he would command a far wider audience if he were to discourse on his vast acquaintance with fine horses and beautiful women (topics where his authority was beyond dispute), and on the divinity that periodically moved his adoring subjects to match his not inconsiderable weight with its equivalent in jewels and precious metals. The Aga said this would be undignified, and the collaboration dissolved amicably. Bryan explained, "The publishers and I wanted a portrait; the Aga wanted a statue."

I myself had already had my own baptism of fire on this treacherous terrain while doubling as a member of the Board of Editors of *Fortune* and a writer for *Life*. In 1947, the Duke of Windsor had invited me to help him with his autobiography, *A King's Story*. In 1955, this time at the Duchess's invitation, supported by his own, I returned to France to help with hers, *The Heart Has Its Reasons*. Now the footing proved less solid. The author of record paid me the distinction—if not the compliment—of firing me out of hand. At the age of fifty, I seemed unable to muster the lightness of heart, let alone the lightness of foot, that she, at sixty, felt was needed to mirror her own. The breach, though painful, was not permanent; I was presently requested to pick up the draft where I had left it, and our relationship was reestablished.

Then, in the 1960's, the Duke having broken the ice of royalty's traditional reticence and finding himself exhilarated by the public's interest, enlisted Bryan and me to collaborate with him in two other literary enterprises. The first was to have been a short, spirited book about King George III and the American Revolution. The thesis (which was Lord Beaverbrook's) was that greedy and reckless British politicians, not Farmer George, were alone responsible for alienating the American colonies. Windsor signed the Beaver's contract with enthusiasm. He liked to think of himself as American by temperament. He even supplied what would have been a superb opening line; "My father, George the Fifth, took quiet pride in never having set foot in the United States." But alas, as time passed, the Duke's incorrigible elusiveness confronted Bryan and me with the probability that he would never settle down to the elementary reading, much less join in the writing, for the book that would bear his name. Even more disconcerting, though understandable, was his tardy decision not to allow anything ill to be said about his subject's sons, that pack of dolts, voluptuaries, and parasites which Queen Victoria herself described as "my wicked Hanoverian uncles." So the redemption of George III's reputation was added to the list of Windsor's unfinished works.

The other book was to have been a frank account of his growing up, first as Prince Edward, Duke of Cornwall, and then (after seventeen) as Prince of Wales. He would have drawn upon the diaries which he wrote faithfully and daily from earliest literacy until after the Great War, and upon the letters which he exchanged weekly with his parents, through the years from his acceptance by the Royal Naval College until he took up bachelor quarters in St. James's Palace. The letters, totaling nearly two thousand, were strung in chronological order on scarlet strings fastened with small brass toggles. The diaries, in a round, schoolboyish hand that never achieved personality, ran to several volumes. Bryan and I read every letter, every entry. Many of them the Duke read aloud to us, to illuminate obscure happenings in the Royal Family half a century before. Neither he nor his father or mother wrote with grace or feeling; the letters on both sides were all but empty of affection, except for the stilted phrases permitted by Victorian reserve. Yet, as he read, the long-submerged memories of his early youth bubbled to the surface: the cramped little cottage at Sandringham, and the genial presence of his grandfather, Edward VII; the Spartan regime at the Royal Naval College; the first explosion of personal freedom at Oxford; and his profoundly affecting discovery, on the French battlefields, of mankind's many, many facets.

I suspect that these readings were the first time that the Duke of Windsor ever bared the innocent and—at times— terrifying sadness of his early years, at least with the thought of putting it on paper. When he came to his accounts of his struggles as a naval cadet, he often broke off to explain how hard—how *very* hard—it was to persuade a scolding martinet of a father that the reason why brother Bertie and he were generally at the bottom of their form was not that they were stupid or lazy, but that their tutor had not taught them much. Once the Duke took us on a tour of Windsor Castle. He showed us the apartments where his family had passed the late spring and early summer after his father's accession, and the room where he himself had made his Abdication broadcast, and the place at the end of the Long Gallery where he had been led as a small, shy boy to take the hand of his great-grandmother, Queen Victoria, in her wheelchair. He told us about the iron ring of governesses, tutors, valets, and courtiers that had constricted his boyhood, and of his introduction to "Uncle Nicky," the Czar of All the Russias, and "Uncle Willy," Kaiser Wilhelm II of Germany, and of his longings for the close family ties that his peers enjoyed. When we had progressed to his first letters from Oxford, in 1912, Windsor suddenly blurted, "I had a *wretched* childhood! Of course, there were short periods of happiness, but I remember it chiefly for the miserableness I had to keep to myself." His parents' four to six pages in return were usually written on a Sunday, and both usually described in almost identical order and terms the events of the past week. The letters were so matter-of-fact, they might have been transcribed from the Court Circular; a dinner for a foreign head of state; a visit to an orphanage or gallery; a weekend at some noble house for a race meet or pheasant shooting; the official opening of a bridge or tunnel; tea at Buckingham Palace for the Archbishop of Canterbury. In the whole dreary canon, there was never a literary quotation, a historical allusion, an amusing anecdote, a *jeu d'esprit*. The dreary flow of parental observation was sometimes salted with reproof, but never sweetened with anything to dissipate a boy's dread of a father who made him feel that he was wanting in common sense, intelligence, and dutifulness. There was no attempt to banish or even balm the uncertainties, the apprehensions, and the abiding loneliness that haunted their firstborn. His unspoken plea for understanding was unheard and unanswered.

Yet beneath his parents' bleak enumeration of royal chores can be sensed the quality and character of this most unusual family—one ruled (as was perhaps no other of their time) by devotion to the state and to the monarchy. Form and usage, custom and constitution, were sovereign with them. What they were, their son would in time become; nothing would change—nothing except Windsor's viewpoint. For as he looked afresh at his letters and diaries through the prism of the independence which he had acquired at such painful cost, the sadness and pathos that breathed from almost every page were filtered out, and what remained now seemed to him appealing, even endearing. He made it seem so to Bryan and me as well: himself and his family in their vulnerabilities along with their strengths, their inner turmoil along with their surface calm. It was history of a sort that only he could have told, and had he persevered, it would have made a delightful, wonderfully revealing little book of royal reminiscence. But he dropped it abruptly, as he had so many other things. "I'd hate for the world to know how illiterate we all were," was the explanation he offered us—us, and Lord Beaverbrook's son, Sir Max Aitken, whose contract he had signed.

By then, illness was crowding him. Perhaps he had a premonition of the cancer that was imminent. There may have been another reason, more compelling. The Duchess had begun to ridicule his poring over old letters. She once taunted him in our presence, "Who'd want to read about a boyhood as dull as yours? It's a waste of time!" She could not bear to have him return in spirit to an era and events in which she had had no part, and between which and the present her own arrival had opened an impassable gulf. One of the reasons why we wrote this book was to salvage some of these experiences, otherwise lost. Frances Donaldson's *Edward VIII* will remain his definitive biography, but she never met the Windsors. Bryan and I have written from a different perspective.

Washington, D.C.
July, 1979

Book I

The Prince
and
His Sweethearts

If you have [charm], you don't need to have anything else; and if you don't have it, it doesn't much matter what else you have.
—What Every Woman Knows, JAMES BARRIE

CHAPTER 1

The Warfields and the Montagues

I got a gal in Baltimo',
Streetcars run right by her do'.
                    —Minstrel song

The British journalist and critic Alastair Forbes, writing about the Duchess of Windsor in *The Times Literary Supplement*, November 1, 1974, made this observation: "She can be said to come from a far higher stratum than, say, Princess Grace of Monaco, Jacqueline Bouvier (Kennedy Onassis) or the Jerome or Vanderbilt ladies of the nineteenth century. By present English standards of birth, she might rank rather below two recent royal duchesses, and rather above two others."

Neither her father's proud family, the Warfields, nor her mother's, the equally proud Montagues, considers the appraisal overgenerous. The Warfields had been patricians in Maryland for two centuries, and before that in England. Her grandfather Henry Mactier Warfield was a member of the state legislature, and was considered so influential that he was one of two Baltimoreans whom Union partisans kidnapped and imprisoned at the outbreak of the Civil War, as hostages against Maryland's secession. The other was his best friend, Teackle Wallis, later provost of the University of Maryland and the acknowledged leader of the Maryland bar. The son who was born to the Henry Warfields in 1869 they named in Mr. Wallis's honor.

In 1895, Teackle Warfield retired to Blue Ridge Summit, Pennsylvania, hoping that the mountain air would arrest his tuberculosis. Pretty young Alice Montague—or "Alys," as she sometimes liked to spell it—had come there in the same hope. She, too, was a Baltimorean, but of Virginia ancestry as ancient and patrician as the Warfields'.

The chronicles of Virginia are thickly sprinkled with Montagues: members of the colonial House of Burgesses, judges, generals, a governor. A cousin of the Duchess's, the late Brig. Gen. R. Latané Montague, U.S.M.C., who began his military career as a private, liked to relate how at his first roll call the sergeant pronounced his name "Mon*taig*." Montague ventured to correct him, only to be told, "All right, *Mont*-a-gue! Four hours' *fat*-i-gue!"

Teackle and Alice met at Blue Ridge Summit, fell in love and were married there, and there, on June 19, 1896, was born their healthy, eight-pound daughter, to be christened Bessie for her mother's elder sister, Mrs. D. Buchanan Merryman, and for her mother's cousin, Mrs. Alexander Brown, and Wallis for her father, and to be known as "Bessiewallis" throughout her childhood.

Alice's hope of a cure was granted. Teackle's was not. When it became clear, soon after their return to Baltimore, that his death was imminent, Alice wanted to take the baby to his bedside, to give each of them a farewell look at the other, but she did not dare, for fear of infection. All she could do was show the young father a photograph of Bessiewallis on a white fur rug, with one foot cocked in the air. Teackle died at twenty-seven, leaving his widow and their five-month-old daughter almost penniless. His mother, herself a widow, had always opposed his marriage; he was the youngest of her seven children; his health was frail; and his only income was from a clerkship. Her resentment now concentrated on Alice. The elder Mrs. Warfield might have been Lady Capulet, for all the love she felt for this fair Montague.

It could hardly have been otherwise; they were different in every respect. The Duchess of Windsor once said, "The Warfields were extremely conservative. They were 'solid citizens,' staid and religious, whereas the Montagues were just the opposite, irresponsible and lighthearted." She added, almost as an aside, "The Warfield in me was always trying to put brakes on the Montague." The two Mrs. Warfields were perfect illustrations of the difference: the mother-in-law tall, dark, and austere, the daughter-in-law small, blond and buxom, fluffy and gay, warm and generous and lovable. Still, the mother-in-law recognized her duty. She opened her house on Preston Street to Teackle's homeless widow and child, and took them in.

Perhaps because it was a time of innocence, and perhaps because it was a time of tidiness and tranquillity as well, the Duchess's memories of the big house have remained clear, even radiant, throughout her life. Her portrait of her Warfield grandmother is the strongest and most arresting in the gallery of her autobiography. Old Mrs. Warfield, then in her sixties, still wore the widow's weeds she had first put on nearly twenty years before: a stiff black dress that rose to a high collar edged with lace, and a tiny white lace cap with three black bows. Her only jewelry was a black enamel bracelet and a small, pearl-bordered brooch that enclosed a strand of yellow hair—whose, Wallis never knew.

When Wallis pictured her, she pictured a vast, darkened room and "a solitary figure with thin features and an aquiline profile . . . in a rosewood rocking chair with green velvet upholstery, so erect that her back never seemed to touch the chair." Convenient to her grandmother's hand was the Warfield family Bible, on a table of its own. She referred to it often—a purple velvet ribbon marked her place—but she was far from being a religious zealot. Rather, she was a Christian lady, dedicated to her family and her faith; and though she was solitary in her ways, her interests were various. She followed Maryland politics raptly; she loved gossip; she was a strict, expert, and fastidious housekeeper. Every morning, her half-dozen servants filed into her upstairs sitting room for their orders. All the cupboards were kept locked, and when coffee, sugar, china, or silver was needed, the proper key had to be asked for first. Precise instructions were doled out with the supplies. Wallis said, "Grandmother's accent was soft, and her enunciation was clear. I never heard her raise her voice, nor did I ever see her unbend. The house was hers; and so, in a matriarchal way, was her family." Her talent for housekeeping became manifest in her granddaughter, but little of her loyalty to her kin, and none of her devoutness.

Old Mrs. Warfield's house also sheltered the third of her five sons, the only one who never married. Bessiewallis knew him as Uncle Sol, a formidable man with sandy hair, a crisp moustache, and keen blue eyes. The rest of Baltimore—pronounced "Ballamer" by its natives—knew him as S. Davies Warfield, a man with position and power. He was city postmaster from 1894 to 1905; president of the Continental Trust Company; president, then chairman of the board of the Seaboard Air Line Railway (now the Seaboard Coast Line Railroad) from 1912 until his death, in 1927; a director of several important corporations; and an adviser and close friend of President Cleveland's. His hobby was opera; a Warfield family legend has him taking the Metropolitan Opera Company from New York every season at his own expense, to perform for the Atlanta Music Festival Association. He could have afforded it, but the records of the Association do not confirm the legend. Again unlike his late brother Teackle, he was cold and silent; but he shared at least one of Teackle's tastes; and when his mother observed his growing interest in Alice, even though Alice did not return it, old Mrs. Warfield made it clear that the welcome—never warmer than tepid—had now chilled, and the young widow and her daughter moved to a modest hotel.

The Warfields never regarded Alice as quite on their social level, and in time would rate her considerably lower; but they did not visit their disapproval upon her child. Bessiewallis was warmly received at her married uncles' houses and at her grandmother's, where the whole family often met for Sunday dinner and always for Christmas dinner.

The Duchess said, "The family ties were very strong." She went on, "I was the youngest, so everybody teased me. When I first put my hair over my ears, one of my uncles used to say, 'We'll all have to speak VERY LOUD, or Bessiewallis won't be able to HEAR ANYTHING!' Then they all *screamed* at me. Mother always wore her hair on top of her head, held there by a barrette, but mine was always being changed. I wore a big bow when I was eight or nine, then a pompadour, then parted on one side, then—when I went off to boarding school—parted in the middle. I liked it that way and I've kept it ever since, except that after the Duke and I were married, I began whittling away the bun in back until I finally got rid of it altogether. Can you believe that I never went to a hairdresser until the year I made my debut?"

Uncle Sol took Alice's indifference without rancor; he gave her an allowance and supplemented it with presents. The allowance came in handy. She was trying to make ends meet by running a boardinghouse. She was an excellent cook and she might have prospered if she had been content to serve staple meals; but no, she had to display her virtuosity with such delicacies as prime sirloins, fancy pastries, soft-shell crabs, and terrapin stew—all at lunch-counter prices. The Duchess said, "I still remember the wagon driving up with the terrapin, and mother picking out the ones she wanted, and how she kept them in a burlap bag in the cellar and fed them on corn meal until she was ready for them." Under the circumstances, income never quite caught up with outgo, and the boardinghouse had to close. Still, there was one valuable piece of salvage: the training that Bessiewallis received in Maryland cookery, which many gourmets consider America's best.

Dismiss any vision of a girl whose plump arms are dusted with flour, and whose forehead, rosy from the stove, is plastered with damp ringlets. Even in adolescence, the cool, immaculate Duchess of Windsor could not have filled such a role. But though she herself was never on intimate terms with the mixing bowl and skillet, she became thoroughly qualified to teach others how to use them.

Alice and Bessiewallis were thrown much in each other's company. The Duchess said, "I loved to talk to my mother. She never talked down to me. We would talk as though we were sisters. She didn't know much about books or music or painting, but she knew a lot about life. The wonderful stories she used to tell about her family and her friends! And what wit and gaiety she had! A cousin of ours said of her, 'Alice was like a sunbeam, always dancing!' I'll never forget the afternoon we went to a five-and-ten-cent store, and mother tripped and fell down the stairs. This clerk rushed up and asked, 'Madam, is there anything I can do for you?' Mother said, 'Yes. Take me to the five-and-ten-cent coffin counter." Half the time, her delightful remarks seemed to surprise her too. Her expression seemed to say, 'Lord, what have I said *now*?' Nothing fazed her. A day with mother was one laugh after another."

Not *every* day. It is almost inevitable for a widow to spoil an only child, and this child had become thoroughly accustomed to having her own way. But there were limits even to the indulgent Alice's tolerance, and when they were exceeded, she did not hesitate to lay down the law and emphasize it with repeated applications of a heavy silver hairbrush. Punishing Bessiewallis was not easy; she was "an explosive package," her mother said—one which the slightest jolt would detonate. Any criticism, especially, was certain to touch off a tantrum. The Duchess said, "I don't know why, but I was always hyper-sensitive to criticism. I could never make myself listen to it. When mother was going to criticize me, she'd have to lock us in a room together, or I'd run away like a coward."

Tantrums and spankings notwithstanding, the happiest years of Bessiewallis's life were probably those when she lived alone with her mother. She had ten of them before she had to share her with someone else: John Freeman Rasin, whom Alice married in 1908. A newspaper account said that "the beautiful young daughter of the bride attended her mother."

The only one of the original United States in which Catholicism is not a bar to social preferment is Maryland, and "Free" Rasin came from a Catholic family long established there. "Nothing is wrong with his background," Baltimore acknowledged, "but his foreground is *awful*!" He was fat, coarse of face and manner, and short of both education and fortune. His father, Carroll Rasin, had been the Democratic boss of Baltimore and one of the most powerful political bosses in the country; the Warfields held this, too, against Free. The Duchess said, "I never heard of him hitting a lick of work. He just sat around the house all day, smoking cigarettes and taking it easy. He was temperamental, hard to get along with, but I must say I liked him. He was kind to me; he gave me a French bulldog and an aquarium with tropical fish. Mother adored him, of course. I often wondered what she saw in him, but that was before I'd learned what an all-out, cap-over-the-windmill infatuation can do to you."

The indolent Rasin making no objection, Uncle Sol continued to be Alice's main support. A girlhood friend of the Duchess's says, "Sol Warfield used to come to lunch with us occasionally when I was a child, because my mother was very beautiful, and he always had a roving eye. He was selfish, though, and I daresay Alice Warfield had a hard time extracting money from him." Maybe so; still, he paid the fees when the time came for Bessiewallis to go off to boarding school—rather, for *Wallis*, as she now asked to be called, "because so many cows are named 'Bessie.'" The school she chose was Oldfields, at Glencoe, Maryland, close to Baltimore, venerable, as American schools go, and fashionable. When she enrolled in the fall of 1912, she brought with her a quick mind, a "twenty-four-hour memory" (her phrase for it), and a willingness to study hard. Her best subjects were English and history; her worst was mathematics; like another duchess, the one in *Alice's Adventures in Wonderland*, she "never could abide figures."

Wallis's schoolmates remember her clearly. She was "clever" . . . "nice" . . . "vivacious" . . . "a worker." She had inherited her mother's wit. "She never took the floor or showed off, but she made funny comments on someone else's performance—not *sharp* comments: kindly." True, there were other voices: "Wallis was an opportunist from the start. She always knew where she was going, and she would have stepped on her grandmother's stomach, if that was the shortest path to her goal." And, "She was not womanly, not maternal." (A strange charge to level against a girl in her teens!) But most of the girls liked her and admired her wholeheartedly. It was their parents who had reservations: "My dear, I hear that the Rasins—"

An out-of-town schoolmate who spent a weekend at Wallis's house wrote an ecstatic letter home to her mother. Her climax was "You ought to see Mr. and Mrs. Rasin on Sunday morning! He comes down late, in a bathrobe, and she wears a chiffon negligee, and what do you think they have for breakfast? Quail and champagne!"

Appalled by these Babylonian debauches, the mother consulted her friend Mrs. Joseph Ames, the wife of the president of Baltimore's Johns Hopkins University. Mrs. Ames replied, "I do not consider that a proper household for your daughter to visit!"

The result was, the tearful daughter, feeling that she had betrayed the hospitable Rasins, was withdrawn from Oldfields and its dangerous proximity to gay, dissolute Baltimore and entered at the Ethel Walker School, then in prim, dull Lakewood, New Jersey.

Wallis's appearance at sixteen was not much different from what it would eventually become. Even then she carried herself beautifully; her smooth skin, which a fashion editor described sixty years later as "flawless, like the inside of one's arm," her big blue eyes, and her high forehead drew attention at once, and diverted it from her prominent chin, her square shoulders, her stubby, knuckly fingers, and her ladylike figure. Her nickname was "Skinny"; in later years she was still signing "S" to informal notes to girlhood friends. "My neck is too long," she once said. "That's why I can't wear big, floppy hats. They make me resemble a toadstool." A magazine writer who rashly used the line "Only her feet were conspicuously appropriate to the Cinderella-role awaiting her" was berated by one of the Montagues, who declared, "She was *not* a Cinderella! She was adored and spoiled from babyhood to her marriage!" Janet Flanner, writing about Wallis in *The New Yorker* for November 14, 1936, a few weeks before the Abdication, described her feet as "beautiful, small and elegant." Alice's were even more so; her slippers were size 2½ A.

Wallis had no illusions about her face. The first time that Jerome Zerbe, the society photographer, took pictures of her, at Palm Beach in 1948, she begged him, "Please pick out the ones that make me look least like a horse!" Her photographs never did her justice; neither did her portraits. Cecil Beaton said, "I never saw a portrait that looked like her. She's very difficult to draw and paint. I'm usually excellent at catching a likeness, but I once spent a whole afternoon with her and failed. In her news photos, the light strikes the tip of her rather bulbous nose. None of her features is classically correct—her nose, for instance; and her mouth is downright ugly—but they all fit together. She's attractively ugly, *une belle laide*. She has an *amusing* face."

The boys in Baltimore found her "interesting-looking." She was beginning to find them interesting, too. Mrs. Merryman—the widowed "Aunt Bessie" who would try to guide Wallis through most of her mature life—enjoyed telling about the red sash that she insisted on wearing with her first white party dress, "so that the boys will notice me." Some of the early costumes she improvised must have drawn notice not only from the boys, but from everybody else in the room. "I had an idea that I was the siren type," the Duchess once said, "so I mustn't dress like other young girls; I must dress differently, in an exotic way. Slinky. 'Vampish.' You know: something tighter or something looser—whichever 'they' weren't wearing—and usually accompanied by heavy earrings and large Oriental beads. Mother had given me a blue and green dress which I was convinced made me too seductive for words. I decided that all it needed was a feather at the back of my head. The afternoon before this dance, I told my mother my idea.

"She said, 'You want to look like Pocahontas?'

"I said, 'Wonderful! A stiff feather at the back of my head will do it. I've *got* to have one!'

"Mother quoted an expression from my childhood: ' "Must-have, got-to-get!" Well, if you want it that bad, you shall have it.' She took a streetcar all the way downtown and came home with this long blue-green feather, and I stuck it in my back hair and went to the dance.

"Can you imagine anything more ridiculous? I must have been the laughingstock of the evening! Of course, I had no idea how silly I looked, and I wore the feather all the time for a long time, until I finally developed enough taste to give it up. I was always inventing clothes, strange sorts of costumes. One of my most dismal failures was a pair of high-button shoes. The bottoms were tan, and the uppers were alternate tan and white stripes, running vertically. Can you *imagine*? The idea had seemed brilliant, but when the shoes were delivered, they were so spectacular that I was ashamed to appear in them."

Her dresses may sometimes have been bizarre in design, but they were always neat and clean, and they always fit. Alice saw to that; she had made them "with the help of a Negress named Ella. I remember that she was red-headed, and how neat and tidy her house was when I went there for fittings. Spotless! Mother also made a complete wardrobe for my favorite doll, Anne. I was so proud of Anne that when we went to a hotel, I insisted that mother register for her too."

It was fortunate that Alice was a fine seamstress as well as a fine cook, because the household was pinched: They had to make do or do without. Some generous Montague cousins in England occasionally sent Alice a hamper of their discarded clothes for her to refit for Wallis; even so, a Warfield cousin remembers that Wallis often had to borrow her stockings, for want of any of her own—"You could make over clothes, but you had to *buy* stockings." Free Rasin's death in the spring of 1913 did not relieve the stringency; his small estate was entailed and went to his three sisters. He and Alice had had no children; she explained that he was "a seedless Rasin."

As a pre-teen-ager, Wallis's first beau had been a choirboy, the son of an Irish fireman. As a graduate of Oldfields, in June of 1914, and a debutante that winter—so certified by her invitation to the Bachelors' Cotillon in December—she could raise her sights. Granted, her Montague mother had become *déclassée*, the Warfield citadel was still lofty and impregnable. Granted, Wallis was penniless, she was still singularly attractive: slim, pretty, intelligent, a buoyant, graceful dancer and always chic. The gown she wore at her debut was "of white satin combined with chiffon and trimmings of pearls. The chiffon veiled the shoulders and fell in a knee-length tunic, banded in pearl embroidery." Another of her gowns was made "with a bodice of cloth of gold, figured with little flowers and a full skirt of crepe de Chine in a shade called 'sunset color.' "[1] Her fellow Baltimorean and lifelong friend, Ambassador David Bruce, looking back to the years when they were in their teens, paid her these compliments: "She was a high-spirited girl, great to have around—in fact, the best company I knew. She read a lot and, young as she was, she could hold her own in a discussion with her elders." Another friend summed it up: "She had everything but money, and money wasn't all that important then." So her choice of beaux was wide. It would have been still wider if her mother had not narrowed it. Alice was determined for Wallis not to repeat her own mistakes, and a youth whose only credential was his face or his fortune, or even both, was not encouraged to call again.

To be sure, a certain imperiousness sometimes crept into Wallis's manner. The orders which she would come to fling at the Duke of Windsor so readily and so brusquely had been practiced on her Baltimore and Richmond swains. One of them remembers her commanding him, "Pick up my handkerchief, Ike!" *She* knew that his name was Eddie, and *he* knew that Ike was a more favored suitor.

Eddie said, smiling, "The barb must have gone deep. It still rankles after sixty years."

Again, when a former schoolmate invited her to Richmond, to stay from the day after Christmas until New Year's, Wallis replied, "If I'm to be told when to come and when to go, I'm not coming!" But she came. Years later, when she was at the peak of her celebrity, the same schoolmate's mother said mildly but murderously, "She's the only girl who ever stayed in my house whom I don't remember at all."

Wallis, too, seems to have had a leaky memory. Apparently, she had already forgotten the monition posted on the door of every bedroom in the school she had so recently left: "Gentleness and Courtesy are Expected of the Girls at all Times." The rival basketball teams at Oldfields were Gentleness and Courtesy; Wallis played on Gentleness. Her lapses from the other rules of deportment were rare. She was liked and admired for the most part, and by girls as well as men—the men for her charms, the girls for, in addition, her precious quality of not being a predator. Everyone who knew Wallis then conceded that she never set her cap at another girl's beau.

For such a paragon, popular and well connected, her debutante season should have been a short, triumphal march from the receiving line to the altar. But the summer of 1914 brought the Great War; and Uncle Sol, who otherwise would have given her a coming-out ball, refused to do so, on the grounds that he did not consider it "a proper time for such festivities, when thousands are being slaughtered in Europe." A deeper disappointment awaited her, one that would leave a scar. Mrs. Alexander Brown, who was not only her cousin (she had been born a Montague) but her godmother, was one of the richest women in Baltimore—three excellent reasons, in Wallis's opinion, for her to give a ball in her honor. "Aunt Bessie" Brown gave the ball, but in honor of another debutante. It was her cruel way of dissociating herself from what Alice Warfield Rasin had come to represent. The slap achieved further sting from the fact that, after Uncle Sol's default, Wallis had counted on this party to help pay off her social debts. There were forty-nine debutantes that season; each was expected to entertain all or most of the others at least once; but Wallis and her mother had neither room nor means to give a proper party unassisted.

A Warfield and one Montague having failed Wallis, another Montague came to her rescue. Alice's first cousin, the widowed Lelia Montague Gordon, had taken a second husband, Maj. Gen. George Barnett, U.S.M.C. As Commandant of the Corps (1914–20), he was now stationed in Washington, D.C.; and there, in April 1915, the Barnetts gave Wallis a tea dance, in Band Hall at the Marine Barracks. The festoons of flags, the officers in their colorful uniforms, the red-jacketed Marine Band, sixty strong—none of this, Wallis's guests from Baltimore agreed, could her godmother have provided, nor her uncle Sol, for all their wealth. The party was a smash success; so was Wallis. A year later, the Montagues stood by her again. Mrs. Barnett's youngest sister, Corinne, whose husband, Lt. Comdr. Henry C. Mustin, U.S.N., commanded the Pensacola (Florida) Naval Air Station, invited Wallis down for a visit. Uncle Sol chose the occasion to raise another obstacle. His mother had died the preceding December, and Baltimore custom, sternly endorsed by the Warfields, required the whole family to go into mourning for several months, during which all public amusement was rigorously forbidden, even in a place as remote from censorious eyes as Pensacola.

Wallis refused to comply. She argued that she was only nineteen; that this was the peak of her second "season"; that if she dropped out of sight now, she "might as well be buried alive." She succeeded in persuading her mother to let her accept the invitation, but Uncle Sol was not to be placated. He notified Wallis that as punishment for her willfulness, he was delaying payment of the five thousand dollars her grandmother had left her (he was his mother's trustee) to the limit that the law allowed: one year—i.e., until that December, 1916. Wallis might have waited out the year in silence and patience but for a totally unexpected development: She fell in love.

* * *

The day after she arrived at Pensacola, she wrote home to her mother: "I have just met the world's most fascinating aviator!" Lieut. (j.g.) Earl Windfield Spencer, Jr., U.S.N., was as handsome and as burly as a fighting bull. His uniform seemed to strain to confine his energy, and the gold wings above his left breast pocket—they were only the twentieth that the Navy had ever awarded—seemed to sparkle with his personal electricity. Beside this eagle, the beaux of Baltimore looked as drab and earthbound as so many barnyard fowl.

Win Spencer was born in Kansas in 1888, the eldest of four brothers and two sisters. Their mother was British, from the island of Jersey. Their father presently moved his family to Highland Park, a suburb of Chicago, where he became a member of the Stock Exchange and made a comfortable living. Win had graduated from the Naval Academy with the Class of 1910, and although he had ranked only 115th among the total of 131, his popularity more than made up for his academic deficiencies. He had "a voice like Caruse [sic]," according to the class yearbook; and he was "brimming with happy spirits, a 'merry devil,' and a good comrade—there could not be a better shipmate." Too soon, alas, Spencer would begin to brim with spirits of a less happy sort, but that was in the future; the present was all roses and rapture.

Or almost all. The announcement of the engagement, on September 19, 1916, brought forward the problem of buying a trousseau and paying for a wedding in the style expected of a Warfield and a Montague. Wallis's pleas for Uncle Sol to release her grandmother's bequest availed nothing; he remained adamant. Spencer could not help her; he had almost no money besides his Navy pay. The Duchess said, years later, "Two facts were in the back of my mind: I was a burden on my mother, and I was in love. What difference did it make if Win and I were poor? Why delay?"

They didn't. The wedding was set for November 8 in Christ Church, Baltimore. Murmurs of surprise and admiration greeted the parade of bridesmaids. Their dresses weren't pink or pale blue, simple, safe, and expected, but pale orchid (Wallis's favorite color) for the faille skirts and cadet blue for the velvet bodices, sophisticated and striking. Wallis had designed them herself. Their hats were the same velvet, and their bouquets were yellow snapdragons. Wallis wore white panne velvet embroidered with pearls and carried lilies of the valley and white orchids. Sol Warfield gave her away.

She and Win spent their short honeymoon at White Sulphur Springs, a luxurious resort in West Virginia, and in New York City. Then, abruptly, they were back at Pensacola; and abruptly Wallis discovered that the man she had married was not the one she had become engaged to. Spencer was a drunkard; a later wife would brand him "a drunken bum." His excuse for uncorking a bottle was "Got to get up flying speed!" When he drank, he became noisy—sometimes enough for the neighbors to complain; and when he was drunk—as he almost always was on Saturday nights, because he did not have to fly on Sundays—he insisted on doing boisterous impersonations. George M. Cohan was his favorite role; a lampshade on his head (no one quite knew why) and a cane in his hand, and he was off, even though the "voice like Caruse" was now almost incomprehensibly blurred.

Worse than a drunkard, he was also a sadist, and jealous to boot. To keep Wallis from going out when he was away from home, he would hog-tie her to the bed or lock her in the bathroom. Once, while she was helplessly bound, he spread all her family photographs on the floor in front of her, and stamped on them, shattering the glass.

She had a reprieve when her mother came down for a visit, thickly painted and powdered, necklines plunging, and more the Merry Widow than ever. The evenings when the Spencers were invited out for bridge or poker were also evenings free from fear and often even from embarrassment. Wallis always protested that she had "no head for figures," but something—instinct, practice—taught her the poker odds and averages, and presently she was making pin money and more.

But even her days were never wholly without fear, though it was not necessarily fear for herself. She had always been superstitious. "Like everybody else who had a colored mammy," she has said, "I was filled with Negro superstitions. Never throw your hat on a bed, never hang anything on a doorknob, never sit down thirteen at table, never start a journey on a Friday, never let a peacock feather into your house. Just after we settled in Pensacola, a package arrived, a wedding present. I opened it, and when I saw it was a peacock-feather fan, I ran and put it on the gate, for someone to find and take away.

"I was *convinced* that if I kept it, Win Spencer would be killed that very day! My ears were always cocked for the sound of the crash-gong. I can still hear it and I still remember the many, many Navy funerals I went to."

The United States' declaration of war on April 6, 1917, briefly distracted Spencer from his two quarries, Wallis and the bottle. He was promoted to full lieutenant, and was feeding himself on dreams of imminent assignment to combat duty when, in June, he was ordered to command the Naval Air Station at Squantum, Massachusetts, near Boston. There were many such posts for him during the next few years, and wherever he was sent, he did well—excellently. He was a born instructor, organizer, and administrator, which was why he was never given his heart's desire, duty overseas, in the combat zone. He was too good at his job to be spared.

The Armistice found him in San Diego, a lieutenant commander, in charge of the new and rapidly expanding air station on North Island. His record there was outstanding: His pilots flew a total of 35,000 hours without a single fatal crash, or even a serious injury, or a single scrubbed plane. Any other career officer would have been proud, but this was not the sort of record that Spencer had wanted, and now it was too late for the other sort: The war was over. He almost envied his brother Dumaresque, who had been shot down and killed in France, while flying with the Lafayette Escadrille. Win was a fighting man left with nowhere to prove his steel. In default, he turned on Wallis again.

He had stopped drinking at Squantum; and peace, if not happiness, had been restored to her life. She was making friends around San Diego, especially in nearby Coronado, where she and Win lived for a while. One friend was Benjamin Thaw, Jr., a young American Foreign Service officer who was enjoying a long leave in California before reporting to the Embassy in Warsaw as second secretary. He was married to Consuelo Morgan, elder sister of the twins Gloria (Mrs. Reginald Vanderbilt) and Thelma (Viscountess Furness). It was through Benny Thaw that Wallis met Katharine Bigelow, recently married, and soon to be widowed and remarried. Time and again the course of Katharine's life and her new husband's would intersect Wallis's, and always to Wallis's comfort and help. Alas, as soon as the end of the war unburdened Win Spencer of his heaviest responsibilities, he began drinking again, and his outbursts of sadism became uglier and more frequent. Often, as before, they were touched off by jealousy, real or feigned. His whips were public taunts and sneers; he also used bludgeons. If she accepted an invitation to dance, she might return to her table to find her husband gone, not to come home, sometimes, until late next day, and then without apology or explanation. For her to be "put in solitary"—locked into her room—became a commonplace. Her only pleasure was in the company of her new friends. She saw as much of them as Spencer's restrictions allowed her.

A civilian electrical expert employed by the Navy remembers her well, from the Saturday-night dances at the Hotel del Coronado. He says, "I noticed her because she was something of a wallflower. Her husband didn't give her much attention, and she wasn't too attractive to the rest of us, besides being rather standoffish. Her face stuck in my memory for some reason, though I never knew who she was until nineteen thirty-six, when her pictures began hitting all the papers."

Senior officers in the U.S. Navy like to ask juniors, "Is it better to know where you're going or where you've been?" Then they answer their own question: "It's better to know where you've been, because the Navy's going to tell you where you're going."

In February 1919—and not a moment too soon for Wallis—the Navy told Lieutenant Commander Spencer where he was going: to temporary duty at another airfield in California, and after that to a third. Wallis refused to accompany him; she stayed on in Coronado; and when he was ordered back to Pensacola in November 1920, she still stayed on. In her mind and vocabulary, Pensacola had become "the home of my error." Something else was in her mind: divorce, but it was shoved into a corner that spring

when Spencer was ordered to the Bureau of Aeronautics—
"BuAer"—in Washington. Wallis decided to join him and
have another try at salvaging their marriage.

Her mother had moved to Washington in 1918, as head
housekeeper at the fashionable Chevy Chase Club. Aunt
Bessie Merryman was already in town, as paid companion
to a well-to-do spinster. Like Alice, Bessie had been widowed early, in 1898, after only four years of marriage. She,
too, had received little from her husband's estate and,
again like Alice, little more when their widower father
died, in 1908. Still, Bessie had enough to let her bring Alice and Wallis to share her home for a while. Childless
herself, she doted on her sister's child, and even before Alice's death, Bessie had established a place in Wallis's life as
counselor (not always heeded), comforter, and chaperone.
Wallis hoped that the proximity of her mother and her
rather more formidable aunt might have a calming, cooling
effect on Spencer's furious temper. It did not. The same
recriminatory bellows began again (provoking the same
protests from the neighbors); so did the sentences to solitary confinement. Spencer locked her into her bathroom
one Sunday afternoon and left her there until late evening.
Next morning Wallis told her mother that her patience was
exhausted; she and Win were tearing each other to pieces;
and for both their sakes, she wanted a divorce. Both were
still young enough, she added, to find happiness with others.

Divorce! The word was a knell for Alice and Bessie's
Montague pride. "Unthinkable!" they declared. "The
Montague women don't get divorced. You must try
again!" They urged her to see Warfield relatives in Baltimore: "If we can't knock the idea out of your head, perhaps they can. Anyhow, you'd better tell your Uncle Sol
about it before he hears it from somebody else." Uncle
Sol's response was what Wallis had expected: "I won't
let you bring this disgrace upon us! From the first Warfield in America, in sixteen sixty-two, right down to the
present day, there's never been a divorce in our family,
and there won't be one now. It's not only a disgrace, it
would be bad for my business. Go back to your husband
and try again!"

She went back and tried again. About a fortnight later,

dinner-time passed with no Spencer and no message. That clinched it. When he finally came home, Wallis told him that she had been considering divorce for a long time, and his behavior that evening had determined her to go through with it.

He said slowly, "I've had it coming to me. If you ever change your mind, I'll still be around."

Wallis moved in with her mother immediately. Before she went to bed that first night, she wrote to Uncle Sol, informing him of her decision. His reply was formal, almost stiff: "Any divorce action you contemplate must be undertaken with your own resources. Expect no help of any kind from me."

❦ CHAPTER 2 ❦
Flings: *Washington, Paris, Peking, Warrenton*

The Spencers separated in the fall of 1921. By the following February, when Win was detached from BuAer and sent to command a gunboat on the China Station, Wallis had found her feet. She had also found that Washington was a merry-go-round where there was ample room for an attractive young "extra woman" who talked well, danced well, and drank well. That summer, she moved out of her mother's apartment and into one of Georgetown's "doll houses" with another lonely Navy wife, who was painting portraits of children to help pass the time while her husband was at sea. Wallis had little money—only the $225 a month that Win allotted her from his Navy pay—but she was *free*, at least temporarily, free from the humiliations, the bullying, and the tortures he had subjected her to; and her natural gaiety and flirtatiousness, so long corked up, began to effervesce again.

At the same time, the pattern of her life changed. In her autobiography, *The Heart Has Its Reasons*,[1] we catch only glimpses of the seven years between her separation from Spencer in 1921 and her second marriage, in 1928.

One of the first glimpses is of a young diplomat in Washington, · a Latin American, a finely fibered fellow, dashing of manner, subtle of mind, an attentive companion who came "to mean much more. . . ." She never divulges his name, but he is dead now, so identifying him will embarrass no one: He was Felipe Espil (1887–1972), first Secretary at the Argentine Embassy. His affair with Wallis began in 1921, when he was thirty-four and she twenty-five. A Washingtonian who knew both of them then describes Espil in terms of the times: "He was a real Latin smoothie, a 'cake-eater,' handsome, sleek, swarthy, beautifully dressed, a beautiful dancer, and brimming with self-assurance. Add a monocle—yes, he actually wore one—and you had a lady-killer from who-tied-the-dog." The "Lady-killer" did indeed come to "mean much more" to Wallis than "only a gay escort." She fell in love with him, headlong and heedlessly; and he—though cautiously—loved her.

He had to be cautious. He was a career diplomat, destined to be appointed Ambassador to the United States and to serve from 1931 to 1943; he was a Roman Catholic, and Wallis a prospective divorcee; lastly, he had only a small income, and Wallis's was smaller. Her lack of a dowry was more important to him than her divorce; the wife he eventually married was twice-divorced, but rich. Considerations of marriage did not hamper them yet. Nothing did. Almost overnight their affair became the talk of the town. It could hardly have escaped being so; Espil himself once acknowledged, "I shouldn't have made it so blatant," and even a prim Montague cousin of Wallis's admitted that it was "flagrant," though how blatant and flagrant Wallis may not have realized until she failed to receive an invitation to Mrs. Lawrence Townsend's annual ball.

Mrs. Townsend was one of Washington's make-or-break hostesses. Her invitations were a social certificate. Being invited to her ball meant that one belonged to the inner circle; not being invited, that one belonged in outer darkness. Worse, all Washington would know about it. Wallis, in desperation, asked Felipe to procure an invitation for her. He was shocked: "I can't ask Mrs. Townsend to invite my mistress! *Ça ne se fait pass!*"

Gallantry seems not to have been among his virtues. He repeated the incident to a "confidant," with the dialogue, and presently the local gossips had another *bonne bouche*. A young hostess who knew Wallis in those days said of her, "She was always asking friends to get her invited to this party or that. She was *pushy*. She had to be, I suppose, because she was on the fringe, never quite *in*. She was a bit fast for us: too many men around her, not top-drawer men, either. When I picture Wallis at a big party, I picture her off in a corner with a group of men, she giggling and they guffawing. We always suspected that they were telling naughty stories."

Wallis's passion for Espil was such that she might have

accepted the humiliation in meekness and silence, if jealousy had not begun to whisper in her ear. Thitherto she had taken it for granted that her lien on his affections was exclusive. When she discovered that it was not, there were scenes which became increasingly violent, and which Espil found it increasingly hard to hide and hush. During one of them, she flew at him like a demon and clawed his face. That did it. An aspirant for an ambassadorship might be forgiven for marrying a quasi-pauper, even one of a different faith; but not if she were, to boot, such a virago that he might have to appear at a diplomatic reception with a lump on his forehead and lacerated cheeks. He broke with her, flatly and forever, toward the end of 1923. Thirteen years later, one of his diplomatic colleagues remarked, "Felipe had a higher regard for his career than Edward the Eighth had."

Spencer had hurt Wallis, but Espil hurt her deeply. A Montague cousin said, "He was the only man she ever wanted and couldn't get." Having lost him, she did the best thing in the circumstances: She left town.

Gossip says that she and Espil had once planned to go to Europe together—that they had engaged a stateroom and had even boarded the ship, and that just before sailing time he "went to get a pack of cigarettes" and never came back. This is sheer gossip. When Wallis left, it was admittedly with the hope that he would join her abroad, all forgiven; but her actual companion was her favorite cousin, Corinne Mustin, recently widowed. Back in January 1918, the battleship U.S.S. *North Dakota* had been steaming off Massachusetts when the heavy sea swept three of her crew overboard. Commander Mustin, her executive officer, grabbed a line and dived after them, and managed to lock his legs around one man's waist and hold him until they were hauled back on deck; the other two men were lost. The terrible cold of the water combined with the heavy burden to strain the heroic Mustin's heart, and he died, a captain, in 1923, at the age of forty-nine. Presently "Rinny" wrote to tell Wallis that she was going to Paris: Couldn't Skinny come along? Skinny wrote back that on $225 a month she couldn't, but perhaps Uncle Sol—one never knew how Uncle Sol would respond. She went to see him. To her aston-

ishment—perhaps more to his own—he gave her five one-
hundred-dollar bills.

Skinny and Rinny sailed in January 1924 and the next
five months were among the happiest that Wallis had ever
known. Twenty years later, her letters would still be reminding Rinny of scenes and incidents from the Paris they
had first known together: How *carefree* they'd been! How
they had laughed! Would Rinny ever forget the Hôtel Matignon? Or the evening at the aviary? She'd love to laugh
like that again! After another five years, Wallis's memories
were still shining: The Matignon (she wrote) still had the
same concierge—imagine!—as when she and Rinny had
shared that hall bedroom. They'd meet again, and again
they'd laugh as they had in those days. It was awful to
grow old and still feel young. . . .

Two such attractive girls—Rinny was a stunning blonde
with huge blue eyes—had no trouble finding company. The
Assistant Naval Attaché at the American Embassy, Comdr.
William Eberle, had been a friend of Henry Mustin's,
and "Imp" Eberle brought along the First Secretary,
Gerry (*G* as in Gertrude, not as in Gerald) Greene. They
made a merry foursome, though Wallis was not quite so
wholly carefree as she later pretended. Win Spencer had
begun to bombard her with letters, begging her to forget
the past, join him in China, and give him one more chance
to rebuild their lives together. She might have ignored his
importunities but for a rude discovery. One reason she had
been so eager to go to Europe with Rinny was the reports
she had heard of cheap, painless Paris divorces. Now that
she was there, she found that the minimum she could expect to pay a local lawyer was several thousand dollars—
for her, an unobtainable sum. The only alternative was to
return to Win. She decided the marriage was worth another
try at salvage. She persuaded herself that the flame that
had died in familiar surroundings might suddenly leap into
life again in a resumed companionship in far-off China.
She notified him of her decision and sailed for home. A
message from him was waiting for her in Washington: She
was to book passage through the Navy on a transport to
the Philippines and there change ships for Hong Kong,
where he would meet her. She sailed in the U.S.S. *Chau-
mont* from Norfolk, Virginia, on July 17, 1924.

A fellow passenger, a Navy captain, "remembered" Wallis's "open romance" with a boyish ensign on the long voyage. He said that when they reached Hong Kong at last, the ensign confronted Spencer and told him he wanted to marry Wallis, and Spencer "threw both of them out." Whether or not the ensign was a factor (if indeed he ever existed), Win and Wallis separated again almost at once. She does not tell us why, or which of them took the initiative—only that their coming together failed, and that on leaving him she bought a ticket to Shanghai, intending to file for divorce in the International Court there, only to discover that, as in Paris, the cost was beyond her means.

Up to this point, the episodes of her life seem to have occurred haphazardly, with a cast of characters largely anonymous and dates deliberately vague. She allows glimpses of strange places and of pleasurable wanderings; of international compounds populated largely by handsome, highly sophisticated diplomats, bankers, soldiers, and traders and where an unattached, pretty young woman could count on a dozen suitors. In Shanghai we are given a misty view of a charming hotel on Bubbling Well Road, the shadowy outline of a gallant Englishman named "Robbie," and a recollection of the stirrings of heart brought on one evening at a supper club on first hearing the cloying strains of "Tea for Two." And in Peking some weeks later, the lens of her memory focuses briefly, but affectionately, on the lingering charm of an Italian naval officer, later an admiral, among whose effects was found a poem in which, before expiring, he bequeathed her, for her private use alone, "the sea, the sky, and the sun." Her "intimates" in Peking also included the French chargé d'affaires, according to a courtier who professed to have seen "the dossier" that King George V had had prepared about Wallis's "China phase."

No doubt she had good reason to paint so lightly on the Chinese screen that is the sole surviving record of the year or so that she spent there. The gossip about her liaisons in China after she became famous aroused her indignation as almost nothing else did. "Venom, *venom*, VENOM!" was her bitter response. Still, there is a hardy rumor that somewhere she fell foul of a Chinese gentleman who began blackmailing her, and some Baltimoreans believe, but groundlessly, that Uncle Sol Warfield made a secret trip to buy him off.

Casual beaux aside, it was also in Peking that Wallis, escorted to a party by one old friend, Gerry Greene, chance-met another, Katharine Bigelow. Gerry was now First Secretary at the Legation; Katharine, whom Wallis had last seen at Coronado, was now married to Herman Rogers. From the moment of this meeting until Katharine's death in 1949 and Herman's in 1957, the Rogerses were Wallis's most loyal and most cherished friends. Indeed, their stories here become inseparable.

Katharine, née Moore, had made a wartime marriage to Ernest A. Bigelow, Jr., also of New York. Soon afterward, she joined the Red Cross and was sent to France. One afternoon in July 1918, a troop train moving toward the front stopped at the Amiens station, where Katharine was handing out coffee and doughnuts. The stop was brief, but it was long enough for an American major on the train to catch sight of the slim blond-haired, blue-eyed woman and feel his heart stumble and leap.

"That's the most attractive girl I've ever seen!" he told a brother officer. "If I ever find her again, I'm going to marry her!"

The major was Herman Livingston Rogers, of the field artillery. His family's estate on the Hudson, Crumwold Hall, adjoined the Roosevelts' Hyde Park. *The New York Times* called it "a showplace" and identified Herman's father, Archibald, as "a sportsman and pioneer railroad builder." One of Archie Rogers's sports was ice-boating; in his *Jack Frost,* which had a mainsail almost as large as a J Class yacht's, he often outsped the Twentieth Century Limited along the frozen river. Herman went to Groton, one of America's most fastidious preparatory schools, and then to Yale, with the Class of 1914. His classmates are few now, but they remember him vividly. They could hardly fail to do so, not only because of his spectacular good looks—he was tall and lean, with wavy brown hair, and he moved with singular grace—but equally because of his versatility and popularity. He was an oarsman, a scholar (Phi Beta Kappa), and a "Bones man" (a member of the eminent senior society Skull and Bones). In short, here in the handsome and muscular flesh were Stover at Yale, Brown of Harvard, and all the other campus-fiction heroes of the moleskin-and-mandolin era. During the spring semester in those days, the senior class at Yale traditionally rated its members in various categories, and "Herm" Rogers's classmates gave him a flattering number of ballots for "Most to be Admired," "Most Entertaining," and "Most Perfect Gentleman." In the years ahead, strangers would mark his grace of manner, with the quiet learning.

Farming had always appealed to him; at one time he had intended doing postgraduate work at the Cornell Agriculture School. But something changed his mind, and he went, instead, to the Massachusetts Institute of Technology, where he studied civil engineering and was awarded the degree of Master of Science. By then, 1917, America was in the war. Rogers enlisted at once, took an officers' training course, and a year later found himself in France and in love with a stranger.

Discharged in the summer of 1919, he joined the engineering department of a New York firm of architects and farm specialists. He also joined, with considerably more enthusiasm, the Knickerbocker, the Racquet & Tennis, and a number of other fashionable clubs. For further diversion, there were parties—parties by the dozen, daily, dusk to dawn—where "the boys" were welcome, along with their girls and their friends and their girls' friends' girls. At one such, Herman was introduced to a lovely young widow. Again his heart tumbled; so did his tongue; but presently he managed to ask her if by any wild, crazy, impossible chance she had been in the Red Cross during the war.

"Yes."

"In France?"

"Yes. Why?"

"Could you have been on the railroad platform in Amiens in July nineteen-eighteen?"

"Yes, but what's all this—?"

"Then," Herman interrupted, *"you* are the girl I promised myself I would marry."

Their engagement was announced—the *New York American* said that "Mrs. Bigelow's future husband is a decided matrimonial 'catch' "—and they were married in November 1920. There was plenty of money, so the honeymooners decided to search the world for what they would agree was its most beautiful spot, and there they would settle. Their first circuit narrowed their choice to Peking, Florence, and the French Riviera—each so uniquely, irresistibly alluring that it was quite impossible to pick one above the others, and there was nothing for it but to let engineering and architecture wait while they made another circuit. They were halfway around, back in Peking, when they met Wallis. In the years to come, they would give her kindness, hospitality, and even shelter in such measure as she would never meet elsewhere. They were her guardian angels from the start, and would so serve her as long as they lived.

Their hospitality began at once. They took her out of the Grand Hôtel de Pékin and carried her off to their big, comfortable house in the Tartar City, its floors deep in Chinese rugs, its walls glowing with Chinese brocades. They engaged a personal maid for her and a personal rickshaw boy, and where the Rogerses went, Wallis went, too. Her new days began with horseback riding before breakfast (Herman had a stable) and shopping afterward, then there was polo to watch, and a late-afternoon swim in the big new pool at the American Legation. The evenings could be counted on for a dinner party, and perhaps a ball, or dancing to the band at some hotel, with Gerry Greene, now her wholly devoted slave, making calf's-eyes and squandering his pay on her. Many of Wallis's evenings ended at the poker table. At her very first session, she won $225—exactly equal to a month's allowance from Spencer. Herman soon saw that she played a cool, strong hand and thereafter he gave her a regular stake of $50—enough to let her sharpen her game and, with luck, to finance her next morning's shopping tour. (When she came to write her autobiography, her editor asked, "What was happening to Spencer in the meanwhile?"

Duchess: "Oh, he was on his gunboat, so I lost myself in the life of Peking and just stayed there until I decided to go home."

Editor: "Did he make any effort to—"

Duchess: "Oh, no, no. . . .")

On weekends, the entire household moved by motorcar and donkeyback to the Western Hills, for an overnight picnic in the abandoned temple that the Rogerses had leased, one with a tiled jade green roof and vermilion eaves strung with bells that tinkled music when the wind stirred them.

The sights and sounds of China made an enduring impression on her, especially the sounds. In her autobiography, she writes with rare feeling about her joy at hearing the temple bells, the soft, mysterious "whee-oo!, whee-oo!" given off by the little bamboo whistles attached to the pigeons' wings as they circled invisibly over the walled houses; the echoing sing-song cries of the hawkers and peddlars; the rhythmic flapping of the rickshaw boys' slippers on the cobblestones; the sweet shrill sounds of the reed flutes and trumpets of the street entertainers. She seems to have heard and noticed everything—the silken livery of the coolie servants, different in every well-appointed villa. It all becomes her, revealing if only in passing, a sensitivity to things outside herself not often in evidence.

Despite her gay and pleasant life in Peking, Wallis began to chafe at the idle, indolent way she spent her days. Not working and making little progress in her study of Chinese, she came to feel the tug of neglected responsibilities. As she was turning twenty-nine, in June 1925, she realized that she had to return to the States and proceed with her plans to divorce Win.

She did not offer Herman Rogers an explanation; she simply left—and so abruptly that both he and Katharine were puzzled. Herman's many virtues included modesty; it never occurred to him, though it did to some of his associates, that Wallis may have fallen in love with him. After all, he was exactly the kind of man for whom her Baltimore breeding had prepared her: patrician, well-to-do, handsome, cultivated, generous, and at ease in whatever milieu chance placed him. But since, in addition, he loved his wife obviously and exclusively, there was nothing Wallis could do, for the moment, but keep silent and take the quickest, safest way out.

So it was good-bye to the charming Herman and the inconvenient Katharine! Good-bye to heartbroken, purse-bent Gerry Greene, and to the suave young diplomats, and the gallant, dashing officers! Good-bye to personal maids and private rickshaws, good-bye to idleness and luxury!

Her lotus year was over: "I left for Japan to take a ship to the West Coast."

There was one more good-bye to be said, and one more murky sequence to suffer through; after that, her life was back on course. Wallis landed in Seattle with "an obscure internal ailment" that required an operation and a period in the hospital. This was one of the few times in her long life that she was ill; for the most part, she enjoyed rude, glowing health. Spencer was in the States, too, on leave, and with his parents near Chicago. He cabled her to come to Chicago where they stayed with his family, and then he accompanied her to Washington. It was the last time she saw him. (Short shrift for his chivalry!) So good-bye to Win Spencer, the poor, boozy flyboy, himself the only casualty of his flying career.

Wallis gives no details of her "ailment" and operation, but they were serious enough to require three months' convalescence, at her mother's apartment, before she had mustered the strength to proceed with her divorce. She could not bring suit in Washington, which recognized adultery as the only grounds; but Virginia, across the Potomac, was more liberal. After the plaintiff's three years' separation from the defendant, and two years' residence (not necessarily continuous), it would grant a divorce for desertion— and at a cost of no more than three hundred dollars in legal fees. What Wallis had been searching for in France and China was right next door the whole time.

A friend recommended that she establish residence in Warrenton, a pleasant, flavorsome little town of some 1,500, only fifty miles away, conveniently near her family and friends, yet not so near that they'd be constantly dropping in. Warrenton was the seat of Fauquier County (pronounced "FO-keer"), and Fauquier was the heart of the Virginia fox-hunting country, which promised a certain amount of gaiety. She took the train from Washington one day in October. It could have been either 1925 or 1926; but a local swain (who admits that he is "still a bit in love with her") says that the actual date of her arrival was June 10, 1926, and he says it as unshakably as if it had been tattooed above his heart on that very day more than fifty years ago. A Negro porter hauled her luggage over to the town's one hotel, the Warren Green, where she would serve her term. The Warren Green was no Grand Hôtel de Pékin, but the modesty of its appearance and accommodations extended to its charges: $70 a month for her room, 75 cents for her dinner.

The room was a single, without bath, "second floor back, fifteen feet by twelve, with faded flowered wallpaper, a high brass bed, battered night table, imitation mahogany bureau, enamelled washstand, large black easy chair in cracked leatherette." So her autobiography describes it. A friend of hers describes its tenant:

"On the physical side, I'd say she was only moderately attractive. Her mouth was too big, her nose was too long, and her clenched-teeth grin was almost grotesque. But her eyes and her hair were very nice; so was her voice; and her figure was trim, though too thin—for my taste—to be exciting. She didn't have enough money to dress really smartly. She was neat rather than chic. She looked her best in country clothes: tweed coat and skirt, sweater, brogues. The important thing was, she was always full of vitality— 'pep,' we called it then. She *shone* at parties! She could dance up a storm and match drinks with anyone—a beau at the Canadian Embassy kept her supplied with liquor. I'm not implying that Wallis was a heavy drinker. She wasn't, not at all. And what she drank never went to her head. She drank *socially,* like the rest of us. When I picture her, it's never with a glass in her hand; it's when she is 'holding forth' to a group of laughing people.

"She was a born raconteur, with an inexhaustible fund of risqué stories. One was a conundrum I still remember: 'What is the difference between a night on the beach at Coney Island and a night on the beach in Hollywood?' Answer: 'At Coney, the girls lie on the beach and look at the stars, and in Hollywood the stars lie on the girls and look at the beach.' "

Wallis's "pep" is the quality that a Warrenton beau of hers also remembers best. Hugh Spilman, then the teller at the Fauquier National Bank, had met her when they were teen-agers in Baltimore. He recognized her strolling through town one day and reintroduced himself, and thereafter he was as constant a companion as she and his job allowed.

Mornings, she'd drift into the bank, and he'd send a boy out for Cokes, and they'd sit and sip and chat until Mr. Tiffany, the president, popped from his office and called, "Hugh, you stop that drinking with Wallis, and get back into your cage!"

Afternoons, they played golf at the Warrenton Country Club. The course had only nine holes, the longest only 225 yards, and the clubhouse was ramshackle, with peeling paint, but nobody cared. They spent a lot of time there. The Negro chef, George Washington, specialized in roast wild duck. "We ate it with our fingers," Spilman recalls. "I can see Wallis now, with the blood running down her bare arms."

Evenings, after the duck dinner, there was almost always a crap game or a poker game, at the club or somewhere else. (When Wallis married the Duke of Windsor, one of her Warrenton friends sent her a pair of dice as a wedding present.) Spilman continued, "She played hard—no quarter asked or given—and she was *good*! One poker night we had a big pot going, and Wallis suddenly jumped up and knocked the table over, and all the cards and chips fell on the floor. She *said* a cat had startled her by rubbing against her leg, but *I* think she saw she was going to lose the pot. As somebody said, 'She saw the kitty, but not the cat.' . . . She was a devil, but man, was she good company!—*wonderful* company! Always up to something. She was invited out a lot because she could make a party go. I don't mind admitting that I was pretty crazy about her, even though she was an awful little flirt. I used to get sore and give her hell for flirting, and she'd say, 'I know, I know, but think of the fun we have making up!' I actually proposed to her. '*Uh*-uh!' she said. 'You're poor, and I'm poor, and we both need money.' "

Spilman laughed. "She was certainly right about *me*! I was making one-twenty-five a month. . . ."

Another tribute to Wallis's vitality is still remembered around Warrenton. In most fox-hunting communities, it is almost *de rigueur* for the horsier houses to be hung with sets of nineteenth-century English sporting prints: "The Moonlight Steeplechase," "Fores's Coaching Scenes," "The Quorn Hunt," and so on. Warrenton was no exception. One house featured a set of "The High-Mettled Racer," by John

Alken. A visitor glanced at them. "What a marvelous title," he commented, "for a biography of Wallis Spencer!"

Girlhood friends occasionally came to visit her, to divert her with talk of schooldays and debutante days. One of the most loyal was Mary Kirk, of the Baltimore silversmithing family. She and Wallis had been classmates at Oldfields; they had made their debuts together, and Mary had been one of her bridesmaids—the favorite, indeed, for Wallis had tossed the bridal bouquet straight into her hands.

Mary, too, had made a war marriage, to a French officer, Jacques Raffray, whom she had met while he was on liaison duty at Camp Meade, near Baltimore. He stayed on after the Armistice and went into marine insurance. The Raffrays lived in New York now, in an apartment on Washington Square, but Mary spent much of her time with Wallis in Warrenton. Mary was a very good looking woman. Freckles gave a hint of *gamine* mischief to her open countenance; her figure summoned a second glance; and her quick mind, her impish wit, her zest for company made her a perfect foil for Wallis Warfield. Their friendship lasted beyond the innocent school years into the far more sharply testing and, where the warring interests of men and women are concerned, dangerously competitive years. Their paths were to cross again and again.

The winter ended, and the spring of 1926 brought a little excitement into Wallis's stagnant life: Her mother, plumping at last for respectability and security, took a third husband, Charles Gordon Allen, a widower who lived in Washington and worked in the Veterans Bureau. He was pleasant, if nondescript; Wallis did not warm to him. Soon after the wedding, Alice brought him to Virginia to meet another Montague, Lelia Montague Gordon, Corinne's aunt, at Wakefield Manor, her estate in Rappahannock County. The weekend happened to be the Fourth of July, and the ebullient Alice wrote in Lelia's guest book, "Here on the Fourth with my third!" (and on a later visit, "Alys Allen, on my last lap"). Except for Bessie Merryman, who married only once, the Montague ladies were a much-marrying lot: three times for Alice, twice for Corinne, twice for Lelia, and—of course—three times for Wallis. Allen had a comfortable house in a pleasant section of

Washington, and there Alice lived happily and respectably for the few years left to her.

Wallis, meanwhile, was trying to turn a penny somewhere else than at the poker table. She competed for a job on the editorial staff of *Vogue*, but didn't win it. In desperation, she briefly entertained the idea of selling tubular steel scaffolding on commission for a company owned by the husband of a friend of hers, but she didn't get that job either. The friend was Elizabeth Key Lloyd; her husband was Morgan Schiller, of Sewickley, Pennsylvania, and Easton, Maryland; the now widowed Mrs. Schiller treasures a home movie, taken fifty years ago, of Wallis and Mary Raffray doing the Charleston together.

Then, the following spring, Aunt Bessie Merryman came to Wallis's rescue, as she would so often. At sixty-three, Aunt Bessie was still slender, with a good figure and tiny feet, like her sister Alice. She was sprightly and eager; the Montague wit was hers in abundance, and its sparkle never dimmed. Once, after the Warrenton Gold Cup race, she climbed into her car and inadvertently sat on a pair of field glasses. "Better hindsight than foresight!" she said. When she was in her forties, a mild stroke twisted her mouth very slightly awry. Far from disfiguring her, it added piquancy to her smile and—as often does a stammer—to her speech. Long afterward, a cousin said to her, "Bessie, I have a story for you that's so funny, you won't be able to keep a straight face!"

"I expect not," Mrs. Merryman said, laughing. "I can barely remember when I had one last."

Since 1914, she had been the paid companion of Miss Mary B. Adams, the largest stockholder in the then prosperous Washington *Evening Star*. The association had proved so agreeable that Miss Adams presented Mrs. Merryman with a generous annuity, which other friends, well-to-do ladies, had supplemented; and since Miss Adams was generous with holidays as well, Mrs. Merryman now had ample means and leisure to share with Wallis and effect her rescue. Soon after Miss Adams's death, in 1953, her niece received a telephone call from the Duchess of Windsor, anxiously inquiring whether the annuity would continue; she seemed relieved to learn that it would.

The rescue was from the triple trap of boredom, an emotional entanglement, and a financial crisis, and it was achieved through an invitation to tour southern Europe, all expenses paid. They sailed to Trieste, traveled by train and car across Italy to Monte Carlo, thence to Nice, Arles, and Avignon, and up to Paris. Here on the morning of October 25 Wallis picked up a copy of the *Herald* and read on its front page the news of Uncle Sol Warfield's death. She started home at once. He had made a few minor bequests to members of the family, she soon learned, but had left the bulk of his estate, which rumor appraised at $5,000,000, for the establishment and maintenance of the Anna Emory Warfield Home for Aged Women, in memory of his mother—the funding to come from the sale of certain stocks in his portfolio. Disappointed, Wallis and a grandniece threatened suit to break the will, but eventually agreed not to do so, upon the trustees' promise to pay Wallis $47,500 and the grandniece $27,500. Alas, by the time the estate was settled, the Great Depression was under way; and some of Sol Warfield's fattest stocks—Seaboard Air Line Railway, for instance, in which at the time of his death he owned about 40,000 shares of common, about 50,000 of preferred, and about $1,200,000 in bonds —had dwindled almost to the vanishing point. As his funeral began, at 3 P.M. on the twenty-seventh, the Seaboard respectfully halted all its trains for two minutes. His pallbearers were a measure of his importance. They included the president of the Pennsylvania Railroad, W. W. Atterbury; Hearst's chief editor, Arthur Brisbane; the president of Columbia University, Nicholas Murray Butler; and one of New York's most prominent legal counsels, Samuel Untermyer. Even after the $75,000 payments, there was a certain amount of salvage—not enough to establish an independent home, but enough to let the trustees comfort a number of aged and indigent women, as Mr. Warfield had wished.

As soon as Wallis had satisfied Virginia's residence requirement, her attorney, State Sen. Aubrey "Kingfish" Weaver, submitted her petition, on December 6, 1927. She and her mother testified to Spencer's intemperance and— doubtless with straight faces—to his having deserted her. A scrawl he had sent Wallis was introduced as evidence of his

implacability: "Sorry we can't make a go of it. Win. PS.
Stop bothering me with your letters." The Spencerian hand
had trembled, though perhaps it was with rage. Four days
later, Judge George Latham Fletcher granted the divorce.
Wallis glanced at his initials on the decree and remarked
" 'G.L.F.'—Good Looking Fellow." (The file on the divorce would disappear, mysteriously, around the time that
Wallis's name was beginning to be coupled with the Prince
of Wales, in the mid-1930's.)

Though she was free of Spencer at last, she was still the
prisoner of her circumstances. The windfall from Uncle Sol
would not be paid until January 1930, so Wallis had to
stay on at her depressing little hotel until she could save
enough from her alimony to buy her passage back to Europe. Two powerful incentives were driving her. Herman
and Katharine Rogers had left Peking for the French Riviera, where they had taken Villa Lou Viei ("the Old
Man," in Provençal), on the Avenue de Vallauris, above
Cannes; the latchstring was out, they had written; her
room was waiting. The other reason was a man, a new one.

During Wallis's two years in Warrenton, her budget had
permitted her an occasional excursion to New York—not
often, but "often enough," she said, "for me to get oxygen-
ated and to recharge my batteries." Mary Kirk Raffray was
always glad to give her a bed and to throw a cocktail party
in her honor. (Her husband, "Jackie" Raffray, was drifting
away, alienated by Mary's extravagance and flirtatious-
ness.) A friend said of her, "She was attractive to men and
attracted by them. When she gave a cocktail party, very
few women were present." A young bond salesman who
knew both girls at the time describes them thus: "Mary
was vivacious and feminine; Wallis was vivacious with a
bite!"

It was the exact word: *bite*. Lilli Palmer, the actress,
writing about an evening with the Windsors, mentions the
Duchess's "voracious vitality." She said, "If she had happened to be hungry, she might have taken a bite out of
you. Whenever I looked at her I was reminded of the nut-
cracker we used for cracking walnuts when we were children. It was made of polished wood in the form of a woman's head which could open its mouth very wide and—c-rr-
ack, the nut disintegrated."[2]

Fifteen years would pass before the bond salesman, by then a successful banker, next saw Wallis, by then the Duchess of Windsor, at a party in Nassau.

"What a *pleasure*, Wallis!" he said, beaming. "I often think of our Sunday evenings in New York—you and Mary and Rodney Williams and I—how we'd have a plate of spaghetti and a glass of dago red at Papa Moneta's, then buy balcony seats at a nabe. Five or six bucks covered the evening's tab for all four. Just as well, because that's about all that Rodney and I had between us! We used to laugh at ourselves as 'a couple of big butter-and-egg men, out on the town.' But what *fun* it was, remember?"

Then, the bite: "No," said the Duchess of Windsor. "I don't." She turned her back and moved away.

A complementary story to the banker's is told by the Baltimore lawyer who helped Wallis break her uncle's will. He said, "She came to our office on July 25, 1929, and my father and I agreed to defend her suit, which we won. Many years later, she and the Duke attended a ball given by the Baltimore Assembly. I introduced myself to her and reminded her of the time when she had employed us. She seemed very much annoyed and vigorously denied that she had ever done anything of the kind."

CHAPTER 3
Wallis in London

This is a spray the Bird clung to,
*   Making it blossom with pleasure,*
Ere the high tree-top she sprung to
*   Fit for her nest and her treasure.*
*   Oh, what a hope beyond measure*
Was the poor spray's, which the flying feet
*   hung to—*
So to be singled out, built in, and sung to!
    —"Misconceptions," ROBERT BROWNING

Mary Raffray's sister Anne published a book about her and Wallis. "Maybe you—Mary—weren't the richest of Wallis's friends," Anne wrote, "nor the most prominent socially, but by golly you were going to be for her the most *USEFUL*! Wallis always had an eye for people who could be the 'most useful.' " [1] Her shrewdness in divining Mary's usefulness was soon proven. On one of Wallis's visits to Washington Square, Mary introduced her to a man named Ernest Simpson. The year was 1926; the date was Christmas afternoon; and sister Anne, who was present, has described the meeting: "We were all lapping up the cocktails when the 'butler,' Jackie Raffray [went to the door], and was nearly trampled upon by two great huge 'grenadiers,' dressed in very shiny top hats and cutaways with the whitest of very broad Ascot ties. . . . They were souls of amiability and glamour. . . . It was such a stupendous event! There, all ready with her open arms, was Wallis, with her heart on her sleeve, and seemingly saying to Ernest [one of the 'grenadiers']: 'You are a gallant Knight on a White Charger, coming to rescue me from the wicked world of poverty and oblivion . . . !' I can see her beautiful blue eyes now, and her square hands clawing the air in ecstasy. . . ."[2]

Ecstasy was not a mood to which Wallis surrendered easily, if ever, and it is doubtful if she did so then. But certainly she liked Ernest Simpson at first sight, and her interest quickened when Mary Raffray told her that he was half English, half American, with an American wife from whom he was separated. The attraction was mutual; they began seeing each other. Ernest soon showed that he met at least two of Wallis's standards: He dressed well and was a good dancer. But there was more to him than this, she discovered—much more. He could offer not only dinners above spaghetti and dago red, and entertainment above neighborhood movies, but topics above the price of bonds. Yet, no matter how stimulating his conversation, his personality was restful. This had become important to Wallis. After being shipwrecked with Win Spencer and marooned by Felipe Espil, she would welcome the smooth, safe voyage that Ernest seemed to promise. Indeed, she would later attribute to him "a temperament as steady and dependable as the trade winds." Their friendship ripened rapidly.

Win Spencer was eight years older than Wallis; Ernest Aldrich Simpson was eleven months younger. His mother was an American, his father English, the head of Simpson, Spence & Young, ship brokers, with offices in London and New York (the firm is still listed in the directories of both cities). A news story in the *American Examiner–Jewish Week* for August 3–9, 1972, quotes a letter in the London *Jewish Chronicle* (no date given) as stating that Ernest Simpson's "family name was originally [sic] Solomon and before that Salaman . . . [according] to the late Dr. Redcliffe Salaman, a noted Anglo-Jewish scientist. . . . Leon Solomon (Salaman) of Dublin married Rose Joseph of Plymouth. Their son was Ernest who took the name of Simpson, and Ernest's son, another Ernest, married Wallis Warfield." Ernest and his sister, Maud, were born and raised in New York. In 1912, when the boy was fifteen, he entered The Hill, a Pennsylvania preparatory school of good though modest reputation, much like the one that he himself would establish in his three years there. He won a prize for poetry, was elected to the school literary maga-

zine, and graduated in the third quarter of his class. Nick-
names are often a significant index to a youngster's personality; Ernest's were obvious and noncommittal: "Simp"
and "My Lord." (Win Spencer's, oddly, was "Duke," a
tribute to his swagger.) Neither of them followed Ernest
from school, and he never acquired another.

He matriculated at Harvard in September 1915, but resigned in the fall of his third year, unlaureled, almost unknown to his classmates, and sailed for England, where he
enlisted in the Officer Cadet Battalion of the Household
Brigade. He was gazetted second lieutenant in the Coldstream in June 1918 and was "disembodied" the following
January as a full lieutenant, mildly ashamed of never having seen action (through no fault of his own), but endur-
ingly proud of having been a Coldstream officer. He wore
the regimental tie or blazer whenever an opportunity offered, and even back in New York affected the "guardee's"
obligatory moustache, bowler, and tightly rolled umbrella.
His American friends, meeting him for the first time since
before the war, hardly recognized the nondescript Ernest
Simpson of The Hill and Harvard in this dapper, bustling,
pink-cheeked chap—so extra-English, even to the accent,
that he seemed to be an American actor playing an Englishman. If they teased him about it, he explained mildly
that he *was* English, half by birth and wholly by law; when
he reached his majority in 1918, he'd had a choice of citi-
zenships and had chosen his father's.

He had already decided not to return to Harvard and
take a degree; he wanted to lose no more time in getting
started at Simpson, Spence & Young. Ship brokerage was
prospering, and Ernest prospered with it. Before long he
found himself in a position to begin collecting *objets d'art*
and first editions. He studied his hobbies (he taught himself to interpret the hallmarks on silver at sight), but he
never rode them at a cocktail party or a dinner table. He
took an informed pleasure in the theatre, the opera, and
the ballet. Another of his recreations was reading the
Greek classics. If he sometimes seemed a bit pompous on
first acquaintance, the impression did not last; men soon
came to like him, and women to find him "sweet." Early in
1923, Mrs. Dorothea Parsons Dechert, a divorcee from
Massachusetts, found him sweet enough to marry. They

lived with his family on West Eighty-eighth Street, Manhattan, for the first year, until their baby was born, then
moved to a brownstone walk-up flat on more fashionable
East Sixty-eighths. They named the baby Audrey. At this
point the Simpsons emerged on the fringes of the mixed
groups of professional people and socialites who made up
the so-called smart set that imparted wit, sparkle and a
new abandon to the speakeasy and nightclub culture of
postwar Manhattan. Here they were briefly in the circle of
one of its most radiant members, the beautiful Clare
Boothe Brokaw, then an editor of *Vanity Fair.* Ernest, she
remembers as "a bustling fellow, somewhat on the pompous side. Well read and very sure of himself." There was
no trace in him then of the mouse that he was made to
appear in the events which would subsequently fix his
sorry place in history. Contrastingly, the first Mrs. Simpson was diffident and withdrawn. The marriage yielded
early to strain; they separated in 1926, and Dorothea
Simpson sued for divorce. The suit was pending when
Ernest met Wallis Spencer. As his final decree drew nearer, and he prepared to take over the management of his
firm's London office, he asked Wallis if she would marry
him when she, too, was free. Though she was now thirty-
one and all but destitute, she refused. It was an act which
she never explained, but which a friend interpreted as
gaining her time enough to "look him up, check on his
financial and social status." Ernest left for London, and
Wallis returned to Warrenton, chafing while her alimony
accumulated.

She seems to have had Ernest much on her mind, because not many weeks had passed before she was hinting
that she was engaged to an Englishman. A Richmond lady
remembers Wallis's announcement that "I'll never have to
sing for my supper anymore. I'm going to live in England
and have a little garden and lead a quiet life. Nobody will
ever see or hear of me again!"

The lady warned her jokingly, "Don't fall in love with
the Prince of Wales!"

Wallis laughed. "What would I have to lose?"

She had her stake by May and left at once for Cannes
and the hospitable Rogerses' Villa Lou Viei. Spring on the
Riviera is always preternaturally enchanting; the spring of

1928 seemed to Wallis especially so, since she presently found herself writing to Ernest Simpson that she had reconsidered: She would marry him after all. This was a daring decision for someone as superstitious as Wallis Spencer, who in her youth must have heard the old jingle, "To change the name and not the letter/Is a change for the worse, not for the better"—i.e., Spencer and Simpson have the same initial. Her acceptance, as she remembers it, was breezy. A friend remembers it as also laying down certain terms: "a Buick convertible and a month's tour of the Continent." Ernest may have heard the breezy note; to the friend, it sounded fairly commanding.

Ernest accepted at once. She joined him in London; and on July 21, a clerk in the Chelsea Registry of Marriages rattled off the contract in a shabby, cluttered office. It was the last shabbiness that Wallis would ever know. Even as a despondent Hugh Spilman, back in Warrenton, was reading the cable she had sent him the night before—"UNEXPECTEDLY I FIND MYSELF MARRYING ERNEST TOMORROW MUCH LOVE"—a chauffeur was stowing Mr. and Mrs. Simpson's luggage in no mere Buick, but a high-powered Lagonda, as yellow as gold, and they were off to the Channel ferry.

Wallis was delighted—and surprised, for Ernest was modest—to find that he knew the Continent well and spoke fluent French. The honeymoon over, they settled down in London. She loved her husband deeply and truly, and not only for the security that promised to be hers at last.

The Simpsons' first address was Ernest's service flat, on St. James's Street. Here they stayed briefly before taking a year's lease on a furnished house at 12 Upper Berkeley Street, while they looked for something permanent. Just as the lease was running out, Wallis had to return to Washington, where her mother had developed cancer of the eye. The pair of silver peacocks which she had always kept on her sideboard, despite her superstition, she had recently removed and buried in the backyard, in a desperate, last-minute attempt to insulate herself from their malignity. It was too late. "Naughty Alice," as the family affectionately spoke of her, died on November 4, 1929.

After the funeral, one of Wallis's cousins suggested that she take her grieving stepfather for a walk. Wallis had never liked Charles Allen. "Can't," she said. "I'm fresh out of leashes."

Allen presently made another marriage, and again it was cut short by his wife's early death. When Bessie Merryman learned that he had thriftily interred Number 2 on top of Number 1, she was outraged; and when Allen's own turn came, in 1931, the earth on his grave was still raw when Bessie had sister Alice exhumed and reinterred elsewhere, in decent privacy.

Early in the winter of 1929–30, the Simpsons finally found what they were looking for, at Bryanston Court, a new apartment building on George Street, not far from Marble Arch. Few romantics make pilgrimages there anymore, but when they do, the West Indian hall porter is proud to escort them up to the next floor and show them the glass door to Number 5, iron-grilled, that had opened so often to the lonely, footloose Prince of Wales and later to the impatient King Edward VIII. The Simpsons' flat comprised a large drawing room, a dining room that seated ten, three bedrooms and baths, a kitchen, and four servants' rooms. The staff consisted of a cook, a chauffeur, a housemaid, a parlor maid, and a part-time maid. There was no shortage of money; the Simpson, Spence & Young ship brokerage was weathering the depression better than most businesses.

Wallis was slow to like London; she found it too standoffish. She missed the free and easy American ways, the telephoned invitations to "come on over," that she was used to at home. She wanted to be on a party list, not a waiting list. Ernest was at his office during the day, leaving her with little to do but work on her budget and read. As yet her only friend in town was her sister-in-law, Maud Kerr-Smiley, whose husband, Peter, was a well-to-do brewer. But the loneliness was only temporary. In 1925, Corinne Mustin had married again, another Navy officer: Lt. Comdr., later Admiral, George D. Murray. Now, in 1930, he was appointed Assistant Naval Attaché at the London Embassy, and his arrival with Rinny meant companionship for Wallis all through his three-year tour of duty. Meanwhile, Wallis found herself devoting more and more of her leisure to decorating her flat. For the first time, she had the means to gratify her maturing good taste and a setting in which to show it. She chose pale-green walls and cream damask curtains for the drawing room; and for the dining room, a glass-topped table, white leather chairs, and white wallpaper with rust-colored figures. The glass-topped table was originally mirror-topped; Wallis said she replaced the mirrors when she "became tired of looking up the noses of the British aristocracy." A friend remembers that "the colors were subdued but cheerful. The flowers were always superb; there was usually a brilliant arrangement on the grand piano. Neither of the Simpsons played, but they often had a guest who did."

There were bookcases in the drawing room, and a number of small tables for bric-a-brac, including Wallis's souvenirs of China: lacquer and porcelain boxes, scraps of brocade, two porcelain fishes, and her collection of "lucky" elephants in ivory, porcelain, and jade. A fine Chinese screen stood in the foyer. For other furniture, she and Ernest combed the antique shops of Chelsea and Kensington, and brought home piece after excellent piece.

Cecil Beaton—a distant, roundabout connection of Ernest Simpson's, in that Beaton's sister's husband, Sir Hugh Smiley, was a nephew of Maud Kerr-Smiley's husband—passed his cold professional judgment on flat Number 5: "Like a thousand other apartments, this one displayed impeccable taste and no originality." Lady Colefax, another professional, would brand "the whole setting" as "slightly second-rate"; and "Chips" Channon, an amateur, would call it "a dreadful, banal flat"; but these were the opinions of critics. Most of the Simpsons' friends expressed theirs in synonyms for "delightful," which they meant so sincerely that a coterie began to gather there regularly, drawn partly by the delicious food and abundant drink, and partly by the chatelaine's unfailingly blithe spirits.

Henry "Chips" Channon II (1897–1958) was more than an amateur decorator; he was a bellwether of *le tout Londres*, recognized and accepted. He was also more than this, though his real distinction did not appear until eight

years after his death. Born in Chicago, the only son of a
businessman whom he did not hesitate to describe as "dull,
charmless, uneducated," young Chips (so nicknamed because he is said to have once had a friend named Fish)
went to France in 1917 with the American Red Cross, and
later became—briefly—an honorary attaché to the U.S.
Embassy in Paris. The war over, he returned to Chicago,
en route spending a few days in London. It was love at first
sight, on Chips's part. Presently he was the most passionate
American anglophile since Henry James. England, he
rhapsodized, was a "land of freedom, where women are all
sincere and men are all gods!" On the other hand, "The
more I know of American civilization, the more I despise
it. . . . Ugh!"[3]

The "uneducated" father had somehow managed to
amass wealth enough to let his son return to England and
enter Christ Church, Oxford, where he formed a lifelong
friendship with Prince Paul of Serbia, the first showpiece in
Chips's eventually enormous collection of royalty. He now
wrote three books—a negligible novel, *Joan Kennedy*
(1929); an entertaining series of Chicago sketches, *Paradise City* (1930); and the authoritative and highly read-
able *The Ludwigs of Bavaria* (1933). With his marriage
that year to Lady Honor Guinness, daughter of the Earl of
Iveagh, he jumped several rungs up the social ladder and
became able to exercise to the fullest his extraordinary talent for giving parties. One of his secrets was to " 'lace' the
cocktails with Benzedrine, which I find always makes a
party go." On the evening of November 25, 1950, two
queens, Victoria of Spain and Helen of Romania, came to
a Channon dinner; Frederika of Greece would have made
a third but for a mission to Germany. W. Somerset
Maugham told Chips, "This is the apogee of your career!"
Maugham was wrong. In 1935, Chips—by then long a
British citizen—had been elected to Parliament, as a Conservative; and in 1957, as a reward for his devoted (if minor) service, he was given a knighthood. *That* was the apogee: "*Sir* Henry!" . . . When he died, the following year,
Paradise must have seemed an anticlimax.

His obituarist in *The Times* wrote that no man in the
House of Commons was more popular, and Lady Diana

Cooper said of him, "Never was there a surer or more en-
livening friend."

One might have dismissed Chips Channon merely as a
snobbish butterfly, or a silver spoonful of whipped cream,
or America's reprisal for the English sparrow—until 1967,
but not after that. In 1967 were published his diaries for
1934 through 1953, and the author was revealed as an
alert, acute observer of the sociopolitical scene, and a
vivid, witty reporter. His cast of characters, nearly nine
hundred strong, includes royalties, of course, but also actors, painters, soldiers, publishers, and musicians, most of
them tagged with an illuminating *aperçu*. No student of the
period can afford to ignore what Chips has written.

The coterie at Bryanston Court (which Ernest Simpson
waggishly liked to call "the Bryanston Courterie") would
eventually include young Foreign Service officers from the
Spanish and Italian embassies (but not the German), and
even an ambassador; William C. Bullitt, later U.S. Ambassador to Russia and France, used to drop in whenever he
came to town. So did the Raymond Masseys and the Vincent Masseys, one brother already an accomplished actor,
the other a future Governor General of Canada
(1952–59).

Ernest's business associates and clients, especially the
Norwegians, were often there; and American friends passing through London—Herman and Katharine Rogers and
a dozen others; an occasional M.P. and journalist—for instance, John Gunther, the London correspondent of the
Chicago Daily News and soon to publish *Inside Europe;*
and an assortment of clever, attractive people from the upper middle class. One of the regular guests was Ernest's
closest friend, Bernard Rickatson-Hatt, editor-in-chief of
the British news service, Reuters. Their friendship had begun in the Guards and had remained steadfast. Rickatson-
Hatt had been the other "grenadier" on that fateful, fruitful
Christmas at Mary Raffray's, and he, too, had an American wife. Ernest and he sometimes read the Greek classics
aloud to each other after dinner, but he was far from don-
nish; indeed, his sharp wit and inexhaustible supply of
fresh political and social gossip quickly entrenched him in

the Courterie—and in Wallis's favor: They liked each other at once.

Wallis herself mixed and served the cocktails, using a coffee table and several small shakers. She could estimate the proportions by eye as accurately as a professional barman; when she had poured, the glass was brimful, and the shaker empty. She herself drank little, and only Scotch. With the drinks she served a variety of canapés, hot and cold, soft and crisp: little biscuits with cheese or sausage or bacon; and big green grapes, pitted, and stuffed with cottage cheese. As in China, everything looked as good as it tasted. If her guests were staying on for dinner, she would have spent the afternoon in the kitchen. Rickatson-Hatt said, "This was what distinguished Wallis. No English housewife of any means would ever have set foot in the kitchen to supervise the preparation of a meal. Wallis did," although she admitted that "I hate to get the smell of bacon in my hair." The basic cuisine that she had learned at her mother's table in Baltimore—it included a chocolate cake which has been described as "historic"—had been supplemented with strange and wonderful recipes picked up in Canton and Peking, and was now receiving its final polish from a Scottish cook trained by the chef of a great London hostess, Lady Curzon of Kedleston. The glass-topped dinner table was always lit by ivory-colored candles; more shone from sconces. On gala evenings, Wallis proudly brought out the pink porcelain dinner service she had inherited from her grandmother Warfield.

After dinner there was usually bridge or a crap game. When Mary Raffray visited Bryanston Court in 1936, she "complained" that "Wallis' parties have so much pep, no one ever wants to leave!" Another early regular was Maj. Martin F. Scanlon, U.S.A., Military Attaché for Air at the Embassy. "Mike" Scanlon did not like Wallis at first; he considered her too aggressive, too eager to be noticed. But she soon won him over, and he still remembers his happy evenings, with the wit sparkling and laughter bubbling. "We had *fun*," he says. Much of it came from Ernest. These gay little parties brought out his lighter side and allowed the winner of The Hill School poetry prize to exercise his modest talent for doggerel. A set of his verses titled

"A Christmas Lewis Carroll: Through the Champagne Glass" includes these lines:

> The Wallis and the Shipbroker
>   Were sitting down to dine;
> They wept like anything to see
>   Such quantities of wine. . . .
> "If ten stout guests with ten stout thirsts
>   Drank it for half the night,
> Do you suppose," the Wallis said,
>   "That they would feel all right?"
> "I doubt it," said the Shipbroker,
>   "But still, I hope they try 't."

An American woman who saw a lot of the Simpsons at Bryanston Court remembered this about Ernest: "Although I was then in my early twenties and totally unimportant, he was always charming and courteous to me. He and Wallis took me to my first Aldershot Tattoo, and I'll never forget how he made me feel a part of the rather chic company and a welcome part at that. He was gentle, yet in no way insipid or flabby. Whatever situation I saw him in, his tact was perfect. I have only the warmest memories of him—warm and delightful, because he was so amusing."

Not everyone who knew Ernest echoed these praises. Another woman described him as "made of cardboard." A third said, "He was very polite, very correct, but an absolute jackass." A man said, "As Wallis's affair with the Prince progressed, Simpson's chief worry was over losing the royal connection—the attitude of a boor, and a *feeble* boor." Another man: "He made no impact." Another woman: "He was good-looking but not in a manly way—more like a puppet."

Among the young Spanish diplomats were Javier Bermejillo, the Second Secretary (known as "Tiger," because of his "pouncing"), and Bernardo Rolland, the Counselor. Ernest celebrated them, too, in his "Christmas Lewis Carroll":

> Beware the Bermejill, sweet one,
>   The eyes that flash, the hands that pat,
> Beware the Javier bird, and shun
>   The dubious Diplomat.

And:

"Will you dance a little faster," said a lady to her beau,
"Mr. Rolland's just behind us, and he's treading on my toe.
He has a way with women, and he's really rather sweet.
He has made a great impression, but alas, it's on my feet."

Bermejillo identified the prime ingredient in the evenings' pleasure as Wallis's extraordinary ability to draw
everyone into the conversation. It took her only a moment
to make the most diffident stranger feel that he had suddenly become a fountain of wit and fascinating information. "She had the instinct of an editor," he said. "She
sensed what interested people." Her familiarity with the
world of affairs sprang from a mind ravenous for information, and fed daily by her assiduous reading of newspapers
and periodicals—a habit she had acquired during her long,
boring hours in the lonely little bedroom at Warrenton.

Ernest was no sportsman; he did not ride, fish, shoot, or
play golf or tennis. On weekends when he and Wallis
weren't "antiquing," he preferred to set out with her in
their car and explore the countryside. He was a well-in-
formed guide to England's cathedrals, historic towns, and
comfortable inns. Later, their tours extended to Scotland
and Ireland; and when business sent him to France and
Norway, he often took Wallis along. One summer he persuaded Aunt Bessie Merryman to join them for a motor
tour through Germany. Some Sundays they stayed in town
and took long walks, usually ending at Grosvenor House,
where they dined with Ernest's father, who was separated
from his wife. He was smaller than Ernest, bearded, and
excellent company. "Ernest was devoted to both of his parents," Wallis said, "so it was painful for him when both
were in London at the same time."

This stimulating new life made Wallis truly happy. Of
the years from 1928 through 1931, she was to say, "I
hoped they would go on forever!" So they might have, but
for a letter that arrived early in January 1932: an invitation to spend the weekend of the thirtieth with the Prince
of Wales at Fort Belvedere.

CHAPTER 4
The Young Prince

Let us pray for the preservation of the King's most excellent Majesty, and for the prosperous success of his entirely beloved son, Edward our Prince, that most angelic imp.

—Pathway Unto Prayer, NICHOLAS BACON

Unlike Wallis Warfield, Edward Albert Christian George Andrew Patrick David, the future King Edward VIII, had never known anything but the material security that goes with wealth and birth at the apex. He was named Edward for his paternal grandfather, soon to become King Edward VII, and for the six King Edwards who had preceded him; Albert (at his great-grandmother Queen Victoria's request) for his great-grandfather, Prince Albert; Christian for another great-grandfather, King Christian IX of Denmark; George Andrew Patrick David for the patron saints of, respectively, England, Scotland, Ireland, and Wales. Though Edward was the Prince's formal, official name—the name he signed—he was David to his family and intimate friends. Born as he was in the direct line of succession to the British throne, the course of his life was fixed from the first: straightaway, unhurried, unchanging, all but unchangeable—and, as he would come to think of it, stiflingly dull.

On the night of June 23, 1894, his grandfather, the Prince of Wales, who was giving a ball to celebrate Ascot Week, interrupted it to announce the birth of his first grandchild, a boy—a "tutsoms baby," Princess Alexandra hailed it. His great-grandmother Queen Victoria (whom he called "Gangan," and whom Kaiser Wilhelm II, her grandson, called "Duck") wrote to her daughter, the Empress Frederick of Germany, "It seems that it has never happened in this country that there shd. be 3 direct Heirs as well as the Sovereign alive!" His twelve godparents, nearly all of them royal, included Queen Victoria, the next Czar of Russia ("Cousin Nicky"), the King and Queen of Denmark, the King of Württemberg, and the Queen of the Hellenes. His childhood was spent in palaces and other great houses. Margot Asquith, the wife of the Prime Minister, remembers him at Sandringham, aged about nine: "Shy and nervous . . . this lovely little boy . . . modest, interested and charming . . . a little shy with his father."[1] Their discomfort in each other's presence had set in already. "Childhood failed to leave me with the happy memories it supplies for most," he once said. "I had few friends, little freedom. There was no Huckleberry Finn around to make a Tom Sawyer out of a stuffy and too timid English prince. Growing up for me was a prolonged misery." Tutors shepherded him through the Royal Naval College and into Magdalen, Oxford. Gibbon wrote in his autobiography, "I spent 14 months at Magdalen College; they proved to be the fourteen months the most idle and unprofitable of my whole life." Prince Edward could say the same. The president of Magdalen found a phrase for him: "Bookish he will never be." Fortunately, the fact that he was an indifferent scholar—Prince Charming, yes; Student Prince, no—as had been his father and grandfather, was of little consequence. Only his death or incapacity could keep him from eventual arrival at the exalted position that awaited him, all the nearer since his father's accession in 1910, and his own elevation to Prince of Wales. Money was never a problem, of course. His family's immense private fortune aside, he himself enjoyed as much as 100,000 pounds a year from the revenues of the Duchy of Cornwall that were his as heir apparent.

So, as the heaven-blessed youth entered his twenties, the broad, safe, sunlit avenue of his life seemed to run straight to the horizon. It did not: A violent detour, unmapped and unforeseen, lay close ahead. When the Great War broke out in 1914, Prince Edward was ending his second year at Oxford. He volunteered at once, took a commission in the Grenadier Guards, and spent most of the next four years in the field with the Allied armies. Not for him a "cushy billet" far behind the lines; he was under fire again and

again—once, and almost fatally, from a British gun firing
short. Another day, his chauffeur was killed. He even had
a go at sniping, and as his shot was immediately returned,
he may have struck his mark. He took as many risks as his
commanding officers allowed him, not because he was
seeking danger, but because he despaired of achieving full
stature as a soldier unless he accepted the same chances as
the men around him. His attitude was "How can I prove
my fitness to be King unless I can hold up my head among
my own generation?"

No one begrudged him his Military Cross, his Croix de
Guerre, and his other decorations and citations, though he
himself insisted that they had been awarded him not because he had earned them, but only because he was Prince
of Wales; and he would not have worn the ribbons if the
King had not ordered him to do so. A distinction that he
did not reject, but enjoyed frequently mentioning, came
when he set foot, in 1917, on the battlefield of Crécy, the
first Prince of Wales to do so since the Black Prince (also
an Edward) fought there in 1346. To his fellow soldiers
who saw him at the front—British, Canadians, Anzacs, In-
dians, and the rest—he was "good old Teddy" forever
after. To the seniors responsible for his safety, he was
"fearless—but a bloody nuisance!" H. G. Wells said of
him, "Nowadays the stuffing is out of princes."

The end of the war found Britian exhausted, its coffers
empty, its world trade shattered. In this emergency, the
Prime Minister, Lloyd George, had the imagination to perceive that among the most precious assets remaining was
the popularity of the Prince of Wales. Forthwith, accompanied by his cousin Lt. Lord Louis Mountbatten, R.N., as
aide, Prince Edward took to the road, lugging his sample
case of British products, and for more than a decade he
traveled the seven seas and to the far corners of the Empire. "Dickie" Mountbatten, born in 1900, was a second
cousin of the Prince's, both being great-grandsons of Queen
Victoria. Dickie's father was Prince Louis of Battenberg,
and his mother was Princess Victoria, the daughter of King
Edward VII's sister Princess Alice, who had married the
Grand Duke of Hesse-Darmstadt. Lloyd George persuaded
King George V early in the First World War that it would
be politic for the three branches of the royal family that

had German names and titles to anglicize them. Hence the King changed his family name from Coburg to Windsor; Queen Mary changed hers from Teck to Cambridge; and Prince Louis changed his to Mountbatten. In 1922, Dickie married the Hon. Edwina Ashley, daughter of Col. Wilfred Ashley, later Lord Mount Temple, and of Maud, daughter of Sir Ernest Cassel, Edward VII's friend and financial adviser.

These Empire tours of the Prince's went from one high spot to the next. In Buenos Aires, a choir of 50,000 boys and girls greeted him with "God Bless the Prince of Wales," to which they had laboriously memorized the English words. In Delhi, he made a speech in Hindustani which *he* had laboriously memorized. At Maseru in Basutoland (now Lesotho), when a sudden downpour forced postponement of the celebration that had been prepared, but broke a long and painful drought, the natives credited him with mighty supernatural powers. On St. Helena, he planted an olive tree near Napoleon's tomb. In Mandalay, a Noah's ark of painted-paper tigers, bulls, elephants, and peacocks, plus thirty-foot dragons and gigantic birds, danced for him through the lantern-lit night, to music from instruments some of which were so ponderous that it took three men to carry them. In Ballarat, Australia, he was presented with a pair of yellow silk pajamas to which every one of the local maidens had contributed a stitch. "He was bird happy in Australia," Dickie Mountbatten recalls. "They *murdered* him with kindness!" In Nigeria, the heralds greeted him with a fanfare on trumpets twelve feet long. In India, among big-game hunts, receptions, and ceremonies, he made a point of driving along the jam-packed streets of whatever city his itinerary took him to, whether friendly or hostile—in response to Mahatma Gandhi's program of *hartal*, a boycott of the Prince—his car moving slowly, slowly, through the crowds that pressed against it, to the despair of the security officers charged with protecting it. Mountbatten said that the Prince and he had greatly wished to meet Gandhi, but could not get the Viceroy's permission. In 1947, he reported this to Gandhi, who remarked, "If I had been face to face with our future Emperor or even our future Viceroy, who knows what might have come of it?"

No movie star or pop singer ever had such a welcome. A correspondent wrote of the "uncontrolled adulation which led his admirers to break through police barriers, to try to touch him—sometimes with a rolled newspaper, he complained, if he was out of hand's reach—and to pillage his clothing of removable objects, handkerchiefs or buttons, as souvenirs." Sometimes handclasp after handclasp swelled his right hand so painfully that he had to withhold it and offer his left. Wherever this "prince of princes" went—to India, the Argentine, South Africa, Japan—his smile, modesty, fearlessness, and boyish good looks won every heart, and orders and commissions blossomed in his footprints. No other member of the royal family ever did more to bolster British commerce and enhance the prestige of British manufacturers.

In the blur that would all too soon obliterate his original, special meaning, this dutiful and truly creative part of what he liked to call the "princing" side of the monarchical business was unjustly forgotten. He used to laugh and say that no hereditary king and few moguls of history could have tramped as many assembly lines as he did, or gone down into so many mines, or inspected so many shipyards, or toured so many farms. There was a time when from the top of his head he could have rattled off the annual gold output of the Rand, the storage capacity of the grain elevators in Winnipeg, the beef exports of Argentina, the tea trade of the Malay Peninsula, and the volume of insurance underwritten by Lloyds. "In my day," he used to say, "I have planted enough memorial trees across the world to fill a national forest, and laid enough cornerstones to construct a good-sized city."

The clothes he wore, and, more importantly, the way he wore them, his marvelous feeling for style, generated an unexpected benefit for British commerce from the imperial travels. His ever-changing wardrobe attracted almost as much attention as his face. The Prince's supreme and unintended artistic success was in selling clothes. He had only to appear in a Fair Isle pullover, or "co-respondent shoes" (i.e., black and white), or a shirt or tie of unusual color or pattern, for half the men who saw him to conclude that the same accessory would instantly make them, too, debonair and irresistible. The appropriate mills and factories in the

Midlands took on night shifts, and exports boomed. It is noteworthy that the popular crosshatched pattern that the English call Glenurquhart, the French call *Prince de Galles*. In addition to his salesmanship, wrote another correspondent, "through the impact of his personality, he helped keep the Empire still loyal to the Monarchy for a decade or so longer in a fast-changing world."

The war years had given him his first sip of independence, and he found it intoxicating. The travel years gave him an even headier draft. Reflecting on them, he remarked to an American friend, "The younger countries overseas taught me newer and freer ways. I became accustomed to being pretty much on my own, to running my own show." He also discovered that he had been drilled in the methods, the manners, and shibboleths of the nineteenth century for a life that had all but vanished in his youth. Mountbatten remembers that "David often got depressed on our tour and said he'd like to change places with me. He was moody—had fits of downright gloom. He made a fine appearance, and was attentive to what was required of him, but then one of his fits would come over him—they came like a flash!—and he'd shut himself in his cabin for days, alone, face drawn, eyes brooding. His staff couldn't go near him. I was the only one who dared intrude, to try to rouse him from his melancholy. He was basically a lonely person, lonely and sad."

At home, the staid ways of the Court had become more galling than ever, so he had begun to spend as little time as possible in Court circles and as much as possible at York House, in St. James's Palace. He had lived there as a child, happily; when his parents gave it to him in 1919, he returned there as a man, even more happily. He loved the old place; it was his town residence for the next seventeen years. The main room, on the ground floor, became his dining room; his sitting room, bedroom, and bath were on the floor above. Most of the furniture was Victorian, dark and heavy; but it could not oppress the Prince, now a carefree refugee from the stuffiness of Buckingham Palace to a bachelor's dream of a pied-à-terre: central, quiet, roomy, and fully staffed—as two other young bachelors were quick to realize. Dickie Mountbatten took over one of the other apartments; and when he married in 1922 and moved out, Prince George moved in.

"Buck House," as Buckingham Palace is flippantly known, has inspired little affection in its modern tenants. It is too magnificent, too stiff, too impractical—the kitchens are a quarter-mile from the table. Queen Victoria's Prince Albert once remarked plaintively, "Food always seems to taste so much better in small houses!" Prince Edward agreed in principle. The relative simplicity of York House, and its independence, were just what he needed. Lord Mountbatten has said, "David was always the progressive in the family. He used to read *The New Statesman*. He wanted to get down to the people. He didn't like the dressing up, the *tamashas,* the fussy ceremonials."

One such fussy ceremonial—one that mortified him deeply and rankled long and sorely—was his investiture as Prince of Wales, in 1911, when he had to appear before ten thousand people in a costume of "white satin breeches, white silk stockings, black shoes with gold buckles, and a purple velvet surcoat, edged with ermine, slashed with black fur, with an outer edging of embroidery in mixed dull and bright gold . . . [and] girt at the waist with a purple silk sash, which had cords fringed with purple and gold." The seventeen-year-old cadet asked himself bitterly, "What would my Navy friends say if they saw me in this preposterous rig?" Mountbatten continued, "He wanted to open the windows and let the frowst and fug blow out. One way he tried to show his independence was by dressing his footmen in the black 'traveling' livery instead of Buck House's formal scarlet, which he'd become tired of.—All well and good, but when the King and Queen made a surprise visit, there was panic while the footmen made a lightning change. Another way was when he, though Colonel of the Welsh Guards, began going out at night in a dinner jacket, despite the regimental custom that required Guards officers to wear tails and a white tie to dinner in a public restaurant and to the theatre." They were also expected to keep their cigarettes in a case, not in the original package; never to carry a parcel in public; and not to reverse when dancing.

King George saw the rebelliousness that was developing in his son's mind and called him onto the carpet for a jobation: "You have had a much freer life than *I* ever knew, but don't think this means that you can now act like other people! Never forget your position and who you are!"

The King had almost certainly received confidential reports that the Prince's behavior—especially during his tours—had not been invariably unexceptionable. For one thing, he had begun to drink—seldom to excess, and not enough to alarm his associates, but he had been almost a teetotaler until Oxford. An American officer who was in Chile during both the royal visits, 1925 and 1931, remembers that "H.R.H. was not popular with the Chileans. Talking to people, he hung his head, mumbled, tugged at his cuffs, or toyed with his necktie or his fly. He smoked cigarettes incessantly, with nervous little gasps. He was boredom personified—restless, impatient to be away. Some of his appointments he broke without warning; others he was late for, without excuse or apology." This chronic tardiness was something else he had in common with Ernest Simpson, whose friends remember it as his only social flaw.

Anthony Weldon wrote of King James I that his fingers were "ever . . . fiddling about his codpiece," and the tendency, dormant for ten generations, may have reawakened in Prince Edward. He had been "fidgety" and "jumpy"—his parents' words—since early childhood. He was just two years old when his mother reported to his father that "David was 'jumpy' yesterday morning, however he got quieter after being out, what a curious child he is." Similarly, he could have inherited his unpunctuality from either or both of his grandmothers. His mother's mother, the Duchess of Teck, thought nothing of returning home two hours late for dinner, and then retiring to her room to change at leisure before coming to the table; Queen Mary is said to have read all three volumes of Motley's *Dutch Republic* while waiting for her mother before meals. As for Queen Alexandra, it was useless for King Edward to remind her of Louis XIV's dictum, "Punctuality is the politeness of kings"; she continued to torment him with her incorrigible tardiness. It reached its climax on the day of their coronation; he paced his room in rising dudgeon until finally he shouted at her door, "My dear Alix, if you don't come *at once,* you won't be crowned Queen!"

* * *

Deep as was the impress that King George's exhortation, "Never forget who you are!" made upon his eldest son, it would have been deeper if the son had appreciated its overtones. Without question the King was indirectly branding not only his unpunctuality, his restlessness, and his obvious public boredom, but also a fault which gave the Royal Family more serious concern: his open and continuing liaison with a married woman.

By 1911, when the Prince was only seventeen, German journalists had already chosen a wife for him: his second cousin, H.R.H. Viktoria Luise, Princess of Prussia, Emperor Wilhelm II's only daughter, aged nineteen. When she came to write her autobiography, she remembered that "David . . . was very nice, but looked so terribly young, younger than he actually was; he always looked youthful." Sir Max Beerbohm wrote in *King George the Fourth*, "Royalties, not being ever brought into contact with the realities of life, remain young far longer than other people." Two years later the Princess married another cousin, Ernest Augustus Prince of Hanover, by whom she had a daughter, Friederike. The autobiography goes on to relate an extraordinary incident that occurred after their visit to England in 1934: "We received a demand from Hitler, conveyed to us by von Ribbentrop . . . that we should arrange a marriage between Friederike and the Prince of Wales. My husband and I were shattered. . . . We told Hitler that . . . the great difference in age . . . alone precluded such a project and that we were not prepared to put any such pressure on our daughter."[2] In 1938, Friederike, or Fredericka, married Crown Prince Paul of Greece, later King of the Hellenes.

The first girl whom the Prince of Wales chose for himself was Lady Rosemary Leveson-Gower, daughter of the Duke of Sutherland, but this was no more than a flirtation, youthful and fleeting. It was not until the last year of the Great War that he really fell in love.

The young lady was Winifred May Dudley Ward, the daughter of an English father, Col. Charles Birkin of Nottinghamshire, a well-to-do manufacturer of lace, and an American mother, Claire Howe of New York. In 1913, "Freda" Birkin had married the Rt. Hon. William Dudley

Ward, M.P. (Liberal) for Southampton and Vice-Chamberlain of the Royal Household. He is remembered today as "charming, but quite vague." His two jobs usually kept him out until late, and his pretty young wife was often left to amuse herself. The circumstances that brought her into the Prince's life make for an odd story—one that she tells nowadays almost wistfully. The instrument which Providence chose for effecting the introduction was a certain "Buster" Dominguez. Freda remembers nothing else about him: neither his age, nor occupation, nor nationality, though she thinks he may have been a young diplomat at some Latin American embassy, and that she met him at a dinner party. The year was 1918—that much is definite—and it was either late February or early March. The evening was warm for the season, so Dominguez offered to walk her home. They were crossing Belgrave Square when the maroons went off, signaling a Zeppelin raid. He drew her to a lighted doorway nearby, Number 31, where a butler was standing. Dominguez asked him, "May we wait under your portico until it ends?"

Just then, a torrent of laughing young people in evening dress and uniform poured down the staircase, led by the hostess. She saw the couple and went toward them. The butler explained, "They wish to stand here during the raid, madam."

She looked them over and was reassured. "Come along to the basement," she said.

They followed her down, and there in the semigloom a young man attached himself to Freda and began chatting. He was still at it half an hour later when the "all clear" sounded, and she told him, "I must go now."

"Nonsense!" he objected. "You *can't* go! The ball is starting again."

The hostess took Freda's arm. "Yes, *do* come upstairs. His Royal Highness is so anxious for you to do so. I am Mrs. Kerr-Smiley," she added.

His Royal Highness was the Prince of Wales, home on leave from France. Mrs. Kerr-Smiley was Ernest Simpson's sister, Maud. The cherub, or imp, in charge of coincidences must have nearly strangled with laughter when he brought off this one—arranging for the Prince to meet his first true love under the roof of the family which before long would supply his last true love. He danced with Freda—her alone—until the music stopped, around three o'clock. Buster Dominguez had served his purpose and was long gone, never to reappear—Freda said with her rippling little giggle, "That was the end of Buster!" The Prince took Freda home, to Lowndes Square. He begged to come in "just for a minute," but she told him, "No, I'm staying with my mother-in-law. Good night. Thank you."

It made no difference. He was already smitten. Before going to bed, he announced to his diary that he had just met the world's most beautiful and most marvelous creature, and he spiked down the statement with ten exclamation marks. From that evening on, for sixteen years, he loved Freda "madly"—in Frances Donaldson's words and italics—"passionately, *abjectly*"[3] (though not exclusively; only time and Wallis Simpson would put an end to his philandering).

Soon after breakfast next morning, a messenger brought a note addressed to "Mrs. Dudley Ward." Since it was on Palace stationery, the mother-in-law, Mrs. Dudley Ward senior, assumed it was meant for her and opened it. The writer asked if he might come to tea, and said he'd be there at five o'clock unless warned off. The signature, "Edward P.," flabbergasted her. Why on earth should the Prince of Wales invite himself to her house for tea? The only possible explanation was that something of dizzying importance and secrecy was in the air. She told Freda that she was having a private interview that afternoon and asked her to be away from home at teatime. Freda had no trouble guessing what had happened, but didn't dare speak out. Nearly sixty years later, she still enjoyed speculating on the Prince's bewilderment when he was greeted by "Mrs. Dudley Ward." Freda ended, giggling, "He and I had a few days of Boxing-and-Coxing around before it was sorted out. The whole thing was *fraught*!"

It remained "fraught"—with laughter, excitement, love. They made a well-matched couple: both of them small and trim and young and a delight to look at, and both of them in love with life and with each other. Shane Leslie's quick sketch of the Freda of those days was "an angelic waif," and Lady Diana Cooper described her as "a dream of beauty with marvelous eyes," only to have a mutual friend protest, "It was much more than her beauty and her charm and her lovely voice. She had—*has*—pride, integrity, dignity." (Her voice is still lovely, though Chips Channon described it as "squeaky.") Lord Mountbatten said, "To me, Freda's greatest charm was always her coziness and warmth"; after a moment he added, "Whatever else Wallis was, she was never cozy."

When the Prince returned to France, he wrote to Freda steadily—"rather schoolboyish letters." When he was back in London on leave, he telephoned every morning and, after she moved into a house of her own, he came to see her every afternoon at five. They played golf and dined and danced. When he went out of town, he left his cairn terriers, Cora and Johnny, at her house, for her to take care of—a responsibility she welcomed not at all. Cairns were his favorite breed for years, until they were supplanted by pugs; early in his association with Wallis, his gift to her of a young cairn, Slipper, struck the Bryanston Courterie as specially significant.

Presently Freda's two daughters, Penelope and Angela, had adopted him as an honorary uncle and were calling him "Little Prince." Sometimes he would stay on for dinner. If he happened to have an official engagement, he would leave to keep it and would return afterward, to take Freda out to a private party or, more often, to a nightclub. For as of Armistice Day, something new was afoot in England; a quest for pleasure as for the Grail, a determined quest, but wild, feverish, headlong.

The end of the Great War brought a lifting of the darkness and an abatement of the cold that had stifled and numbed English spirits for the past four years. They were the worst years the English had ever known. Years of dreading to answer the door for fear of being handed a War Office telegram announcing the death of a husband, father, brother, son. Years of hesitating to open the daily newspaper, with its long and ever longer casualty lists. Years of anxiety about poison gas, the "flu," invasion, Zeppelin raids—"It passed *right over* our house!" Years of feeding hope with myths: the angel of Mons, "Kitchener still lives!," the Russian battalions in transit through England—"My neighbor has a cousin who *saw* them! He *saw* the snow on their boots!" Years of having to learn strange new words: blighty, ack-ack, *Boche* and *poilu,* dugout, U-boat, Anzac; and strange new phrases: over the top, gone west, no-man's-land, *spurlos versenkt.* Years that brought unknown people to the front pages: Edith Cavell, Lawrence of Arabia, Pershing, Von Richthofen, Mata Hari; and unknown places: Passchendaele, the Somme, Przemysl, Jutland, Ypres ("Wipers"), Kut-el-Amara, Verdun.

Those terrible four years consumed too much of the Empire's youth and too many of the older men who were needed to put things right in peacetime. But now it was all over, the immediate fear and pain and worry, even most of the petty discomforts and inconveniences. The searchlight batteries vanished from the parks. The streetlights came on. Butter and sugar were back on the grocers' shelves. Khaki and navy blue faded from the restaurants and clubs. The *honk-honk!* of the taxi replaced the *clang-clang!* of the ambulance. To be sure, some eyes still filled with tears at the first five notes of "There's a Long, Long Trail," but otherwise almost everything was soon just as it had been in the sunny summer of 1914—everything but the unslakable grief for loved ones lost or maimed, and the gooseflesh memories of the moment when a deathblow missed by a hairsbreadth, and the necessity for picking up a thread to follow out of the ugly, overwhelming past into the calm, golden future. Some never found a thread at all; some chose one tagged "work"; some chose religion; some chose travel or hobbies; some chose play, with jazz music to drown out the clamorous memories, and iced champagne to cool the burning sorrow. These last, the merrymakers, whose cry was "On with the dance!" (and away with all restraints), included the Prince of Wales and Freda Dudley Ward. The Prince, wrote James Pope-Hennessy, swiftly came "to personify for millions the longings and aims of the new post-war generation, with its driving wish for freedom from tradition and convention, whatever the cost. This was, to say the least of it, an unusual role for any member of the British Royal Family."[4] Malcolm Muggeridge added, "It was the generation who, youthful, were required to be mature, and in maturity persisted in being youthful."

The Duke of Windsor looked back on the parties in

those first post-war years and said, "Two of them still
stand out in my memory: the Wimbornes', for their beautiful ballroom lit by candles; and the Derbys', for their
champagne. One's taste certified that it was a marvelous
vintage, but there was no other way to tell—Lord Derby
had had the labels washed off and the bottles polished.
Chic, I always thought."

Freda Dudley Ward said, "There were parties every
night, in Mayfair or Chelsea or somewhere else"—she
went to one costume party as a little girl, and the Prince as
a member of the Ku Klux Klan—"and if we didn't feel like
a private party, we went to a nightclub." The smartest
were the Embassy, Ciro's, Quaglino's ("Quag's"), and the
Kit Kat. During the season, almost every Thursday evening found the Prince and Freda at one or another, usually
the Embassy, "the Buckingham Palace of nightclubs,"
which stood at the Piccadilly end of Bond Street. Its proprietor was the famous Luigi; its maître d'hôtel, the
equally famous Poulsen (who later opened the rival Café
de Paris); and the leader of its band was Ambrose. Few of
its regular clientele, which included not only the Prince of
Wales but also the King of Spain and Winston Churchill,
recognized or cared to remember that its decor had been
copied from the Palm Court of the *Lusitania;* and certainly
none was aware that one of its dance hostesses, Miss
"Queenie" Thompson, was soon to be better known as
Merle Oberon.

The Kit Kat featured the singing and piano-playing of a
Negro team, Layton and Johnson. The Prince and his
party often picked them up, when the club closed for the
night, and took them back to York House for an hour or
so of private entertainment—the first blacks ever to be so
honored. Another black, a West Indian named Leslie
Hutchinson, who entertained at the Café de Paris, was also
a favorite. "Hutch" played his two signature songs, "Where
the Lazy Daisies Grow" and "These Foolish Things," at
York House so often that a sharp ear could probably hear
them seeping from the walls today. The "in" spot for final
nightcaps was the Cavendish Hotel, in Jermyn Street,
where the ribald proprietress, Rosa Lewis, would interrupt
her outrageous stories only long enough to slop more
champagne from a "cherry-bum" (her idiom for "jero-

boam") into everyone's gorbellied goblets, and then babble on: ". . . Take 'is gran'father now, the Earl. 'The Wormy Bird,' *I* call 'im! An' the old Countess: *barkin'* mad! Thought nothin' of goin' to the Palace wearin' 'er false teeth for a brooch. . . ."

Freda and the Prince saw the same people over and over again: Sheila Chisholm, the Colin Buists, Poppy Baring, the Eric Dudleys, Hugh Sefton, Esmond Harmsworth (the future Viscount Rothermere and chairman of the *Daily Mail*), Ali Mackintosh, Edwina d'Erlanger, "Porchy" Porchester (the future Earl of Carnarvon), Perry and Kitty Brownlow. . . . An outsider summed them up thus: "All the girls had slim, lovely legs. All the men were rich, and some were flashy. They were golf- and bridge-players, party-givers and party-goers." Miss Chisholm, an Australian, became Lady Loughborough, then Lady Milbanke, then Princess Dmitri. Freda said of her, "She had auburn hair and a lovely figure—the most beautiful girl I've ever seen." Buist had been at the Royal Naval College with both the elder princes and later served as extra equerry to King George VI, 1937–52, and to Queen Elizabeth II, beginning in 1952. Miss Baring, in whom Prince George was much interested at one time, became Mrs. Peter Thursby. Dudley, the third earl (1894–1969), was Wales's oldest and closest friend; for long years they telephoned each other at least once a day. Dudley's early attachment to Freda having come to nothing (her husband, Dudley Ward, was his kinsman), he married first, in 1919, Lady Rosemary Leveson-Gower (once the Prince's puppy love), who was killed in an air crash in 1930; second, in 1943, Laura, the former Viscountess Long—they were divorced in 1954; and third, in 1961, Grace Marie Kolin, a Yugoslav, whose first husband had been Prince Stanislas Radziwill, later to marry and divorce Jacqueline Kennedy Onassis's sister, Lee Bouvier, who had previously married and divorced Michael Canfield, who then married Laura Lady Dudley. Grace Lady Dudley would become a close friend of the Duchess of Windsor's and would help sustain her through the Duke's obsequies.

Freda said, "Everyone knew everyone else—everyone but H.R.H. He'd gone straight from the nursery to the Royal Naval College and from there to the war [after

Magdalen], so he was entering the London world almost as a foreigner. He was innocent at first, but after he got to York House, he learned fast. He bloomed late and he never quite came to full bloom. He stayed a little naïve, a little childish to the end.

"All this running about worried the King, especially because it was with another man's wife—me. He was convinced that David had inherited old King Edward's randy streak, and he was trying to curb it. No use. His strictness only chafed David and led to rows. He became more bitter—David, I mean—and more despondent as time passed, and the rows became hotter. He was a grown man now and he resented his father's *ordering* him to button his jacket and straighten his tie."

Alden Hatch has written in *The Mountbattens*, "A palace official heard [George V] giving his son a dressing down. In his best storm at sea voice, the old King roared, 'You dress like a cad. You act like a cad. You *are* a cad. Get out!' " [5] And Hector Bolitho has written in *A Century of British Monarchy*, "It is said that [in the fall of 1926], on the way back to Britain from South America, [the Prince] dreaded the discipline awaiting him so much that he sent a letter ahead to the King, saying that he had decided to renounce his rights and settle in one of the Dominions unless he were allowed his own way." [6] Yet Queen Mary's lady-in-waiting, Mabell Countess of Airlie, has written in *Thatched With Gold*, "As the heir to the throne grew older the stream of paternal criticism increased but the Prince's behaviour when his father hauled him over the coals for being 'the worst dressed man in London,' and laid traps for him with orders and decorations, showed the utmost forbearance." [7]

Freda Dudley Ward remembers that "at times his parents humiliated him to the point where he actually burst into tears. I tried to put some stuffing into him. After one really angry row with his father, he came to my house and flung himself into a chair and shouted, 'I'm fed up! I've taken all I can stand!'

"I told him, 'You don't *have* to take any more! Stand up for yourself!'

"He went on, 'I want no more of this princing! I want to be an ordinary person. I *must* have a life of my own!'

"I said, 'Ah, that's different! You *can't* be an ordinary person. You were born to be king. It's there waiting for you, and you can't escape it.'

"Again and again I heard him grumble, 'What does it take to be a good king? You must be a figurehead, a wooden man! Do nothing to upset the Prime Minister or the Court or the Archbishop of Canterbury! Show yourself to the people! Mind your manners! Go to church! What modern man wants *that* sort of life?'

"David loved his mother more than his father, but he was terrified of them both. All the boys were. They used to drop in at my house and tell me their troubles. George remained my friend to the last." The fourth son of King George V and Queen Mary, Prince George Edward Alexander Edmund was born at Sandringham in 1902 and was created Duke of Kent in 1934. Gifted, wild and charming, handsome, with wavy brown hair and bright-blue eyes, Kent, slightly the tallest and stockiest of the brothers, was Wales's favorite among them. Freda continued, "He was shallow and frivolous but a nice man. He called on me the day before he left for Prestwick [and the R.A.F. mission on which he was killed, in 1942]. The boys used to tell me a lot about what went on in the family. I'll never forget a story about Harry—"

The third son, Prince Henry William Frederick Albert, was born at Sandringham in 1900. He attended Eton, the Royal Military College and Trinity College, Cambridge, hoping to make the Army his career; when circumstances prevented, he was lastingly disappointed. His family and close friends knew him as "Harry"; certain others referred to him privately as "Potty" and, after his elevation to the dukedom of Gloucester in 1928, as "Glossipop." He was often described as "Hanoverian"—i.e., stodgy and slow of mind—but he was kind and courteous, and was well liked, though not by Wales. Lilli Palmer has told how Webster once asked her:

"Do you know my brother Gloucester?"
"No, sir, I've never had the pleasure."
"Pleasure!" he said, rolling his eyes heavenward.
"Did you know my brother Kent?" . . .

"Unfortunately not." . . .

"Pity," he said. "He was a fine chap." [8]

"—This was about a year after the war," Freda went on, "so Harry would have been about nineteen. Anyhow, he crept out of the Palace one night with his dancing shoes in his hand and crept back again around five in the morning. A courtier saw him, and Harry knew he'd be reported to the King. It was a rule—an absolutely *unbreakable* rule!— that the boys came down to breakfast at five to nine and stood around until their father came down exactly as Big Ben began striking the hour. Then they all sat. Well, this particular morning, Harry was a few minutes late. When he came in, his father just *looked* at him—and Harry *fainted*! Imagine it: at *nineteen years old*! The strange part is that instead of being sympathetic, the other boys were delighted!"

A courtier commented on this incident, "I can well believe it. The brothers were all jealous of one another. The only time they were happy was when one got in trouble with their father. He considered them dolts, the lot of them, until Bertie married [Prince Albert, later Duke of York, and King George VI]. After that Bertie was his favorite. He could do no wrong in his father's eyes."

Freda continued, "David never wanted to dine with his parents. He never wanted to tell them where he was going or what he was going to do, which didn't ease things. They knew about us, him and me. I learned from friends of mine at Court that the King referred to me only as 'the lacemaker's daughter,' so they started calling me Miss Loom, after the weaver's daughter in *Happy Families*. I never met either the King or the Queen. They regarded me as a scarlet woman. They were always after David to leave me and marry within his rank—some princess or other. Nothing below a princess was considered suitable for a prince to marry until Elizabeth Bowes-Lyon came along. I hardly had the Archbishop of Canterbury's blessing, either. Not that I expected it, but neither did I expect him to write me poison-pen letters, which he did. Imagine it: the *Archbishop of Canterbury*!" Her laugh bubbled up.

"Heavens, it wasn't as if I were *trying* to marry David!

Or even wanted to. He asked me often enough, ardently, too. But just as often, I said, 'No!' The whole idea was ridiculous. I was already married, of course, so there'd have to be a divorce, and his parents and friends and the Church would never have allowed it. I kept telling him, 'I'm not going to let you do such a stupid thing!' and finally I persuaded him. He was very suggestible. Someone said of him, 'He reset his watch by every clock he passed.' It was true.

"Many people have pointed out that David was three different men, in personality as well as rank: the Prince of Wales was one man, the King of England another, the Duke of Windsor a third, and no two of them alike. I knew him only as Prince of Wales, and what he was then was certainly nothing like what I heard he became. He was the kindest, gentlest, most thoughtful man you can picture! My daughters adored 'Little Prince.' He never forgot their birthdays. He and I never had a row, never exchanged ugly words. And *generous?* Whenever I asked for anything, he gave it to me immediately. He couldn't do enough for me. Once, I remember, I asked him to rescue a friend of mine who had gone head over heels in debt to bookmakers. It wasn't a matter of a few pounds, but of several thousand. David wrote out a check without a question or a murmur. All he ever said was—and he *always* said it when I asked a favor—'You know I aim to please.'

"He had his faults. Who hasn't? The worst of them was moral cowardice—he was weak—but I knew nothing about that until our sixteen years together came to an end. It was abrupt, all right, but I can't say it was a surprise. He had always strayed a bit. There were other girls, quite a few, but it never made any difference to me. Our friendship remained, and I loved him, even though I realized all the while that no good would come of it, that there was no future in it, and that when it ended, it would be to my disadvantage." A feature of the British Empire Exhibition at Wembley in 1924 was a statue of the Prince modeled in butter. The medium proved symbolic.

But during those sixteen years—at least as they began—there is no doubt that he loved Freda Dudley Ward exactly as Frances Donaldson describes: "madly, passionately, *abjectly.*" Lord Mountbatten relates how, in March 1920, he picked up the Prince at Freda's house, en route to the train for Portsmouth, whence the cruiser H.M.S. *Renown* would take them to New Zealand and Australia:

"He was then twenty-five and he'd just been given his fourth stripe, but he looked a baby and he was crying, blubbering, like one, because he was leaving Freda for six months. 'Dickie,' he said, 'did you ever see a post captain cry? No? Well, you'd better get used to it!' He cried all the way to Victoria Station.

"There was something religious, almost holy, about his love for her. She was the only woman he ever loved that way. She deserved it. She was sweet and good, a good influence on him. None of the others were. Wallis's influence was fatal."

CHAPTER 5
Mrs. Simpson Meets the Prince

One of the first girls whom the young Prince of Wales "strayed" towards, he met while fox hunting. He had ridden as a boy and had hunted a few times at Oxford, but after the war he became serious about horsy sports in every form. The famous Pytchley Hunt, in Northamptonshire, were his first hosts, in the 1920–21 season. Next he hunted with the equally famous Beaufort, in Gloucestershire. From there he went to Leicestershire, the home country of three other famous packs: the Quorn, the Cottesmore, and the Belvoir. A friend who often hunted with him said this:

"My most vivid recollection of H.R.H. in the hunting field dates back to an afternoon with the Quorn in February nineteen twenty-four. It was latish. Dusk was beginning to fall when the fox came to the Whissendine and slipped in and swam across, the hounds after him. The stream was more than twenty feet wide just there, with an oxer [a low fence with a single rail] guarding the near bank, and a drop of some six feet on the far side. The field—we were about two hundred strong—didn't like what they saw ahead, and wavered and held hard, myself included. The huntsman made as if to attempt the jump, but the Master, Algy Burnaby, signaled him not to. Just then H.R.H. pulled out of the crowd and dashed forward, on a handsome bay. They fairly soared over the fence and stream, landed in the muck on the other side, scrambled up to firm ground, and away they went, after the hounds. The rest of us had to ride two miles upstream to a cattle bridge and cross over, shamefaced. This was the only time in my whole hunting life that I ever saw anyone 'pound the field.' The story was in all the papers next morning, as it deserved to be.

"Yes, H.R.H. was a bold 'un, no argument! When he

came to a daunting obstacle, he threw his heart over—as the old expression goes—and jumped after it. His chief fault in the hunting field was poor judgment. If you keep putting tired horses at five-barred gates, sooner or later you'll come a cropper, no matter how good your hands and seat. That's what H.R.H. often did."

He did not do it to forestall someone's accusation of faintheartedness, but to forestall his own. John Jorrocks acclaimed fox hunting as "the sport of kings, the image of war without its guilt, and only five-and-twenty per cent of its danger." The danger was what attracted Wales. Just as in the Great War, he had to test himself, to prove his "fitness." For the same reason, he would take flying lessons; and once he had "proved himself" by soloing, he lost interest. His falls, both in hunting and in racing, were no more frequent or more severe than normal, but because he was the heir to the throne, they were widely publicized and he himself widely denounced for jeopardizing the succession. He did not retort, but privately he liked to declare that "There's nothing better for the inside of a man than the outside of a horse," and blithely he galloped on.

Then, soon after his feat at the Whissendine, his luck ran out. Riding in a point-to-point, he took a purler that left him unconscious for half an hour, gave him a concussion, put him in a dark room for a week, and kept him in bed for three weeks more. That tore it. First, Prime Minister Ramsay MacDonald wrote him ("Pray do not put me down as an interfering person, but—"), and then the King ("*I must ask you* to *give up* riding in the future steeple chases and point to point races—"); only the Archbishop of Canterbury held his pen. The Prince surrendered and hung up his racing silks for good. He was allowed to continue fox hunting and polo, though, and it was at a meet of the Belvoir Hunt that he met the lovely Audrey James.

Her father, "Willie" James, was an American industrialist who had a large estate, West Dene Park, in Sussex. Her English mother was a famous hostess whose populous and gala house parties, and her intimacy with King Edward VII, were the subject of much speculation.

A contemporary said of Audrey, "She had very blue eyes and a face like a violet. That's as far as the resemblance went, because under her aristocratic loveliness she

was a tough cookie. It showed in her voice, which she deliberately made harsh and rasping. She was brassy, too—
loved to make an entrance, have herself announced as 'Mahatma Gandhi's mother,' that sort of thing. I'm talking
about the first postwar season, nineteen-nineteen. Perry
Brownlow was one of her heaviest beaux [Peregrine Francis Adelbert Cust, sixth Baron Brownlow, 1899–1978;
lord-in-waiting to King Edward VIII, 1936; Lord Lieutenant of Lincolnshire, 1936–50; "Perry" Brownlow would escort Wallis Simpson when she fled to Cannes in December
1936], but then Dickie Mountbatten caught sight of her.
That was in November. He wasn't yet twenty, and Audrey
was a year or two younger—"

Their romance was gathering speed when the Prince invited Dickie to come along on the New Zealand-Australia
tour. They would go out via Panama, San Diego, and Ha-
waii, and return via Panama again and the West Indies.
Dickie accepted; it would be an experience he could not
afford to miss, even though it meant a seven months' separation. Home again in October, he and Audrey became informally engaged, and again the romance was interrupted:
The coal miners struck in April 1921, and Dickie, a Navy
officer, was plucked out of gunnery school and sent on
strike duty with the rest of the military. Only rarely could
he get leave to see Audrey, and Audrey soon made it clear
that she was not a girl to suffer neglect in silence, however
worthy the cause. Helpless, desperate, Dickie appealed to
his friend and cousin to intercede for him. The Prince
called on Audrey; they discussed the engagement and
agreed that it could never prosper—better to break it off at
once, which they did.

A year later, she married Maj. Dudley Coats, of a rich
cotton-spinning family. London wits said that she "preferred the arms of Coats to the coat of arms." Her marriage did not discourage her suitors, among them now the
Prince himself. A mutual friend said, "He had seen a lot of
her in the hunting field, and presently they were having a
merry little caper together—merry, but brief. If I had to
guess what cooled him off, I'd say that Audrey was too
possessive." Coats died in 1927. In 1930, she married another millionaire, Marshall Field III, of Chicago and Long

Island, and divorced him in 1934. Her third marriage, in 1938, was to Peter Pleydell-Bouverie; not long before she divorced him, too, in 1946, she impressed Evelyn Waugh as "a strained, nervous, cross-patch of a woman,"[1] but her friendship with Queen Elizabeth the Queen Mother remained warm and firm. In 1968, Audrey, of the "face like a violet," died.

The Prince's next "caper" was more serious and more lasting. Again it was with a married woman. Both Freda and Audrey were half American, but Thelma Morgan Furness was American on both sides. Born in Lucerne, one of the twin daughters of Harry Hays Morgan, a Foreign Service officer, Thelma eloped at sixteen with a black sheep twice her age and already once divorced; his second divorce soon followed. At twenty-one, she repeated the pattern by taking another husband twice her age: the widowed Marmaduke Viscount Furness (1883–1940), a coarse-grained, stocky man with red hair and the temper that is popularly believed to accompany it. His father's hair and beard were so flaming that he was known as "the Fiery Furness." "Duke" had inherited the Furness shipping lines, but devoted most of his attention to brandy and his special, foot-long cigars, and the rest of it to the pursuit of foxes and women—he liked to boast that Peggy Hopkins Joyce was among his "conquests." The mercenary and widely available Miss Joyce's struggles to escape so rich a peer must have resembled those of a boa constrictor in the toils of a rabbit.

Thelma's second marriage was also brief. She and Duke would not be divorced until 1933, but their bonds had slacked long before. When Bruce Lockhart recorded in his diary for September 12, 1931, "The Prince of Wales . . . has been going great guns with Lady Furness at Bayonne," he was two years late with the news.[2] Thelma's beauty had carried her into the Prince's set, and indeed into his arms, in the summer of 1929, when she was still only twenty-three. It could have carried her anywhere. Sir Cecil Beaton, a connoisseur of lovely, fashionable women, wrote that she and her twin sister, Gloria, "alike as two magnolias, with raven tresses, flowing dresses, slight lisps and foreign accents . . . diffuse an atmosphere of hot-house elegance and lacy femininity."

Some who knew both Thelma and Freda wondered if "elegance" was quite the right word; to these, the new love seemed slightly "tacky," slightly à côté, when compared with the old. Thelma was also less protective of Wales's reputation. A few weeks after Bruce Lockhart's first entry about her, he wrote a second: "Millie [Millicent Duchess of Sutherland] and Tommy [Vera Mary Countess of Rosslyn] both say that the Prince is more irresponsible than he was. They blame Lady Furness, who has a bad influence on him. Freda . . . could keep him under restraint. She could get him back tomorrow if she wanted to, but apparently she does not want." The end of their sixteen years together was approaching. When it arrived, it was not because of Thelma, but it was through her. Thelma would introduce the Prince of Wales and Wallis Simpson.

The members of the Royal Family are like so many planets revolving around the monarch sun. Each of them is highly visible, and though few are important or attractive in their own right, all are institutionally remote from ordinary earthlings. Moreover, each moves in an ordained orbit that was thought immutable until the Prince of Wales began breaking the laws of royal astronomy. Under an alien influence that has never been identified (but was probably the leveling of class distinctions brought on by the Great War), his orbit became less and less predictable, more and more erratic. He wandered into new quarters of the sky. Strange satellites clustered around him. Then a comet crossed his path, close by; and suddenly, almost before he was aware, it was dragging him helplessly after it, out of his own familiar solar system, and into far, cold emptiness. The cataclysm that followed, the disruption of the immense forces involved, and their readjustment were Velikovskyan in scope. But where Velikovsky's specialty is retrospection of the behavior of heavenly bodies, so two other specialists, no less renowned, used heavenly bodies to predict the behavior of Wallis Simpson and Edward Prince of Wales. The course of their lives was prophetically outlined, in dramatic detail, years in advance.

The Duchess of Windsor's autobiography relates that

when her divorce from Win Spencer was in progress, in the latter 1920's, the celebrated New York astrologer Evangeline Adams (1872–1932) told her that there would be two more marriages, plus "several serious emotional crises"; that she would have a "normal life-span"; and that "between the ages of forty and fifty," she would "exercise considerable power . . . this power will be related to a man."

At about the same time in London, the equally celebrated English astrologer Cheiro was writing this: "[The Prince of Wales's] chart shows influences . . . that . . . point to changes . . . greatly affecting the Throne of England. . . . [He] was born under peculiar astrological circumstances which make his character a difficult one to understand: . . . intense restlessness, a lack of continuity of thought, a difficulty of concentration, and an absorbing love for . . . travel, and a lack of . . . 'a sense of danger.' . . . [He] is determined not to 'settle down' until he feels a *grande passion* but, it is well within the range of possibility. . . that he will fall a victim of a devastating love affair. If he does, I predict that the Prince will give up everything, *even the chance of being crowned* [italics supplied] rather than lose the object of his affection."[3] Within nine years, it so befell.

At the time of Prince Edward's birth, a prediction no less astonishing had been made in the House of Commons by Keir Hardie, the founder of the Labour Party. He said it was impossible to foretell how the boy would turn out—this boy who would some day be called on to reign over the Empire; but "from his childhood onward this lord will be surrounded by sycophants and flatterers by the score and will be taught to believe himself as of a superior creation. A line will be drawn between him and the people he might be called upon some day to reign over. In due course following the precedent which has already been set he will be sent on a tour round the world and probably rumours of a morganatic marriage will follow; and the end of it will be that the country will be called upon to pay the bill." And a few years later, the Hon. Ralph Stanley predicted that Prince Edward either would not accede at all or, if he did, would abdicate soon afterward, in favor of the Duke of York.

* * *

Momentous as were the consequences of Mrs. Ernest Simpson's first meeting with the Prince of Wales—momentous not only for the principals, but for the whole British Empire—it is notable that each of the three persons most intimately concerned remembered it differently.

The third person was Viscountess Furness, the Prince's then current love. Thelma Furness sets the date somewhere between latter 1930 and early '31, and the scene at her London townhouse, 21 Grosvenor Square. Her eldest sister was Consuelo Morgan Thaw, whose husband, Benjamin Thaw, had been a friend of Wallis's from her Coronado days and was now in the London Embassy as First Secretary. "Connie" Thaw telephoned Thelma one morning to ask if she might bring some American friends for cocktails that afternoon. The friends proved to be the Simpsons. Here is the impression that Mrs. Simpson created on her hostess: "She did not have the chic she has since cultivated. She was not beautiful, in fact, she was not even pretty. But she had a distinct charm and a sharp sense of humor. Her dark hair was parted in the middle. Her eyes [were] alert and eloquent. . . . She was not as thin then as in later years . . . merely less angular. Her hands were large; they did not move gracefully, and I thought she used them too much when she attempted to emphasize a point."[4] Cecil Beaton also was seeing Wallis for the first time about now. He remembers that "she looked coarse. Her back was coarse, and her arms were heavy. Her voice had a high nasal twang. She was loud and brash, terribly so—and rowdy and raucous. Her squawks of laughter were like a parrot's."

As chance could have it, the Prince dropped in at the cocktail party. The other guests were presented to him, and Lady Furness makes this further comment: "Wallis Simpson was as nervous and as impressed as any woman would have been on first meeting the Prince of Wales."[5]

A King's Story, the Duke of Windsor's autobiography, dates it in early 1931, at a house party at Melton Mowbray, in Leicestershire, where he and Prince George had gone for a weekend's fox hunting. He remembers the weather as "damp and foggy," and Mrs. Simpson as suffering from a heavy cold. Her obvious wretchedness drew from him a conjecture that she must be missing the central heating which America possessed in such abundance. His recollection, refreshed for the purposes of composition by her clearer one, went like this:

A mocking light came into her eyes. "I am sorry, Sir," she said, "but you have disappointed me."

"In what way?"

"Every American woman who comes to your country is always asked that same question. I had hoped for something more original from the Prince of Wales."

I moved away . . . but the echoes of the passage lingered.[6]

The third account, the Duchess of Windsor's,[7] sets the date in 1930, but agrees that the scene was the same house party. However, she supplies a provocative detail which the Prince's delicacy had omitted: The party was held at Burrough Court, a hunting box belonging to the Furnesses, and Thelma Furness was the hostess. Again the Simpsons' invitation had come through Connie Thaw, who had suddenly found herself unable to chaperone the party and had begged Wallis to take her place. Wallis demurred, partly because of her cold; but Ernest finally persuaded her that the opportunity to meet the Prince was not to be lost. Her curtsey and the Prince's bow seem to have comprised their only exchange. She was too miserable to develop it: she was feverish. The headache returned, and her one desire was to go to bed and suffer in privacy. After dinner the Prince and Thelma joined the poker table, while Wallis played bridge. It was not until the following day, when Wallis found herself seated next to the Prince at luncheon, that their dialogue began.

Believers in *grandes passions* insist that when a magnetic woman meets a magnetic man, a field of irresistible force instantly envelops them. If any such phenomenon now occurred, the voltage was too feeble to register on the Prince. That Monday, when the Simpsons had left for London, one of the ladies in the party asked him what he thought of Wallis. He dismissed her with an airy wave and "Oh, she's just another ——— ———," naming a hard-bitten American girl to whom he had paid noticeable attention in New

York in 1924. Wallis, for her part, had no recollection of what she and the Prince had talked about. But she did recollect—and with painful clarity—that she was "petrified." Maud Kerr-Smiley had warned her always to let the Prince lead the conversation—"a restraint," which Wallis, by her own admission, was "ill-equipped to exercise" by habit and temperament.

The Prince's chatter may have made no impression; but his looks and manner did: "I remember thinking how much like his pictures he really was—the slightly windrumpled hair, the turned-up nose, and a strange, wistful, almost sad look about the eyes when his expression was in repose. . . . I decided that he was truly one of the most attractive personalities I had ever met." Dr. J. H. Plumb would call it "his foolish, harlequin charm." Freda Dudley Ward said, "Every woman who saw that sad little face felt she had just the shoulder for him to cry on."

His impact on Ernest was so overwhelming that it restimulated his pride in being English. Ernest teased Wallis that evening, "You Americans lost something when you dispensed with the British monarchy!" He little foresaw that it was a loss which she would to some extent recoup.

Despite the wealth of detail in the Duchess's account of the "first" meeting, she was not telling the truth. Punctured vanity long refused to let her admit that the actual first meeting had taken place ten years earlier, during Prince Edward's New Zealand-Australia tour with Dickie Mountbatten. On April 7, 1920, H.M.S. *Renown* put in to San Diego; and that afternoon the acting Commander in Chief of the U. S. Pacific Fleet, Vice Adm. Clarence Williams, U.S.N., gave a reception on his flagship, the battleship U.S.S. *New Mexico*, in the Prince's honor. Among the guests were Lt. Winfield Spencer, U.S.N., and his wife, Wallis. They were presented to Wales and Mountbatten, they shook hands, and the line moved on. Naturally, the American woman remembered; understandably, the Englishman forgot. There was a ball for the Prince that evening at the nearby Hotel del Coronado, and although the Spencers did not attend, legend insists that this was really the scene of the momentous meeting. The hotel itself encourages the legend with a "Prince of Wales Grill," featuring a portrait of the Duke and Duchess.

Years afterward, Wallis Windsor chided Mountbatten about the incident. He said, "She never got over our not noticing her. She told me, 'I was dressed to kill! I shook hands first with the Prince and then with you, and neither you nor David remembers it!' She couldn't seem to accept our not being able to remember her, but it's quite true. She had something, as events were to prove—something not immediately visible perhaps, but it was there, and we missed it."

In mid-January 1931, soon after the Burrough Court house party, the Empire's star salesman left for South America and was gone for nearly four months. No word came back to Wallis, not even a postcard. She had no reason to expect any. She knew, as did all London, that the young and beautiful Thelma Furness had been his *maîtresse en titre* for more than the past year.

To celebrate his return at the end of April, Thelma gave an afternoon reception. The Simpsons were invited. In the crush, the Prince seemed barely to notice them, but when he saw Wallis in June, at Court, his awareness was acute. She was one of several women, British and American, being presented to Their Majesties. From the Prince's post behind their thrones, he watched her advance in the queue of white gowns, nodding plumes, and gorgeous jewels. Wallis's were aquamarines: a band of them to hold her plumes, and an aquamarine cross on a thin gold necklace. The Prince was to remember her thus: "When her turn came to curtsey, first to my father and then to my mother, I was struck by the grace of her carriage and the natural dignity of her movements." Wallis's train, fan, and plumes had been lent her by Thelma, who had worn them at her own presentation, in 1927.

The popular belief is that divorce disqualifies a woman for presentation at Court—or did so in George V's reign. How, then, did Thelma and Wallis, both of them divorcees, manage to be presented? Did the Prince of Wales intervene for them? No, says the Lord Chamberlain's office: "Viscountess Furness submitted her divorce papers to the Lord Chamberlain, from which it was apparent that she was the innocent party. Likewise Mrs. Ernest Simpson was the innocent party." A former courtier comments, "Much weight was attached in those days to what the Law Courts considered the innocence of one party or the other in a divorce case, and anyone coming under that heading was eligible for presentation. No intervention would have been needed."

Immediately after the Court, Thelma was having a few friends in for drinks. Again she had invited the Simpsons, and again the Prince appeared. Thelma Furness was as smart-clever as she was smart-chic; it was most uncommon for her to make a tactical blunder. But in throwing the Prince and Wallis together for the third time, she served—in her own words—"as an unwitting catalytic agent in the historical events that followed."

Nothing showed yet on the surface of the relationship. Over a glass of champagne, the Prince complimented Wallis on her Court gown. That was all. Presently he took his leave. The Simpsons lingered briefly, then they, too, left—to find the Prince outside, standing by his car with Brig. Gen. Gerald F. Trotter, his groom-in-waiting, extra equerry, and Assistant Comptroller.

The Simpsons' surprise was succeeded by pleased astonishment when the Prince hurried forward and asked if he might give them a lift home. They were happy to accept. The ride took only a few minutes. Ernest invited them in for a nightcap, but the Prince declined: He had to be up early. He added, "I'd like to see your flat one day. I'm told it's charming. Good night!"

Though seven months would pass before he and Wallis met again, the fuse that had been lit at Burrough Court had now begun to burn briskly. Wallis still did not realize it, but much later she would write of that evening in June 1931, "That was how it all began."

CHAPTER 6
The Fort

Finders keepers!
—Old saw

Fort Belvedere, to which the Prince of Wales had invited the Simpsons for the weekend of January 30, 1932, stands on the edge of Windsor Great Park, six miles from the Castle and twenty-five from London. "The Fort," as it would be known, had laid its enchantment on him in boyhood. When his family moved to nearby Frogmore for the early summer, his tutor, Hansell, or his valet, Finch, would sometimes take the Royal children down to Virginia Water for a row on the quiet pond. Viewed from that distance, the Fort had the look of something lingering on from a forested past—the tallest tower floating above the trees like a mirage of Camelot. It had been built nearly two centuries before for George II's third son, William Duke of Cumberland, as a defense against a possible raid by "the Young Pretender," Charles Edward Stuart. Sir Jeffry Wyatville had adapted it for George IV, but it had fallen vacant again. Enlarged to fourteen rooms, rebuilt, and frequently altered, by 1932 it was a mock-Gothic hodgepodge of towers and battlements in beige-colored stone, shadowed by yews and beleaguered by weeds—a miniature castle, complete with even "cannon and cannon-balls and little furnishings of war," wrote Lady Diana Cooper. "The sentries . . . must be of tin. . . . The house is an enchanting folly and only needs fifty red soldiers stood between the battlements to make it into a Walt Disney coloured symphony toy."[1]

Lady Diana, a frequent guest at the Fort with her husband, Duff, was the daughter of the eighth Duke of Rutland, and as the most famous of contemporary English beauties, starred in Max Reinhardt's production of *The Miracle* in 1924–32. Duff Cooper was a hero of the Great War, and later a statesman whose many high offices included First Lord of the Admiralty, from which he resigned in disgust with Chamberlain's deal with Hitler at Munich.

The Prince's remembrance of a misty, distant beauty remained with him; and in his early manhood, after he had left his parents' roof, he was tempted more than once to return for a closer look, since here—he thought—might be an ideal country house, private, yet within easy reach of London. He did not go. At that period he was not disposed to settle anywhere for long. Moreover, the Fort was already occupied by a courtier, a close friend of the King's. It was a period, too, when the way of life at Windsor, mirroring the father's interests, had few attractions for the son. First fox hunting and steeplechasing, and afterward golf, had become his absorbing recreations; he was satisfying his need for lodgings in support of them with rented flats in the hunting country and with rented houses at either Sandwich or Sunningdale, two of England's finest links.

Then, in 1929, the Fort fell vacant, and the Prince decided to drive out and see what it was like inside. Sir John Aird, his equerry (and later King George VI's and Queen Elizabeth II's), went with him. This is Jack Aird's recollection of what they saw:

" 'An unstately ruin' is the only proper term for its condition. The dust was inches deep. Splintered floors, sagging doors. No more than two or three w.c.'s in the whole establishment. The servants' quarters would have disgraced a prison ship. But the Prince fell in love with it even before he crossed the threshold and he was blind to the rot within. His excitement mounted as he rushed from room to room, to peer through the grimy windows. He was then thirty-five years old. His only permanent residence was York House. It was a lovely place and useful for his work in town, but he had been longing for a home in the country, and York House could not satisfy that hunger, whereas the Fort well might. A vision of what could be made of it seized his imagination. One afternoon's look convinced him. 'This is what I've always wanted,' he said over and over. 'I *must* have it! I shall ask Papa for it the instant I return to London!'

"He did. The King demanded, 'Why do you want that queer old place? Those damn weekends, I suppose! Well, if you want it, it's yours.' "

From the day that it became his own, and for the seven years that he lived there, "Toyland," as one cannot help thinking of it, meant more to him than any other material possession. It was the focus of all his interest and the source of his innermost joy—not only because it represented a reprieve from the jail of the Court and the arid formality of the great royal residences, or because the very word "fort" suggested impregnability and therefore promised him—for the first time in his life—a measure of isolation (he would come to speak of it as "my get-away-from-people house"), but also because this ramshackle ruin so warmly invited a restoring hand.

For all his eagerness, he could not start renovations until the following summer, 1930. Ahead of everything else came the long, exhausting, official tour of Africa, from Capetown to Cairo. It would not begin until early in January and it would end late in April, but he needed two months to prepare for it and another two to rest from it. Thereafter, every hour he could spare from his duties, he devoted to repairing the "blemish'd fort," cleaning it and decorating it—with the professional help of the firm of Lehmann and the quiet good taste of Freda Dudley Ward, who had also helped him at York House. Indoors, his objectives were comfort and convenience, not chic. Even so, Lady Diana found a "pink bedroom, pink-sheeted, pink Venetian-blinded, pink-soaped, white telephoned and pink-and-white maided." Outdoors, he enlisted his friends, willy-nilly, as assistant groundsmen and gardeners. Each was handed a sickle or a billhook, shown a tangle of undergrowth, and ordered to fall to. Not even Prince George was encouraged to come unless he promised to swing a scythe. Mike Scanlon, a recruit from the American Embassy, remembers that "a weekend at the Fort meant blisters and a sore back."

Aird recalled, "H.R.H. threw himself into the remodeling with the same enthusiasm he had shown for golf. In the course of felling trees and clearing the grounds, he conceived a passion for gardening. His favorite flowers were the old-fashioned ones: phlox, sweet William, nasturtiums, delphiniums; and his favorite shrubs were rhododendrons. One evening he was putting in an appearance at the Chelsea Flower Show when a beautiful rock garden caught his eye. It seemed made to order for the Fort, so he bought the whole exhibit on the spot, with the proviso that every rock, every plant, every last trowelful of earth be delivered and reassembled in the original pattern. The day after the show closed, a convoy of vans drew up at the Fort, and the landscape architect who had designed the exhibit began directing the installation of its components. Just then H.R.H. arrived, too, and at once began issuing a contradictory set of orders.

" 'I want those rocks moved *here*,' he told the workmen, pointing to a spot ten feet from where the expert had placed them, 'and I want the foxgloves and Canterbury bells over *there*.'

"The result was, the pattern so carefully designed for the connoisseurs at the flower show was knocked hopelessly awry. The expert flung off, speechless with indignation. His workmen followed. H.R.H. quickly lost interest, and when I last saw the rock garden some years later, it was still unfinished."

One of the Fort's most powerful attractions for the Prince was its nearness to Windsor. He said, "Mama knew more about the Castle and its treasures than the official guides did. When we were children at Frogmore, she used to have my tutor give us little lectures as he escorted us around, and try to impart some notion of the waves of history that had rolled there. I never had much interest in that sort of thing as a boy, but after I moved into the Fort, I came to love Windsor—the great gray walls, the meadows, the Long Walk with the lovely elms which Charles II had planted, and the copper statue of George III, my great-great-great-grandfather, dressed like a Roman emperor and riding a copper horse. That statue always made Papa snort! He couldn't understand why his Hanoverian forebears had to pretend to be something they weren't, when they should have been everlastingly grateful for the good fortune that had made them Englishmen.

"I also loved St. George's Chapel. Often, on Sunday afternoons, I'd leave my guests at the Fort, and slip over there for Evensong, in the stall reserved for me as a Knight of the Garter. The service was short and mostly choral, and the choir was excellent. Henry VIII is buried there, you know, with Jane Seymour who was perhaps the nicest of his wives, and one of Queen Anne's children—'a mixed grill,' Papa used to say, 'a strange busload to be traveling through eternity together!'

"It was wonderfully peaceful. I'd whisper the prayers, join in the hymns, and confide to God the most urgent of the matters—and they weren't few at that stage—in which I needed His guidance."

When Wallis and Ernest Simpson arrived at the Fort for their first weekend, they noticed a strange flag flying from the staff on the topmost tower. It was certainly not the Union Jack; nor was it any royal standard they had ever seen before. An inverted pyramid of fifteen golden balls on a black background—in heraldic terms, "Sable fifteen bezants or in pile 54321"—what *could* it be? They were still puzzling over it when their host bounded out to greet them.

"Oh, *that*?" he said, following their gaze. "That's the flag of the Duchy of Cornwall. I fly it to show that this is to be regarded as a private house, not as a royal residence."

He himself escorted them to their bedroom, "Number 2"; Lady Furness was in "Number 1." Connie and Benny Thaw were also of the party, as was Brigadier Trotter. Ernest knew that he had lost his right arm in the Boer War, and wondered how he had managed his evening tie. He would have been even more admiring if he had known that "G" was an expert fly fisherman. After an excellent dinner, at which the host helped wait on the table, he marched around and around the room with two pipers, squealing and squawking until the walls, if they had ears, must have wished for fingers to stuff into them. He always put on correct Highland costume—bonnet, kilt, silver-buckled shoes, and the rest—before playing the pipes. Lady Diana once saw him in a "tartan dress-kilt with an immense white leather purse in front." His mother had complained that he was a "fidgety, jumpy" child. Lady Diana noticed the same characteristic: He was "over-restless, fetching unnecessary little things, jumping up for the potatoes or soda-water." At another Fort dinner, he wore "a pale dove-grey [tartan] with black lines, and his exquisitely fitting jacket rather Tyrolled-up in shape . . . and instead of that commonish white lace jabot . . . the most finely pleated Geneva bands, like John Wesley. On Sunday by request he donned his wee bonnet and . . . [played] 'Over the Sea to Skye' and also a composition of his own." [2]

This was the climax of his evening; he would merrily puff himself into exhaustion, then settle down to his gros point, and Thelma to her petit point, while others played bridge or red dog or fiddled with a yard-square jigsaw puzzle. Later there was dancing to a Gramophone in the octagonal hall, originally the guardroom. The mood was like the sofas and chairs: easy, informal, comfortable. Stiffness and ceremony were left at the door. The party broke up before midnight. Ernest went to brush his teeth—the bathroom for Number 2 was on another floor—and came back to tell Wallis, "Most embarrassing! As I crossed the hall, I saw the Little Man disappearing into the shadows of the stairway. He was tiptoeing up to Number 1. I didn't dare move until I was reasonably sure he was well bedded down for the night." "The Little Man" was a sobriquet of convenience which the Simpsons had picked up from Thelma; Ernest would continue to use it until one even more derisive occurred to him: "Peter Pan." It was Peter, of course, who said, "No one is going to catch me and make me a man. I always want to be a little boy and have fun."

The maid who brought their breakfast next morning reported that His Royal Highness was already working in the garden; there was an unspoken suggestion that his guests join him. They found him with a machete in his hand and two cairn terriers at his heels; he was wearing a beret, a Fair Isle pullover, and plus fours down to his ankles—so grotesquely long that someone whispered the obvious comment, "They look more like plus sixteens!" As he guided the Simpsons around—and his tour included not only every room but every closet, even the ones where he kept his suits and shoes—he explained how he had installed central heating, had built a bathroom with a shower for each bedroom, plus a steam bath for his own, and had made a swimming pool from a former lily pond. The pool, with its chaises longues and Lilos, its trays of drinks and cigarettes, was the summer center of the Fort's social life. As soon as anyone was allowed to down tools, he broke for the cool water and the cold drinks.

The Simpsons' visit was the first of many they would make—two more that fall and four more that winter. Sometimes Anthony Eden, later Prime Minister and first Earl of Avon, would be there, and usually half a dozen members of the Prince's suite and circle: Perry and Kitty Brownlow, Eric Dudley, Colin and Gladys Buist, "Poots" Butler and her husband, Sir Humphrey, a tall, thin equerry to Prince George. If Prince George himself was along, the others wouldn't let him leave the piano. Prince Edward had by now forsaken the "eukulele"—as it was then spelled—for the bagpipes, despite the fact that Lorelei Lee, of *Gentlemen Prefer Blondes*, had praised his skill: "Even if he were not a prince, he would be able to make his living playing the ukulele if he had a little more practice." When the Mountbattens came, Dickie never failed to bring some toy or gadget for his host's amusement.

Another of Wales's intimates was "Fruity" Metcalfe. Formally and officially, he was Maj. Edward Dudley Metcalfe (1887–1957), but he had been addressed and referred to as Fruity for so long that not even his wife knew where or when the nickname had originated. Irish by birth—he never lost his brogue—and a graduate of Trinity College, Dublin, he joined the 3d Bengal Cavalry in 1909, fought with distinction in Mesopotamia and France during the Great War, and returned to India in time to take part in the Waziristan Campaign of 1919–22. His fine military record recommended him to the Viceroy; and when the Prince of Wales arrived in Bombay on his Indian tour of 1921–22, the Viceroy in turn recommended Metcalfe as an equerry *pro tem,* emphasizing his thorough knowledge of horses, in addition to his attractive personality. One of the highest compliments in the Royal Family's repertory, "He's easy to get along with," might have been coined with Fruity Metcalfe in mind. The Prince immediately responded to the lean, handsome Irishman's gaiety and charm, and the upshot was an invitation to join his permanent staff. Metcalfe accepted. "We clicked," he said.

From then on, as Metcalfe would prove again and again, the Prince had no more loyal friend, nor any whose loyalty would be more meagerly rewarded. Lord Brownlow has written of the "rich, warm smile of enthusiasm and devotion" which the Prince's name always called to Fruity's face. The pair of them were inseparable. Fruity was at the Prince's side during his conquest of Long Island in the late summer of 1924; but they had to part the following spring when the Prince left on another of his Empire tours—this one to Africa and South America—and Fruity stayed behind to marry Lady Alexandra Curzon, Lord Curzon of Kedleston's younger daughter. The Prince would have been best man but for the tour, and Fruity would have gone on the tour but for his wedding.

Fruity now went back to India to serve on the Commander-in-Chief's staff. When his three years there were up, and he was home again, he and the Prince quickly resumed their old, affectionate companionship, and before long a weekend that did not see the Prince with the Metcalfes at their country place, South Hartfield House, at Coleman's Hatch, Sussex, saw Fruity and "Baba" with the Prince at the Fort. The fun and games seemed as if they would never end, but they did, with the arrival of Mrs. Simpson. From then on, and almost before the Metcalfes were aware of it, she had built a palisade around the Prince with her own intimate friends, and—said Lady Alexandra—"Since we had never been among them, our intimacy with him ended. Some of the *ancien régime* stayed on and made the adjustment. We didn't try to." Not that there was any resentment on the Metcalfes' part; resentment could not survive in the climate of Fruity's disposition; and when Windsor went into exile in 1936, Fruity, ever loyal, ever forgiving, voluntarily left his own circle to keep him company in his loneliness.

The Metcalfes first met the Simpsons in the spring of 1933. Fruity remembered the occasion clearly and twenty years later gave this account of it: "I called on H.R.H. at York House one Friday afternoon. He said, 'Some Americans are spending the weekend with me at the Fort. If you and Baba have nothing better to do, why not join us?' So we motored out. Except for us two and, of course, H.R.H. himself, the party was one hundred percent American: Thelma Furness, the Simpsons, and a couple from the American Embassy. Ernest Simpson was the one who caught my eye, chiefly because of a boil on his neck. He had broad shoulders and he was wearing a bright-yellow sweater. All these years I have carried a mental picture of the shoulders, the yellow wool, the scarlet neck, and that huge boil showing under an inadequate poultice.

"The dinner was delicious as usual [Bruce Lockhart quotes the menu at one of the Prince's informal dinners: 'Two cocktails, melon, soup, lobster cutlets, cold grouse, ice, and savoury: sherry, champagne, port and brandy— and whisky!' [3]]. Luncheon at the Fort tended to be sketchy, if it was served at all. H.R.H. was not a lunch man. Besides, he had a lifelong dread of getting fat. After dinner there was bridge. He disliked the game, so he worked on his needlepoint, his fair hair shining under the lamp beside him. When the rubber ended, Mrs. Simpson asked would he mind if she played some dance music on the Gramophone. 'Not at all,' he said. 'Go to it!' She swirled over to me and invited me, in a challenging way, 'Come on, Major, let's liven things up a bit!' I kicked back the rug. We danced a fairly brisk fox-trot, and another couple joined in. When the record was turned, the Prince put aside his work and took my place. I wasn't conscious of any strong attraction between him and Wallis. On the contrary, Thelma was still the focus of his interest." The focus was not unwavering. Late in the Duke of Windsor's life, he let drop that during his state visit to Sweden in October 1932, there occurred "something involving a girl" which caused "quite a stir." When pressed, he changed the subject at once and never returned to it. Mary Duchess of Buccleuch remembers how he fussed over Thelma—how he made sure that the straps on her life jacket were securely fastened before taking her out in his motorboat, which was slow and safe, on Virginia Water, which was safe and shallow.

Thelma was always present at the Fort. The Simpsons were now more than mere acquaintances of hers, they were

her friends—close friends. Ernest composed a flattering little quatrain in her honor:

> Twinkle, twinkle, Thelma dear,
> How I love to have you near!
> Glory of the British nation,
> You're a blinking constellation!

Thelma was to write, "I came to regard Wallis as one of
my best friends in England." Wallis, at this time, never
stinted the expression of her gratitude for Thelma's sponsorship. They lunched together often, at Claridge's or the
Ritz. Thelma drew the Simpsons into her little nightclub
supper parties for the Prince. If he applauded after a
dance, the orchestra played again; if he did not, it did not.
If he had just met his partner, and wanted to see more of
her, he stopped in the middle of the floor, took out a small
gold pencil, and wrote her telephone number on his white
cuff. He was too short to make his dancing partners look
their best. They used to complain also that he exhausted
them by pump-handling their right arms. It may have been
at Thelma's generous suggestion that the Prince gave a
party for Wallis at Quaglino's that spring, on June 19, her
thirty-seventh birthday. His present to her, his first—he
called it a "prezzy"—was an orchid plant. He warned her,
"It won't bloom for a year!"

Wallis knew from her visits to the Fort that any *objet
d'art* there that he had tired of, or taken a dislike to, he
sent down to the cottage of his butler, Osborne.

"A year?" she repeated. "By that time, sir, I'll be in Osborne's cottage!"

She was wrong. When the orchid bloomed a year later,
exactly on schedule, it was Thelma who found herself "in
Osborne's cottage." Her relegation came about in a matter
of months. Her marriage, precarious in recent years, collapsed during a safari in Kenya in the fall of 1933. On her
return to London, she notified the Prince, whose affectionate response was, by her account, "Oh, my darling, I am
sure you have made the right decision. I am so very, very
happy."

Comforted, unapprehensive, she began packing for a

visit to America, where her twin was disputing custody of her ten-year-old daughter, also named Gloria. One of the last persons whom Thelma saw before sailing was her great friend Wallis Simpson.

In 1958, in her *Double Exposure*, Thelma recounted their meeting:

> Three or four days before I was to sail, I had luncheon with Wallis at the Ritz. I told her of my plans. . . . She said, "Oh, Thelma, the Little Man is going to be lonely."
>
> "Well, dear," I answered, "you look after him while I'm away. See that he does not get into any mischief." [4]

Cecil Beaton was a fellow passenger of Thelma's. He went into the ship's bar just before sailing time and found her drinking champagne. At once she turned the conversation to the Prince's devotion. "Come out on deck," she said. "I'll show you something." She pointed to a small plane circling overhead. "There he is now! He's telling me good-bye."

As things turned out, he was indeed.

That was in mid-January. Soon after she landed at New York, a luncheon was given for her. Presently the butler whispered to the hostess, who announced, "Thelma, you have a call from the Prince of Wales."

She was gone some time. When she returned, everyone wanted to know what the Prince had said.

"He said it's raining in London," she reported sweetly. Then, "He's having a small dinner party at the Fort, and guess who's with him? The Simpsons, little Ernest and Wallis."

They were spending the weekend there. A few days later, the Prince came to Bryanston Court for dinner. Another few days, and he telephoned Wallis—the first time he had ever done so—to invite her and Ernest to a dinner party he was giving at the Dorchester on January 30. It would prove to be a memorable evening for the Simpsons and, for the Prince, the turning point in his life.

He seated Wallis on his left and presently found himself,

to his later embarrassment, describing the side of his "princing" that satisfied him the most: his imperial tours, his attempts to promote trade, his enthusiasm for boys' clubs, his efforts to prod the Government and the bankers into providing more and better housing for the poor.

"I know about the poor," Wallis remarked. "I was one of them."

She pressed him with questions—"hard questions," the Duke of Windsor would remember, "the questions of a woman who had read a lot and knew something about the new forces at work in the world. Usually, my partner at a dinner would open with something like 'I see by the papers, Sir, that you've been to Leeds.'

" 'Yes,' I'd say, 'I went there to visit a new housing project.'

"Then she'd say, 'Oh, Sir, how tiresome!,' and the talk would turn to something equally fatuous. Talking with Wallis was different. Her interest was genuine, and her outlook was new to me. It was a wonderful mixture of warmth, curiosity and independence of spirit, with an attractive trace of impudence."

For perhaps the first time in his life, he was being treated without the least tinge of obsequiousness—as a man, a person in his own right, and not as a royal puppet. He decided that her attitude was "wholly American." So it remained. Even as Duchess of Windsor, she never became anglicized in the least. She remained American and she always defended America against any criticism. The Duke also decided that he liked her loyalty. Encouraged, he went on to tell her about his heavy burden of duties, his hopes for the monarchy, and his frustration in trying to realize them. Suddenly he broke off: "But I'm boring you!"

"On the contrary!" she assured him. She said he reminded her of American men, the men of her own family: "I come from a country where businessmen are folk-heroes. You care for achievement the way they do. I am truly interested in what the British Heir Apparent thinks and does."

The Duke of Windsor remembered, "Right then I made an important discovery: that a man's relationship with a woman could also be an intellectual partnership. That was the start of my falling in love with her. She promised to bring into my life something that wasn't there. I was convinced that with her, I'd be a more creative and more useful person."

"Wallis," he told her gravely, "you're the only woman who has ever been interested in my job!"

His statement reflects an unchivalrous forgetfulness that must have been deliberate. Not long before—a matter of months at most—he had urged Freda Dudley Ward to help him organize the Feathers Club Association—named for the Prince of Wales's emblem—to aid the unemployed. She consented; indeed, she served as chairman of the Association, unpaid, for thirty years, went to its office daily, and even solicited funds to run it.

When the party ended, the Prince asked Wallis if he might stop by "now and then" for a cocktail: "Perhaps you'll be good enough to telephone me at York House and invite me?" Not only Thelma, but the Prince himself evidently felt that he needed looking after.

"Sir," Wallis said, "Baltimore women are brought up very strictly. They never telephone men."

The reply delighted him. "A pity more women didn't learn the same lesson," he said, laughing.

"But any time you are free," she added, "or feel lonely, please come in. I'm usually at home in the afternoon. If you'd like to come to dinner some night, just say so."

He lost no time in snapping up her offer. January 30, the date of the Dorchester party, was a Tuesday. The very next afternoon, the Prince turned up at Bryanston Court for cocktails and stayed for dinner. On Thursday he was there for cocktails again, and again on Friday, and again he stayed for dinner. Saturday he had the Simpsons to the Fort for the weekend. On Wednesday, February 7, he dined at Bryanston Court, then took the Simpsons to a nightclub. On Friday, the Prince and Wallis dined in a restaurant, alone, and next day she and Ernest went to the Fort for another weekend. Various sources count at least six more meetings with the Prince between then and March 22, when Thelma returned. Plainly, he was infatuated. The "love affair of the century" had blossomed from the rubbly ground of mass housing.

CHAPTER 7
A Victory and a Surrender

The evening of Thelma Furness's return from America, the Prince invited himself to her house. She found him distant. Presently he blurted, "I hear that Aly Khan has been very attentive to you!"

She was stunned. Where on earth had he heard such a thing? A few nights before sailing back to England, she had dined with some friends in New York. Prince Aly Khan was there and, in her own phrase, had "turned his battery of charm" on her. It was quite a battery. When it came to maneuvering the light artillery of love, Aly was a master tactician, a boudoir Bonaparte, the victor in a thousand silken skirmishes. The only child (born in 1911) of the multimillionaire Aga Khan by his second wife, an Italian ballet dancer, Aly was handsome, dashing, fearless, and— to be sure—rich. He drove expensive cars at furious speeds; he rode his horses against professional jockeys; he piloted his own plane; and he spoke half a dozen languages, though none so fluently as Cupid's, for he was above all else a ladies' man, catnip to the kittens. When the encounter with Thelma Furness took place, she was twenty-nine and he only twenty-three. Because of her experience, particularly in the art of defense, the advantage should have rested with her. Until then, her romances had all been with older men. But Aly, in the prime of his young manhood, was adept in attack, the peer of the young Napoleon who took the bridge at Arcole.

Elsa Maxwell, best remembered for her indefatigable party-giving, and for the intensity (while it lasted) of her relationship with the Duchess of Windsor—sometimes adoring, sometimes vituperative, but always highly publicized—thought that "a good deal" of Aly's magnetism for women stemmed from animal vitality: "I'm convinced he was born with a built-in Benzedrine plant." Juliette Greco said that he was "charming in a very special way. He takes you to a restaurant, and if the most beautiful woman comes in, he doesn't look at her. He makes you feel you are a queen." After a moment's reverie, she added, "Of course, his love-making had a lot to do with it. . . ." His biographer, Leonard Slater, went straight to the point: "In the precise and complex art of love, Aly had no peer." [1]

As soon as Aly learned that Thelma was about to sail, he pressed her to delay for ten days, until he would be free to accompany her. She refused; her return was urgent, she said. However, she agreed to dine with him the following evening. Next day brought flowers and a note, and that evening "We dined, we talked, we danced." Aboard ship were more flowers—red roses crowding her stateroom; and among them, more notes, billets-doux: "You left too soon, Aly," and "Love, Aly," and "See you in London, Aly." She was breakfasting in this seagoing bower when her telephone rang: "Will you lunch with me today?" It was Aly, a fellow passenger, she was astonished to learn. She dined with him that evening, and their remaining evenings aboard. [2]

The duel must have been a pretty one to watch, with the Prince of Wales's lovely mistress defending her honor against Society's wiliest, most tireless, and most notorious swordsman. Aly's suit was flattering for another reason: Here was the champion Beau Sabreur daring to challenge the paramount Beau Idéal for her favors. Whether he won them is of no consequence now; the Prince of Wales had already decided that she had surrendered. The evidence was strong that he had had her watched, and that word of the dinners had been flashed to him. The stain on his pride was darkened by his loathing for his rival, whom he remembered as a child in rabbit skins—"a swarthy little Baby Bunting"—being presented to the King and Queen at Buckingham Palace by his father, the Aga.

Baffled by the Prince's sudden coolness, Thelma again sought her "best friend," Wallis, and asked if she could explain it. If history is to accept Thelma's account of the confrontation, Wallis said only, "Darling, you know the Little Man loves you very much. The Little Man is just lost without you." [3]

If, on the other hand, Wallis's is the true account, the dialogue went somewhat further. Thelma asked her bluntly if the Prince was keen on her. Wallis had expected the question and was "glad to be able to give her a straight answer." She said, "I think he likes me, but if you mean by 'keen' that he is in love with me, the answer is definitely no." [4]

The "straight answer" failed to allay Thelma's apprehensions, and they were confirmed the following weekend, when she and the Simpsons were at the Fort again. She noticed early in the dinner that Wallis, seated next to the Prince, seemed to share "little private jokes" with him; but not until the salad course did Thelma grasp what they really shared. To anyone else, the tip-off would have seemed innocent byplay. The Prince, whose table manners were occasionally Tudoresque, picked up a scrap of lettuce in his fingers, and Wallis slapped his hand, lightly, as would a governess reproving a child. Thelma was shocked at the lese majesty; one simply did not take these liberties with royalty!—especially with the Prince of Wales, who was famously quick to resent any trespass on his dignity. Joseph Kingsbury-Smith, then the head of the Hearst Services in London, said of the Prince, "He could get goddam *regal* in a hurry!"; and a secretary, Dina Wells Hood, told in her book, *Working for the Windsors* (at twenty pounds a month and living expenses), how she had to take the Duke's dictation, respectfully standing, "sometimes for over an hour at a stretch" and usually with an armful of papers, unless he happened to invite her to be seated. [5] Thelma caught Wallis's eye and threw her a friendly frown of warning. What she got back was this, in her own words:

"Wallis looked straight at me. One cold defiant glance told me the entire story. I knew then she had looked after him exceedingly well." [6]

Long past were the days in Baltimore when Wallis's girl friends could commend her "precious quality of not being a predator, of never setting her cap at another girl's beau."

Thelma retired early, without "good nights"; and next morning early, without "good-byes," she quitted the Fort forever, bag and baggage, leaving Wallis mistress of— among other things—the field.

The fourth figure in the drama, Prince Aly Khan,

stepped up the pace of his life until he became a blur in the public eye. His flamboyant marriages, his countless other romances, and his spectacular sporting exploits kept him in the headlines up to his death, which came in a motor crash (to no one's surprise) in 1960, when he was forty-nine. Though he passed his life in a blaze of publicity, the most important role he ever played was scarcely recognized. But for Aly, Thelma Furness might never have lost the Prince's favor; King Edward VIII might never have abdicated; and almost certainly he would have died at home in England, full of years and honors, and beloved by his Empire.

Though Wallis's "cold defiant glance" made it clear that she was now in command, Thelma failed to grasp the psychological significance. The Prince's unprotesting acceptance of the slap, playful though it was, meant that he had already begun to subject his will to Wallis's. All these years the world has asked, "What grip does she have on him?" The answer was written on that lettuce leaf: He was waiting for the woman who would dominate him. German by descent, temperament, and preference, he was happiest under a despot. All his life, his decisions had been readymade. His character was the product of constant direction and correction. He had grown up in the fear of a martinet father who raked him fore and aft for a waistcoat button left undone, and continually tried to catch him out on petty details of military insignia. From this incessant harassment and diminishment, he sought comfort from his mother, only to learn that all she could give him was perfunctory sympathy, with exhortations to try harder. Thus, denied the "security blanket" of mother love, he developed a personality deficiency. Deep within him grew a desperate need for a woman to supply the fiber that he himself lacked—in short, a mother-mistress. He liked to prate about how much he enjoyed running his "own show," but what he was really longing for was a woman to tell him how to run it—better yet, to run it for him. And who better than "the perfect woman"?—as he would acclaim her again and again in the years ahead. Some who heard him must surely have caught the echo of Wordsworth, and if they silently completed the couplet

>A perfect woman, nobly planned,
>To warn, and comfort, and command,

they could not be blamed if they found themselves emphasizing the final word.

Freda Dudley Ward understood Wales's psychology. She said, "I could have dominated him if I had wanted to. I could have done *anything* with him! Love bewitched him. He made himself the slave of whomever he loved and became totally dependent on her. It was his nature; he was a masochist. He *liked* being humbled, degraded. He *begged* for it!" There were no restraints on the brash, square-jawed American woman. As soon as she discovered his vulnerability, she did not hesitate to exploit it.

Thelma was banished in April 1934; a month later it was Freda's turn. By then she had long been legally separated from her husband, so their divorce in 1931 had made small difference in her relations with the Prince; he continued to telephone her and to visit her almost daily. Gossip and the press had made her aware of Wallis Simpson's existence, but the Prince never mentioned her, and Freda felt no concern. Then, in May, her elder daughter, Penelope, fell ill, and Freda stood several days' vigil at her bedside. When the crisis was past, and she had leisure to resume her routine, she rang York House and asked the telephonist, William, to put her through to His Royal Highness. She says, "There was a dreadful silence. At last, William said in a broken voice, 'I'm most dreadfully sorry, Mum, but I have orders not to.' . . . It had to end sometime, of course, and perhaps it was better to end like that. But I can't help wishing he'd had the courage to tell me face to face, instead of leaving me to find it out from a servant."

She added this: "*His* servants continued their friendship with *my* servants, who told me that they—his—were terribly upset. They told mine, 'You don't *know* what's going on. You don't know what's *going on*!' "

Freda's friends would blame "the Simpson woman" for lowering this summary, heartless curtain on the long and tender affair; they were persuaded that it was the price she had exacted from the Prince for her favors. But Wallis

Simpson, speaking as the Duchess of Windsor twenty-five years later, protested that she deserved the blame for neither Freda's fall nor Thelma's. "Something had happened between her [Thelma] and the Prince; the former warmth and easiness of their relationship had gone." Wallis could hardly have been in doubt where the warmth, at least, had gone to. Such gratitude as she may have felt she owed Thelma, for introducing her into circles where she might not have been bidden for herself alone, was that of one poacher to a fellow, for sharing a secret pathway into a closed preserve. That each had taken the other's measure was implicit in Thelma's suggesting, and Wallis's accepting, the compact whereby Wallis would "look after the Little Man" during Thelma's absence—the purpose of the arrangement being to make sure that the Prince, in boredom and idleness, did not fall prey to a third poacher on the prowl.

As for Freda, the Duchess said she never realized that the Prince was tiring of her until the breach was final. Further, "I scarcely carried enough weight with him that early to try exerting any serious influence, even if I had wished to. We were little more than new acquaintances. Of course, I was aware—as was almost every other woman in the West End—that he was greatly attached to the beautiful Freda Dudley Ward, and I had no reason then to suspect that the attachment was ending. On the contrary, I remember clearly that well after he had begun ringing up Bryanston Court and asking permission to stop by of an afternoon, he'd often phrase it like this: 'May I stop by on my way to St. John's Wood?' [where Freda Dudley Ward then lived]. At the same time, I could hardly help noticing that whenever I saw him with a companion, it was not she, but Thelma.

"I also noticed, when it came about that *I* began being invited to cocktail parties and suppers as his companion, Mrs. Dudley Ward was never present. This made me uncomfortable. It didn't take much imagination to figure out what the others were thinking. They had known her long and well; then they'd had to get used to Thelma; and here, suddenly, was a new woman—another American at that. I suggested to one or two hostesses that it would be nice if they invited Mrs. Dudley Ward too. I said the Prince would be pleased. Well, they knew him better than I did. If she was ever invited, she chose not to accept."

It was plain, as the Duchess talked, that the jilting of Freda still troubled her—especially its aftermath, when the Prince visited his coldness upon her younger daughter. The occasion was Angela's marriage to Lt. Robert Laycock, in January 1935. (Her sister, Penelope, married Sir Carol Reed.) Laycock would become a hero of World War II, the youngest general in the British Army, and eventually a major general, a knight, and Governor of Malta. Until the severance of communications with the Little Prince the preceding May, the two sisters had seen (and adored) him almost daily for sixteen years; so "Angie" begged her mother to ignore the rift and ask him to the wedding. An invitation was sent out, but nothing came back: no present, not even a reply. The Dudley Wards never attempted to see him again.

The Duchess of Windsor, looking back on the incident from 1955, said this: "When I read that her daughter was to marry young Laycock, I mentioned to the Prince that it seemed to be a splendid match, and that I supposed he was greatly pleased. He brushed my remark aside with something to the effect that he no longer saw the family and wouldn't be going to the wedding. I asked if he had sent a present. He glared at me and grunted, 'No!' It was my first encounter with that side of him. A shutter would close, and no power on earth could open it.

"I saw Mrs. Dudley Ward once," the Duchess went on, "only once. It was at a movie house. The Prince and Ernest and I were crossing the foyer when a woman came up—quite tiny, beautifully dressed—and touched his arm. He introduced us. She spent a moment with us, then went back to her party. That was all."

Freda, now the widow of Wing Commander the (Spanish) Marqués of Casa Maury, R.A.F., has no recollection of the meeting. Nor has she any tangible souvenirs of her long romance—no jewelry or other keepsake from the Prince, no photographs, not even a snapshot, nothing but a few of those "rather schoolboyish" letters he sent her from France and from his tours. She did not go to his funeral. She mentions Wallis rarely, and then without bitterness.

But once she remarked, "She got him by witchcraft. There's no other possible explanation. I blame him for nothing. He was a doomed character." The same explanation would suggest itself to Stanley Baldwin during the Abdication crisis. He wrote to his niece that the King "seemed *bewitched.* . . ."

Breaking off two liaisons and embarking on a third, all within a few months, would leave a more sensitive man emotionally exhausted. Not the Prince. Cheiro had written, "Persons born under such peculiar astrological conditions [as he] exhibit remarkable fluctuations of feeling—they pass from ardor to indifference in a few seconds, and they are very liable to be charged with inconstancy." [7] If sacking his old loves ever brought him even a twinge of remorse, he never showed it. Unlike the Duchess, he had little to say about her predecessors. Jack Aird observed that when their names bobbed up in conversation, his only response was annoyance. Freda is not mentioned at all in *A King's Story*, and Thelma only in passing, as an acquaintance of Mrs. Simpson's. But of his new liaison, he once said this:

"I didn't have much official business to occupy me just then—early 'thirty-four. My only important engagement was a trip to Brussels in February, to represent my father at the funeral of King Albert, who had been killed while mountain-climbing. I also made excursions to Scotland for a Boy Scout Jamboree; to Glasgow, to look at the new *Queen Mary,* almost ready for launching; and take the salute of the Royal Scots Fusiliers at a review at Ayr. [In Scotland he insisted that his route to Clydeside be changed to pass through Glasgow's slum areas, among the most notorious in Europe. Then, looking at the ship, he remarked sadly, "Isn't it strange that we can afford money to build this beautiful toy, but can't afford money to eliminate slums?"] There was the usual round of 'princing,' of course—fairs, exhibitions, factory openings, charity balls, memorial services and the like—but I was able to shift some of these jobs onto my brothers. My all-absorbing desire at that point was to work on the Fort, and to decide what was to become of me.

"I was forty that year, and forty is the now-or-never

birthday, the outermost limit of youth. If a man isn't in control of his fate by then, chances are he'll never be. By forty, I had sown my wild oats—a fairly meagre planting, if I say so myself. I had been away from England too much. My hope was to put down roots [one of his favorite phrases] where I could create a private life of my own—not as at Sandringham, nor Balmoral, nor as on the great estates of some of my friends. I wanted something simple, a place in the country where I could garden, entertain congenial people, and play golf when I felt like it—in short, a place like the Fort.

"Another thing: for some fifteen years, starting with my Empire Tours after the Great War, my calendar had always been laid out a full twelve months in advance. I had become a performer in what Jack Aird called 'the Decorated Circus'—that mobile, ever-ready company of princes, politicians, and retired field marshals and admirals whom the Empire drew upon to lay foundation stones, cut ribbons for opening bridges and highways, plant memorial trees and so on. It was part of my job. I knew I had to do it, and much of it fascinated and even excited me; but I was always glad to get home again, especially as I now had a home of my own to come to.

"So the 'roots' part of my program was taken care of. But something was still lacking: a partner to share my life. Presently I began to cherish a hope that this might be taken care of too."

Early in June, he invited the Simpsons to join him at the Fort before Ascot, which would start on the nineteenth, her birthday, and to stay over for his, on the twenty-third. The Simpsons arrived on the sixteenth and she stayed for ten days. Whether Ernest was with her throughout, no one remembers; nor does a record survive of her thoughts about an item in the *Sunday Express* which was brought up on her breakfast tray the morning after her arrival:

Edward, Prince of Wales, the most eligible man in the world—and the loneliest—will be forty years old on Saturday.

The Prince is the center of attraction everywhere he goes. Cheerful, smiling, charming, whether surrounded by officialdom or in a circle of friends.

But always, in reality, alone with the burden of responsibility which there is none to share.

That is the secret of the Prince of Wales today. He echoes in the present the cry of the widowed Queen Victoria in the past—"I am alone." "Heir to half the world," in Dean Stanley's phrase, "he is less free to do as he likes than the humblest of the millions who may one day be his subjects. . . ."

Nearly six years ago when the King lay for weeks between life and death, the shadow [of the throne] came nearer and nearer than it had ever been, and from that day the Prince has changed.

Those who know him best say that the Prince is much more serious in his outlook, more settled in his ways, and more stable and mature in his judgment since those days. . . .

One subject only rouses the Prince to anger . . . no one must talk to him of marriage. . . .

Golf and gardening, the pursuits of a man who has settled his way of life, are the two hobbies which appeal to him. . . .

The Prince has numerous friends . . . but even those who are his intimate friends never learn to know the Prince completely.

He is constantly springing surprises, even on his staff and entourage who see him and work with him daily. That is one more facet of his many-sided charm.

He is one of the most popular figures in the world today. And one of the most enigmatic.

Wallis must have smiled when she finished reading. The Prince was hardly an enigma to her by then, although at this stage only the equerries who had known both Freda Dudley Ward and Thelma Furness suspected the shift in the balance of power around him—they and one other: the Fort's butler, Osborne, who was dismayed to see how quickly and surely Mrs. Simpson was taking control of the household. Orders for running it no longer came from the Prince or his aides; they came from her. She usurped not only their authority, but—and this made the situation particularly irksome for Osborne—his own. He had been the

Prince's soldier-servant batman in the Great War and was accustomed to getting his orders direct, not through an intermediary. Yet he found himself arranging the flowers and rearranging the furniture at Mrs. Simpson's instructions, and relaying to the chef the weekend menus which she had dictated by telephone. His patience wore thin. What broke it was a collapsible tea-table which she had foisted on his pantry, until then his personal domain. Osborne inspected the newfangled contraption and judged it flimsy, not to be trusted. He balked at using it, but when the Prince asked where it was, he had to produce it. He brought it in, snapped the legs down, and muttered, "Your Royal Highness, this thing won't last twenty-four hours!"

Resentment at the intrusion of an alien authority was felt even more explosively by Osborne's opposite number, Finch, the butler-valet at York House. Finch was senior to all the other servants, having entered King George V's employment as valet to David and Bertie soon after their graduation from the Sandringham nursery; and he had been in charge of York House ever since the Prince moved in on his return from the Great War. There was nothing of the cringing menial about Finch. A rawboned, big-fisted Yorkshireman, he was—in Windsor's own words—"very much an autocrat. He never hesitated to find fault with the way things were run at York House, or how I entertained."

Even after the Prince had entered manhood, and Finch was promoted to butler, he continued to regard his former charge as a headstrong youth who needed a tight rein. In this respect, he and King George were of the same mind. Finch said, "His Majesty would scold me: 'Why can't you make my eldest son dress as a gentleman should?' and 'Why can't you make him remember that he's a gentleman?' "

Finch tried. Whenever the Prince stayed up too late or seemed to be drinking too much, Finch sternly rebuked him; and if he did not care for the guests whom the Prince brought home for dinner, or for the menu the Prince proposed, he said so forcefully. He was never mutinous or impertinent; he simply wanted the future King, whom he had served since childhood, to conduct himself as his father did.

During Freda Dudley Ward's gentle reign, Finch's occasional truculence merely amused the Prince. It did not make for trouble until an American woman, Thelma Furness, introduced an American innovation, cocktails, at York House. At first, Finch refused even to mix one; he finally agreed to do so only on condition that he would not have to commit the un-English offense of using ice. He would bring the shaker into the drawing room, but there the Prince would take over and add the ice himself. (This dramatic demonstration of the separation of powers often supplied a useful conversational gambit—an icebreaker, so to speak.) But when Wallis supplanted Thelma, she insisted that while it was permissible for the Prince to hand around cocktails at Bryanston Court, it ill became him to be his servant's servant in his own residence. Finch tried to make it plain to her that regardless of how matters were managed elsewhere, at York House the only valid orders came from H.R.H. himself. In the showdown, Finch lost out, another casualty of 1934. Windsor, looking back, said of him, "He had become obstinate. He'd been with me too long. I had to pension him off." His place was taken by Fred Crisp, the son of a gamekeeper at Sandringham. Crisp, like Finch, would stand only so much. In two years, he, too, would be gone.

Now that Wallis had secured the Fort, the Prince's weekend retreat, she confidently took over his weekday social life in London. Her own account of the improvement in the Simpson fortunes is modestly inaccurate, so much so as to be an understatement. According to her, she and Ernest had been pulled so deeply and irresistibly into the Prince's own world that they had all but lost a lodgment in their own. Actually, it was the other way around. By then, the spring of 1934, his aides and equerries, his staff at York House, his family and his friends recognized that Bryanston Court was being raised to his unofficial London seat.

He has said that his royal duties were light at that time. Sometimes they took him to the provinces, but whenever he was in London, he would hasten to the Simpson flat at the end of the day, often to no more purpose than a brief chat, a cocktail, or a potluck dinner—"chicken pie or a stew," Wallis remembered. "He'd never had dishes like that before, and they amused him." She was fussy about details. She knew how to mix piquant sauces. All this made such a strong impression on the Prince that he often followed her into the kitchen, to watch her assume command. Rickatson-Hatt heard her tell him, "My staff objects to my trespassing in their kitchen, but all good American wives hold themselves responsible for the meals, and I shall continue to do so here." Presently the Prince considered himself so much a part of the Simpsons' lives that he no longer bothered to "propose himself," in the royal phrase. They seldom knew when he would turn up or how long he would stay; evening after evening, Wallis would eventually have to whisper to the parlormaid, "Tell Cook there will be three for dinner."

Ernest "dearly loved a lord"; he was never content to write merely "H.R.H."—it was always the full, rolling splendor of "His Royal Highness"—and when he spoke of something the King had done or the Queen had said, it was always (according to Wallis) "with hushed breath." Still, flattering though these princely stops-by were, they could be vexatious when Ernest had brought home a briefcase full of work. On such evenings, the host had no choice but to ask his guest's permission to retire to his room. Permission was never withheld.

The Prince's attentions imposed other penalties as well. The Simpsons had to entertain for him—at first, with cocktail parties and impromptu suppers; later, with formal dinners, which meant heavy bills for wine and food and flowers, new frocks and extra servants. Harold Nicolson's diary records a dinner at Bryanston Court: "Black tie . . . butler and maid at door . . . many orchids and white arums. The guests consist of Lady Oxford, Lady Cunard, Lady Colefax, Kenneth Lindsay, the Counsellor of the U.S. Embassy at Buenos Aires plus wife, and Alexander Woollcott. Mr. Ernest Simpson enters, bringing in [the guest of honor]. We all bow and curtsey. . . . Mrs. Simpson is a perfectly harmless type of American, but the whole setting is slightly second-rate. I do not wonder that the Sutherlands and the Stanleys are sniffy about it all." [8]

Rickatson-Hatt said, "I always thought that Wallis was rather unimaginative about the people she had in to meet the Prince. Once he became a fixture, she invited only those she judged would amuse him—what we later called 'café society.' I urged her to mix them up—politicians, bankers, industrialists, publishers, and editors—people of substance and influence. She waved me off. She said, 'He spends his days in the company of stuffed shirts. He comes here to be amused.' For my taste, the company tended to be fairly frivolous and lightweight, yet I have to give Wallis credit for this; that through the Prince's interest in her, he encountered many unusual minds he might otherwise have missed. I remember sitting up with him and her until past four one morning—Ernest had long since gone to bed—while he pumped an architect from Chicago for details of a mass-housing scheme. He wanted to know if it might be applied in the British slums, financing and all."

It was at the Prince's request—and still more so, later, at the King's—that the Simpson parties came to be made up largely of Americans. He liked them and their country. He once remarked that he envied Winston Churchill the American half of his blood; and after the Abdication, he confessed to Lilli Palmer, "My trouble is that I never really felt at home in England. When I first set foot on American soil as a very young man, it came to me like a flash: This is what I like. Here I'd like to stay." Now he told Wallis that he was eager to widen his acquaintances among Americans, so that he could discuss the New Deal, the forsaken gold standard, and the political leaders he had met on his several visits. Edward VII enjoyed Americans "of the right sort," but George V did not share his father's and his son's enthusiasm. The only Americans he felt comfortable with were Pierpont Morgan and Walter Hines Page. The Prince urged Wallis to bring her friends to the Fort, where the Simpsons were now spending almost every weekend. Before long, his Americanization had proceeded to the point where his accent was American, and Americanisms studded his conversation. He plumed himself especially on his mastery of American slang, and enjoyed startling his staider English associates with "Okey-dokey!," "making whoopee," and "hot-diggety-dog!"

Clearly, an osmotic process had set in: The Prince was being absorbed into Wallis's milieu, and she into his. By midsummer the process was complete. He had taken a house in Biarritz for August, and had invited the Simpsons to visit him. Ernest declined; business, he said, would require his presence in New York. Wallis, too, declined; she had invited Aunt Bessie Merryman to keep her company while Ernest was away. The Prince promptly expanded his invitation: "Bring her along! From what you've told me about her, I'm sure she'll be the life of the party."

Wallis wrote her, and she accepted. This is what she remembered of her first meeting with the Prince: "I knew from Wallis's letters that he had been extremely kind to her and Ernest, but I had no idea how close they had become until he appeared at Bryanston Court, unannounced, the afternoon I arrived. He passed around the drinks and canapés, and was plainly very much at home. No question, he was handsome and attractive. Amazingly young, almost boyish. Beautiful manners. Before he left, he said to me, 'I hope you'll come to the Fort with Wallis and Ernest tomorrow, for the weekend. I've heard you're a very wise and witty lady, and I look forward to spending some time with you.'

"He sent his car to my hotel next day. When we pulled up at the Fort, toward dusk, he took me to my room, and looked around to see that everything was as it should be. We all met at the pool for cocktails. I remember the bright wall of roses and delphiniums and polyanthus that bordered the path. The other guests were charming. I counted myself lucky to be among them. But I couldn't dismiss a sense of apprehension. Ernest was a fine man, intelligent, good company, but he was hardly the reason why Wallis and I were there. The Prince's attentions were centered on *her.*"

A visit by a member of the British royal family would be no novelty to Biarritz. Queen Victoria had gone there in 1889 and had driven around town in a donkey cart. Ten years earlier, Edward VII, as Prince of Wales, had been there briefly; but in 1906, as King, he spent most of March and April there and continued to do so until his death, in 1910. Biarritz, in gratitude and pride, sprinkled itself with names commemorating these royal favors: Avenue de la Reine Victoria, Avenue Édouard VII, Boulevard du Prince de Galles, Hotel Victoria, Hotel Édouard VII. Hotel Victoria frowns on Avenue Édouard VII just as mother frowned on son—and as she would have frowned even more disapprovingly on her great-grandson with his intended mistress.

The royal party set out on August 1: the host, Mrs. Simpson and Mrs. Merryman, the Colin Buists, and three aides, including Jack Aird. Their days on the sunny Basque coast passed in swimming, golf, and bridge; some evenings the Prince and Wallis dined alone, in a restaurant. One evening he gave a dinner, then took his guests on to the Casino. "Everyone was home by three," he enjoyed remembering, "except Wallis's Aunt Bessie. *She* didn't get in until broad daylight!" After a month, the original eight became nine, with the arrival of Mrs. Kenelm Guinness, young and pretty and known as "Posy." Lord Moyne, another member of the Guinness family, put into a nearby port just then in his yacht *Rosaura*, and invited them all to join him for a fortnight's cruise in the Mediterranean. Mrs. Merryman preferred to set out for Italy on her own, but the rest climbed aboard, and the *Rosaura* headed along the Spanish-Portuguese coasts. A former Channel steamer, she was big (2,000 tons), fast, and luxurious, but her powerful engines consumed so much fuel that she could stay at sea only a few days on end. The Prince did not complain; he was a prey to seasickness, and he was always happy when they dropped anchor for a dip in a sheltered cove or for a picnic ashore. He never forgot Moyne's two stewards: "They were elderly men, more like clowns than servants, and they stayed in a state of genial drunkenness day and night, seldom bothering to make the beds or wash the dishes. Depending on their whim, our dinner might begin with the cheese or a sweet and end with the soup, or the soup might be poured over the sweet, and the roast served with the ice cream."

Nor would he forget Formentor, on the island of Majorca, where they spent three days, "Sept. 6–9," according to the log in which he scrupulously recorded his lifetime travels. This bare notation is the only mention his autobiography makes of the interval that, by Wallis's blurry account, brought their budding relationship to full flower. Under a new moon, a new enchantment overwhelmed them; and it was then, Wallis confesses, that they "crossed the line that marks the indefinable boundary between friendship and love."

When they reached Cannes, the Prince bought her a small diamond-and-emerald bangle for her bracelet, the first substantial gift he had ever given her, the first pebbles of the gorgeous, glittering avalanche soon to follow. A more tender memento would be given presently: a slow march which he composed for the bagpipes and called "Majorca."

One evening a year later, as the pipers were circling the dining room at Windsor, King George V realized that their tune was unfamiliar. He reached for the program and read "*Majorca,* by the Prince of Wales."

" 'The Prince of Wales,' " he repeated. " 'The Prince of Wales.' . . . What Prince of Wales could possibly have written *that*?" He scowled at his eldest son. "Could it be *you*?"

"Yes, sir."

"I didn't know you played the pipes. Imagine a member of the Royal Family playing the pipes! . . . It's not bad, you know." He thought for a moment, then added—lest he be guilty of paying his son a compliment—"But it's not good either."

The *Rosaura* dropped the Prince's party off at Genoa, and he, Wallis, and Jack Aird made their unhurried way to Paris, where Mrs. Merryman rejoined them. The Prince and Aird left for London next day, to keep official engagements, while Wallis and her aunt boarded the *Manhattan* at Le Havre—Wallis to disembark at Southampton and meet Ernest, Mrs. Merryman to keep on to New York and Washington.

As soon as the aunt and niece were alone, Mrs. Merryman put this question: "Isn't the Prince rather taken with you?"

Wallis tried to answer evasively, but when her aunt held her to the point, warning her that a deeper involvement might be dangerous, she flared up, "You don't have to worry about me! I know what I'm doing!"

Did she know? If she did *not*, she was showing a foolhardiness and obtuseness alien to one who, since her schooldays, "always knew where she was going, and would have stepped on her grandmother's stomach" to get there. But if she *did* know, she was deliberately allowing a flirtation with the heir apparent to progress so far that he would insist on marrying her, regardless of the consequences to himself, to his family, and to the monarchy. There is no doubt that she knew—that at the end of the Majorca interlude, both she and the Prince were definitely committed to marrying, if "the job," as he was to dub it, "could be brought off." Clear as is the evidence in their separate autobiographies, it would have been still clearer if the authors had not been restrained by their fear—and their British lawyers by the knowledge—that further candor would support the suspicion that collusion had been present in Wallis's divorce.

Mrs. Merryman's misgivings were quickly intensified. No sooner had the *Manhattan* touched at Southampton than there jovially burst into her stateroom not only Ernest but the Prince, too, followed by his chauffeur, Ladbrook, with a huge hamper of fruit, chocolates, and other delicacies, as well as several bottles of chilled champagne.

Ernest's friend Bernard Rickatson-Hatt, who was also a passenger, later gave this account of an incident at the sailing:

"I had dined with Ernest in London the evening before, so I knew he'd be meeting Wallis. He spied me as I was about to mount the gangway and told me she was already ashore, and urged me to go over to their car with him. 'Besides,' he added, 'a rather important friend wants to say hello.' He took me through the shed to where a big car was parked, its lights dimmed and a chauffeur at the door. He opened it, the saloon light came on, and I saw the Prince sitting beside Wallis. We had exchanged only a few words when the ship's siren sounded the 'all ashore,' and I had to leave. Ernest walked me back to the gangway.

" 'What's going on?' I asked.

" 'Aunt Bessie's aboard,' he said. 'The Prince has become very fond of her. He insisted on driving me to Southampton so that he could say good-bye to her, and now he insists on taking Wallis and me back to the Fort for the night.'

"I said, 'Strange . . .'

" 'What's strange?'

" 'It's strange that our favorite prince should become so attached to an elderly lady he has known so little time.' Ernest did not comment."

Rickatson-Hatt had met Mrs. Merryman at Bryanston Court. Next day he invited her to dine. They had a number of chats during the voyage, he said later, "and on every occasion, she led the conversation around to the Prince's interest in Wallis. She told me, 'I don't like it. I'm worried. He's crazy about her—I'm not exaggerating. It was in the air at Biarritz. It's an infatuation he makes no attempt to conceal. If this goes on, something terrible will happen.'

"Mrs. Merryman was fond of Ernest. She respected him. What she feared was a liaison, an affair, that would wreck his marriage and leave Wallis high and dry at the end. It never occurred to her that things would go the other way, and *Ernest* would be left high and dry. It never occurred to me, either. Nor, most of all, to Ernest."

CHAPTER 8
The Launching of Wallis

*The young Prince led Cinderella onto the ballroom
floor. She danced so gracefully that the Court whispered about her more than ever. The Prince never left
her side; all evening he paid her compliments.*
— "Cinderella"

The peppery passage with her aunt upset Wallis. After it,
she reviewed her association with the Prince, and eventually she would decide that above and beyond the undenia-
ble charm of his person, he was the open sesame to a new
and glittering world. A world where the royal command
could cause crack trains to be held, yachts to materialize,
suites to be flung open at the finest hotels, airplanes to roll
up to the tarmac. It all seemed so incredible, so enchanting, that it produced in her a "happy and unheeding acceptance."

The Prince, for his part, though no less happy about
their future, was rather more heedful. Four enormous ob-
stacles stood in his way.

The first was the Royal Marriages Act of 1772, which
forbade a member of the royal family to marry without the
consent of the sovereign and ultimately of Parliament. It
was inconceivable that his father would accept this marriage, and unlikely that Parliament would.

The second was the Church of England's stern opposition to divorce. Not only did Wallis Simpson have a lawful
husband already, but a previous husband, divorced, was
still alive.

The third was the problem of the succession. In order to
marry Wallis, the Prince would have to withdraw from the
line, since he could not expect to be crowned King and

Defender of the Faith if married to a woman whom he had taken from her husband.

The last obstacle was financial. If he withdrew, he would lose the royal perquisites and services and even his beloved Fort. Worse, he would lose the bulk of his income, including the revenues from the Duchy of Cornwall (some 100,000 pounds a year), which are reserved for the heir apparent. This would mean the instant evaporation of those trains, yachts, suites, and airplanes which Wallis found "part of the natural order of things."

Nonetheless, the Prince still cherished the hope that "one day I might be able to share my life with her, just how I did not know."

If he was ever to find out, the first obstacle had to be surmounted at once: He had to disclose his intentions to his father, which—he acknowledged—was "not going to be easy." This was an understatement; he would find it not only difficult, but impossible. When the old King died, seventeen months later, the Prince still had not mustered his courage; nor had he ever advanced the argument which he had painstakingly framed and rehearsed—that his brother Bertie, so much more like their father in both temperament and habit, would make a capable, dutiful monarch.

Prince Albert ("Bertie"), the second son, was doomed from his birth in 1895 to Queen Victoria's disfavor, for the offense of having been born on December 14, "Mausoleum Day," the anniversary of the death of her adored consort in 1861. In an attempt to appease her, the infant was named for him. Prince Bertie's childhood was unhappy; he had to wear corrective braces on his crooked legs, and the stammering that embarrassed him through his whole life began when he was only six or seven, probably as a result of his father's unwise attempt to break him of his natural left-handedness. Lady Airlie has written:[1] "Intensely sensitive over his stammer, [Bertie] was apt to take refuge either in silence—which caused him to be thought moody—or in naughtiness. He was more often in conflict with authority than the rest of his brothers." He was also given to nervous rages which sometimes drove him, even as a mature man, to stalk off the tennis court or the golf course after a poor shot, abandoning his partner or opponent in midgame.

In his early teens, he followed his elder brother to the Royal Naval College, but was seldom able to struggle higher than one or two slots above the very foot of the class. Handicapped by his slow wits, his stammer, and his frail constitution, he nevertheless chose the Royal Navy as his career, and he was serving as a midshipman on H.M. battleship *Collingwood* when the Great War broke out. His tour of combat duty was short; after three weeks, an attack of appendicitis put him ashore for an operation and a long, slow convalescence. Ill health continued to dog "Mr. Johnson," as the Navy knew him, from then on. He rejoined the *Collingwood* in February 1915 only to be soon knocked out again, by a gastric ulcer; and days after he rejoined her a second time, in May 1916, as a sublieutenant, the ulcer had him back in sick bay. He was there on the thirty-first when the *Collingwood* opened fire in the Battle of Jutland, but he insisted on manning his battle station in "A" turret, and he stayed there until ordered below. Later he would have the distinction of qualifying as an airplane pilot.

Created Duke of York in 1920, he married Lady Elizabeth Bowes-Lyon, daughter of the Earl and Countess of Strathmore, on April 26, 1923, in Westminister Abbey—the first British prince to be married there since the fourteenth century. Just before their wedding, his father wrote him, "You have always been so sensible and easy to work with and you have always been ready to listen to my advice and agree with my opinions about people and things that I feel we have always got on very well together. Very different to dear David." Father and second son were alike in more than temperament. Queen Marie of Romania wrote to George V (her first cousin) in 1922 that Bertie, who had been visiting her, "reminded me so much of you, though he has exactly May's [Queen Mary's] smile, but his movements were yours, and his hands." Presently father was to write son again, "The better I know and the more I see of your dear little wife, the more charming I think she is." Princess Elizabeth of York (now Queen Elizabeth II) was born on April 21, 1926, and Princess Margaret Rose (now Countess of Snowdon) on August 21, 1930.

* * *

A courtier who knew the royal family intimately said of them, "They were not given to talking things out together, even *en famille*. If anything was wrong, the subject was carefully avoided. They would talk about shooting, the weather, a friend's marriage, the shocking behavior of the French—but never a word about the subject gnawing their souls."

Prince Edward had no trouble rationalizing his default. When he returned from the *Rosaura* cruise, his parents and the Court were already absorbed in preparations for the marriage of his youngest brother, Prince George (newly created Duke of Kent), to Princess Marina of Greece, on November 29. The lovely Marina, daughter of Prince Nicholas and Grand Duchess Helena of Russia, and sister of Princess Olga, who had married Prince Paul of Yugoslavia, was a first cousin of King George II of the Hellenes and of Prince Philip Duke of Edinburgh. As had Princess Friederike of Hanover (now ex-Queen Mother of the Hellenes) and Princess Ingrid of Sweden (now Queen of Denmark), Princess Marina had been pushed forward for the heir's approval. None of the three had aroused his interest, but Prince George had fallen in love on the spot. Wales had deep affection, tinged with envy, for Bertie, the devoted family man who was next to him in the line, and he was happy to realize that Bertie's marriage meant his escape from their father's authority; but he had more in common with George, despite the gap of nearly eight years between them. They had discovered their special compatibility during the winter of 1911, when they were left together at Sandringham while their parents went to India for the Durbar, and ever since then George had been David's favorite. They shared much beside their notable good looks and charm. No less notable was a rebelliousness that the other brothers lacked, a wildness that these two seemed unable to control. Lady Willingdon, the wife of the Governor General of Canada, long remembered the evening in 1927 when the two princes disappeared from a ball in their honor at Government House, in Ottawa, and reappeared some hours later at a private party elsewhere.

The Bruce Lockhart diary for September 6, 1929, records that "The Prince of Wales turned up at the Casino in

Le Touquet the other night quite drunk and incapable of standing." Those who knew the Prince during that period find this tale unlikely. To be sure, he never had a strong head for liquor. His diary for his first term at Magdalen, in 1912, fragments of which he read aloud one festive evening to these authors, is studded with callow confessions of drunkenness and nausea at regular fortnightly intervals, almost as if he had bound himself to a barbaric rite of passage into manhood. Years later, he would tell Cyrus Sulzberger, the *New York Times* columnist, that he had found Oxford quite agreeable "because we were drunk all the time."[2] This is part braggadocio and mostly nonsense; his diary also shows a regimen of jogging, hacking, and hunting that he could not have sustained if he had indulged himself in anything much more debilitating than an occasional spree. He continued to drink throughout his life (usually Scotch and soda before dinner, and brandy afterward), but with both a stronger head and increasing moderation. Lord Mountbatten never saw him "more than a bit tiddly, never so sloshed that he couldn't have instantly pulled himself together." Thelma encouraged him to run loose, but Wallis soon brought him back to heel and kept him there. After his marriage, few ever saw him even "a bit tiddly" until his last years, when alcohol helped numb his almost constant pain. However severe it became, he never, never broke his rule against drinking before seven in the evening.

A friend of Wallis's remembers a tiny incident when cocktails were being served before a luncheon on Maryland's Eastern Shore. The butler asked the Duke, "What may I give you to drink, sir?"

"A glass of milk, please," the Duke said, smiling. "Silly, isn't it?"

Barring his cold, callous discard of an outworn friend or a superseded mistress, his social offenses were seldom worse than unpunctuality or a broken appointment or another such incivility. Prince George's were more extreme, more frequent, and more alarming, as Wales seemed to realize. Watching them together, Wallis did not have to look closely to perceive that the Prince of Wales was becoming gravely alarmed that Kent had gotten out of hand—that he had not only become reckless to the point of wildness but that he was losing control over his appetites. Although Raymond Mortimer, writing in *The Sunday Times*,[3] submits that "The Duke of Kent was the only child of Queen Mary to grow up without serious handicaps," he would find it hard to defend his thesis if "handicaps" included defects of character. According to a lady who knew all the princes, "George had a clear tinge of narcissism. He frankly loved to be loved and admired. When he visited an old nurse of his who had retired to Roehampton, it was partly out of kindness, but chiefly because she loved him and often told him so."

A late equerry of Prince Edward, both as Prince of Wales and King, agreed with the lady's analysis. "Self-esteem was a strong trait in the whole royal family," he said, "especially in Kent. He had more brains than any of the other brothers and more taste, and was more interested in intellectual affairs, but he was a scamp. He was always in trouble with girls. Scotland Yard chased so many of them out of the country that the Palace stopped counting. Whenever I heard about a new caper of his, I was reminded of Jingle's remark in *Pickwick*: 'Kent, sir—everyone knows Kent—apples, cherries, hops, and women.'" One of Kent's women, an American, seduced him into taking drugs and so corrupted him that he was led to the brink of suicide. The corruption was abetted by a rich young South American roué whom the Prince of Wales ordered brought to St. James's Palace. "You are to leave England *at once*," the Prince told him curtly. "Where do you wish your baggage sent?"

"To Paris," the boy sneered. "To the Hôtel Prince de Galles."

Wales persuaded Kent to take a cure; and for his eventual rescue and redemption, George had his brother David to thank—and only David.

Marriage to Princess Marina would steady George, but it would mean that David saw less of him. He had always enjoyed showing his guests at the Fort the room permanently reserved for George (who also had his own room at York House). "It's full of the most *dreadful* birds!" he would warn them beforehand, and then fling open the door on a wallpaper with a garish pattern of toucans.

There seemed to be no intermission between the Kent wedding festivities and the King and Queen's preparations for Christmas, the season when, more than at any other, the royal family became an English family, and always gathered around the hearth at "dear old Sandringham," as the King called it, "the place I love better than anywhere else in the world." Edward VII had loved it, too; he spent not only his Christmases there, but his birthdays, November 9, and Queen Alexandra's, December 1. As Prince of Wales, he had bought the 7,000-acre estate in Norfolk for 220,000 pounds in 1861 and had spent an additional 80,000 pounds building up the shooting and refurnishing the huge, mock-Tudor mansion before he considered it fit to receive him, in 1870. Since then, the property has been enlarged to 19,000 acres and is now valued at 6,000,000 pounds. Considering Wales's passion for Mrs. Simpson and his commitment to her, why did he not take this ideal opportunity to inform his father of his intentions? What warmer, more sympathetic atmosphere could he hope for, than the family hearth at Christmastide? The question still hangs over the whole Simpson affair. There are only two plausible explanations. One was his hope, nourished by his natural procrastination, that a Micawberish solution would present itself if he waited until he mounted the throne—an elevation which his father's rapid decline seemed to make imminent. The other was that he was too terrified of his father—as were his mother, his sister, his brothers, and the entire Court—to expose to open air a subject which, like phosphorus, would thereupon instantly ignite.

They all had reason to be terrified. The King's hair-trigger temper and his often abrasive manner were combined with insensitivity and invulnerability. He was utterly indifferent to whose feelings he trod on, or how heavily. Sometimes he was merely sarcastic, as when he remarked to the courtier who was rashly affecting the new style of cuffs on his trousers, "I was not aware that my Palace is damp!" Sometimes he was brutal, as when he snarled at a servant who had dropped a tea tray at Windsor, "That's right! Break up my whole bloody castle!" Sometimes he was insulting, as when Emir Amanullah of Afghanistan was taking his leave, and the King called to the lord-in-waiting who was ushering him out, "Shut the door! I can

smell that damned nigger from here!" Sometimes his
brusqueness sent Queen Mary from the dinner table in
tears; and when his mortal illness was upon him, and she
tried to cheer him with "You look better today! Soon
you'll be able to go back to Bognor and rest," his only
response was "Bugger Bognor!"

Once when his wrath had scorched all his sons unfairly,
Dickie Mountbatten urged them to lay the facts before
their mother: "She'll make him see your side of it."

"No," said Prince Edward. "It wouldn't do any good.
She's as frightened of Papa as we are."

It was true. She never dared to cross him or to stand up
for the children in the face of his fury. After his death, she
drew somewhat closer to her younger sons and became
more tolerant, more forgiving, but the softening was too
late to help her eldest.

Lord Mountbatten has said, "The King loved his children—make no mistake about it! But he was a martinet,
gruff, unbending on matters of form and etiquette." It cannot be wondered, then, that they spent in his company as
little time as they could manage—especially the Prince of
Wales, tortured as he was already by his desperate,
laboratory-rat attempts to thread the blind maze and reach
his reward. Naturally, he turned to Wallis for balm. Ever
since Formentor, he had been telephoning to her several
times a day, often on the pretext of consulting her about
his princely duties or about some housekeeping problem at
the Fort. It was less that he wanted suggestions than that
he wanted instructions, *orders*. More often than not, the
consultations were continued at a twosome dinner in some
secluded restaurant. Before long he had abandoned all pretense at discretion and was parading her openly, until there
was scarcely an evening when they were not seen together
at the theatre, or a State ceremony, or an embassy reception. Plainly, he was thrusting her upon London Society,
and Society—quick to realize that a new favorite had been
given his accolade, and that therefore a new and unknown
power had to be deferred to—was forced into a rapid re-
alignment.

A small group of loyalists privately deplored his desertion of Thelma Furness. A far larger group was too busy
enlisting under the new banner to spare Thelma even a

tear. Of these latter, the leaders, whom the Prince had astutely commissioned as his field commanders, were London's two smartest hostesses: Lady Cunard and Lady Colefax.

Emerald Cunard's friends liked to discuss whether the
ideal artist to have painted her was Nattier, Boucher, or
Fragonard. Tiny and wrinkled, heavily *maquillée*, with a
silvery powder brushed through her hair, squirrel-toothed
and incessantly gabbling, she made Cyril Connolly think of
"a little parakeet in her pastille-coloured plumage" [pas-
tel?]. To Chips Channon, she was "a twittering, bejewelled
bird." To Kenneth Clark, she was as "neat as a Clodion
with tiny bones and brilliant blue eyes." To Mary Craws-
haw, she was "the daughter of Puck and Madame Tussaud." To Harold Nicolson, she was "a third-dynasty
mummy painted by an amateur." But Nicolson hated
Americans, and the celebrated Lady Cunard was indeed an
American: She had been born a Burke in San Francisco
and christened "Maude"; the "Emerald" came later, on the
advice of a numerologist. At twenty-three she had married
Sir Bache Cunard, twenty years her senior, and had moved
to London, where she caught the eye of King Edward VII
and, in time, of his grandson, the Prince of Wales. The
grandfather would have agreed that her step had lost none
of its buoyancy.

The two loves of her life were George Moore and Sir
Thomas Beecham. Moore mooned over her "fern-like"
hand; Beecham broke her heart. Until the rivalry ended,
with Moore's death in 1933, one or the other of them often
starred at the luncheons and dinners she gave several times
a week, first at Carlton House Terrace, and later at 9
Grosvenor Square. The circular table was made of lapis
lazuli, the food was delicious, and the conversation (which
she led) was brilliant. No one noticed her wrinkles and
paint after she began to talk. An excellent education, a
sparkling wit, and a huge fund of miscellaneous information let her discuss subjects that ranged from cockfighting
to Webster's *Duchess of Malfi*. Her specialty was the
"throwaway shocker," a small bomb dropped with the utmost casualness; one such as "Christ had a very unpleasant
face, and John the Baptist's was little better"; another was

"Christmas is only for servants." She particularly enjoyed posing mischievous questions, embarrassing to answer. She asked Prince Friedrich of Prussia, "Which do you think are the more unfashionable, the Connaughts or the Gloucesters?"; and she cooed at the German Ambassador, Von Ribbentrop, "Tell us, dearest Excellency, *why* does Herr Hitler dislike the Jews?"

There was usually an ambassador at her table, a cabinet minister and his wife (the Churchills, the Duff Coopers, the Anthony Edens), a writer or two (Shaw, Somerset Maugham, Sacheverell Sitwell, Peter Quennell, Evelyn Waugh), and assorted other celebrities, often including royalty (Wales or the Kents). She never bothered to have equal numbers of men and women because "I invite my friends for conversation, not for mating." She may have led the conversation, but she never monopolized it. One of her most attractive talents was for making shy, dull people rise and shine.

Shane Leslie said that she "could flick her guests into animation like a practiced ring-master"; someone else said that she was like "a spiritual dowser in a desert." Her generosity (usually anonymous) was as proverbial as her charm and wit; it was Emerald Cunard who organized and led off the fund that let James Joyce live out his last years in financial peace. Her friends spoke of her affectionately as "the Pocket Venus" and "the Lollipop." Almost her only faults were her unpunctuality, and the sympathy she sometimes professed with Nazism. Even then, those who knew her best thought that she was influenced more strongly by Von Ribbentrop's dimples than by his creed.

Early in 1940, with the war refusing to abate, she moved to the Ritz and gave up 9 Grosvenor Square, "the house where"—Chips Channon lamented—"we have all been made so exquisitely and elegantly happy . . . where the great met the gay, statesmen consorted with society, and writers with the rich—and where, over a year, the drama of Edward VIII was enacted. . . . The conversation in the candlelight, the elegance, the bibelots and the books. . . . It was a rallying point of most of London society."

A few years after the war, she died, in her latter seventies. Her ashes were scattered over Grosvenor Square.

* * *

Her rival, Lady Sibyl Colefax, was much like her, professionally. In her beautiful Argyl House in Chelsea, and then at 19 Lord North Street, Westminster, she, too, served memorable luncheons and dinners to celebrated people. According to Alastair Forbes, writing in the *Times Literary Supplement*,[4] "Someone once said that Sibyl's dinner parties looked like a lot of lunatics having a rotten time in the charge of a very strict unsmiling matron-cum-wardress, while Emerald's more often resembled a lot of jolly loonies enjoying themselves under the leadership of the maddest mad hatter of them all." Although her guest list largely overlapped Lady Cunard's in politics and diplomacy, Lady Colefax drew more on literature (T. S. Eliot, the Kiplings, Rebecca West, H. G. Wells, Max Beerbohm, André Maurois), the stage and screen (John Gielgud, Tilly Losch, Granville Barker, Alexander Korda, Charlie Chaplin), and America (Mrs. Otto Kahn, Alexander Woollcott, Walter Lippmann, the Thomas Lamonts); but almost any international face card was likely to turn up at her table sooner or later. Woollcott loved "the enchanting odor of burning pinewood that greets the guests as they step across the threshold," and suspected "some kind of tea smouldering in the umbrella stand." It wasn't unusual for Arthur Rubinstein or Noel Coward to come to dine and remain to play. Soon after Edward VIII's Accession, Lady Colefax even arranged to have a key scene from a current drama about divorce and remarriage, *Storm in a Teacup,* staged in her drawing room, so that he and Mrs. Simpson could see it in privacy, without having significance attached to their presence together.

"The Coalbox," short and slender and prisoned in an "iron cage of curls" (according to Osbert Sitwell), was quite as garrulous as "the Lollipop," but neither so kind nor so witty; and yet, in one of the few instances where they crossed swords, Sibyl Colefax drew the blood. Lady Cunard remarked that she had just received "a very nice letter" from Count Dino Grandi, the Italian Ambassador in London. "Have *you* heard from him, Lady Colefax?"

"Only by telegram," Lady Colefax said. Her own letters were notoriously illegible; Kenneth Clark said that they "looked like a bicycle race"; and Woollcott reported to Noel Coward during the war, "I have heard with exquisite pleasure that the overworked censors are compelling Sibyl to use a typewriter."

She reminded Channon of "obsidian or onyx—shiny and metallic." (Ronald Tree, M.P., applied the second adjective to Wallis: "Her somewhat metallic elegance did not attract me.") [5] A few thought Lady Colefax too "hostessy"; but she could be cozy and interesting tête-à-tête or in a small group. A point on which there was no disagreement whatever was her skill and taste as a decorator. Her famous (and famously expensive) shop, Sibyl Colefax and John Fowler, Ltd., was represented in many of the smartest houses in London, and indeed is still thriving, just off New Bond Street.

During the war, she, too, gave up her house and moved to a hotel, the Dorchester. She died in 1950, having scored off her rival yet again in surviving her by two years.

Once this clever, pushy pair took up Wallis Simpson, invitations from the lower ranks cascaded into Bryanston Court. To be sure, the truly great London families, those of stately homes and venerable names—the Devonshires, the Derbys, the Sutherlands, the Salisburys, the Londonderrys, the Stanleys, and the haughty rest—continued to keep their distance. They had no need, or even the inclination, to jockey for position in the circle forming around the Prince's controversial new favorite—not least controversial because she was now seen seldom with her husband and seldom without her lover. Mayfair wits were saying that Ernest Simpson had become "the little man who wasn't there."

Lady Colefax and Lady Cunard launched their protégée well, and by January 1935, four months after Majorca, the promotion campaign was well under way. Presently the Baltimore girl was quite used to finding herself at the same table with half the most important names in England. She was far from dazzled by this galaxy. She herself shone, too, quietly, in manner, wit, and dress. She was an ornament to the table and to the Prince. Though he and Freda had been a conspicuously "well-matched couple," he and Wallis were quite as much so. Both were slim and small, about five feet six, with her perhaps half an inch the taller. Both had blue eyes; hers were deep and lustrous, unquestionably her best feature; his were pale and slightly bulging, the "poached" eyes of the Hanoverians. Both were neat; it was as impossible to picture her with soiled gloves or a sagging hem as to picture him unshaven or with frayed cuffs. Both had a flair for fashion, both were vivacious, both liked to laugh, and both enjoyed frivolous, raffish companions. Such were some of their similarities; their dissimilarities were fewer, slower to be recognized, and grave.

Several of her new acquaintances have testified to the impression she made upon them:

Channon's diary for January 23, 1935, recorded his invitation to meet her at a luncheon at Lady Cunard's. Although he too despised everything American, as only self-exiled Americans can, Wallis struck him as "a nice, quiet, well-bred mouse of a woman with large startled eyes and a huge mole" (below the right corner of her mouth; it was usually painted out in her photographs). But "quiet"? Prince Christopher of Greece said that she "never stopped talking." "I think she is surprised," Channon went on, "and rather conscience-stricken by her present position and the limelight which consequently falls upon her." When he saw her next, two months later, at a luncheon he and his wife gave for her, his judgment had matured. Wallis was still a "quiet, unpretentious, and unprepossessing little woman, but . . . she already has the air of a personage who walks into a room as though she almost expected to be curtsied to. . . . she has complete power over the Prince of Wales, who is trying to launch her socially." Plainly, the "mouse of a woman" had gained authority and gained it fast.

Channon, himself a climber, was fascinated to watch his compatriot's swift, assured, adroit arrogation of power. Another month, and his diary recorded that Wallis had banned Thelma Furness's group from York House: "It is war to the knife between the past and the present. . . . The Prince of Wales . . . is obviously madly infatuated. . . . Never has he been so in love. She is madly anxious to storm society, while she is still his favourite, so that when he leaves her (as he leaves everyone in time) she will be secure."

They met again in Emerald Cunard's box at the opera;

and Channon noted the "extraordinary hold Mrs. Simpson has over the Prince." Aghast, he watched her make him "take a cigar from his breast pocket. 'It doesn't look very pretty,' she said." Frances Donaldson wrote of this incident in her *Edward VIII*,[6] "One has only to visualize Mrs. Keppel [King Edward VII's last mistress] pulling at the King's cigar, and ordering him about with the confidence which only intimacy can give, to realize how little Mrs. Simpson was equipped to be Queen of England or even for the role of King's mistress." The unabashed authority that Thelma Furness had seen exhibited in the privacy of the Fort, Wallis no longer scrupled to exercise in public. The Baltimore canons of etiquette, having reformed the royal handling of a lettuce leaf, were now addressed to the royal display of a cigar. Janet Flanner's article about Wallis in *The New Yorker* would note her "American woman's tendency to reform men in small ways."

Harold Nicolson met Wallis and the Prince at a theatre party given by Sibyl Colefax. What impressed him most strongly, as it had Channon, was again her open demonstration of the nursery one-two: reproach and correction. "She forbade [him] to smoke during the *entr'acte* in the theatre itself." Nicolson saw her as "bejewelled, eye-brow-plucked, virtuous and wise," but he also sensed something that troubled him: "I have an uneasy feeling that Mrs. Simpson, in spite of her good intentions, is getting him out of touch with the type of person with whom he ought to associate. . . . I think the P. of W. is in a mess."[7]

CHAPTER 9
The King Dies, the Question Unasked

While we are postponing, life speeds by.
—Letters to Lucilius, SENECA

Nicolson's opinion was far from being the P. of W.'s own. He was never livelier, busier, or happier than in the opening months of 1935. While he was making it known to Society (which "the Prince of Wales's set" had led for so long) that Wallis Simpson had become his new love, Wallis was making it known to Ernest, with something of her lover's own indirectness. One January evening at Bryanston Court, she told him that the Prince was organizing a party to go to Vienna and Budapest in February, and had invited them to join him.

"I can't possibly," Ernest said. "I've already planned a business trip to New York. In fact, I was rather hoping you'd come with me."

Wallis laughed. "And miss Vienna and Budapest? I wouldn't dream of it!"

Ernest went to his bedroom, slamming the door. It was not a scene to inspire the composition of more doggerel.

The fun lasted for better than three weeks. Thereafter, whenever Wallis heard a melancholy little song called "Chi, Chi, Chi," about rain on the roof, she would remember Budapest and the gypsy violins. Another song, a waltz,

Ich weiss auf der Wieden ein Kleines Hotel
In einen verschweigenen Gässchen.
Die Nacht ist so kurz und der Tag kommt so schnell . . .
Komm mit mir, du Kleines Countesschen!

[I know a small hotel in the Wieden
On a small, hidden street.

The night is so short, and the day comes so quickly . . .
    Come with me, my little countess!]

would always recall for her Vienna and more violins.

Vienna, in turn, would recall the Prince's visit for more practical reasons. Sir Walford Selby, the British Minister, wrote, "The Austrian authorities . . . appreciated the political significance, in support of Austria, deriving from a visit from the British Heir Apparent. . . . H.R.H. enjoyed great personal popularity in Austria. The Austrians were unquestionably grateful to him for his presence in Vienna at a time when they were under so much pressure from Hitler."[1]

Back in London as the month turned, he found the King's calendar crowded with a round of celebrations for the Silver Jubilee, so it was hardly "a propitious time" for him to raise the nettlesome question of marriage to Mrs. Simpson. Doubtless to his relief, he had an excuse for postponing the confrontation once again.

Like Queen Victoria's schedule, George V's was ordained and inflexible. Each successive year was cut to the identical pattern of the year preceding. But unlike hers, his accommodated sporting events: the Derby, the first Wednesday in June; Royal Ascot, the week afterward; Goodwood, the third week in July; Cowes, the third week in August. The grouse season opened on August 12, but even though the King had a passion for shooting, he enjoyed Cowes too much to leave for Balmoral before the twenty-fifth; then he stayed until October, when he returned to town for the opening of Parliament.

Nothing except illness and the Great War was allowed to alter this schedule in any respect. Even Court functions—two levees, two garden parties, two Courts—had second priority; they had to be meshed with the sporting fixtures as best they could. The Jubilee celebration, which ran from March into July, meant additional pother almost daily—official luncheons, dinners and receptions, audiences, parades, reviews and other ceremonies, such as the State Ball on May 14, each requiring the Prince of Wales to be at his father's shoulder. Wales's obligations were increased by the King's failing health, which loaded all four princes —particularly the heir apparent—with extraordinary public appearances. To husband the King's strength for major occasions, Wales stood in for him at the first levee, on March 22; again at the Court ball on June 13; and again at Windsor, where he received the Queen's state visit on the fifteenth. On top of all this, he launched the King George V Jubilee Trust Fund with a reception for all the lords lieutenant, lord mayors, and provosts of Great Britain, on March 1 at St. James's Palace; and there again, on May 7, he and his sister gave a party for twelve hundred in honor of their parents.

The levees, which always took place at St. James's Palace at eleven in the morning, were stag affairs. The King sat on his throne, and a line of men passed before him, each pausing and nodding, receiving a return nod, and passing along. Jack Aird, standing behind the King, found his own head nodding in unison. He said, "The operation became so mechanical, so like a sausage machine, that we could 'process' a man every six seconds, six hundred men an hour." Wales considered levees a bore, but he knew they were a necessary bore. Unless a man had been invited to a levee as a bachelor, he could not be invited to a Court function. Before the Second World War, young women and newly married wives were presented to the King and Queen at one of the Courts. Queen Mary ran them with great style. They were much more serious than levees and were a magnificent spectacle, the women in their most beautiful gowns and jewels, the men in their most splendid uniforms, with decorations.

The Prince drew his new love into as many of these affairs as protocol—and prudence—permitted. He even dared dance her past his mother and father at the State Ball. According to Wallis, it was then that she felt "the King's eyes rest searchingly" upon her.[2] According to a cynical courtier who happened to be watching, "The King always knew when there was a girl somewhere in Wales's background. Now he knew that the main drain was open." Her friends felt in her an undisguised exhilaration, the emergence of an unexpected taste for command, for the kowtow. And little wonder. When they inquired about her, it was to be told by the maid and increasingly often by Ernest alone that she was out for supper with the Prince. Her own calendar confirms it. They had already spent most of February together in Vienna and Budapest, and they would return there for August and September as well. In addition, they had more than seventy meetings in England, including almost every weekend at the Fort and a full week at Ascot in June. (But Wallis's name never appeared in the Fort guest book.)

The summer of 1935 would prove even less propitious than the spring for the Prince to face up to his father, in whose bad graces he was now freshly and triply embedded. His first "offense" was a proposal to the British Legion that it send a delegation to visit German veterans of the Great War—a proposal which the Legion's chairman had urged upon him, and which the Legion later adopted. His second "offense" was committed in another address, this one at a public school, where he deplored the London County Council's pacifistic ban on the further use of even wooden rifles by the cadet corps. His third was his announced intention to wind up his Riviera holiday with a cruise to the resort ports of Italy and Greece. This drew from his father a blast which began, "You don't seem to read the newspapers!" referring to the well-known strain in Anglo-Italian relations over Ethiopia, and ending with "When you have made new plans, please let me know *for my approval*" (italics added). That said, the King left for Balmoral, and the Prince hastily scrapped the cruise for another visit to Vienna and Budapest.

He invited Ernest on this excursion, too, but again Ernest declined; he was planning to go to New York and on to Washington, to consult Mrs. Merryman about his disintegrating marriage. Aunt Bessie's sympathies were with Ernest, whom she had always liked and respected; moreover, she disapproved her niece's bold behavior. Ernest told her that he "adored" Wallis—was "crazy about her" and did not want to "lose her for any reason." (The sincerity of his devotion seemed unquestionable at the time, though developments in the next few months would put it in doubt.) He said, "This thing has hit both of us like an avalanche. Wallis can't seem to stop it. I'm a British subject, and it's an honor for me to have the Prince sit at my table and accept us as his friends. Wallis isn't alarmed." He added unconvincingly, "Neither am I."

But Mrs. Merryman was. She had seen Wallis emerge from a wretched marriage into a happy one, and she did not wish this one also destroyed. She warned Ernest, "No woman can resist for long the attentions the Prince is paying Wallis. I've watched her. There is no possible outcome but unhappiness for the three of you."

"Perhaps," Ernest said. "But both Wallis and I have profited from his friendship." It was the only self-serving remark that Mrs. Merryman ever heard him make.

The Prince's spirits quickly recovered from his father's blasts. A cousin of Wallis's saw him at Bryanston Court "wearing a German helmet and goose-stepping around the living room, for what reason I can't imagine." Chips Channon saw him there on another afternoon, gaily shaking cocktails and pouring them for Emerald Cunard, David Margesson, and others; he seemed very much at home— "very much the 'jeune homme de la maison,'" though it pained the American-born Chips to observe that his voice was now "more American than ever."[3] Wallis's voice was changing, too. Her gentle, unobtrusive Maryland accent was becoming overlaid by a peculiar, flat *quack* which sounded like an Americanized adaption of the British accent then in increasingly unintelligible evolution in Mayfair drawing-room comedies, a rare specimen of which survives in the speech of Katharine Hepburn. When the Duchess of Windsor was asked whom she would choose to portray her on the screen, she said without hesitation, "Katharine Hepburn!" The Duke, to portray himself, chose Rex Harrison. Her voice made different impressions on different people. In 1939, Anne Morrow Lindbergh would see the Duchess in Paris and noted her "strange exaggerated drawl."[4] Eighteen months later, one of William Randolph Hearst's star reporters, Adela Rogers St. Johns, met her and wrote of her "lovely voice, the *English* English, as the English speak it . . . but the Southern accent gets all mixed up with it. I was to discover that one or the other predominated according to mood or situation, and now I wonder if that was one reason she gave me *always* a slight feeling of artificiality."[5]

*   *   *

With Ernest in America, the Prince's party took off on August 5. Besides the host and Wallis, it included Perry and Kitty Brownlow, Colin and Gladys Buist, Helen Fitzgerald (Lord Beaverbrook's sister-in-law), Hugh Sefton, and Jack Aird. The first stop was Paris, then Cannes, Geneva, Budapest, Vienna, Salzburg, Munich, Paris, and home again, early in October. The current and all-absorbing topic, they found on their return, was Ernest's absence. What had been until recently a tactful *ménage à trois* was now down to two, except on those occasions when Ernest's failure to appear would have spread the gossip outside the "set," and hastened the scandal that was making up around the Prince.

It would break soon enough, as it was. Indeed, his infatuation with Mrs. Simpson was already causing concern in the three most exalted quarters of the realm: Buckingham Palace, Lambeth Palace, and 10 Downing Street. Cosmo Lang, the Archbishop of Canterbury, had brought his misgivings to Balmoral on his usual September visit; he found the King depressed by "certain family troubles," which the two old friends discussed freely but painfully. No such misgivings would beset the soon-to-be Prime Minister, Stanley Baldwin. He had never liked the Prince, and had no confidence in him; should the scandal destroy him, Baldwin would not grieve. In *King Henry VI, Part II,* the Earl of Warwick declares, "York is the worthier"; Baldwin privately agreed.

If the Prince had hoped that two months in Wallis's company, uninterrupted, would strengthen him for the dreaded parley with his father, he was wrong. He postponed it still, justifying himself on the ground that "a remarkable concatenation of events left me no opportunity to talk things over." The first event was the marriage, on November 6, of his third brother, Prince Henry Duke of Gloucester, to Lady Alice Montagu-Douglas-Scott. Her father, the Duke of Buccleuch, was George V's oldest friend, and his death on the eve of the wedding was a heavy blow to the King. It did not comfort him to reflect, next day, "Now all the children are married but David."

His parents were baffled and troubled by their "child's" reluctance to perpetuate the royal line. He was forty-one. For more than twenty years, Mama in particular had been

nudging him to choose from the dwindling pool of candidates. The night before he started on his first trip to Germany, in March 1912, when he was not yet eighteen, he
had dined alone with her and had recorded in his diary
how thoroughly she had briefed him on the relatives he
would meet; how she had traced for him the intricate
bloodlines that linked her House of Teck with Papa's
House of Hanover, and both with those that crisscrossed
Hohenzollern Germany; and how she had laid special emphasis—it struck him—on the comeliness and eligibility of
certain young *Prinzessen*, as a hint that he should begin
thinking about the fulfillment of his dynastic duties.

Mama and Papa could not understand his failure to do
so, any more than they understood his liaisons with married women, and his preference for fast (to them) associates and American ways. It would have availed nothing to
remind them of Edmund Burke's dictum, "Kings are naturally lovers of low company," or for them to recall that
Edward VII, too, had enjoyed just such people; they
thought rather in terms of Proverbs 28:7: "He that is a
companion of riotous men shameth his father."

Had the parents but known, David was ready to marry,
even pledged to marry. Unhappily, his consort-to-be was so
patently unsuitable that he had dared bring her into their
presence only twice, and then in a press of people, and gin-
gerly. The first time was at a Palace reception before the
Kent wedding; he escorted the Simpsons to the dais and introduced them. An equerry remembers that Ernest, unac-
customed to Court dress, seemed fearful of tripping over
his sword. The second time was at the State Ball, when
Wallis had felt the King's eyes upon her. But for Wales, the
leap from arranging these casual encounters to announcing
that he intended *marrying* the woman was one that, as time
passed, he felt himself less and less capable of making.

Ever since George V's return from Balmoral, those closest to him had noticed the slow, steady waning of his
strength. The Duke of Buccleuch's death had hastened it.
Now, four weeks later, he suffered another blow, even
heavier, in the death of his favorite sister, Princess Victoria
Louise. "Toria" was born in 1868, the fourth child of King
Edward VII and Queen Alexandra, and the second of their
three daughters. The eldest, Princess Louise (1867–1931),

married the Duke of Fife; the youngest, Princess Maud (1869–1938), married her cousin Prince Charles of Denmark, who was elected King of Norway and took the name Haakon VII; Princess Victoria, the most intelligent, was never allowed to cut herself loose from her mother's apron strings. Even when she fell in love with Lord Rosebery, "Darling Motherdear" clung to her—and continued to cling until poor Toria took refuge in hypochondria and drink. Her brother once wrote to his wife, "Mama . . . is one of the most selfish people I know." During the twenty-five years of his reign, Victoria never failed to ring him up every morning that he was at home. The most cherished anecdote about them has her opening one of their telephone chats with "Is that you, you old fool?"

"No, your Royal Highness," the operator answered. "His Majesty has not come on the line yet." He wrote in his diary, "How I shall miss her and our daily talks on the telephone."

The day of her death, he was scheduled to open Parliament. He subordinated his duty to his emotions for the only time in his life, and canceled the ceremony; he never appeared in public afterward. Meanwhile, a general election having brought Stanley Baldwin back into power, and the Italian-Ethiopian situation having come to a head, the King's State papers demanded more and more of his time. Then another Sandringham Christmas was upon them, and the Prince left the family hearth with his gnawing question still unasked. He would never have another chance to ask it, nor to withdraw from the succession without damage to the throne itself.

King George VI's official biographer, Sir John Wheeler-Bennett, believed that Wales never seriously intended telling his father about Mrs. Simpson; he would not have dared to. His brother Bertie agreed; he said to a friend, "It was difficult for David. My father was so inclined to go for him. . . . It was a pity that David did the things which he knew would annoy my father. The result was that they did not discuss the important things quietly."

Lord Mountbatten thinks otherwise. "If George the Fifth had lasted one more year, I'm positive the Prince of Wales would have mustered the courage to announce that he intended marrying the lady, and was prepared to retire from the succession to do so. Look how easy it would have been: The old King would still be on the throne, with the Duke of York warming up on the sidelines. Then, when the time came, there'd have been no violent dislocation, only a smooth, painless transition. The Prince would have remained in England to help his brother, if need be, and Mrs. Simpson would have become a royal duchess."

Opinion also differs on whether Wales really wanted to be King at all. Elsa Maxwell has written that as far back as 1927, he had declared to her, "I don't want to be King. I wouldn't be a very good one." An American woman is steadfast in her recollection of an evening in 1930—she was a guest of the Metcalfes at the time—when Wales rang up and asked Fruity to be at Buckingham Palace next morning at nine-thirty, as he intended telling his father then that he had no wish to inherit the throne. Lady Alexandra Metcalfe, however, does not recollect the incident. Again, in 1931, he is reported to have made the same statement to his father—or to have threatened to make it. And Kent told a friend of a confession of Wales's in 1934, the year he first became infatuated with Mrs. Simpson: He would never be able to endure Court life, with its outmoded restraints and suffocating ceremoniousness; indeed, his independence of spirit, Wales had added, might well make him a "bad" king. He could not help measuring himself against his father, of whom Harold Nicolson wrote that in his twenty-five years as King, he never said or did a wrong thing; and of whom his close friend Sir Derek Keppel, who served as a courtier from 1893 until his death in 1944, said, in phrases that might have come from Sir Thomas Malory, "His was the straightest court there ever was and the cleanest, and King George was the straightest man I ever knew."

The strongest probability is that Wales wanted to be King, but on his own terms, which he knew that the Court, molded by his father in his own uncompromising image, would almost certainly reject. He also wanted to marry Mrs. Simpson, but she would have been twice divorced, and he knew that for this and other reasons, the Court, the

Church, and the Government would almost certainly reject her, too.

While he hesitated, the gulf between himself and his family widened and by now was almost unbridgeable. His brothers Bertie and Harry, dissuaded by their prim wives, rarely visited the Fort anymore; George alone was still a companion. Among his other relatives, only the Mountbattens continued to turn up for weekends. He had lost his mother's sympathy. His father could not be approached. At a time when he needed wise, affectionate, and disinterested counsel, he had no one to turn to. The historian Clarendon wrote of another popular favorite, the second Duke of Buckingham (1628–87). "His single misfortune was (which indeed was productive of many greater) that he never made a noble and a worthy friendship with a man so near his equal that he would frankly advise him, for his honor and true interest, against the current, or rather the torrent, of his impetuous passions." True, Churchill, Duff Cooper, and Beaverbrook stood ready to advise the Prince—and indeed did advise him—but they were not vintage friends of his; and the few such that he had were hardly celebrated for their acumen. He was trapped, distraught, desperate.

Such was the heir apparent's plight, and such was his mood, when, on January 17, 1936, King George V made the last entry in his diary: "I feel rotten." It was almost illegible. Three more days, and—in the gentle phrase of Lord Dawson of Penn, the senior Court physician and the King's friend—his life "moved peacefully to its close." It came just before midnight, as had his father's. An improbable anecdote says that one of his dying whispers was "The Empire?" and that his private secretary answered, "It's absolutely all right, sir."

The Queen and all their children except the Duke of Gloucester, who was ill, were present in the chamber, as was the Archbishop of Canterbury. When death was pronounced, the Queen stooped before her eldest son and took his hand and kissed it; so did the Duke of Kent. The Archbishop noticed that the sons, "especially the Prince of Wales [sic], were painfully upset—I suppose they had seldom if ever seen death." A lady-in-waiting also noticed the new King's anguish; she thought it "frantic and unreasonable," far exceeding that of the other members of his family. Perhaps it was intensified by his awareness that he now had no escape from the succession. Lang went on, "It was the Queen . . . who supported and strengthened" them all. But her friend Lady Airlie observed that "behind her facade of self-control was passionate grief for the husband who had been the center of her life for over forty years."[6]

Presently the new King composed himself enough to slip out and telephone to Wallis; the rest separated for the night, leaving Kent to prepare telegrams for kinsmen, other royalty, and heads of state. Next morning, the King and the Duke of York flew up to London for the Accession Privy Council—the first reigning British monarch ever to fly. John Betjeman commemorated the precedent with some verses, "Death of King George V," which express the puzzlement of the old King's contemporaries when "a young man lands hatless from the air."[7] The Sandringham carpenter made a simple coffin; that afternoon it was taken through the garden, with Forsyth, the King's piper, playing a lament, and laid before the altar in the village church. There it rested, watched over by employees of the estate, until the morning of the twenty-third, when it was loaded onto a gun carriage, and a team from the Royal Horse Artillery drew it the three miles to Wolferton Station. A small procession followed on foot: the four sons and the son-in-law, Lord Harewood; tenants, gamekeepers, neighbors; a groom leading the favorite shooting pony, Jock; and Forsyth, playing another lament. The widowed Queen and the Princess Royal rode in a carriage.

A special train for London waited at Wolferton. When it reached King's Cross, the imperial crown, brought over from the Jewel House in the Tower, was fixed to the lid of the coffin, which another gun carriage, black-draped and hauled by hand, bore to Westminster's Great Hall for the lying-in-state. En route, an ominous incident occurred: The Maltese cross that topped the crown—a cluster of two hundred diamonds and one large square-cut sapphire—became loosened by the jolting and fell, sparkling as it tumbled along the street. The King saw it from the corner of his eye. "Christ!" he muttered. "What's going to happen next?"

The Minister of Agriculture, Walter Elliot, overheard him and remarked to a companion, "That will be the motto of the new reign!"

A Grenadier sergeant major, marching beside the carriage, also saw the flash. Without missing a step, he scooped up the cross and trousered it. The Duke of Windsor would write, "It was one of the most quick-witted acts I have ever witnessed."

During the five days and nights of the lying-in-state, officers of the Household Troops, along with the Gentlemen at Arms and the Yeoman of the Guard, stood a continuous vigil at the bier, four at a time, in turns of twenty minutes. Nearly a million mourners filed past, but it is doubtful if any of the hundreds who came just after midnight on the twenty-seventh noticed that among the silent officers in full-dress uniform, heads bowed over arms reversed, stood the late King's four sons, paying him their last tribute. Queen Mary commissioned a painting of this "Vigil of the Princes," and she and the rest of the royal family presented it to King Edward on his next birthday. He in turn gave it to Lord Brownlow, who bequeathed it to Prince Charles.

The interment was that day, in St. George's Chapel, Windsor. The Archbishop of Canterbury recited, "Earth to earth," and slowly and silently the coffin sank into the vault where King George V's forefathers awaited him.

A. J. P. Taylor wrote of George V, "He never made an interesting remark, never hit on a fresh belief. . . . He was unfailingly ordinary." Here he echoed the King's own words, for George V once remarked to the Archbishop of Canterbury, "I am only a very ordinary fellow."

He was right. When he met Charles Lindbergh, he at once put a question that had sprung to every ordinary fellow's mind, though perhaps not to his lips: "What did you do about peeing?" An ordinary fellow is matter-of-fact, humorless, imprescient. Yet on July 11, 1881, the naval cadet who would someday become the "matter-of-fact" King George V entered in the log of H.M.S. *Inconstant* that he had sighted, only two hundred yards away, the legendary *Flying Dutchman*, her hull, sails, and spars vivid and unmistakable in the brilliant phosphorescent light.

And when the infamous Hoare-Laval Treaty was revealed in December 1935, the "humorless" George V remarked, "No more coals to Newcastle, no more Hoares to Paris!"

Finally, the "imprescient" George V said to Stanley Baldwin, "After I am dead, the boy will ruin himself in twelve months." The process actually took less than eleven. (Just before Edward VII's death in 1910, he is said to have predicted, "My son may reign, but my grandson never will."[8])

Wallis Simpson was at a cinema in London on the evening of the King's death. The film was interrupted at nine-twenty-five for the "peacefully to its close" bulletin from Sandringham; and when it resumed, she saw and heard none of it. Her thoughts had already raced elsewhere. Years later, she described the turn they had taken:

"I was sure I had a big hurt coming. I liked the world that David had introduced me into—being taken to fine houses, meeting important people and having them suck up to me. My eyes were popping. My head was spinning. But something kept telling me, 'It's going to end now. You're going to know heartbreak.' I remembered my Navy days with Win Spencer. The commandant's wife is the queen bee. She has the best quarters, houseboys, a car with a driver. The other wives kowtow to her. But when her husband is ordered to sea, it all vanishes, and she moves into a little flat—no car, no houseboys, and definitely no kowtowing.

"Was this going to happen to me now? Was I about to revert to being plain Mrs. Simpson, a discarded woman? Nobody believes that David had never asked me to marry him. He just took it for granted I would. I often felt that he thought a woman was only to be enjoyed, not to be taken seriously. Ernest warned me that I was just the froth on David's champagne. Was the monarchy going to close around him and wall me out, as his parents had already done?"

She had part of her answer within hours. Her telephone rang, and a familiar voice said, "It's all over, darling! Papa died a few moments ago." Outside the death chamber, she was the first person to know. The new King went on, "Bertie and I will be flying to London first thing in the morning, for the Accession meeting of the Privy Council. I must see you. I'll break away as soon as I can."

Immediately after the meeting, he came to Bryanston Court. They dined together, and he gave her the rest of her answer: She was not to fear; he would allow nothing between them to change. If any doubt lingered in her mind, it was dispelled next day, when he insisted that she come to a room in St. James's Palace overlooking Friary Court, and watch him be proclaimed King Edward VIII. Traditionally, the monarch does not attend this ceremony; but to Wallis's astonishment, he presently joined her. A newspaper photographer snapped him through the window, and when the picture was printed, it showed at his side the shadowy figure of a woman. She was not identified, but the King's staff and his intimates, recognizing her, felt an icy premonition.

Book II

The King
and
His Mistress

All agreed that he would have been a great ruler, if only he had not ruled.
                    —Histories, TACITUS

CHAPTER 1

The Secret That Was No Secret:
Marriage on the Throne

Being royal has many painful drawbacks.
—The Young Visiters, DAISY ASHFORD

No other public man of this era ever entered upon a climactic duty in middle age with the universal upwelling of goodwill that attended the Accession of King Edward VIII. As Prince of Wales, he had attracted the best press of any figure in the first third of the century. Fame and high expectations had singled him out in youth, not only because he was heir apparent to the world's most powerful throne, but also because of the singular comeliness of his English face, with its shadow of melancholy, especially in repose, that made people linger over his photographs. Through his long maturing as Prince of Wales, he had shown himself courageous in sport and war, solicitous about the poor, eager for instruction in new and promising technologies, and reasonably conversant with, if not sympathetic to, the radical political and social notions that had vexed and baffled his kingly father. In many parts of his vast dominions, he was more than merely admired, he was adored. When a carping voice was raised, it was seldom heard above the worldwide chorus of laudation. The fountain of hero worship bade fair to continue flowing as long as he lived, and the British were disposed to prepare a niche for him in the national pantheon, alongside such demigods as Alfred the Great, King Arthur, Richard the Lion-Hearted, Robin Hood, Nelson, Wellington, and Dr. W. G. Grace.

True, there were his occasional incivilities—tardiness, restlessness, manifest boredom; his unbecoming and inconsiderate parsimony; his cruel dismissal of mistresses and

servitors. There were also rumors—though few and faint—
of certain clandestine irregularities, but these had currency
only in an inner circle. The great mass of his subjects
found him wholly without foibles, much less faults; and
they did not stint the expression of the love they bore him
or the sunny hopes they entertained for him and for themselves. The alarm, the indignation, the wrath that gripped
the Palace Secretariat, and the senior members of the York
House staff who were being absorbed into it, had barely
been sensed, let alone felt, at 10 Downing Street. Scarcely
a hint, even, had yet sifted down to his subjects; so far as
they were concerned, nothing was amiss at the Palace or
could be.

"To the men and women of his generation," wrote Sir
John Wheeler-Bennett, "he typified all that was best in the
twentieth century, and they looked forward to the promise
of a modern monarch, cognizant of the problems of his
peoples and closely identified with their interests and aspirations."[1] Windsor's autobiography, describing his Accession, wryly quotes several of the unqualified encomiums
that gushed from exalted quarters where, before the year
was out, the rage and abuse would be no less unqualified.
The Times perceived in his character and behavior "an
unerring eye for the distinction between dignity and solemnity," a concern for the underprivileged which "more
democrats profess than feel," and a commendable pragma-
tism—"men, not books, are his library." The Archbishop
of Canterbury was inspired to a prediction that the
speeches the new King had made as Prince of Wales would
represent to future historians "the best that can be said of
the industrial, social and commercial life of his day and
generation." And the Prime Minister acclaimed his sovereign as possessing "the secret of youth in the prime of age."

At that juncture, a secret of far more importance was,
What did the King contemplate for Mrs. Simpson? The answer, known only to himself and her at this stage, was, "I
shall marry her." He had so decided some eighteen months
before, at Majorca. But now, having meanwhile acceded,
implementation of his decision had been made immeasur-
ably more difficult. Mrs. Simpson, in becoming his wife,
would also have to become his Queen Consort. No matter;
marriage on the throne had been his heart's most ardent

desire from the moment he knew of his father's death. The
evidence cannot be denied, though neither principal ever
confessed—except privately, and long afterward—to the
course on which they were determined from the first day of
the reign.

The new King had cogent reasons for disguising the true
state of his romance. To have acknowledged it would have
exposed the intended collusive—and therefore illegal—
nature of the Simpson divorce before it had been set in
motion, or even broached to the party of the second part,
Wallis's husband. Windsor said, "The thought always in
the forefront of my mind was to arrange matters so that I
could marry before the Coronation. The trouble was, I
didn't know just how the job could be brought off. It was
because of this uncertainty that nineteen thirty-six was
such a prolonged agony for me." But once on the throne,
he lost no time in making the vital initial deployments for
what he knew in his bones would be a struggle which
would test his resolution to the utmost and which he
sensed he could well lose. To prevail, he would have to win
the assent of the Prime Minister, the Primate of All England, the Parliament, and the governments of the Dominions over the sea. The task called for a negotiator of subtle
talents, solidly grounded in constitutional law and usage
and sensitive to the flux of politics. He already had in his
sights a man of these gifts: Walter Monckton, fortunately a
friend and widely marked as one of the most brilliant
young barristers in the realm; and it was Monckton whom
the King—over the heads of the Palace Secretariat long in
place—reached for as his first counselor.

Walter Turner Monckton (1891–1965) would become
Minister of Information, 1940; Minister of Labor and National Service, 1951–55; Minister of Defence, 1955–56;
chairman of the Midland Bank, 1957–64. He would be
knighted in 1937 and created first Viscount Monckton of
Brenchley, 1957. His was a starring role in the Windsor
drama and he played it superbly. The son of a venerable
Kentish family, he entered Harrow in September 1904 and
soon began to show the dazzling versatility that would dis-
tinguish him thereafter. He captained the cricket eleven,
played football for his house, and won the fencing champi-

onship of the school, in addition to being awarded a scholarship for "sound learning" and being acclaimed the best debater. One of his schoolmates and closest friends was Harold Alexander, later Field Marshal Alexander of Tunis. More laurels awaited him at Balliol, notably the presidency of the Oxford Union, an office which could be a springboard to the highest political posts, if the incumbent so desired. Monckton did not so desire. He preferred the sporting life: fox hunting and steeplechasing (he was a superb horseman), cricket, and gambling and drinking with the richer and racier dining clubs (encouraged by champagne at five shillings the bottle). This was the milieu where he and the Prince of Wales met. The Prince's diary for June 12, 1913, records that he was photographed with the Vincent's Club at Merton at one o'clock and went on to lunch with "Walter Monkton" (—the spelling of Monckton's name gave him trouble all his life).

Beyond that both young men were "bloods," they had little in common. The Prince was Monckton's junior by three and a half years. He was addicted to regular, vigorous exercise—running and beagling, for instance—but he did not care for team sports, especially contact sports. He found cricket a bore; he was too slight for football; and despite arduous practice, he was never better than merely competent at shooting, golf, and riding. Though he rode boldly, even bravely, he would not have ridden at all but for his father's insistence that a good seat was indispensable to his appearance in parades and reviews; his passion for riding did not develop until the 1920's. In contrast to Monckton, his education was paltry and his intellectual interests few. Perhaps the widest disparity between them was in their social address; the Prince was awkward with strangers, whereas Monckton was the most popular man in Balliol, if not in the whole University. Yet, for all his gifts, he achieved only Second Class Honors. When asked why he failed to get a First, he answered gaily, "I was too busy fox hunting, steeplechasing and playing cricket!" His preference doubtless helped redress his unequal friendship with the Prince.

It was slow to flower. After Monckton's gallant service in the Great War, he was called to the bar by the Inner Temple, and within short years had emerged as one of its luminaries. The princes of India chose him as their chief legal adviser; the richest of them, the Nizam of Hyderabad, made him a specially intimate confidant. (Monckton was not easily impressed, but he never forgot being shown the blue safe for the Nizam's sapphires, the red safe for his rubies, and the green safe for his emeralds.) He did not reenter Wales's life until 1928, when George V became critically ill, and Wales summoned Monckton to advise him on the constitutional matters which he now had to face, as the heir apparent, for the first time. The Prince's old admiration was renewed, although their contacts were few and formal. Then the urgency imparted to his private problem by reason of his sudden accession to kingship made a closer association desirable, and he arranged this by appointing Monckton Attorney General of the Duchy of Cornwall, a fiefdom now vacant because the King had no son of his own. The appointment, on its face, was an innocuous one. In the job, Monckton would handle such legal matters as might arise between the vast estate and its numerous tenants and employees, as well as dicker with the Treasury over the fraction of the Duchy's revenues (by now running in excess of 100,000 pounds a year) to be applied to the Civil List, the State's contribution to the sovereign's general expense. But beyond that routine chore, the King wanted to have Monckton close by, to be able to call on his sinewy brain to mastermind the constitutional challenge that he was bent on making, come hell or high water.

Years later, when the Windsors were working on their autobiographies, with Monckton sitting in on the discussions to straighten out or reinforce their fading recollections, the Duke surprised him on one occasion by confiding laughingly that he had resolved as early as 1934 to marry Wallis. Thereafter he was waiting all the while for a favorable opportunity to broach his enterprise when his father's death forestalled him. Monckton, for his part, was utterly innocent of any foreknowledge of the King's intentions when he was first brought onstage. His only thought, on receiving the summons to the Palace a week or so after the great funeral, was one of pleasure at the prospect of being asked to serve his sovereign, in a role that promised not to be an unduly arduous one. He had never met the

Simpsons, and while he had caught whiffs of the gossip attaching to the Prince of Wales's friendship with Mrs. Simpson, he had dismissed the affair, if such it was, as a familiar and ephemeral phenomenon where his friend was concerned.

Thus the association began with the King believing that he was harboring a precious secret from the man he had chosen to be his adviser. It was nothing of the sort, of course, as Monckton himself was soon to learn, and from a most unexpected quarter. The sagacious Lord Wigram, who had doubled as both private secretary and Keeper of the Privy Purse to King George V, let Monckton know that the Palace not only was fully aware of the Prince's infatuation, but did not doubt that marriage was on his mind, if the divorce were arranged. This development, Wigram intimated, had grieved the old King and perhaps had impaired his health. Further to the point, well before the onset of his final illness, he had been sufficiently alarmed by the swelling rivulets of gossip to summon the Archbishop of Canterbury for a long, intimate talk; and Dr. Lang's impression, according to his biographer, J. G. Lockhart, was that the King's "closing days were clouded with anxiety for the future," because of his son's conduct.

Nor were Wigram and the Primate the only outsiders who were privy. According to Sir Samuel Hoare, who had been Baldwin's Foreign Minister until just before the Accession, two of the most senior members of the Palace Secretariat (he never identified them) met privately with the Prime Minister after King George's funeral, and notified him that the new King was marriage-bent. Baldwin responded that he was aware of "the trouble brewing," but Hoare suppressed the fact until the appearance of his memoirs, *Nine Troubled Years,* in 1954. The British Labour leader and later Prime Minister, Clement Attlee, revealed tardily in his own memoirs, *As It Happened,* in 1954, that King Edward had looked "very nervous and ill at ease" at the Accession Council. Attlee remembered, too, that following the Council, Baldwin, "depressed and distinctly nervous," had expressed anxiety about events and had doubted "whether the new King would stay the course." (Baldwin's depression was doubtless due in part to the death three days earlier of his first cousin, Rudyard Kipling.) Anxiety was besetting the Chancellor of the Exchequer, Neville Chamberlain, also, as the new reign began; he wrote in his diary, "I do hope [the King] pulls up his socks and behaves himself now he has such heavy responsibilities, for unless he does he will soon pull down the throne." Chamberlain succeeded Stanley Baldwin as Prime Minister in 1937, but was forced to resign in May 1940 and was in turn succeeded by Winston Churchill. Six months later, Chamberlain died. He is best remembered for the Munich Pact of September 1938 and for his umbrella.

Ernest Simpson himself can be pinpointed as a source of some of the intelligence flowing into the Palace and 10 Downing Street. Within days of the old King's death—possibly even while he lay dying—Simpson sought out a trusted adviser of Baldwin's, Sir Maurice Jenks, a former lord mayor of London, and told him that Windsor was in love with Wallis and had proposed marriage. The peculiar and unedifying set of circumstances that surrounds Simpson's call on Jenks, whom he knew, are described at some length by Baldwin's biographers, Keith Middlemas and John Barnes, in their *Baldwin*.[2] In their account Jenks saw the Prime Minister on February 4, barely a fortnight after the start of the new reign, and the story that he told was supported by an earlier bizarre experience involving both Simpson and the then Prince of Wales. Simpson was up for membership in the Masonic Lodge of which Jenks was the head. His application had been rejected, despite his being strongly supported by the Prince. On the Prince's demand for an explanation, Jenks replied that it would have been a breach of Masonic law to admit to membership a man whose wife was known to be the mistress of another member. The Prince assured him that his friendship with Mrs. Simpson was an innocent one, and the blackball was withdrawn. When therefore Simpson sought out Jenks, with his sponsor on the throne, it was, in the biting words of Messrs. Middlemas and Barnes, in the role of " 'the mari complaisant' [become] the sorrowing and devoted spouse" whose overriding interest was to save his marriage. Baldwin heard Jenks out, but he brushed off a suggestion that he hear the whole story from Simpson himself, saying that he was adviser to the King, not to Simpson. Still, he was sufficiently disturbed to ask Wigram to come to see him that same evening. They were agreed that whatever hopes the King might cherish, marriage to Mrs. Simpson was "unbelievable" and therefore unthinkable, and Baldwin let the matter rest there.

A somewhat less lurid version of the King's situation was given to Walter Monckton by one of Baldwin's senior lieutenants, Sir Maurice Gwyer, First Parliamentary Secretary and Counsel to the Treasury, and soon afterward by one of the new King's staff, his Comptroller, Admiral Sir Lionel Halsey. The two informants had chosen Monckton because he was in a better position than they to inform the King what Simpson had reported, and thus alert him to "the possibility of blackmail upon an extravagant basis."

Monckton did not mistrust the intelligence, but he was too sensitive to the unprecedented constitutional implications to believe that the King, at the very onset of his reign, would issue such a challenge to the Establishment. Monckton was also too astute to relay thirdhand information in so private a matter, especially as the King had not confided in him. Even then, twenty years after Oxford, their friendship, though firm, was still formal. The Moncktons had never been weekend guests at the Fort, nor had they ever been invited to the cozy suppers at Bryanston Court. It is not surprising, therefore, that when the storm warnings of the emotional crisis in the making could no longer be ignored by Monckton, he chose to bottle them up. Perhaps it made it easier for him to continue to serve the King unswervingly by holding to the belief that nothing could ever come of a scheme so manifestly hopeless of accomplishment in terms of the real world. In the papers that he left behind, he wrote:

> I am free to confess that I always underestimated the depth and strength of the King's devotion and of their united will. I thought throughout, long before, as well as after, there was talk of marriage, that if and when the stark choice faced them between their love and his obligations as King-Emperor, they would in

the end each make the sacrifice, devastating as it
would be.[3]

So the secret that was no longer a secret lay undisturbed
between the King and his adviser. The formality that had
previously governed their relationship did not last. More
and more the King began to lean on Monckton as a private
counselor. In a manner both unexpected and alarming,
Monckton was made aware not only of the changed relationship, but of how profound was the King's discontent.
Monckton had called at the Palace to discuss a problem in
the Duchy of Cornwall, and the King proposed that they
walk to its offices, close by at Buckingham Gate, and examine the pertinent papers. They were halfway across the
great courtyard when he suddenly stopped, seized Monckton's arm, and pointed to the Palace's calm gray mass.
"Walter," he exclaimed, "I'm not going to let them lock
me up in that place! I'm not going to sit like a monkey in a
golden coach. The world has taught me other things. I
must have a life of my own!"—the exact words he had
used to Freda Dudley Ward.

He then related an unhappy exchange with Clive Wigram over his right to an independent life. Wigram had
chided him for flaunting his association with "persons" not
normally in the sovereign's company. The King told
Monckton, " 'What is at issue,' I said to him, 'is that I
don't take pains to conceal my private life.' 'Sir,' Wigram
retorted, 'Sir, you *have* no private life! The *King* has no
private life. You are mistaken if you believe otherwise' "—
almost the exact words that Freda had used to him.

The duchy's problem was not mentioned again that afternoon. The King would talk only of his conviction that his
mother, the Palace Secretariat under Wigram, and the entire Establishment were determined to make him over in
his father's image, and to imprison him in a past that had
never really been his.

"Wigram told me," he went on, "that if I were so unwise
and reckless as to insist on conducting my affairs on two
planes—one in the proper circumstances associated with
my father's habits and style, the other in the company I
favor—then he hoped I would keep the second associations
discreetly out of public view. He suggested that I not be

seen any more in nightclubs, and that if I was determined to persist in certain companionships, it would best be done in the privacy of the Fort or at Sandringham, and that the companions not be named in the *Court Circular*."

The breach that Wigram, by custom the sovereign's senior adviser, opened with his excellent but unwelcome advice on the decorum of kingship was never repaired.

The King, trapped in his dreadful quandary, would have been inhuman if he had not asked help from someone he could trust, someone outside his personal staff. (It was said of Monckton that he received and guarded more confidences than any other man in London.) Until that moment, he had never been cognizant of Windsor's private affairs; their previous consultations had been only on the duchy's investment and land policies. Now he was astounded to hear the King declare that the course of his reign would be different from his father's. They must take him as he was: He would faithfully execute the duties and ceremonials required of him, but he was determined to be himself.

Monckton said, "From the very start, he was torn between his genuine desire to exercise the influence and prerogatives of kingship and an equally strong desire to live as he pleased. It took me a long time to understand what was happening. Only toward the end, with the throne lost to him, was I persuaded that he had actually all but made up his mind, well before his father died, to abdicate in favor of the Duke of York. He was wildly in love with Wallis Simpson and was bent on marrying her, whatever the cost, as life without her would be unendurable. He had brooded over making a clean breast to his father and asking permission to step aside from the Succession. He went so far as to declare this to the Duke of York and the Duke of Kent. Both of them looked up to him; he was their leader. The Duke of York, especially, was appalled. The last thing he wanted was to become King. But it happened anyway."

When Monckton was reminiscing with Windsor in later years about his autobiography, he recalled the conversation they had had while walking to the duchy offices. He mentioned his subsequent reflections, adding that he had failed then to see the significance of what he later recognized as an open declaration of independence. "It struck me at the time, Sir," Monckton said, "as nothing more than the forthright statement of a new king who was insisting, as all kings before have done, on retaining a measure of privacy."

"It was that all right, Walter," Windsor acknowledged, with a laugh. "But the other was there, too, only I couldn't tell you then." *

The other was, of course, his marriage.

The fact has been established that in the last weeks of Windsor's princeship and the first weeks of his kingship, his intention to marry Mrs. Simpson had been discussed with concern and foreboding in Buckingham Palace, in Lambeth Palace, Downing Street, and in Whitehall. The Prime Minister was to confess to Sir Samuel Hoare that he had refrained from bringing the issue before the King straightaway only because he felt that his "intervention might be resented by the public," and because he hoped "the young man would see sense." Not so the Archbishop of Canterbury. As the one dignitary in the Empire privileged to challenge the sovereign on a point of moral conduct, he now ventured to do so, though warily.

The day after King George's funeral, Dr. Lang called at Buckingham Palace to comfort Queen Mary; and while there sent word to the new King that he wished to pay his respects. The encounter was one that King Edward did not welcome. He detested Lang, even though he had been one of his father's closest friends. The Primate was approaching seventy then. In the King's eyes, he was, like so many members of the Sandringham and Balmoral "little" Courts, an anachronism—a gaitered, black-garbed "medieval Churchman," given to "the pursuit of power and prestige" and marred by "an over-anxiety to please." One of the Cecils considered him "a middle-class Archbishop." Certain High Church circles suspected him even of being "a renegade Presbyterian."

True, Lang possessed an unattractive side, but he had others, worthier. He was a vastly learned man, steeped in the classics, and a superb preacher and commanding orator. In political matters (toward which all successful prelates must cock a sensitive ear) he was alert, well informed, and, when occasion demanded, responsive. He was pain-

fully aware of the King's personal antipathy and of his utter lack of interest in the Church of England. His breach of
the kingly custom of fairly regular churchgoing was only
the most conspicuous evidence of his aversion from religion. He had seldom attended family gatherings at which
the Archbishop was the favored guest. He had failed to
show even perfunctory curiosity about either the troubled
affairs of the State faith, of which he was now the sworn
defender, or the problems of the large ecclesiastical establishment, of which he was the principal ornament and con-
veyance of authority. Save for occasionally dropping in at
St. George's Chapel at Windsor for Evensong, his church
attendance in recent years had been limited to weddings,
christenings, funerals, and the Crown and State ceremonials which he could not easily evade. Without consciously
rejecting religion, he had in fact become an agnostic (as
was Wallis Simpson). All these bleak signs, together with
the past personal slights, warned the Archbishop that he
was in for heavy weather in the new reign.

The harsh contemporary judgment of Cosmo Lang's performance as intrigant and executioner in the Abdication
crisis has been softened by the passage of time. He did
right in seeking that first audience; his motives were
straightforward; the conflict which his Church could not
possibly have composed to the King's satisfaction had not
yet been revealed. Yet both parties had expected tension,
and it was present. The King tried to ease it by directing
the talk toward his new duties as head of the Established
Church. In a naïve effort to suggest that he was not wholly
unconversant with ecclesiastical affairs, he brought forward
the names of several clergymen—mostly military chap-
lains—whom he knew and liked. Lang did not respond.
Instead, he changed the subject with a tactless abruptness
that cost him whatever opportunity he might later have
had for exerting his influence.

From Windsor's account, Lang began by regretting that
they had had so little in common through the years when
his association with the rest of the Royal Family had been
so warm. Then, with a candor that proved disastrously ill-
timed, he blundered ahead, admitting that George V had
on occasion—"as you no doubt realize, Sir"—acknowledged the worry caused by his heir's waywardness. "But it

would be a pity, Sir," he pressed on, "if you were to misjudge me in this connection." For his part, he had attempted to persuade the King that the son possessed a different temperament and bespoke the interests of a different generation, and his actions should therefore be viewed in a kindlier light.

Frederick Locker-Lampson wrote in *My Confidences*, "The sons of George III all of them swore lustily; but I think the Duke of Cumberland was the only scion of royalty who habitually swore when conversing with the Archbishop of Canterbury." Edward VIII must have wished for some of his great-great-great-uncle's impudicity during this interview.

When Lang spoke of "your conduct," it is unlikely that he had only Wallis Simpson in mind. He was aware of her existence; he and Stanley Baldwin were in close, constant touch; moreover, the late King had almost certainly discussed her with him. But to believe that the phrase "your conduct" was a veiled warning to the new King not to pursue the relationship to the danger point is to believe that Lang was inviting a head-on collision at their first meeting—a risk he was much too cautious to run, even though the atmosphere of the audience had already degenerated into one of mutual distrust. As for the King's wish, and intention, to marry Mrs. Simpson, if Lang had heard the rumor, as Baldwin already had done, he had probably dismissed it as not merely impracticable but impossible. After all, he, the Primate of all England, would preside over the Coronation; the holy sacrament of communion would be his to administer. The sovereign, backslider or no, was still bound by the Act of Settlement of 1701 to be a member of the Established Church and the Defender of its Faith. The presumption that he would require the Church to include in the ceremony, and recognize as his consort, a woman not only once divorced already but remarried, and so obliged to negotiate yet a second divorce on the eve of the Coronation—this must have struck even the worldly Lang as beyond the bounds of reality.

Yet the conviction that Lang was making an oblique declaration of his antagonism to Mrs. Simpson instantly leapt to the King's hypersensitive mind. He would later claim, but with pale conviction, that it was his first intimation that he might be approaching a showdown with the Primate. He already knew that he was embarked upon a desperate course and that his landfall might be nonexistent. Nevertheless the menacing implication which his innate suspiciousness read into Lang's remarks sharpened his resolve to move forward. "The Archbishop was clearly against my continued friendship with Wallis," he decided. "He would undoubtedly muster powerful forces in opposition to my project when I came to press it." His project was, of course, to make Mrs. Simpson not only his wife but Queen of England.

A fortnight later, Dr. Lang sought a second audience. Apart from his personal responsibility as the King's spiritual adviser, he was urged toward immediate fence-mending for practical reasons as well. He and the House of Bishops were mounting a major campaign to increase the Church's dwindling membership, to recall strays and backsliders, and to assert with fresh vehemence their adherence to the marriage laws. Nothing, therefore, could have been more disconcerting to Dr. Lang, at an hour when he was struggling to slow the divorce rate, than to have the role of Defender of the Faith pass to a sovereign whose open preference was for married women; and to whose circle of friends divorce was a convenience, and the Church an institution useful chiefly as a custodian of the dead.

The second audience was no more fruitful than the first. Dr. Lang recorded of it that the King "knows little and, I fear, cares little, about the Church and its affairs." He would tell his biographer, "I noted at the time—and the facts seemed strangely significant now—that he summoned his brother ('Bertie') to be present, and when . . . I gave him a book of the Service as used at his father's Coronation he gave it to his brother, saying, 'I think *you* had better follow this.' I wonder whether even then he had in the back of his mind some thought that the Coronation might not be his, but his brother's."[4] There was never a third audience, though Lang may have tried to reach the King during the duel with Baldwin. He could have gained nothing. Marriage, however it was to be accomplished, was the only outcome the King would accept. After the crisis was upon him, he tried to rationalize that the question whether he could marry on the throne was political, not religious—one to be hammered out with the Prime Minister, not the Primate. According to Monckton, the King's argument was that "there was for him no other way of meeting the situation than by marrying"; the leaders of the Church, his own family, his ministerial advisers alike were hopelessly wrong and given to "cant"; and he had "no time for the shufflings and humbug which he saw in constitutional morality."

CHAPTER 2
Divorce: How the Bargain Was Struck

When an earlier David became infatuated with another man's wife, he merely sent orders for the husband to be "set . . . in the forefront of the hottest battle . . . that he may be smitten and die." Alas for the later David's impatience, superfluous husbands were no longer disposable so briskly. The law now insisted on the tiresome, long-drawn-out, and often embarrassing formality of divorce. Moreover, unless Ernest Simpson were willing to acquiesce in the role of the guilty party, there could be no divorce action and no Coronation of Queen Wallis. The timing was also critical. The controlling date was Coronation Day: May 12, 1937. If the King was to savor the joy of having Wallis crowned alongside him, seated on the same throne that his mother had graced when she was crowned alongside his father, then she would have to have been a free woman for a seemly interval beforehand.

Under the British law of those days, the finding for divorce was a two-stage process. First came the granting of a decree *nisi*, a decree "unless"—unless, that is, during a six-month waiting period the King's Proctor is shown evidence that the action was brought through improper collusion or through a miscarriage of justice. On the expiration of the six months, and in the absence of any damaging evidence, the decree *nisi* was followed by the granting of an absolute divorce. The waiting period therefore required Mrs. Simpson's petition to be filed not later than the fall of 1936.

The Duchess's autobiography is carefully misleading about the first steps toward her divorce. Exactly who took them and precisely when are never disclosed. Nor is her account even half-complete. The fact that her intimate friend Mary Kirk Raffray was one of the four principals is all but suppressed, and Mrs. Raffray is kept offstage nearly until the Abdication, although there is little doubt that her status was a powerful factor in Wallis's strategy. The full extent to which Mrs. Raffray was involved is only now becoming known outside the "family circle." The details of what follows, Mary herself merrily related a few months before her death, in 1941:

At some point during Ernest's trip to America in late 1935—probably after his visit to Mrs. Merryman in Washington—he returned to New York and called on Mary, who had left her husband and Washington Square sometime before for an apartment uptown, on Madison Avenue. Wallis had written ahead, alerting her to his arrival and inviting her to visit them at Bryanston Court the following spring. The letter ended with a plea to treat Ernest kindly, as she herself had not been the best of wives—a strange echo of Thelma's "Look after the Prince while I'm away, dear!"

Wallis had taken Thelma at her word; now Mary took Wallis at hers. Evenings that began with a cozy little dinner often continued on to a nightclub and presently did not end until just before Mary's maid arrived to prepare her breakfast. One morning when Ernest tiptoed out, he forgot to take along his hat. The maid found it in the foyer and, obviously disapproving, brought it in with the breakfast tray. The lovers were already past being flurried by such little contretemps. Heedless in their rapture, they even went to Atlantic City for a weekend; and when Ernest sailed back to England, pledged to Mary, his feelings must have been a bittersweet mixture of the pleasures of a new love and a gloating, triumphant satisfaction with his one-in-the-eye for Wallis.

Did his conquest screen out second thoughts about Wallis? Had Mary told him about the strangely permissive, almost provocative letter? Did he question its motives, and did it occur to him that he and Mary had been lured into a trap where Wallis could now count on his gallantry to further her divorce? The answer can be no more than "Possibly," but at least the ingredients in the pot are known.

Possibly he told Wallis at once of his commitment to Mary, and invited her to proceed with the divorce at her convenience. *Possibly* she at once told her glad news to the Prince of Wales (or perhaps he had recently become King;

there are few definite dates in the chronology of the divorce). By her own account, the King had stopped by Bryanston Court late one afternoon, as he did so often, and there received her tidings, without surprise. She then asked him how she might engage competent legal counsel. Needless to say, he recommended his own solicitor, the able and resolute George Allen, of Allen & Overy. The situation was eased by the fact that George Allen and Walter Monckton were old friends. They had met in the Great War, when Allen was in the 8th South Staffordshire Regiment and Monckton in the 4th West Kent. Monckton's glasses had been blown off by a shell burst, and he was blindly stumbling across no-man's-land when Allen caught up with him, turned him around, and led him safely back.

As for suggesting how Wallis should proceed legally, her recollection is that the King's advice was limited to a mild observation that she should do what was best for her. One likes to picture the quick, light, often shy smile that was so much of his charm, as it must have played across his face when he came upon that sentence in the draft of her autobiography.

The fact is that the King stage-managed the divorce from beginning to end, with Wallis as his active collaborator—despite her bland assurance to Chips Channon a few months later that the divorce was "at Ernest's instigation, and at no wish" of hers. Precisely when the King decided to start preparations for her suit is not clear. The vague, but best available, date is "one evening in February 1936." It is established by Walter Monckton's papers, which relate how Bernard Rickatson-Hatt took him to luncheon at the Guards Club on August 13, 1940, and told him a story which is without counterpart in the annals of lovelorn royalty—a story which Rickatson-Hatt retold some years later to one of the authors of his biography. "One evening in February" 1936, Rickatson-Hatt said, Ernest Simpson asked him to come to York House for a private supper with the King. Whether it was Ernest or the King who had sought the meeting, Rickatson-Hatt seems not to have told Monckton; but he later stated firmly that it was the King. The more that Rickatson-Hatt considered the role in which Ernest had cast him—a witness—the less he relished it. Indeed, when the King entered the room, Rickatson-Hatt excused himself and started to leave, "but Simpson asked him to stop"—according to Monckton's notes—"and in his presence told the King that Wallis would have to choose between them, and what did the King mean to do about it?—'Are you sincere? Do you intend to marry her?' The King rose from his chair and said, 'Do you really think I would be crowned without Wallis by my side?' "

This was all that Ernest needed; he would promise not to contest the divorce if the King would promise to marry Wallis. And Ernest's promise was all the King needed. The bargain was struck. And kept.

Rickatson-Hatt remembered that Ernest was "profoundly unhappy, even outraged, but it was impossible for him, a loyal Englishman, to obstruct the plan without damaging his Sovereign, and this he would not do. Having no choice, he consented to stand aside." In view of Ernest's commitment to Mary Raffray, one wonders if his stand-aside was quite as selfless and noble as Rickatson-Hatt represents. After all, the divorce would free not only Wallis to marry the King, but Ernest to marry Mary. Rickatson-Hatt may have been gullible, but he was discreet and he respected a confidence. This one, unquestionably the scoop of the century, he, though a professional journalist, kept locked in his breast for more than four years—i.e., until the luncheon with Monckton. Later he became the Bank of England's first public-relations officer, a position demanding the tact and reticence which he was outstandingly equipped to bring it. He discharged his duties in exemplary fashion up to his retirement in 1958 and died in 1966. If he left any memoranda for posthumous publication, they have not yet appeared. Windsor, for reasons immediately understandable, omitted the dramatic little incident from his own narrative of the Abdication; so did the Duchess from hers, thereby suggesting that she and the King were helping each other in all innocence.

The implications of Rickatson-Hatt's story fascinated Monckton, as it bore upon the characters of Windsor and Ernest Simpson. Monckton was convinced that it was true; after all, a divorce petition could not be drawn up in any confidence of success unless Simpson were first persuaded to come forward as the guilty party. His inducement had to be the King's word that his intentions toward Wallis were, in an unconventional sense, honorable. The story also established that blackmail was not in Ernest Simpson's thoughts. On the contrary, the two motives he seems to have had—marriage to Mary Raffray aside—are much to his credit. First, he felt it his duty to warn the Government that unless timely action were taken, the Coronation might be subjected to extraordinary stresses. His other motive, strangely, was a chivalrous desire to protect the reputation of his wife, as best as this could be salvaged where the cuckolding had been so overt as to make the consideration academic.

Finally, it accorded with the King's self-adjusting sense of honor that he should face Simpson, in the presence of a witness, and proudly assert that he envisaged Wallis not as his mistress (no mean station, incidentally; countless wellborn women had informally shared the lives of his gallant forebears), but as his Queen Consort. In the whole protracted, contorted sequence of the Abdication, no other single incident discloses so much about the state of the King's mind, the erosion of his pride and self-respect, the intensity of his "passion"—as Winston Churchill put it—"to marry the woman he loved," as does Rickatson-Hatt's casual lunch-table revelation to the King's negotiator of the bargain struck at York House.

Meanwhile, the Duchess's autobiography—still prudently evasive about dates—notes that Ernest had sailed to New York again. This is doubtful; but it is certain that Mary Raffray came to London, to Bryanston Court, in response to Wallis's invitation from the autumn before. The facts that Wallis did not cancel it, and that Mary felt no compunction about accepting it, nor Ernest any about welcoming his mistress under his wife's roof, make an eloquent comment on the sensibilities of the persons concerned. What is not clear is when Mary arrived, though a rough fix is given in the diary kept by Mike Scanlon, who had returned to the London Embassy that February for a second tour of duty, with a promotion to Military Attaché and with a wife, Gladys. During his first tour, his friendship with the Prince of Wales had been warm and informal, but now, when he unexpectedly met the *King* at Bryanston Court, he suddenly realized that he had no idea how to address him. In his quandary he blurted out, "Sire—" His diary finishes the story crisply:

> Emerald Cunard was there. She heard me and giggled. I had never liked her before. Now I *dis*liked her, actively.

The King picked up their friendship where it had left off in 1933, and before long the Scanlons were fixtures on his list. Here is the second of many similar entries in the 1936 diary:

> *26 March.* Dinner at York House. The Simpsons. The Herman Rogers, over from France. A piper came in with the coffee. Movie afterwards: Marx Brothers "A Night at the Opera." Mary Kirk Rafferty [*sic*] was there. The King looked tired. We should have left earlier.

By the end of March, then, the cast of characters was complete.

Mary's lighthearted preparations for the reunion with her lover had included the purchase of a chic black straw hat trimmed with buttercups, from New York's most fashionable milliner, John-Frederic. The first time she wore it in London, she was instantly dubbed "Buttercup" and was so addressed throughout her stay. (Another "dear little Buttercup" would bob up in Ernest's life a few months later.)

Wallis lost no time in hauling Mary onto the giddy heights where the Simpsons now frolicked: "Guess where we're all spending this weekend? With the King, at Fort Belvedere!"

Mary was duly impressed, but as soon as she and Ernest were alone, he grumbled, "*Damn* Fort Belvedere! I know that I'm the biggest cuckold in the world, and I swore I'd never go there again. . . . Well, we'll go. I want you to see it and to meet him."

The following weekend, Wallis announced that they were going back. Ernest protested that Mary had just been there and might prefer going somewhere else. Wallis shrugged; she would go without them. As soon as she drove off, Ernest told Mary, "I know a hotel in Dover—"

If Wallis suspected hanky-panky, she gave no hint of it when she returned on Sunday; she merely mentioned that the King would be dining with them on the Monday. That evening, perhaps in his eagerness, he arrived before she had quite finished dressing, so she asked Mary to entertain him. Mary found him sitting on a couch. As she rose from her curtsey, he asked her abruptly, "How were the chalk cliffs?"

Long afterward, relating the story to a friend, Mary said nothing about her shock or her embarrassment or her stammered reply; she was still too angry. "What do you think?" she fumed. "That nasty little King had put detectives on us!"

Despite the exposure, Ernest defiantly (or cooperatively) kept another tryst that April, this time in Cornwall and possibly—*possibly*—not with Mary Raffray. Walter Monckton and George Allen, spending a holiday on Dartmoor, chanced to spy him outside a hotel at Two Bridges, with a lady whom they could identify only as "other than Mrs. Simpson."[1]

No closer identification was necessary. Wallis now had all the evidence she needed. There was no longer any reason to tolerate Mary's presence. In a climate that had fast become arctic, Mary packed and left for Cannes shortly after Easter (April 12). Her first morning there, in her bedroom at the Carlton Hotel, she addressed two envelopes—one to Wallis, the other to Ernest—and took them down to the beach, where she sat in the sunshine and wrote two letters—a bread-and-butter letter to Wallis, a love letter to Ernest. And then put them in the wrong envelopes and posted them! Almost at once she realized her mistake and sent a telegram to Wallis: "DO NOT OPEN LETTER ADDRESSED TO YOU AS IT IS NOT FOR YOU." There have been few people on earth to obey such an injunction, and Wallis was not one of them. Inside the envelope was enough more evidence for half a dozen divorces.

Mary's letter made Wallis realize that her marriage to Ernest was finished and done for. It was unfair to continue carrying on the pretense of their relationship, when she was already launched on an unpredictable trajectory that didn't include Ernest and prevented him from following his own course. The circumstances of her divorce from Win Spencer were different: Wallis had felt that he was ruining his life, and she had feared for her own safety.

Mary returned to London and took a flat overlooking Hyde Park, where she could be near Ernest and bide her time until Wallis's divorce freed him. Mary, too, would have to get a divorce, from Jackie Raffray, but Reno was only forty-eight hours away, and the decree only six weeks further. One day she rang up Wallis, who refused to see her. The break was final. On June 14, Mary wrote to her sister Anne, "On the outs with Wallis, but for God's sake keep that under your hat. So do not move in Royal Circles any more."

Neither did Ernest. He had done so only intermittently for several months. As far back as March 31, Mike Scanlon's diary was carrying this sort of entry:

> Gave a cocktail party and invited the Simpsons. Wallis appeared with the King but no Ernest. The King teased Gladys for not having included him.

Scanlon commented on this passage long afterward, "I had no idea how serious the King was. We were all aware that Ernest was fading into the background, that he was becoming less and less visible in the triangle and that the King was seeing Wallis every day. We also sensed that Ernest was unhappy about the situation, but was unable to do anything."

Again, two months later:

> 31 May. Another weekend at the Fort. Wallis there, but not Ernest. The Rex Bensons, the Duke & Duchess of Gloucester, the Duchess most nervous and fidgety. On Monday, Gladys and Wallis set off for Paris to buy hats. The King drove Wallis to Victoria Station.

And a month after that:

> 3–5 July. On the 3rd the king, Wallis and Laura Ramsay [Lord Beaverbrook's sister] came for tea. On the

4th we drove to the Fort. Wallis already there, the George Hunters too. No Ernest.

The King never told either Monckton or George Allen of his bargain with Ernest Simpson; nor did he ever even hint that marriage was its reason. Monckton said later, in Windsor's presence, that not until the Abdication crisis was upon them all, the following November, did he finally accept the truth that marriage on the throne had been the King's first and all-controlling goal throughout. Monckton, himself attracted by and attractive to beautiful women, was inclined for a long time to regard his sovereign's relationship with Mrs. Simpson as a natural one between a man and a truly cherished mistress. Monckton liked her, and the friendship between them lasted—except for at least one acrimonious passage—until his death, in 1965. To the King, Wallis "was the perfect woman," Monckton wrote, in a judgment both generous and accurate of the King's feelings (indeed, he was borrowing the King's own pet epithet for her). "She insisted that he should be at his best and do his best at all times, and he regarded her as his inspiration. It would be a great mistake to assume that he was merely in love with her in the ordinary physical sense of the term. There was an intellectual companionship, and there is no doubt that his lonely nature found in her a spiritual comradeship." He felt that they "were made for each other."

Only Rickatson-Hatt, Wallis Simpson, Ernest Simpson, and Mary Raffray knew as early as February 1936 that the King was at last in a position to make their matching complete. His plan for doing so, as yet shared only with Wallis, depended on disguising his real intentions while appearing to let the divorce take its natural course. Meanwhile he had the unstinted help of his allies Emerald Cunard and Sibyl Colefax in bringing Wallis before an ever-widening audience of the socially and politically influential. He congratulated himself—on rather flimsy evidence, it turned out—that she was making a happy impression. Because he had decreed six months of full mourning in his father's memory, he could not yet exploit the balls and galas that normally would have accelerated the process of easing her into London's most fashionable circles. But the chic little parties that alternated between 9 Grosvenor Square and 19 Lord North Street rippled along unabated, presenting her to changing and always fascinated groups, sometimes with Ernest, more often not, but always in the King's company, though they were never any longer alone together in public. The amplitude and evident expensiveness of her wardrobe became the West End's Topic A and remained so until succeeded by her apparently bottomless jewel boxes. A goggle-eyed Chips Channon confided to his diary: "Mrs. Simpson was literally smothered in rubies." A little later, he sighted her "dripping with emeralds." And Lady Diana Cooper would presently return from a dinner at the Fort to declare that Wallis was "glittering, and dripped in new jewels and clothes."

When word of this bedizenment reached a certain fashionable prelate with a gift for apt quotation, he cited II Samuel 12:4: " 'The rich man took the poor man's lamb'— his 'one little ewe lamb,' I remind you—'and dressed it.' . . . I further remind you that the rich man was a king named David."

What neither Channon nor Lady Diana knew was that most of these rubies and emeralds—and sapphires and diamonds and pearls—were the property of the Royal Family, left to Wales by his grandmother, Queen Alexandra, for the eventual adornment of his wife, the Queen of England. Even though some of the larger pieces had been dismantled and reset, certain individual gems were of such distinction that sharp-eyed old friends of the late Queen had no trouble recognizing them, and murmurs of disapproval began to be heard: "Even if they were *his* to give her, my dear— which they are *not*—should she be flashing them in nightclubs, do you *really* think? Can you *imagine* dear Alice Keppel being so vulgar?"

No, no one could.

In King Edward's day, the ideal woman was soft and sweet and creamy, like an éclair. She had dimpled shoulders and a gentle voice. A corsage of Parma violets was pinned to her Worth gown, and her hat—a huge, fragile confection of satin and tulle—was pinned to her pompadour. She wore a pearl choker or a rope of pearls. She carried a ruffled parasol, and her handkerchief was "a wisp of lace."

Alice Keppel more than matched this ideal woman; she was the ideal mistress, "the most perfect mistress in history." She had met the then Prince of Wales in 1898, when he was fifty-six and she twenty-nine (and for seven years the wife of the Hon. George Keppel, a younger son of the Earl of Albemarle). It was not long before everyone knew whom the Ambassador from Austria-Hungary, Count Albert Mensdorff, meant when he spoke of "la Favorita." Her face was lovely, with sky-blue eyes and a pink-and-white complexion, framed by chestnut hair. She was slender, with a billowy bosom above a tiny waist. Her voice was deep and throaty, and she had a "faint personal odor, of spring blossoms and fresh green sap." Her physical charms first caught the King's attention, but it was something more that held it: She was gay and vivacious, witty and intelligent, never possessive or jealous—"so restful, so understanding," wrote Anita Leslie, "the perfect mistress for an ageing man."[2] Still more, she was *discreet*. The King trusted her implicitly (as he did his daughter-in-law, Princess May, and no other women). His official biographer, Sir Philip Magnus, wrote that he surrounded himself with a circle of seven highly placed, trusted, and congenial friends: Sir Ernest Cassel, his financial adviser (and grandfather of Lady Mountbatten); Viscount Esher, his adviser on military affairs; Lord Fisher, the First Sea Lord; Lord Hardinge of Penshurst, twice the senior career head of the Foreign Office as Permanent Under-Secretary of State, and soon to be Viceroy of India; Sir Francis Knollys, his private secretary; and the Marquis Luis de Soveral, the Portuguese Ambassador; the seventh was Mrs. Keppel.

Immediately after Edward VII's death, Lord Hardinge wrote in his private file: "I take this opportunity to allude to a delicate matter upon which I am in a position to speak with authority. Everybody knew of the friendship which existed between King Edward and Mrs. George Keppel. . . . I used to see a great deal of Mrs. Keppel at that time, and I was aware that she had knowledge of what was going on in the political world. I would like to pay a tribute to her wonderful discretion and to the wonderful influence which she always exercised upon the King. She never utilized her knowledge to her own advantage (though Cassel gave her some highly profitable tips on Canadian stocks) or to that of her friends, and I never heard her repeat an unkind word of anybody. There were one or two occasions when the King was in disagreement with the Foreign Office, and I was able, through her, to advise the King with a view to the policy of government being accepted. She was very loyal to the King and patriotic at the same time. It would have been difficult to find any other lady who would have filled the part of friend to King Edward with the same loyalty and discretion."

Princess Daisy of Pless wrote of her, "Inimitable! What spirit, wit and resilience that woman has!" Margot Asquith, who seldom had a compliment for anyone except herself, had several for Alice Keppel: "She is always large-hearted and kind . . . a plucky woman of fashion; human, adventurous, and gay, who . . . has never made an enemy"—including Queen Alexandra. "Large-hearted and kind" herself, the Queen took Alice as a friend and often invited her and her husband to dinner and receptions at the Palace, and even to stay at Sandringham—a welcome she never extended to the Princesse de Sagan or the Countess of Warwick or Lillie Langtry or any other royal mistress. Alice played an excellent game of bridge, which was important to the King; but her mere presence kept him in good humor, which was important to everybody.

Following the Queen's lead, the King's hosts often included the Keppels in the weekend house parties that were so ritualistic a part of Edwardian Society. There were prudish exceptions, to be sure: The Salisburys never invited them to Hatfield, nor the Norfolks to Arundel. Otherwise, the relationship was recognized and accepted not only by the royal circle, but by the general public. As John Pearson has written, "A rakish king was what the people wanted. . . . For his subjects there was vicarious pleasure in applauding this happy hedonist whose aim in life was still quite plainly to enjoy himself as much as possible."[3] Far from begrudging him his affair with Mrs. Keppel, the public rather relished being in on it. The King made no secret of it. When he named one of his race horses "Ecila," the cipher was something less than impenetrable. Vita Sackville-West has told how, as a girl, she would go to spend an afternoon with Mrs. Keppel's daughter Violet at the house in Portman Square, and "I used to see a discreet little one-horse brougham waiting outside and the butler would slip me into a dark corner of the hall with a murmured, 'One minute, miss, a gentleman is coming downstairs.' "[4] Alice accompanied the King to Cowes and sailed on the royal yacht, *Britannia*. He always went to Biarritz for Easter, and the Keppels and their young daughters Violet and Sonia (who called him "Kingy") always joined him there. "Kingy" enjoyed children and spoiled them; Sonia was allowed to "race" bits of bread and butter down the stripes of his trousers. But the holiday can't have been quite so carefree for poor George Keppel. Biarritz still remembers a large luncheon at which a Portuguese duchess, seated next to him, picked up his place card and read it aloud—very much aloud: "Kep-*pel* . . . Kep-*pel* . . . How very odd of you to have the same name as the King's mistress!"

Painful incidents of this sort had to be expected by husbands on whose wives royalty had looked with satisfied longing. "Guelpho the Gay" had given not only George Keppel, but many other *maris complaisants,* the dubious privilege of wearing a cuckoo's feather in their caps; and now his grandson and namesake was giving the same privilege to Ernest Simpson. Although Wallis thus belonged to the same sisterhood as Alice Keppel, they had little else in common. Vivacity and gaiety, yes; discretion, no—alas for Edward VIII, and alas for Wallis herself. Increasingly she would be compared with Alice, and always to Wallis's disadvantage.

When Edward VII was dying, on May 6, 1910, Queen Alexandra, "large-hearted" as ever, sent for Alice and led her to his chair, but some say that he was already too far gone to recognize her. He died a few minutes before midnight (as would his son and successor). Sonia Keppel was to write of the next day, "A pall of darkness hung over the house, blinds were drawn, lights were dimmed, and black clothes appeared, even for me, with black ribbons threaded through my underclothes."[5] She was not quite ten years old. When the Edwardians mourned, they mourned indeed.

*   *   *

All fashions change, and fashions in mistresses are not an exception. The contrast between King Edward VII's and King Edward VIII's was especially emphatic. Where one woman was modest, the other was brash. Where one was yielding, the other was brittle. Where one was lacy, the other was sleek. Wallis was not wholly to blame for the facade she now presented. The exhausting years with Spencer, the knockabout years in China, and the frustrated years with Espil had all taken toll of her emotions; and a heavier one was now being levied by the strain of keeping her footing on the tightrope she had chosen to walk. Frail in itself, it was strung high—perilously high—in the gusty air that blows upon a king's favorite. The warm, soft, Montague side of her nature had been abraded away forever; she would need all her cold Warfield toughness to survive.

CHAPTER 3

"A Bad Beginning," Said the Deputy Comptroller of Supply

*All I say is, kings is kings, and you got to make allow-
ances. Take them all around, they're a mighty ornery
lot. It's the way they're raised.*
          —The Adventures of Huckleberry Finn,
                                    MARK TWAIN

Edward VIII was no fool, but he was capable of folly; and
when one sets what he was prepared to risk against the
most that he could hope to gain, it was folly at full length.
He was aware that the lines of battle were already being
drawn, and that the marriage he was determined to celebrate on the throne would, once declared, be fiercely opposed in the very quarters where strong support was crucial for success; yet he was resolved not to yield an inch on
his determination to marry. Nor could he bring himself to
open his heart to anyone, least of all to the courtiers who
had spent a lifetime in the service of his father and grandfather, and who alone might have pulled him back from
the brink. He may already have been past saving. Dawson
of Penn had a surer appreciation of what was befalling him
than had the rest of the Court. He wrote to Princess Mary
after the Abdication, "A *first* absorbing love coming after
40 or so is apt to take possession. . . ."

Finally, the King knew that neither could he count on
support from the Lords Temporal—the stalwarts of the
Court and the old aristocracy upon which the Court rests.
Senior officers retired from the military or foreign services
hold most of these positions. At the time of Edward VIII's
Accession, some still on the scene had served with his fa-

ther in the Navy or had been with him at the Delhi Durbar in 1911. Almost without exception, they were sprung from patrician families which had attended the monarchy for generations. The richest component in their lives was the ceremonials and usages associated with King George V: the Courts and levees, investitures, garden parties at the Palace, and royal progresses; the ritual expeditions to New-market and Ascot, to Cowes for the Royal Yacht Squadron Regatta, to the hills of Scotland for stag, to its moors for grouse, and to Sandringham and the estates of friends for pheasant.

The bright, cynical "sets" that clustered about the new King would be looking instead for their seasonal change and refreshment to the nightclubs of the West End, to the *boîtes* and bistros of Biarritz and Cannes, and to the ski slopes of the Austrian Alps. His abandonment of his fa-ther's stately, measured ways had long been remarked and, in Court circles, deplored. Lambeth Palace's distress at his loss of faith, the Court echoed with wrath at his loss of Britishness. To the Court's mind, he had been obnoxiously Americanized by Mrs. Simpson and by the irreverent, mot-ley coterie which he and she had recruited from café so-ciety and the international set, and which had spilled over into York House and the Fort.

The foreboding which infused the Palace bureaucracy on Wales's rise to sovereignty has been described by the late F. J. Corbett, who was deputy comptroller of supply at Buckingham Palace when the old order yielded place. Mr. Corbitt wrote in his *Fit for a King*: "You could set your watch by [King George V]. When he came in sight in the Grand Hall on a Tuesday morning, his 'stamp day,' it was invariably fourteen minutes past ten o'clock. He was on his way to the room where his stamp collection was kept. He would spend the whole day in the room, sometimes with the Keeper of the Royal Philatelic Collection, Sir Edward Bacon. He took his lunch and tea there. The same punc-tuality extended to every movement in his well-ordered life. Wales was completely different; a lunch ordered for 1:15 might not be eaten until perhaps half past two. He suffered from insomnia and was fonder of late parties at restaurants and night clubs than he should have been. He would return to York House at 1, 2 or 3 in the morning, bringing half a dozen gay friends; he would ring and order sandwiches and drinks, and tea for himself."[1]

Corbitt remembered saying of the start of the reign, "It's a bad beginning, and it will be a bad ending."

Despite the obvious desirability of building up goodwill in all possible quarters, especially in his own household, King Edward took a number of summary actions that fretted and alarmed the Palace bureaucrats. He ordered an immediate wage cut of 10 percent for everybody in the royal service—this at an hour when his Government, harking to the counsel of Maynard Keynes, was trying to generate more demand in Britain's slowly rising economy by making more work. The King followed this dismaying step with another: He announced that he was reducing the game-raising at Sandringham, and had commissioned his brother York to audit the property and plan for its more efficient administration. All that the King really wanted was to submit his estate, especially its costly game-raising, to the systematic controls that were being introduced on large estates elsewhere. Inevitably, the announcement was construed as concealing the dismissal of more old retainers; and unfortunately, this was the truth.

Yet another of his early executive acts—indeed, his very first—was to order Sandringham's clocks, which ran a half hour ahead of Greenwich time, turned back to true time. Edward VII had set them ahead in a desperate but vain attempt to compensate for his Queen's chronic tardiness; and George V had continued the little deception, out of respect for his father's days. Putting the clocks back changed nothing; everybody at Sandringham always knew the true time, and guests enjoyed the make-believe. But because Edward VIII abolished the custom so precipitately, the Palace bureaucracy, responsive to the prevailing mood of suspicion and apprehension, took it as symptomatic of his determination to dismantle everything his father had cherished. Through the snug little offices ran the fear that they would be upended and shaken out; and Sandringham and Balmoral, demoded as symbols of the Prince Consort, Edward VII, and George V, foresaw themselves doomed to the scrap heap. The Duchess would comment years later, "The Duke is very quick-moving. Maybe he made some changes too quickly." If her remark ever reached his ears, it may have awakened an echo of a similar remark made by his father, after the two of them had contributed to the massacre of 3,937 pheasants in one day, at Lord Burnham's: "Perhaps we went a little too far today, David. . . ." Lang, learning about the clocks, asked his diary, "What other customs will be put back, also?"

For such unwelcome agitations, including a complaint—which he would repeat in exile—that the household was using too much soap, and most certainly for the de-Anglicization of the King's Saxe-Coburg-Gotha character, the Palace held Wallis Simpson solely responsible. The King himself never expressed regret for a single change. On the contrary, he declared later that if he had had more time "on the job," he would have "let a breath of fresh air into the whole suffocating system—a *whirlwind* of fresh air." He considered Mrs. Simpson the world's most imaginative authority on styling and organizing a household, and he credited her with inspiring many of his ideas for refurbishing the monarchy, the Palace, and the Secretariat.

After he became King, there was no overestimating her influence on him and over him. The privileges she had assumed after displacing Thelma Furness as the Prince's favorite were exercised even more freely after her elevation to the King's favorite. She telephoned him again and again during the day, to offer counsel, or merely to call his attention to an item she had read or heard about. The busiest channel on the Palace switchboard was the one to Bryanston Court. Associates who remembered the King's demeanor as Prince of Wales were sensible of a psychological change. Geoffrey Bocca, an early biographer of the Windsors, wrote in *The Woman Who Would Be Queen*, "The King had become two persons, one person when the enigmatic Mrs. Simpson was at his side, and another person altogether when she was gone. The first Edward was assertive, wayward: his ministers found him difficult to handle. . . . Away from her he would deflate."[2]

For nearly three hundred years, it had been the custom for British coins and, later, postage stamps to show successive monarchs in alternate profile. Those of Queen Victoria's reign showed her left profile, Edward VII's showed his right, George V's his left. Thus Edward VIII's would have shown his right if he had not refused. Possibly because his hair was parted on the left, he felt that his left profile was more photogenic, and when he was being photographed, he usually maneuvered to put the camera on his left. He notified the Royal Mint and General Post Office that the left it must be. They yielded, grudgingly, but the postal authorities neglected to change the background they had already prepared for the right profile, which meant that the King faced away from the crown, in the upper right corner, and into a shadow. After the Abdication, *The Times* recalled "the superstitious anxiety of those who shook apprehensive heads at the new stamps, because the head of King Edward VIII was turned away from the light, and looked forward into the gloom—apt symbol of a reign which began with everything in its favor and moved onward into calamity."

Only four denominations were issued: ½ d., 1 d., 1½ d., and 2½ d. They are by no means rarities; a set of the four, used, can be bought for about 25 pence today. The only coin issued was a three-penny bit, and only fifty were struck. Because they were made of nickel-brass and were dodecagonal, the mint sent them out to manufacturers of vending machines, to test their suitability. Twenty-two of the fifty were returned; twenty more found their way to collectors; the remaining eight have disappeared. The last one offered for sale, in 1961, fetched 2,500 dollars; numismatists agree that a specimen would bring several times this much by now.

The bickering over the profiles was a small matter, but the bureaucrats scored this, too, against him. They had forgotten, or were ignoring, the fact that his father had indulged a similar vanity without exciting their criticism. According to Sir Kenneth Clark's *Another Part of the Wood*, "[Charles] Sims was chosen [in 1924] to paint an official portrait of George V. . . . It was a brilliant work; but unfortunately Sims had been fascinated by the King's very elegant legs and turned-out toes, and had given them undue prominence. King George thought he had been made to look like a ballet dancer and ordered the canvas destroyed. It was . . . burned on the academy premises. . . . A year later Sims committed suicide."[3]

* * *

Members of the Secretariat, even the middle-aged companions of his princely travels, found themselves walled off from the King's business, except for minor and often disagreeable chores. A breach opened between him and the seasoned courtiers who had managed his affairs from York House. Within weeks after the Accession, the most senior member of the York House staff, Sir Godfrey Thomas, who had been Wales's friend and private secretary for seventeen years and was first in line for promotion to be the King's principal officer and official link with Downing Street, made up his tormented mind that the role would demand a duplicity of which he was incapable. He declined the honor, stepped down in the Secretariat, and soon resigned.

Thomas never explained why he turned his back on the imminent promotion for which his whole career had been preparatory, but his colleagues knew why: He was disquieted, even alarmed, by his master's indiscretions, his extravagances, his secret schemes for Mrs. Simpson. One reason for the resentment caused by his callous hacking at the meager salaries of Secretariat and backstairs staff was that the jewels being showered on Mrs. Simpson were fast depleting the customary surpluses from the Civil List and the income from the duchies of Cornwall and Lancaster. The King grabbed at the extra money—it was widely gossiped—in order to heap more gifts on "that woman."

Where, then, in the face of such opposition, did he expect to find support? The answer is, among the good-tempered, fair-minded "blokes" of Britain—the Welsh miners, the Scottish crofters, the shipbuilders on the Clyde, the machinists of the Midlands, the working men who gave him a rousing welcome whenever he appeared among them. As he liked to say, "I had seen the workers at their jobs and in their homes: I had some idea of what was in their minds." He also counted on the millions of former Tommies, now middle-aged as he was, with whom he had served in the Great War and with whose ordeal in the trenches his own youth had been unforgettably bound. Finally, he counted on the revolutionary change in the moral and social outlook of all classes of Englishmen, brought on by the Depression: the collapse of confidence in the established order. He persuaded himself that the new acceptance

of divorce as the solution for lost marriages, the demand
everywhere for a more liberal scale of values, would make
the likely consequences of his own proposed arrangement
far less catastrophic than the Primate and the Prime Minister believed. "What I needed to make the thing go," he
remarked in the aftermath, "was all there, a favorable climate, a friendly mood. But it proved to be a tide that was
too late in flooding."

In view of his earlier misgivings about his temperamental fitness—even his desire—to mount the throne, the alacrity with which he took command, at least of the Palace
bureaucracy, was little short of astonishing. He was to say
afterward that once Crown and Sceptre—that is, the sovereignty and the duty—passed to him, he felt an exhilaration,
a flash flood of pride and self-confidence which swept away
the doubts that had once beset him. No longer did he need
consult and defer to his father's wishes. Now it was his
own wishes that galvanized the staff. "Brief as the experience was," the Duke used to say, "perhaps even because of
its brevity, I enjoyed being King. What it did for my ego
was altogether agreeable."

The Duchess also made light of the gossip that he was
uncomfortable on the throne. "All that talk of his not
wanting to be King makes me angry," she said in the
1950's. "He wanted very much to be King. He often discussed with me, before his father died, what he proposed to
do. He intended to be not so much a new kind of King as a
King who would reign in a more modern way. This didn't
mean he intended to stand on his head in Piccadilly Circus
at high noon every day. All it meant was, he was convinced that the Monarchy would be more useful if he could
introduce some of the ideas he had learned as Prince of
Wales. In saying this, I'm not being critical of the way
King George the Fifth and Queen Mary conducted themselves. What they did was just right for their times. But
there was good reason for David in his turn to seek
change, to try to bring the Monarchy up to date. My husband would have made a good King. I'll always believe
that."

Windsor himself was never explicit about his moderniza-
tion process. His autobiography admits that he took on
"the job" with no blueprints in his pocket, no grandiose

schemes that might earn him the sobriquet "Edward the Reformer." His simple—perhaps even simple-minded—goal was to be a king in a modern way, and he would have been gratified if his subjects had come to speak of him as "Edward the Innovator." One could not retrace with him the dusky, rough, crooked path that led to his abdication without being chilled, somewhere along the way, by the conviction that what had made the prospect of kingship most stimulating for him was the certainty that its splendors, its pageantry, the adulation, and the luxuries would be shared with Queen Wallis.

Walter Monckton, in his conversations with Edward VIII through the early months of the reign, never heard him express "any doubt or hesitation" about going on with the kingship. Still, Monckton formed a strong impression that his brisk, naïve though always absolute self-confidence in his handling of affairs welled from his faith in Wallis Simpson's judgments on almost everything. Whether he would have been a good king, with or without her, is a speculation past proof. Monckton was doubtful, because of his "restless and impatient" nature. "He abhorred the tedious functions," Monckton wrote. "Such obligations would have been irksome to him even with a wife beside him."

Luckily for the King's composure, the half-year of State mourning spared him many of the ceremonials. His worried ministers, however, did not lack for serious issues to keep the sovereign advised about. In March, when he had been on the throne only six weeks, Hitler's *Wehrmacht* goose-stepped into the Rhineland, thereby demolishing the Anglo-French alliance's barrier against armed aggression in Western Europe. Mussolini had also dispatched his fascist legions into Ethiopia, to scatter Emperor Haile Selassie's spear-brandishing tribesmen. These and other ominous foreign developments were a natural part of the King's daily business. They brought Anthony Eden, who had succeeded Sir Samuel Hoare as Foreign Minister, to Buckingham Palace. Duff Cooper, as Secretary of State for War, was another frequent caller. Britain was beginning to rearm, because of the upsurge of German militarism; and Duff Cooper, who loathed Hitler, had to report his feeble progress to a sovereign—in other matters an amiable listener—who was convinced that the Nazi menace was exaggerated.

In Windsor's dealings with his ministers, as in his cocktail and dinner conversations with congenial friends, he never suppressed his belief that the revival of German power would serve Europe as a bulwark against bolshevism. He also favored a martial injection of fascist efficiency into the medieval economy of Ethiopia. These private opinions, so long as they remained private, presented no immediate embarrassment to the Government, since Baldwin was maneuvering to avoid a showdown with the fascist powers. But the King's pro-Germanism was marked enough to have drawn the attention of the press. It noted that when he visited a school, he made a point of inquiring whether German was taught there as well as French. He had fostered a meeting between the chiefs of German and English ex-servicemen's organizations. At his first diplomatic reception, in February, he had devoted considerably more time—a half hour—to the German Ambassador, Leopold von Hoesch, than to any other. (Von Hoesch's sudden death in April would be publicly attributed to a heart attack, but privately to Nazi murderers, since he had never joined the party. He was succeeded in London by Joachim von Ribbentrop.) The press's apprehension was premature. Considering that the King was a confluence of so many streams of German blood, his sympathy with his ancestral homeland could be excused as no more than normal—at least up to this point.

Such State business as occupied the new King during his first six months on "the job" was mostly routine. He liked to say that perhaps his most vexing decision was whether to abrogate the Tudor requirement that all the Yeomen of the Guard—the "Beefeaters" at the Tower of London—had to wear beards. His signature was required on each of the multitudinous flakes in a daily blizzard of paper: on the commissions of officers in the armed forces; on the awards of decorations and the honors of knighthood; and on the appointments of ambassadors and ministers in the Foreign Service, of governor-generals to the Dominions and governors to the Colonies, and of bishops and clergy to crown livings.

He did not shirk this chore. Still, his distaste for any intellectual exercise combined with his procrastination to provoke grumbling in the Secretariat. Worse still, he was scandalously careless in scattering about York House and the Fort the contents of "the King's boxes"—the handsome red leather cases, opened by keys possessed only by the sovereign and his private secretary, that carry the most confidential information between Whitehall and the Palace. The Mike Scanlons spent the weekend of July 4 at the Fort, and the entry in Scanlon's diary for Monday the sixth ends, "I was taken aback when, as we were starting back to town, the King asked me to take his 'Boxes' to Buckingham Palace and deliver them to [Alex] Hardinge [Major Hardinge, the King's Private Secretary]. I had a feeling that Hardinge did not approve of the King's practice of confiding State papers to the care of an American intelligence officer."

The German Foreign Ministry in Berlin boasted that its London Embassy needed no secret agents; thanks to the King's cavalier attitude toward security, Britain had no secrets. H. Montgomery Hyde wrote in his biography of Stanley Baldwin that the Prime Minister "was already worried about reports . . . from the head of the secret intelligence service about leakages of the contents of state papers which had been traced to the King." Robert Lacey had this to say in the *Sunday Times Magazine* for August 3, 1975: "Things had reached a stage . . . where the Government were withholding confidential papers from the King because there were serious doubts over national security. It was no good the Cabinet trying to bluff Mussolini over Abyssinia when the King was secretly telling the Italian Ambassador that the League of Nations, which was trying to impose sanctions, could from the British viewpoint 'be considered dead.' " And Lacey would add this in his book, *Majesty*: "Alarm began to be felt in the Cabinet Office when highly confidential documents began to return obviously unread, occasionally marked with slopped cocktails and the rings of wet glass bottoms and, worst of all, after extraordinarily long delays. Discreet inquiries were instituted through his principal Private Secretary, Alexander Hardinge, and it was discovered that red boxes containing crucial Cabinet discussions were going down to Fort Bel-

vedere to be left unguarded there while an unsupervised
and cosmopolitan selection of guests came and went."[4]

In addition to the boxes and the paper work, there were
too many other demands of the King's time to sustain any
imputation that his days were idle. He made, though not
always cheerfully, the calls that the major military commands, the staff colleges, and other establishments required
of a new Commander in Chief. As honorary Colonel in
Chief of all seven regiments of the Household Troops, he
called at all seven regimental headquarters. On Maundy
Thursday, with the Archbishop of Canterbury beside him,
he distributed alms to seventy-one poor aged men and an
equal number of poor aged women.

He gave audiences to the miscellany of emirs, sheiks,
sultans, maharajas, princes, and other chieftains from British possessions in Africa, the Near, Middle, and Far East,
and elsewhere, who had journeyed to London to pay their
respects to the British Raj. He appeared at the annual
flower shows, industrial fairs, and charitable gatherings of
which his father had been a patron. William H. Davies
might have had Edward VIII in mind when he wrote:

> God's pity on poor kings,
>   They know no gentle rest;
> The North and South cry out,
>   Cries come from East and West—
>
> "Come, open this new dock,
>   Building, Bazaar or Fair."
> Lord, what a wretched life
>   Such men must bear.

This was a familiar road, well trodden by generations of
British monarchs. A courtier said, partly in admiration,
partly in pity, "All of them—and their consorts, their sisters and their cousins and their aunts—buzz about like so
many bees!" (During three consecutive war years, King
George VI, the Queen, and the two Princesses would make
a total of just over 3,000 public appearances, an average of
some 250 apiece per year.) What was new was the detour
that now ended the royal workday.

Practically every evening, on his way home from the Palace, he stopped at Bryanston Court for a cocktail with Wallis. He could count on an audience fascinated by his description of a king's day. He was made to feel that he was embarked on a historic mission to modernize the monarchy and refresh its traditional glory and strength. She would remember that he talked about little else, and was at times indignant and enraged that his modest initial innovations were being frustrated by the Court functionaries who wanted nothing changed. Or so she would have history believe.

What they both failed to perceive, and what was to bring on their early ruin, was that the issue between the Crown and its custodians was not what was to be culled from the monarchy, but what was to be preserved. The British journalist Malcolm Muggeridge—no friend of the Establishment, and certainly none of humbug—rightly perceived the King's mistake. The father's Court had been dull, respectable, solid. But—Muggeridge wrote—solidity "was the most necessary quality of all in a sovereign and his way of life. So much thought solid had proved unsubstantial; and now was the Monarchy itself to partake of the same unsubstantiality? Was the gold of the Imperial Crown to suffer the same fate as the Gold Standard? To be a Prince Charming suited a Prince, but a King Charming would never do; firmly and properly had Prince Hal put away Falstaff, along with other princely things when he became King Henry. Let King Edward do likewise. . . .

"He showed little inclination to do so, in that sharing the fate of so many of his generation, who, youthful, were required to be mature, and in maturity persisted in being youthful. His position demanded of him that he suffer pomposity gladly, and bear the dull burden of authority without the delight of exercising it; whereas his inclination was to dispense with the ceremonial respect and make his own will felt; to be both less and more than the King who ruled before him."

The miscalculation would doom him.

By King Edward VIII's own account, he was braced from the start for trouble, and not alone over Mrs. Simpson. Instinct had warned him that his Prime Minister, Stanley Baldwin, had little use for him. Uncongeniality had characterized their first meeting, in 1927, when Prince Edward and Prince George represented their father at the celebration of Canada's Diamond Jubilee. Baldwin, who had been Prime Minister for three years, led the British delegation, and he and the two Princes crossed the Dominion together. The young men found him a bore, given to long-winded disquisitions on the apple husbandry of Worcestershire and the revision of the Book of Common Prayer. Others who had also been exposed to Baldwin at length sometimes became not only impatient with his loquacity, but skeptical of his competency. Sir Kenneth Clark quotes Neville Chamberlain as remarking, "S.B. is always talking about his love of nature and the English countryside. He couldn't recognize five common English birds or English trees."[5] And Sir Oswald Mosley wrote, "I am always inclined to distrust men . . . [like] the bucolic pig-fancier, too honest to be true stuff, of the Baldwin school."[6]

Baldwin, for his part, resented the low esteem in which Wales openly held politicians. Wales may have contracted his contempt from his father, of whom Jack Aird remarked, "If King George the Fifth had one clear conception, it was that politicians must be kept in their places—both because he realized that the monarchy was receding into political desuetude, and because he himself detested the breed." The unfavorable first impression then was later darkened by Wales's practice of expounding his personal prejudices in sensitive political issues, indifferent alike to the traditional constraints on royalty and to the position of the Government. This failing hardened Baldwin's judgment that he was deficient in certain fundamentals which the exercise of kingship demanded. Well before the breach became open, Baldwin privately expressed these misgivings and added, "The Yorks will do it very well."

The King was aware of this disaffection. He further realized that he faced another formidable foe in the Archbishop of Canterbury, a powerful personality in his own right and made doubly so by his close friendship with the Prime Minister. Church and State found comfortable alliance in their temperaments. The King's two meetings with the Primate had been, on his side, less than cordial, though the lack of rapport did not trouble him. He had drifted away from the Church. After his Accession, he sometimes occupied the sovereign's stall in St. George's Chapel, but he never returned to the little church at Sandringham where he had worshiped with his parents. In exile, he would forsake churchgoing almost entirely. On one of his postwar visits to England, he would ask a friend, "Am I still prayed for by name?" The answer was, No; he was now merely lumped under the heading "other members of the royal family."

Clerics were seldom among the company he gathered around himself and the Duchess for instruction and example. What he became in old age was foreshadowed in the last years of his princeship and the eleven months of his kingship: a living contradiction, a faithless Defender of the Faith. Leaving his Church was for him a Faustian bargain, the price he paid for a marriage that would cut all his ties with the kingly past forever.

Additionally, he knew that he could count on no support from the Lords Temporal—those personages who manage and help staff the pageantry that lends the monarchy its splendor.

To take on these redoubtable personalities and institutions was rash enough. Worse still for the King, he neither trusted, nor was wholly trusted by, many members of the Palace Secretariat, including veterans of his personal staff. Without their unique skills and experience, and equally their loyalty, he could not begin to discharge the day-to-day duties of kingship, much less manage an unobtrusive meshing of his public regime with the increasingly demanding private schedule that centered on Mrs. Simpson.

The ranking officer on the King's staff is the private secretary—at once senior adviser and counselor, director of intelligence, chief administrator, conscience, and link with the Cabinet, the agencies of Government, and (in Edward VIII's time) the Empire and Commonwealth. He directs the unceasing flow of paper between Whitehall and the Palace—a flow requiring, on the one hand, the King's constitutional assent and, on the other, his continuing cognizance. The private secretary is also the King's eyes and ears; he keeps track of whatever happenings may affect British life, whether in politics, economics, or foreign affairs; and, within politics, he is expected to bring to his sovereign the opinions and programs not only of his ministers, but those of the Loyal Opposition as well.

Sir Clive Wigram, later first Baron, had served George V in all these capacities for twenty-six years, having entered his service from the Indian Army in 1910, four years before the start of the First World War. During the last months of the reign, he had doubled as Keeper of the Privy Purse, a job he had shouldered after Lord Sysonby's death in October. In the line of accomplished senior courtiers that began with Sir Henry Ponsonby, who was Queen Victoria's private secretary for a quarter of a century, through Sir Francis Knollys, Edward VII's shrewd counselor, to Sir Arthur Bigge, later Lord Stamfordham, a Royal Artillery officer who had fought the Zulus before joining the Palace Secretariat under Ponsonby and who stayed on to be George V's good right hand—men who, like Foreign Ministers, had been the channel between the monarchy and Whitehall since Victoria's day—Clive Wigram was the last. When George V acceded in 1910, he invited Wigram, who had been Stamfordham's understudy, to be his assistant private secretary, and Wigram stayed with him for twenty-six years. He was a courtier of unusual versatility and poise.

But Wigram, at sixty-three, had had enough. What made him loath to serve the son was not alone the difference of twenty-two years in their ages. It was a conviction that the new King was headed for disaster, and that such counsel as a private secretary was dutybound to proffer would fall on deaf ears. Unlike Lord Stamfordham, who with the father's approval had never hesitated to rectify the young Prince of Wales, and whose admonishments were softened by affection, Wigram had had little contact with the son. When Wigram achieved seniority, Wales was thirty-six, too old for scolding. Their relationship was therefore friendly but distant, since Wales considered him "elderly." As Edward VIII he needed him badly, and he banked on Wigram's staying on for a year or two longer, long enough for him to get a firmer grip on "the job" and to assemble a staff of his own.

Custom allows a late King's staff to remain undisturbed

in its offices through the six-month period of mourning. To the new King's surprise, Wigram came to him soon after the funeral to say that he wished to retire at the King's earliest convenience. "He gave me no impressions of animosity," Windsor said of their talk. "His reasons were that he had put in twenty-six years of hard work, that my father had promised to make him Archivist of his papers, and that he wanted to tackle them and putter in his garden."

But Wigram's real reason for dissociating himself was the desperate one that impelled him to impress upon Baldwin the "perils" that awaited, if the King persisted in his course. An excruciating debate over where his loyalties truly lay must have preceded this extraordinary step. Its justification was obvious: If the monarch could not be saved from himself, then the Prime Minister must save the monarchy. Wigram's account of that meeting, if one exists, has never been published. A discreet passage in Baldwin's biography reveals only that Wigram himself doubted whether "against a passion so overmastering . . . words of reason would be of any avail." Baldwin ignored the appeal; no such words were uttered. It suited his strategy, as well as his temperament, to let the King sink deeper into the quicksand of his own making. The diarist Thomas Jones, to whom Baldwin confided much, wrote that Wigram "found the King's temper and habits so irregular that he resigned and told the P.M. his reasons." His distress notwithstanding, Wigram finally agreed to stay on until the mourning ended, in July.

For his successor, after Godfrey Thomas declined the promotion, the King should have logically chosen one of the two highly experienced assistant private secretaries on the Palace staff. The senior was Maj. Alexander Hardinge, later second Baron Hardinge of Penhurst, son of the famous diplomat who had been Edward VII's close friend, Viceroy of India, and twice Permanent Under-Secretary of State in the Foreign Office. Hardinge had inherited none of the conviviality that might have drawn him, as it had drawn his father, to the favorable notice of another convivial King. He was a Buchmanite (a member of the Oxford Group) and a ramrod-straight civil servant, sure of himself and of the right way to manage the monarch's business. Having been Wigram's deputy at the Palace, he was at home with the machinery of kingship, if not with the King himself. Windsor judged him "stiff, humorless, almost wooden. I never cared for him, even before I broke with him. My mother didn't like him either. She thought him defeatist, an obstructionist, and tiresome."

The junior assistant private secretary, Alan Lascelles, was no stranger. He was a first cousin of Lord Lascelles's, the King's brother-in-law; and had been assistant private secretary during nine boisterous Prince-of-Wales's years, 1920 until 1929—years that "Tommy" Lascelles decided at the end had become altogether too boisterous. He quit cold, but not before he had given the Prince a tongue-lashing which was a model of schoolmasterly rebuke, scari-fying and irrefutable. Although Lascelles never revealed what had aroused him, Lord Mountbatten said, "The rela-tionship was doomed to fail. Their temperaments were in-compatible. David was boyish and buoyant. Tommy was difficult, disapproving, prissy." A courtier who also knew both men added, "Lascelles had disapproved the Prince's behavior in the nineteen twenties—the drinking, the late hours, the rowdy friends. He was afraid that for all of the Prince's good qualities, he was on the verge of losing his moral and ethical principles; that ordinary words bearing on a man's conduct—*honor, responsibility, family feeling, good taste, gentlemanliness,* even *affection* and *gratitude*—were ceasing to mean anything to him. Something strange happened between him and Wales only a year after George the Fifth's nearly fatal illness in nineteen twenty-eight—a blow-up of sorts—over the heir apparent's behavior when he should have been steeling himself for the succession. Lascelles was sure that the corruption was related to the Prince's war experiences, but if he knew what went wrong then, he never said. He simply felt that an older man, such as himself, had to step forward and try to pull him back from the brink."

For Lascelles to find himself once again serving the man, now King, whom he had dressed down, was an un-comfortable turn of events. Yet neither side seemed to bear a grudge; the relationship was resumed in an atmosphere of cordiality, and it would remain cordial through the brief kingship. When Windsor in exile was admiring the skill with which Lascelles had guided King George VI through ten years of cold war, hot war, industrial unrest, and the crumbling of the Empire, he praised him as "a great secretary, perhaps better even than Stamfordham."

Still, because the King regarded Lascelles along with Hardinge as "a George the Fifth man"—relicts overdue for abolishment—he had made up his mind to dismiss them in the summer, when he would be free to start a general shake-up. He liked and trusted no one who came to him with his father's stamp. He was like Commodus, of whom Gibbon wrote, "The friendship of the father [Marcus Aurelius] always insured the aversion of the son." Meanwhile, since neither Hardinge nor Lascelles figured importantly in his grand plan, he would leave them in their offices at the Palace, where they would be occupied with kingship's public chores. The private side—the advancement of Mrs. Simpson—he proposed to handle alone. He thus began his reign by isolating himself from all the sources to which a constitutional monarch by custom looks for advice—not only the courtiers who had long served his father, but also the Prime Minister and the Primate. His isolation from them was widened by his decision to manage the kingship not from the Palace but from York House and the Fort. Wigram's prophecy was being fulfilled. The King was moving out of reach and past reason.

Ernest Simpson having bowed to his monarch's conception of the proper etiquette in a situation where the conventions of chivalry had been turned upside down, the squalid, perfunctory business of assembling evidence to satisfy the divorce court was no longer a problem. That would be arranged in the early spring, on Simpson's return from the United States.

In consequence, the King now had room to maneuver within his strategical plan; and Mrs. Simpson, relieved of the risk of a possibly scandalous trial, could confidently put off filing her petition until late summer or early fall, and still be free to marry her lover before the Coronation and to be crowned with him. This hazardous gambit having come off satisfactorily thus far, the King turned his attention to other matters.

His dominant concerns were that Wallis never be at a loss for excitement and never have cause to fear the outcome of their compact. Beyond range of his father's ire at last, the King was free to concentrate on propelling her, with the help of Emerald Cunard and Sibyl Colefax, into the influential circles that revolved around Parliament and Whitehall, where the charm that had enslàved him would, he was sure, again carry all before it. He also had a third concern: how best to prepare his subjects for the changes, even surprises, ahead. His outburst against an Establishment which he imagined was conspiring to make him over in his father's image bespoke a rebelliousness that ran much deeper than Walter Monckton appreciated. He was obsessed with the notion that he had to make clear his determination to be King in his own way. In later years, he would argue that he gave Britain fair warning that his style of kingship would be different from his father's; and as an example of his candor, he cited a broadcast that he made on St. David's Day, March 1, five weeks after his Accession.

This was his first statement to the Commonwealth and Empire, and the Government urged him to make it. The prolonged depression, the growing menace of Hitler, Mussolini's lunge at Ethiopia, and the ebbing influence of the League of Nations all conspired to darken Britain's prospects. The hope in Whitehall was that the fresh accents of the new, still youthful monarch would revivify the tired British blood and reawaken the loyalties of the Dominions and possessions beyond the sea. Windsor welcomed the invitation, but for a different reason: It provided a pulpit for what he called a private declaration of independence from outmoded kingly usages of the past, a personal declaration of purpose.

By custom, the Home Secretary (then Sir Samuel Hoare) prepares and reviews the King's official statements, thereby keeping him from straying outside the policies and interests of the Government. Well in advance of the St. David's Day broadcast, the Palace received the Home Office's draft— a piece of standard Whitehall rhetoric, eulogizing George V's long reign and declaring the son's intention to carry on the father's work.

"Privately," Windsor recalled, "I found the language

pompous—heavy with references to 'my people' and 'my realm.' Naturally, I wanted to pay tribute to my father, but I wasn't inclined to be so specific so early about what I myself would or would not do. I decided it would be enough to suggest that I had neither the temperament nor the desire to fit myself into the mold favored by my father, and that things would be somewhat different with me. I was trying to word this smoothly when Wigram notified me that the Home Office was wondering why I hadn't returned a finished draft. I said I wasn't quite happy with a paragraph of my own that I wanted to work into it. Wigram was insistent: The Home Office *had* to know what I intended saying. My answer was, The speech is mine to give, and I'll say what I damn please. The Home Office could rest assured that the text would give no offense."

It did not. Read today, the contribution which the King regarded as significantly his own sounds altogether harmless, even wistful. All he said was: "I am better known to you as Prince of Wales—as a man who, during the War and since, has had the opportunity of getting to know the people of nearly every country of the world, under all conditions and circumstances. And, although I now speak to you as King, I am still that same man who has had that same experience and whose constant effort it will be to continue to promote the well-being of his fellow men. . . ."

In Windsor's later reflections he conceded that these mild allusions to the princely example hardly constituted a challenge to the Establishment, and even less a warning of the apocalyptic actions that he had in mind. Far from setting alarm bells ringing, the speech was acclaimed everywhere as a promise that Edward VIII would bring the throne closer to the real world, while keeping everything as it was. His public conduct could not have been more reassuring. That same day, he took the salute of the Welsh Guards at their parade at the Tower of London, and attended the coming-of-age St. David's Day services at the Church of All Hallows nearby. A few weeks later he would be even more reassuring in another speech: "As Prince of Wales I bore a device with an ancient motto: 'I serve.' As King I shall hold this in constant remembrance; for a King can perform no higher function than that of service."

One is left with the unanswered question: What did Edward VIII really mean when he told Britons that they could expect from him as King the qualities and interests he had displayed as heir apparent? What kind of king did he intend to be? Did he seriously entertain any schemes for modernizing or democratizing the ancient institution of the monarchy? He died without supplying the answers.

🐝 CHAPTER 4 🐝
"Mrs. Simpson Has Stolen the Fairy Prince"

The King's responsiveness to the remote control being exercised from Bryanston Court, coupled with his increasing distaste for routine chores, further hastened the disintegration of his personal staff. Yet he seemed oblivious to what was happening before his eyes. Two of his stoutest and most senior lieutenants—the groom-in-waiting, Brigadier "G" Trotter, and the Comptroller, Admiral Sir Lionel Halsey—were dismissed in the space of a few weeks. The cause was the same for both men: their unwillingness to connive at making Wallis Simpson Queen of England.

"The Old Salt," as Halsey was affectionately known to the household, had seen action ashore in the Boer War and in all three North Sea battles in the Great War. During them, he wore over his uniform a robe of kiwi feathers which a Maori chieftain had presented to him when he commanded H.M.S. *New Zealand,* and which he had promised he would always wear in combat. When, now, he not only ventured to protest the extravagant levies on royal funds to meet Mrs. Simpson's soaring bills, but warned the King that the public would never accept her as his wife, the King told him, "I'm sorry, but I no longer want your services."

Lord Mountbatten had been Halsey's flag lieutenant during the Prince of Wales's cruise to Australia and New Zealand in 1920. He couldn't believe the news of the sacking: "The Old Salt fired? It's not true! I admire that marvelous man more than anyone I know!"

The break with Trotter came over his continued friendship with Lady Furness. When the King told him, "I am through with Thelma and very keen on Wallis, so please cut Thelma," Trotter answered, "Sir, I made friends with Thelma at your request. I don't sack my friends."

Trotter's stubborn loyalty was an echo from 1876, when the Prince of Wales (later Edward VII) reprimanded the Marquess of Blandford (soon to become Duke of Marlborough) for his affair with Lady Aylesford. Blandford's brother, Lord Randolph Churchill, called on the Prince and pointed out that it ill became *him* to censure an adulterer, especially as he, too, had flirted with Lady Aylesford, among many others. The Prince, enraged, announced that he was blacklisting the Churchills forthwith, and would no longer enter any house where they were still welcome; ten years would pass before he spoke to them again. In all society, only two persons dared stand up to him. The Duchess of Manchester told him, "I hold friendship higher than snobbery"; and John Delacour (now identifiable only as "a Yorkshire country gentleman") said ringingly, "I allow no man to choose my friends!" Thus Trotter. His obituary in *The Times,* written by "an old friend," includes this significant passage: "As to what his intimate friends knew of 'G,' it is a story that cannot be told here. It is a story of . . . loyalty to his friends, and loyalty to those he served. The value of friendship ranked very highly with him."

A courtier said bitterly, "He was a fine man, G was, proud and spirited. Because a cad had no compunction about scrapping a mistress, he assumed that a gentleman had none about scrapping a friend!"

Sir Max Beerbohm had written a clear warning into his *King George the Fourth*: "Remember that a Great Personage, like a great genius, is dangerous to his fellow-creatures." Still, the brusqueness and injustice of their dismissals wounded both Halsey and Trotter, though Trotter found some compensation in being released from what had been a cruel trap. Royalty never carries cash, even when it is host at a restaurant or nightclub. When the party ends, an equerry quietly pays the bill, expecting his account to be settled in due course. The system had worked smoothly during Edward VII's forays into Paris, but when his grandson took it over, he allowed it to develop a disastrous flaw: The equerries continued paying the bills, but the Prince discontinued repaying the equerries.

Some were men of such wealth that a few dozen bottles of champagne mattered little more than so much ginger beer. Lord Dudley and Lord Brownlow, for two, could have brought Quaglino's, Uncle's, or the Embassy and tossed it to the maître d'hôtel as a tip. But others, like Trotter and Metcalfe, had shallower purses—indeed, Trotter's main income was his meager pay as groom-in-waiting—and night after night of fielding bills first for the Prince, then for the King gravely depleted their bank accounts. A few of Windsor's former intimates excuse him on grounds that he had no idea of the value of money—one said, "I honestly don't think he knew whether a ten-shilling cigar was expensive or cheap"—and therefore never realized that he was imposing on men who not only couldn't afford it, but couldn't avoid it. Another theory (which time would reinforce) was that he was simply stingy. As Gibbon wrote of Vespasian, his "virtues were disgraced by a strict and even sordid parsimony." The correct explanation is academic. When poor Trotter was dismissed, he had almost exhausted his modest resources; by scrimping, he stretched them over his last few years—barely. When he died in 1949, he was bankrupt.

Halsey fired, Trotter fired; it looked as if the King were clearing decks in preparation for the storm. The only persons now admitted to the Fort for weekends and to York House for suppers were those who wore Wallis Simpson's colors: the George Hunters, Helen Fitzgerald, the Mike Scanlons, Sibyl Colefax, Emerald Cunard, and "Foxy" Gwynne—so nicknamed because of her rufous hair (she was American-born and had married an American, Erskine Gwynne, a connection of the Vanderbilts). In the small circle of the fashionable West End set, these intimates of the King's favorite had come to constitute a smaller inner circle of their own. If occasion demanded, the parties were filled out from the handful of friends remaining from the past: Dickie and Edwina Mountbatten, Hugh Sefton, the Colin Buists, and notably the slender, saturnine Jack Aird, the last of the gallant galaxy of princely aides still to enjoy the royal confidence.

The cast of characters was different, but weekends at the Fort were otherwise much as before, with cards and dancing, and light talk over the excellent table which Mrs. Simpson now ruled. It was she who gave the chef and butler their orders; and as she directed the flow of conversation, the King visibly rejoiced; he was like a soloist waiting confidently for the conductor's nod. An observer described the scene to the writer Geoffrey Bocca: the King "watched her happily as she laughed, joked, talked, spread her strong expressive hands in acute, sharply defined gestures. Then the King would be restored to his old bouncy self."

He passed the weekend afternoons pottering in the garden, usually in bright-colored shorts and a white jersey, with a black mourning band on the sleeve. Yet the atmosphere of bucolic ease which had been engendered in his first joyful creation of the Fort had all but vanished. The tension, the anxiety, that were infusing the host could not help being communicated to the company. During Jack Aird's last summer evenings there, listening to the Gramophone while the others danced in the little octagonal room, he had the sensation of being "aboard a doomed ship, with the orchestra playing a fox-trot in the saloon, and six feet of water in the engine room." Aird had already arranged for his recall to the Grenadier Guards in the fall, and was hoping that the action would not be read for what it was: *Sauve qui peut.*

By now the Government, the great merchant houses, and London's hotels were stepping up the pace of their preparations for the Coronation. The date fixed for it, May 12, was still nearly a year away, but its approach increasingly dominated the King's still secret arrangements for Mrs. Simpson. Inasmuch as Court mourning would not end until July, he was not yet making the public appearances where he could have established her discreetly and with progressive familiarity as a permanent companion. Still, under his covert sponsorship, and her overt co-sponsorship, the quasi-private dinners of introduction and social rehabilitation being organized by Sibyl Colefax and Emerald Cunard went on apace. Bruce Lockhart's diary for June 10, 1936, records one of these parties, where the ostensible purpose was to allow the other guests to meet the King, but the real one was to introduce Mrs. Simpson as his prospective consort. Wrote Lockhart: "Dined at [Lady Colefax's] . . . King came in rather late with Mrs. Simpson—very neat in black. [He] looks older and harder—a little stiffer perhaps since he became King, defi-

nitely more confidence in himself since he met Mrs. Simpson. . . . He did not leave until nearly one. Came and left
with Mrs. Simpson. Quite unattended. No A.D.C., etc."

The campaign, for all its skillfulness, persuasiveness, and
cost, was not an unqualified success. Of the aristocratic
families who are truly influential in English Society, none
had yet opened its doors to this stranger whose only credential was the King's love. To him, it was a minor concern; at that point he was more bent on overcoming his
Prime Minister's still undeclared resistance.

One May day at the Fort, he told Wallis that he was
inviting the Baldwins to dinner at York House and
wanted her to be there. "It's got to be done," he said.
"Sooner or later my Prime Minister must meet my future
wife."

Mrs. Simpson says she protested, "David, you mustn't
talk this way! The idea is impossible. They'd never let
you."

"I'm well aware of all that," he said almost gaily, "but
rest assured, I'll manage it somehow."[1]

The dinner was on May 27. In addition to the Baldwins,
the fifteen other guests included the Simpsons, Lady Cunard, the Mountbattens, and Col. and Mrs. Charles Lindbergh—an astonishing mixture. Emerald Cunard was there
because the King wished to show her his gratitude for
shepherding Wallis through the bright new world where
her style would be displayed to best advantage. The
Mountbattens were there because Dickie, the King's
cousin, would be proof to the Baldwins of family solidarity.
The Lindberghs were there because they had just returned
from a tour of Germany, where the colonel had been impressed by German vigor and purpose, and even more by
the power of the nascent *Luftwaffe*. The King shared Lindbergh's favorable impression of Germany and his respect
for German might, and wanted to have available, in the
after-dinner talk, an authoritative voice against a Prime
Minister who had been slothful about rearming Britain and
contemptuous of Hitler's intelligence. As for Ernest Simpson, he was there for the sake of appearances; the King
was not yet ready for the Prime Minister and his straitlaced wife to come to his dinner and find no Mr. Simpson
in sight and a vivacious Mrs. Simpson presiding.

She had planned the menu and chosen the table decorations, but though the meal was doubtless a splendid one, nobody seemed to remember the courses. What the guests remembered was that the party did not come off. Baldwin was to remark, "My wife was well placed, but I own it surprised me to see Lady Cunard at one end of the table and Mr. Simpson at the other." The King was in the middle, with Mrs. Baldwin on his right and Wallis across from him. A remark of Lucy Baldwin's also survives: "Mrs. Simpson has stolen the Fairy Prince."

Yet the dinner became memorable for extraneous reasons. The *Court Circular* mentioned Wallis Simpson for the first time and Ernest for the only time. As she put it, "This was the last time Ernest and I were publicly together in David's company."

Soon afterward, to Walter Monckton's astonishment, even consternation, the King telephoned to say that he and Mrs. Simpson would soon arrive at his chambers in Harcourt Buildings, in the Temple. It was an extraordinary indiscretion, considering the obvious inference which anyone who chanced to spy them there might draw about the King's role in the Simpson divorce. The risk, far from discouraging the happy pair, did not keep them from repeating the visit several times. It was too much to hope that the spectacle of the King and an unknown woman flitting down the narrow, crooked alley behind the Harcourt Buildings, leaving the royal motor at the curb, would pass unnoticed, and it didn't. (The frequent presence of the royal motor outside Bryanston Court had been exciting comment since 1934.)

The object of these conferences was to settle on a solicitor to lay the groundwork for the case. The King's solicitor, George Allen, did not take divorce cases, but Monckton found a topnotch substitute, Theodore Goddard, a large man with a large, pale face. Soon after the arrangements had been made, Monckton learned that the King and Mrs. Simpson had instructed Goddard to engage Norman Birkett, K.C., to argue the case. Monckton was stunned. Birkett was the most famous trial lawyer in England, known everywhere for his wit and his flamboyant courtroom style. To bring Birkett's big guns into action on what any prudent couple would hope to carry off as a simple marital split-up would, Monckton foresaw, attract acute interest and be instantly taken as evidence of the King's concern with the divorce.

Even so, Monckton remained convinced that the divorce was not a prelude to the King's marriage. The King assured him, "I do not propose to let my friendship with Mrs. Simpson prevent her from obtaining a divorce." The lady herself was candor personified. "She told me in answer to a direct question," Monckton wrote, "that she wanted to be free of her present marriage; that she was getting older; that she might well meet someone whom she might happily marry. She told me . . . that it was ridiculous to imagine that she had any idea of marrying the King." To this Monckton added wryly, "I thought so, too."

He said later, "I also thought that the King had no idea of marrying *her*. He seemed too absorbed in his work, in the affairs of State, and in his plans for simplifying and lubricating the machinery of the Monarchy. But before long, I suddenly realized for the first time the depth of his feelings for her. He and I were making a quick trip to inspect a vacant holding in one of the Duchy [of Cornwall] properties. While we were being shown around the house, I noticed that he was no longer with me. I found him in an empty room, standing as if transfixed, staring out the window, his face aglow. I asked him, 'What are you looking at, Sir?'

"He said, 'Nothing. Nothing at all.' Then he said happily, 'But *she* is there, in that direction.'

"His gaze was roughly toward London. I asked, 'How far?' being unable to come up with anything more intelligent.

" 'Don't know,' he said. 'Perhaps a hundred miles. But I've been thinking of her. She is in my mind.' "

While tidying up the legal preparations, the King had brought Mrs. Simpson back onstage at York House on July 9, at another star-studded dinner. This time the guest list was heavily weighted with politicians whose goodwill needed cultivation. They included three members of Parliament: Winston Churchill, temporarily "at liberty"; David Margesson, Conservative chief whip and a power in the

Commons; and Sir Samuel Hoare, senior statesman of the conservative Party, one of Baldwin's chief lieutenants, and newly appointed First Lord of the Admiralty—all these with their wives. A member of Parliament not present was Lady Astor. The invitation would have been wasted. Her biographer, Christopher Sykes, says that she had already declared her views to the King "on the subject of his possible marriage. This she did in June 1936. . . . She gave two accounts in letters. According to one, 'I went to see him myself and begged him not to do as he was doing.' According to the other she spoke 'hotly and loudly.' The circumstances of the encounter are not recorded."[2] The facts that both she and Mrs. Simpson were Americans, both were of Virginia descent, and both had been divorced evidently did not sway Lady Astor's sympathies.

The most recent Viceroy of India was there, the Marquess of Willingdon, with Lady Willingdon. The Duke and Duchess of York supplied the family connection. Filling out the table were the King's banker, Sir Edward Peacock, with Lady Peacock; Lady Diana Cooper, of the porcelain loveliness; the new private secretary, Major Hardinge, with Mrs. Hardinge; Lady Asquith, a considerable force in politics; and Lady Colefax, here being rewarded for her fieldwork in Mrs. Simpson's benefit, as had been her co-commander, Lady Cunard. The last name on the list was Wallis Simpson, unpaired. Hoare noted that she was "very attractive and intelligent, very American, and with little or no knowledge of English life." She in turn noted that the Yorks were cool and remote—a mutual, enduring dislike had instantly sprung up between Wallis and the Duchess— but she remembered the evening chiefly for her sensation of being under steady scrutiny—the object of "well-bred but not so well-concealed curiosity." She remembered it also for marking her second recognition by the *Court Circular*. There was still another reason why she might have remembered it: Winston Churchill blandly and impishly introduced the topic of Mrs. Fitzherbert's clandestine marriage to the Prince of Wales (later King George IV) in 1785.

The Duchess of York said sharply, "That was a very long time ago!"

Churchill, not to be turned from his mischief-making,

jumped to the Wars of the Roses, and the Houses of Lancaster and York.

"*That*," said the Duchess, still more sharply, "was a very, *very* long time ago!"

The end of Court mourning, in July, meant that the King could resume a more open existence. He welcomed the change. It suited his strategy of bringing Mrs. Simpson before larger audiences, but still at a decorous distance from him, at least until his subjects became accustomed to her as his consort. Three important public ceremonies now loomed ahead: on the sixteenth, the King's birthday parade and the ritual Presentation of Colors; on the twenty-first and twenty-second, garden parties at the Palace for the season's debutantes; and on the twenty-fifth, a state visit to Vimy Ridge, near Arras, with President Lebrun of France and Prime Minister Mackenzie King of Canada, to unveil a memorial to the Canadian dead of the Great War.

The Simpsons—it would be their last appearance in public together—were in the stands in Hyde Park, in the section reserved for the families of officers of the Household Brigade and former officers, when the new sovereign presented new colors to the three senior regiments of the Brigade of Guards: the Grenadiers, the Coldstreams, and the Scots. He rode out from the Palace with an escort of the Blues under Lt. Bob Laycock, Freda Dudley Ward's son-in-law. (The irony of the changed circumstances was not lost on the King's attendants.) The park was in full leaf, the sun shone, the air was warm, the stands were packed; and six battalions of Guardsmen, magnificent in scarlet tunics and bearskins, bayonets flashing, formed three sides of a square in front of the platform on which stood the King, in the dress uniform of Colonel in Chief of the Grenadiers, his beloved wartime regiment. To the young ensigns who came to kneel before him, he passed the colors two by two: the King's, of blood-red silk embroidered with his cipher, and the regiment's silken Union Jack, with its battle honors. At the conclusion of the solemn ritual, he gave a brief but moving speech that Winston Churchill had polished for him, then remounted, to lead the battalions down Constitution Hill toward the Palace, where he was to take the salute.

The commander of the London District, General Sir Bertram Sergison-Brooke, rode on his right; on his left was the Duke of York, the Colonel in Chief of the Scots Guards; Sir John Aird, a major in the Grenadiers, rode a length or two behind. They had just passed through Wellington Arch when the King glimpsed "something bright and metallic" flying at him from his left. It clattered on the pavement under his horse and skidded under the general's. The King said to him quietly, "We'll know in a moment if it's a bomb." It wasn't; it was a loaded revolver which an alert policeman had wrested from an onlooker just as he raised it. The man, a lunatic Irish journalist named George McMahon, was not seriously bent on regicide; it developed that he merely wished to draw attention to a fancied grievance. The scene was not far from where another lunatic, young Edward Oxford, had fired on Queen Victoria in June 1840. Accordingly, McMahon was charged with nothing more heinous than "intent on alarming His Majesty," and his sentence was a lenient twelve months at hard labor. Even so, no one could have been sure of his intent at the time, and the King's coolness fully met Ernest Hemingway's definition of courage: "grace under pressure."

In later years, when the Duke of Windsor and Jack Aird recalled the afternoon, they always made light of what they had laughingly dubbed "the Dastardly Attempt." Aird insisted that his first impulse had been to dismount and examine the object, but he had not done so because "my uniform was so tight, I could never have got back on my horse."

Windsor reminded him that afterward they had put on golfing clothes as quickly as possible, and had gone out to Coombe Hill.

"Yes," Aird said, "and you were in fine form. I remember remarking that you had to have something thrown at you, to reach the top of your game. I've often thought that if a similar Dastardly Attempt could have been staged every week or so, you might be King today."

Still later, Aird added this: "Sometimes he'd dash in with only a few moments for changing into one of his elaborate uniforms. Once was a previous Trooping the Color.

The full-dress trousers of the Grenadiers—dark blue, with a red stripe—were extremely tight, and when he tugged them on, they split down the whole length of one leg. His valet, Crisp, snatched up a bottle of blue ink and painted as much of the flesh as showed, and he went through the ceremony with nobody the wiser."

The Dastardly Attempt was unique. Never before or afterward did anyone make even a perfunctory attempt on the Prince-King-Duke's life. But an American friend of his, Dr. Henry Field, remembers a milder parallel from an afternoon at the Melton Races in the middle 1920's:

"We were walking through the gates to the paddock—I between H.R.H. and Fruity Metcalfe—when a woman in a shawl and shabby clothes came forward and bowed. As she raised her head, I saw that her face was contorted with rage, and before any of us could move, she whipped out a hatpin and drove it into H.R.H.'s right arm. The police dashed up and dragged her away, screaming, but H.R.H. simply walked on, so calmly that I asked if such incidents were common. He said yes, they were. Very often a woman would pop out of a crowd and stick a pin into him, or pinch him with all her might. He thought it was probably because they had lost someone in the Great War and were taking revenge on him as the living symbol of the Crown. He said, 'They could get no satisfaction from kicking the Houses of Parliament, whereas I was both handy and responsive.' "

Alas, the image of dauntlessness which the King thus impressed on the public mind was all but washed away five days later. He had changed his role from Warrior King to Fountain of Honor, and as such could reasonably have been expected to endure a sprinkle, even a wetting. Instead, a rain shower put him to inglorious flight. The occasion was the formal Court presentation of debutantes and distinguished women. In George V's day, his lord chamberlain, Lord Cromer, would divide the annual crop into quarters and run a different quarter through each of the four Courts that were held in May and June. Cromer was still lord chamberlain, but now his task was more difficult, the usual spring Courts having been postponed because of the six months' official mourning. As a result, an accumulation of some six hundred girls was waiting to receive the royal accolade—and waiting impatiently, since these parties traditionally marked the end of the London season, and Society was about to scatter for the summer. In the interests of speed, Cromer decided to "process" the candidates in two extra-large garden parties, to be held on successive afternoons; and here at the first of them, three hundred debutantes, accompanied by parents, fiancés, and friends, crowded into the Palace gardens.

The King sat in a thronelike chair in front of the main tent—the "Durbar" tent, upheld by lances of hammered silver—which sheltered the Royal Family and members of the peerage, the diplomatic corps, the household, and their guests (including Mrs. Simpson). From the chair, a Persian carpet stretched across the garden, and at its far end, the debutantes in their white picture hats and billowing white frocks began to advance. The Duke of Windsor described what happened:

"The line had hardly started past when a shadow fell on the lawn, and I looked up to see a huge black cloud coming straight at the Palace. There was a spatter of rain, then a deluge. I was prepared to wait it out. After all, I had dry clothes only a few yards away. Meanwhile, all I had to do was sit in that silly gilt chair, keep my hands folded and try not to fidget, and acknowledge each curtsey with a smile and a bow, and pump up another smile for the next girl, ten seconds later. If she happened to be the granddaughter of some friend of my parents', Lord Cromer was there to alert me. So I had no problem. But the poor girls were soon in a dreadful state. You'd have thought it was a reception for the survivors of a shipwreck. Their hats and gowns were soaked, their slippers stained, their rouge smeared, but still they pressed on. About half of them had gone by when I turned to Cromer and asked, 'Isn't this becoming ridiculous?'

"He said, 'It is indeed, Sir!'

"I said, 'Then I'll stop it.' I did. I went into the tent"—where he collected Mrs. Simpson and carried her off to the Fort.

Word of his departure was slow to reach the bedraggled girls who were still in line. Their disappointment on learning that they would not be given the accolade, and their anguish over the ruin of their finery, were matched by their parents' indignation at what they considered the King's discourtesy. The second garden party, next afternoon, went off sunnily, and hurt feelings were balmed to some extent by Lord Cromer's assurance to "those ladies who [had been] unable to pass the King's presence" the day before that they might consider themselves "officially presented at Court." Even so, many of the ladies—and their parents and friends and the general public—would long remember a photograph in that morning's newspapers: the King, hunched in his gilt chair, twisting his ring and scowling with boredom.

He knew that he had behaved badly. He said later, "My mistake was not in leaving the party, but in the manner of my leaving. What I should have done was walk down the line and give each of those woebegone girls a smile and a word, and urge them all to run for shelter; but I didn't have the presence of mind to do it." After a moment, he added happily, "I showed good sense' in one respect, though. When I'd first taken my seat, I put my bowler down beside me; and when the rain started, I turned it crown-up. If I hadn't, I'd have got a double-drenching when I clapped it on my head and ran."

Almost as he and Wallis Simpson were arriving at the Fort, Ernest Simpson was arriving at the Hotel de Paris, in the village of Bray, with another woman, a professional co-respondent. They signed the register as man and wife (he was "Ernest Arthur Simmons"), they shared bedroom Number 4 overnight, and breakfast was served to them in bed together—all this under the eyes of agents whom the King's solicitor had engaged to verify Ernest's "turpitude." The solicitor added their report to that of the agents at Dover, and to Mary Kirk's misdirected letter, and he saw that sufficient evidence for launching—and almost guaranteeing the success of—Wallis's divorce action was now comfortably in hand.

The King's failure to salvage something—anything— from the disaster of the debutantes was intensified by the abundant endowments he brought to the conduct of a ceremony: charm, good looks, a winning smile. He might have outshone his father in time, if these natural assets had not been canceled all too often by his obvious boredom and his indifference to public opinion. But that he could, when an occasion interested him, rise to it triumphantly, he proved within the week, when he and President Lebrun met at Vimy Ridge. King Edward happened to arrive a few minutes early and took advantage of the interval to circulate among the six thousand Canadian pilgrims—veterans, officials, and their families—who were assembled at the soaring monument. He remembered many from having served with them in the field, and plainly they remembered him. Wherever he moved, his smile drew cheers and shouts of "Good old Teddy!" just as it had twenty years before, in the trenches and in the villages behind the front. The press photographs that showed him being all but mobbed by the adoring crowds restored his public standing to its zenith, if but briefly.

True, he bobbled once, but only once, and then harmlessly. While he was introducing his entourage, the name of his father's last Governor-General of Canada, the Earl of Bessborough, refused to come to his lips. Windsor recalled it as "one of the worst moments of my life. Half a dozen similar names flashed wildly through my mind—*Loughborough, Marlborough, Scarborough,* and so on—but I knew that none of them was the right one. As I floundered, Bessborough stepped forward, shot me an icy glance, and said to Lebrun, *'Monsieur le Président, mon nom est Bessborough, Lord Bessborough.'* "

Otherwise the King staged a performance as masterly as that at the birthday parade. His dedicatory remarks were eloquent. Lascelles had drafted them, and Churchill had refined them; Windsor said, "I trimmed the speech a bit to make it glitter more. It's always easier to strike out someone else's adjectives than one's own." Before flying back to London, he yielded to a happy impulse and invited a whole lot of Canadians to drop in for a "cuppa" on their way home. They took him at his word. Three afternoons later, to the consternation of the Master of the Household, the Canadians poured through the Palace gates, flooded the gardens, and even overflowed into the Palace itself. When the King appeared among them, again to glad cries of

"Good old Teddy!" the tide engulfed him—the men eager
to shake his hand or clap his shoulder, the women longing
to buss him. He spoke his words of warm welcome; Queen
Mary came out on a balcony to wave; and the multitude
sang "For He's a Jolly Good Fellow" and "God Save the
King." The uproarious, tumultuous reception was "without
precedent in the dignified history of Buckingham Palace,"
according to the *Chicago Tribune;* and the *Toronto Star*
reported that the London newspapers of the day were "full
of sly winks and snickers about the way we mobbed His
Majesty in his own backyard and even in his house."

During one of Wallis Simpson's visits to the Fort that
July, there occurred a small but significant incident. It
transpired when, shortly afterwards, a London hostess ad-
vertised for a footman. One applicant seemed especially
well qualified, so she asked him, "Who was your last employer?"

"His Majesty, at Fort Belvedere, madam."

"So? And why did you leave?"

"Well, madam, one afternoon the butler, Mr. Osborne,
sent me down to the swimming pool with two drinks.
When I got there, what did I see but His Majesty painting
Mrs. Simpson's toenails. *My Sovereign, painting a woman's toenails!* It was a bit much, madam. I gave notice at
once."

🐚 CHAPTER 5 🐚
The Cruise of the Nahlin

The Owl and the Pussy-Cat went to sea
* In a beautiful pea-green boat:*
They took some honey, and plenty of money
* Wrapped up in a five-pound note.*
The Owl looked at the stars above
* And sang to a small guitar,*
"O lovely Pussy, O Pussy, my love,
* What a beautiful Pussy you are,*
*   You are,*
*   You are!*
What a beautiful Pussy you are!"

Pussy said to the Owl, "You elegant fowl,
* How charmingly sweet you sing!*
Oh! let us be married; too long we
* have tarried. . . ."*
  —"The Owl and the Pussy-Cat,"
                    LEWIS CARROLL

Looking back toward the summer of 1936, the Duke of Windsor said, "My father's mistrust of most things foreign had persuaded many Britons that it was a Royal tradition for the Monarch to begin his summer holidays at Cowes, then move to Windsor, and on north to Balmoral, where he would stay until October, when Parliament opened—always among his own people, except for foreign relatives and a handful of foreign statesmen invited for the sport. The fact is, an older tradition had the Monarch making excursions to Biarritz, the French Riviera and the German spas. There's a charming statue of Queen Victoria in Nice, commemorating her visits, and one of grandfather on the Croisette in Cannes.

"I'd enjoyed the stalking at Balmoral when I was a youth, but after I'd seen the French and Italian Rivieras and the Austrian Tyrol, Balmoral began to appear stodgy and parochial. I had another reason for wanting to get away from home that summer. Wallis's companionship had become my only solace in a job which otherwise would have been intolerably lonely. I was aware that we had begun to excite talk, and I knew that if we went to Balmoral, there'd be a maximum of buzz and a minimum of privacy, whereas we could be reasonably secluded on the Continent—say, in a villa on the French Riviera. I had the ideal one in mind: Château de l'Horizon, at Golfe-Juan, just east of Cannes." L'Horizon then belonged to Maxine Elliott, an American actress renowned as much for her beauty as for her talent. Aly Khan later bought it, and it was here that he and Rita Hayworth would hold their wedding party in 1949. Windsor said, "I'd been there a few years before, and I'd never forgotten its odd pigeonhole façade, its large cool rooms, its terraces and swimming pool, and the long marble chute from the lower terrace down to the sea. *Zzzzzip! Splash!* Wonderful!

"I'd opened negotiations to rent it for August when, early in June, Léon Blum and his Socialists came into power, jointly with the Communists in the Front Populaire. I sent for George Clerk, our Ambassador to France, and asked his advice. George was a good friend of mine, and highly knowledgeable about French politics. He laughed off my apprehensions. He said, 'The French Government are *delighted* that you may take l'Horizon! Your presence there will put millions of francs into the pockets of local *hôteliers* and *restauranteurs*.'

"Still, he suggested that before I sign the lease, I wait until July fourteenth, Bastille Day, when the demonstrations would give us a clue to the national temper. I agreed that this was prudent. The next time I saw him was when he met me at Calais, en route to Vimy. Now, he said sheepishly, he had to advise me *against* my August visit. He said that the Côte d'Azur, the 'Blue Coast,' was blazing with red flags. One, indeed, had been raised in full view of l'Horizon.

"George went on, 'The French Government are very upset, but if Your Majesty insists on coming, they are quite

sure they can spare you any inconvenience or embarrassment. Premier Blum is prepared even to post a battalion of
infantry at the villa.'

"That was hardly my idea of a vacation. I asked George
to thank Monsieur Blum, and turned to Jack Aird. 'Jack,' I
said, 'it's too late now to line up another villa. When we
get back to London, your first order of business is to
charter a yacht, a big, comfortable one, around two thousand tons. She must be in tiptop condition. I want nothing
to spoil our cruise. *Nothing!*"

The slow, old-fashioned royal yacht *Victoria and Albert*,
4,700 tons, was at the King's disposal, but he was looking
for something splashier to impress Wallis. Aird found it for
him in the sleek new *Nahlin*—all-steel, 1,574 tons, 250 feet
on the waterline, with a beam of 32 feet (and a price tag of
720,000 dollars). Her four steam turbines and twin screws
drove her at twenty knots without strain. She had a gymnasium and a dance floor; and her eight luxurious state-
rooms, each with its own bath, were so disposed—two
master's forward, six guests' aft—as to invite, said one
giggly guest, "a certain amount of unsanctioned pairing."
Her officers and the crew of fifty were Scots almost to a
man, naturally taciturn, little given to gossip either at the
scuttlebutt or ashore. Even so, her owner, the widowed and
enormously rich Lady Yule (her husband's fortune came
from jute) had drilled into them they were never to disclose where they were going or who was aboard.

In retrospect, the kindest thing to be said about the
cruise is that it was beyond doubt the most exuberant, the
most reckless, and, in terms of its consequences for the
King, the most costly gratification of a royal whim that
England had witnessed since 1814–17, when Caroline
Princess of Wales, accompanied by her lusty "chamberlain," Bartolomeo Bergami, and a roistering troupe, made
a tour of Europe and the Mediterranean "worthier of a
circus," Shane Leslie wrote, "than of the Court circular."
Just so, the *Nahlin*'s course was laid with an eye not to
statecraft, but to frivolity. The King did not bother to consult the Foreign Office beforehand. He and Wallis simply
invited their guests to rendezvous in Venice for a glorious
bash before sailing. Only the year before, his father had

scolded him for putting pleasure before policy in proposing to visit Italy. Now, at a time when Mussolini's assault on Ethiopia and his meddling in the Spanish Civil War had strained Anglo-Italian relations almost to rupture, the King was rescheduling the very visit his father had forbidden. Not until the last minute was Alex Hardinge made privy to the itinerary. When he communicated it, the Foreign Office was aghast. For the King of England to turn up in Italy with a party of revelers just then would have undermined his Government's efforts—feeble enough at best—to bridle Mussolini's imperial ambitions. Vigorous protests from the Foreign Secretary persuaded the King to bypass Venice, but he did so with poor grace. He said sulkily, "Eden was probably afraid that I'd get a fine hand in Italy, which wouldn't have pleased the British Government, or that I'd have onions thrown at me."

The bypass was the last point on which good sense, let alone good taste, governed the excursion. To lend it a gloss of State business, the King scheduled formal calls on King George II in Greece, Czar Boris III in Bulgaria, and Prince Paul, the regent in Yugoslavia. The real purpose of the cruise was far more romantic. It was to give the girl from Baltimore a foretaste of the excitement, the adulation, and the luxury that go with a royal progress abroad; and to stage a dress rehearsal of the role that would be hers in the years ahead as Queen Wallis: the eye-filling pageantry, the joyful bands and fawning attention; the cheering crowds, the red carpets and barrages of roses, the special trains and honor guards. In short, it was to be "Wallis in Wonderland." Moreover, the *Nahlin* was ideal for the ardent pursuit of courtship. For Windsor himself, a large, well-found yacht had the attraction of enabling him as sovereign to combine the comforts of the Ritz and the protocol of a royal progress with a well-heeled beachcomber's vagabondage. The *Nahlin* alone did not supply the magic; Ernest Simpson would have recognized its inexhaustible source as "Peter Pan," a king abroad on holiday.

Except for three of the King's aides—Jack Aird, Godfrey Thomas, and Tommy Lascelles—most of the guests were those comparatively recent English friends of Wallis who already knew that the King was "besotted" with her (the Duke of Kent's word for it): Emerald Cunard, the

beautiful Helen Fitzgerald, the Buists, the Humphrey Butlers. Several of the King's old friends—Hugh Sefton and
Foxy Gwynne (they met on the *Nahlin* and were married
in 1941), the Duff Coopers, the Brownlows—were in the
party off and on, as was the British golfer Archie Compston, the King's favorite instructor and winner of the British
PGA in 1925 and 1927. The King had had the strange
insensitivity to invite Ernest Simpson, too, and—as the
incredulous Ernest told Rickatson-Hatt—"seemed genuinely surprised when I declined." The only Americans
whom Wallis asked along were Herman and Katharine
Rogers.

The first cadre assembled in Paris to await their host,
traveling under the wholly transparent incognito of "the
Duke of Lancaster," who arrived on the morning of August 8 in a plane of the King's Flight. That evening they
boarded a private car attached to the Orient Express. They
had expected to reach Zagreb, in Yugoslavia, the following
night, but Prince Paul blocked their path with a barrage of
telegrams urging them to stop off at his country seat for
tea. The King had known him and liked him at Oxford—
"He was something of a dilettante, but he was quick and
bright and very knowledgeable in the arts"—but had allowed their acquaintance to wither of late, probably because Paul missed no opportunity to warn him against
Germany's threat to the peace of Europe, a subject on
which the King's mind was closed. Grumbling, he accepted
the invitation in behalf of family concord, since Paul's
wife, Princess Olga, was the Duchess of Kent's sister.
There would be repercussions four weeks later, but for the
present all went smoothly. New timetables were meshed,
and after a bone-jarring ride over rails that trembled along
precipices, the royal party arrived at the tiny Dalmatian
port of Sibenik, where—huge, trim, gleaming white, and
filling their view—the *Nahlin* lay at anchor.

Twenty thousand peasants in bright costumes swarmed
around them, shouting glad greetings, as they mustered on
the quay. The crowd also included scores of reporters and
press photographers. Two nights before, when the Orient
Express had paused at Salzburg, and the King and Wallis
had incautiously strolled down the platform, photographers
had sprung from ambush, and the royal "cover," flimsy to

begin with, had been shredded. Any hopes of its integrity that might have survived Salzburg perished on the quay at Sibenik.

Wallis was to say later that, to her surprise—if no one else's—she instantly found herself almost as much the center of attention as was the King.

If the world's press had not been so starved for tidbits just then, the *Nahlin* might have escaped much of the attention that now focused on her. As it was, an epidemic of curiosity began to rage over southeastern Europe, and every port in the area was alert for the sight of the big white yacht with "Youth on the Prow and Pleasure at the Helm." The lovers should have been alarmed, but in their trance they noticed nothing. Everywhere that the golden-haired King of England (a former mistress said his "buttercup-colored" hair was "the most attractive part of him") went with his new mistress—from Sibenik around to Istanbul, and back through the Balkans—the festive air, the innocent, unstinted rejoicing that surrounded them, seemed normal, a reflection of their own happiness. Jack Aird was moved to wonder "if perhaps the same explosions of emotion occurred—but with the leading roles reversed, of course—when Anthony floated down the Nile on Cleopatra's barge."

Wallis Simpson's most vivid memory of the embarcation was a strange one: "The King had a wonderful valet, Crisp. That morning—it was only about ten o'clock and glorious weather—Crisp was there on deck, trying to sort out the hundreds of bags belonging to the twelve people coming on board, the eight guests and their maids and valets. While he was struggling, Poots Butler asked him—I'll always remember it, because it rather shocked me—Poots asked him, 'Could I have a Martini, please, Crisp?' I thought to myself, 'A Martini at ten o'clock in the morning! How extraordinary! And to stop Crisp right in the middle of his battle of the baggage, too!' He brought the Martini, this wonderful servant, and ten o'clock became known as 'Martini time.'"

In this blithe mood, the *Nahlin* sailed. Ahead stretched an exhilarating prospect: a full month of poking around ancient coastal villages, climbing over mossy forts and temples, shopping at bazaars, and supping in dockside cafés.

Also ahead, thanks to the King's defiance of convention, lay the ruin of his scheme for slipping Wallis Simpson's divorce quietly through the courts before their names were publicly coupled.

In Trogir, a few miles down the coast, hundreds of students materialized out of nowhere to surround the lovers walking hand in hand, and to wish them happiness and long life. In Dubrovnik (August 17–19), they were caught up and borne through the town by a mob chanting, *"Zivila ljubav!"*—"Long live love!" In Ragusa, Diana Cooper was fascinated to see a whole village "cheering their lungs out with looks of ecstasy on their faces."[1] And there is Wallis's own account of the starlit evening at Kotor, when she and the King watched spellbound from the *Nahlin*'s deck while the dark mountainside began to shimmer, as thousands of torchbearers filed down the steep trails, like a slow cascade of glowworms.

The King asked her teasingly if she realized for whom the bewitching pageantry of light and movement was being given. For him, was her modest reply. Not at all, he insisted: It was all for her, because the simple mountain folk were pleased that a King had found his true love.

If Aird had happened to overhear, he might have been reminded anew of Cleopatra's barge, where even "the winds were love-sick."

The warm sun of the Ionian Sea melted away not only the few remaining constraints that royal discretion had laid upon the King, but the years themselves. To Lady Diana, he suddenly seemed a boy again—"radiant in health, wearing spick-and-span little shorts, straw sandals and two crucifixes around his neck." His sunniness was clouded afresh at Corfu, by another royal invitation. This one, for dinner on August 21, came from King George II of Greece; and like Prince Paul's, it could not easily be declined. Moreover, he was not a favorite; King Edward regarded him as "a poseur affecting a monocle and a walking-stick; he was also a glad-hander." He added, "But I grant that he was a good mixer and had a high sense of duty about his hopeless job." Although they were double second cousins, being great-grandsons both of Queen Victoria and of King Christian IX of Denmark, Edward never spoke of him as "George" or "my cousin," but coolly—and inaccurately—

as "the King of Greece." George was nothing of the sort;
being of non-Greek (i.e., Danish) descent, he was "King of
the Hellenes"—and that only intermittently. They had de-
posed him in 1923 and had not brought him back until
1935. Most of the years between, separated from his wife,
he had spent at Brown's Hotel, in London, and mostly in
the company of "an exceedingly good-looking English-
woman" (Diana Cooper's description) named Mrs. Jones.

She was with him now, at his villa on a small island just
offshore from Corfu proper. They dined on the terrace, the
host between Wallis and Mrs. Jones, and King Edward on
Mrs. Jones's other side. The Duke of Windsor remembered
that "the King of Greece [*sic*] was in a very low frame of
mind. He told me that he was 'a King in name only,' and
that he was reconciled to a life of absolute loneliness and
discontent. For the first time, I felt sorry for him." His
sorrow could not have been overwhelming; at least one
guest noted the animation of his table talk, for Wallis complained to him, on their way back to the *Nahlin*, "You
never spoke a word to the woman on your left, but only to
the King's mistress!" Then, "He's divorced, isn't he? And
so is she. Why doesn't he marry her?"

Nobody rushed to answer. Finally somebody broke the
painful silence and explained that it wasn't all that easy for
a reigning king to marry a commoner, especially one who
had been divorced. . . . (Mrs. Jones was already becoming known as "the Mrs. Simpson of Greece.")

Lady Diana gives another vignette of King Edward next
day, when they were off Cephalonia: He "appeared with
an old shrimping net on his shoulder, looking like a child
of eight. He ordered out a dinghy and set about catching
jelly-fish, while we all leant over the ship's side shrieking,
'There's a big one, Sir!' " Sometimes, barechested, and clad
in trunks, he would row the dinghy around and around the
yacht. When the *Nahlin* transited the narrow Corinth
Canal on her way to Piraeus, the port of Athens, thousands
of Greeks on either bank saw the King of England at close
hand, hatless, golden hair rumpled, naked except for
shorts, socks and espadrilles—an unroyal impropriety that
scandalized Jack Aird. He was worse scandalized a few
evenings later at Piraeus, when the King and Wallis dined
at a small waterfront café with Eric Dudley, who had pre-

ceded them there with a yachting party of his own. For the King of England to be seen enjoying himself in such surroundings at a time when only martial law was propping up his cousin's throne would be to suggest that he was indifferent to the fate of a kingly cousin. Aird called this to the King's attention; his counsel was rebuffed; fuming, he dined aboard the *Nahlin* alone.

Before the King left home, the Palace had asked Fleet Street to respect his privacy on holiday, as usual. Fleet Street acquiesced; throughout the cruise, it made no open reference to Mrs. Simpson's presence aboard, though *The Times* hinted at it by preaching that a sovereign "should be invested with a certain detachment and dignity." But the American and Continental press, aware of Mrs. Simpson's status and of the London rumors, deployed their battalions to keep the *Nahlin* in close sight from start to finish. They missed no scrap of news within earshot or within range of telephoto lenses, or that could be bribed from a guard or a waiter. Their newspapers and magazines printed it all: the King and Mrs. Simpson strolling hand in hand; the King and Mrs. Simpson in swimming; the King, Mrs. Simpson, and members of their party shopping, lunching, chatting with friends; the King and Mrs. Simpson side by side in an open car. In the United States, particularly, the newspapers and newsmagazines had been digging out everything they could find about the "Royal Romance" for many months, as Wallis knew. Her Christmas card for 1935, from Bryanston Court, had begged Rinny Murray not to believe the press: It was all libel! She renewed her entreaty the following June: Don't believe what you read! Wallis assured her that she was still the same "nut" that Rinny had always known. The "nasty" way her fellow Americans were talking about her made her "sick," whereas the English were being "kind" and "lovely."

Friends she had made at Coronado in 1918–20 seemed to have read and believed the same "libel." They telephoned to her in London to ask if the rumors were true. According to a newspaper account,[2] "Her answers . . . were in the old Wallisarian manner—quick, amusing, to the point [but apparently noncommittal]. The bill . . . was $75 and there was no one present who did not insist that

the talk was worth it." So in America, at least, there was
mounting confidence that a relationship which the King
seemed perversely determined to bring into the open, after
evading marriage so long and being so discreet about his
earlier mistresses, was about to burgeon.

Although little of what was reaching Corinne Murray
and the Coronadans was being reported in Britain, some of
Fleet Street knew even more than the foreign press. True,
photographs of the King on holiday were appearing regularly, but they always showed him in sedate circumstances,
usually alone, and never with Mrs. Simpson. The American press clippings that were winging home from Britons
in America and from British loyalists in Canada were under no restraint and were frankly sensational. The embassies and consulates were sending a more selective sampling
to Whitehall; and the Palace Secretariat was receiving
much the same intelligence, as was Queen Mary. Anxious
questions were being raised in ever widening circles—and
the King, far off on his yacht, was oblivious to their pur-
port.

From Athens, the *Nahlin* doubled Cape Colonna, and
stood northwest up the Euripus Channel. All this while she
was being accompanied by two Royal Navy destroyers,
Grafton and *Glowworm*, which had been detailed partly to
protect her, partly to provide cipher communication with
London, and partly to shuttle from *Nahlin* to shore and
pick up the State papers which couriers were delivering to
the nearest ports almost daily. The nickname that Wallis
(or it may have been Lady Diana) coined for them, "the
nanny-boats," reflected the breezy climate of the cruise.
When they reached Chalcis (August 31), *Grafton* and
Glowworm behaved less like nannies than like ruffians.
Chalcis is where the Euripus Channel, which separates the
island of Euboea from mainland Greece, is so narrow that
a swing bridge spans it, and the current is swift and capricious. The *Nahlin* nosed into the channel cautiously—*too*
cautiously; she did not have speed enough to maintain
steerageway, and the current shoved her against a lock,
staving in her motor launch (this had also been given a
nickname, *Queen Victoria*, for reasons unspecified). The
heedful destroyers shot through at twenty knots—safely,

but unaware until too late that their reverberating wakes had capsized fishing smacks and pleasure craft right and left.

Jack Aird, still resenting his rebuff at Athens, was overheard to mutter, "This is a visit by a British King that the Greeks will remember for a long, long time!"

The convoy entered the Dardanelles on September 3. At their northern end, Gallipoli, the King went ashore to see the beaches where appalling losses had been suffered in 1915–16 by (among other forces) a number of British territorial regiments. One of these was the 6th Norfolks, which included the Sandringham company, drawn largely from tenants and workmen on the estate, and their male relatives. Their commanding officer, the estate manager, fell in the assault; his body was never recovered.

Early on the morning of the fourth, the *Nahlin,* the two British destroyers, and two Turkish destroyers in line ahead steamed into the Bosporus, to find both its shores clotted with hundreds of thousands of cheering Turks, many of whom had been there all night. Streamers with the legend "WELCOME EDUARDE REX" hung between minarets, and nearly every building along the waterfront displayed the Union Jack crossed with the Star and Crescent. As soon as the *Nahlin* dropped anchor off Dolmabahçe Palace, the British Ambassador, Sir Percy Loraine, came aboard. He was somewhat surprised to be received by his monarch in flannel trousers, an open shirt, and espadrilles, and he may have wondered if this extreme—almost insulting—informality was a royal rebuke for a recent clash. What had brought it on throws an extraordinary light on the King's character.

Back in Athens, he had been told (wrongly) that there was a superb golf course at Istanbul, so he had wirelessed Loraine that he intended playing a round there—that, indeed, he was putting in to Istanbul for this purpose alone, and did not wish either an official reception or to meet any members of the Turkish Government, even the dictator, Mustafa Kemal Atatürk. Loraine was horrified and alarmed. At the time, there was a nascent pro-Nazi party in Turkey as well as the traditional pro-British party. Atatürk himself was pro-British, not so much from love of England as from the conviction that she would continue to play a dominant role in Europe, and he therefore wished to associate his country with her. If the King of England chose this moment to turn his back on President Atatürk, it would be a diplomatic disaster. How Loraine averted it was related by Christopher Sykes in the January 1975 issue of *Books and Bookmen,* and is here condensed. It is important to bear in mind that not all authorities agree with Mr. Sykes's version of events.

[Loraine] insisted that as the first European sovereign since Kaiser Wilhelm II to visit Turkey [and as the first British sovereign ever] he must meet the head of State and should also visit Ankara [the capital] if Atatürk wished him to. The King was enraged, and when Loraine continued to protest, the King asked the Foreign Secretary, Anthony Eden, for his dismissal from the service. Loraine had in the meantime kept the Foreign Office informed of these negotiations and insisted that if the King persisted in his golfing plans, he would resign and leave Turkey before the *Nahlin*'s arrival. The Foreign Secretary was in complete agreement with the ambassador and gave him full support. He let the King know, and the King found himself cornered. [Eden is reported to have said of him, "Whereas his father knew much and interfered little, he knew little and interfered much."] For all his political ignorance he recognized a danger signal: the ambassador's resignation would involve first the Foreign Secretary's and then the Government's, after which the throne would have to survive the Percy Loraine General Election! He had disagreeable food for thought on the voyage between Athens and the Golden Horn: he had been harshly and abruptly shown the limits of his power. He had been told where to get off. For an egocentric this is always especially painful. He had been humiliated and entirely through his own silly fault. . . . In the end the King met Atatürk. . . .

Mustafa was his given name; Kemal—"Perfection"— was bestowed on him at school, some say as a tribute to his extraordinary proficiency in mathematics; Atatürk—

"Father of the Turks"—was a title voted him by the National Assembly in 1934. (King Edward liked to pretend that it had an arcane cognation with "Attaboy!") He was waiting on the quay with a perspiring group of dignitaries when the *Nahlin* party stepped ashore. According to Loraine, the president "at once felt the King's uncommon charm . . . simplicity and directness." According to the King, the president impressed him as "a tough city-politician surrounded by hooligans." Nonetheless, according to Aird, the two of them "got along swimmingly." Atatürk usually rode, dictator-style, in a bulletproof limousine, but that day he had chosen an open car as a compliment to his royal visitor, and they drove to the British Embassy through streets jammed with crowds roaring a welcome.

That afternoon, the King had Atatürk aboard for cocktails—"an enormous success," Loraine wrote thankfully. A dinner at the Embassy followed. The evening ended with a sort of regatta, in which the *Nahlin* was circled by a myriad of small boats, all of them brilliantly lit with lanterns and torches, and all, wrote Loraine, "loaded down to the line with passengers packed into them absolutely sardine-wise. On catching sight of the King the passengers started waving, cheering and clapping in a frenzy of excitement, and King Edward, who appeared delighted, went from side to side of the bridge, raising his cap and waving his handkerchief in acknowledgement. . . . The Turkish public, normally undemonstrative, had taken [him] to their hearts." Patrick Kinross added, in his *Atatürk*, "For many years afterwards the walls of coffee-houses in Istanbul and throughout Anatolia were adorned with a bright colored picture of the two rulers, seated together beneath their respective national flags."

This was the first time that Wallis had starred in so huge a production, and she never forgot it. Also vivid in her memory were Istanbul's bazaars, where she bought eight tortoiseshell spoons and some jewelry of curious design. But most vividly of all she would remember Atatürk himself. She was to say later, "I've met Hitler, and Atatürk was fifty Hitlers. He was the most fascinating man I've ever met. A *strong* man! And *alive*! His eyes were magnetic without being fanatic. Bluish-grey, with dark rims around the irises. Grey hair. A grey suit. They called him 'the Grey Wolf,' you know." He was also a libertine, so his sobriquet was doubly apt.

Jack Aird said, "The King's first concern was to show Wallis a good time, and he did; but he never neglected an opportunity to advance British interests. Percy Loraine had informed him privately that Atatürk was eager to rebuild his fleet, which consisted mainly of German vessels from before the Great War. British shipyards were bidding for a share of the new business, and the King, who prided himself on being a born salesman, invited Atatürk to bring some of his admirals aboard his destroyers for a closer look at the fine British arms and armor. I tagged along. The King was so enthusiastic about our ships' fighting and sea-keeping qualities, and so persuasive in his promise of the generous terms our shipyards would offer, that I found myself making plans to send the crews home by commercial transport, fully expecting to have their ships sold out from under them before the King returned to shore."

Loraine's firm stand paid dividends that were almost incalculable, even though (Sykes's account of the episode ends) the King

> couldn't be bothered to go to Ankara. The results were out of all proportion to the effort. . . . The visit . . . made so lasting an impression on Turkish opinion that it manifestly influenced events in that country during World War II. Without that visit the German party would have been stronger and the British party weaker. . . . It was Edward VIII's finest public action, and it is mournful to have to recognize how mean was his own part in it.

Atatürk died in 1938, aged fifty-eight, from cirrhosis brought on by his inordinate consumption of raki. If he had lived a year or two longer, he might have led Turkey into World War II on the Allies' side.

The *Nahlin*'s charter having expired, she sailed for England, whence she would presently be sold to Carol II of Romania, who had anticipated Edward VIII by renouncing his throne, in 1925, for the sake of his divorced mistress.

The final flowering of Atatürk's hospitality was to start the King and his guests home on September 6 in his white-and-gold private train, the most luxurious that any of them had seen. Czar Boris of Bulgaria met them at the frontier with his brother Kyril, and escorted them to his capital, Sofia, where he gave them lunch in his gloomy palace. Its ballroom, Wallis would remember, had "a dry, stale smell—the smell of a room little used." Windsor said of him, "Bulgarians are mostly Slavic, but Boris was of German blood, a Coburg, and so distantly of my own line. I liked him." He was a likable man, brave and accomplished: a linguist, a botanist, and a first-class engine driver. Atatürk's train was returning to Istanbul, so Boris put his own at the party's disposal for the run to the Yugoslav frontier—more than that, he took the throttle himself, and somehow prevailed on the King to join him in the cab. The ride, Windsor said, was "mildly exhilarating."

Prince Paul's private train—their third—was waiting for them at the frontier. They had scarcely begun to roll again, and were settling down with their books, when Jack Aird came in with a telegram. The Duchess of Windsor told the story:

"It was from Paul, *insisting* that we dine with him in Belgrade—he wanted to show us the palaces, he said. The King told Jack, 'I had tea with him on the way down, remember? I'm paid up. I don't have to see him again.' He went back to his book.

"Jack waited a moment, then whispered to me, 'This is going to be very, very dicey! Paul expects to come aboard in Belgrade. After all, it's a natural courtesy for him to pay the King of England as he goes through.'

"I whispered back, 'Why don't we get the King to have him to dinner with us, instead of our going to dinner with him? That would leave us still on the train.'

"Jack said, '*You* approach him.'

"I did, but he only demanded, '*Why* must I have him again? I've already had him. He's'—this, that and the other, all very petulantly.

"I persisted: 'I think you're wrong, Sir. He's only trying to be polite to you.' [Lady Diana Cooper noted that Wallis never addressed him in public as "Darling" or even "David," but always and only as "Sir."]

"Anyway, Jack and I finally won him over, and Prince Paul was invited to dinner. He was delighted to accept, but it was a very difficult affair, since the King had made up his mind he didn't want to see him. The rest of us talked like mad while the King sat in royal silence. It wasn't a success."

Wallis would always remember the incident as "one of the really bad points of the trip," and she liked to cite it as an example of "David's mulishness" and the difficulty of persuading him against his will. That she succeeded must be entered on the credit side of her ledger, together with the fact—also noted by Lady Diana—that she disciplined him: "You *must* read your telegrams, Sir!"

Why was he so "mulish"? Was this what he meant by being "a modern king"? In later years, he sometimes hinted that the explanation was his desire to show Wallis that royal life did not have to be as stuffy as his parents had made it. This hardly justifies his indifference to the basic proprieties—the unroyal exhibitionism, the dockside dinner at Piraeus, the vindictive attempt to ruin Sir Percy Loraine's career, the rudeness to Prince Paul—whom he never thanked for all the trouble and expense the Yugoslavs had been put to. He may have been simply trying to convince Wallis that his will was his own, and that he would carry forward what he was disposed to do. If this hypothesis is valid, it helps confirm two independent judgments: Baldwin's, that the King, unmarried, could never have endured the petty obligations of kingship; and Monckton's, that he might have found the tedium unbearable even with a wife.

A further reason for the King's disgruntlement with Prince Paul was that because of having to wait over in Belgrade while they dined, their arrival at Vienna was delayed a day, until September 8. For Wallis Simpson, the last days of their holiday, in this ancient and urbane capital on the Danube, where the very stones and boulevards breathe romance and veneration of things imperial, represented the "high noon" of the courtship. She liked to think of Vienna in terms of violins and candle-lit restaurants, but as she came into the Hotel Bristol that day, she seemed to have something harsher on her mind, for an observer recorded the scene thus:

"The King's entourage entered, led by a small, beautifully dressed woman. Her sullen expression and the purposeful way she walked gave me the impression that she would brush aside anyone who had the temerity to get in her path."[3] The observer was Elsa Maxwell, soon to become one of the Duchess's closest friends and later one of her most scorned and scornful enemies. This brusqueness, this sea-change arrogance newly emerged, had already impressed itself on her fellow passenger Lord Sefton, the King's intimate friend and his lord-in-waiting. "We Molyneux came to England with William the Conqueror," the seventh Earl complained, "and Mrs. Simpson still treats me as if I were a serf!"

The party began to dissolve now and return home. Jack Aird, relieved at having survived what he mockingly called "my last crusade," left to command the Grenadier Guards; he had no wish either to continue in the King's service after the marriage which he saw "clearly on the horizon," or to delay his resignation until the reason for it became rudely obvious. (Aird once said that the British Army was composed of "the Grenadier Guards and the attached troops.") Most of the rest stayed on in Vienna a few days more. Wallis, though not especially musical, and the Rogerses wanted to hear Kirsten Flagstad in *Götterdämmerung*. The King did not. But torn between boredom and separation from his love, he finally went, on her promise to let him sneak out of their box from time to time for a cigarette, if he would return for a final curtain and applaud with extra vehemence. He left and he did.

He also wanted a chat with young Dudley Forwood, formerly a subaltern in the Scots Guards and since 1934 an attaché on the staff of Minister Selby. He had been seconded from the staff the year before to attend the Prince of Wales on his skiing trip to Kitzbühel and had impressed him as a possible future equerry. The King now sent for him, to discuss the appointment. Forwood said later, "Everyone at the Embassy was on tenterhooks to learn how far the King was bent on carrying the affair. That never came up in our interview, of course. But I found him happy and composed. I doubt that he realized how much the gossip churned up by the *Nahlin* was hurting him. He loved England and adored the throne, and all he wanted was to adorn it with a perfect thing, Mrs. Simpson."

On the thirteenth, the remnants of the party took the night train west. Crowds gathered in the Ring to cheer the King off. "Come back again!" they shouted affectionately. "Come back again!" He would come back within a few months, unexpected, and no longer as King. Next morning he left the train at Zurich, where he was met by a plane of the King's Flight. En route to London, his thoughts (as he later recollected them) were these: "I have no regrets for having chartered the *Nahlin,* though I may have been a bit indiscreet. Clouds seem to be rolling up—not only clouds of war, but clouds of private trouble. I'm in for some bad weather. The American press has discovered my relationship with Wallis and is convinced of its importance, so we're sure to be under its eyes from now on. Well, we'll cross that bridge when we come to it. . . ."

Wallis and the Rogerses continued on to Paris, where she planned to replenish her winter wardrobe. Ernest Simpson met her there. To explain his absence from the *Nahlin* cruise, he had dutifully gone through the motions of a business trip. Now he was dutifully waiting. According to Rickatson-Hatt, "Ernest wanted to make one last effort to stave off the disaster that threatened both his marriage and the King, so he asked Wallis to return to London with him. She refused; she said that the King had invited Ernest 'privately' to join them at Balmoral. Ernest would have no part of that, of course, and begged Wallis not to go either. She defied him and went. He stayed on in Paris a few days. When he got back to Bryanston Court, the flat was almost empty. Wallis had already begun moving her things to her new house in Cumberland Terrace." Although Rickatson-Hatt was Ernest's closest friend, he seems to have had no inkling of the current and ardent affair with Mary Raffray.

Wallis was to say that she had an exultant feeling that "my wave was still far from reaching its crest." Actually, it was almost ready to break and ebb. The King returned to London no longer the invincible figure he had appeared to be when he left to join the *Nahlin.* The world publicity had done him in. Within the Establishment his reputation was in ruins.

❧ CHAPTER 6 ❧
"The King Is Cross," Twitted Mrs. Simpson

Ask yourself my love whether you are not very cruel to have so entrammelled me, so destroyed my freedom.

—JOHN KEATS to Fanny Brawne

The King dashed from his plane straight to the Fort, changed to a white tie, and dashed on to the Palace for dinner with his mother. The old King had been dead for nearly eight months now, but Queen Mary still had not found time to pack and send over to Marlborough House, where she was about to take up residence, the last of her notable collections of furniture, silver, porcelain, paintings, and *objets d'art*, especially her Chinese jades, enamels, and miniature tea sets. The truth was, her twenty-five years in the Palace had thoroughly accustomed her to its grandeur and luxury, and she was in no hurry to move out. Just so had Queen Alexandra, the Queen Mother, lingered on alone in the big house at Sandringham, keeping Queen Mary and her large family cramped in York Cottage.

Her son embraced her nervously. The question uppermost in his mind was: How much did she know about the tales appearing in the American press? She did not raise the subject. Nor did she mention the divorce action, although she must have known that it was in preparation, since Monckton was keeping Downing Street and the Secretariat informed. True, her son thought her somewhat distrait at dinner, but this he attributed to her sadness at having to give up the rooms she had occupied for so long. He took his leave under the impression, which was ill-founded, that he had comforted her with the news that he was about to spend a fortnight at Balmoral, in the castle that she and her husband had loved. (In truth, Queen Mary was no

doubt seething inside, because she knew that the Prime
Minister, the Archbishop of Canterbury, and various senior
courtiers had not received the accustomed invitation to
join the sovereign in the Highlands.) An odd aspect of this
quiet, strained evening is that the Queen's biographer,
James Pope-Hennessy, came upon nothing in her papers or
letters, or in her children's and friends' recollections, even
hinting at the anxiety that must have filled her as her son,
in his father's chair, made light chatter from behind his
sunburned mask.

He left for Balmoral almost at once, to make sure it was
in fit shape to receive the friends (especially Wallis) who
would join him there in a few days. He had not thought it
either necessary or politic to show the guest list to his
mother; almost certainly it would have made her reel.
Aboard the *Nahlin,* his staff had actually prepared the
usual formal invitations to his father's dignified cronies,
only to have the new King cancel every one of them in
favor of some frivolous but more congenial freethinker.

Not that he was turning his back on the whole Establishment. His guests would also include, though briefly, the
Duke and Duchess of Marlborough, the Duke and Duchess
of Buccleuch, the Duke and Duchess of Sutherland, and
the Earl and Countess of Rosebery. The Yorks, in residence at Birkhall Lodge close by, and the Gloucesters, at
Abergeldie Mains, would be asked over for dinner once or
twice, and the Kents would spend several nights. Finding
Wallis in the role of informal hostess intensified, on the
Duchess of York's part, the mutual dislike they had conceived at the York House dinner two months before. But
when the *Court Circular* presently began to be sprinkled
with names from the *Nahlin* and Fort sets—Rogers,
Hunter, and Mrs. Simpson again ("Mrs. Ernest Simpson
. . . arrived Balmoral Castle on the 23rd")—the Establishment, scanning the mists over the Scottish moors for clues
to the King's mood, would perceive that he was renewing
his challenge to them in yet another tradition-bound
quarter. Providentially, the mists shrouded the fact that he
had ensconced his guest of honor in the suite long reserved
for his parents.

Windsor maintained to the end that he never meant to
profane the old usages of Balmoral, dull and silly though

some of them seemed. His excuse for bypassing the dignitaries of his father's day was that he would soon enough be
seeing his fill of them at official ceremonies in London. For
him, Balmoral was the last part of his holiday; and as laird,
he wanted to share its amenities with friends who had
never been there before, to show it to them when the deer-
stalking would be at its best, and the moors still held
plenty of grouse. Shooting—especially bird-shooting—had
been George V's passion; he deserved his reputation as one
of the world's finest wing shots. But his eldest son never
really enjoyed it; he shot chiefly to please his father and
earn his applause. The awkward, frail-seeming, left-handed
York was a far better shot than Wales. For instance, a
game book records that he and five other guns killed 495
ducks on the morning of January 4, 1938.

It was the King's tactlessness that gave the worst offense.
When Balmoral first learned, earlier in the summer, that—
contrary to its apprehensions—the King would be coming
to the Castle after all, joy surged through the household
staff, the gillies and gamekeepers, the farmers and foresters.
Then followed the dampening announcement that he did
not wish the servants to line the drive to welcome him, as
theretofore they had always welcomed the monarch. He
meant only to show consideration for them by dispensing
with a tedious and unnecessary piece of frippery, but he
failed to make this clear; and the staff's interpretation was
that in abrogating the old custom, he was preparing them
for a regime of austerity like the one already imposed on
Sandringham: Superfluous jobs would be lopped off, main-
tenance would be skimped, and a close audit of accounts
inaugurated. On all sides were heard strained jocosities
about "Balmoral's bad morale."

The cold drizzle of dismay that this assumption—a correct one—produced at Balmoral was almost forgotten in
the greater storm that presently burst over the King. He
committed an act of selfishness and discourtesy for which
his neighbors never forgave him. The trustees of the Royal
Infirmary at nearby Aberdeen had asked him, that spring,
to preside at the opening of some buildings to be completed in September, but he had begged off on the grounds
that Court mourning forbade his making public appearances. His excuse was specious: Mourning had not kept

him away from Ascot in June; moreover, it had ended
in July, well before he went to Scotland. Worse for him,
almost at the hour when his deputies, the Yorks, were
filling in for him at the Aberdeen ceremony, he was
spotted on the platform at Ballater, the station for Balmoral, his face partly concealed by a heavy wool scarf,
waiting for the train bringing Wallis Simpson and the
Rogerses up from London.

Two months earlier, Walter Monckton had become worried over the "damage" the King might suffer from the increasing conspicuousness of his association with Mrs.
Simpson, and had consulted Winston Churchill, who "particularly said that Mrs. Simpson ought not to go as a guest
to Balmoral." Here she was, and the damage was done.

The sense of outrage that convulsed Scotland would
have kept the occasion fresh in her memory, one would
think, but she later affected vagueness about it all: "We got
off at—I don't know *where* you get off. I don't think the
King came to meet us, but somebody came."

On the way to Balmoral, their car broke down, and
"somebody" gave way to temper. Wallis laughed him out
of it by chanting,

> "King's Cross!
> King's Cross!
> The King is cross!
> The King is cross!"

She could not have laughed the Aberdonians out of their
temper. The King had insulted them, and they were furious. His gaffe was yet another in the lengthening list of
those he was making in his blind desire to show Wallis
Simpson that her interests had top priority in the kingdom.
Most of all he was wounding his brother Bertie. Shocked
and grieved by David's seemingly callous treatment of the
Balmoral staff, Bertie wrote to their mother in London:
"David only told me what he had done after it was over,
which I might say made me rather sad. . . . I never saw
him alone for an instant." Though heir presumptive to the
throne, he felt that he no longer enjoyed his brother's
confidence; unwanted and ignored, he was being denied access. The feeling had taken hold of him, his biographer

learned, that "he had lost a friend and was rapidly losing a brother."

The King himself, apparently unaware how deeply he was troubling the hearts of his family and the Balmoral staff, romped around the vast estate with his ladylove and their retinue. Where Queen Victoria had made a point of serving haggis, bannocks, and other native dishes, Wallis introduced the American three-decker sandwich. But there was one Balmoral custom which the King not only preserved but uniquely enriched: After dinner every evening, he would don a rakish and ribboned bonnet, and with his dress kilt of the Balmoral tartan swinging, he would lead five other pipers out of a gallery and round and round the table, the six of them skirling some Scottish "tune." Neither his father, his grandfather, nor his great-grandfather could have done *that*! It was said of him, "He piped while the Establishment burned."

The King left Balmoral on the evening of September 30, never to see it again. Accompanied by Wallis and the Rogerses, he returned to London on the royal train. Once again he went straight to Buckingham Palace, which Queen Mary would be quitting forever within a few hours. That morning, for the first time since George V had left his Palace for Sandringham, where he would die, the royal standard flew from the Palace mast, a signal to London that the King was once again in residence. Queen Mary stayed for lunch with him as did Princess Mary. Afterward he escorted them out through the garden gate into the Mall, and on to Marlborough House, where he let his mother show him around the well-remembered rooms and explain the changes she had made since they had all lived there nearly twenty-five years earlier, when she had been Duchess of York. He pleased her by saying that her changes "delighted" him.

There was little ahead that would delight his mother. Late in July, on the eve of departing for the *Nahlin* cruise, Wallis Simpson had instructed her solicitor, Theodore Goddard, to proceed with the divorce action as quickly as possible. The King, too, was impatient. Although Goddard would later deny any attempt at deception, he chose—with the approval of both his client and the King—not to enter the petition in the London courts, knowing that to do so would touch off a sensation. Instead, he was first disposed to put the case on the docket of the Reading Assize, at Maidenhead, a court which had the double attraction of being at a protective distance from London, yet comfortably close to Bray, and thus convenient for the servants from the Hotel de Paris there, who would testify that Ernest Simpson had observed the formalities of misconduct. But the Reading Assize, it developed, was not hearing divorce cases that sitting. Goddard then chose the Ipswich Assize, in Suffolk, seventy miles from London, only to learn that the earliest opening on its calendar was the last week in October. This meant an extremely close run for the King's marriage plan; barely a fortnight would elapse between the day the divorce became absolute, at the end of April, and the Coronation on May 12.

Even so, "the last week in October" had struck the King as pleasantly vague and distant; but hard on his return from Balmoral came the announcement that *Simpson v. Simpson* would be heard on Tuesday, October 27, and the firm, definite date, less than four weeks off, gave him a touch of panic. He and Goddard agreed that it would be prudent to have Walter Monckton close by, in case matters should come unstuck. Monckton was then half the world away, in Hyderabad, but he cabled back that he would fly home as soon as possible. Matters were, in fact, already beginning to slip. Whitehall and the Old Guard at the Palace had long known that Ipswich would be the venue, and were alert for the case to appear on the docket. When the exact date was published, Queen Mary, the Prime Minister, and Alex Hardinge, among others, learned of it as soon as did the two lovers. In Queen Mary's bewilderment and pain, according to her biographer, she first sought advice from "one or two extraneous persons"; then, seeing no other way to head off the onrushing catastrophe, she dispatched an emotional appeal to the Prime Minister, pressing him to take "action" through the cabinet to prevent the case from coming to trial.

A divorce such as this required the plaintiff to be residing within the court's jurisdiction at the time of the hearing. Wallis had therefore reserved a cottage at Felixstowe, a middle-class seaside resort ten miles from Ipswich; and on her arrival from Balmoral, on October, 1, she moved there, after first spending a few days at 16 Cumberland Terrace, Regent's Park, the handsome, spacious Georgian house which she had rented some weeks earlier, in response to the King's desire for her to have a "more suitable" address at which to prepare for their marriage. Lady Cunard had ruled that "A lady or a gentleman lives in Mayfair or Belgravia"; Regent's Park was neither, but it was a thick cut above Bryanston Court. Although Number 16 had been rented furnished—significantly, the lease ran for eight months, until just after Coronation Day—Wallis had invited Syrie Maugham, one of London's most fashionable decorators and former wife of W. Somerset Maugham, to make a few temporary additions, especially in the L-shaped white and olive-green drawing room, and —wrote the waspish Sir Cecil Beaton—"Mrs. Spry [London's most fashionable florist; she would do the flowers for the Windsor wedding] contributes her arrangements of expensive flowers mixed with bark and local weeds."[1] The bark and weeds may have been removed when a later guest arrived; he noticed only "lilies, roses and tiny orchids in shades of yellow and white," and "seven lamps shaded in rosy vellum . . . 'Exquisite,' he said, 'is the only word.' "

Beaton had called at Number 16 to show Wallis the proofs of some photographs of her. In 1930, he had found her "coarse" and "brawny"; now she looked "immaculate, soignée, as fresh as a young girl. Her skin was as bright and as smooth as the inside of a shell, her hair so sleek she might have been Chinese." Still later, he said of her, "She is attractively ugly. In her new photos, the light catches the tip of her rather bulbous nose. She has an amusing face. None of her features is classically correct—her mouth, for instance, is downright ugly—but they all fit together."

He and she were shuffling through the proofs when the butler announced, "His Majesty."

"Wallis gave a caw of surprise. 'Oh, sirrrr,' she drawled. . . ."

The King took the proofs from her and glanced at them. "I want the lot," he told Beaton.

Mrs. Simpson protested, half-jokingly, "Oh, sir, wouldn't that be too much of a Wallis collection?"

Beaton went on, "The King talked very fast, darted about the room, rang bells, busily untied parcels. . . . Wallis' eyes sparkled; her brows lifted in mock-pain. . . . her mouth turned down at the corners as she laughed."

But that was later, after the ordeal at Ipswich. Those early days at Cumberland Terrace, before the last of her favorite and familiar chattels had been transferred from Bryanston Court, and before Mrs. Maugham and Mrs. Spry had laid their healing hands on the raw rooms, the house seemed lonely and depressing. Beech House, at Felixstowe, would be worse.

She took up residence early in the second week in October. George and Kitty Hunter, an amiable and undemanding English couple whom Wallis had met through Ernest's sister, came along to keep her company. A cook and a maid went too—all in a new Buick, a gift from the King. According to Geoffrey Bocca, the cook had been plucked from the Palace kitchens by the King himself; he had also detailed his personal bodyguard, Chief Inspector David Storrier of Scotland Yard, to escort Wallis and protect her from harassment. To ensure that she lacked no comforts, he sent after her a station wagon loaded with hampers of grouse and venison from Balmoral, cases of wines and other delicacies, and even her own bed linen. It was quite an *au revoir* for a lady on her way to shed her second husband; her new circumstances must have struck her as a happy improvement on those attending her lonely arrival, nine years before, at the Warren Green Hotel in Warrenton, where she had gone to shed her first.

Still, as the long autumnal days dragged by, Wallis turned bored and restless. No community is so lifeless as a seaside resort out of season. The only sounds were the swish of the sea on the empty beach, the sigh of the wind in the leafless trees, and the banging of shutters on the deserted cottages. There was nothing for her and the Hunters to do except take walks by the sea, or into the village for mail and newspapers, and pass the evenings at cards in a tiny parlor. A divorce, Wallis would reflect out of the experience distilled from two, is "a disagreeable, a heartbreaking experience."

One scarcely less disagreeable had meanwhile threatened the King. Marlene Dietrich, who was making a film in England just then, became convinced that it was her appointed mission to save him from Mrs. Simpson, and that she could accomplish it if given a chance to focus her charm on him, face to face. Accordingly, she begged mutual friends, including the Metcalfes, to arrange an introduction. Their refusals did not daunt her; she began telephoning the Palace and the Fort direct; and though it was always in vain, not until she had presented herself at the door of the Fort, only to be rebuffed there, too, did she abandon her hapless and irrelevant intrusion, the motives for which would have better befitted a Balkan farce. Bruce Lockhart, hearing of it, was amazed at the confidence that Hollywood stars have in their personal power: "There is apparently no limit to what they think they can do."

The King still spent his weekends at the Fort, but he was gradually settling into the Palace. Not wishing to suggest impatience to assume his father's place, he refused the King's rooms on the second floor, and moved instead into those reserved for visiting monarchs, the ground-floor Belgian Suite, named in memory of Queen Victoria's uncle, Leopold I. Tall French windows opened upon the garden, and there was private access through the garden entrance, used only by the sovereign. An extra switchboard was put in for his private use, and a private line was run to the Fort from the Palace. He installed a shower, and replaced the vast four-poster bed favored by Victorian and Edwardian monarchs with a simple pallet, but these were the only changes he made—perhaps because, as he was to say, he had a feeling he might not be there very long.

The silence of the press, its false calm, was becoming more unnatural daily. It could not continue and it did not. On October 12, Lord Beaverbrook's *Evening Standard* learned of the approaching action at Ipswich, and its editor, Percy Cudlipp, at once recognized the implications of the news. Before breaking the story, he consulted his chief. This was (William) Maxwell Aitken, first Lord Beaverbrook, known worldwide as "the Beaver." Born in Maple, Ontario, in 1879, he had made a fortune through the amalgamation of Canadian cement mills, and had moved to England in 1910; but it was not for more than another decade that he found his metier, when he bought control of the *Evening Standard* and the *Daily Express* and founded the *Sunday Express.* He had been Minister of Information in 1918 and would be Minister of Aircraft Production and of Supply in 1940–41. When he died in 1964, his son Max, who had been a heroic fighter pilot in World War II, disclaimed the title, saying, "There can be only one Lord Beaverbrook."

Peter Howard, a biographer of the Beaver's, capsuled him as "Divisive—often. Damnable—frequently. Dynamic—always. Dull—never." He was not a big man; he stood only five feet seven, and his figure was slight, with a small paunch. A staff writer, Tom Driberg, described him as having a "powerful head, broad, rather flat-topped, bulging"; a face "dark in hue, a mottled tan, permanently sunburned"; and "a satchel mouth, bisecting the face in an enormous grin." Lady Diana Cooper wrote of "this strange attractive gnome with an odor of genius about him . . . with his humor, his [Ontario] accent, his James the First language . . . his poetry and his power to excoriate or heal." Elizabeth Longford emphasized his "monkey-like charm and delight in mischief." The key words are "grin" and "mischief." No other publisher of the twentieth century, with the exception of Henry R. Luce, of *Time, Life,* and *Fortune,* and Herbert Bayard Swope, of the New York *World,* derived more demonic joy than Lord Beaverbrook from exposing the follies and rascalities of the exalted and overexalted. He told Cudlipp to proceed; the King's name could not be brought into a private action between two of his subjects, but London gossip would fill the gaps.

Beaverbrook was in a better position than most newspapermen to find out what was really afoot at Ipswich: Mrs. Simpson's solicitor, Theodore Goddard, was an old friend of his. Though Goddard was a cold fish, in the demeanor cultivated by British solicitors, Beaverbrook's telephoned warning that the *Standard* would report the divorce petition so startled him that he asked for a conference at once. They met that evening at Cherkley, Beaverbrook's house in Surrey; and for two hours Goddard argued that Mrs. Simpson was entitled to privacy before the action, lest the publicity prejudice her case. He declared that the King had no intention of marrying her—the rumor was baseless.

Beaverbrook saw him to the door without having committed himself.

That same day, the twelfth, brought Walter Monckton's return from India. Goddard and George Allen picked him up the next morning and, en route to the Palace, explained the choice of Ipswich and Birkett's preparations for the hearing. Monckton was appalled. In a few moments he found himself exclaiming to the King, "If Birkett had set out to *stimulate* public interest in the divorce, he couldn't have taken a surer route! It was rash enough to engage Birkett, but *Ipswich!*—a place that could hardly be more remote from Mrs. Simpson's world! Everyone will assume it was chosen for purposes of concealment."

The King was upset, but there was no repairing the damage at that late hour. His agitation was not soothed by Goddard's warning that the *Standard* would probably break the story. The King had at last awakened to the danger that premature disclosure of the suit would invite hot speculation about his romance, especially in the foreign press. At Goddard's suggestion, he telephoned Beaverbrook and asked him to come to the Palace. "Name your own time," the King said—a clear sign to Beaverbrook that he was "exceedingly anxious" to stop the story; but the Beaver had to beg off; a toothache would keep him out of action for several days.

The King would look back on that Tuesday, October 13, as the true beginning of the Abdication crisis. Nothing damaging occurred; nothing unmanageable materialized; nevertheless, uneasiness was in the air. Monckton, Goddard, and Beaverbrook had each added to his anxieties; and still ahead, at the end of the day, awaited an ordeal that would be tedious at best and painful at worst: an interview which the Prime Minister had requested the day before.

They had not met since the start of the summer holidays. While the King was cruising in the *Nahlin*, Baldwin had retired to Wales for a three-month rest cure, only to interrupt it, pay a brief visit in Norfolk, then suddenly, unexpectedly, turn up in London a full month ahead of schedule. His pretext for the audience was to discuss the Fleet Air Arm, a branch of the service which the King was eager to strengthen; but his real concern (as the King doubtless surmised) was with something quite different: the Simpson Affair.

By now, with the divorce action in train, it had begun to tower over everything else on the Prime Minister's calendar and on his mind. Queen Mary's appeal for "action," the fireworks in the American press, the letters pouring into Whitehall from alarmed Britons aboard, the panic and fury that were suffusing informed circles in the Court and the Church—all these were urging Baldwin to move forward strongly and without further delay.

His friend Geoffrey Dawson of *The Times* had passed on to him Sir James Barrie's dour remark, that at any moment some Scottish churchman "might feel called upon to take the place of John Knox and denounce the sins of the Court." (Dawson, born "Robinson" in 1874, was *The Times*'s editor twice: in 1912–19 and again in 1923–41.) According to John Gunther, he was "certainly one of the ten most important men in England." Lord Beaverbrook wrote of him, "He was a man of middle height, with a good head, going a bit bald, and a rather flushed face. He walked with a firm tread. He would have looked well, and he would have done well, on the bridge of a battleship . . . he was a *somebody*." Beaverbrook also wrote that Dawson "was the most important factor—with the sole exception of . . . Stanley Baldwin—in compelling the King to abdicate."

Time, too, was pressing Baldwin. If marriage was the King's secret goal, Baldwin would have to shoulder almost immediately the dreadful, delicate task of trying to turn him back before the Ipswich court removed the last civil barrier between him and his lady. When Baldwin presented himself at the Palace that evening, he was hoping that the King would devote a few perfunctory minutes to the Fleet Air Arm, then open his heart and volunteer a frank statement of his intentions. He did not; and Baldwin, whose colleagues had recently begun to find him newly lazy, indifferent, and craven, did not muster the nerve to press him. A painful week would pass before either adversary would face the issue.

The King had no wish to face it ever. Indeed, he was pretending that it did not exist, that *Simpson v. Simpson* might have been *Jones v. Jones* for all he cared, except that this particular "Mrs. Jones" happened to be his friend—or so he would insist on the sixteenth, when Beaverbrook's toothache abated enough to let him go to the Fort and hear the King's plea for press silence. Though Beaverbrook—who had a lifelong weakness for frauds, rogues, and con men—would eventually decide that the King had staged a brilliant tour de force, he felt at the time that the plea had been made "calmly and with considerable cogency." The King said that his only reason for requesting suppression of the news of the divorce petition, and for restricting news of the findings to the bare details, was that Mrs. Simpson was "ill, unhappy and distressed by the thought of notoriety" which had been unfairly brought on simply because she had been his guest aboard the *Nahlin* and at Balmoral. He was intervening in her behalf, he continued, from an obligation to spare her further pain resulting from their association.

Beaverbrook was won over—for the moment. He agreed to try to persuade the rest of the British press to print only the simple facts of the finding, with no mention of the King's friendship; and next day, the seventeenth, he set about meeting his word. Taking Monckton along as *amicus curiae* of the King, he called on his Fleet Street rival, Esmond Harmsworth, whose father, Viscount Rothermere, owned the powerful *Daily Mail* and *Evening News* group, and was chairman of the Newspaper Proprietors' Association (now the Newspaper Publishers' Association). Harmsworth, who knew and liked the King, agreed that the press's discretion was desirable. Monckton and the two solicitors, Goddard and Allen, also had enlisted in the campaign and, also with Monckton's help, had peddled the King's case over the telephone to scores of publishers in the provinces, even before Beaverbrook and Harmsworth began peddling it in Fleet Street. Beaverbrook then approached the leading papers in Scotland, Ireland, and Paris. The British publishers accepted, including *The Daily Worker*, though not always with enthusiasm; so did the Irish and some of the French. *Figaro* had tactfully ignored *l'Affaire Simpson* throughout. *Paris Soir* had not; every drop of juice it could squeeze from the scandal it had gleefully served to its readers. (It is an axiom of French journalism that no story sells more newspapers than a scandal involving British royalty.) But now its publisher, Jean Prouvost, agreed to desist, out of trust in Beaverbrook's judgment.

Beaverbrook's spell of innocence did not last long. Afterward, he would hold that even if he had known the King wanted the divorce in order to marry, he would have favored stifling the news, out of sympathy for a lady in distress. The issue was academic until the divorce; no harm was done to the press by its brief self-restraint, or to Britain itself; the only losers were the King and Mrs. Simpson. The American press had already reported that divorce was imminent; in the absence of hard facts, its accounts of the King's interest in the unknown girl from Baltimore were ardent and imaginative. Envelopes from Wallis's friends in Washington and Baltimore were fat with clippings. Aunt Bessie's weekly letter included several of the gaudier reports, and she did not disguise her apprehensions.

Although the King had succeeded in temporarily gulling the press barons, he had not allayed the deep mistrust now flooding Whitehall, Lambeth Palace, and the part of the royal household which centered around Queen Mary. The mistrust was breeding a strategy, and the strategists' scheme was to maneuver him into declaring himself before he had laid a base of popular support for his enterprise, or had completed his campaign to manufacture acceptable social and moral credentials for a woman still very much a stranger to the British public.

The critical question—whether he proposed to marry Mrs. Simpson and make her his Queen—he had managed to evade so far. His mother might have got his answer by appealing through love; the Primate might have got it by appealing as his spiritual adviser; but neither dared approach him. The only person with authority to demand (if necessary) the answer—to challenge the King's wisdom in this unique matter, semipublic, semiprivate—was the Prime Minister; and the King's adversaries now set about persuading Mr. Baldwin that his duty would brook no further delay.

They made their approach through the King's personal private secretary, Major Hardinge, the bridge from the Palace to Marlborough House and Whitehall. By Hardinge's own account, written many years later, he first "leaned on" Baldwin in an informal conversation just before or just after the audience of October 13. If the marriage was to be blocked, Hardinge argued, there had to be an immediate intervention. Baldwin objected that the time was not ripe; besides, he had no constitutional grounds for interfering while the lady was still married. However, he added that he and Mrs. Baldwin were spending that weekend with Lord Fitz Alan at Cumberland Lodge, a Grace and Favour house in Windsor Great Park; why didn't Hardinge look in there on Saturday morning, quietly and privately, and present his case? (Lord Fitz Alan of Derwent was the younger son of the fourteenth Duke of Norfolk, an M.P. from 1894 to 1921 and Viceroy of Ireland, 1921–22.)

Hardinge agreed to look in. Though he had an impression that his urgency was lost on Baldwin, this was not so. That the question was actually haunting him became evident when, about this time, his Foreign Minister, Anthony Eden, called at Downing Street to report on developments in international affairs during Baldwin's two-month rustication. One of Baldwin's biographers, H. Montgomery Hyde,[2] relates how Eden found his chief distrait, inattentive. Apropos nothing, he suddenly asked Eden if much of his mail concerned the King. Without waiting for an answer, he continued, "I fear we may have difficulties there. . . . I hope that you will try not to trouble me too much with foreign affairs, just now." He could have added, "—or at any other time." Foreign affairs simply did not interest him. But the Simpson affair had begun to grip him.

That Saturday morning, the seventeenth, while Mrs. Simpson chafed in her dreary cottage at Felixstowe, and the King prepared for a four-day shooting party at Sandringham, the action that Queen Mary had called for was developing on two different fronts: At Cumberland Lodge, Baldwin was being pressed by Hardinge and several of the most eminent members of the Establishment to beg the King to have *Simpson v. Simpson* dropped, and to make his association with the lady less conspicuous; meanwhile, in Whitehall, Theodore Goddard was being pressed by several of the most influential civil servants to beg Mrs. Simpson to abandon the divorce, *whatever the King's wishes*.

The other guests at Cumberland Lodge included Lord Cranborne, Under-Secretary of State for Foreign Affairs, and later to succeed as fifth Marquess of Salisbury; the Duke of Norfolk, senior peer among the Lords Temporal and, as Earl Marshal, the *régisseur* of the Coronation; and Lord Kemsley, who, with his brother, Lord Camrose (their name had been Berry until Baldwin arranged peerages for both of them), was the proprietor of *The Sunday Times*, the *Daily Telegraph*, the *Financial Times*, and other "quality" newspapers. Their conversation, which was led by Hardinge, centered on the King and Mrs. Simpson. Although Hardinge owed the King his official loyalty, his sense of shock and outrage had transformed him into Baldwin's man at the Palace; and he had come to regard himself as the conscience of the Palace Secretariat. Fitz Alan's guests all knew about Ipswich, and not one was sympathetic with the King's intention. Despite their unanimity, Baldwin would not promise to confront the King; the furthest he would go was to suggest that Hardinge return for dinner and continue the discussion. Hardinge left. During the afternoon, Baldwin found an opportunity to draw Kemsley aside and inquire where his newspapers would stand on the royal marriage.

Kemsley gave a stout answer: "Prime Minister, the Nonconformist conscience is not dead!"

Relieved and amused, Baldwin commented, "I believe that you ought to be in charge of this, not I."

Baldwin meant this sincerely. He would gladly have shifted to Kemsley—or to anyone else—the showdown which he now realized was inevitable. At the end of the second discussion, the majority prevailed; Baldwin not only agreed to see the King, but asked Hardinge to fix an audience forthwith. The King had informed Hardinge that he would arrive at Sandringham that same day, Saturday. Hardinge rang him there, but was told that His Majesty was not expected until sometime after midnight. Puzzled, Hardinge left a request that the King call him immediately on his arrival.

* * *

In Whitehall, Goddard was holding a firmer line. He had been summoned there by the head of the Treasury, Sir Warren Fisher, who demanded point-blank what could be done to stop the Simpson divorce. Fisher stated that the Government had reason to believe that the King meant to marry Mrs. Simpson—something that no one wanted. Goddard retorted that the divorce was undefended and straightforward, and that it scarcely devolved upon him to advise his client about a future marriage, least of all about one which he had been assured was not in the cards. The discussion became heated. Fisher called in several colleagues, including Lord Vansittart, the Permanent Under-Secretary of the Foreign Office, and the formidable Sir Horace Wilson, a civil servant closely associated with Baldwin and by him put into the Treasury to be his liaison. Wilson attacked strongly, but Goddard maintained that marriage was not Mrs. Simpson's intention.

He had yielded nothing when he left, but his confidence was shaken: There had been no mistaking the Government's hostility, or the implication that steps to block the divorce were being considered. He telephoned Monckton to report this "jarring development," and Monckton relayed it to the King. How Monckton could reach him, and where, when Hardinge, acting for the Prime Minister, could not, is a piquant item for chroniclers of the Abdication. Frances Donaldson, drawing on private sources which she has not disclosed, states that "it was assumed [presumably by Hardinge]—correctly—that [the King] had gone to see Mrs. Simpson at the house at Felixstowe." Lady Donaldson encourages that assumption by her confident statement that the King did not actually reach Sandringham until four o'clock on Sunday morning the eighteenth. The King's autobiography skips across this gap and does not bother to mention the "jarring development" that Monckton reported. If the King had in truth made a lover's detour to Felixstowe—which would have meant a hundred-mile drive by night from there to Sandringham—it was foolhardiness of the most arrant sort. Any one of a thousand mischances might have exposed him and virtually

corroborated the suspicion that Mrs. Simpson's divorce
was collusive, and therefore invited the court's denial.

He returned Hardinge's call at nine on Monday morning, to be told that the Prime Minister was spending the
weekend at Lord Fitz Alan's and wished to see him on
"urgent and important" business. The King realized at
once that coincidence did not account for the Prime Minister's presence so near the Fort; he must have gone to
Windsor to seek a private talk, disguised as a casual neigh-
borly visit. If Mr. Baldwin's business was so urgent, the
King said, he would be welcome at Sandringham at an
hour of his choosing. Hardinge hesitated before suggesting
that the Prime Minister might be reluctant to interrupt the
King's shooting party, since so conspicuous an intrusion
would raise questions; the matter had best wait until both
returned to London. The King agreed to cut the party
short; he would be back at the Fort late that evening and
would see Mr. Baldwin there at ten o'clock next morning.

Hardinge's ominous message, coming so soon after
Monckton's, and at a time when the King had a dozen
guests on his hands, distracted and worried him. He read
the messages as two clear warnings that the Government
was preparing to force him to declare himself. He had no
way of knowing precisely how far the Prime Minister was
prepared to go, or how much he really knew, though he
felt in his bones—one of his favorite phrases—that Baldwin, like Fisher and Wilson with Goddard, would try to
persuade him to keep the divorce from coming to trial.

It was his habit to telephone Mrs. Simpson every noon
and evening. This Sunday evening he told her that at the
Prime Minister's request he was returning to London for a
meeting, and he mentioned that it might involve Ipswich.
"But don't let it bother you," he soothed her. "Forget
about it! There's nothing Baldwin can do."

Lightly though he dismissed the Prime Minister's entrance into the situation, Mrs. Simpson remembered the
call as "shattering."

Sir Samuel Hoare was in the Sandringham shooting
party; he was privy to what the Cabinet knew; and watching his host at the table and in the coverts, Hoare saw that
he was drawn taut. The King never forgot those last hours

he would ever spend at "dear old Sandringham." The birds flew fast and high; the coverts were in what his father would have described as "capital" condition; but he shot badly.

Small wonder.

Queen Mary as Duchess of York with Prince Edward, Princess Mary, and Prince Albert

The Duke of Windsor as
Colonel of the Welsh Guards

Mrs. Winfield Spencer

The Duke of York's wedding to Lady Elizabeth Bowes-Lyon

The Prince of Wales wins a point-to-point race at Tetbury, 1926.

Freda Dudley Ward

Thelma Lady Furness

Mary Kirk Raffray and Ernest Simpson, 1938

Aunt Bessie Merryman, center, celebrates her 100th birthday.

The Fort

Inspecting troops, World War I

During the cruise of the *Nahlin*, with Katharine Rogers

Thirty days before the Abdication, with his mother

The Royal Family at Whitehall, November 20, 1936

King Edward VIII at Westminster Abbey with the Archbishop of Canterbury

Lord Louis Mountbatten
aboard the aircraft carrier
H.M.S. Illustrious, August 1941

Prime Minister and Mrs.
Stanley Baldwin

Lord Beaverbrook

"Mrs. Simpson" at Madame
Tussaud's

Sir Walter and Lady Monckton

Lady Alexandra Metcalfe

Lady Diana Cooper

With Wallis are, from left to right, Lord Brownlow, Katharine Rogers, and Herman Rogers at Cannes, 1936.

The wedding party, with Herman Rogers on left and Fruity Metcalfe on right at Château de Candé

The Duchess of Windsor, 1937

CHAPTER 7
"She's Going to Be Queen?"

When Joy and Duty clash,
Let Duty go to smash.
—Rebecca of Sunnybrook Farm,
KATE DOUGLAS WIGGIN

Sharp at ten on Tuesday morning, October 20, Stanley Baldwin's little black car pulled up at the door of Fort Belvedere for his second audience. The King, refreshed by sleep, ushered him to an armchair near the fire. He had speculated on Baldwin's gambit widely and nervously, but the one forthcoming surprised him: "May I have a whisky and soda, please?" Unlike the King, Baldwin was exhausted; he had been up half the night, pacing. The King's autobiography mocks the mild request, made as it was by an otherwise austere Prime Minister and at an hour when the sun was still well short of the yardarm. The King's derision was all the more ungenerous since he himself had only recently stiffened his will to postpone his day's first drink until seven in the evening. He was also ungenerous in another respect. Though he may have forgotten the incident entirely, his autobiography skips over Baldwin's preamble to their discussion. Eight years earlier on December 11, 1928—"a prophetic date," Windsor's autobiography called it, as it was exactly eight years before his Abdication—they had come up together from Fokestone to London, where King George V lay ill with pleurisy.

"You said to me then, sir," Baldwin now began, "that I might speak freely to you about everything. Does that hold good when there is a woman in the case?"

"Yes," said the King.

It could well have been at this point that Baldwin, facing a Beecher's Brook of a topic, asked for an emboldening tot.

His own account of the incident is at considerable variance from the King's. He seems to have suffered some embarrassment afterward over his need for support so early in the morning. He told his son Oliver (who repeated it to Harold Nicolson, who put it into his diary) that their conference had taken place in the garden: "They had walked round and round . . . discussing the business, and then retired to the library having agreed that H.M. must abdicate. [Baldwin] asked for a whisky-and-soda. . . . [He] raised his glass. 'Well, Sir, whatever happens, my Mrs. and I wish you happiness from the depths of our souls.' At which the King burst into floods of tears. Then S.B. himself began to cry. What a strange conversation-piece, those two blubbering together on a sofa!"

Both accounts agree that the meeting lasted an hour, but the King's maintains that the question of marriage was raised only indirectly, and that there was no discussion of abdication. He insisted, in fact, that Baldwin never asked him straight out if he meant to marry the lady. Instead, the King's impression was that he was subjected to a pious preachment on monarchic manners and morals—one that left him feeling that instead of being helped by a kindly Prime Minister through a personal problem, he was being fitted by a "political Procrustes . . . into the iron bed of convention."

All the same, Windsor agreed that the report of their discussion which Baldwin delivered to Parliament was substantially correct. The purpose of the Prime Minister's visit did indeed concern the King's friendship with Mrs. Simpson. The Prime Minister reminded the King it had become a continuing scandal in the world press, and that complaints and criticism of his behavior were clogging the Government's mail; he even produced a sheaf of "representative" letters for the King's inspection. He went on to declare that this course, if persisted in, must degrade the meaning of the throne; and he ended, "You may think me Victorian, sir. You may think my views out of date, but I believe I know how to interpret the minds of my own people ["my people"? Surely he should have said "your"?]; and I say that although it is true that standards are lower since the war, it only leads people to expect a higher standard from the King than they did a hundred years ago."

On this particular point, the King could and did make reply, arguing that the aim of his kingship was to supply his subjects with what he had decided that they expected from a king in the twentieth century: "I know there is nothing kingly about me, but I have tried to mix with the people and make them think I was one of them."

Baldwin would take from the meeting a conviction that he had gripped the divorce issue hard, that he had even urged the King to send Mrs. Simpson out of the country for at least six months. Without yet mentioning the marriage, Baldwin warned the King, "I don't believe you can get away with it."

To the end of the King's life, he affected to remember none of this. What he did remember was his growing realization, as the talk proceeded, that Baldwin's "object was to persuade me to prevail upon Wallis to withdraw the divorce petition."

Baldwin finally asked him, "Must this case really go on?"

The position that the King now took with the Prime Minister was much the same as he had taken with Monckton, Beaverbrook, Goddard, and Allen—one of cool, distant judiciousness: Mrs. Simpson's divorce was her own business; "I have no right to interfere with the affairs of an individual. It would be wrong, were I to attempt to influence Mrs. Simpson, just because she happens to be my friend." As the King measured the outcome, their first meeting was a Mexican stand-off. He successfully evaded Baldwin's round-about attempts to smoke out his true intentions toward Mrs. Simpson, and the Prime Minister, for his part, had astutely avoided revealing to him the strategy which he proposed to follow if faced with the issue of marriage head-on.

That same night, he told Mrs. Baldwin that the King had said that Mrs. Simpson was "the only woman in the world, and I cannot live without her."

Baldwin never claimed to have accomplished more at this audience than to have "broken the ice" and to have made the King aware of the terrible danger that he faced. Actually, he had buttressed the King's determination both to ignore his counsel and to bank on muffling the press until he was ready to unfold the larger plan. How monstrously and tragically the King was mistaken would become plain within the week.

On October 27, the case of *Simpson W. v. Simpson E. A.* was called for hearing in the early afternoon. American journalists had been pouring into Ipswich; its hotels, inns, and pubs were full. A number of British reporters were also at hand, but under the "gentlemen's agreement" with the King, they had come only as observers. What they first observed was unprecedented. Police took up positions in and around the courthouse. Newsreel cameramen were hustled away from the vantages whence they had expected to photograph the plaintiff entering and leaving. The public seats in the courtroom were rearranged; the ones that normally allowed spectators to face a witness in the box were roped off. The few reporters who were admitted found themselves shunted into a corner with a view of the witnesses' backs. A chair had been placed in the box for Mrs. Simpson's comfort, although custom required a witness to stand while testifying. The King's invisible hand was sheltering her as no other woman had been sheltered in an English court.

The presiding judge, Sir John Hawke, swept in, an ominous figure in his robes of red and black and ermine, and took his seat under the claret-colored canopy. He had not been consulted about the security precautions; they plainly surprised and irritated him; and his temper was not softened by a streaming cold. Mrs. Simpson, wearing a severe blue suit, entered between Sir Norman Birkett and a young solicitor from Theodore Goddard's office. It was noted that she looked "pale, haggard and miserable." Goddard had called for her that morning at Felixstowe, and they had driven over in a hired car, in order to mislead reporters alert for the Buick. Here is her story of that afternoon:

"An English court is a terrifying place, and the judge himself was terrifying, terribly severe-looking. His wife had come to see the show. She brought a friend and they sat in a balcony, the only other women in the room. I hadn't slept for two nights, and the stares made me nervous before I was even called. I became convinced as I waited that the judge had already made up his mind not to grant the divorce, that he would try in every way to trip me up about my residence, my intentions. Then I was put into this little box, and questioned as if I had committed the most horrible murder. . . ."

Birkett asked her, "Did you live happily with the respondent until the autumn of nineteen thirty-four?"

"Yes."

"Was it at that time the respondent's manner changed toward you?"

"Yes."

"What was the change?"

"He was indifferent and often went away for weekends alone." Some of Simpson's trips were presumably while his wife was in Biarritz, or aboard the *Rosaura* or the *Nahlin*, or at Balmoral, or in Budapest or Vienna.

Birkett then asked, "On Christmas Day, nineteen thirty-four, did you find a note lying on your dressing table?"

"Yes."

The note was produced and handed up. Although the dates do not match, it was almost certainly the one that Mary Raffray had meant for Ernest, but had misaddressed to Wallis. Also put in evidence was a copy of the letter Wallis had written to Ernest after his little rendezvous at Bray, notifying him that it was "conduct which I cannot possibly overlook."

Wallis said later, "The judge was very rude—rude to Birkett, who was terribly clever; and rather rude to me." Accounts in the American press mention Justice Hawke's irritation, but not any hostility. Wallis felt that "it was touch and go for awhile. I could see that he was absolutely against me." His preliminary statement of his decision raised her hopes: "I suppose I must come to the conclusion that there was adultery in this case."

"I assume," said Birkett unctuously, "that is what your Lordship has in mind."

Hawke swooped on him at once: "How do you know what is in my mind? What is it that I have in mind, Mr. Birkett?"

Birkett, flustered, hastened to explain that he presumed the court to have in mind a finding on "hotel evidence"— allegations in which the other lady's name is not disclosed.

He had taken care that the hotel servants did not mention it, for fear that its improbability—"Buttercup Kennedy"—would ignite Hawke's suspicions.

"That is what it must have been, Mr. Birkett," Hawke acknowledged icily. A moment later, he found against Ernest Simpson, charged him with the costs, and granted his wife—the "innocent party" for the second time—a decree *nisi,* though "with obvious reluctance." The hearing had taken a mere nineteen minutes. The King's protective hand hovered over the plaintiff to the end. As Wallis and Goddard left the courtroom, its doors were slammed and locked behind them, and the reporters clamoring to follow were shouted down by the bailiffs' cries of "Silence! Silence!" Outside, the police smashed two news cameras, and blocked off all traffic until Wallis and Goddard were safely away in their car.

They returned to Beech House to pick up her bags and to telephone to the King, then headed for London. Minutes after they arrived at Cumberland Terrace, he was at her door, to thank Goddard, see him off, and dine with her alone.

Their reunion was a mixture of joy and fear—joy that they were safely past the first barrier to their marriage, fear of the implications of Baldwin's intervention. She told him she was frightened; the atmosphere in the courtroom, the behavior of the press breathed hostility and unshakable curiosity.

The King consoled her. "I'm sure I can fix it," he said.

But he couldn't fix it. There was no possible way he could fix it, least of all as King. He was on reasonably solid ground in maintaining that his relations with Wallis Simpson were a private matter; they did not engross or even interest the majority of his subjects, although the gossip in the clubs and drawing rooms was spicy and amusing. His *marriage,* on the other hand, would be a public matter, all the more so as it involved a woman twice divorced; further, in Queen Mary's disdainful remark, "Two of the former husbands are still living." This—not Mrs. Simpson's being American—was the bone that would stick in British throats.

By now the King was realizing that the odds were overwhelmingly unfavorable. He had loaded the dice against himself by the folly of the *Nahlin* cruise. The day before the divorce hearing, the *New York American* had predicted, on the authority of "an unidentified Palace source," that the King would marry Mrs. Simpson. The secret was out of the bag, and the King was now vulnerable. Next day, he had to receive Mackenzie King, the Canadian Prime Minister. King had recently been an overnight guest of Stanley Baldwin's at Chequers, where Baldwin had briefed him, hoping he would voice to the King the misgivings that newspapers from across the border were spreading over the Dominion. At the audience, Mackenzie King evaded the major issue, but his oblique references to the affection which Canadians bore for the Crown, and for Edward VIII himself, fed the King's growing apprehensions. They swelled larger when he learned that the divorce decree was front-page news in the French press. One newspaper had greeted it with this jubilant and unequivocal headline: *"L'Amour du Roi Va Bien!"*

A long evening with Lord Beaverbrook a week later did not restore the King's peace of mind. His lord-in-waiting, Lord Brownlow, whom Beaverbrook knew and liked (and who would become his principal private secretary in World War II), gave a dinner on November 5 with the purpose of subjecting the Beaver to Mrs. Simpson's charms. The King was present, and a number of other guests. This was the Beaver's first meeting with the lady, and here is the impression she made on him: "She appeared to me to be a simple woman. She was plainly dressed, and I was not attracted to her style of hairdressing. Her smile was kindly and pleasing, and her conversation was interspersed with protestations of innocence of politics and with declarations of simplicity of character and outlook, with a claim in inexperience in world affairs. Throughout the evening she only once engaged in political conversation, and then showed a liberal outlook, well-maintained in discussion, and based on a conception which was sound. I was greatly interested by the way the other women greeted her. There were about six women who were present at the dinner or who came in afterwards. All but one of them greeted Mrs. Simpson with a kiss. She received it with appropriate dignity, but in no case did she return it."

Such political talk as there was, the King led. He spoke "very plainly" about Baldwin and his Cabinet, and Beaverbrook took this as probably preparatory to a frank disclosure of the marriage plan, and an invitation to help him maneuver it through. By then, Beaverbrook felt certain that the King had been less than forthright at their meeting two weeks earlier; the intensity of his concentration on Mrs. Simpson gave him away, and the Beaver wanted "to stand down from intimate consultations with the King and to regain my liberty of expression in my own newspapers." But the tender topic was not broached, though at the end of the evening the King let the Beaver know that there was "something" further he wished to discuss. A few days later, having heard nothing from the Palace, Beaverbrook recommended to Perry Brownlow that a practical policy for the King to adopt, if marriage were truly in prospect, was candor with those whom he consulted.

If this hint ever penetrated the King's cocoon of self-absorption, the evidence has not appeared. When he finally opted for candor, his first move was characteristically oblique: He summoned Monckton and confided the "secret" that until then only three persons—Wallis Simpson, Ernest Simpson, and Bernard Rickatson-Hatt—had heard from his lips: He was going to marry her. Monckton wrote in his notes of the meeting, "Although I had not taken the view that his mind was made up, I cannot say that the news came as a shock."

The King need not rush to disclose his intention, Monckton submitted: The decree would not become absolute for nearly six months. But the King said No, the disclosure could not wait: He could not go forward to the Coronation on May 12 unless his intentions were made known; he did not intend to—and would not—deceive the Government or the people. He added that he would tell the Prime Minister in good time.

Aunt Bessie Merryman sailed for England on November 4, the day after President Roosevelt's landslide reelection. She had intended joining Wallis there during the summer, but Wallis asked her to wait until fall, when she might "have need" of her. Mrs. Merryman had not liked the sound of this; it had strengthened her suspicion that divorce was in the air, and she dreaded what might follow.

A probably apocryphal exchange is attributed to their first few minutes together at Cumberland Terrace:

Wallis (indignantly): "They're calling me a boarding-house-keeper's daughter!"

Mrs. Merryman: "Perhaps it's because you're acting like one."

They had time for little more. The King was at the door only minutes after Aunt Bessie arrived and carried both of them off to the Fort for the weekend. Except for that single association, he carefully avoided any public intimation that his life had been even mildly affected by the Ipswich verdict. Indeed, the whole fortnight that followed the verdict seemed devoted exclusively and almost continually to public affairs. On October 30, he received the new German Ambassador, Joachim von Ribbentrop, in a full-dress ceremony at the Palace. On November 3, he rode in his Daimler to the House of Lords, and opened Parliament. On the eleventh, Armistice Day, he went to the Cenotaph, to lay a wreath of remembrance for the war dead. That evening at Albert Hall, amid massed flags and brilliant uniforms, his comrades of the Great War gave him a hero's reception: six long cheers followed by a sustained roar. And that night he took the train to Portland, for a visit to the Home Fleet.

It was raining next morning, so the First Lord of the Admiralty, Sir Samuel Hoare, who was in attendance, turned out in a waterproof. Not so the King; he scorned to wear one; and the men noticed it, with pleasure. On hand to welcome him were former term-mates at Osborne and Dartmouth, and officers who had accompanied him on the long imperial cruises—all seniors now, with cuffs heavily laced. The memory of that visit lasted into old age: He spent a happy two days going from wardroom to wardroom, coming upon a friend and being reminded of some cheerful, distant incident. Hoare was awed by the enthusiasm which the King kindled: "He seemed to know personally every officer and seaman in the Fleet"; and after the King's impromptu speech on the huge hangar deck of the aircraft carrier *Courageous,* Hoare added, "In my long experience of mass meetings, I never saw one so completely dominated by a single personality."

That was the high-water mark of the kingship of Edward

VIII. His exhilaration lasted until he rejoined Wallis and Mrs. Merryman at the Fort early in the ill-omened evening of Friday, November 13. To his anger and dismay, he was instantly faced with the stunning fact that time and the Prime Minister had not waited for him. They were forcing a showdown before he was ready for it.

What brought on the crisis was an "urgent and confidential" letter waiting atop the pile of red boxes on his library table. It was from Alex Hardinge, who had instructed the butler to bring it to the King's attention immediately on his return. Its few short paragraphs were like hammerblows. They informed the King that the British press's silence "on the subject of Your Majesty's friendship with Mrs. Simpson" was about to be broken, probably in "a matter of days"; that the effect would be "calamitous"; that the Prime Minister and the senior Cabinet members were meeting to choose the course to be pursued, in the light of the "serious situation"; and that the King must reckon on the possibility of the resignation of the Government, to be followed by a general election in which "Your Majesty's personal affairs would be the chief issues." Hardinge's advice—"the one step which holds out any prospect of avoiding this dangerous situation"—was "for Mrs. Simpson to go abroad *without further delay*" (Hardinge's italics).

As the King's link with his ministers, Hardinge was obliged to keep him informed of the Government's actions and intentions as they bore on constitutional issues. Although he had let his language become overheated by his outrage, and by his indignation over the King's conduct and his contempt for what Mrs. Simpson represented, the letter was accurate. Long after the Abdication, it became known that on the eve of Ipswich, Dawson of *The Times* had brought Hardinge a summary of what the American press and British subjects and Anglo-Americans were saying about the King's affair, and it was then that Hardinge had taken up his pen. Baldwin's biographer would later admit that the Prime Minister had approved both the Dawson-Hardinge meeting and the Hardinge letter, though he had not initiated either. Hardinge also saw Queen Mary at about this time, and there is reason to suspect that his recommendation to expel Mrs. Simpson was the unspecified "action" that she had wanted the Cabinet to take some six weeks earlier.

A similar action had produced salutary results in breaking off Kent's reckless liaisons. Hardinge's mistake in framing the cruel recommendation that closed his letter was in not foreseeing that it would flick a raw nerve in the King's memory. It enraged him that his fiancée—his nonpareil, his "perfect woman," the intended glory of his kingship—had been lumped with Kent's doxies—doxies whom he himself, as an indignant elder brother, had helped the Palace boot out. The King might properly have retorted to Hardinge in the same terms that Queen Elizabeth I had retorted to Robert Cecil: *"Must*? Is *must* a word to be addressed to princes? Little man, little man! Thy father, if he had been alive, durst not have used that word."

But the phrases that Windsor used in his autobiography were restrained; he wrote merely that he resented the pressure to ship off from "my land, my realm, the woman I intended to marry." But to a friend he confided: "Hardinge was a tool, a catspaw. I doubt if he ever knew how the family got rid of my younger brother's girls. Scotland Yard could be quick, silent and invisible in those little jobs. No strong-arm measures, mind you—only a firm suggestion. Then a bank address in a foreign land or a packet of five-pound notes. A stateroom reservation and a departure in the dead of night, with an unobtrusive stranger a step or two behind, to make sure that the tearful, 'misunderstood' lady was on her way. I was having none of that." His resolution became him. It would also destroy him. In meeting Hardinge's challenge, the King decided to be a gentleman, in the chivalric sense of the word. Having pledged his troth to Mrs. Simpson, he would now declare it to his ministers and to his mother, brothers, and sister.

On Sunday afternoon, November 15, he met Monckton secretly at Windsor Castle, in the second-floor rooms that had been his as Prince of Wales. He showed him the letter, swore he would sack Hardinge, and promised to send for the Prime Minister first thing in the morning and present his ultimatum: marriage or no coronation.

Monckton urged him not to bring matters to a head, and certainly not to sack Hardinge out of hand: "Wait and be patient, sir!" But anger had stopped the King's ears. He telephoned to Mrs. Simpson at the Fort and repeated, in Monckton's presence, what he had just said. Mrs. Simpson liked to believe that she begged the King to send her out of the country, as Hardinge urged; but Monckton's clear impression was that she volunteered nothing of the sort. The King put down the telephone and asked him to take Hardinge's place as his representative in the negotiations between the Crown and Government that he wanted to begin next day. Monckton consented, though it meant enormous financial sacrifice, since barristers and physicians do not bill the Royal Family for their services.

The following evening, Monday, the King and Baldwin had their third session. For privacy, Baldwin used the garden entrance to the Palace. As before, the two men met like strangers viewing each other across a toe-drawn line. Baldwin, approaching seventy, symbolized for the King a past that had overstayed its welcome, a symbol behind which he discerned, "shadowy and malign," the presence of the Archbishop of Canterbury. The King, at forty-two, still struck Baldwin as what he had originally judged him to be: a headstrong, spoiled, shallow playboy, unfit for sovereignty. In the struggle now joined, the King would exaggerate Baldwin's hostility and even more the balefulness of his alliance with Dr. Lang.

Baldwin was carrying a heavy handicap. His popularity was nothing, compared with the King's; his health was failing; he wanted to retire from politics and was planning to do so after the Coronation. All the same, he had the whip hand, chiefly because he had done his homework. Five days earlier, he had unofficially sounded out three close colleagues in the Cabinet: the Chancellor of the Exchequer, Neville Chamberlain; the Lord Privy Seal, Lord Halifax (former Viceroy of India and later Ambassador to the United States, 1941–46); and the Home Secretary, Sir John Simon (later Chancellor of the Exchequer and Lord Chancellor). Sir Oswald Mosley rated Simon as "the leading lawyer of the age," but Lloyd George once spoke of him as "lending one of his countenances to a measure." The measures he is now best remembered for supporting were those to appease Nazi Germany.

All three men were opposed to the King's marrying Mrs.

Simpson. Indeed, Chamberlain's agitation had already led him to draft a letter scolding the King so harshly, and advising him to "reorder" his private life, that Baldwin pigeonholed it, fearing that if it were released, it would have the contrary effect of generating a wave of sympathy. When, therefore, Baldwin's talk with the King turned toward the marriage—and this was the first time that the subject had been broached between them—the Prime Minister was not daunted. He knew he was on firm ground in warning the King that it would not meet with Cabinet approval.

"I mean to marry and I am prepared to go," the King said.

"Sir," said Baldwin, "this is grievous news."

The Conservative Party's chief whip, David Margesson, was waiting for him at 10 Downing Street. Baldwin told him, "I have heard such things from my King tonight as I never thought to hear. I am going to bed." Later, he told his son, "I never saw such a look of beauty on anyone's face. He was like some young knight who had just been given a glimpse of the Holy Grail. No reasoning or pleading by family or friend could penetrate that rapturous mist. He was alone with his vision."

The King, meanwhile, changed to a white tie and went across to Marlborough House, to dine with his mother. He had decided in the morning that she should be next after the Prime Minister to know his intentions, and so had proposed himself for dinner. Queen Mary had asked Princess Mary to join them; in her widowhood, she had come to count on her daughter more and more. Alice Duchess of Gloucester had also been included. For the King, the meal seemed interminable. After dessert, Alice excused herself, to the King's relief (he barely knew her; she had been his sister-in-law for only a year), and he and Princess Mary followed their mother to her boudoir.

He remembered, or chose to remember, little of their searing discussion, beyond that his mother and his beloved sister could not seem to follow his argument that his marriage was a part of his right to be a king in a modern way. His mother yielded not an inch. She simply could not believe that her eldest son was so blind, so insensitive, as to surrender of his own free will something as precious and exalted as the Crown. Having acquiesced, herself, first in an arranged engagement, and then in an arranged marriage to her late fiancé's brother, she considered a royal marriage for love alone to be indefensible and almost incomprehensible. His choices, she argued, were but two: Give up marrying Mrs. Simpson or give up the throne, and his duty was to stay on the throne. Duty was her theme: duty, *duty*, DUTY! She was the personification of Wordsworth's "Stern Daughter of the Voice of God." Robert E. Lee might have been speaking for Queen Mary when he said, "Duty is the sublimest word in our language." Lady Airlie, for fifty-one years lady-in-waiting and extra lady of the bedchamber to Queen Mary, quotes her as having once defended Catherine the Great of Russia on these very grounds: "She loved her kingdom. She was prepared to make any sacrifice for it, to go to any lengths—even to commit terrible crimes for it." [1] (Lady Airlie also shows the old Queen in merrier moods: laughing at the jokes in *Punch* and even *La Vie Parisienne*, sending comic postcards, and learning the words to "Yes, We Have No Bananas." [2])

The King argued that kingship would be intolerable without the woman he loved, and if he could not marry her on the throne, then he would surrender it. The impasse was such that at the evening's end, Queen Mary refused her son's request even to receive Mrs. Simpson. When he pressed for the reason, she said coldly, "Because she is an adventuress!" There was no changing his mother's mind. He never forgot that Victorian epithet, "adventuress." He could not bring himself to put it into his autobiography, and he may never have mentioned it to his wife; but it echoed in his memory for years, and when he finally told a friend what she had said that evening, the epithet seemed to lie there like a coiled malevolence.

Walter Monckton theorized later, "If only Queen Mary had received [Mrs. Simpson], the crisis might have been avoided. Queen Mary alone of all women had the power and the love to make her understand what was involved. Instead, the Royal Family had all but expelled her."

One of Queen Mary's lifelong little pleasures was to whistle when she was alone. It can be presumed that few merry tunes rose to her lips when she was finally alone that bitter evening. Still, she is reported to have acknowledged at least one good quality in Mrs. Simpson: Whereas Thelma Furness is widely blamed for having encouraged the Prince to drink, Wallis Simpson is widely credited with having encouraged him to abstain. His mother may have heard this, for Bruce Lockhart recorded in his diary for November 13, 1936 (four days before the "adventuress" dinner), "Queen Mary is supposed to have said: '. . . The one thing I have always feared for David is drink. I was afraid it would ruin him or make him a laughing-stock. And [Mrs. Simpson] has been a sane influence in that respect.'"

By the afternoon following their dinner, Queen Mary had unbent to the extent of writing him a note. Years later, he showed it to her biographer, James Pope-Hennessy: "As your mother, I must send you a line of true sympathy in the difficult position in which you are placed—I have been thinking of you all day, hoping you are making a wise decision for your future. . . ." But her exasperation would remain undiluted, even by the passage of slow time. In July 1938, when her son had been in exile for nineteen months, she wrote him (in part): "You will remember how miserable I was when you informed me of your intended marriage and abdication and how I implored you not to do so, for our sake and for the sake of the country. You did not seem able to take in any point of view but your own. . . . I do not think you have ever realized the shock, which the attitude you took up caused your family and the whole Nation. It seemed inconceivable to those who had made such sacrifices during the war that you, as their King, refused a lesser sacrifice. . . . All my life I have put my country before everything else, and I simply cannot change now."

The Prime Minister called at Marlborough House that same afternoon to inform her of developments and to seek her counsel. As she entered the room where he was waiting, her hands held out before her in a gesture of despair (according to Pope-Hennessy), there burst from her lips a cockney phrase she had picked up years before from her brothers:

"Well, Mr. Baldwin, *this* is a pretty kettle of fish!"

Beyond doubt, Queen Mary was the noblest figure among the dramatis personae of the Abdication. She was "oriflamme and guidon" for the royal family, as Wheeler-Bennett put it—a compound of steel and sympathy. She once admitted to Sir John Gielgud that as a girl she, too, had taken the stage in a Shakespearean role: She had played Wall in *A Midsummer Night's Dream*. Rehearsing for it must have served her well during the battering weeks now upon her. Few outsiders saw her while the King's ordeal and her own were running their separate courses; but the King, the Archbishop, the Prime Minister, and the members of his Cabinet, her sons and her daughter, and—most excruciatingly—Mrs. Simpson all knew that she stood like a strong wall, a wall against Wallis: immovable, unbreachable, insurmountable.

Monckton's King and client having now settled on the road he would take, Monckton himself was impelled, most unwillingly, toward a private crossroads of his own. About this time, November 16 or 17—the exact day is not clear—Baldwin asked him to come to his office in the House of Commons. They had been governors of Harrow at the same time, and so were old acquaintances; yet Monckton's notes show that the meeting was painful. Baldwin told him that Britain, and even less the Dominions, would not tolerate the marriage to Mrs. Simpson, and begged him to dissuade the King from a course that could only prove fatal. Alarmed, Monckton called at the Palace immediately, and reported what Baldwin had said. The King seemed not to hear. Later that evening and through the next day, Monckton sought out friends and acquaintances in the Commons, the City, and the press, to test the temper of London. His poll convinced him that the Simpson Affair was Topic A, and that all England was certain that the King was marriage-bent. Monckton also found something beyond the gossip: If the King were to abandon his job for the sake of Mrs. Simpson, Englishmen everywhere would look on him as "letting the whole side down irretrievably in the eyes of the world."

When he had finished his poll, and well knowing that he was consigning his words to the wind, he nevertheless wrote a long letter to the King. He described the attitudes he had encountered, and moved on to a veiled warning: For him to be seen so much in Mrs. Simpson's company was feeding a suspicion that "the divorce was for the King's convenience"; moreover, their intimacy could jeopardize the petition by prompting the King's Proctor to intervene before the decree became final. The King did not answer; he was too busy burning his bridges.

In the several days that followed the dinner at Marlborough House, the King sent for his three brothers separately and told them each in turn what he had told their mother. Gloucester, the middle one and least close, accepted the decision calmly; what seemed to disturb him most was that Abdication might burden him with more "princing," at the expense of his Army career.

Kent, the youngest and closest, was sympathetic, fascinated, and appalled: "What will she call herself?"

" 'Call herself'?" the King echoed. "What do you think? 'Queen of England,' of course!"

Kent gasped, "She's going to be *Queen*?"

"Yes," the King assured him joyously, "and Empress of India—the whole bag of tricks!"

The scrap of dialogue raced through Mayfair; Chips Channon heard it and embalmed it in his diary for November 19.

The King's meeting with the brother who would succeed him was poignant. York did not want the throne. He was sincerely a Man Who Would Not Be King. In his own phrase, he was not "Palace-minded"; he would have been content to pass his life in the quiet backwater of Sandringham, and he dreaded being dragged from York Cottage before a world that, he feared, would parrot and deride the stammer which no therapy seemed able to cure. The King's disclosure so affected him that he could not express the tumult inside him. When the right words finally came, days later, they were words of trust in a brother he loved. The King seems not to have been responsive to Bertie's anguish, and perhaps not even aware of it. Only a few days before, Bertie had written to Queen Mary: "I have been meaning to come and see you but I wanted to see David first. He is very difficult to see & when one does he wants to talk about other matters. It is all so worrying & I feel we all live a life of conjecture; never knowing what will happen tomorrow, & then the unexpected comes."

Owing to a rigid schedule drawn up months before,

there now occurred an event which, though not momentous in itself, was to impart an air of grace and humanitarianism to the dying hours of the kingship, yet which was to infuriate the King's critics. Two days before his November 16 meeting with Baldwin, and before he had quite finished indoctrinating his brothers, he was obliged to go to South Wales for a quick tour of the impoverished, woebegone, and depression-idled mining villages among the black hillsides of the Rhondda and Monmouth valleys. He was no stranger to the misery of the Welsh. He had visited them often, and they looked on him, by reason of his old title, as their patron prince. Now that he was returning as King, there was a surge of affection for him—a singing of hymns, and impulsive pressing forward of the townsfolk as he walked their streets, under their welcoming arches strung with leeks and past their thousands of miners' lamps winking a friendly greeting in the November gloom.

"Had I been brought up among them," he said afterward, "I doubt that I would have been so civil to a head of State that had done so little for me."

There was little he could do for them now, except appear among them. But he was moved to say, first, "I am going to help you," and then to add, as he progressed into the desolation, "Something must be done to find work for you!" His enemies would accuse him of having organized the trip to incite the miners against the Government that had neglected them; but it had, in fact, been undertaken at the Government's suggestion, and two ministers were in attendance.

Was the King seriously considering measures to improve the miners' lot? It is unlikely. But his promise brought comfort to the poor, the broken, and the hopeless; and the Welsh never forgot it. The Government was in his debt for that.

CHAPTER 8
"The Morganatic Job"

The political crisis, as it embraced the King standing on his avowed intention in late November, was still entirely hypothetical in a constitutional sense. He was still, by the grace of God, Ruler of the Realm. His ministers could neither impeach him for saying that he was resolved to marry Mrs. Simpson, nor toss him into the Tower, nor resign in protest against his declaration, since marriage in England was legally impossible for her before April, five months away. Inasmuch as the King had not threatened to whisk her off to Gretna Green for a hasty, lamplit ceremony, State and Church were powerless to bring him down until he offered them an explicit proposition to oppose. In that sense, he was still out of reach. On the other hand, so long as he persisted in his intentions to marry her and have her accepted as Queen, the only weapon left him was a not-too-subtle form of blackmail. "No Marriage, No Coronation" now became his cynical slogan. It was both vow and threat. Its effectiveness in a struggle with his ministers would depend upon his boldness and skill in exploiting his strongest asset—his popularity—though its true value was yet to be assayed in the crucible of public opinion.

The King began by asking the Prime Minister's permission to see two members of the Cabinet with whom he was on good terms—Sir Samuel Hoare, First Lord of the Admiralty, and Duff Cooper, Secretary of State for War—and invite their views on the feasibility of his intentions. Baldwin offered no objection. The King then added a third adviser on the side: Max Beaverbrook, whose counsel he was free to seek, as Beaverbrook was not in the Government. The King's private, unvoiced hope was that his inquiry would produce influential support for his contention that, even in the upper strata of the Establishment, divorce was ceasing to be the unforgivable social sin which the Primate, the Prime Minister, and the Queen Mother believed it to be.

In the turmoil, the King and Monckton had failed to keep contact with Beaverbrook. They had looked for him on November 16, the day the King presented his ultimatum, and had been dismayed to learn that he was aboard the *Bremen*, already two days at sea en route to New York; thence he would visit his native Ontario, and later Arizona, where he hoped that the dry air would relieve his chronic asthma. The King called him by radiophone: Affairs were fast approaching a crisis, and he needed counsel on how best to put Baldwin down. His dominant fear was that the press would spring a leak; he wanted Beaverbrook home for the additional task of keeping a finger in the dike. The upshot was Beaverbrook's decision to sacrifice his holiday and stay aboard for the *Bremen*'s return trip.

He was still on the high seas when the King sounded out the two ministers. He accomplished nothing with Hoare, who warned him that his cause was hopeless; that the Cabinet was solidly behind Baldwin; and that if he persevered, he would meet "a stone wall of opposition." Duff Cooper agreed with Hoare's assessment, but advanced a subtle and ingenious proposal for avoiding the stone wall, thus: "I suggested postponement [of the marriage]. . . . I thought that if [he and Mrs. Simpson] would agree not to meet for a year, during which he would be crowned and perhaps attend a Durbar . . . he would . . . have grown more accustomed to his position and more loath to leave it. I also secretly thought that he might in the interval meet somebody whom he would love more. . . . He refused to consider the suggestion for a reason that did him credit. He felt it would be wrong to go through so solemn a religious ceremony as the Coronation without letting his subjects know what it was his intention to do. I could not argue against such scruples, but could only respect them." [1] This was a point that the King had raised with Monckton earlier; to have done what Duff Cooper proposed would have meant, as he said, "being crowned with a lie on my lips."

Yet stopping short, temporarily, of the stone wall was the only course that might have saved his throne and left him a chance to marry on it later. Beaverbrook, on his

return to London, would press much the same argument.
So would Winston Churchill. "I . . . did my utmost,"
Churchill wrote, "to plead both to the King and to the
public for patience and delay." [2] The strategy they endorsed was Fabian: Let Mrs. Simpson withdraw into the
background until the furor had subsided; let the King lend
himself wholeheartedly to the preparations for the Coronation in May; let him be anointed, given Crown, Sceptre,
Orb, and invested with the mystique of kingship; and then,
all in good time, after Mrs. Simpson had made herself favorably known throughout the realm by modesty and good
works, the marriage proposal could be raised again,
calmly.

This strategy had a firm basis in logic. Just as there was
no constitutional requirement for the King to seek his Government's permission to marry, so nothing empowered the
Government to deny him his right to do so. The Royal
Marriages Act authorized the sovereign to keep any member of his family from marrying someone he disapproved
of, but the only restraint on his own freedom of choice was
that he might not marry a Roman Catholic. All the shrewd
advice, from worldly and highly politicized minds, went
unheeded. The King was obsessed with being married before settling with the final ceremonial pomp into the kingship. Without waiting to hear out his panel of advisers on
the wisdom of delay, he recklessly sanctioned a compromise form of marriage that would cost him his throne, and
Mrs. Simpson her place as King's favorite.

The new proposition was that they should marry morganatically—that is, not as equals, but in their respective
stations. By such a marriage, the King would retain his
exalted rank, but his wife would not be Queen. Rather, she
would be a consort of lesser rank, perhaps a duchess—of
Cornwall or Lancaster, say—certainly a peeress; and their
issue, if any, could not enter the line of succession, nor
succeed to the King's styles and titles, nor inherit from
him. The English line had never sanctioned these "left-
handed marriages" (so-called because the left hand was
sometimes given in the ceremony), but they were fairly
commonplace with lesser European royalty, especially in
the nineteenth century. Nevertheless, there was nothing in
the Constitution to prevent the King from contracting such

a marriage, and nothing to prevent Parliament from sanctioning it.

The *Encyclopaedia Britannica* points out that the wife in a morganatic marriage "often . . . received some gift, transmissible to her children: such for instance was the origin of the houses of Teck [Queen Mary's family] and Battenberg. Morganatic marriages became quite common in the house of Hohenzollern, but the most remarkable was that of the Archduke Franz Ferdinand"—Emperor Franz Josef's nephew, who married Gräfin Chotek in 1900 and was assassinated with her at Sarajevo on June 28, 1914. King George III's sixth son, Prince Augustus, contracted a morganatic marriage with Lady Augusta ("Goosey") Murray in 1793; and after her death in 1830, contracted another with the widowed Lady Cecilia Underwood, née Gore, next Buggin, and finally (by Queen Victoria's grace) Duchess of Inverness—a step up for her in euphony as well as rank.

Baldwin's biographer suspected Winston Churchill of having fathered the morganatic idea; so, for some time, did the King. The real author was an associate of Lord Rothermere's. This intelligent, public-spirited man passed it on to his son, Esmond Harmsworth (himself now Lord Rothermere), not as something desirable in itself, but as a possible solution or escape. Harmsworth, a friend of the King's, decided to broach it to Mrs. Simpson and invited her to lunch at Claridge's—on November 19 by her account, on the twenty-first by the King's. Harmsworth had studied the subject, and explained to her the advantages and disadvantages of morganatic wifehood. Mrs. Simpson was greatly taken with the idea; so was the King; he summoned Harmsworth, questioned him about the origins of the proposal, and briskly authorized him to carry it to Baldwin and to report then on Baldwin's response.

Harmsworth went to Downing Street on Monday, November 23. Baldwin had expected him to discuss the newspaper publishers' increasing discomfort, seated as they were on a throbbing valve, with Fleet Street's boilers close to rupture. He was startled to be confronted with the morganatic proposition and stunned by Harmsworth's disclosure that he had sought the meeting at the King's behest. In reporting back, Harmsworth described the Prime Minis-

ter's response as "surprised, interested, and noncommittal."
Baldwin had promised to ponder the proposal, and had
suggested that if the King were serious about it, he—
Baldwin—would present it to the Cabinet. In some second-
hand accounts, the Prime Minister is further said to have
warned Harmsworth that he doubted if the Commons
would pass the enabling legislation and, rather than sponsor it, he would himself resign. Baldwin's friend and associate Thomas Jones quotes a postscript to the interview:
The Prime Minister exclaimed that he could "quite understand why people were put in the Tower in the old days,
and he would gladly put Mrs. Simpson there if he could."

The King was too distracted to heed the warning implicit in Harmsworth's report. In his impatience, he determined to extract from Baldwin a straight Yes or No. On
Wednesday the twenty-fifth he summoned him to the Palace for a fourth audience and asked him point-blank
whether a morganatic marriage would be acceptable. To
Baldwin's credit, he tried to turn the King from this dangerous course. First explaining that he had not yet weighed
the merits, he vouchsafed the confident opinion that Parliament would balk. By the King's recollection, a crucial exchange followed.

The King asked Baldwin if he was on sure grounds.

The Prime Minister, knowing he was, countered by asking whether the King wished him to sound out the sense of
the Parliament formally.

The King, furious at being drawn into a chancy test of
strength, went on, unthinkingly, to say yes.

Baldwin reminded the King that the Statute of Westminster of 1931 provided that "Any alteration in the law
touching the Succession of the Throne or the Royal Style
and Titles shall hereafter require the assent as well of the
Parliaments of all of the Dominions as of the Parliament of
the United Kingdom." Since their allegiance to the Crown
was the sole political circumstance binding them to the
mother country, anything affecting the King's traditional
situation had to be approved by their governments and, if
opinion was split, by their Parliaments. Baldwin flagged yet
another warning: If the King were to force the issue, and if
the "fury" of the British people were aroused, the King
should not count on being able to shield Mrs. Simpson

with his own popularity. This was the only time in their several encounters, Baldwin would admit, that "something like anger" roiled the surface politeness. The King, on being shown that small revelation years later, merely shrugged and said, "*All* of it angered me! I've put it out of mind."

The launching of the morganatic proposal is one of the strangest episodes in the melancholy annal of Edward VIII's kingship. It is also marvelously revealing of the mother-child, mistress-slave relationship that had developed between Mrs. Simpson and himself. The King's heart was never in what he came to call "that morganatic job," and he "never set high hopes"—Monckton wrote—on its winning popular support. Before the fourth meeting with Baldwin, Monckton had advised the King to drop it, and he was ready and eager to do so. He knew that his guns were spiked, but he continued to stand to them at Mrs. Simpson's urging. Yet she herself would blame him and Esmond Harmsworth for championing the fatal cause! Even while the issue was still in the air, she chose to believe in her reconstruction of the sorry event that the idea of a morganatic union had been unpalatable to her and that she never would have accepted so "ambiguous" a status.

Beyond any doubt, the prime mover in the scheme was neither the King nor Harmsworth, but Wallis Simpson. The King let slip her decisive offstage influence when Lord Beaverbrook drove to the Fort, immediately after landing at Southampton from his twelve-day round trip. The King met him at the door and took him into a small room where the table was already laid for lunch, prepared in accordance with the Beaver's diet. Here the King finally declared to him his determination to marry Mrs. Simpson or to abdicate if the Government instructed him. He related what had passed between himself and Baldwin at their meetings, and blamed Baldwin for inspiring the Hardinge letter. Then, toward the end of his long recital, he outlined the morganatic proposal, winding up with the disclosure that he had sent Harmsworth to broach it to Baldwin.

Beaverbrook realized instantly that the King, by asking his ministers' advice, was bound to accept it. If he did not, they would have to resign, no longer enjoying the sovereign's confidence. It would then fall upon him either to form a new Government or, failing the required parliamentary support, to dissolve Parliament and call for new elections.

Beaverbrook strove to alert the King to the perils of the gambit: "If you leave the proposal where it rests now, with Baldwin, you will be placing your fate as King in the hands of the politicians, foremost among whom is Baldwin himself. . . . Sir, you are putting your head on the executioner's block!"

Not only were the five dominions—Canada, Australia, New Zealand, South Africa, Eire—almost surely opposed to a morganatic marriage, but each of the several Prime Ministers would frame the language of the bill he would submit to his Parliament and set the time it would come up for debate. Beaverbrook, understanding the political realities, knowing in his heart that the Dominions would never accept Mrs. Simpson, urged the King to retrieve the proposal from the Cabinet before it acted against him. The advice was sound. A strategy for survival on the throne, Beaverbrook argued, put a premium on flexibility: The King should stand on his prerogatives and avoid letting the Cabinet box him in on any issue.

When Beaverbrook left for London, to muster support for the King's cause, he believed that the King had accepted his advice and would abandon the proposal. His assurance was reinforced by a talk later that same day with Walter Monckton, who also was against submitting the morganatic plan; and he turned in at Stornoway House that night confident that their counsel had prevailed. That it had not, he learned a few hours later, at two o'clock, when he was roused to take a call from the Fort. It was the King, now informing him for the first time that the proposal had already been committed to the political process. Further, Mrs. Simpson "preferred the morganatic marriage to any other solution. Indeed, if the choice were between becoming Queen and being a morganatic wife, she would choose the latter." In his reminiscences of the Abdication, Beaverbrook wrote: "When he made that statement I knew the agreement between us was null and void. Whatever [the King] might assent to in his mind, it would not have the agreement of his heart. . . . A morganatic marriage was what Mrs. Simpson wanted, and what Mrs. Simpson wanted the King wanted." Yet *The Other Mrs. Simpson* says that when the morganatic marriage was discussed, and Wallis was asked what she would think about that as a solution to all their problems, her reply was, "How inhuman!"[3]

By that blunder—one which the King may have deliberately abetted from lack of courage for a head-on clash with the Government—control of the issue passed to Baldwin. He never lost it thereafter. While he had been gauging the King's intentions, he had also been gauging the mood of Parliament, among not only his fellow Tories, but the leaders of the Opposition. All were abreast of the gossip. The King had hoped that the working classes would rally to him; he was mistaken. Clement Attlee, the leader of the Labour Party, was not among his admirers. When Baldwin asked him privately how his Socialist colleagues in the Shadow Cabinet and the parliamentary members of the Labour Party felt about the marriage, particularly a morganatic one, Attlee gave an unhesitating estimate: The Labour Party—"with the exception of a few of the intelligentsia who can be trusted to take the wrong view on any subject"—would refuse to have Mrs. Simpson as Queen, or as the King's morganatic wife. The parliamentary leader of the Liberal Party, Sir Archibald Sinclair, gave Baldwin a like answer. He would later explain that the proposal would "offend Puritan opinion which still survives in this country (especially in the Liberal Party)." A thoughtful man, Sinclair saw the morganatic marriage as a potential source of controversy and mischief in perpetuity, with the present King and his successors ever pressing to enlarge the rights and improve the status of the consort. Baldwin called this aspect to the attention of the Cabinet, remarking, according to Geoffrey Bocca, that he doubted if the King (and even less Mrs. Simpson) would be satisfied for long with inferior status. His opinion was shared by two ministers: Chamberlain, who wrote that the morganatic marriage would be "only a prelude to a further step of making Mrs. Simpson Queen with full rights"; and Simon, who reasoned that "the lady the King married necessarily becomes Queen and her children would be in direct succes-

sion to the Throne." Monckton, as a lawyer, had anticipated such constructions and had warned the King that
they constituted an additional obstacle to the plan. Sir Archibald Sinclair's graver fear was that marriage to Mrs.
Simpson in any form "would weaken the position of the
Monarchy not only at home but as a link between the nations of the Empire."

The Prime Minister was armed and armored by the
moral force, as he saw it, of his cause; but before joining
battle, he tallied his support. In the Cabinet, his fellow
ministers had pledged themselves to his banner; so would
the Dominion governments, as he had elicited by a private
poll of their high commissioners in London. In Parliament,
the Socialist and Liberal-opposition for once would present
a united front with his own Tories. In the Anglican Church
and in the Royal Family, his support was unanimous and
unswerving.

The lines were drawn. Baldwin gave the signal and
moved forward, to force the King to surrender either Mrs.
Simpson or the throne.

A special meeting of the Cabinet was called on Friday,
November 27. The principal order of business was the
morganatic proposal; it was quickly agreed to transmit the
King's request to the Dominion premiers at once, and to
offer them these three choices:

1. The King to marry Mrs. Simpson as Queen Consort.
2. The King to marry morganatically (a solution requiring special legislation).
3. The King to abdicate.

In the accompanying messages, Baldwin reviewed his conversations with the King and invited each premier to recommend the best solution, and to give his estimate of how
his Dominion would react to the King's intentions, once
they became known.

Beaverbrook remained convinced to the end of his days
that Baldwin had stacked the cards—that to prompt the
answer he sought, he had phrased the key question something like this: "Do you recommend the King's marriage
to a woman with two husbands living, or do you recommend abdication?" For the suspicion to take root in Beav-

erbrook's mind was for him to give it voice; and having
put the monkey on his enemy's back, he was not disposed
to remove it, lest confession of having falsely accused
his adversary of a minor deviltry might be taken as con-
doning his "career of unrelieved political rascality." Actually, the messages had been composed not by Baldwin at
all, but by the Secretary of State for the Dominions, Malcolm MacDonald, and were a fair, unslanted representation of the blunt terms that the King had himself laid
down: either marriage with the lady as Queen, or political sanction of a morganatic marriage; otherwise "no
Coronation"—that is, abdication. The situation had finally
come down to this: The King had recklessly and unequiv-
ocally put the precious inheritance of his sovereignty in
hostage to the democratic political process, an art in which
he was a novice.

After having staked so much so soon, the King suddenly
felt the spur of panic. He became alarmed that some of his
wilder subjects, in an outburst of the fury which Baldwin
had warned him about, might try to assassinate Mrs. Simpson. She was already receiving anonymous letters, many of
them abusive, and some of them threatening. Though the
majority bore English postmarks, a considerable few originated in the United States and Canada. A series of half a
dozen, arriving in quick succession, warned her that the
writer was coming to London to kill her. Alarmed, and for
the first time fearful for her person, she sent these last to
the King, who immediately dispatched a courier to Cumberland Terrace with a handwritten note telling her that
the letters were the work of a madman and had to be taken
seriously; she and her aunt must be ready to move to the
Fort that afternoon—it was November 27, the day of the
letters to the Dominions—and under no circumstances was
she to notify her staff where she was going or for how long.

A Daimler slid up to the door of Number 16 at dusk,
and an elderly lady came down the steps, followed by a
younger carrying a small dog—the cairn, Slipper, which
the King had given her. A slight figure, dim, but not to be
mistaken by the passersby, helped the ladies into the car.
Less than an hour after their final farewell to Cumberland
Terrace, they were at the Fort; Wallis was being resettled

in the room that had been hers since Thelma Furness's eviction; and Aunt Bessie was making herself comfortable in the one where her niece and Ernest Simpson had spent their first visit there a long, long five years before.

The King's concern, aroused by the "madman's" letters, had been intensified by an incoherent telephone call to the police, warning them that a bomb was about to be planted at Number 16. Scotland Yard ignored the call as a crank's, but the King used it as an excuse to fetch his fiancée under his roof again. If ever proof was lacking that the Simpson divorce had been for the King's convenience, that open act of possessiveness supplied it. To be sure, he wanted to protect her, but he also wanted something from her. As the demons of his fate crowded in, he had to have her close by, not merely because of what she meant as a tender companion and comforter, but because he was no longer able to act without her. He needed her as a diabetic needs insulin.

His horizons were contracting. He was cutting himself off from his staff. State papers requiring his signature or his tacit concurrence had piled up, unread. "I feared for him," Monckton said. "Outwardly, he remained charming, polite. But he was like a man who had taken leave of the real world. He was seldom alone at this stage. One or another of us was always rushing in or out. And whenever anything arose requiring a decision, or some action, he would hurry off to ask what *she* thought. She was the reality. We were shadows."

That weekend of November 27–29 advanced in a frenzy of activity—there were constant comings and goings, between the Fort and London, of advisers, aides, and couriers. The telephone never stopped ringing. The King, curiously, remembered it as the last period of comparative calm before "the pent-up storm broke." And Max Beaverbrook, about to emerge as the principal strategist and recruiter of what would be called "the King's Party," remembered it as the time when Baldwin sent an emissary to try to persuade him to desert the King.

At first glance, Beaverbrook seemed miscast as king's champion. He was no Royalist; unlike his cherished friend Winston Churchill, descendant of the great Duke of Marl-

borough who won Queen Anne's battles, he was not emotionally bound to the monarchy. He was more amused
than dazzled by royal affairs, and by the pomp attaching to
the Court and the rest of the Establishment. What drew
him to Edward VIII—according to A. J. P. Taylor, who
edited Beaverbrook's own account of his part in the Abdication—was largely a feeling that the King was being unfairly harassed by the Establishment of which he was the
main adornment. Beaverbrook was moved by the spirit of
"charity, the desire to help a human being in distress"—a
recurring impulse which caused Churchill to dub him "my
foul-weather friend."

He entered the battle also because he loved a rousing
political clash and, all the more eagerly, because the issue
of the King's marriage gave him a stick to belabor Baldwin
with. Tories both, they were implacable enemies. Baldwin
had fought down Beaverbrook's dream of a vast Empire
locked together in a common market and allied with the
United States. To the further detriment of their relations,
Baldwin had undermined the influence that Beaverbrook
had exercised in Conservative councils when his friend and
mentor Bonar Law was head of the party (1911–21) and
briefly Prime Minister (1922–23). The insult that crowned
these injuries, Baldwin had hurled in a by-election only
five years earlier when he slurred Beaverbrook as a back-
room operator seeking "power without responsibility, the
prerogative of the harlot throughout the ages"—a wither-
ing characterization which he had borrowed from his
cousin, Rudyard Kipling.

There was, then, in Beaverbrook's loyal zest to do battle
for his King, a collateral desire to square accounts with
Baldwin. When Randolph Churchill asked Beaverbrook why
he did it, the impish answer was "To bugger Baldwin!"
Late as the hour was, he was convinced that if the King
would only withdraw from the Cabinet the question of his
marriage, and let the issue be fought out in public on a
straight political basis, "the King must prevail and Baldwin
must be destroyed." The strategy crystallizing in his
shrewd mind was an amplification of what he had suggested on his return from America:

1. The King should pull back, forcing Baldwin to take
   the offensive in pushing him off his throne.

2. The King should then refuse to accept the Government's advice on marriage, forcing Baldwin and the Cabinet to resign.
3. Lastly, the King would form a new government, possibly around Winston Churchill.

Churchill was the most formidable debater in the Commons, and a statesman head and shoulders above the run of politicians. Also, he was slowly regaining public favor by his telling attacks on Baldwin for not rearming Britain faster. Beaverbrook reasoned that a new government with Churchill as Prime Minister would attract support to the King from backbenchers in all parties. He reasoned further that the threat of a "King's" party that cut across party lines would paralyze Baldwin, and perhaps even scare him into accepting the marriage—should he still be in power when the King found the hour opportune for raising the issue.

"Time, sympathetic treatment, patience and endurance would bring the King safely through the crisis of his love story," Beaverbrook thought. Time was also needed to prepare "judicious propaganda." Lord Rothermere stood ready to wheel his mass-circulation *Daily Mail* and *Evening News* alongside Beaverbrook's *Daily Express* and *Evening Standard*. The Beaver was sanguine that the heavy artillery represented by their combined readerships could "blast and frustrate the knavish tricks of the enemies of the King." What he was not so sanguine about was the King himself—whether he possessed "the resolution, determination, and steadfastness of purpose" for open warfare.

The Beaver was primarily occupied with two tasks that crucial weekend: to find a distinguished man who would speak up for the King in the Cabinet, and to abate the King's obsessive desire for an immediate ruling on the marriage. Sir Samuel Hoare, his first choice for spokesman, declined the honor as dubious; he dined at Stornoway House on Sunday the twenty-ninth and brought two interesting items of intelligence: The Cabinet would meet on Wednesday to vote on the marriage proposal, and the press's silence would soon be broken. The second item was hardly news; but the information about the Cabinet was momentous, as its decision would certainly go against the King. With catastrophe imminent, Beaverbrook saw the

King next day and induced him to withdraw the morganatic proposal, and the King promised that Monckton
would so inform Baldwin. As for the right man to put the
King's case to Baldwin, Beaverbrook finally settled on an
old friend, Lord Hewart, the Lord Chief Justice, with
whom he had served in Parliament and in Lloyd George's
coalition Cabinet. The King, too, liked Hewart.

That same Sunday night, the Duke of York took the
train to Edinburgh, to be installed the following day as a
substitute for the King as Grand Master Mason of Scotland, a ceremonial dear to his forebears, but one which the
King himself was not in a mood for. Next day, the thirtieth, Harold Nicolson, no longer charmed by the King, no
longer approving of Mrs. Simpson, made this sorrowful entry in his diary: "I go to see Ramsay MacDonald [lord
president of the Privy Council, with a seat in the Cabinet].
He talks to me in deep sorrow about the King. 'That man,'
he says, 'has done more harm to his country than any man
in history.' It seems that the Cabinet are determined that
he shall abdicate. So are the Privy Council. But he imag-
ines that the country, the great warm heart of the people,
are with him. I do not think so. The upper classes mind
[Mrs. Simpson's] being an American more than they mind
her being divorced. The lower classes do not mind her
being an American but loathe the idea that she had two
husbands already. Ramsay is miserable about it. The effect
on America, the effect on Canada, the effect on our prestige. . . ."[4]

🎘 CHAPTER 9 🎘

Mrs. Simpson Flees the Fort for France

> *The Kirk an' State may join, and tell*
> *To do sic things I maunna:*
> *The Kirk an' State may gae to Hell,*
> *And I'll gae to my Anna.*
> *She is the sunshine o' my e'e,*
> *To live but her I canna;*
> *Had I on earth but wishes three,*
> *The first should be my Anna.*
> —"Yestreen I Had a Pint o' Wine,"
>   ROBERT BURNS

The press had a banner year in 1936. A succession of tremendous news stories of worldwide interest broke at convenient intervals—a fresh sensation almost every month. On January 20, King George V died and was succeeded by King Edward VIII. On March 7, Hitler's troops marched into the Rhineland. On April 3, Bruno Hauptmann was electrocuted for the kidnap-murder of the Lindbergh baby. On May 5, Italy completed its conquest of Ethiopia. On June 18, Max Schmeling defeated Joe Louis. On July 16, the Spanish Civil War began. On October 27, the Rome-Berlin Axis was formed. The pace was getting faster now: On November 3, Franklin D. Roosevelt was reelected; on the twenty-fifth, Germany and Japan signed the anti-Comintern treaty; on the thirtieth, the Crystal Palace burned. But all these were merely appetizers for the story that December would bring, a story that front pages around the world would headline in what newspapermen call "Second Coming type," the biggest and blackest in the shop—so big, indeed, that many headlines ran to only a single word: ABDICATION!

Up to the last day of November, no word of the King's association with Mrs. Simpson had appeared in the British press, and all references to it had been censored from the foreign press before English distribution was permitted. Thomas Jones wrote, "The silence of our Press is extraordinary and is not enforced by the Government but by a sense of shame."[1] Westminster, the Court, Fleet Street, and Mayfair knew something of what was happening, but the "outer public" was still in the dark. An agent who made an informal poll for Baldwin in the north of England reported that the gossip had begun to permeate the middle classes, but not the working classes. Away from public view, the issue was gnawing at Baldwin's vitals. As a version of the perennial "American Problem," the King's infatuation with Mrs. Simpson was becoming, from the Cabinet standpoint, a unique political experience; yet it was already ranking in sheer vexatiousness with the Boston Tea Party, the *Trent* Affair, the Venezuela Boundary dispute, and the war debts. Now, as December wheeled in, gray and depressing, the whole situation was violently transformed. A relationship which the King thought he was entitled to keep private exploded into the most shocking royal scandal since George IV was crowned alone, while his legal wife, Caroline, wailed and beat her fat fists against the barred doors of the Abbey.

The explosion was detonated by the Right Rev. A. W. F. Blunt, Bishop of Bradford, in the West Riding of Yorkshire—a chubby, smooth-faced, and quite obscure cleric who had a local reputation as a scold. In an address before a diocesan conference on Tuesday, December 1, Dr. Blunt discussed the religious meaning of the approaching Coronation service. If he had stopped at these generalities, he would have received small attention from the laity. But he pushed on to ask the conference to commend the King "to God's grace which he will so abundantly need . . . if he is to do his duty faithfully. We hope that he is aware of his need. Some of us wish that he gave more positive signs of his awareness."

It was all true enough and to the point, as far as concerned the Church's responsibilities for the Coronation; and when the conference broke up, its members probably

judged the address for just what it seemed: a homily on the
King's need for divine guidance. But in the charged atmosphere of Fleet Street and Westminster, Blunt's language
took on portentousness. Rumor represented the address as
an oblique attack, slyly inspired by the Archbishop of Canterbury, in the hope that this little additional pressure
would burst the dikes that held back full exposure of what
he always called "the King's matter." There is no evidence
of Lang's hand. On the contrary, Blunt himself later insisted that his words were wholly his own; when he wrote
his draft, some weeks earlier, he had never heard of Mrs.
Simpson; and when the gossip finally reached him, he decided to stand on what he had already written. Malcolm
Muggeridge's explanation of the cataclysm thus brought on
likened Blunt to "an elderly visitor at a Swiss mountain
resort, who, wandering amiably along in knickerbockers,
carelessly kicks aside a stone and releases an avalanche."

Dr. Blunt had spoken in the forenoon, and that afternoon's Bradford *Telegraph and Argus* carried a full report,
which the Press Association picked up and forwarded to
Fleet Street. Beaverbrook realized at once that the dikes
must now give way. From his professional sources, he
learned that two of the most influential provincial newspapers, the *Yorkshire Post* and the *Manchester Guardian*,
were going to break the truce next day, Wednesday, and
print leaders that would reveal the tip of the constitutional
deadlock and the dim, massive bulk of the scandal below.

On Wednesday the second, while the provinces buzzed,
the great London dailies kept silent; they merely excerpted
Dr. Blunt's address without dwelling on what it implied.
But all that day their newsrooms seethed with preparations
for what they would print next morning. In hundreds of
photographs, especially those of the *Nahlin* cruise, Mrs.
Simpson had been snipped or airbrushed from the King's
side before publication; now she was restored and clearly
labeled. Reporters invited attention to the peculiar appro-
priateness of Dr. Blunt's name. From the meager facts that
subeditors and feature writers had been able to gather in
England, the United States, and China about the previously unimpressive, but singularly complicated, life and
marriages of Wallis Warfield Spencer Simpson, they hur-

riedly patched together the tale of the King's incredible romance; and Beaverbrook telephoned him that the gentlemen's agreement was about to go "with a whoop."

That same Wednesday, the last of the cables from the Prime Ministers of the Dominions were laid before the Cabinet. The ministers were Joseph Aloysius Lyons of Australia, William Lyon Mackenzie King of Canada, Eamon de Valera of Ireland, Michael Joseph Savage of New Zealand, and Gen. James Barrie Munnik Hertzog of South Africa, and their cables read much as Baldwin had wanted and Beaverbrook had expected: Forthright and uncompromising, they declared that the King must give up the marriage or abdicate. Lyons's was particularly strong; he felt that the King should go anyway, marriage or not; the Crown having "already suffered so grievously" from his association with Mrs. Simpson that he could not now reestablish its prestige or command confidence as King. Lyons was a Roman Catholic; he had no sympathy for divorce as an institution, or for divorced people; and as a Socialist politician and union organizer, he had only scorn for both the monarchy and its most conspicuous ornament. Savage and Mackenzie King concurred, but were less condemnatory. Savage, who was also a Roman Catholic, managed to avoid damning the morganatic marriage without actually giving it his blessing. Mackenzie King made a reply that was feeble but satisfactory—thanks to prodding by the Governor-General (Baldwin's close friend Lord Tweedsmuir, better known as John Buchan). De Valera, with a constituency 90 percent Roman Catholic, replied as expected. Hertzog made it unanimous.

Baldwin's confidence in his judgment of the political balances had meanwhile been reinforced by another poll of parliamentary opinion. The Tory whips assured him that at worst only a handful of backbenchers would break away from the Cabinet line and go to the King's side—doubly reassuring, because Attlee, too, was "satisfied that the Labour Party would be wholly unanimous" (sic) against the King's marriage.

Baldwin went to the Palace late that day for his fifth meeting with the King, to inform him of the Dominions' stand. Though the King could hardly have been surprised, he remarked bitterly that the Dominions were his Water-loo. Baldwin had ignored his request, which Monckton had presented two days before, to withdraw the marriage question from consideration. His excuse—a hard one to discredit—was that the King had not renounced the intention to marry. As Baldwin now put the issue to him, his choice was straight-forward: Since neither the British Government nor the Dominion Governments would accept Mrs. Simpson as his wife, either he must give her up or he must abdicate.

As Baldwin remembered the King's answer, it was "I have known that all along."

As the King remembered it, it was that his Prime Minister had left him with only one choice.

Both parties agreed in their future accounts that Baldwin urged the King to stay on the throne. The Cabinet, Baldwin said, wanted him to remain ruler of the realm. The King had the final word: He was determined to marry Mrs. Simpson and would abdicate if he could not otherwise have her as his wife.

The King was distant and outwardly defiant during the audience, but it was a defiance that acknowledged defeat. The hard tone of the provincial press had disheartened him. He had glanced at the Birmingham *Post* and remarked, "They don't want me." As if reconciled to his self-destruction, he now moved, heedless of his pride, to shield Mrs. Simpson from being destroyed along with him. From a source she never divulged (it was probably Rickatson-Hatt), she had learned that Geoffrey Dawson was readying a story that would "tear me to shreds." She appealed to the King, and the King now begged Baldwin to "forbid" *The Times* to publish it. Baldwin, who must have found smug satisfaction in being asked a favor that the King was no longer able to command for himself, reminded him of the independence of the press and pointed out, perhaps as a rebuke for the "gentlemen's agreement," that he had no more control over *The Times* than over any other newspaper. The King, rebuffed, was driven to make an even humbler proposal: Would the Prime Minister read the story before it went to press? The King trusted Mr. Baldwin's sense of fairness to keep the lady from being defamed. Baldwin consented. A proof was delivered to Downing

Street at midnight, well before the presses were to start, but
Baldwin had not waited for it; he was already asleep. No
doubt he knew in advance that Mrs. Simpson's fears were
groundless. Dawson's leader was high-flown, but devoid of
invective; he hewed to the constitutional aspects of the
King's dilemma, and left Mrs. Simpson unshredded.

Although Baldwin was sanctimoniously upholding the
press's right to report what it had picked up about Mrs.
Simpson, he was not scrupling to manipulate it wherever
he could. He was organizing a solid front of editorial opinion in favor of abdication, even as the news columns were
bringing to the general public its first confirmation of the
King's intention to marry. Beaverbrook had excellent
sources of intelligence throughout the British press; he
knew that emissaries from Baldwin had invited a number
of newspaper proprietors to come forward in his support.
Beaverbrook was himself approached by his old friend Sam
Hoare. His answer was "I've taken the King's shilling. I am
a King's man."

The gloom that had settled on the King during his conversation with Baldwin darkened as the evening of
Wednesday the second wore on. He telephoned to Beaverbrook several times, to ask what the leading newspapers
were preparing to publish. Beaverbrook warned him to
brace himself. The King's voice was trembling as he declared that only one road was left open to him: retirement
to private life. Beaverbrook, whose relish for battle was in
direct proportion to the length of the odds against him,
urged him to hold on: The battle had just begun.

"Whether [the King] made his declaration in a mood of
momentary depression or [as] a half-threat," Beaverbrook
wrote, "I did not take it as final, for he had shown that he
was most unwilling to leave the Throne and had taken no
practical steps toward abdication."

Both observations were accurate, but incomplete. They
failed to weigh the King's psychological collapse, the ebbing of will, the inability to reconcile his resolution to
marry with the certainty (which he privately expected)
that marriage would cost him the kingship. Beaverbrook
watched Hamlet emerge on the royal battlements: "The
strain of the crisis was telling heavily. . . . He showed it
in many ways. He smoked incessantly, sometimes a ciga-

rette, and sometimes a pipe. He kept on saying 'No marriage, no coronation,' repeating this phrase more and more often and with increasing emphasis as the days wore on. Sometimes he would sit with his head in his hands. Occasionally he would wipe the perspiration from his brow with an unfolded handkerchief, or hold his handkerchief against his head, as if to ease some hidden pressure or pain. If he continued to be subjected to this intolerable strain, it was clear to me that some rash and fatal and quite unnecessary decision would be taken."[2]

The reason the King had made no preparation for abdication was that, having decided not to engage Baldwin and the Establishment in open battle, he dared not face the fact that his kingship was doomed. To acknowledge that he could not be both King and husband would mean admitting to Wallis that the glorious imperial prospect which he had assured her would be theirs forever was on the verge of dissolving. The admission would have been all the more difficult for him because she was far from persuaded that the struggle was lost, or that abdication was inevitable, and even less that it was imminent.

Throughout the last weeks of Edward VIII's kingship, his principal financial adviser, Sir Edward Peacock, trusting and wholly deserving of trust, was beside him—at the Fort, at the Palace, and in the tiny offices of the Duchy of Cornwall, where they could be sure of privacy. Wherever they were, Peacock observed the surrender to a stronger will. The King did not disguise his dependence on Mrs. Simpson; at the Fort, he called her into discussions with members of his staff; he *wanted* to be influenced by her; and away from her at the offices, Peacock could not help but overhear his unresisting, even eager assent to the counsel she was imparting in their interminable telephone conversations.

Monckton's biographer, Lord Birkenhead, found among Peacock's papers a clarifying judgment of Mrs. Simpson's previously hazy role in the abdication process. Earlier, a number of the King's friends had noted her disciplining of his manners, his public behavior, his civility; Peacock was struck by her hold on his spirit. One of his notes read: "The lady [kept insisting that the King] should fight for his rights. She kept up that line until the end, maintaining that he was King and that his popularity would carry everything. . . . The lady persisted in her advice until she saw that her tack was hopeless. . . ."

Alex Hardinge, who was closer to the King than even Peacock, held a similar and even more vigorous opinion. The Palace staff was slow to realize, he wrote, "how overwhelming and inexorable was the influence [Mrs. Simpson] exerted. . . . As time went on it became clearer that every decision, big or small, was subordinated to her will. . . . It was she who filled his thoughts at all times, she alone who mattered, before her the affairs of state sank into insignificance." The second Baron Hardinge's respect for King Edward VIII's mistress fell somewhat short of the first Baron's for King Edward VII's.

The deepening of the King's thralldom, which these two senior courtiers had witnessed in private, was increasingly manifest in public—so much so that a quip from his father's reign, "King George the Fifth and Queen Mary the Four-fifths," was revived and revised: "King Edward the Eighth and Mrs. Simpson the Seven-eighths." A week after the divorce proceedings at Ipswich, the ubiquitous Chips Channon had encountered the King and Mrs. Simpson at a dinner party. The fact of her sure ascendancy did not escape him, and the velvet-glove style that she affected in the presence of the King's subjects rather pleased him: "The King's attention to Wallis," he wrote, "was very touching. He worships her and she seems tactful and just right with him. Always prefacing her gentle rebukes with 'Oh, Sir. . . .'" Channon further noticed, without comment, that Mrs. Simpson had begun to relax her pose as the demure, starry-eyed damsel, unworldly, innocent of politics. She wanted her friends to recognize that she had become the power behind the throne, that the King took the lead from her. Channon's entry for that evening went on: "She confessed to Honor [his wife] that she always kicks him under the table hard when to stop and gently when to go on."

A few weeks earlier at Balmoral, Herman Rogers, too, had witnessed the effective control exercised by this engine-room telegraph: "Suddenly remembering from our China days together how absolutely indifferent Win Spencer had been to her bossiness," he remarked, "I found myself say-

ing to Katharine, 'Our little Wallis has certainly come a
long way! Fifteen years ago, Lieutenant Winfield Spencer
had mutinied under her. Now she is giving sailing orders
not only to the Admiral of the Royal Navy, but marching
orders to a Marshal of the Royal Air Force, and instruction in politics and behavior to the Liege Lord of Great
Britain, Ireland, and the Dominions. I can't believe it!'

Only a woman foolishly vain, or supremely self-
confident, would have flaunted her power so. Mrs. Simpson had become both, obviously. The King's acquiescence
in the disastrous morganatic proposal, against the prompt-
ings of his own more sophisticated judgment of British psychology, was but one example of her influence. A second
was her scheme, born from his demoralization by the publicity in the provincial press, for him to take to the air with
a broadcast to Britain and the Commonwealth, in which he
would put his case eloquently and directly to the people.

In her naïveté she persuaded the King that he could
sway British public opinion to his side as President Roosevelt was doing in the United States with his "fireside
chats" over the radio. To a man in desperation, a broadcast modeled on the temper and solicitude of George V's
immensely admired Christmas greetings to the Empire
seemed to offer a quick, effective way to rally the support
of the British people. Walter Monckton, summoned to the
Fort to help with the draft, found him already scribbling
out a message which would present his situation "not
merely as a knotty and constitutional issue," but rather as
a simple declaration of his intentions. The broadcast would
end with his offer to go abroad for a while, and give the
people time to reflect on what they expected of their King.

It was by no means a harebrained idea. The King did
not lack powerful allies on that Thursday, December 3,
when the whole press of London and other British cities
broke loose with the astounding revelations. The "quality"
newspapers—*The Times,* the *Morning Post,* the *Daily Telegraph*—were for abdication, but not yet vehemently. So
were the Kemsley newspapers and, as foreshadowed by
Clement Attlee's hostility to the King, the *Herald,* controlled by the Labour Party. By contrast, the *Express* and
the *Mail* spoke up emphatically for the King, as did certain

of the provincial dailies. On the following day, to the astonishment of Fleet Street, the *Catholic Times,* a journal of
considerable intellectual repute, also declared for the King,
putting its objections to Baldwin's politicizing above its distaste for the divorce. Beaverbrook's assessment of the opposing newspaper forces confidently concluded that "support for the King was certainly more powerful in the
country than was support for the opposition." He so reported to the Palace, hoping that this auspicious showing
in the opening skirmish would hearten his man.

But his man was listening only to the woman. In
Monckton's judgment, the King was suffering from the delusion that the entire Establishment—Lambeth Palace, the
Tory leadership, the "quality" newspapers, and the
Court—was united in a plot to drive him off the throne.
Beaverbrook's argument that his popularity would prevail
in the long run was lost on him. The last thing he was
emotionally geared for was the long run—"a tiresome,
hopeless stern chase" were his words for it. His mind was
fixed on making the broadcast at the earliest hour, preferably the following evening, Friday the fourth—and if that
failed, striking his flag.

Mrs. Simpson's American approach—to solve a British
constitutional problem by a public-relations scheme—had
one flaw: It was utterly unworkable. For the King to go
before the Commonwealth on a political issue required the
consent of the Government; and it was plain to Monckton
and the Palace staff that Baldwin would refuse it, the Cabinet and the Dominions having already advised to the contrary. Beaverbrook, whom the King had invited to lend eloquence to the draft, knew that Baldwin would veto the
scheme out of hand. So did Churchill, whom Beaverbrook
had brought over to the King's side and to whom he read
the draft by telephone.

Beaverbrook, the chief recruiting officer and field commander of the "King's Party," remembered that Thursday
as "a day of spectacular ups and downs." For the Duke
and Duchess of York, who returned to London in the
morning on the night train from Scotland, it was a day of
shock and unending suspense. As they left the train at Eus-
ton Station, they were confronted with this newspaper
poster: "THE KING'S MARRIAGE." The Duchess, horrified,

forgot her usual public smile; she could only pat her husband's hand. The Duke still refused to believe that his brother would loose the monarchical cord. For Churchill, whose support of the King first came into public view that evening, it was a day that ended in heady satisfaction. His loyal and affectionate reference to Edward VIII during a speech in Albert Hall brought on "a storm of applause." For Mrs. Simpson, it was a day of panic; by evening she was fleeing to France—her last excursion under the King's protection. And for the King himself, it was the day his defeat became all but final.

At nine o'clock that Thursday evening, the King was back at the Palace, for his sixth meeting with Baldwin. In Baldwin's account, the King read him the draft of the broadcast. Whether or not this was so, the text came as no surprise. Baldwin had already acquired a copy, probably from Monckton. When the King asked if he could go on the air, Baldwin said that it would be unconstitutional, but volunteered to ask the Cabinet for a ruling—hardly a generous offer, considering that that very afternoon the Cabinet had rejected the copy he had passed around.

The King retained little memory of what passed between them. The strain was beginning to tell on him. Perhaps he chose to shut his mind to the memory of another failure. Baldwin's recollections of the encounter celebrate a modest moral triumph for his side—presenting himself as a kindly, avuncular Prime Minister instructing a naïve sovereign where his duty and his best interests lay:

> King: You want me to go, don't you? And before I go, I think it right, for her sake and mine, that I should speak.
>
> Prime Minister: What I want, Sir, is what you told me you wanted: to go with dignity, and making things as smooth as possible for your successor. To broadcast would be . . . telling millions throughout the world—among them a vast number of women—that you are determined to marry one who has two husbands living. They will want to know all about her: the press will ring with gossip, the very thing you want to avoid. You may, by speaking, divide opinion; but you will certainly harden it.[3]

The broadcast lost and his love in flight, what little remained of the King's purpose wilted into nothingness. He had never had much backbone for a fight. He was never seriously tempted, for all the siren counsel of Beaverbrook and Harmsworth, to pit his popularity against Baldwin's political reputation, battered though it was. The Duchess of Windsor denied for the rest of her life—though only in public—that she had ever pushed the King into the duel with Baldwin, yet she enjoyed twitting him for not having learned the fundamentals of public relations when he was Britain's foremost salesman abroad. "If you had brought in a first-class public-relations man from New York," she told him one evening, in the presence of friends, "there'd have been no abdication. He'd have turned things around in short order. If he couldn't have kept you on as King, you'd certainly have ended up as Prime Minister!"

Heavily as he leaned on her advice in other matters, he alone chose the style of his going. To his credit, he was animated by a resolve not to lift the issue between himself and Baldwin out of private channels and, above all else, not to split the country further. Sir Edward Peacock was sure of this: "The King realized the falsity of [Mrs. Simpson's] position. He wanted no part in deepening the constitutional crisis, nor in causing more trouble between King and Ministers."

How far gone in defeat he was, as "that terrible day" approached its end, was visible to his mother and his brother Bertie, when he visited Marlborough House after the meeting with Baldwin. Earlier, Queen Mary had sent a note to the Palace: The morning newspapers were "upsetting" and, as she had not seen him in ten days, would he "look in sometime?" Bertie was with her.

The King explained that he meant no neglect by his aloofness: "I have no desire to bring you and the family into all this. This is something I must handle alone."

Bertie was agonized. His private narrative reports: "David said to Queen Mary that he could not live alone as King and must marry Mrs. S——— . . . a dreadful announcement." He could not bear to spell out her anathematic name. Mother and brother realized then, for the first time, that David was about to abdicate.

The obvious and odious parallel between his behavior and King Carol II's, each of them abdicating for love of his mistress, drew from Queen Mary an outraged "Really! This might be Romania!"

From Marlborough House the King returned to the Palace for the day's last piece of business: a conference with Monckton and Allen. They had been with Churchill and Beaverbrook at Stornoway House most of that evening, planning the course to be pursued if the King should steel himself to try saving the field. The two Tory leaders were spoiling for a fight; all that they asked from their man was time—time to dispose of Baldwin.

On balance, Thursday was indisputably Baldwin's day. The tide had set strongly in his favor, as public opinion absorbed the import of the King's intentions. Harold Nicolson, who had been in the House of Commons through the afternoon and evening, wrote in his diary: "That note or feeling of expectancy which is unmistakable hangs over our dear old aquarium. Baldwin rises to answer some unimportant questions, and is received with cheers from every part of the House. Members crowd in . . . and the galleries and gangways are packed. Attlee gets up to ask if the P.M. had anything to tell us. Baldwin rises in a hush of stillness so marked and so immovable that the House suddenly looks like a print of itself, row upon row of immovable faces. He looks ill and profoundly sad. He said that no constitutional crisis 'has yet' risen."[4]

The public, by contrast, was not yet of one mind. Thomas Jones concluded that "The country is divided between those who see in the King's conduct the action of a brave and honest man who will have nothing to do with humbug or hypocrisy and is a pattern to previous monarchs, and those who prescribe a thrashing for bringing all this trouble on the country." Nicolson, on longer thought, was sure that England was blaming the King: "I do not find people angry with Mrs. Simpson, but I do find a deep and enraged fury against the King himself. In eight months he has destroyed the great structure of popularity which he had raised."

It was an hour past midnight when the King left the Palace for the Fort, with Monckton. The handful of spectators who had gathered outside the Palace gates on learning of his return to London, had grown into a crowd. A cheer went up as the Daimler rolled out. "Ah, that's better," Monckton murmured, and the King agreed, acknowledging the cheer with a wave.

As they drove through the wintry night, Monckton began summarizing the results of his transactions; halfway along, he realized that the King had not heard a word—his mind was groping for answers that would not come. Monckton fell silent; he, too, had much to ponder. He had accepted, with misgivings, the duty to serve the King. In negotiating for the King's right to marry, he had resorted to every wile that he could muster, and every legal argument that precedent afforded. He had always known that marriage on the throne was hopeless; his overriding concern was to keep the King on the throne, after the case for the marriage failed. While he still pondered, the Daimler drew up at the Fort. The two men chatted a moment, then Monckton gave the King a sleeping pill, wished him pleasant dreams, and turned in, exhausted.

The King never again set foot in the Palace as King, or in London. He would not risk being made the nucleus of a demonstration that might explode and further damage the nation. In the seven days that remained to him in England, he shut himself up in the Fort, which was now under siege night and day by photographers, not only British, but also the more tenacious and daring Americans. His bedroom and bathroom were on the ground floor, so he had to live with their curtains drawn, lest a telescopic lens intrude on his privacy. Otherwise it was complete. He told his equerries he would have no further need of them for a while. He cut himself off from the Palace staff, depending upon Monckton to represent him in his transactions with them, and to bring him whatever State business demanded his attention. Only two matters dominated his thinking from this point on: negotiating the Abdication, and making sure that Wallis Simpson was not prized or cajoled away from him while he was engaged in the legal formalities of transferring his sovereignty to his brother Bertie.

A strange threat to the entire structure which he was painfully struggling to hold together was emerging in the quarter where he had least expected trouble. The friends who were most determined to keep him on the throne and to throw Baldwin into the dustbin of history had managed, by an incredible stroke of luck, to bring Mrs. Simpson under their influence. Their aim now, having failed to make the King give up marriage before the Coronation, was to induce her to give up the King—at least until the crisis had ebbed.

CHAPTER 10
"Our Cock Won't Fight!"

Show what you're made of! Now is the time, before all is lost! This is your moment to say the word, set the pace, show your utter lack or your real power. Emerge from the wings. No more promises, it's time to act. Your apprenticeship is over!

—HENRI FREDERIC AMIEL

In the game of chess, the most powerful piece is the queen. So it was in the final struggle over the throne, though with two differences: The queen in question was not a Queen Crowned, but a Queen Pretender; and, oddly enough, both opponents maneuvered to sweep her from the board, though not for the same reason. To the Baldwin camp, Mrs. Simpson was a nonperson. The King's camp, tardily, sought to sacrifice her in the last hour, to stave off certain checkmate. No one close to the King was in doubt of her hold on him. Peacock, Hardinge, and Monckton had observed her dominance when the King transacted daily business. Diana Cooper, too, whenever she was with them in the company of friends: The King relaxed, not bothering to hide his feelings toward Wallis. "She was his oracle," Lady Diana remembers. "He never disputed her. If she had said, 'David, I would never *dream* of marrying you!' he'd have accepted it meekly and unquestioningly and stayed on the throne—her influence over him was that absolute." Lady Diana thought this true in 1936; so did her husband. Early in the crisis, the two of them, one evening at the Channons', tried delicately to persuade Mrs. Simpson to put aside for a year or two any plan to marry. She brushed off their suggestion as irrelevant, even absurd; the King, she insisted, had never breathed the word "marriage" to her. She was deceiving the Duff Coopers as she had deceived Esmond Harmsworth.

Beaverbrook had also recognized, in the King's irrational embrace of the morganatic proposal, that Mrs. Simpson was the key to any plan for keeping him from abdicating—all the more now that his troth was publicly plighted. Honor bound him to that pledge, but—in Beaverbrook's interpretation—it did not bind *her*. She could back out on the noble justification that if marriage to her meant the loss of kingship to him and of its King to England, not only would she release him, she would herself insist on being released, in the service of interests higher than her own.

On the chance that the lady would see the logic of a quick retreat, and be grateful for a plausible escape from humiliation, Beaverbrook had forehandedly drafted, on the Thursday when all Britain learned about Mrs. Simpson, an experimental lead story making these points. He wanted to clear it with her alone and get her permission to run it in the next day's *Express*; but when he asked the King if he might show her something he had written, the King demanded to see it first. Knowing that his article would get no further, Beaverbrook drew back and, with the concurrence of Monckton, Harmsworth, and Allen, tried another approach.

Though they themselves were unable to evade the King's protectiveness and reach Mrs. Simpson at the Fort, where she was sequestered, they had a perfect double agent in Lord Brownlow, who had free access there. Beaverbrook dispatched him to see her, on the pretext of offering assistance; then, when the time was ripe, he was to take her aside and beg her to renounce the marriage immediately. It was no plot, although the King would later refer to it lightly as a "conspiracy." Beaverbrook wrote, "Never at any time did I have a desire to prevent [the King's] marriage to Mrs. Simpson. The renunciation I was looking for was never intended to be a final and irrevocable decision. . . . My sole purpose was to ease the tension and to gain time." However, when Brownlow went to the Fort that day, it was unexpectedly at the King's own command; and, far from having to contrive a moment's privacy with Mrs. Simpson, he found himself charged with the extraordinary

mission of spiriting her out of England and down the
length of France to the Herman Rogerses' villa, Lou Viei,
at Cannes.

Mrs. Simpson's sudden departure was her own decision.
When she entered the drawing room after breakfast on
Thursday, December 3, the King hastily tried to push out
of view the stack of newspapers he had been skimming—
papers whose front pages were ablaze with the Simpson
story.

She had already seen them. What she had seen frightened her; she had become notorious, an American stranger
and divorcee who was imperiling the world's strongest
monarchy. In her panic she told the King that she had to
leave England that day. He agreed. She had no friends in
the United States who could put her up in the style to
which she had become accustomed, and she knew she
could expect no protection from the U.S. press. Lou Viei
was the obvious haven. There remained the question of her
escort. When the King chose Perry Brownlow, who was
delighted by both the honor and the opportunity, the "con-
spirators" could hardly believe their luck: Their man
would be not only in close proximity to the lady, but responsible for taking her out of the King's surveillance and
over to the Continent!

As a chapter in the chronicles of high romance, Mrs.
Simpson's careening, headlong flight through France might
have been plagiarized from *The Perils of Pauline*. The
Duchess of Windsor has narrated the story at length, so a
summary will suffice here. She and Lord Brownlow, then,
left the Fort in his Rolls-Royce early on the Thursday evening. His chauffeur drove; beside him, "riding shotgun,"
was Inspector Evans of Scotland Yard, charged by the
King with seeing them safely past all inconveniences and
hazards, foreign and domestic. Slipper stayed behind, as an
involuntary pledge that his former master and present mistress would one day rejoin. The reporters outside the Fort
failed to notice the Rolls. Lights dimmed, it raced to the
far side of Windsor Great Park and away. Brownlow
wasted no time in opening his campaign. He had his chauffeur stop at the roadside, then turned to Wallis: "Wouldn't
it be better if you stayed in England? Kitty [Lady Brown-
low] and I can put you up at Belton [their home at Gran-

tham, in Lincolnshire] and look after you. You'll be close
to him, only a hundred miles away. He won't yield to a
reckless desire to follow you. He can think his way through
the matter with you close by. What about it?"

Wallis hesitated for a moment, then answered, "If I stay,
and the King quits, then I'll be blamed. They'd say I was
afraid of losing him, that I'd lost heart after leaving the
Fort and stayed close, so he wouldn't forget me. I'll be
damned if I do and damned if I don't."

The car took the road again.

Meanwhile, Mrs. Simpson's own car, the Buick that Ernest had given her for their honeymoon—*not* the one that
the King had given her for Felixstowe—had been driven
from Cumberland Terrace to the Newhaven–Dieppe ferry
by Ladbrook, the King's chauffeur. The two cars made
their rendezvous, the fugitives changed over, and, as "Mr.
and Mrs. Harris," they boarded the ferry unrecognized.

So far everything had worked perfectly. But on their arrival in Dieppe, at midnight, their flimsy disguise came
apart. A customs inspector noted that the registration for
the Buick bore an electrifying name, "Mrs. Ernest Simpson"; and "Mrs. Harris," on his closer look, bore an electrifying resemblance to the Mrs. Simpson whose photographs were adorning the front pages. After the first shock
of joyful surprise, he made a profound bow and waved
them through, gallantly dispensing with formalities. Brownlow, peering back, saw him pointing out the Buick to other
passengers coming off the ferry. That tore the cover apart.
At Rouen, a few hours farther, they stopped at an inn for a
nap. When they came out, a crowd was clustered around
their car, alerted by the press.* A girl thrust a camera at
Mrs. Simpson, and Evans struck it down. Wallis cried,
"Why did you do that?"

"I am under the King's orders," Evans said. "How could
I be sure it wasn't vitriol?"

Vitriol! The word chilled her. She asked herself, "Can I
be so hated that a stranger would throw acid in my face?"

Brownlow decided that by now the press would have

---

*Several newspapers ran photographs of the car's license plate—
three letters and three numbers—but forbore to sniggle over the
fact that the letters happened to spell an indelicate French word.

surmised that they were headed for the Rogerses' villa, and would have posted lookouts along the fastest road south, Route Nationale No. 7, so he ordered Ladbrook to take a roundabout road well to the west. Meanwhile, he kept after Wallis: How much better for everyone, really, if the King stayed on the throne, and she broke off their affair!—better for herself, the King, and the Empire. She listened and wavered. Finally she agreed to beg the King to seek advice, preferably from someone outside his household and intimate circle, someone older and greatly respected, like Lord Derby. He had long been one of George V's closest friends, and his son Edward Stanley had been the King's friend since childhood. Another adviser might be the Aga Khan, whose worldly wisdom (though not whose son) the King admired.

Her first opportunity to telephone came at Evreux. They stopped at the Hôtellerie du Grand Cerf for a light lunch and, while it was being prepared, Wallis put in her call to the Fort from a booth near the bar. The King had drawn up a code-list of names for her to use in emergencies like this. He was "Mr. James" (from his previous residence in St. James's Palace); she was "Janet"; Lord Beaverbrook was "Tornado"; Baldwin, "Crutch"; the Aga, "Mr. A"; and Churchill, "WSC." Wallis had written out her message. Mr. James was not to step down, whatever befell; he must consult Tornado, Mr. A, and WSC; he must stand firm— but the crackling, sputtering static on the trans-Channel circuit defeated her. The frantic King understood only that his love was calling him from a town well off her scheduled route, and was pressing him to do something utterly unintelligible. Again and again he demanded, "Why are you in Evreux?" The louder she screamed her explanation, the louder screamed Brownlow and Inspector Evans, to keep the customers in the bar from overhearing her. The situation was impossible. Wallis had no choice but to hang up. In her haste and agitation, she left the code in the booth. The proprietor of the hotel found it and put it aside; and years later gave it to Harold Nicolson, who had chanced to stop in. Nicolson chivalrously returned it to the Duchess of Windsor, who mislaid it for good.

The fugitives pushed on for Orléans, where Wallis again

tried to telephone the King. Again it was useless; she could not get through to England, even. At Blois, they broke their trip to dine at the Hôtel de France et de Guise. Now Brownlow resumed his argument, and before long he had won his overtired, overwrought companion close to the position that Beaverbrook and the other leaders of the King's Party were hoping for: She agreed to sign a telegram urging the King to postpone his marriage plans until a good six months after his Coronation—thereby giving Britain almost a year for debating the desirability of the marriage.

Brownlow had planned to put another fifty miles behind them before stopping for the night, but he changed his mind when he saw that a heavy snow had begun to fall, and that the lobby of their hotel had filled with a score of reporters and photographers who were deploying to block all exits. He booked rooms for himself and Wallis, then called over Ladbrook and Inspector Evans and loudly "reminded" them that departure time next morning would be nine o'clock *sharp*. Lastly, he took the night concierge aisde, out of earshot, and gave him two assignments: to bring coffee to their rooms at three in the morning and to be ready to sneak them out of the hotel without rousing the pack. A tip of 10,000 francs assured his cooperation. At that time, 10,000 francs was roughly equivalent to 100 pounds or 470 dollars. Brownlow later remarked that although it was his custom to tip like a lord, this sum seemed in retrospect rather more than either his rank or the emergency called for.

Their escape, backstairs and through the kitchen, came off brilliantly. Snow and sleet made the unlighted roads doubly dangerous, but they covered the 150 miles to Moulins in time for breakfast and for Brownlow to send Wallis's telegram to Walter Monckton, and his own to Herman Rogers at Cannes, alerting him to expect them late that evening. Another hundred miles brought them to the outskirts of Lyons. The route was poorly marked, so Ladbrook drew up to ask directions. A passerby peered into the Buick. What he saw paralyzed him for an instant. Then, *"Voilà la dame!"* he shouted. *"Voilà la dame!"*

That shout would echo down the corridors of Wallis's memory. It was picked up and flung ahead of them, relayed from tongue to tongue. A hubbub of horns broke out. Cars sprinted up alongside, and more faces peered in. Happily, Brownlow's goal, the world-famous Restaurant de la Pyramide, where they would lunch, lay only a few miles ahead, at Vienne. The view-hallooing press followed them inside, while the *patronne*, Mme. Point, took Brownlow and Wallis into a private dining room for a snack so quick that it was blasphemous; and her husband, Fernand, bought time for them by serving the pack a sumptuous, torpor-inducing feast and giving his assurance that their quarry had retired to rest. But while the pack gorged, the quarry tiptoed downstairs to the kitchen (again!) and squeezed through a window opening onto the alley where the Buick waited.

That was Saturday afternoon, December 5. At two-thirty next morning, the Buick climbed a last sleet-slick hill, and its lights picked out the gates of Lou Viei. Brownlow saw a mob surge forward. "Damn it, Wallis!" he said. "Those reporters have beat us to it! We're for it!—No, wait a minute. Get down on the floor!"

She crouched, he covered her with the lap robe, and the car crawled up to the steps of the villa where the Rogerses were waiting for the friend whom they had sheltered years before in Peking. Katharine Rogers opened her arms. "*Dear* Wallis! Welcome!"

Wallis's telegram to Monckton at the Fort would go through Beaverbrook, who interpreted it as a reliable signal that Mrs. Simpson was ready to withdraw from the marriage. He was jubilant. "The future was bright with promise," he decided. "Victory seemed to be within our grasp." The Crown could still be saved for the King, and— far more to the Beaver's satisfaction—Baldwin's "seemingly impregnable position had been overturned."

Beaverbrook had good reason to be sanguine. On Friday the fourth, his and Rothermere's campaign to support the King had picked up eloquent recruits. The highly respected *News Chronicle*, a Liberal newspaper grounded in Nonconformist opinion, argued forcefully for the morganatic marriage, and the intellectual *Catholic Times* came out strongly for the King's right to marry. London and the provinces began to ring with other sympathetic voices, including those of the crackpots and extremists: Harry Pollitt, chairman of the British Communist Party; Dame Fanny Lucy Houston, the eccentric millionaire philanthropist and owner of the *Saturday Review*; and Sir Oswald Mosley, founder and leader of the British Union of Fascists, who wanted to save a King devoted to friendship with Germany. While crowds outside Buckingham Palace and Number 10 were singing "For He's a Jolly Good Fellow" and waving placards bearing such slogans as "God Save the King—from Stanley Baldwin," Mosley and his bullyboys were marching up and down Whitehall chanting:

> "One, two, three, four, five!
> We want Baldwin, dead or alive!"

Most inspiriting of all, for the "King's men" at their battle stations in Stornoway House, was the cheer that went up in the Commons when Churchill rose to ask Baldwin's "assurance that no irrevocable step will be taken before a formal statement is made to Parliament."

These scattered and spontaneous manifestations disturbed Baldwin. If they were to coalesce, they might easily result in the emergence of a King's Party, with calamitous results for his leadership, as well as for the unity of England. That he was still unsure about how best to demolish the King's petition in public was evident in his performance in Parliament that same Friday afternoon. Attlee, having first given the Prime Minister warning that he could not put the question off, rose from the Labour front bench to ask for the second time if the Government were able to make a statement in the matter occasioning so much public anxiety. For the second time, Baldwin replied he was unable to do so. He was bent on resolving the issue privately between the King and himself; toward that end, his strategy was to keep pressing the King to make up his mind—if possible, before that first weekend was out. Toward the close of their painful meeting at the Palace the evening before, Baldwin had nearly stampeded him to a decision by reminding him that some "muddle-headed busybody" might try, by intervention through the King's

Proctor, to keep Mrs. Simpson's divorce from becoming final.

As Baldwin hoped, that seedling of a nightmare took rapid root in the King's harrowed mind. All next day, Saturday the fifth, it haunted him, withdrawn at the Fort, unheeding of the affection that so many of his subjects were trying to express in the streets, the parlors, the pubs. And it alarmed Monckton, the only person close to him who was now absolutely certain that, with Wallis Simpson gone from England, nothing short of the Government's capitulation would keep him from abdicating and dashing after her. "I was desperately afraid," Monckton wrote, "that the King might give up his Throne and yet be deprived of his chance to marry Mrs. S." The Bills of Abdication were already being tentatively drafted in Whitehall. To protect the King from losing everything, Monckton asked him if he might offer a bargain to the Government: that the bill expressing his intention to renounce the throne be accompanied by one making the divorce absolute forthwith. Monckton believed that by taking the case out of the courts, there would be left "no ragged ends or possibilities for further scandal." During his negotiations with Baldwin's lieutenants, he had been led to understand that if the King would not prolong the uncertainty, the Cabinet was prepared to make "due provision" for an appropriate income and title in his retirement. The King grasped eagerly at what he hoped would be a life raft but what proved to be a straw.

The trumpet was giving an uncertain sound. The King had surrendered, at least in his soul, before Baldwin drove out to the Fort early on Friday evening, for their seventh meeting, to get what he hoped would be a positive answer. The excuse for the meeting was to advise the King formally that the Cabinet had rejected his two petitions: to broadcast and to contract a morganatic marriage. The Home Secretary, Sir John Simon, speaking for the Government in the Commons, had finally slain the morganatic idea with a masterly brief: "The lady whom [the King] marries . . . necessarily becomes Queen. She herself, therefore, enjoys all the status, rights and privileges which . . . attach to that position . . . and her children would be in direct line of succession to the Throne. The only possible way in which this result could be avoided would be by legislation dealing with a particular case. His Majesty's Government are not prepared to introduce such legislation. Moreover, the matters . . . are of common concern to the Commonwealth . . . and such a change could not be effected without the assent of all the Dominions. I am satisfied . . . that this assent would not be forthcoming."

None of this surprised the King; he had been reconciled to the loss of both projects. When the Prime Minister had disposed of these points, he begged the King to reconsider the whole question of marriage and abdication—"the prayer of His Majesty's servants" was that he would. In any case, could not the King, mindful of the anxiety and strains being experienced not only by Britain but by the Empire as well—"a paralyzing preoccupation," wrote G. M. Young,[1] "had settled over business and private life, and it could be dispelled by only one man"—could he not give the Prime Minister an early answer, perhaps now, before he started back to London?

The King said only, as he rose to end the interview, that he would let the Prime Minister have his decision when he came to it.

Before surrendering his last chip, he wanted Monckton to bargain for the sanction of an immediate marriage. Monckton had already arranged to explore the "two bills" scheme with Baldwin's lieutenants next morning. If the Government would agree to make the divorce absolute immediately, that would be a consoling brand plucked from the burning.

Baldwin had barely taken his leave when Winston Churchill whirled up at the Fort, to dine. Walter Monckton, George Allen, and Ulick Alexander, Keeper of the King's Privy Purse, were also at the table. Early in their negotiations, Baldwin had frowned on the King having formal consultations with Churchill, since he was not a Minister of the Crown and therefore not a proper source of advice. However, Baldwin had finally withdrawn his objections, and Churchill descended on the Fort like a relief column, with banners flying, arriving to raise a siege. Any dinner at which Churchill was present was likely to be memorable; this one was especially so. The man who four years thence would rally a defeated Britain with the strong

cry, "We shall never surrender!" was inspired to give a
dress rehearsal of the same splendid rhetoric, in an effort to
keep his King from surrendering. "We must have time for
the big battalions to mass," Churchill told him. "We may
win. We may not." Be patient, his advice went. Retire to
Windsor Castle! Summon the Beefeaters! Raise the draw-
bridge! Close the gates! And dare Baldwin to drag you out!

Churchill was back at the Fort on Saturday evening,
bristling with confidence. Between dinners, he had issued
an eloquent public statement that was a plea for "time and
patience," for "chivalry and compassion." He also had
written for the King's eyes only a longer and more passionate appeal not to abdicate. In yet another message, he appealed to Baldwin not to press the King further: To expect
a decision from a man "in no fit state" to make one would
be "cruel and wrong." All the fine words went for nothing.
That very morning Monckton carried to Whitehall, along
with the request for a special divorce bill, the answer that
Baldwin was poised for: The King was ready to abdicate
and would himself so inform the Prime Minister at the
Fort that afternoon.

Sometime in the morning, the King finally remembered
to notify Beaverbrook of what he had told Baldwin. He
was a trifle late. Baldwin, hopeful that the King's decision
to abdicate would induce Beaverbrook to silence the bugle
of the *Daily Express*, had already dispatched Sir John Simon to Stornoway House with notice of what impended.
But no one remembered to tell Churchill until an hour before noon, when Beaverbrook went to his flat in Westminster to report that the King was leaving the field. "Our cock
won't fight!" Beaverbrook said.

Churchill, wholly committed to the attack, refused to believe his friend. Smacking his lips and thumping his thighs,
he read aloud the press statement he was about to fire off
at Baldwin.

"No dice" were Beaverbrook's parting words. Even
when the King confirmed the dismal news that evening at
the Fort, Churchill still refused to give up.

Baldwin had meanwhile come to the Fort and gone. Before leaving London, he had examined the "two bills"
proposition in a general way, Monckton having outlined it
in the morning during the course of a private talk at the

Windham Club with Baldwin's right bower, Sir Horace Wilson, and his parliamentary private secretary, Maj. Thomas Dugdale. They agreed with Monckton that the King deserved consideration, and Baldwin was no less favorably disposed when Monckton reviewed the terms for him in the King's presence. In fact, Baldwin even promised to resign if the Cabinet rejected the divorce bill.

Next morning, Sunday, Monckton was back at Number 10 for the Cabinet's decision. For two hours he cooled his heels outside Sir Horace Wilson's office before being invited into the Cabinet Room adjoining. The dozen frozen faces that confronted him around the green baize table told the story: The "two-bill" project had foundered. Because it "smacked of a bargain where there should be none," the ministers would not have it. They also rejected the special divorce bill, because it would "affront the moral sensibility of the nation."

One minister asked Monckton what the King's response would be. Monckton, taken aback by the Cabinet ruling, murmured that the King would undoubtedly need time for further reflection—possibly weeks. The ministers were as practical as they were principled. Baldwin said that the King must decide before Christmas. His colleagues objected that the country could not safely wait even that long; the protracted uncertainty was already hurting Christmas shopping, and there was risk of panic on the Stock Exchange. Baldwin, properly, took Monckton aside after the meeting to say that he would resign if the King wanted to hold him to the promise he had made at the Fort the evening before. And the King in his turn, properly, nevertheless sent Monckton back to Number 10 to say that he appreciated Baldwin's effort in his behalf and that he was standing on his word: He would abdicate as soon as the essential legal instruments were in hand.

His decision came none too soon. The several days of his dilly-dallying had not only divided England over his right to marry, but had splintered the divorce opinions. As Malcolm Muggeridge wrote, there were "the romantically inclined who saw the King as one who must choose between love and a kingdom, and chose love; Socialists who saw in him an incipient Fascist leader, and other Socialists who held that he was being victimized for his proletarian sympathies; persons themselves in matrimonial difficulties whose hearts went out to a fellow-sufferer, and persons fearful of matrimonial difficulties whose hearts hardened against one who might by his example encourage a more lenient attitude towards divorce; the snobs who, even though they might never have occasion to, could not bring themselves to envisage curtseying to Mrs. Simpson; and the anti-snobs, fond of quoting Burns, who would welcome a Queen without rank's guinea stamp, and whose mother had once, it was said, taken lodgers in Baltimore."

Then, over the weekend, as if a clearing wind had blown across England, opinion hardened against the King. The change was instantly perceptible in the House of Commons, as the members returned from their constituencies in the provinces. When Churchill rose to make yet another plea on the King's behalf, there were hot, impatient shouts of "Sit down! Shut up!" *The Times* called it "the most striking rebuff in modern parliamentary history." Baldwin's lined face and heavy-lidded eyes showed no emotion while he watched the silencing of the adversary he most feared. Only three days before, after agreeing to the King's seeing Churchill, he had confessed to the Cabinet, "I have made my first blunder." But the weekend's mysterious reversal in British thinking proved that he had not blundered. After the House responded on Monday as Baldwin had predicted it would, his friend Thomas Jones congratulated him on his prescience. The Prime Minister remarked, "I have always believed in the weekend. But how they do it I don't know. I suppose they talk to the stationmaster." His sense of triumph showed in a faint smile.

It was the womanly distaste for Mrs. Simpson's matrimonial past, and the stain of scandal on her incomplete divorce, that doomed the King's Party. A country girl condensed the feeling into a neatly balanced sentence: "It's a pity he can't marry the woman he loves, and a pity he doesn't love a better woman." A Paris taxi driver told an English fare, "As long as your King is going to buy a *tacot* (jalopy), he should pick one with less mileage on it." A lady M.P. spoke for British women in harsher words when she said, "We are not going to acknowledge two sorts of women, one a wife, but a wife not good enough to be a Queen." And *The Times* savagely flogged the dead donkey

that the morganatic marriage proposal had become: "The
Constitution is to be amended in order that she may carry
in solitary prominence the brand of unfitness for the
Queen's Throne."

Something even more ruinous to the King's case than
the moralistic view had begun to yeast in the British character: Wit was debasing the solemn affair into a near farce.
The first quips were flickering and ricocheting from cocktail party to Stock Exchange, and from club to pub and
vice versa.

> Seen the new play? *The Unimportance of Being Er-
> nest.*

> Talk about being busted in the service! The King,
> who was once Admiral of the Fleet, is now third mate
> on an American tramp.

> There's absolutely nothing between the King and Mrs.
> Simpson—*nothing*, not even a sheet.

The same vulgarity had been printed about his grandfather
and Mrs. Langtry. Even children took up the irreverence
and began to chant:

> "Hark, the herald angels sing,
> 'Mrs. Simpson's pinched our King!' "

Even so, the King and the Simpsons were fortunate that
they lived in the 1930's and not at the turn of the eighteenth century, the heyday of the scurrilous broadside. Far
better a few quips passed from lip to ear than peddlers
hawking lewd verses by "Peter Pindar" (perhaps straining
to rhyme "W-ll-s" with "B-ck-ngh-m P-l-ce") and bawdy
cartoons by Rowlandson, Bunbury, and Gillray (perhaps
showing Ernest blindfolded, while his wife cuddles the
King, over some such forthright title as "The K-ng and his
D-xy").

Here the political side of the Abdication narrative
should by rights have ended. The wits and romancers had
taken over; Monckton and the Cabinet were drawing up
the Article of Abdication; in spirit, the reign of Edward

VIII had closed on Saturday, December 5, even though a small bank of partisans from the Fort and the Bryanston Court sets refused to believe that their cause was lost. On Monday morning, their leader and standard-bearer, George Hunter, rang Mike Scanlon at the Embassy and submitted that, true, the situation was desperate, but it was not beyond hope of salvage; would he and Gladys come to dinner that evening and help them try to find some solution? They accepted, with misgivings. Mrs. Merryman was there, along with several others whom Scanlon no longer remembers. Their first proposal was that Mrs. Merryman redouble her efforts to draw from Wallis a gesture that would relieve the King of any obligation to her. Mrs. Merryman protested that she had already done everything in her power towards just that, but without avail. Here more recruits came in, friends of the Hunters. Scanlon said, "Everybody in the room was a King's man. All we needed were rapiers, plumed hats, and long cloaks, to personify Fealty Afire." Presently he was astonished to find himself being urged to fly to Cannes and take command of the situation on the spot. He begged off, convinced that it would merely waste his time and Wallis's. When the discussion finally broke up, far past midnight, Mrs. Merryman was exhausted and distraught, and—just as Scanlon had expected—nothing had been accomplished.

But even as George Hunter's cohorts were laying down their arms, there had been an extraordinary development in Cannes. After hours of a drama which deserved to be titled *Simpson Agonistes,* Lord Brownlow and Herman Rogers had persuaded Wallis to beg the King publicly not to give up the throne. The following statement, written largely by Brownlow, was read to the reporters waiting outside Villa Lou Viei: "Mrs. Simpson, throughout the last few weeks, has invariably wished to avoid any action or proposal which would hurt or damage His Majesty or the Throne. Today her attitude is unchanged, and she is willing, if such action would resolve the problem, to withdraw forthwith from a situation that has been rendered both unhappy and untenable." In London, the statement created a sensation in the few remaining precincts where hope of averting abdication persisted. The quality newspapers that were taking their line from Baldwin, knowing that the

King had passed the point of no return, dismissed the dispatch as an interesting though puzzling irrelevance. Dawson of *The Times* printed it without comment, but appended directly beneath it an item—otherwise of no consequence—which was as close to a slur on Mrs. Simpson as he dared come, yet which delighted those able to appreciate the juxtaposition: "Thelma Viscountess Furness arrived at Southampton in the liner *Queen Mary* yesterday from New York." Tom Driberg, a columnist on the *Express,* thereupon charged *The Times* with "feline malice and vulgar frivolity that can scarcely have been paralleled in the worst of the gutter press."

Mrs. Simpson's apparent renunciation proved to be nothing of the sort, when one perceived what was missing from the substance. Brownlow had tried to make her realize from the start of their journey that only one action could now keep the King from abdicating: her unequivocal statement that she would not marry him and was giving up her residence in England. Brownlow urged her again and again to make the statement *at once,* before the process of abdication moved through the legal machinery past recall. But she was loath to withdraw by her own will; and lacking her flat renunciation, the King could not and would not in honor release her. The language of the statement— the strongest that Brownlow could extract—was the subject of agonized telephone conversations between Cannes and the Fort during that fateful weekend. The King objected at first, then relented, according to Sir Edward Peacock, because he realized that her gesture was hollow: "It would divert criticism from her to him, which he wanted." The King decided to let the statement pass. His own mind was made up.

The frail scheme foundered. So did a last-hour attempt by Goddard, her solicitor, to persuade her to withdraw the divorce action and thus block the possibility of immediate marriage. Goddard (and the Government) also learned on Monday the seventh that a citizen's action calling upon the King's Proctor to intervene and keep the decree from being made absolute was imminent, and would probably be accompanied by an affidavit supplying "evidence" of collusion. Goddard promptly informed Monckton, who agreed that he should go to Cannes and acquaint his client with the threat. But first, Goddard motored to the Fort to clear the trip with the King. The King ordered him to stay away from Mrs. Simpson; he was sure that neither the Proctor, being his own official, nor any private complainant could lawfully hale him into court, let alone cite alleged misconduct to halt the divorce. Baldwin, however, conceived a notion that the threat might be exploited, if Mrs. Simpson's statement represented her genuine desire to keep the King on the throne. Sir John Simon took the same view. As a result, Goddard found himself summoned to Downing Street directly on his return from the Fort. When he entered the Prime Minister's office, Baldwin was brooding over the press report from Cannes. He asked Goddard what he made of it. Goddard said he had not been in touch with Mrs. Simpson; her motives puzzled him, too. The renunciation, Baldwin observed, was hardly "categorical." Goddard must see Mrs. Simpson at once, to determine her intentions and warn her of the danger of intervention. Baldwin would take responsibility for countermanding the King's orders.

It was already past the dinner hour. Goddard collected his toilet articles and a few extra clothes for the trip and presently was on his way to Croydon, expecting to take off for Cannes at two o'clock next morning, Tuesday. The airplane provided for him was one normally used by the Prime Minister's couriers. It was small and flimsy, and that night it was dangerously overloaded to boot, since Goddard, who was in his middle fifties and mindful of the strain that a long, uncomfortable, and hazardous night flight would impose on his weak heart, had brought along his personal physician, Dr. William Douglas Kirkwood, in addition to a junior member of his legal staff. At Croydon, they found that the weather was too stormy to permit 'a takeoff in darkness. By daylight, at seven, it was still raining; worse, fog was settling in; but Goddard did not dare delay longer. They had barely crossed the Channel when engine trouble forced them down for the first of several times. The air stayed bumpy; the overcast stayed thick. When they finally approached Cannes, the airport was socked in, and they were waved back to Marseilles, one hundred miles behind them.

Goddard tottered off at once to notify Brownlow of their

arrival, only to get—instead of the praise and sympathy he felt he deserved—a furious reprobation. It appeared that the press had spotted him and his two companions at Croydon; and when investigation established that Dr. Kirkwood had once been attached to a London maternity hospital, it was instantly assumed that he was an obstetrician and the other man his anesthetist. Word was flashed to the newsmen keeping vigil at Lou Viei. Their further assumption, incredible but inescapable, they had brought to Brownlow for confirmation. His rage was still white-hot when poor Goddard telephoned. He had managed to announce that he would hire a car and drive over early next morning, when Brownlow broke in to shout a series of emphatic orders: Under no circumstances—he repeated it: *under no circumstances*—were any of the party to be carrying bags, briefcases, satchels, parcels, or anything whatsoever that might be suspected of concealing obstetrical instruments. Is that clear? Yes. Is it *absolutely* clear? Yes. (There was also speculation that Goddard's mission, assigned him by the Royal Family no less, was to retrieve Queen Alexandra's jewels, which Mrs. Simpson was rumored to have taken with her.)

So, on Wednesday morning the ninth, poor Goddard, his large face paler than ever, presented himself at Lou Viei; he passed Brownlow's scowling inspection, and they joined Mrs. Simpson in the drawing room. The critical point, Goddard said, was this: If she decided to call off the divorce suit with the private intention of reinstating it at some later date, he had to warn her that it could be "untidy." Before giving her answer, Mrs. Simpson telephoned to the Fort, and returned to instruct Goddard to let the divorce proceed. He bowed and left.

One last testing remained for her. That evening, she and Brownlow had another long talk, on the way back to Cannes from dinner in Monte Carlo. He told her that she was at her Rubicon. If she were serious about keeping the King from abdicating, she could not let another moment slip by; she would have to cut herself off from him completely—sail for some far-distant land at once, before he could overtake her. In her exhaustion, she seemed to accept the argument; she would return to China; the long voyage would interpose an obstacle that the King could not cope with. She allowed Brownlow, who had volunteered to see her safely into oblivion, to advance her plans to the point of hiring a car to take them to Genoa on the morrow, booking her a stateroom on a ship for Shanghai, and drafting (again with Rogers's help) a brave farewell to the King, to England, and to love.

But it was not in her temperament to leave the stage without the classical parting. Once the message was in hand, she had to call the King and read it to him, tearfully. He told her it was too late now—there could be no turning back; he would be gone from the throne, and from England, in twenty-four hours. He had something to read to her, too: a sentence that George Allen, who was helping draw up the general settlements, wrote out for him as he talked: "The only conditions upon which I can stay here are if I renounce you for all time." Allen repeated to her the same momentous words. The King then took over the telephone, and what she said caused him to say, "The void between us disappeared."

"For all time" was too long for her.

The narratives of the various principals deal delicately with the real purpose of Goddard's excursion. Was it to frighten Mrs. Simpson into abandoning the divorce action, under threat of a ruinous scandal? The King thought so, but for obvious reasons never made a point of it. If so, was it at the Government's behest? Beaverbrook suspects this. Goddard told him later that the direct question he put to Mrs. Simpson in Cannes was one the Prime Minister wanted answered: "Is it wise to continue with the divorce proceedings and obtain the decree absolute?" Mrs. Simpson claimed that Goddard asked her authority for recession—"I believe [that] was the term he used"—of the divorce action. Was the Government covertly involved in the intervention? That was Beaverbrook's residual suspicion, but he could never prove it; and in an account which Goddard wrote for Beaverbrook, he saw to it that a fog enveloped his role.

CHAPTER 11
"I Don't Think
I Could Have Changed His Mind"

Walter Monckton disagreed with Lady Diana Cooper's opinion that Wallis's influence over the King was "absolute." He believed that there was nothing she could have done to keep him from abdicating. "The easy view," he wrote, "is that she should have made him give her up, but I never knew any man whom it would have been harder to get rid of." That was her explanation, too. Again and again she protested, "You don't understand! The King would never have let me go. He would have followed me wherever I went."

She wanted to believe that it was her innocence of British psychology that lulled her doubts, disarmed her, and led her unsuspectingly to catastrophe. Her recollections of the course of events were seldom the same, but here is what she said over two decades later:

"It's possible that if I had stayed in England instead of going to France, I might have persuaded the King not to abdicate, but I don't think I could ever have changed his mind. The truth is, he never told me until the storm broke in the press how serious was the issue between him and Baldwin. He assured me that he could manage things. I was not to worry. He would be crowned, everything would come out all right, he and I would be together. It all sounded so certain, so easy.

"I never dreamed I could be Queen. Let me be positive about that. The idea didn't rhyme with anything. It would have been preposterous—the King as Defender of the Faith, the Queen a divorced woman. There were ways around the Queen problem. Morganatic marriage was one. But there seemed to be no hurry to settle the problem. The

King was matter-of-fact about it all. Then the thing hit. For me the turning point was seeing my picture on the front pages. I was hurt deeply and I was desperate. I told the King I couldn't stay at the Fort. At first he tried to keep me from going. He said I was unduly upset. But I said I had to leave; my position had become impossible. 'I am leaving England at once and I intend to go as far from this country as I can go.' He said, 'Wherever you go, I shall follow and I shall find you.' We were both in a daze. Neither of us was thinking well. . . .

"Yet while I think I did the right, the only, thing, I was to realize all too soon that the minute I put my foot inside France, I had ceased to exist, so far as my being able to affect events was concerned. The telephone circuits in France roared with static. I couldn't make myself understood. Nor was the King in a mood to listen to me. He was hard-driven himself. The people around him were pulling him apart. A time came when he could endure the pulling and hauling no longer. His one thought was to get away, away from the Prime Minister, away from the Government, the newspapers, his own family.

"He could be influenced and persuaded, but it had to be done a certain way; his reason had to be appealed to. Try to force him, and he'll slide from your grasp. He'll walk out of the room and shut the door behind him, and that's the end of it, until he lets you know what he has decided by himself. He is *Royal*, you know. Royals are not like other people. Royals don't wrestle with problems; they only acknowledge them. The Duke can be very kingly, abdicated or not.

"Where Baldwin, where the Cabinet, erred, was in pushing the King into a decision. If Baldwin hadn't pushed him so hard, the idea of marriage might have gone from his mind. He had a strong sense of duty. He had worked hard for Britain. He wanted to do the right thing, but he was new in the Kingship. He was trying to change from being the Prince of Wales, with all the accustomed independence and privacy, and becoming the Monarch. He was in love with me, and it saddened and angered him that others disapproved. He never reacted well to criticism. He wasn't used to it. He felt he was being censured, like a wilful boy. This infuriated him.

"Could I have kept him from doing what he did? The thought haunts me still. There was a time when, if someone wiser than I was about things British had come to me and told me what was at stake—had told me why the Dominions, the Church, the gentry, the whole Establishment were acting as they did—I might have gone to the King and said, 'Let's stop it.' But no one ever came forward to tell me. In Cannes, I could only say no to a man who wasn't listening.

"Somewhere I missed a warning sign. Because the King had convinced me that I understood him as no one else had done before, I was deceived into thinking I understood England. And the fawning and kowtowing of the people who flocked around because I could bring them into the Prince of Wales's circle, then into the King's, made me think I had found the key to English character.

"Perhaps my worst mistake was in leaving England. Yet as I left, I was sure in my own mind that the English people—the Establishment—would never let him go; they would work on him and hold him. He himself seemed glad to see me leave the Fort. He kept saying that last morning, 'I must fight this thing out alone.' He didn't want me involved. He also kept his family out of it. He moved to the Fort because he didn't want the issue to be decided by the mob in the streets of London. He said to me afterwards, 'I was alone on the bridge. I even sent my navigators below.'

"That's the way it happened. If my British friends drew away at the end, if the British Government ignored me, they at least paid me the compliment of not trying to buy me off. It was the only insult that was *not* tried."

That is how the Duchess of Windsor explained the loss of the throne—a loss that she might have averted had she only taken Perry Brownlow's advice when they stopped to hash things over on the road to Newhaven. She had been overpowered by the King's love; and in her ignorance of English ways, she did not have the sense to move in time to prevent the disaster. Lady Monckton, who saw much of her after the Abdication, says, "She would say over and over again, whenever the talk returned to the Abdication, that she had never imagined the outcome. It all blew up with a speed and violence that undid her. She once told me, 'It came upon me with devastating force that I didn't know England very well, and the English not at all.'"

Lord Beaverbrook also believed that the battle was lost because the King isolated himself from all influential sources of help. Reflecting on the situation that developed after the King insisted on pushing the morganatic proposal, Beaverbrook had come to this judgment: The King "had mixed more freely with the people than any Heir Apparent before, but he had hardly mixed at all with politicians. . . . He was now facing a grave political problem quite unprepared for the task, and he was neglecting to follow the advice of his own counsellors and was also neglecting to consult sage and experienced friends to whom he might have turned. . . . He was anxious about the wrong things—all of his energies should have been devoted to the main issue, which was the struggle to remain on the Throne and be married in due time. . . . But he was preoccupied . . . principally with protecting Mrs. Simpson from hostile publicity, or indeed from publicity of any kind, at whatever cost or sacrifice. . . . There were suicidal errors of judgment."

The Archbishop of Canterbury, hovering in the wings, also thought he might have helped stave off the Abdication. "I am disposed to think," he confided to his diary, "I might have written to King Edward VIII, if only to liberate my conscience." He chose not to, and no doubt wisely: "Almost certainly this would have evoked, even if any reply had been given, the sort of slight which *I* personally would have understood, but to which the Archbishop of Canterbury ought not to be exposed." The Primate, according to his biographer, J. G. Lockhart, made "repeated" efforts through third parties for a meeting, but the King kept the door closed. On the issue of Mrs. Simpson, he was given to understand, only the Prime Minister "had a right to speak to the King and advise him." Although Dr. Lang was aware of what was going on, and was kept advised by the Prime Ministers, by members of the Royal Family, and by his friend Geoffrey Dawson, he remained offstage throughout the King's ordeal. All the same, there is reason to believe that the King would have done better if he had permitted the marriage question to crystallize as a moral choice, and had sought the counsel of his Primate.

The Archbishop let it be known much later that he would have conducted the Coronation service even if the King had married Mrs. Simpson before. He had arrived privately—and reluctantly—at this decision, according to Lockhart, on the theory that for him to refuse would mean retiring from his great office and yielding the leadership of the Church to another prelate, of "fumbling and suspected" hands. The King, to his disadvantage, never sensed this strange ambivalence in the Primate's character.

Bernard Rickatson-Hatt, who, after Ernest Simpson, knew Wallis probably better than any of the embroiled political strategists, believed that the whole episode was quite unnecessary; it was a case of the eternal triangle getting askew, all because of the "obstinacy" of the King. Rickatson-Hatt's friendship was reinforced, if anything, by the social ostracism which Simpson had to endure as the crisis mounted. He and Ernest saw a lot of each other; he was convinced, and Ernest was disposed to agree, that but for the King's insistence on having her completely to himself, the affair would have run its course, without breaking up the Simpson marriage.

Rickatson-Hatt was probably right about the lady, but Baldwin was certainly the one who best understood the King. The King lost his job, and Baldwin saved his, and this outcome baffled Churchill and Beaverbrook, along with Baldwin's not inconsiderable body of critics. If it was indeed Baldwin's aim from the start to push the King from the throne and clear the way for the Yorks, he must be credited with having brought off a masterly feat. He transformed an inherently moral issue into a political one, and on that terrain his superb tactical skills prevailed. As Winston Churchill had properly argued, no constitutional question had arisen—there could be none until marriage became a practical possibility on the completion of the divorce, in April 1937. Yet simply by taking skillful advantage of the King's impatience, by making it appear that the pressure was from the King on the Cabinet, not the other way around, Baldwin succeeded in fostering the illusion of a constitutional crisis forced by an obstinate and wayward monarch. On that murky but troubling non-event, he was able to rally the Dominion Governments, lure the Liberal and Socialist opposition into a tacit agreement not to lend themselves, if called upon, to an alternate government, and thus to solidify parliamentary opinion on his side.

Yet even at this remove, with the memoirs and papers of most of the principals in public view, it is impossible to be certain about Baldwin's guiding motives. Was it the King he wanted to be rid of? Or was it to rid the King of Mrs. Simpson? Monckton, who dealt with Baldwin throughout the crisis and hid nothing from him, was convinced that he wanted the King to stay and would have gladly reversed the abdication process at the last hour, if the King had only been willing to give up Mrs. Simpson as a wife. On the Tuesday that Goddard was making his slow and dangerous way to Cannes, the Prime Minister asked Monckton to inform the King of his wish to come out to the Fort that evening for a long talk—better still, for dinner, if the King would have him. He wanted to make one last try at persuading him not to abdicate, and he was prepared to spend the night helping him come to terms with his conscience—"He must wrestle with himself in a way he has never done before, and if he will let me, I will help him. We may have to see the night through together."

Baldwin's biographer heard "something of the old Wesleyan strain" in these words. In Beaverbrook's view, Baldwin was "a man of pretenses"; he could be two-faced. He would say later of this last call on his King, "Only time I was ever frightened. I thought he might change his mind." For the Prime Minister's admirers, this was "the red earth showing through also"—the shrewd side. To the King's friends, Baldwin's self-invited visit to the Fort had a sinister motive: If he was sincere about helping the King to exorcise his grotesque passion, he was also bent on casting out the King with the sin. Monckton, trying to walk the narrow line between the two principals, was himself unsure about Baldwin's purpose. They drove out to the Fort late that afternoon, cramped in the rear seat of the Prime Minister's small car, with his parliamentary private secretary, Sir Thomas Dugdale. For some mysterious reason, Baldwin had told his driver to go at a snail's pace. Monckton would long remember the tedious trip, with Baldwin, strangely nervous, pulling on his pipe, humming tuneless little snatches, cracking and snapping his fingers, with a quick flip of the hand past his right ear, and relapsing into long silences, while the car, its windows closed against the night chill, filled with a smoky fug.

Baldwin had puffed his pipe even while calling on Cosmo Lang to offer him the Archbishopric of Canterbury. "Different though he [Baldwin] was from Edward," wrote Brian Inglis in *Abdication,* "they shared one common experience, a childhood under a stern Victorian father. . . . Stanley as a boy was much in awe of his father, and he remained so most of his life, finding the same difficulty of communication that Edward was to find with George V. One consequence . . . of this strange inhibited childhood was nervous strains which 'left their mark in the twitching of the facial muscles . . . and a habit of involuntarily snapping his fingers which conveyed to the observant a revealing comment on the public image he managed to impose on his followers'—that public image being a placid, pipe-smoking countryman, always in command of his emotions."[1]

Baldwin seemed to be dreading the meeting, perhaps from fear that the King might reverse everything. Monckton, too, was fearful, though not about a change of mind; he knew that the King's resolution was set in concrete. It was his physical condition that was disquieting. He was exhausted when he set out from London that forenoon, and he looked even more so as he came forward to greet his guests. He made two facts plain, instantly but politely: He wanted to be spared further argument, and—having caught sight of a valise being brought in—he did not propose for Mr. Baldwin to spend the night under his roof; not only because he wished to be spared Baldwin's company, but also because he suspected the Prime Minister would make use of the hospitality in his own account of their transactions to show that he had labored to the last hour to bring a wayward monarch to his senses and back to his duty on the throne. Then he led them into the octagonal drawing room. The curtains had not been closed, and through the tall windows they could see the garden in the moonlight and the loom of the woods beyond. The King sat facing the fire, Baldwin on a sofa, and Monckton on a chair between them. Baldwin was not dismayed by the King's stony-faced rejection of further counsel. "He returned to the charge with renewed vigor," Monckton said, "and, I thought, put the case even better than before." His brief was wasted. When Baldwin finished, the King shook his head: Exhaustion did not affect his obduracy. He excused himself, saying that he would rejoin them presently in the drawing room for a drink before dinner.

Two of his brothers, York and Kent along with Ulick Alexander, Sir Edward Peacock, and George Allen, had been summoned to spark the cheerless table, which otherwise would have been occupied only by four men with nerves drawn dangerously taut. When the King reappeared, it was as if the Fort's amenities included a hot-and-cold Fountain of Youth, and he had bathed in it. Monckton was astounded by "his boyish smile and a good fresh color." He was wearing his favorite evening clothes, a white kilt, and from its brightness he seemed to take his mood. Following his lead, the table was presently "rippling with light conversation," Monckton recorded, yet the King kept a "careful eye to see that his guests were being looked after."

For York, only three days from kingship, it was "a dinner I am never likely to forget. . . . My brother was the soul of the party, telling the P.M. things I am sure he never heard before about the unemployed centers [for the Welsh miners]. I whispered to W.M., 'And this is the man we're going to lose!'" York was on Baldwin's right. Monckton remembers him turning toward his brother and exclaiming, "Look at him! We simply cannot let him go!" And Peacock remembers him saying afterward, "I would never have been able to do that. I can't do this job. . . ."

Baldwin, Dugdale, and Peacock left for London as soon as the table rose, at nine-thirty. Baldwin had no reason now to regret his visit to the Fort; his apprehensions had proved groundless. He told a friend, "The King had given his word, and that was enough." He would even tell the Cabinet next day that "The King appeared happy and gay, as if he were looking forward to his honeymoon."

York left at eleven-thirty, and the others turned in soon afterward, all except Monckton, who stayed up to see the King safely in bed. The strain on his emotions was showing through now. His face was drawn and pale; his hands shook. He impressed Monckton as being on the brink of disintegration. There was no suggestion that he was having second thoughts about the wisdom of his decision—"no wavering, no looking backward." Rather, the probability was that he had suddenly, belatedly, become aware of the disaster about to engulf his personal affairs, and was stunned, even frightened, by the realization that he had no idea what awaited him, except that he had to leave England. His alarm infected Monckton; might the King, exhausted and desperate, kill himself in the night? Leaving him brooding before the fire, Monckton excused himself and, with the help of the Valet Crisp, searched the bedroom, to assure themselves that no gun was temptingly at hand. They found none.

Lurid stories were abroad. One had the King exploding with rage and hurling an inkpot at Stanley Baldwin during one of their interviews. It was widely gossiped that York had refused the job; that Queen Mary had agreed to act as regent for Princess Elizabeth; that the King had locked himself into the Fort, dead drunk, and that the senior physicians attached to the royal household had been summoned to certify his unfitness to conduct State affairs. *Time* dared to print: "So much brandy and soda was continually taken by His Majesty during the early stages of the crisis, particularly after the steadying influence of Mrs. Simpson was removed, that . . . it was necessary once to apply the stomach pump (Reportedly on December 4, by Lord Horder, the King's physician.)"[2] Though there is no word of truth in the whole passage, Upton Sinclair, a distant cousin of Wallis's on her Montague side, quoted it in his *The Cup of Fury* and introduced it with "He ruled the whole British Empire, but could not quite rule himself. He was known . . . as 'a brandy man.' "[3] Walter Monckton's reminiscences firmly dismiss this irresponsible slander: "There were more half-consumed whiskies poured than I have ever seen. . . . Among all the great men who saw us constantly through those days, I never heard of one who thought that either the King or myself had been drinking." Stanley Baldwin agreed; he told Lady Airlie that the King was "absolutely sober, though certainly in a very exalted state. Just a romantic boy, all for marriage."

Churchill, dining at the Fort on the fourth and fifth, had seen him in a state that was the very opposite of exalted: "He appeared to me to be under a very great strain and very near the breaking point," he wrote. "He had two marked and prolonged blackouts, in which he completely lost the thread of his conversation."

The emotional crisis passed overnight. When the King came downstairs on Wednesday the ninth, after breakfast in his room, he was again in control of himself. It was well; there was work to do. That morning, his ministers had expressed their reluctance "to believe that Your Majesty's resolve is irrevocable, and still venture to hope that before Your Majesty pronounces any formal decision, Your Majesty may be pleased to reconsider an intention which must so deeply distress and so vitally affect all Your Majesty's subjects." The King wrote out in his own hand an eighteen-word reply: "His Majesty has given the subject his further consideration but regrets he is unable to alter his decision." As the reigning monarch, there being no higher authority in the realm, he also supplied Parliament with a paper conveying his royal assent to his own Act of Abdication.

The ancillary business connected with liquidating the kingship fell to the solicitors. The King would later describe the very private, necessarily hurried negotiations over family real estate, capital, furniture, *objets d'art*, and other possessions as resembling "not so much a receivership or a bankruptcy, as a kind of fire sale." Though he was ceasing to be King, he would remain head of the House of Windsor. The principal family properties, the most valuable being the great estates of Sandringham and Balmoral, had descended to him, the eldest son, as they had to his father. During these last days, negotiations for transferring them to York occupied the brothers' solicitors. Clive Wigram was brought out of retirement to advise York on these transactions and on his preparations for assuming and exercising the kingship. Walter Monckton and George Allen continued to represent the King.

These complicated deals had the happy side effect of reuniting the two brothers. From childhood through youth they had been extraordinarily close, the older shielding the younger and weaker from the harshness of a father who had small liking and less respect for either of them. Now, in the brief interval of warmed-over mutual affection, it was the younger who tried to save the elder—"Because he loved him and admired him and trusted him," Colin Buist said, forty years later. "And when the elder became King, the younger's love and trust deepened. David would make a *fine* King! He could do no wrong! To the end of his life, George the Sixth never understood what had made David do what he did."

After the meeting in their mother's presence at Marlborough House the previous Thursday, the King shut his brother out for four tension-filled days. They did not meet again until Monday evening, and then only because Bertie, who had spent the weekend at the Royal Lodge so as to be close by, pressed the staff at the Fort to let him come over, until they consented. His simple account of the evening follows: "My brother rang me at 10 minutes to 7.0 p. to say, 'Come and see me after dinner,' I said, 'No, I will come and see you at once. . . .' The awful and ghastly suspense of waiting was over. I found him pacing up and down the room, and he told me his decision that he would go. I went back to the Royal Lodge for dinner and returned to the Fort later. I felt having got there I was not going to leave. As he is my eldest brother I had to be there to try and help him in his hour of need."

The following evening was the dinner with the Prime Minister. Early next afternoon, Wednesday the ninth, David visited Bertie at the Royal Lodge. Their mother and sister drove out from London to join them, and an odd thought crossed the King's mind: En route to Windsor on the Great West Road, they must have passed Monckton en route to London with the draft of the Instrument of Abdication. He told them of the arrangements in progress: The succession would pass formally to Bertie on Friday, and he himself would leave England that night. In the King's account, his mother felt for him, prompting her to say with tenderness, "And to me, the worst thing is that you won't be able to see her for so long." Queen Mary's diary for the day, by contrast, was laconic: "At 1:30 with Mary to meet David (on business) at the Royal Lodge. Back before 5."

Walter Monckton made three round trips between the Fort and Whitehall that Wednesday, shuttling the successive drafts of the documents between the principals. A thick fog had settled in the Thames Valley, slowing traffic and making driving dangerous. Harassed though he was, he nevertheless called at Marlborough House, on his final trip back to the Fort late that evening, to show Queen Mary and the Duke of York the draft of the Instrument of Abdication which the King would sign in the morning. The document was one which York, according to Pope-Hennessy, "regarded with revulsion and his mother read with incredulity." Queen Mary wrote in her diary, "Mr. W. Monckton brought [Bertie] and me the paper drawn up for David's abdication of the Throne of this Empire because he wishes to marry Mrs. Simpson!!!!!" (Unlike her second son, Queen Mary did not shrink from spelling out Mrs. Simpson's name; and unlike Queen Alexandra and Queen Victoria, she seldom used exclamation marks. In these circumstances, however, she seems to have considered a salvo of five not excessive.) "The whole affair has lasted since November 16 and has been very painful—It is a terrible blow to us and particularly to poor Bertie." Before Monckton took his leave, he outlined the provisional terms of the settlements. Queen Mary listened, aghast. Then, tapping the paper she said as though disbelieving her eyes and ears, "To give up all that for *this*—!"

While the transfer of the Crown was proceeding between the King and his ministers, the transfer of the private properties was proceeding between him and the brother who would succeed him. It could hardly be an altogether amicable process, with so huge a fortune in contention (Sandringham and Balmoral, each of some 30,000 acres, together would be knocked down for approximately one million pounds); indeed, York would remember "a terrible lawyer interview." Preliminary negotiations would end "quietly and harmoniously," but in the months to come, acrimony would foil attempts to arrive at a final settlement. York generously offered to leave Fort Belvedere as it was—except for its American power mower, which he admitted coveting—and to reserve it as his brother's proper residence. For the younger brother dearly, even desperately, wanted the older one back in England, to be close by with the counsel and support that had helped to sustain him through a sad boyhood and an awkward youth, and indeed to lend a practiced hand to the grinding chores of the monarchy. It was generously agreed between them, in the upwelling of recovered affection and mutual need brought on by the painful realization of the imminent separation, that David would be free to return to England to live. A two years' absence abroad struck them as quite long enough for Bertie to settle into the harness of kingship, for the bitterness of the day to dissipate, and for the two of them to decide on the line of work that would be most suitable for the former monarch. It was also Bertie's inspiration to remind his brother that a new title would have to be created for him, since he would presently revert to the status of a Prince of the Blood Royal. In 1917, at the height of the war with Germany, George V had decided that patriotism required the reigning house of Britain to purge itself of all the "degrees, styles, dignities, titles and honors" deriving from the ducal House of Saxony and the princely House of Saxe-Coburg-Gotha, and that descendants in the male line should thereafter bear the family name of Windsor. It was now the inspiration of *Rex Futurus* to offer *Rex Quondam* the first dukedom of Windsor. The elder brother was pleased with his new title, his eighth (and last). (The progression was from Prince Edward of York through Prince Edward of Cornwall and York, Prince Edward of Wales, Duke of Cornwall, Prince of Wales, King Edward VIII, Prince Edward of Windsor, to Duke of Windsor. "Edward of Windsor" had once been a title of Edward III's.) "His Royal Highness Prince Edward Duke of Windsor" had a fine orotundity and resonance. But there was a critical defect, as the Duke would discover on the eve of his wedding. It did not stipulate that the Duchess, too, would be a Royal Highness. The Duke's lawyers, rushing to complete the negotiations, either failed to notice the omission or, more probably, assumed that provision for his Duchess was implicit, as it had been for the wives of his brothers. By the time he learned that an equal status would be withheld from his wife-to-be, the climate of trust and forbearance had changed; he was no longer in a position to impose his terms: and the result was the permanent envenoming of the Duchess and the permanent estrangement of the hitherto affectionate brothers.

This intangible aside, Windsor fared well. He was not leaving England as a poor man, by any standard. Though there is no accurate way for an outsider to measure his fortune at the time, members of his staff judged that it was close to three million pounds sterling—and this when the pound stood at $4.90. The main source of the wealth was successive legacies from his great-grandmother, Queen Victoria, his grandfather, and his father. Another was accumulations from the unspent revenues of the Duchy of Cornwall—these alone amounted to between 90,000 and 120,000 pounds a year, and they had flowed into his personal account for some forty years.

Baldwin and Neville Chamberlain, Chancellor of the Exchequer, assured Monckton that Parliament could probably be induced to make "a substantial provision" for the King on its own, supplementary to his income from his private fortune. His ministers retained little sympathy for him, but they did not want him either to become a remittance man on the shabbier fringes of Continental society or to be in a position to disturb the new reign. They therefore stipulated, in their negotiations with Monckton, that the two years of absence proposed by the brother be honored.

The negotiations were still under discussion when a development in another quarter greatly strengthened the Government's hand. On Wednesday the ninth, the threatened intervention in the Simpson divorce—which the Government had learned of a week earlier—was in fact made. An obscure solicitor's clerk, one Francis Stephenson, aged seventy-four, appeared alone at the Divorce Registry at Somerset House and petitioned for an intervention, claiming to possess supporting evidence which he would present to the King's Proctor. Had the intervention's original purpose been, as Goddard implied, to keep the King from abdicating, it was now a cocked pistol pointed at his head. It could keep Mrs. Simpson from marrying anybody. The Prime Minister and the Home Secretary, in their meeting next day with Monckton, took note of the threat. The Government's proposal to provide an annual allowance for the King was to be presented to the Parliament in the next Civil List. The ministers instructed Monckton to warn the King that if he attempted to join Mrs. Simpson directly after leaving England, or did anything whatsoever to sharpen the suspicion that the divorce had been collusive, "he would not get a penny, because Parliament would not pass" the money bill.

It was in the ominous shadow of these warnings that the King had to fulfill the constitutional requirements for his Abdication. As he finished a light breakfast on the morning of Thursday the tenth, the dukes of York, Gloucester, and Kent arrived at the Fort. Precisely at ten o'clock, the four brothers, the King's lawyers (Monckton and Allen), and the two courtiers (Peacock and Alexander) assembled in the drawing room. Monckton had brought out seven copies of the Instrument of Abdication the evening before—one for the Cabinet, one for the Parliament, and one for each of the Prime Ministers of the Commonwealth, and eight copies of the Abdication "message." While he was laying out the papers on the King's desk, the brothers talked in subdued voices and smoked; the only discordant noise was a sudden, hysterical guffaw from Gloucester. Silence fell when the King took his seat, dipped his pen, and prepared to start signing. Then, "There's no ink in the damn pot!" he said fretfully. Someone handed him a fountain pen, and he started again. His hand was firm. The Instrument said:

I, Edward the Eighth, of Great Britain, Ireland and the British Dominions beyond the Seas, King Emperor of India, do hereby declare my irrevocable determination to renounce the Throne for Myself and for My descendants, and My desire that effect should be given to this Instrument of Abdication immediately.

York would remember the occasion as "a dreadful moment and one never to be forgotten by those present." Said Monckton, "I had helped him to bring this about, because he commanded me to do it, but to see it happen was like witnessing a death." When the King had finished, he smiled wanly and yielded his chair and pen to York, and went outside for a last turn around the garden, while the brothers were adding their signatures, fifteen times apiece, according to their order in the succession. George Allen held the papers steady and blotted each one. After Kent had signed the last, Monckton gathered them up and folded them into one of the red dispatch boxes, and the King, back from his stroll, half-mechanically locked it with the gold key he had inherited from his father. By noon the papers were at 10 Downing Street. Minutes more, and courier and cable were carrying the official notice of King Edward VIII's abdication to the other parties concerned.

Baldwin made his Abdication statement to the Commons that afternoon. It was a masterpiece of reminiscence, lent additional fascination by his candid disclosures of what had passed between him and the King. At its end, his spellbound audience was half convinced that the King had not been pushed from the throne, but that a kindly, devoted Prime Minister had not been able to save him from himself. "I am convinced that where I failed," Baldwin concluded humbly, "no one would have succeeded." H.G. Wells would later say that Baldwin had cunningly transformed what should have been a political disaster into a triumph: He had "collared the martyrdom."

Because constitutional procedure required the King to give his royal assent on the morrow to the Act which Parliament would pass that Thursday evening, Edward VIII would remain King into Friday, after which tact would require him to quit England with all possible expedition. Meanwhile, a rare stillness was descending on the Fort. The telephones stopped ringing. No more motorcars dashed up, spattering the gravel on the driveway. The King took advantage of the hush to sit down with Monckton and prepare a draft of the broadcast—a farewell to his former subjects—which he insisted on making the next evening, to the displeasure of most of his ministers. The hush had become almost oppressive by the time of his last, and least joyful, dinner within the walls he loved. One would have thought that on an occasion so solemn and melancholy, he would have surrounded himself with members of his family, and his oldest and most cherished friends—Eric Dudley, Godfrey Thomas, Duff and Diana Cooper, Fruity and Baba Metcalfe, Jack Aird, and Edward Stanley. Instead, his four guests had all been brought into his life by Wallis; they were her aunt Bessie, Mike Scanlon, and George and Kitty Hunter.

As Scanlon drove up with Mrs. Merryman, the butler,

Osborne, flung open the door and growled at them, "What brings you damned Americans back here? Haven't you done enough harm already?"

Mrs. Merryman, seeing the King come forward, expected him to dress his servant down for this insolent outburst, but he seemed not to have heard it; he was in a trance. Scanlon said that the incident marked the beginning of a "dreadful" evening. The Fort was dark and depressing. The footmen were as surly as the butler; none bothered to conceal his distaste for the friends of the woman who had brought their King to this sorry pass. The food, half cooked and cold, they flung onto the table. It was doubtless the worst dinner ever set before a king since the pie of live blackbirds.

Mrs. Merryman said, "He tried to keep the talk gay, but he failed. He was absolutely tuckered out." Perhaps in the hope that his exhaustion had opened him to persuasion, she repeated an argument that she had often used to him before: "You can always find another woman to love, but you can never find another throne!"

He told her gently that the Abdication papers had already been signed, and that he would be gone from England by the next midnight. "Anyhow," he added, "the throne means nothing to me without Wallis beside me."

Sir Edward Peacock, who had dined earlier with the Duke of York at the Royal Lodge, returned to the Fort before the guests left for London. He found little remaining of the "eat, drink, and be merry spirit" of the evening before. Both Hunters, he noted, had "wept into their soup"; and "Kitty, in a conversation with us while the King was out of the room, burst into tears and explained how Mrs. S. had fooled her to the end, declaring she would never marry the King." When Peacock left, they were still crying; Scanlon, too: "I couldn't hold back my tears. We all wept copiously."

The King embraced Mrs. Merryman and kissed her good-bye. She was quiet on the drive home, but just before they arrived at Cumberland Terrace, her Montague pride found consolation. "It isn't as if the King were giving it all up for nothing," she told Scanlon. "After all, Wallis *does* have background!"

CHAPTER 12
Exit in Darkness and Cold

Bare-footed came the beggar maid
    Before the King Cophetua.
In robe and crown the King stept down,
    To meet and greet her on her way. . . .
Cophetua sware a royal oath:
    "This beggar maid shall be my queen!"
—"The Beggar Maid," ALFRED TENNYSON

English weather showed its virtuosity on Abdication Day. The early morning fog at the Fort lifted to become a low overcast; this yielded to an icy drizzle; and at nightfall there was a shower of hail, scattering the watchers in Downing Street. The King spent his last morning as King in supervising his packing, and in helping mothball the Fort for what he hoped would be only a short interval. Winston Churchill presently arrived to work on the broadcast. He asked for a bottle of Chablis; then, sipping and pacing, he read aloud and savored the draft which Monckton had composed and the King had fiddled with.

The dining room at the Ritz was jammed that afternoon; "all London" was lunching there, including Alice Keppel. According to Janet Flanner, writing in *Travel & Leisure,* Mrs. Keppel now made the "devastating" remark: "Things were done better in *my* day."

In 1930, Chips Channon had found the grandfather's mistress "still magnificent and charming." Now, six years later, Bruce Lockhart thought she looked "rather formidable and slightly coarse." Another six years, and Channon would record that she was "very Edwardian in her veil and gloves . . . full of charm and vim." But when he saw her in 1944, she seemed "a touch tiddly," and had begun coloring her hair. Both she and her husband died in 1947.

One other quotable remark survives her, though the attribution may be false: "A royal mistress," she is reputed to have said, "should curtsey first, then leap into bed."

Churchill and the King were still at table when a clerk in the House of Commons arose to read the royal assent. His voice faltered as he spoke the last phrase: *"Le Roi le veult."* The succession had passed. The exact moment was 1:52 P.M. The shortest reign in English history was Edward V's: seventy-seven days, in 1483. The next shortest was Edward VIII's: 326 days. Long before, King George V had warned Stanley Baldwin that within twelve months of his death, his son David would "ruin himself"; in Alastair Forbes's metaphor, he had "spotted the kick in this Thorobred's gallop." Later, George V told Lady Airlie, "Bertie has more guts than the rest of his brothers put together." He told her again, "passionately," a few weeks before he died, "I pray to God that . . . nothing will come between Bertie and Lilibet and the throne!" Nothing could now. His prayer had been granted. Bertie had become King George VI; King Edward VIII had become the Duke of Windsor, though he was left in possession of the now hollow and meaningless ranks of Admiral of the Fleet, Field Marshal of the Army, and Marshal of the Royal Air Force—and Ernest Simpson, said the twopenny wits, should become a marquis, since he was between an earl (i.e., Spencer) and a duke.

After luncheon, Churchill worked on, pausing to brighten a phrase with his lapidary skill, and brightening the King's spirits with his own. When they said their goodbyes at four o'clock, Churchill's eyes filled, and he muttered a couplet of Andrew Marvell's about the beheading of Charles I:

> He nothing common did or mean
> Upon that memorable scene.

Windsor turned from the door and rang for his valet, Crisp. "How's the packing coming along? . . . Good!

Collect what you'll need for yourself. You'll be going with me."

Crisp said, "Sorry, Sir, but I'm not. I'm staying in England. I shall be leaving your service when you leave the Fort." The only explanation Crisp ever offered was a gruff "He gave up *his* job, I gave up mine."

"No matter," Windsor said. "I'll get you a job here." He telephoned the King: "What about taking on Crisp? He's the best authority on medals and decorations in the world!"

Bertie agreed to engage him, and the junior piper, too.

It reveals much about Windsor's state of mind that he had devoted almost no thought to how he would take up life in exile. Just as he had assumed that Crisp would accompany him, so he had assumed that everything else would also go smoothly—that someone, somewhere, was making the usual arrangements for his care, comfort, and privacy. Kipling wrote in "The Sons of Martha":

> It is their care that the wheels run truly;
>   it is their care to embark and entrain,
> Tally, transport, and deliver duly the Sons of
>   Mary by land and main.

All his life, Windsor had been a "son of Mary," figuratively as well as literally. Now, with exile only a few hours away, he had done nothing for himself beyond adopting an aide's suggestion that he book a suite in a hotel at Zurich—this being as close to his ladylove as he yet dared approach. When he informed her of his bleak plans, she indignantly refused to let him pursue them. The Eugène de Rothschilds, she said, had invited her to spend Christmas at their *Schloss* at Enzesfeld, near Vienna, and she proposed that he go in her place. The Rothschilds considerately transferred their invitation; the exile would have his accustomed comfort and privacy after all. He said later, "It was the first time in my life that I had no place to go. Until that last day, I'd taken it for granted that my staff would take care of me. But my staff was evaporating. . . ."

Bertie spent Friday in London at York House, preparing for his Accession Council next morning. He had asked David, their two brothers, and other members of the family to dine at the Royal Lodge that evening before the broadcast, which was scheduled for ten o'clock from Windsor Castle. On their way to the dinner, all the brothers were to meet at the Fort for a drink. Dickie Mountbatten remembers joining the abdicating King in his bedroom, and watching Crisp pack "dozens" of photographs of Mrs. Simpson, and noticing that the big double bed was "a foot deep" in telegrams and cables from all over the Commonwealth, most of them pleading, "Stay with us! Please don't desert us!"

When Bertie arrived at the Fort, and the servant who bowed him in addressed him as "Your Majesty," and another told him, "His Royal Highness is in his bedroom," he seemed startled: Surely they had the titles backward? He blurted to Mountbatten, "This is terrible, Dickie! I never wanted this to happen. I'm quite unprepared for it. David has been trained for it all his life, whereas I've never even seen a State paper. I'm only a naval officer. It's the only thing I know about."

Wheeler-Bennett tells how Mountbatten heartened the new King: "This is a very curious coincidence!" he said. "My father once told me that when the Duke of Clarence died, your father came to him and said almost the same things that you have said to me now, and my father answered, 'George, you're wrong! There is no more fitting preparation for a King than to have been trained in the Navy.'"

David, too, consoled Bertie: "You're not going to find this a difficult job at all. You know all the ropes and you've almost overcome that slight hesitation in your speech that used to make public speaking so hard for you."

The brothers finished their drinks and left for the Royal Lodge at eight, to meet their mother and sister and the others. Mountbatten stayed to dine at the Fort, with Monckton, Peacock, and Alexander. Monckton took the opportunity for a last look around. On the King's bed table, he saw "Wallis" penciled, with a telephone number. He wet his handkerchief from the water jug and wiped the tabletop clean. Shortly before his death, he told the little story to a friend, who observed, "Pity the whole wretched business couldn't have been expunged as easily."

The brothers were surprised to find their mother in a

bright-colored gown—the first time they had seen her out of mourning since their father's death. Her attempt to dispel the gloom that the evening could not help generating was brave but futile; the gown only emphasized her pallor and her recent loss of weight. Her hair had turned white during the Great War; the Abdication crisis—a far shorter strain, but one far more severe for her—drained her of twenty-five pounds. Windsor's favorite uncle and aunt, the Earl and Countess of Athlone, completed the table. His sisters-in-law had not been invited, by his express request; he would always resent their siding with his mother and barring their doors to Wallis Simpson.

The family was still at dinner when Monckton arrived to escort Windsor to the Castle whose name he now bore. They were going alone; Windsor wanted no one else with him. They drove in silence down the deserted Long Walk, turned into the huge Quadrangle, and stopped at the sovereign's entrance. The director general of the B.B.C., Sir John Reith, was waiting there. Windsor got out of the car, holding a cigar in one hand and Wallis's cairn, Slipper, in the other, and introduced Monckton, whom Reith had never met. Windsor had asked to make the broadcast from his former living quarters, the little suite in the Augusta Tower, though this meant that most of the electrical equipment had to be set up in the corridor, so as not to cramp the technicians. Windsor greeted them affably—Reith thought that he seemed more relaxed than they were—and went into the sitting room, where the microphones stood on a table, with a chair facing them and an evening newspaper beside them. Reith handed him the paper and requested him to read a few lines aloud, to test his voice level. The passage Windsor happened to choose was about a lawn-tennis meeting at which Sir Samuel Hoare had remarked that the new King was a keen player.

The former King commented, "They'll like that!"; then, to Reith, "How much time have we?"

"A few minutes, sir."

"In that case, I'd better go in here." He closed the door behind him; there was the noise of a flush, and he reentered, smiling: "I expect that's the last time I'll use that place."

At thirty seconds before ten o'clock, Reith sat down at the microphones, waiting for the red light to flash and "bring the ears of the whole world into that little room." The light flashed. Reith leaned forward and said, "This is Windsor Castle. His Royal Highness the Prince Edward."

As Reith slid out of the chair, to the left, Windsor was to slide into it, from the right; doing so, he inadvertently gave the table leg "an almighty kick." The microphones picked up the sharp sound, and Reith was widely accused of leaving the room in a temper, and slamming the door to express his disapproval of the whole abdication business.

Then began the most moving and most memorable broadcast in the history of radio—one relayed around the world, wherever the English language was understood. It opened, "At long last I am able to say a few words of my own." He went on to praise, in noble language, his brother the new King; to speak generously of the Prime Minister and the other ministers of the Crown; to express his gratitude for the kindnesses that the British people everywhere had shown him in his service as Prince of Wales; to absolve Mrs. Simpson ("the other person most nearly concerned") from all responsibility for his leaving; and to explain that he had given up the kingship because its burdens would be too heavy "without the help and support of the woman I love." That phrase will be long remembered.

In New York, taxi drivers pulled over to the curb and stopped, to hear him through. The whole English-speaking world all but stood still for seventy seconds. People wept. There has never been its match for pathos: a king—a King of *England*!—renouncing his imperial splendor for love alone! Nor its match for drama: H. L. Mencken, the sardonic sage of Mrs. Simpson's Baltimore, declared it "the greatest news story since the Resurrection." To Lady Ravensdale, it was "hot-making and melodramatic,"[1] but she was writing long after the event, when her judgment may have been discolored by Windsor's ungracious treatment of her brother-in-law, Fruity Metcalfe, in World War II. Nor was Archbishop Lang wholly satisfied. He wrote in his diary: "It was well done: his voice was under good control. It had some real pathos, but there was one passage which jarred: it was when he said that he had been 'denied' the

happiness of his brother in having his wife and children—
as if he might not at any time have honestly possessed this
happiness if he had chosen."

One American's response was unusual: "Give up being
Defender of the Faith? All right! Give up being King of
England? Maybe! But how could *any* man give up being
Emperor of India?"

Arthur Bryant spoke for most of the audience when he
wrote in the *Illustrated London News,* "With touching simplicity, he made his renunciation, and nothing in his whole
brilliant and generous career of service became him like
the leaving it."² The rest of Duncan's report on the Thane
of Cawdor's death (*Macbeth,* I, iv) is equally pertinent to
Windsor, and Bryant might have continued the passage to
advantage:

> He died
> As one that had been studied in his death,
> To throw away the dearest thing he ow'd,
> As 'twere a careless trifle.

Monckton had been standing behind Windsor's chair
throughout the broadcast. As he stepped forward to collect
the pages, Windsor rose and laid his hand on his shoulder.
"Walter, it's a far better thing that I go."

The family heard him over a special instrument in a
drawing room at the Royal Lodge, and Queen Mary wrote
in her diary, "David made his private broadcast to the Nation which was good & dignified."

Some of its dignity was debased in recordings which
were presently being bootlegged in New York. The text
was immaculate until the very end, when, immediately
after "God bless you all! God save the King!" what seemed
to be still Windsor's own voice continued without a pause,
"—and as for you, Prime Minister Baldwin, and you,
Archbishop of Canterbury, both of you may—" etc. New
York's largest department store, Macy's, had rushed an authentic, inviolate version on sale within a few hours, at one
dollar apiece. But England did not record the broadcast
commercially in any form, to the astonishment of—among
many others—John Gunther, who wrote: "It is somewhat
shocking . . . that a country which traditionally prides it-

self on free speech and fair play should submit to the stupid censorship which prevented phonograph records of this speech being bought anywhere in England. Of course, the ruling classes, trying desperately to 'build up' the Duke of York, did everything possible to bury Edward and his memory at once."[3]

Windsor returned to the Royal Lodge at ten-thirty, to say his adieus. Mountbatten had driven over from the Fort; he remembers that "Everybody was still in tears when David came in, but David himself was jubilant. He was like a schoolboy going off on holiday. 'It's all over!' he kept saying. 'It's finished, thank God!' He had no job to take up, nowhere to go except to a stranger's house, no one, not even his valet, to bear him company on the way: nothing, nothing at all, to look forward to, except marriage."

The hour was late. Queen Mary and the Princess Royal left first, at eleven-thirty, with the Athlones. "Came the dreadful good-bye," the mother would write. "The whole thing was too pathetic for words."

The Duke of Windsor stayed on with his brothers and Mountbatten a short while longer. The Government's indifference to his comfort and convenience would begin as soon as he was out of Britain, but at least it would see him off in becoming style: He had been notified that the Admiralty yacht *Enchantress* would stand by at Portsmouth to take him across to Boulogne. *Enchantress*! Eventually, someone with unindurated sensibilities awoke to the connotations of the name, and the destroyer *Fury* was assigned to substitute. Sailing time would be two o'clock Saturday morning, which meant leaving Royal Lodge at midnight. The others walked him to the door. Now it was the eldest brother who bent over the hand of the younger: "God bless you, Sir! I hope you will be happier than your predecessor."

George VI remembered, "We kissed, parted as Freemasons, and he bowed to me as his King."

Kent, his eyes red and swollen, sobbed, "It isn't *possible*! It isn't *happening*!"

The least stable of the brothers and the one most devoted to Windsor, Kent was gravely upset by the Abdication and had difficulty regaining his emotional balance. Within a few weeks, rumors of his divorce began to fly, and presently Bruce Lockhart was describing him to his diary as "A nervous wreck. . . . Capable of doing anything. Wants to kill Mrs. Simpson."

Mountbatten had arrived with two cars: his Rolls, in which he himself would run Windsor to Portsmouth, and his station wagon and a driver for the luggage. Windsor told him, "Thanks, but no. Walter Monckton is going with me. We have unfinished business to attend to. Why don't you follow with my bags?"

Mountbatten was furious. "I came to keep *you* company, not your damned bags!" he said, and stormed out.

With Inspector Storrier on the box as bodyguard, the Duke and Monckton set out soon after midnight across the Hartford Bridge Flats, shrouded in fog. Here the two of them, as Oxford undergraduates in the Officers' Training Corps, had drilled on the hot, dusty plain in the summer of 1914, on the eve of the Great War. Though they talked mostly about the past, because it was rich in shared memories, Monckton could not keep his thoughts from straying into the future. He wondered to himself how the man beside him—so composed, so seeming at ease—would survive in a world in which he had renounced so much. The man beside him had no apprehensions; he was going, he wanted to believe, into the world of his choice. Sir John Reith, at home by now, "sat late . . . thinking of a car speeding through the dark on such a journey, with such a purpose, as never car sped before."

Ill chance led their driver to Portsmouth's Main Gate instead of the Unicorn Gate, where a guard of honor had been posted. Worse, he soon became utterly confused as he crisscrossed the vast, darkened base in search of the royal jetty, where the *Fury* was moored. The Duke took it calmly. Every now and then he would recognize a warship he had sailed in and point it out to Monckton. As they passed the silhouetted spars of Nelson's flagship, "There's *Victory!*" he exclaimed. Suddenly cheerful, he went on, "I think Nelson would have understood what I am doing. He too loved—loved *deeply*." It seems not to have occurred to him that Nelson also had certain expectations of every Englishman.

The sentry at the Main Gate had seen the royal motor flash by, and had passed the word to the Commander in

Chief, Adm. Sir William Fisher, R.N., who finally caught up with it and led it to the royal jetty. Two other admirals and the *Fury*'s captain saluted the former King as he stepped out of the car, with Slipper tucked under his arm. The remaining members of his household—Ulick Alexander, Godfrey Thomas, Sir Piers Legh—were waiting in the cold at the gangway. "Joey" Legh had volunteered to carry on to Enzesfeld, after discovering that his former master would otherwise go into exile alone. Legh had been his equerry from 1919 until the Abdication; in 1949, he told Bruce Lockhart that the Duke of Windsor's charm was "still so great, I would thrill with emotion if he entered the room just now."

Windsor insisted that they all have a last drink, in the wardroom. There was bounce in his stride as he went aboard. At the approach of 2 o'clock, they drained their heeltaps. Admiral Fisher's eyes were brimming, and his voice was thick. "Good-bye, sir," he managed to say. "Not from me alone, but from the Royal Navy." Alexander stayed aboard to receive Windsor's final instructions during the cross-Channel run; the *Fury* would bring him back to Portsmouth. Thomas went up to London with Monckton. He was heartbroken; he had given seventeen years of his life to Windsor as Prince of Wales and King, and it had all ended up, "my life's work, in a shipwreck."

It was past four when Monckton was finally let off in front of the Windham Club. He had been up for twenty-two hours; indeed, he had had little sleep and no respite for four weeks, ever since the King had summoned him to show him the bomb from Alex Hardinge. But before going to his bedroom, he wrote a letter to Queen Mary and left it with the night porter for delivery by hand after breakfast. He described the drive to Portsmouth and told her that her son had spoken affectionately of her, saying "how grand you are, how sweet to him." For himself, he added: "There is still and always will be a greatness and a glory about him. Even his faults and follies are great. And he will, I am sure, never lend himself to any such dangerous courses as some, not unreasonably, fear. He has shown that he cares for unity; and he felt deeply the unity of the Family with him last night."

By the time he had sealed his letter, the *Fury*, which had

anchored in St. Helen's Roads (a shipping lane in the English Channel) so that its passenger would not have a long wait for his train in Boulogne—and could also send some radiograms at Navy expense—was making ready to sail. The Duke of Windsor was put ashore soon after daylight. His first act was to telephone Mrs. Simpson in Cannes.

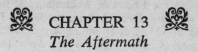

CHAPTER 13
The Aftermath

The anxiety and outrage stirred by King Edward VIII's infatuation were perversely misdirected, many feel, when they assess them in the present climate of permissiveness. Considering the ominous events on Britain's horizon, the passions expended on that affair could have been devoted more profitably to coping with the issues of war and peace. Malcolm Muggeridge, for one, would have been more amused than scandalized had his King taken up with a Siamese twin. What vexed him most about the uproar was the convenient excuse it offered the Prime Minister and his senior colleagues to evade the real crisis: Hitler's threat to the peace of Europe. Muggeridge would decide that if Baldwin had but "devoted a quarter of the ingenuity required to unseat his King to unseating Hitler, the decade he largely dominated might have ended less precariously." And a Member of Parliament, after listening to the Prime Minister's final oration, properly inquired whether it made sense to let the King go, if he truly merited such praise. The hard fact is, of course, that moral standards expected of men in high places were sterner then than today, and Mr. Baldwin judged the British temper better than did his sovereign. For as soon as the King chose not to make a constitutional issue of his right to marry, the flame of political crisis flickered out as swiftly as it had flared.

An elderly courtier sighed, "We have seen the last of the Stuart charm in the Royal Family!" but elsewhere sorrow over the summary and bloodless ending of the rogue reign was all but invisible. Bruce Lockhart, baffled by the ruin of a King he had admired as a Prince, interpreted the dismal finale as the product of an aberration—the irrational behavior of a man afflicted with "*dementia erotica*." In the City, where the barometer of Britain's health is calibrated

in pounds and pence, the Stock Exchange started to climb
on the Thursday afternoon, as Baldwin prepared to announce to the House the resolution of the crisis. It climbed
even higher on the Friday of Abdication. At the close of
trading on that day, December 11, the index of industrial
shares stood at 121.6, after sinking from 122.3 to 119.1
during the week. Consols regained their wonted robustness;
and sterling, which had slackened against the dollar, recovered to slightly over $4.90. Again according to Bruce
Lockhart, one Rothschild remarked incredulously to another, "If anyone had said two years ago that a King of
England had abdicated, and that on the same afternoon
there had been a boom on the Stock Exchange, he would
have qualified for the lunatic asylum." Evelyn Waugh, with
his usual savagery, recorded in his diary that "The Abdication crisis has been a great delight to everyone. At
[Mrs. Hollis's] nursing home, they report a turn for the
better in all adult patients. There can seldom have been
an event that caused so much general delight and so little
pain."

Two of the many places in London where this jubilation
awakened no echo were 19 Lord North Street and 9 Grosvenor Square. A contemporary couplet said:

> The Ladies Colefax and Cunard
> Took it very, very hard

—and the latter the harder. In her disappointment, she
wailed, "How could he *do* it to me? How *could* he?" It
transpired that little Maud Burke of San Francisco had
been dreaming of succeeding Lady Airlie as Mistress of the
Robes. Now there was no earthly chance of it. Someone
asked the new Queen if she and her husband had ever been
invited to a party of Emerald's when they were the Yorks.
"No, *indeed*!" she said. "We weren't smart enough for
her."

As things turned out, it was Emerald who had not been
smart. Nor had Sibyl Colefax, who had counted on being
Queen Wallis's chief handmaiden in nurturing a splendid
efflorescence of the arts and letters to ornament the neo-
Edwardian Era. Nor had Chips Channon, who dolefully

predicted to his diary, "We will be out of the royal racket, having backed the wrong horse."

Still, in ringing down the curtain on Edward VIII, the British as a whole have seldom employed to better advantage their propensity for putting a saving face on disaster. Their monarch dies, instantly his heir steps forward, and the continuity remains unbroken: "The King is dead! Long live the King!" The calendar year 1936 is unique in the millennial span of British monarchical annals, in that three kings, all in direct succession, occupied the throne in less than eleven months. Nothing like this had happened in a civilized nation since A.D. 68–69, when Rome had five emperors—Nero, Galba, Otho, Vitellius, and Vespasian—in eighteen months. Edward VIII's personal uniqueness came from his having achieved almost instantaneous oblivion while his life had nearly thirty-six years yet to run. Just as Britain's first weekend of reflection, after Bishop Blunt's diatribe, turned popular opinion against the marriage, so further reflection over the second weekend—the interval that followed the Abdication—would find the departed King himself rejected. It was as if by quitting the throne and Britain both, he had ceased to exist in any significant way for his former subjects. He had become a nonperson.

Thus on the second Monday, December 14, *The Times* allotted only twelve inches on page 14 to his arrival in Vienna the day before, noting merely that the British Minister, Sir Walford Selby, had met him at the railroad station and escorted him to Schloss Enzesfeld. Mrs. Simpson's continued presence in Cannes was not even mentioned, so swiftly did the curtain fall. Even as Edward VIII made his exit, *The Times* saw to it that George VI entered with the credentials that the situation called for. Its leading article on Abdication morning, signed by "A Friend" (unidentified), attributed to "a senior industrialist" (also unidentified) the gratifying judgment that no lay visitor to his works had ever asked "more sensible questions" or displayed a quicker grasp of its complicated technical processes than had the former Duke of York. "He does like getting to the bottom of things," the estimate concluded. The brothers' old tutors at the Royal Naval College would have smiled wryly.

Even while Windsor's train was taking him across Europe, the British press, which had hailed him through a quarter-century as the supreme embodiment of royal charm, determination, and fitness, was redeploying to exploit many of the same virtues in his successor. That the transfer of sovereignty took place with so little and such brief commotion was impressive evidence of the British capacity for accommodation—for making the best of a mess. What helped ease the transition was the impalpable, even romantic, strain in the otherwise practical national temperament. It was not so much any perceived differences in the characters of the brothers as it was the hold of the throne itself on the imagination, the earthly faith, of the British people. By now, nearly thirty-six years after Victoria, loyalty to the monarchy had ceased to reside in a blind devotion to an individual, or in an irrational confidence that the random workings of the hereditary principle would invariably cast up worthy sovereigns. For Britons, corporate fealty in its grandest, most selfless meaning had come to center upon the throne itself—the throne as an institution, half fantasy, but deathless, exemplifying the beneficences and constraints that together regulate civilization's oldest ongoing social order.

The larger moral of the Abdication, as Denis W. Brogan has observed, lay in its unequivocal revelation that "the King held his Crown on tacit conditions, one of which was that he should represent, publicly, certain standards which his subjects expected to be respected, if not obeyed." The Abdication thus resembled the American Watergate calamity, in that the occupants of the highest offices in their respective societies each went down for defects of character; each had breached a great trust.

King Edward VIII's failure notwithstanding, a few found it in their hearts to commend him for having smoothed the succession for his brother. Even the Prime Minister was impressed by the King's behavior at the end. Baldwin told his biographer, "Whoever writes about the Abdication must give the King his due. He could not have behaved better than he did." But Baldwin's gratitude seems to have been limited to an appreciation of the King's cooperativeness in lessening the troubles attaching to his riddance.

That was certainly the impression he conveyed to Lord Brownlow, when they met at Chequers over the Christmas holiday, on Brownlow's return from his escort duties at Cannes and from a brief call on the Duke of Windsor at Schloss Enzesfeld.

Baldwin was curious to learn what had taken place at Cannes during those frantic days when Mrs. Simpson's last-minute gesture at withdrawing her divorce petition threatened to derail the abdication process. Brownlow undertook to convince him that the conjoined efforts to secure her renunciation had been sincere, and that he himself had been thrust onstage solely to spirit her away. He had rather expected a hero's welcome from the Prime Minister. "In fact," Brownlow said later, "I was confident that he wouldn't consider a dukedom an excessive reward for my services, with perhaps even a State allowance of a hundred thousand a year." Instead, after he finished the dramatic tale of his adventures, Baldwin asked coldly, "You did all *that*?"

"Yes, sir."

Baldwin said, "Had you succeeded, I'd have sent you to the Tower for life!"

Brownlow was aghast. "But *why*?"

"You had no way of knowing the King's highly emotional state," Baldwin explained. "He would have called for his airplane and followed you and her to the ends of the earth, and never come back to England. No documents would have been signed. The legality of the succession would have been clouded. The monarchy might well have gone down the drain."

The gallant Brownlow left Chequers without even his Prime Minister's thanks, let alone a dukedom. He had already suffered a similar rebuff from Queen Mary, to whom he had sent word asking if she would like a firsthand account of his journeys and his "clients."

"No," she sent back.

In the aftermath of the Abdication, while the Baldwinites were congratulating themselves on the dignity and reasonableness with which they had held throne and Empire together, the Archbishop of Canterbury, alone among the principals, was moved to belabor the already beaten monarch. In a radio broadcast on December 13, the first Sunday after the Abdication, he embarked on what Malcolm Muggeridge describes as "a malignant attack on a fallen adversary," and Frances Donaldson as "a self-indulgent and uncharitable flight of fancy," during which he likened the former Edward VIII's departure from England to James II's, 248 years earlier to the day. "In darkness he left these shores," were Lang's guilt-implying words. For the King's surrender of "a high and sacred trust," he blamed "a craving for private happiness" pursued "in a manner inconsistent with the Christian principles of marriage, and within a social circle whose standards and way of life are alien to all the best instincts and traditions of his people." (Archdeacon Lamble of Melbourne also weighed in with a criticism of the King's "exotic entourage.") That alien circle, Lang went on, now stood "rebuked by the judgment of the nation which had loved King Edward." He ended with Othello's cry to Iago: " 'The pity of it, O the pity of it!' To the infinite mercy and protecting care of God we commit him now, wherever he may be."

The Archbishop later attempted to explain that his primary purpose had been to acknowledge the nation's debt to the banished sinner for "the high hopes and promise of his youth" and "his years of eager service," but he felt he could not in conscience do so without also admonishing him for the sins themselves. Whatever the motive, the admonition backfired: It was Lang who drew the rebukes. Lambeth Palace was bombarded with indignant letters; Walter Monckton, for one, took offense at being included in that "alien," un-British company; Brownlow, for another, extracted a grudging private apology from Lang by threatening to sue him for slander; and Lang himself was pilloried in an impromptu quatrain that circulated among a vast and vastly appreciative audience:

> My Lord Archbishop, what a scold you are!
> And when your man is down how bold you are!
> Of charity how oddly scant you are!
> How Lang, O Lord, how full of Cantuar!

A variorum reading of the second couplet is

In Christian charity how scant you are!
You auld Lang swine, how full of cant you are![1]

There was some truth in Lang's arraignment. Moreover,
it was an echo of Geoffrey Dawson's savagely phrased
leader on Abdication morning, which in no small measure
blamed the King's fall from grace to the presence of "an
exotic society," not lacking in men and women of high
birth, "all of them remote from the 'people,' who cared less
for his welfare than for their own amusement." A collateral
phenomenon of the oblivion already engulfing the former
center of that circle was the instantaneous fragmentation of
the circle itself. The story went around that after Windsor
left England, it was impossible to find in all London anyone who had really liked Mrs. Simpson, or had enjoyed the
company at Bryanston Court or the Fort. The shameless
alacrity with which the lost Court was deserted inspired
another item of Abdication verse, "Rat Week," by Sir Osbert Sitwell:

> Where are the friends of yesterday
>   That fawned on Him,
>   That flattered Her,
> Where are the friends of yesterday
>   Submitting to his every whim,
>   Offering praise of Her as myrrh
> To Him? . . .
> Oh, do they never shed a tear
>   Remembering the King, their martyr,
>   And how they led him to the brink
> In rodent eagerness to barter
>   All English history for a drink?
> What do they say, that jolly crew?
> Oh . . . Her they hardly knew,
> They never found her really *nice*
> (And here the sickened cock crew thrice). . . .

And so on, for fifty-six scourging lines.

Not all the King's supporters foundered with him. Walter Monckton, who had never been part of the Fort and
the Bryanston Court sets, was King George VI's personal

choice for a knighthood in the first New Year's Honors
List, announced only a few weeks after the Abdication. It
was a reward for having served not only the royal brothers,
but also Queen Mary and indeed the monarchy, with fastidious care and insight through the always hazardous negotiations with the Cabinet and the press.

The comfortable relationship that had grown up between
Monckton and the new King is implicit in a note of
Monckton's describing how he was knighted. Because
George VI insisted that he stay on as a personal counselor,
and so provide a private bridge to the brother abroad,
Monckton was not subjected to a formal investiture. Instead, the King suggested that he "stop in" one afternoon
for a chat and small ceremony at 145 Piccadilly—the cozy
house where the Yorks had entertained as they pleased,
and had got their own supper after returning late from the
theatre, and from which they were already moving with
their two daughters into the cheerless magnificence of
Buckingham Palace. After he and Monckton had exchanged a few words, the King pointed to a yellow foot-
stool and said, "We'll be needing that." Monckton pulled it
to the center of the room, knelt, and the King tapped him
lightly on the shoulder with a sword he took up from a
table. Monckton started to rise. "No," the King protested.
"I haven't done yet." He then tapped the other shoulder
and said, smiling, "Well, Walter, I didn't manage that very
well, but then neither of us had done it before."

Monckton's legal associate and lifelong friend George
Allen would be similarly honored in 1952. Both men continued to serve Windsor without pay to the end of their
lives, and Allen in addition handled the Duke of Kent's
legal affairs. In 1957, Monckton was raised to the peerage
as the first Viscount Monckton of Brenchley, the village in
Kent where his family had had its seat for generations.
Lady Monckton is a Scottish peeress in her own right,
Lady Ruthven of Freeland. The Duke of Windsor, whose
demands on Monckton's time and talents had been far
heavier than his brother's, gave him nothing in recompense
except a pair of cuff links—later stolen by a laundryman in
India—and a silver cigarette box inscribed in a facsimile of
his handwriting:

Walter Monkton [*sic*]
from
Edward R.I.
11th Dec. 1936

For Lord Beaverbrook, the heady business of counseling
a distraught King, and commanding a private line into the
Palace, had ended abruptly a week before the Abdication.
The break cost him no sleep. He had relished the excitement while it lasted, and his only regret, other than the
curbs which the relationship had temporarily placed on his
journalist's verve, was that his man had chosen not to
make a fight of it. But Churchill in defeat fell prey to remorse and alarm. The hostility vented upon him by Baldwin's triumphant cohorts persuaded him for the nonce that
by championing the King, he had ruined his career. A day
or so after the Abdication, Beaverbrook went to Paris on
business. Churchill telephoned him there in the middle of
the night to ask if he might fly over for a late breakfast.
Beaverbrook ordered his plane, and Churchill arrived a
few hours later, morose and embittered. The man who in
less than four years would be summoned to save England
was convinced that he had blundered—not in taking on
Baldwin or in standing up for the King, but in having been
slower than Beaverbrook to perceive that their man had
quit the field before the battle was fairly joined.

"I'm through, Max," he announced, as he drained the
glass of champagne that followed a hearty meal. "I'm retiring from politics."

"Oh, no, you're not!" said Beaverbrook. "Not while
Baldwin's still there!"

It was low tide for Ernest Simpson, too. In a Christmas
note to Wallis in Cannes, expressing his sympathy for her
isolation, he remarked that his own lot was scarcely happier. Certain of his business acquaintances had become distant; certain members of the Guards Club had turned their
backs when he entered the bar; there had even been talk at
the India Club of asking him to resign.

Nor was there rejoicing at Marlborough House. It would
be long before Queen Mary could choke down the indignation that surged in her at any reminder of her eldest son's
defection. She remained furious with him not just because

he had failed as King, but because he had callously thrown upon his younger, unprepared brother the onus of redeeming the failure. A friend who called on her, expecting to find her grieving, instead heard her storm, "The person who most needs sympathy is my second son! *He* is the one who is making the sacrifice!" Bruce Lockhart would presently make this entry: "Someone said to Queen [Elizabeth] that the Duchess of Windsor had done much for the Duke—stopped his drinking—no more pouches under his eyes. 'Yes,' said the Queen, 'Who has the lines under his eyes now?' "

Though the new King's good character, his sincerity, and sense of duty were never in doubt, there were valid apprehensions about his capacity to master "the job" quickly enough to avert invidious comparisons with his brother. Prince Bertie's mental action had never suggested a gallop or even a brisk trot. His fund of knowledge was small, his interests parochial; he advanced his opinions in a timorous, diffident manner, made more halting by the stammer that he had not yet subdued. It was known, too, that George V had never seen fit to have his counselors instruct his second son in even the rudimentary arts and styles of kingship, let alone the daily methodology. He was the King whom almost everyone had overlooked.

To his great credit, he did not lack the wisdom to surround himself with experienced courtiers, and the will and the patience to learn from them. His immediate decision to build his own staff on the two most seasoned survivors of his brother's—Alex Hardinge as personal private secretary, and Ulick Alexander as Privy Purse—proved to be shrewd. Their presence restored authority and the lost continuity with his father's reign. The quiet remuster at Court and within the Palace Secretariat of venerable personages who had been shouldered out, the swift resumption of the "olden ways," the sedate jollity of the family gathering at Sandringham for the first Christmas, even the diction of the new King—all these signs were widely construed as evidence that the tempest had passed, and the monarchy was back on an even keel.

The Archbishop of Canterbury, after an audience at 145 Piccadilly on December 21, admitted to his diary, "What a relief it was, after the strained and wilful ways of the late [*sic*] King, to be in this atmosphere of intimate friendship, and instead of looking forward to the Coronation as a sort of nightmare, to . . . [be] sure that to the solemn words . . . there would be a sincere response." A Christmas note from George VI, Lang joyfully professed to find indistinguishable, in handwriting and even signature—"George R.I."—from like notes from his good friend George V. *"Prosit omen!"* he prayed. He had already received a "long and delightful" letter from the Queen, to which she signed herself "for the first time and with great affection, Elizabeth R." The Archbishop's cup ran over.

The shutters were going up, meanwhile, at the Fort. A skeleton staff under Osborne's direction stayed on to shroud the furniture, roll up the rugs, crate the china, silver, and linen, and return to Windsor Castle the odd pieces and paintings which had caught King Edward's fancy there. In Cumberland Terrace, the movers who had transported Mrs. Simpson's possessions in September from Bryanston Court were packing them again, for a move to an address not yet known. In these and other ways, the more conspicuous vestiges of Edward VIII were being erased, one by one, whereas Wallis Warfield Spencer Simpson, on the other hand, was being memorialized in at least one place: Mme. Tussaud's Baker Street pantheon of the notable and the notorious.

The craftsmen at Tussaud's generally need as much as four months to achieve the precise, authentic realism which is their hallmark; but so intense was the public's curiosity about Mrs. Simpson that Bernard Tussaud (Madame's great-great-grandson, and the last member of the family to work as a sculptor) undertook to model her figure himself, in the interest of speed. He began the job in mid-November, and though he had only photographs to guide him, plus some crude notes for the head and face—"High forehead, firm jawline. Skin smooth, opaque. Hair is long, dressed in plainest possible style, parted in middle and fastened in a bun at nape of the neck"—he managed to complete the wax dummy in a record-breaking four weeks, and only one week after the ex-King had left England. Three weeks more for makeup (heavy, to withstand the strong lights), costume (a scarlet gown, skin-tight, an exact replica of one of her own), and accessories (a matching purse, with the diamanté initials "WS"), and "Mrs. Simpson" was ready to go on display.

The stage chosen for her was a pedestal in an isolated niche in the Grand Hall, somewhat apart from the Royal Family, among whom stood the Duke of Windsor, wearing a worried and lonely look. Only Napoleon stood in similar isolation. Mme. Tussaud's does not reveal the basic measurements of its effigies, even those modeled by eye, but contemporary estimates put "Mrs. Simpson's" height at five and a half feet, her bust at about thirty-four inches, her waist at about twenty-eight, and her hips at about thirty-seven. Scrupulously accurate representation did not matter here; the typical visitor who stopped and stared at her said only, "So *that's* Mrs. Simpson! *That's* the woman he gave up the throne for! Gracious, what high cheekbones she has!" A few years after her debut, her scarlet evening gown was changed for one of pale-blue satin, with a high neck and long sleeves; and her husband was moved to her side. Another few years brought her a third gown, low-necked and sleeveless, but with a jacket. In 1956 she was put in storage, and the Duke was returned to the Royal Family group.

Fifteen more years would pass before Mrs. Simpson would close the distance in the real world that symbolically separated her from the Royal Family in the wax world. It was not alone a question then of their detesting her for what she had done to their David. They simply did not trust her. They doubted that he would find happiness with her, or that she would be faithful to him, or that their marriage would last. The misgivings in the minds of them all were revealed by Baldwin in a sad talk with his niece: "His family are all wondering what will become of him when at last he opens his eyes and sees the sort she really is." What no one perceived then—neither his advocates nor hers— was that it would be his unwavering fidelity, his refusal to find in her anything other than what he wanted to find, that would make the union last.

Book III

The Duke
and
His Duchess

At thirty, man suspects himself a fool;
Knows it at forty, and reforms his plan;
At fifty chides his infamous delay,
Pushes his prudent purpose to resolve;
In all the magnanimity of thought
Resolves; and re-resolves; then dies the same.
— Love of Fame, EDWARD YOUNG

God helping us all, who could have forseen,
imagined, been made to believe anything so
pitiful and paltry as their End?
— ADELA ROGERS ST. JOHNS

CHAPTER 1
"Never Have I Seen a Man More Madly in Love"

The king's but a beggar, now the play is done.
 —All's Well That Ends Well, SHAKESPEARE

The Duke of Windsor, accompanied by an equerry, Sir Piers Legh, and Chief Inspector Storrier, caught the train from Boulogne to Vienna on December 12, 1936. The following night, they motored the eighteen miles to the village of Enzesfeld, where the single turret of Eugène and Kitty de Rothschild's *Schloss* jutted from the crown of a woody hill now thick with snow. The Rothschilds welcomed their guests and showed the Duke to his apartment, which overlooked the wintry garden. He was traveling light, they noticed. Indeed, he confessed that he had brought "just clothes to last a week or so, and a few treasured photographs and mementos."

When Edward VIII, in his last hours as King, accepted the invitation to Schloss Enzesfeld, he planned to stay only long enough to catch his breath, clarify his financial affairs, and arrange for a residence in France, as close as he dared be to Wallis Simpson. The Duke of Westminster had offered his splendid hunting lodge in Normandy, Château St. Saëns; Windsor had been tempted to take it, but his lawyers stopped him; they warned him that if there was even a whisper of his being seen in Mrs. Simpson's company before her divorce became final, some four and a half months hence, the pressure on the King's Proctor to invalidate the decree could become irresistible. More than this, the mysterious intervention by Stephenson, the solicitor's clerk, still before the King's Proctor, made it advisable for the lovers to keep at least one national frontier between them during the quarantine, and Windsor's residence in Austria had the merit of interposing not one but two.

He bowed to the inescapable. "What had looked to be a moderately inconvenient exile," he later complained, "turned into a shipwreck. I found myself adrift, with all friendly ports closed to me. You might say I had become a man without a country."

Considering his actual circumstances, he was by no means a castaway and even less a Philip Nolan. To begin with, he was scarcely alone; the faithful but not wholly approving Joey Legh attended to his wants. Nor could he be considered isolated, so long as several hundred letters and telegrams continued to arrive each day. Nor is it probable that any Rothschild home, be it ever so humble, would call to mind either a raft or a desert island. Finally, Windsor himself seemed to forget both that his isolation was his own choice and that he was no longer the sovereign.

The host stood by briefly, to see that his guest's considerable needs would be satisfied, then left for Paris, so as not to be in the way. Born in 1884, Eugène de Rothschild had had a leg shattered on the Russian front during the Great War, and while convalescing had studied mathematics to such effect that he was eventually able to identify— and report to the grateful author—a printer's error in a treatise by Einstein. He had tested the rising winds of Europe some months before the Duke's arrival, and had begun to move his fortune from Austria to France. Now he himself followed. His wife, Kitty, stayed on for several weeks, to supervise the large staff, the senior members of which had been summoned from the Rothschild residence in Paris. Anne Morrow Lindbergh met her in 1939 and describes her in *The Flower and the Nettle* as "a tall and rather majestic woman of middle age, quite good-looking, with pride and courage in her face."[1]*

A shrewd and fascinated observer of Windsor's unenthusiastic efforts to accommodate himself to a lesser station was Dudley Forwood, the newest addition to his household. Two winters before, when Windsor as Prince of

---

*Born Wolff, in Philadelphia, the daughter of an immigrant Austrian school teacher, her first husband was Spotswood Dandrige of Petersburg, Virginia. Rothschild was her third.

Wales was in Kitzbühel for the skiing, Forwood, a Foreign Service officer, had been detached to serve as an aide. He recalls, "I expected to be given a room in H.R.H.'s hotel and told to sit there and answer the telephone. Instead, he said, 'Dudley, get a pair of skis and come with us.' Very heady!" It was even headier when Windsor took him onto his staff as an extra equerry, an honor that carried with it invitations to all Court functions. Later, Windsor, as King, had asked Forwood to look after the *Nahlin* party as they passed through Vienna on the way home; and now, on his return there after abdication, he again asked for him, to spell the overworked Joey Legh.

Forwood said, "I thought it prudent to ask the King if he had any objections. He sent word, 'None at all. Nothing would give me greater pleasure than to have you serve my brother.' All the same, I reported to Schloss Enzesfeld with some apprehensions, wondering just how one dealt with an abdicated monarch. I found out soon enough that the Duke was not altogether reconciled to his new status. Although he was plainly a broken man, a shell, he still expected full service, a monarch's service."

From the day of the Duke's arrival at Enzesfeld, he was constantly on the telephone to London, ordering clothes, arranging for funds, directing the collection of his property, papers, and records; and providing for the comfort of Mrs. Simpson in Cannes. His confident expectation that largesse and services would continue to flow from their wonted sources fell, naturally enough, on Walter Monckton, George Allen, Tommy Lascelles, Godfrey Thomas, Sir Edward Peacock, and others so long associated with his official and personal affairs. But the one on whom he leaned most heavily was his brother Bertie, the King. At first, Windsor's main concern was gathering up and storing his possessions at the Fort and in the Palace, and handling Mrs. Simpson's household goods. Bertie patiently took on these chores and lent him Frogmore, in Windsor Great Park, as a storage place. But their daily telephone chats, which had begun in mutual affection, were rapidly soured by a dispute between David's solicitors and Bertie's, over the financial settlement that had been hastily drawn by the lawyers and accepted by the brothers just before the Abdication. Hardly less vexing to the younger brother, increas-

ingly burdened by State duties, were the elder's lectures on
the proper stance he should take on political issues of the
hour, and the tactics he should employ in controlling his
more troublesome ministers. David had also begun pressing Bertie to recognize Mrs. Simpson formally, and to prepare to welcome her into the Royal Family.

Much though Bertie admired and loved David, he could
not exercise a free hand in many of these matters. He
could not publicly oppose the policies of the Government,
however much he might privately deplore them. Nor was it
for him to fix the amount of the Duke's annual remittance;
since the money would come out of the Civil List, the
Treasury held the purse strings, and there was already a
strong feeling in Treasury quarters that the Duke was
proving more avaricious than was justified by the manner
of his default.

When it came to welcoming Mrs. Simpson, Bertie was at
an impasse. The other brothers, their mother, and the three
sisters-in-law had set stony faces against her, whether wife
or no. The family simply would not accept her. As tactfully
as Bertie could, he tried to make David understand this,
but the older brother professed not to hear. Monckton, at
once go-between and trusted adviser to both men, had to
listen to first one of them, then the other, and his heart
ached.

"The Duke," he wrote, "was particularly quick in understanding and decision, and good on the telephone, whereas
George VI had not the same quickness and was troubled by
the impediment in his speech." Bertie, all but driven to
distraction, finally had to remind the dictatorial David of
their relative positions.

The Duke's close friend, Fruity Metcalfe, could not
help overhearing the Enzesfeld end of the exchange. Metcalfe had not been part of the King's inner circle during
the Abdication crisis; in fact, he had rather drifted away
from the Fort Belvedere set after Mrs. Simpson's institution; nor had he been encouraged by the King's ungrateful
and (to many) incomprehensible failure to appoint him to
his household. But it was not in Fruity's generous nature to
bear a grudge; and finding himself on holiday in Austria a
month after the Abdication, he rang up the Duke and proposed himself for a visit. The Duke was delighted; he urged

his old friend to join him at once; and Metcalfe arrived toward the end of January, exactly as matters between the brothers reached a climax. Halfway through his first dinner at the *Schloss* came a telephone call from London: The King wished to speak to the Duke. Windsor could not be bothered just then; let the King call later. The King sent word coldly that the only time he would have free for their business would be at 6:45 P.M. next day, and *the call would come through precisely then.* Metcalfe, in a chatty letter home that same evening, described the Duke's reaction: "It was pathetic to see HRH's face. He couldn't believe it! He's so used to having everything done as he wishes. I'm afraid he's going to have many more shocks like this."

Even so, the Duke continued his importunities until the King, exasperated and desperate, sent Monckton to Austria to explain that more urgent business—affairs of State—demanded his attention. Monckton was further charged with assuring the Duke on the King's word that the financial arrangements they had agreed upon would be confirmed in good time, as soon as details could be worked out. So impatient was the King to have the telephoning broken off that he asked Monckton to set out at once in a plane of the King's Flight. Somehow Monckton was able to persuade the Duke that his daily calls were exasperating his brother, and they stopped abruptly. In Windsor's version, his brother himself told him that the calls would have to end; the Queen and the staff had made the King put his foot down, Windsor suspected, in order to scotch his influence forever.

Monckton was less successful in relieving Windsor's anxiety about money. The haggling went on for months more, to the King's embarrassment and the Duke's rising rage. At one point, the Duke threatened not to sell Balmoral and Sandringham back to the Royal Family after all, claiming (probably out of sheer mischievousness) to have received from what he gleefully described as a "syndicate of Seventh Avenue sportsmen" in New York such a handsome, long-term offer for the shooting rights that he would be enabled to retain ownership of the properties, while drawing rentals that would support him in proper style.

About this time, Windsor also made gestures toward the

famous stamp collection that his father had founded. The future King George V had conceived an interest in philately during his cruises to far lands as a young naval officer, and had bought his first stamps from his own pocket. Then, when he became King, and word of his interest spread, post offices throughout the Empire began sending him single specimens and even whole sheets of their new issues, as a matter of courtesy. The result was that at the time of his death, the collection was rated one of the two or three most valuable in the world, and was unmatched in its British representation. Although George V in later years had appointed a royal philatelist and an assistant to help catalog and refine the collection, the family—and indeed the King himself—assumed that it was his personal property, not the Crown's or the State's. As Windsor cast about for untapped sources of capital that he might claim as his inheritance, he suddenly remembered the stamps; and having learned from private soundings that their value might run to five million dollars, he decided to grab for them, and asked his lawyers to establish his claim, under the doctrine of primogeniture. Their dismal finding was that George V's original rights, if any, had been nullified when the King called in the two specialists and began paying them from the Civil List. Moreover, the bulk of the stamps had been gifts of British post offices, and were in fact Government property.

Windsor was never in the least embarrassed by his obsession with money. He used to say, "The profession into which I was born has been losing ground for centuries. I have better cause than most to make provision for a rainy day. For me, as for Noah, it would mean a deluge." Walter Monckton maintained that his royal client had reason to feel angry and frustrated by the snarls that had developed in the negotiations with the Privy Purse and the Treasury. They would not be untangled to his satisfaction for months, and then it would be only because the King honorably insisted that his side of the contracts with his brother be kept to the letter.

Windsor's peremptoriness was doubtless caused in no small part by the commencement of an ordeal for which he was wholly unprepared. Truly on his own for the first time in his life, he soon found himself no longer a master of the smooth dialogue of command and response to which the Palace staff had accustomed him. To be sure, his own requirements were now fairly modest. He was well looked after and he had few grounds for complaint. But he had scarcely settled in at Schloss Enzesfeld before a series of anguished appeals began reaching him from Wallis, some six hundred miles away in Cannes. Beset by the press, still in a state of shock, and still unwilling to accept as final her lover's loss of his kingly prerogatives, she persuaded him to join her in a clumsy, unworthy effort to redeem a publicity blunder of the kind that would dog them through much of their lives together.

The beginnings of the contretemps, which Wallis herself was chiefly to blame for precipitating, were certainly innocent, if unwise. Long before matters got out of hand in Britain, letters and clippings from the United States had made her aware of the excitement that she was stirring in the press. By her own account, she had enjoyed the publicity at first: rising from obscurity to sudden prominence was intoxicating. But the outburst of press speculation engendered by the *Nahlin* excursion showed her that she was on the verge of also becoming notorious, and that if Britons were to welcome her as a suitable consort for their King, a very different image of her background and interests would have to be projected. Her confidence in the power of public relations to mend mistakes and influence opinion was naïve in the extreme. As soon as she realized that the dispute between the King and the Prime Minister over her marriage was hardening into a deadlock, she decided that the best way to preserve her prospects was to stimulate (if she could) a more favorable press in her own country. Her "wild hope," as she put it, was that if her countrymen—the women especially—could be convinced that the Britons' only real objection to her as Queen was her American birth, then the wave of indignation that would roll across the far larger rest of the English-speaking world would force the Palace and Whitehall to back down. Her letters home during her last months in England became shrill with complaints about the unfairness, as well as the inaccuracy and sensationalism, of the American news stories, and she urged her friends in America to help put things right.

Nearly a fortnight before the dam gave way in the British press, an influential opinion-molder offered himself as her champion: Newbold Noyes, associate editor, director, and part owner of the nationally respected Washington *Evening Star*, the city's largest and most prosperous daily. The son of Frank B. Noyes, president of the Associated Press (and himself later president of the North American Newspaper Alliance), he had recently married Lelia Dickey, née Gordon, whose mother and stepfather, Major General and Mrs. George Barnett, U.S.M.C., had given the tea dance for Wallis, their first cousin once removed, in 1915. On November 20, Noyes had sent a cable to Aunt Bessie Merryman in London, proposing "a frank discussion from one whom [sic] you know and Wallis knows would not abuse any confidence." His intention, he explained, was to write a series of friendly articles for worldwide distribution by the *Chicago Tribune–New York News* syndicate, to help counter the ugly publicity that Wallis was inviting. He had been a member of the Washington group in which Wallis had circulated during her Warrenton interregnum; he liked her; to praise her as a proper Baltimorean would put no strain on his professional ethics. At the same time, his interests went beyond a quasi-cousinly concern: He hoped the connection would give him an inside track to an exclusive story.

The reply to his cable came directly from Wallis herself: "Delighted to see you. W." He signaled the syndicate to crank up its distribution machinery and sailed for England at once. He had expected to dine with her on the evening of his arrival, Monday, November 30, but when he presented himself at 16 Cumberland Terrace, he learned that she had been whisked off to the safety of the Fort three days before, so he and Aunt Bessie had dined alone. Next evening, the King had sent his car to bring them to the Fort, and the four dined together.

Though the King's nerves must have been raw, his behavior gave no clue. On the contrary, he impressed Noyes with how easily he led the table talk, how reasonably he

discussed the sensitive issues that were still unknown outside the little groups that were negotiating them; and, as
course succeeded course, how surprisingly candid he was
prepared to be. Whatever doubts Noyes had entertained
about his determination to marry Wallis were dispelled
long before the savory appeared. To Noyes's surprise, the
King presently introduced the topic of morganatic marriage and analyzed its advantages and disadvantages, objec-
tively, without emotion. He even invited Noyes's suggestions, "man to man," for achieving marriage with the
minimum of embarrassment to Wallis.

That Noyes responded with equal candor is plain both
from his subsequent correspondence with the Duke of
Windsor and from his account of the discussion, as related
to his family on his return home. He urged Wallis, "in the
interests of Empire," to renounce King Edward at once, if
temporarily; and to quit England for the Continent or the
United States. The King, Noyes continued, should proceed
to his Coronation alone, and should resume the courtship
in good time, under the less tindery circumstances—
precisely the same advice already given by Beaverbrook,
Duff Cooper, and Monckton. (Later, Noyes would realize
with astonishment that, full and forthright though the conversation had been, abdication had never been mentioned.)

He and Aunt Bessie motored back to London, sharing
the belief that disaster was avertible. They assured each
other that the King, despite the depth of his infatuation,
remained mindful of his higher duty; and that Wallis was
prepared to make a graceful exit and stay offstage until her
lover's conflict with his Government could be resolved.

Next day, Wednesday, December 2, Noyes went to the
Palace, where an office had been put at his disposal—an
unprecedented accommodation for the Crown to provide
for the Fourth Estate—and telephoned to his father at the
New York headquarters of the Associated Press, assuring
him that the rumors afloat about Wallis were utterly false
(one had it that she was pregnant), and urging him to
instruct his editors to brand them as such. When he had
reported this to the King at the Fort, Wallis came on the
line. She apologized for the abrupt change of plans, but if
he would return to Cumberland Terrace, Aunt Bessie

would welcome him (this would be his third consecutive dinner with her); moreover, it had been arranged for Mr. and Mrs. Rickatson-Hatt to be there, too, and Bernard could tell Newbold almost everything he wanted to know about her life in London.

Wednesday was, of course, the day that the King suffered a double blow: word that the Dominions had refused to countenance his morganatic marriage, and warning that the great London dailies were about to reveal his plighted troth. Noyes knew from his contact with the local office of the AP that the King's affairs were at climax. He did not mind Wallis's putting him off for another day; did he not have a private path to her thoughts and to the King's as well? Moreover, his imagination was soon fired by Rickatson-Hatt's disclosure at dinner, based upon "reliable information," that Queen Mary was to receive Wallis on the morrow at the Palace, for either luncheon or tea. If the Royal Family was thus softening its obduracy, the King might still go forward to the marriage; and the story all but in Noyes's grasp would be infinitely more valuable. He congratulated himself on the good luck and the good connections that had placed him at the right time so close to the heart of things.

As matters turned out, he would never be so close again, nor did he ever see either of the principals again. Wallis, far from being received at the Palace that Thursday afternoon, spent it preparing for her flight to Cannes with Perry Brownlow. This much is certain, but the darkness that covered her flight also covers much of the narrative from here on. Some say that she never notified Noyes of what was afoot, but left him high and dry in London; others, that he had been thoroughly alerted—that, indeed, he and not Brownlow had been the King's first choice as escort. A prime source of this persistent rumor was Lord Beaverbrook, on whose authority Geoffrey Bocca wrote:

The selection was odd, though not quite as odd as it sounded. Noyes was married to a second cousin of Wallis's, so he could be considered remotely "in the family." But Noyes, who was deeply respectful of the monarchist tradition, and felt himself personally and emotionally involved in the crisis, declined.[2]

The *Washington Herald*, a rival to the Noyes family's *Evening Star*, went so far as to report his actual presence in Cannes. The story, with his photograph, identified him as the mysterious "gray-haired gentleman who accompanied as her 'secretary' Mrs. Wallis Warfield on her automobile dash across France."

Did the King ask Noyes to be Wallis's escort? The question has a certain historical interest, though minor. Noyes's widow (he himself died in 1942, aged fifty) and their son firmly declare that never once in his remaining years did he even hint at any such commission. They also declare that had it been offered, he would have accepted without hesitation. The son says, "His chivalry would have made him do it"; the widow agrees, and adds, "If there was ever a knight in shining armor, it was Newbold." A carbon of a letter he wrote to the Duke implied that he had been of additional service in certain "intimate matters," but this alludes to probably nothing more than his suggestions for phrasing the renunciation that Brownlow was struggling to draft for Wallis.

By then, the journalist in Noyes had displaced the solicitous kinsman. He realized that he could not count on further conversations with the King, and that Wallis could not receive him at Cannes without detonating a riot among the newsmen besieging the villa. After waiting a day or two more for a possible summons, either to the Fort or to Lou Viei, he booked passage home for the eighth. He was satisfied that his dinner at the Fort had given him the substance of a tremendous journalistic scoop, and he so notified his syndicate.

He wrote the first two articles before leaving London and sent them off by cable. He was pleased with his start and pleased even more with this telegram from Cannes: "Goodbye and thank you so much for coming over to see me. Wallis." He had originally planned to work on his series at leisure during the voyage, but Wallis's melodramatic dash down France, and the obvious fact that the King was reeling toward abdication, had intensified the syndicate's impatience as well as its interest. More than fifty American and foreign newspapers, with combined circulations of more than ten million, had signed up and were clamoring

for copy. (Noyes had stipulated that the series not be offered to any Hearst paper or to "Cissy" Patterson's *Washington Herald,* both publishers being, in his opinion, vulgar
sensation-mongers.) Once aboard ship, he shut himself in
his cabin and turned to at top speed, rushing each article
up to the radio shack as fast as he finished it. Before they
docked at New York, he had written and radioed eight
more articles, for a grand total of 14,000 words. Bearing in
mind that the only time he had spent with Wallis and the
King was those three hours at the Fort, and that in addition he had talked with them by telephone for certainly less
than another hour in all, Noyes's series is a high-water
mark in American journalism.

To read it today is to be awed both by the author's skill
at squeezing the last drop of significance from all but juice-
less items, and by the naïveté with which he viewed the
lovers. He seems to have donned for the occasion specta-
cles that were not only rose-colored, but soft-focused.

The first article introduced Wallis: "She was as I remember her. . . . Still as gay, still as witty, but now she
smiles more than she laughs." She had "refined and matured." The scene—the living room at the Fort—was "comfortable, almost cozy . . . calm and serene." There was an
open fire. The butler announced "in a ringing voice, 'His
Majesty!' "

The second: The King entered in a plaid kilt and went
straight to Wallis, who rose and curtseyed. He bent over
her hand, then went to Aunt Bessie; then he greeted
Noyes, to whom he said, "I have heard of you from my
friend Mrs. Simpson, of course." He impressed Noyes as
"the perfect host," courteous, thoughtful, gay.

The third: "In my opinion, Wallis Simpson is well fitted
for a throne—in character, poise, and mental attributes—
as any woman who ever lived. . . . The five chief characteristics which, I think, predominate in [her] personality
are companionability, loyalty, simplicity, vitality and natu-
ralness."

The fourth: "One of [the King's] most marked characteristics [is] informality. He could win the love of almost
any woman or the sincere friendship of almost any man.
. . . He likes gardening, a glass of Burgundy, dancing,

sleight of hand, thought-provoking books, the heads of woodcocks [to eat], all blooded animals except cats, old snuffboxes, very crisp bacon and people who can make him think or laugh. He dislikes pomp, stiff shirts, overdone beef, Wagnerian opera, hypocrisy, off-color stories, and all tedium." Astonishingly, the King remarked to Noyes, "I understand in your country there are certain marriages where the bridegroom has to be—shall we say—*cajoled*? You didn't by any chance bring a shot gun with you, did you?"

The fifth: "I have watched the eyes of King Edward VIII as they followed Wallis Simpson. I have watched the play of expression upon her face as she looked at and talked about the man she loves. And if ever I saw two people wholly, deeply, almost unbelievably lost in each other, I saw them then."

These were the highlights of the first half of the series. To pad out the other half, Noyes was reduced to describing the Cumberland Terrace house, reprinting the dinner menu at the Fort, and so on, the fare becoming thinner with each succeeding article—thinner, but still altogether inoffensive, still quite unexceptionable (fulsomeness aside), and only slightly misleading—Wallis's previous marriages were glossed.

The series began to run on December 16, to such editorial tuckets and sennets as "Stamp of authenticity. . . . Remarkable and intimate sketches. . . . Delightfully written. . . . Firsthand information. . . . The famous lovers talk with their own lips of their romance. . . ." Noyes, back at his desk at the *Star*, was basking in these compliments when his eyes fell on a page-one story datelined "Cannes, Jan. 5," in which Mrs. Simpson flatly repudiated the articles "published under the signature of Mr. Newbold Noyes, styling himself her cousin." Noyes was not her cousin, her statement continued; she had not asked him to come to England; his articles had never been shown her, so it is obvious that she had not approved them; she had authorized him only "to publish a 'Portrait in Words' of herself with the object of rectifying many fantastic reports"; however, the actual articles had "far exceeded" the "portrait in words"; finally, the talk at the Fort had been "solely of a general nature and at no time took the confidential turn indicated."

Noyes, stunned and mortified, fired off a protest to Wallis and issued a statement of his own: The King and Mrs. Simpson had indeed asked him to write the articles; he possessed papers to prove it. The exchange could have ended here, to the advantage of both parties; but Wallis's return cable protested that the King had thought that Noyes, far from intending to write any series, was planning merely "to use press connections to correct [the] picture of me in America. Neither of us dreamed that you would bring his name into your story capitalizing on your presence for a few hours in his house as a guest. . . ."

Noyes cabled back that her repudiation was "an act of incredible unfairness and ingratitude"—she and the Duke had known all along that he was writing the series and had never requested that it be submitted for approval. He ended:

> There is no word in these articles which is not accurate. . . . no disclosure of confidence implied or given. . . . I have never claimed to be your cousin, but I have been proud to call myself your friend and have sought to prove my friendship. I can only tell you that if . . . you go forward with a repudiation . . . I shall use every legitimate means to protect my name and professional reputation. . . .

While he was awaiting her reply, an official of the syndicate rushed to his side and sent subscribers a confidential bulletin which ended:

> Her protests don't carry much weight with people who know the facts—though they are not surprised at the disavowal. The British campaign to make of the Duke of Windsor the world's prize forgotten man will miss no trick.

What had inspired the disavowal was not hard to determine. The editors of the newspapers frozen out of the syndicate had put angry pressure on their stringers in Vienna and Cannes to cajole or force the lovers to give them equal time. The British press was the most indignant. Never before had a British king granted an interview, far less admitted the journalist to his table and given him the use of a private office in the Palace. Fleet Street was all the more galled that the first to be so favored was an American. The hungry pack at the gates of Lou Viei forthwith redoubled their badgering of Herman Rogers, until he begged Wallis for a morsel to throw them. She poured out her anxieties to the Duke. The Duke consulted Monckton. And it was presumably on Monckton's for once injudicious recommendation that he instructed Rogers to put onto Wallis's tongue the words impeaching Noyes's reliability.

Considering the pot of melted marshmallow in which Noyes had dipped his pen, Wallis's resentment struck him as unduly bitter. The reason for it became clear on January 10, when he received the first cuttings of his series as printed in the foreign press. Most of the English-speaking subscribers had respected his text, but others—notably the French and Italians—had not. Certain among them had turned it over to rewrite men for "sexing up." The grossest offender was *Paris Soir*, which had shifted the scene of one article to Wallis's boudoir and with smirks and leers had brought in the King not merely to "bend over her hand" (as Noyes had written), but to embrace her. Unfortunately, *Paris Soir*'s version, and not Noyes's original, was the one which had been laid before Wallis in Cannes. He cabled her immediately.

> I have just read the first installments of what purports to be a translation of my articles in *Paris Soir*. . . . A large percentage of these stories is pure bilge I never wrote.

The explanation was wasted. The truth could not overtake the lie. Try as Noyes might, he never succeeded in absolving himself in Wallis's eyes and the Duke's. Protestations of "misunderstanding" met with accusations of "betrayal." As late as December 16, 1937, exactly a year after the first article had appeared, the Duke was writing to Noyes, "The incident is closed and I would prefer not to revive it." And a month later, on January 22, Noyes was retorting quite as stiffly, "I have no wish to continue this correspondence."

As the onetime King and the woman from Baltimore made their way through life together, they would leave a trail of broken and discarded friendships. On the long roster that began with Freda Dudley Ward and Thelma Furness, G. Trotter and Lionel-Halsey, and included almost the entire Royal family, Newbold Noyes now had the unsought distinction of being the first American in the post-Abdication section. By no means would he be the last.

CHAPTER 2
Pyramus in Enzesfeld and
Thisbe in Cannes

Our leader's led,
And we are women's men.
            —Antony and Cleopatra,
                    SHAKESPEARE

In later years, Windsor would remember the stay at Enzesfeld as an "unspeakably wearying ordeal, just waiting, waiting, waiting for the English law to run its measured course." But Fruity Metcalfe and the other former aides 'and equerries—Douglas Greenacre, Charles Lambe, Jack Aird, and Godfrey Thomas—who, unsalaried and at their own expense, traveled there in turn to spell one another at warding off cranks, keeping their former master diverted, and answering the telephone and the mail, all found him, the nettlesome money question aside, in a mood of exuberance, the mood of a man marvelously released from the confinement of unwelcome duties and unwanted tasks.

Fruity stayed on through two full months. The gossipy letters which he wrote home to his wife and which she opened to Frances Donaldson for her *Edward VIII*, paint an extraordinary picture of adolescent euphoria in middle age.

Fruity wrote on January 24, "Never have I seen a man more madly in love." Winston Churchill agreed. Two months earlier, he had told Lady Airlie, "The King's love for [Mrs. Simpson] is one of the great loves of history. I saw him when she had gone away for a fortnight. [Presumably this was her trip to Felixstowe.] He was miserable— haggard, dejected, not knowing what to do. Then I saw him when she had been back a day or two, and he was a different man—gay, debonair, self-confident. Make no mistake, he can't live without her."

Now, at Enzesfeld, the lovelorn Pyramus was on the telephone to his Thisbe in Cannes every evening, often for two hours at a time. He kept a calendar by his bed, and before going to sleep he would draw a line through the day just ended, saying aloud, "That's one less to April twenty-seventh!" (when the divorce would mature). Fruity reported—as later would Dickie Mountbatten—that if the Duke had any regrets over giving up the throne, or missed England and his associations there, he showed no evidence of it. Indeed, "He seems glad to be free of it all." Fruity's impression was that he had been magically reinvested with the spirit of youth: "He is at his very best and quite like his old form."

Perry Brownlow had recognized earlier, and with consternation, his friend's detachment from reality. In mid-December, Brownlow had made a detour to Enzesfeld on his way home from Cannes, bringing messages from Wallis and an assurance that all was well with her. They told him at the *Schloss* that the Duke was resting. The bedroom door was ajar, and in the wintry afternoon light Brownlow saw Windsor asleep, on a bedspread strewn with photographs of his adored. He was smiling beatifically and clutching a small yellow pillow that had belonged to *her*. "It was quite frightening," Brownlow said.

An air of buoyant fantasy enveloped the Duke during his first weeks in exile. Good afternoons he spent on the ski slopes. He had ordered his bagpipes sent on from London and he played them with spirit after dinner. He kept his aides and occasional visitors up until three in the morning with poker games and rambling reminiscences. He attended a number of dinners and receptions at the British Embassy, where he gossiped happily in German with German and Austrian diplomats. The Germans were continuing to cultivate him, and he responded by inviting them to Enzesfeld for drinks. Once a week he drove into Vienna for a haircut at the Bristol Hotel; afterward, he bought presents for Wallis, or wandered through Schönbrunn Palace or a museum, puttering about much like another duke, the one in *Measure for Measure*, who was "a looker-on here in Vienna." All this make-busyness was calculated solely to sustain his impersonation of a man untroubled in heart or soul, and with much to attend to. On Sundays he even went to services at the English church with Minister Selby and read the lesson from the pulpit. "A great peace came over me," he confessed to Elsa Maxwell, "and I felt comforted."[1]

If true, this was the only occasion in his life when Windsor ever acknowledged drawing solace from the Scriptures. The fact is that he was a defeated man, even if he could not bring himself to admit it. The instant that Jack Aird entered the *Schloss* to take his turn as a volunteer equerry-in-waiting, he sensed the unuttered and unutterable despair. He had not seen Windsor since quitting his service after the *Nahlin* cruise, and had arranged for leave from the Grenadier Guards in order to help his friend through the first difficult months of exile. "The Abdication had finished him," Aird decided. "When I saw him again at Enzesfeld, he had turned into something quite different, something apart. It was as if he had crossed an alien frontier. He never again thought for himself or had a mind of his own."

Fruity Metcalfe, too, was aware of the insecurity and anxiety under the Duke's thin armoring of gaiety, and soon pinpointed its principal source. Their rooms adjoined; the door between was ill fitting, the common wall was thin; and Fruity could not help overhearing the Duke's side of the long conversations with Wallis. As the winter dragged on, the lady plainly became more demanding, more critical. Fruity wrote home, "He's on the line for hours and hours every day. I somehow don't think these talks go so well sometimes. It's only after one of them he ever seems a bit worried and nervous. She seems to be always picking on him and complaining about something he hasn't done or ought to do." When Windsor came down to dinner, his guests often found him edgy, flustered, even shaken. He might have been still more shaken if he had known the tenor of his daily mail. Fruity informed his wife that it was "enormous—sometimes 300 letters, etc., mostly from mad people! Gosh, but some of them are abusive. We never show him any of those, of course. They come from all over the world. . . . The things they write about W are unbelievable."

Enzesfeld was a bad patch for Windsor on many counts. Pricked and prodded and made to seem ineffectual by a mistress hardly less beleaguered than himself, galled by his family's refusal to acknowledge her existence, and enraged by the interminable bickering over money and property, he yielded to a near-paranoid suspicion that his brother was fostering a conspiracy to wall off him and his beloved and to deny them what was rightfully theirs. His frustration darkened his hours alone; he railed against old friends who had not spoken up for him in his struggle with Baldwin; and the notion that he—and Wallis—had been betrayed and abandoned injected a mutual misery into the long colloquies with Cannes.

But for Walter Monckton's calm presence and wise counsel on his frequent visits that winter, Windsor might have disintegrated. "It was the sense of powerlessness," he once admitted, "that brought me close to the breaking point. I could do nothing there but wait and count the days." Fortunately for the stability of the family, Monckton still held the confidence of both brothers across the widening breach between them. Although he had not been able to soften the attitudes of the Queen Mother and her daughters-in-law, he persuaded the King to encourage Princess Mary and her husband, the Earl of Harewood, to pay David a visit. They came for a week early in February; Kent soon followed, but alone; Dickie Mountbatten arrived in mid-March to offer himself, with the King's blessing, as best man at the Windsor wedding. David had been best man at Dickie's marriage to Edwina Ashley, in 1922, and Dickie hoped the compliment would be returned. It was a happy coincidence that Fruity was still on the premises when he arrived, inasmuch as Dickie had been Fruity's best man—"so," Mountbatten said, "my being David's would complete a happy triangle." The three old friends passed their first day together in laughter and gossip and reminiscence. Late that afternoon, Mountbatten found—as had Fruity—that his room, too, adjoined the Duke's and that he, too, was an unwilling eavesdropper on the conversation with Cannes. It began, he still remembers, with "Darling, I've just spent the happiest day of my exile! Dickie's here!" Then a pause. Then this: "Oh, no, *no*, darling! I could never be _really_ happy with _you_ not here, but this was the nearest thing to not being _un_happy!"

A day or so later, Mountbatten found an opportunity to tell the Duke, "I have special permission from Bertie to offer myself as your best man."

"Thank you, but no," the Duke answered. "I want a proper royal wedding, with my two younger brothers as supporters." (There is no best man in royal weddings, only personages of rank, called "supporters.")

Mountbatten knew that the members of the Royal Family had agreed not to associate themselves publicly with the wedding, so he changed the subject: "What are you going to wear?"

"Why, my uniform as colonel of the Welsh Guards."

"You can't do that, David! The Welsh Guards are getting a new colonel." The monarch is automatically Colonel in Chief of each of the Guards regiments—the title passes with the Crown; but the _colonelcy_ is by appointment, and always goes to a member of the Royal Family or to a distinguished officer.

Windsor bit his lip. "You're right. I've lost that, too."

Mountbatten remembers the remark because this was the only time during his visit that he heard the Duke say anything suggesting regret for what he had left.

Windsor's depression and sense of injury were slow to lift. "He is frightfully close about money," Metcalfe wrote. "He won't pay for anything—it's become a mania with him." When Kitty de Rothschild departed early in February, leaving him in sole occupancy of the castle, Fruity wrote:

Kitty left yesterday!! _Terrible show_! as HRH was late getting dressed owing to his infernal telephone call!! _& missed her_! Never saw her to say good-bye or thank her! She was _frightfully hurt_ & I don't blame her. . . . I went down to the station with a letter I got him to write & that made things a bit better—He also never saw the servants to tip them and thank them etc!! (all due to more d--n talking to Cannes. It never stops)

An American journalist who came to the castle for dinner presented him with a box of expensive cigars. The Duke exclaimed over their fragrance, then shut the lid. "No need to be extravagant," he said. "We'll smoke the Rothschild cigars instead. They go with the *Schloss*." Metcalfe, far from receiving an equerry's salary for those two months with his royal master, had to hire a valet and pay his wages from his own pocket; and when he and the Duke lunched or dined at a restaurant, it was usually Fruity who had to pick up the bill. "HRH pays for as little as he can when we go anywhere," he complained to his wife.

Aird had remarked the difference that the Abdication had wrought in Windsor. Here Metcalfe pointed to one aspect of it: A notably generous man had suddenly turned stingy. As bad—or worse—a bold horseman stopped riding; and a man who had soloed became reluctant to fly in an airliner. It was as if his character had reversed itself.

Although Fruity kept assuring his wife that Windsor was "the most delightful companion to be with," and was even moved to add, "If he'd remain as he is, I'd give up everything to serve him for the rest of his life," he finally had to admit that "it is not a very restful life, to say the least of it." He left Enzesfeld late in March, and was not surprised at having to buy his ticket home. His sister-in-law, Baroness Ravensdale, wrote in her *In Many Rhythms*, "The Duke of Kent told me some months later that the King and he would not forget my brother-in-law's selflessness in at once going back to his old chief's side when he was in distress,"[2] but if King and Kent did *not* forget, they gave no sign of their remembrance to either Metcalfe or his wife.

By then, Dudley Forwood had quit the Foreign Service to become the Duke's permanent equerry. Forwood had watched Metcalfe and had conceived an admiration for him: "Fruity had nothing, neither position nor money. In a way, he was the Duke's kept man, a devoted attendant. He never left his master's side, difficult though the master made things for him. But then, he made things difficult for everybody." Forwood was therefore under no illusions about what he himself was in for. "I am a romanticist," he would say. "My whole desire was to serve my former King in his time of trouble." The paltry pay—under two thousand dollars a year, plus expenses—the lack of warmth, of even the most elementary and grudging appreciation, did not deter him. "I never tried to understand the Duke or the other members of the Royal Family. I doubt if their character can be penetrated. My pleasure came from serving them, from being near them, near the throne."

Forwood's dedication, worshipful though it was, must have been taxed at times, as when Windsor capriciously decided that managing the *Schloss* was too much of a bother, and had him move their household to a small pension, the Villa Appesbach, near Ischl, not far from Salzburg. For recreation they tramped the hills and meadows or played golf. Forwood never achieved Fruity's relationship of easy, comradely chaffing. One evening he showed up in a new dinner jacket with the shawl collar that was just coming into favor. Windsor examined the innovation, then remarked coldly, "When I want you to wear something different from what *I* am wearing, I'll give you warning."

At Cannes, a day and a night's journey distant, Wallis Simpson was also enduring a hard winter, as therefore were her hosts, Herman and Katharine Rogers. Not long after Perry Brownlow left, Aunt Bessie Merryman, who had remained at Cumberland Terrace for a fortnight or so after the Abdication, arrived with Wallis's clothes, her Irish maid, and a comfortable shoulder for weeping on. She took rooms at the Carlton Hotel, and from there she wrote Corinne Murray on New Year's Day, 1937:

> The events of the past month are too big for my feeble pen to tackle. I find Wallis looking very well—too thin of course—she has been through a frightful ordeal. . . . The mail is colossal literally tons and very few disagreeable letters. I come in for a few of these but I will have to take them in my stride. . . .

Wallis immediately offered to join her at the Carlton, but Katharine Rogers refused to hear of it, knowing that she would become the prey of sightseers and possibly of vengeful cranks, bent on insulting and perhaps injuring her.

By then, the reporters had melted away, but for a few

stringers on watch for any unexpected turn of events. Wallis and the Rogerses were now able to take long drives through the hills, but the commotion she aroused on the one occasion when she slipped into Cannes to shop kept her fearful of being accosted. Somerset Maugham gave her and the Rogerses Christmas supper, with Sibyl Colefax, in his villa at Cap Ferrat, and the Rogerses had friends in for dinner and bridge at Lou Viei. Elsa Maxwell has an anecdote about one of these games which is often cited (perhaps unfairly) as typical of Wallis's wit. Maugham asked her why, holding three kings, she failed to support his bid of one no-trump.

"My kings don't take tricks," she told him. "They only abdicate."[3]

A cousin-by-marriage of Wallis's said, "She can't be correctly described as 'witty.' I never heard her make a single really witty remark; but she was quick and alert, always ready with a wisecrack or a 'one-liner.' " Alexander Woollcott said that her wit was "of a purely topical variety; it won't travel."

She has been credited with a maxim of sorts: "You can always handle another woman, if your husband is after her, but you can't handle another man." A remark she made to George Allen, who had come over to dine with the Windsors in Paris, has a gentler, more memorable quality. She had asked what he expected to see during his visit.

Allen said, "Frankly, I want to go to the Lido"—a nightclub with a floor show that featured a spectacularly bare-bosomed chorus.

"George," the Duchess told him, "the only woman worth seeing undressed is one you have undressed yourself."

On the long interval between the Abdication and the divorce, the Duchess of Windsor later made this comment: "I was really a prisoner at Cannes. It was the next thing to not living at all. Yet the truth is, I really didn't wish to show my face in public. I was always afraid that someone, probably an English person, might say something ugly to me on the street. I was made to feel that I had committed some horrible crime, worse even than murder. I have never had any spite in my make-up, nor any envy of others. But at this point, I came to feel that the majority of people in the world were not kindly and well-wishing, but jealous, crazy and spiteful. At one swoop, I discovered how much evil and bitterness lies just below the surface of life. Of all the outgrowths of the whole affair, nothing shook me so much or hurt me more than discovering the scorn, even hatred, that so many strangers felt for me."

No one kept count, but Herman Rogers estimated that close to five thousand letters addressed to "Mrs. Ernest Simpson" were delivered to Lou Viei during her first month there. In contrast to those pouring into Enzesfeld, most of which deplored the Government's injustice and ingratitude to a beloved public servant, those to Lou Viei were flung like stones. Despite Mrs. Merryman's report that "very few" were "disagreeable," the truth is that nearly all were abusive, and many were foul and even threatening. Some bore only her name and the address, "France." One, which from the postmark had met with no appreciable delay in the French postal system, was addressed to "King Edward's Whore." There was a sequence of half a dozen, each from a different London borough and spaced a day or so apart, from a man claiming to be an Australian, who swore that he was on the way to Cannes to kill her. Because of this threat, Inspector Evans stayed on until he could be relieved by a colleague from the Sûreté. At one time, five Sûreté men were assigned to guard Lou Viei.

The day's mail would be brought with Wallis's breakfast, and over Rogers's objections, she insisted on opening every letter. "Each morning," she said, "my private world blew up on the breakfast tray. Sometimes I had to wait till I got a little stronger before I'd reach for the paper knife. You can't imagine the fantastic stories that were abroad about me!—stories about my upbringing in Baltimore and my alleged affairs in China. My own country was against me. So were the Dominions. The whole damn British Empire, in fact. They blamed me for not preventing the Abdication. I couldn't *possibly* have done it! They didn't stop to think of the Duke's make-up—whether you can influence a man of his character to do something or not do it. They never said, 'Well, maybe she tried.' They never gave me one break. No one stood up to say, 'Oh, stop it! She can't be *that* bad!' No, people just got out their whips and lashed.

"In the Europe of that day, an American was a nobody if he wasn't an Astor or a Vanderbilt, or an officer of General Motors, or had a shooting box in Scotland, but I didn't even have a father or a mother, much less a connection with anyone of influence—anyone who could have said to someone in power, 'Listen, let's tone this thing down! It's getting pretty rough!' I felt I couldn't go out and show my face. As for the Duke, they thought of some devilish thing to hurt him about every six weeks during the six months we were separated. And they saved their atom bomb for the end, for the eve of our wedding."

The unhappy lovers were convinced that the Palace had their mail under surveillance. "We never dared send a letter through the post," Wallis said. "It would certainly have been intercepted. But if a good friend—Daisy Fellowes was one—happened to be going to Vienna, I'd ask her to take a letter for me." Mrs. Reginald Fellowes, renowned for her beauty and chic, was the daughter of a French duke and of an American mother who had inherited a share of the huge Singer sewing-machine fortune. Whenever she saw one of the ubiquitous Singer advertisements, she is said to have crossed herself.

Lacking a regular courier, the Windsors had to depend on the vagaries of the international telephone circuits. It was revealed after the war that German Intelligence had monitored all calls to and from Schloss Enzesfeld, hoping for a clue to Windsor's views on foreign affairs, but the "tap" proved unprofitable; about all that the monitors could have heard was a fresh installment in the endless serial of woe.

"I was alone in Cannes," Wallis remembered, "and the Duke was pretty much alone at Enzesfeld. Two people combatting a common danger are stronger together than the same two people apart. The Duke had the worst of it. Before they had built him up to the sky; he could do no wrong. Now they were out to flatten him, by taking away a colonelcy, or some post he had held for years. They didn't have to do all that. He had left in good grace. Talking to him was heartbreaking; and it was hard on him, I imagine, to have to listen to *my* troubles, though we both tried to keep things buttoned inside ourselves."

It was not only heartbreaking; it was ear-straining and patience-exhausting. Many years later, the Duchess described her daily ordeal thus: "The French telephones are bad enough today, but back in nineteen thirty-seven—! The only phone at Lou Viei was in the dining room, by the fireplace, and when the Duke rang me late every afternoon, I'd bring it over to the table, so that I could sit on a chair during our long talks. The trouble was, the table was already laid for seven-o'clock dinner, usually including some soup spoons Katharine had bought in China, with pretty coral handles. Well, I'd be screaming into the phone—I'm sure they could hear me in Cannes—and just as I'd be getting across to the Duke, we'd be cut off, and in my rage I'd slam my elbow down on the table, and *crack!* would go a coral handle. I'd apologize to Katharine, but the next day it would happen again, and finally she wouldn't let the butler lay the table until our conversation was over.

"She was an angel to put up with me! I must have been the most exasperating guest in history, what with breaking her spoons and monopolizing her dining room just when dinner was ready to be served. I blame it all on the French telephone system. Sometimes I'd have to wait half an hour or more for the Duke's call to come through, and if I didn't grab up the phone the instant it rang, the connection was broken. My French was very weak in those days, so I'd have to get Katharine to come help me, and poor Katharine would drag herself up the narrow stairs to the dining room and start screaming at the operator.

"It was *maddening*! But those talks, difficult as they were, were what the Duke and I lived for—and *on*, really, during the six months we were separated."

Still, a friendly hand or two went out to her. Ernest Simpson, for instance, had sent Christmas greetings to her and to the Duke, and during the winter he wrote Wallis several tender letters. She kept them through the years and produced them for her editor when she started work on her autobiography. One was especially touching. She read it aloud one afternoon in her suite at the Waldorf Towers, in the Duke's presence: Ernest deplored the criticism howling around her, and wondered if it might not have been best for her in the end if she had broken with the King. In the next sentence, he decided the argument against himself: She had come under the spell of her royal "Peter Pan," and there was no drawing back. She had no objection to including the letter in her autobiography, but as the editor was picking it up, the Duke intervened to say that he would prefer to copy it himself, rather than have it shown around. A day or so later, when the Duchess asked him for the copy, he claimed that he had not been given the original. It could never be found. The Duke protested innocence, but he had not hidden his displeasure at being labeled "Peter Pan" by the husband he had ousted, and there is no doubt about what he did with the sad little letter. It was the last one she ever received from Ernest.

In both Enzesfeld and Cannes, spring brought a quickening not only of flora, but of apprehension. Was there any chance of intervention by the King's Proctor before April 27, when the decree *nisi* would otherwise become absolute? Monckton and Allen were quite sure that the danger was past, and their confidence proved well founded. In March, some weeks before the threshold date, Francis Stephenson's notice came up for action in the divorce court. He was present at the hearing, a bent, frail old man with drooping moustaches. The Attorney General, Sir Donald Somervell, representing the King's Proctor, moved swiftly to close the matter. The court was told that Stephenson had confessed to having no firm evidence that the divorce had been collusive; his allegations had all been based on rumors and newspaper reports. At the court's direction, he rose and declared in a tremulous voice that he was withdrawing his notice; it was thereupon ordered struck out, and Stephenson dropped from public view as mysteriously as he had appeared. He lived on into his nineties, in a boardinghouse in South London; to the end, he never revealed what had inspired him to act and why he had called back the affidavit. He said only, "Because I was told to."

Others, too, had been apprehensive about Stephenson. On January 7, Mary Raffray, in London, had written to her sister Anne, in the States: "I am leading such a quiet domestic life you wouldn't know me. . . . My flat is really a little gem, E[rnest] such an angel—if only that damn King's Proctor doesn't upset the divorce. We are staying very quiet on purpose. This is not the time to launch myself on the unsuspecting London[ers]. I have been mentioned many times as having been the corespondent in the Simpson divorce, which is unpleasant but actually would not throw people off, they are very broad-minded about such things here; but even the rumor might prevent my being present [at Court] if I ever wanted to. But everyone has been sitting tight waiting to see what would happen before they'd come out as loyal to Wallis or tear her to bits. Many of the people who sucked up to her when the King was the King, now claim they hardly knew her. And no one would have wanted to take a chance on being nice to me if they [Wallis and Windsor] hadn't left the country, which is a great break for me. There is plenty of time to make friends and it won't hurt me to play possum now. That to me seems the smart thing to do. But I see a few people and love my life and E. and am happy—"[4]

Stephenson's withdrawal removed the last major obstacle to Mary's marriage as well as to Wallis's; now it was only a matter of waiting for the court to make the decree absolute. That done, and Mary divorced from Raffray, she could rush into Ernest's arms. But Wallis and Windsor found that other problems were arising to confront them: Who would perform the ceremony? And where? And where would they spend their honeymoon? The first problem was shelved, in the hope that time would bring a solution. The third was answered by Count Paul Münster, a cousin of Eric Dudley's, whose offer of Castle Wasserleonburg, his sumptuous establishment in Carinthia, the Duke quickly accepted. The remaining problem came down to two choices. One was to rent the Château de la Croë, at Cap d'Antibes, a few miles from Lou Viei. The other was to borrow the Château de Candé, at the village of Monts, near Tours. Neither the Duke nor Wallis had seen or heard of Candé, yet they plumped for it—and thereby set off a chain reaction of blunders that cast grave doubts on their common sense, not to mention their integrity and taste.

Candé came to them (and they to it) through Herman

Rogers, who had stayed there several times. Soon after Wallis's flight, the owner of Candé, Charles Eugène Bedaux,[5] cabled Herman from the United States, putting his estate at her disposal until she and the Duke could find a place of their own. Herman thanked him, but gave him no more thought until an evening when Wallis mentioned, after a particularly painful telephone discussion with Enzesfeld, that "David" was impatient to find a house fit for them to be married in. Candé returned to Herman's mind. He described it to Wallis as a sprawling, sixteenth-century gray stone castle that was classified as a *monument historique* despite its having been rebuilt and restored with an eye to mass rather than to beauty. Granted it was no Chenonceaux or Blois, it offered a repertory of amenities seldom found in old châteaux: American bathroom fixtures, for instance, a brigade of servants, and a telephone switchboard large enough for a hotel, plus such recreational facilities as a nine-hole golf course, a swimming pool, a billiard room, stables, a croquet lawn, an archery range, an indoor badminton court, and a 40,000-dollar pipe organ.

Wallis was enthusiastic, but Herman persuaded her to wait until he could get a line on Bedaux before she told the Duke about Candé. Herman's brother Edmund, a New York banker, was Bedaux's principal financial agent in the United States. In response to a question from Cannes, Edmund assured Herman that so far as he knew, there was nothing in Bedaux's character or associations to embarrass the Duke; in fact, he himself had found Bedaux a man of probity. Herman thereupon urged Wallis to relay the offer, pointing out that among the château's other attractions were its remoteness from tourist byways, and a surrounding park, large and wooded, that assured privacy.

The Duke himself favored being married at La Croë, both because its nearness to Lou Viei would be convenient for Wallis as well as for the patient Rogerses, and because the backdrop hills would be awash with the golden foam of mimosa, borne on the flooding tide of the Mediterranean spring. He telephoned the King once more, to list the advantages and disadvantages of both places, and to ask his preference. The King must have assumed that his brother had investigated Bedaux to his satisfaction, because he plumped firmly for Candé. The Riviera, he explained, was

thought of as a playground, whereas there was dignity
about an old château in central France. So Candé it was—
and when the storm of criticism began to rise, Wallis did
not fail to insist that "King George the Sixth made the
choice, not us."

The critical mistake was in not running a fine check on
Charles Bedaux's record. It eventually transpired that he
was a rich and arrogant entrepreneur-promoter who,
though well regarded in certain industrial sectors, exuded
an aroma of mystery. Born in France in 1887, the son of a
civil engineer, he had never completed his schooling, preferring to serve a hitch in the French Foreign Legion. He
was still in his teens when he was invalided out, and at
twenty he emigrated to the United States, where, after a
succession of odd jobs, he was naturalized in Grand Rap-
ids, Michigan, in 1917. A few years later he devised the
"Bedaux system," which used time-and-motion studies as
the basis for formulae applicable to the individual worker's
output, rewarding high producers and penalizing laggards.
The workers opposed it as a form of stretch-out and speed-
up (and were supported by Charlie Chaplin's 1936 satire,
Modern Times); but because Stalin adopted it as the pilot
model for his far harsher Stakhanovism in 1935, the leftists
in American labor made only perfunctory protests, and Bedaux's American clients presently included such giants as
Diamond Match, General Electric, Campbell Soup, du
Pont, and Eastman Kodak, and his companies were introducing the system into Europe, too, and the Middle East.

Along the way, Bedaux himself had acquired both fortune and an international reputation as an industrial engineer, an amateur explorer, and a prodigal spender. His son
had graduated from Yale. He had a second American wife,
the former Fern Lombard, and New York apartments in
the Ritz and the Plaza. When he first stepped onstage in
the Windsor drama, he was fifty-one years old, a squat,
solid, energetic man with an unusually large head, a battered face, bold eyes, and an engaging smile which he exercised freely, despite the worrisome reverses which his affairs had begun to encounter. For one thing, the Hitler
Government had shut down his operations in Germany,
and he was clandestinely maneuvering among powerful

Nazis for authority to start them up again. Before long, his ambition and cupidity would make him their collaborator, a traitor to two countries: that of his birth and that of his adoption. But this dark side of his character had not yet come into view. His approach to the Nazis had only just begun when the former King of England instructed Herman Rogers to inform Bedaux that his offer of the château was accepted. That careless decision proved, if nothing else, how unprepared was Windsor for the real, the continuing world.

CHAPTER 3
The Wedding

Anne Bullen: By my troth and maidenhead
I would not be a queen. . . .
No, not for all the riches under heaven.
Old Lady: 'Tis strange: a threepence bowed would
hire me,
Old as I am, to queen it: But, I pray you,
What think you of a duchess? have you
limbs
To bear that load of title?
—King Henry VIII, SHAKESPEARE

Early in March, well before the winter rains had relented in the valley of the Loire, Wallis Simpson left Cannes, to prepare the Château de Candé for her wedding. The party traveled in two cars: Wallis, the Rogerses, and a French security officer in the Buick the Duke had given her; two maids, a second security officer, a secretary, and the luggage in another. At dusk on the second day, they drove into the château grounds through a rear gate, to evade the press already watching the main gate, and after skirting files of poplars and clusters of willows, pulled up at an elaborate Gothic doorway. Fern Bedaux was there to make them welcome. She struck Wallis as "an unusually handsome woman, graceful and poised and charming." She gave them tea in the paneled library, in front of a fireplace with great logs blazing. Later, she showed them around. There was a large drawing room with an organ, and off it a small salon with pale walls and Louis XVI furniture—"typically French," Wallis thought. Here, she decided, was where she would be married. The dining room, in the cellar, impressed them particularly, with its vast oak table flanked by low benches, and the hams and sausages hanging from the thick old beams that spanned the ceiling. Wallis took the master bedroom; because her life was still being threatened, Rogers, still the faithful sentinel, took the small sitting room adjoining, as had become his habit, to sleep on a daybed with a pistol under the pillow. As soon as the party was settled in, the Bedaux moved out—they were landlords, not hosts; Windsor paid rent and the servants' wages—and did not return until just before the wedding.

Despite the occasional arrival of friends to fill out the bridge table, time dragged. To help it pass, Katharine Rogers made frequent trips to Paris, but Wallis dared not, and Herman would not quit her side. Things improved in April, when the early spring that they had left behind on the Côte d'Azur caught up with them. They could take walks then and lunch at nearby restaurants and play golf, and even visit the famous Loire châteaux. The Duchess remembered that "when we made one of our little expeditions, Herman always told the reporters exactly where we were going, and they never followed us. They trusted him, because he always told them the truth. He used to take me out just to divert me," she added, "so that I wouldn't always be sitting in the house just staring into space, which is what I did most of the time."

One game of golf had a pitiful ending. A courier from the Duke had brought Wallis little Slipper, who had gone to Enzesfeld with him. The day after he arrived, Wallis, Herman, and the Rickatson-Hatts took him along with their foursome to give him some exercise. He was nosing in the rough when a viper struck him and killed him. Wallis never forgot Slipper's death. She said, "The duke's telephone call usually lasted close to an hour. That afternoon it was much shorter. We were both too grief-stricken to talk. Another thing: I suddenly remembered that woman who had read my horoscope so many years before in New York [i.e., Evangeline Adams]. She told me that I'd die unexpectedly, some place like a golf course. Poor little Slipper brought her prediction to mind, and I seldom played golf afterwards. In fact, I may have stopped then and there." To solace her, Bedaux bought her another cairn, Pookie.

Some weeks later the Duke, himself tortured by tedium, addressed an impatient and impassioned appeal to his lawyers to find legal grounds that would let him visit Wallis, if only for an afternoon. Thorny problems had to be settled— engaging a priest, choosing the friends they wanted at the wedding—things that, he argued, could best be done vis-à-vis. The lawyers were sympathetic, but did not yield. The Duke later reminded George Allen, "You told me very, very seriously that if I went to Candé, it would be at my own risk." So, frustrated, he stayed on in Austria.

The six-month waiting period fixed by the decree ended on April 27. At ten-thirty on the morning of May 3, George Allen telephoned from London, first to Candé, then to Villa Appesbach that the court had finally acted: The decree was now absolute. Wallis got through to the Duke in minutes. Joyfully he shouted the tidings that he was already booked on the Orient Express, which would pass through Salzburg that afternoon and would arrive at Verneuil, a station some thirty miles east of Paris, after breakfast. He was bringing with him, he added, the new equerry, Dudley Forwood, Inspector Storrier, a valet, and Thomas Carter, a small, precise, elderly clerk from the Privy Purse office of Buckingham Palace, who would double as private secretary.

Wallis met them at Verneuil and curtseyed to the Duke, addressing him as "Sir"; the household at Candé noticed that she continued to do so when they first met every morning. She thought he looked "very thin and strained, but I hadn't expected it otherwise. He'd been through a great deal. He was absolutely struck down by his family's behavior. He had left them in a very friendly way, but no sooner was his back turned than they began to attack him. It was a terrific shock to him and it showed on his face." A shock far more terrific would befall them on their wedding eve—one that would nearly demolish their marriage.

The Duke's intention had been to marry Wallis the moment she was free, but he had discovered that a number of troublesome factors opposed him, not the least of them being that under current Anglican doctrine on divorce, no church would receive them and no priest would administer the sacrament. Moreover, the Coronation of King George VI and Queen Elizabeth on May 12 was now but a week off, so the Duke generously decided to postpone his wedding until later, lest it trespass on his brother's day of greatest glory. Coronations were customarily scheduled for late June, with its warm weather: Queen Victoria's was on June 28 (1838); King Edward VII and Queen Alexandra's would have been on June 26 (1902) if his illness had not forced its postponement until August 9; and King George V and Queen Mary's was on June 22 (1911). But this one had been advanced more than a full month, to give spectators above street level along the Coronation route a better view than if the trees had come into full leaf.

The lovers' first hours together after their long separation were scarcely easy for either one. Wallis said, "That afternoon David and I took a walk. He began by impressing on me that he was now cut off from his family, his old work, even from most of his friends, so it was important for the two of us to plan our married lives on the assumption that we would be quite on our own. Little help would be forthcoming from the once bountiful sources in England. He was sorry for the way the British people had acted towards me. He intended to devote his life with me to mending the hurt, as best he could.

"I answered that I knew well what we were in for. I accepted the situation and was braced for the difficulties. I told him I was even sorrier for the way my own country had acted towards me. No one there of consequence had spoken up for me; no one had had the kindness to say that this Mrs. Simpson is one of us, an American, that she is a good woman, that she comes from good stock. We'd been over it before, but the idea would not let go, and I had to tell David again, 'I have ceased to be an American. I'll make my life with you outside the boundaries of a nationality. Nothing is going to crush me—not the British Empire, not the American press. You and I will make a life together, a good life.' "

He had warned her once that he was taking her into a void. It was already enveloping them.

It was a peculiar void—a void of the spirit, of purpose, of personal meaning. The Duke realized by now that his desire to be married with his brothers as supporters, and in his sister's approving presence, would not be fulfilled—the Royal Family steadfastly refused to participate in the wedding of divorced persons. Moreover, Kent's wife, Marina, and Gloucester's, Alice, would not have accompanied their husbands to Candé under any circumstances. In the end, Windsor settled on Fruity Metcalfe, his friend and faithful aide of sixteen years.

Windsor's bitterness over what he called the "Palace boycott" led him to limit the formal invitations to fewer than twenty. His attitude was, Let friends who still loved him show their loyalty by proposing themselves. The few that did included Hugh Lloyd Thomas, who had been his assistant private secretary in 1929–35 and was now the British Minister in Paris. But the Brownlows did not go to Candé; Perry had little wish to celebrate the sad outcome of an abdication he had tried to prevent. Nor was Sibyl Colefax or Emerald Cunard there. Nor was Hugh Sefton, or Eric Dudley, or the Duff Coopers, or the Mountbattens.

Years would pass before the defaulters were forgiven, although the Duke himself may have unwittingly encouraged their absence by his decision to send out so few invitations. Dudley Forwood has no recollection of their being sent to anyone, not even to the King or to Queen Mary. Wallis and the Duke apparently asked certain friends to invite certain others by word of mouth, but—says Forwood—"Most of the people who came proposed themselves. I know for a fact that many of the Duke's old friends, especially those who valued their places at Court, stayed away rather than risk offending the Palace. The Duke was always suspicious of the ones who sought him out later. He'd remark, 'All they want is to be able to return to England and to say they'd seen me.' "

A rumor popular at the time was that an unspoken order had gone out from the Palace: The wedding was to be ignored, on pain of reprisal. The truth is that the King held no one back from Candé, and bore no grudge against anyone who went there.

On May 8, the Duke announced that his marriage would take place on Thursday, June 3. That same day, the bride-to-be did something that must have summoned wry smiles to the faces of Win Spencer and Ernest Simpson: She had her name changed back to Wallis Warfield by deed poll— back to her virginal beginnings, as it were—and thereby prepared to defy again the old superstition against changing the name but not the letter. She did this, she has written, to please her fiancé, who was hoping that the expedient would help exorcise the disturbing thought that she had loved and been loved by other men. Far away in London, at this time, Emerald Cunard would insist to Bruce Lockhart that she was "sure that the Duke of Windsor has not yet lived with Mrs. Simpson, and that he worships her as a virginal saint." Bruce Lockhart made the entry in his diary and added, "I doubt this." His skepticism may have been ill founded, along with the Duke's jealousy; and Lady Cunard's confidence may have been more thoroughly justified than she realized. For if Wallis Simpson herself is to be believed, she had indeed come to the Duke as a virgin: "I have had two husbands," she told Jack Aird on the *Nahlin*, "and I never went to bed with either of them." (So much for her often repeated assertion that the greatest disappointment in her life was her childlessness.) When Aird was asked if he had made any comment at the time, he said, "It did not occur to me to find a parallel with the Virgin Mary."

The date set, Candé was besieged by the international press. Its curiosity was nowhere so intense as it had been first at Felixstowe, then at the Fort, and most recently at Cannes; still, the press associations and the leading British, French, and American newspapers posted their flashiest writers to the scene. Kenneth T. Downs, chief of the International News Service's Paris bureau and soon to be commander of O.S.S. Field Intelligence in the European theatre in World War II, went on watch immediately after the Duke's arrival from Villa Appesbach. The preparations, he recalls, had an air of carnival. No one seemed to be fully in charge, or to know just how the wedding was to be brought off. Herman Rogers gallantly took on the thankless task of press secretary, as he had done at Cannes. Every afternoon at five, he walked down to the gatehouse to issue a brief report on how Mrs. Simpson—as everyone continued to think of her—had passed her day. It was always a mob scene, with the reporters, men and women, crowding around to ask how much of an allowance George VI had settled on his brother, and if Mrs. Simpson was pregnant, and what the trousseau had cost. Rogers answered as best he could and always with tact and good humor. No one thought to ask what would prove to be the crucial question: What title would the King bestow upon her? Everyone took it for granted that she, like the wives of the other royal dukes, would become "Her Royal Highness." The "press conference" over, the reporters would race back to Tours, twelve miles away, file their stories, then dine at the Hôtel Univers and play poker. They went to Tours because Monts, the hamlet nearest Candé, had only one telephone. It was capricious and it screeched, but Downs forehandedly leased it, expecting to scoop his rivals with the wedding *FLASH!* Alas, on the great day a French reporter discovered his scheme and cut the wire.

Downs had come to know Rogers at Cannes, and to like him. Calling on him now, he reconnoitered the ground and later was able to interpret a little scene that escaped the other reporters. The château's only radio, he had learned, was in the gatehouse. On Coronation Day, just before the broadcast began, Downs found a point of vantage and focused his binoculars on the château driveway. Wallis's autobiography paints an affecting picture of the Duke raptly listening to the solemn service, and presumably brooding on the thought that it had so nearly been meant for him and the woman beside him. But Downs counted only Herman and Katharine Rogers, Wallis, and Forwood entering the gatehouse. The Duke's absence, he decided, was further evidence of the ill feeling between the brothers, and he implied as much in his story. He added, "In a splendid gesture to prove to the whole world the unity of the British Royal Family, and contradict malicious rumors which had cropped up since the Abdication, [Queen Mary] broke the tradition by which no English Queen Dowager is present at the Coronation of her husband's successor, and attended the ceremony at Westminster Abbey."[1] In London, meanwhile, Ernest Simpson and Mary Raffray had turned their radio to the service, and Mary would write to her sister Anne, "Ernest said to me, 'I couldn't have taken it if it had been Wallis.' "

As June 3 drew closer, the number of reporters standing by in Monts swelled to more than two hundred. The Havas Agency was represented by a young Frenchman, Maurice Schumann, who would eventually become Foreign Minister. Cornelius Vanderbilt, Jr., drove up in a luxurious

trailer and offered his credentials as a roving correspondent
for an assortment of minor press services and magazines.
The most splendiferous figure was Randolph Churchill,
whom Esmond Rothermere had engaged at a gaudy price
to report the wedding for the *Daily Mail*. Downs remembers him for a "shock of golden hair, blue eyes, an engaging smile, and a determination to shake up Britain and
arouse it to an appreciation of Baldwin's folly in letting a
great king go." Young Randolph's connections gave him
an immediate entrée to the château; he would dine there
every few days, yet during his three weeks on the scene,
he never wrote a line until toward the end. Then, having
composed a paean to the noble works and splendid character of Edward VIII, he telephoned his father in London
and read it to him. He was strangely subdued when he
met Downs for a drink at the end of the day. His father,
he explained, had urged him to be more sparing in his use
of the famous phrase "the woman he loves." Its undoubt-
ed author warned his son that it had "become a trifle shopworn. . . . Nowadays when the plumber is late, he says
it's because of the woman he loves." Rothermere had another objection: The piece "lacked balance." He dropped
it, but Max Beaverbrook picked it up; he liked the light
flavor of malice in young Churchill's regret for the Government's mishandling of the Abdication.

All this while, a final problem, still unsolved, was bedev-
iling the bridegroom and gnawing at his pride: Who would
perform his marriage? The civil ceremony that French law
requires would be conducted by the mayor of Monts, but
the Duke longed for a religious ceremony, too, conducted
by a priest of his own Anglican faith, and none had volunteered. "It was an important thing with him," his wife said
later. "I imagine it was because this was his first marriage.
As for myself, I'd have been content with just the mayor's
blessing." On the rare occasions when the Duke could be
induced to probe into his motives afresh, he was always
candid about his reason for insisting on a priest: "Marriage
to Wallis would be the fulfillment of such meaning as life
possessed for me, and I wanted the union sanctified."
It was not uncommon even then for Anglican clergymen
to remarry the innocent parties in a divorce, yet George

Allen had beaten the ecclesiastical bushes for weeks without finding a priest willing to marry the quondam Defender of the Anglican Faith. Then, with the wedding day less than a week off, one came forward: the Rev. Robert Anderson Jardine, vicar of a church in the working-class district of Darlington, in the diocese of Durham. Out of the blue, Jardine wrote to Herman Rogers that he would happily go to France if his former monarch wished a church service. Rogers showed the letter to the Duke, who telephoned to Allen, who telegraphed to Jardine, asking him to ring back.

If Allen had checked on Jardine's reputation, he would have learned that though his own congregation liked him well enough—he gave them four services every Sunday—his brother ministers did not. He had been an agnostic in his youth; after his conversion he had served as a missionary to the fishermen in the Shetland Islands and now, at nearly sixty, was something of an "activist"—contemptuous of old religious customs, impatient to thrust the church into vexing social questions, quarrelsome with his bishop, and—beyond any doubt—greedy for publicity. His pleasure at defying his bishop—Jardine said loftily, "I consulted only my own conscience"—probably explains his overture to Rogers. Allen knew none of this. He had no time to establish anything beyond that Jardine was an ordained priest, as represented. And when Jardine rang back, reaffirming his offer, Allen, glad to be rid of a distasteful chore, gave him a round-trip ticket to Tours, plus a fee, and accepted his promise to be at the château in good time. Jardine never bothered to ask his bishop's permission, knowing that it would be refused; thus there was no announcement of his role until he appeared in Tours.

The press at Candé had sensed that the lovers were having trouble recruiting a clergyman, and its cynical speculations inspired Kenneth Downs to sponsor a harmless hoax. On Tuesday morning, two days before the wedding, he happened to meet a friend in Tours, a Hearst reporter on holiday. Their conversation turned to the goings-on at the château, and Downs mentioned the Windsors' problem of a proper wedding ceremony.

"No problem at all!" his friend assured him. "In a pinch, I'll offer to perform the ceremony myself. Look—"

He whipped off his necktie, turned his stiff collar, and—his natural talent for mimicry supported by a florid complexion and a resonant voice—launched into one of his favorite roles, that of a bibulous, wenching Scottish pastor, trying to explain why his bishop had unfrocked him.

Downs knew genius when he saw it. He persuaded his friend to retire and stay out of sight until sent for. Meanwhile, Downs went to the regular five-o'clock conference, where he floated a rumor that the chosen clergyman had arrived in Tours; and later, as the Univers bar was filling, he gave the signal. In a few minutes, a stranger entered. The reporters quickly noticed his somber clothes and clerical collar, and crowded around him: Was it he who would officiate at the wedding? The "pastor," speaking in a strong Scottish burr, righteously refused to answer; he was bound by secrecy, he said. As if this were not confession enough, he allowed a drink or two of whisky to loosen his curbs, and soon—as burr became slur—he was frankly acknowledging the reasons for his presence. What was his parish? the press inquired. Ah, this was a tender subject! His parish had been a proud one, but evil tongues had accused him—not without reason, alas!—of drinking and philandering. His bishop had hearkened and removed him; his only congregation now was that of "all lovers, sinners, and dissenters." Still, there were compensations: His worldly outlook had come to the Duke of Windsor's attention, and the invitation to Candé had followed.

A fortified toddy in hand, the "pastor" was well launched on a Rabelaisian account of his transgressions, interlarded with his somewhat unorthodox ideas for injecting into the Windsor ceremony "a livelier spirit, a jocund air," when there was a commotion outside. The authentic Jardine, escorted by a member of the Duke's staff, was registering at the desk. . . .

In the realm of the spirit, Jardine would presently prove to be as deplorable a guide as Bedaux would be in the political realm. Indeed, before 1937 ended, some of the reporters who had been in the Univers bar that evening would wonder if the Windsors might not have been wiser to have scratched him in favor of Downs's friend, the Hearst man, whose impersonation of a cleric, unlike Jardine's, was flawless throughout.

* * *

By Tuesday, June 1, the preparations were complete. Aunt Bessie Merryman arrived, the sole representative of either side of the bride's family; others had offered to come, but Wallis had cabled them, "Unfortunately have had to refuse family. Terribly sorry." Many of her cousins and old friends, including bridesmaids from her first wedding, did not receive even announcements, to their surprise and hurt. George Allen, grave of mien, flew over from London to rewrite the wills and draw up the marriage settlement. Alexandra and Fruity Metcalfe arrived that same day. Bedaux, down from Paris several days earlier, hovered about. Wallis noted that he was "small, full of energy, not particularly attractive looking"; Alexandra Metcalfe found him "brilliant and very astute, but unattractive." On an earlier weekend visit, the Duke had discovered that Bedaux seemed to share his own interest in urban housing and improving the workingman's lot. Now, as Bedaux expanded on his multifarious international operations—particularly those under way or in prospect for the United States and Germany—the Duke let himself be persuaded that association with this dynamic man, even visiting Germany with him, might be a stimulating escape from idleness.

Mainbocher came down for the final fitting of the crepe-satin wedding dress. Born in Chicago, and originally "Main Bocher," he did not weld his names together until he became a professional couturier—one of the world's greatest, with a clientele that included Mary Martin, Gloria Vanderbilt (Mrs. Wyatt Cooper), and, conspicuously, the Duchess of Windsor. He was proud of having designed uniforms for the WAVES, for the women's auxiliary of the Marine Corps, and for the Girl Scouts, but he is perhaps best known as the sponsor of the decorated sweater and of the "basic black" dress. The unusual shade of blue of Wallis's dress, which he had chosen (and had had the cloth dyed in secret) to match the pale, watery green of the salon where the ceremony would be held, was at once press-christened "Wallis blue" and at once copied and sold around the world. Reboux made a matching hat of straw, feathers, and tulle in a design that impressed at least one observer as "halo-like." Wallis explained, "Like any other woman who has been married before, my idea was to have a perfectly simple dress and a perfectly simple hat to go with it." From Paris arrived, as well, a manicurist and a hairdresser. Constance Spry, who had often supplied the flower arrangements for Bryanston Court and Cumberland Terrace, came from London to convert the somber château into a glorious bower. With her arms full of peonies, she told Cecil Beaton, whom Wallis had chosen as court photographer, "I'm going to make the flowers as beautiful as I can. I'd do anything for her. I adore her!"

Beaton always watched Wallis through two lenses: one friendly and soft, the other professional and hard. From the visit to Candé, he would remember that "she twisted and twirled her rugged hands. She laughed a square laugh, protruded her lower lip. Her eyes were excessively bright, slightly froglike, also wistful." While she was posing for him, she made the revealing admission that she was "very much like a man in many ways," and that Katharine Rogers, her best friend, shared the same authoritative traits. Wallis once said, "I had a surer idea of what I wanted than most women do, and so had little trouble making up my mind on most matters"—providentially for the Duke just then, since his attempt to act as the Man in Charge was even less convincing than usual, though Alexandra Metcalfe found him in "marvelous form, obviously happy, much easier to talk to" and determined to make "no allusion to England, family, staff, or friends." She also observed that "he sees through Wallis's eyes, hears through her ears, and speaks through her mouth."

Jardine presented himself on the morning of Wednesday the second. Wallis would remember him as a simple sort, a country parson. Windsor thought him rather ordinary: "stocky, ruddy-faced, a bulbous nose, and quite assertive." He remained for lunch and passed the afternoon rummaging through the château, under Bedaux's guidance, for articles to lend a semblance of religious meaning to the ceremony. A church in the village gave candles, but a cross acceptable to the Protestant service was not to be found in this Roman Catholic community. An appeal to the British Embassy in Paris brought assurance that the Embassy chapel would send one down in care of the Minister— diplomatic, not Anglican—Hugh Lloyd Thomas. This would be the second favor that Thomas had done for the

Duke that spring. As the owner of a valiant horse named
Royal Mail, he had tipped Windsor to back it in the recent
Grand National; and when Royal Mail won, at 20–1,
Windsor happily boasted that he had cleared enough to
pay the "formidable" bill, nearly four thousand dollars, for
the telephone calls between Enzesfeld and Cannes. He
liked to add, "In 1935, I went to Aintree for the Grand
National and backed the winner, Reynoldstown. Next year
I backed him again, and he won again. And the next year I
had Royal Mail. Never before or since did I win a race
three years running." Less than a year after Royal Mail's
victory, Thomas was killed steeplechasing.

For an altar, Jardine selected an ornate chest carved
with a row of fat caryatids. Wallis said gaily, "We must
have something to cover up those extra women!" and produced from her own linen a beautiful organdy tablecloth
with a design of lilies, which Lady Alexandra pinned up to
resemble an altar cloth. Some of the guests observed that
Bedaux and Jardine were developing a warm rapport in
the course of their rummaging. George Allen said, "They
quickly perceived that they were birds of a feather." Fruity
Metcalfe, too, was sure that each recognized the other as
"a privateer sailing under false colors." Wallis would insist
later that the pair had never been members of the wedding
party and that Bedaux had little to do with the preparations: "Neither he nor Fern was then running the house. I
had made it clear that I would engage the servants who
would look after us and our guests during our stay. I paid
their wages and all the running expenses—food, wine, telephone, electricity. Everything. None of us," she added,
"not the Duke, not George Allen or Walter Monckton, not
Herman Rogers, ever forsaw how Mr. Jardine and Mr. Bedaux would manipulate the publicity they got simply from
being with us. I mean, you have to trust strangers some
time. But nearly everybody seems to have had one motive
or another for trying to exploit us just then."

On Wednesday afternoon, the organist, Marcel Dupré,
arrived. He had been borrowed from Notre Dame and was
reputed to have an inexhaustible repertoire, but when he
learned that he was expected to accompany the ceremony
with "O Perfect Love," he looked blank; and Alexandra
Metcalfe had to hum it for him until he could pick it out.

Cecil Beaton had spent most of the day photographing the bridal couple in their wedding clothes, which they had put on despite the tradition that it is bad luck to do so. Finished at last, he left for London with his precious film. Walter Monckton arrived at teatime. The Duke was resting in his room, but Monckton asked to see him at once: He was bringing a letter of extreme importance, from the King. As Windsor read it, his hands began to shake. Monckton said later, "He was transfixed, as if poleaxed. Then an oath burst from him: '*Damn* them! Damn them *all*! I'll make them pay for this!' "

The letter notified him that the King would, by letters patent, "be pleased to declare that the Duke of Windsor shall, notwithstanding his Act of Abdication, be entitled to hold and enjoy . . . the title, style or attribute of Royal Highness," but that the same attribute was not being extended to his wife or descendants, if any. The King, as Fountain of Honor, had thus brutally marked the Duchess of Windsor as the inferior in the union—had excluded her, in her view, as a member of the family. Unlike the wives of the other royal brothers, she would be simply a duchess, whereas her sister-in-law's names were preceded by the magic initials "H.R.H." Accordingly, other women curtseyed to them, and men bowed. They were conduits authorized to transmit the blood royal to the next generation. But none of this was to be Wallis's.

"What a *damnable* wedding present!" Windsor shouted.

His first impulse was to suppress the letter until after the ceremony, but he quickly realized that it was an abridgment of the official notice that was about to be published in the *London Gazette*, and that the story was bound to come out next day. In any case, it is doubtful whether he could have bridled his fury that much longer. He raced up the turret stairs to tell Wallis the crushing news, and when they all gathered for cocktails, everyone was aware of it. Still, Windsor felt that something had to be said. He began, "My brother—" but choked, and there was a painful moment before he went on, almost sobbing, "My brother *promised* me there would be no trouble over the title! He *promised* me!"

One who refused to condemn the broken promise was Donald Blythe, who says in his *The Age of Illusion*,[2] "Per-

haps Royalty, having to spend so much of its time foun-
taining honor and magnanimity over its inferiors, has to be
indulged when it turns on the cold tap over its equals."

The Duke, his heartsickness struggling with the rage,
told Alexandra Metcalfe that he would like to give up his
own title, and that he had already sent off a letter warning
his brother that he would fight the ruling. He swore to
Herman Rogers that he would make the King withdraw it,
adding, "I hope that you and all of Wallis's friends and
mine will recognize her after tomorrow as 'Her Royal
Highness,' and that the ladies will curtsey to her." He told
Forwood, "Notify the staff to address my wife as 'Your
Royal Highness.' I expect you to do the same."

While they were dressing, he poured out his resentment
in front of Fruity. It seemed to calm him, for when Jardine
led the wedding party through a brief rehearsal just before
dinner, the Duke picked up his cues promptly. M. Dupré
finished his last embroideries on "O Perfect Love," and
they went in. It was to have been a gay table, but the affront to the bride from the family of the bridegroom cast a
heavy pall over the company.

The evil tidings had not been unexpected; it was the
form they took that made for shock. A day or two earlier,
Ulick Alexander had telephoned from the Palace to warn
the Duke that Monckton would be bringing him an envelope which would contain "not very good news." Monckton was familiar with the contents; the King had shown
him a draft, apologetically remarking that "This isn't going
to make a nice wedding present for my brother." It remained Monckton's strong conviction that the King was
torn in two directions. He recoiled from raising to royal
rank a woman whom the family loathed; he and his mother
could never convince themselves that David would long
abide such a woman, twice married and, on her record,
faithless. In fact, the King mentioned to Baldwin that the
reason he himself was reluctant to confer the title on her
was that she would remain a Royal Highness forever, even
if the marriage broke up. Suppose that it did—or that the
Duke died—and she remarried and bore children: What
would *their* titles be? Or suppose that the marriage failed,
and the Duke remarried: What would the royal family do

about *two* unwanted Royal Duchesses? Or suppose that the marriage endured and was fruitful: Might this not encourage a line of pretenders? All these considerations weighed with the King and his advisers. On the other hand, he shrank from wounding so grievously a brother truly beloved. This, Monckton felt, was the stronger pull; and with the advocacy of which he was a master, he urged his sovereign to forbear.

As in so many other cases where the interests of family, Church, and State converged upon the Duke, it is all but impossible by now to identify with any assurance the prime movers in the affair of Wallis's title. Twenty years after the event, the Duke declared that "The letter was obviously written by Sir John Snake [i.e., Simon], probably with the help of someone in the Palace Secretariat and God knows who else. My brother just took a piece of paper that was handed to him and copied it. It was not an idea he'd have thought of himself. Even less was the language his own—legalistic, no loopholes. I never blamed him. I've always given him the benefit of the doubt. Without question, other influences were working on him—somebody close to him, perhaps, others possibly of ministerial rank, and I daresay the Archbishop of Canterbury. Yes, the Primate almost certainly had a hand in it."

—The Primate only possibly, but, almost certainly, the Royal Family. On Coronation Day, Chips Channon had written in his diary, "[Queen Mary] and the Court group hate Wallis Simpson to the point of hysteria, and are taking up the wrong attitude: why persecute her now that all is over? Why not let the Duke of Windsor, who has given up so much, be happy?" Whoever first raised the question of royal rank for Wallis had quickly passed the hot potato on to the Cabinet; and the Cabinet, nervous about handing down the decision on its own, sounded out the Dominions. It was Baldwin's responsibility to sign the cables, but he used his failing health and his imminent retirement from office as an excuse for not doing so; instead, he directed Simon to induce Neville Chamberlain, already designated to succeed him as Prime Minister, to take on the squalid chore. Monckton tried to dissuade Simon from making a Cabinet issue—and indeed an Empire issue—of what was basically an act of private retribution. He failed; the cables went out; and later he was given to understand that none of the Dominions favored raising Mrs. Simpson to royal rank, Canada and Australia opposing it with special vigor.

Monckton, fastidious in the way he served the two parties without breaching confidences, never fully revealed to the Duke either the adverse machinations that in the end gained the King's grudging consent, or his own efforts to spare the Duke and Wallis the humiliation in store; but he never disguised where he felt the equities—and his sympathies—lay. Among his papers was found this note, rephrasing the case he made to the King and to Simon and other members of the Cabinet: "When [the Duke] had been King he was told he could not marry Mrs. Simpson because she would have to take his status and be Queen, so he gave up his Kingdom and Empire to make her his wife. He could not give up his Royal birth, or his right to be called 'His Royal Highness' which flowed from it. It was a little hard to be told, when he did marry her, that she would not have the same status as himself."

It was worse than hard: It was all but unbearable. Wallis Windsor always insisted that the blank in her title never vexed her. It would have ill become her to quarrel over the rank withheld from her, considering what he had given up to be her husband. But quibble she did, and not only quibble but rage within. Privately she wailed with Salanio, "O that I had a title good enough to keep his name company!" Publicly her pose was one of superiority to these petty gauds and vanities. Whenever the subject of the title arose, she protested that it meant nothing to her, "but it was an insult that gave my enemies a stick to beat me with. This wounded the Duke deeply. He saw it as a blow aimed past him at me."

That was so. No one would converse with him long about his post-Abdication life without realizing that the breach with his family, his interminable bartering with the British Government, his stubborn insistence on his Duchess's being rendered nonetheless the civilities that accompany "H.R.H."—all had their roots in the title denied. What he could never bring himself to admit, but what she—especially when in a foul humor—never let him forget, was that he had failed again. He had led her to believe that she would become Queen Empress on their wedding day, and she awoke to find that she was not to be even a royal duchess. This was the secret source of the shame and sorrow that awaited the poor Duke: the dreadful realization of his ineffectuality.

The wedding day, Thursday, brought "bride's weather"—warm and sunny—and the bridegroom's spirit lifted. Soon after luncheon, the mayor of Monts, resplendent in his tricolor sash, performed the civil ceremony in the presence of the sixteen guests: Mrs. Merryman, the Rogerses, the Metcalfes, the Bedaux, Lady Selby, the Rothschilds, Walter Monckton, George Allen, Hugh Lloyd Thomas, Randolph Churchill, Forwood, and Mr. Carter. Then, while the pipe organ wheezed "O Perfect Love" for M. Dupré, Mr. Jardine's religious service began. Herman Rogers gave the bride away. Fruity Metcalfe, as best man, stood at the groom's right, holding a prayer book that Queen Mary had presented to her eldest son on his tenth birthday; written in it was "To darling David from his loving Mother." Three reporters from the press associations, self-conscious in morning coats and striped trousers, watched from the back of the room. The candlelight sparkled on the bride's jewels: a magnificent brooch of sapphires and diamonds at her throat, with a sapphire-and-diamond bracelet (the groom's present) and sapphire earrings, their deep blue accentuating the blue of the long dress, and the short, tight-fitting jacket. Mr. Jardine read the service "simply and well," in Lady Alexandra's judgment, but the patent artificiality of the scene moved her powerfully: "It could be nothing but pitiable and tragic to see a King of England of only six months ago married under those circumstances. And yet, pathetic as it was, his manner was so simple and dignified, and he was so sure of himself in his happiness, that it gave something to the sad little service which it is hard to describe. He had tears running down his face when he came into the salon. . . ."

There was a brief, whispered debate among those ladies who would curtsey to the new Duchess and those who would merely bow, but it was broken off by a summons to the wedding breakfast, with champagne, toasts, and music for dancing. The bow-or-curtsey dilemma would perplex

many ladies from this moment on, and those who tried to
evade it by pretending not to see the Duchess were sometimes brusquely jerked to attention by the Duke.

Telegrams came from the King and Queen, Queen Mary,
and Winston Churchill, among many, many others. Queen
Mary's must have been a strain for her to write, since June
3 was also the birthday of her late husband. She noted in
her diary, "Alas! the wedding day in France of David &
Mrs. Warfield." A letter from Stanley Baldwin paid the
Duke a tribute that was guarded but fair: "Through all
that time in the early winter, you ran dead straight with
me and you accomplished what you said you would do:
you maintained your own dignity throughout; you did
nothing to embarrass your successor, nor anything, as
might so easily have happened, to shake the monarchy
more than was inevitable under the circumstances."

Among the presents was one from Charles and Fern Bedaux: a statue entitled "Love," by a German sculptress,
Frau Anny Hoefken-Hempel, who was under the protection of Dr. Hjalmar Schacht, Hitler's Minister of Economic
Affairs and president of the Reichsbank, and a man whom
Bedaux was sedulously cultivating. There was even a present to Herman Rogers from the press: a gold fountain pen
and a testimonial to his patience and evenhandedness.

For Monckton, the events of the day brought an agony
of spirit. He was still haunted by his recollection of Windsor's refusal to be deflected from renunciation of the kingship. More sharply than most, Monckton had felt Wallis's
hardness, her selfishness; he and George Allen, after all,
had observed her cold-blooded casting-off of Ernest Simpson. After the ceremony, finding himself alone with the
new Duchess, he yielded to an impulse and led her into the
garden, where, in his quiet way, he gave her a lecture on
behavior—perhaps the only reasoned lecture she had heard
since Uncle Sol tried to lay down the law to her in youth.
"I told her," Monckton wrote in his notes, and later repeated to her almost the same words, when she was re-
freshing her memory in preparation for her autobiography,
"that most people in England disliked her very much because the Duke had married her and given up his Throne:
but if she made him, and kept him, happy all his days, all

that would change; if she failed, the British people would never forgive her. She took it all very simply and kindly, just saying, 'Walter, don't you think I've thought of all that? I think I can make him happy.' "

It was all over by half-past three. "The last toast quaffed, the last measure trod," the newlyweds set out in the Buick, Ladbrook at the wheel, for the night train to Venice, where their summer-long honeymoon would begin.

Cecil Beaton had told himself, "She loves him, though I feel she is not in love with him." Alexandra Metcalfe would not concede even that Wallis loved him; she wrote in her diary that evening, "If she occasionally showed a glimmer of softness, took his arm, looked at him as though she loved him, one would warm toward her, but her attitude toward him is so correct. The effect is of a woman unmoved by the infatuation of a younger man."

Next day's *Times* devoted an entire column to the wedding. The *Court Circular* ignored it.

Jardine, the turbulent priest, lost no time in trying to exploit his fleeting prominence. He took his wife to America and, expectably, headed straight for Los Angeles, in a small car studded with medallions of Edward VIII, struck off before the Coronation aborted. He liked to show acquaintances the cuff links he had been given as a memento of the wedding—gold, initialed "EW"—and to hand out his new business cards:

Rev. R. Anderson Jardine
(The Duke's Vicar)

He had hoped for a lecture tour, but even with the help of a Hollywood agent he could not muster enough interest to warrant one. In 1941, he was given the temporary pastorate of a small Los Angeles church which he immediately renamed "Windsor Cathedral"; and on his first day in the pulpit, he read to the congregation a letter from the Duke, authorizing him to choose a gold altar cross "as a remembrance." He displayed a model of it and said it would cost about five thousand dollars.

Windsor Cathedral did not prosper; nor did Jardine. In desperation, he began to talk of going into the movies, and of writing a book about the Windsor wedding. Neither plan worked out. He and his wife had moved into a one-room apartment when help came at last: an appointment as presiding bishop of the South African Episcopal Church, an independent sect, not directly related to the Church of England. They returned home and were preparing to sail for his diocese when he died, in 1950.

The Windsors told the press that they would "always remember with gratitude his Christian charity in coming forward to marry them."

Candé, too, returned briefly to the news, in a capacity which few could have foreseen. Just before the French Government fell in June 1940, Ambassador Bullitt and his staff moved south from Paris and made Candé the American Embassy in France *pro tem.*

CHAPTER 4
An Embittered Honeymoon

"Yours has been a very steady rise in the social scale,"
said Lord Ickenham admiringly. "Starting at the bot-
tom with a humble baronet—slumming, you might
almost call it—you go on to an earl and then to a
duke. It does you credit."
> —Uncle Fred in the Springtime,
> P. G. WODEHOUSE

The honeymoon began tenderly and traditionally. Between
trains in Venice the day after the wedding, the happy couple fed the pigeons in St. Mark's Square and rode in a
gondola, as thousands of honeymooners had done before
them. Passersby clapped and waved to see the famous lovers, and the lovers waved back, bowing and smiling.
Rather less traditional was the retinue in attendance just
offstage: the Duke's valet and the Duchess's maid; the
equerry, Dudley Forwood, to deal with protocolary problems; and Chief Inspector Storrier to smooth the party's
passage across frontiers and through customs. The Duchess's new secretary, Mrs. Melville Bedford, who was bi-
lingual in French and English, had gone ahead; so had Mr.
Carter, to manage the staff and supervise the transfer
of the honeymoon baggage.

Carter's job, judging from the newspaper accounts, did
not invite the term "sinecure." Somehow the press had discovered that the Windsors found it necessary to travel with
266 pieces, including 186 trunks*—an inordinacy that

---

*When the Duchess's old Warrenton beau, Hugh Spilman, read
this item, he burst out, "I can't believe it! I simply *can't* believe
it! Why, when Wallis and I were going to spend the weekend
with friends she just threw a nightie and a toothbrush into a
paper bag, and away we went!"

seemed thoughtless, even shocking at a time when most of the Western world was still struggling out of the Great Depression. Even so, the statistics had their value. Not only did they provide a convenient standard for measuring the scale of the Windsors' future travels, but they proclaimed—promptly, loudly, and *coram populo*—the Duchess's resolve never to let her husband's demotion to ducal rank choke off, or impede in the slightest, the cornucopia flow of luxuries, privileges, and special attentions which she had come to expect from his previous eminence as King. Her resolve was adamantine; in the years that followed, it would corrupt her sense of values and impart a hardness and ugliness to her personality.

That evening, their train crossed the border into Austrian Carinthia and presently dropped them off at the mountain village of Villach, the station for Schloss Wasserleonburg. It was close to midnight, but the entire local populace in gay Alpine garb had waited up to welcome them and to see the mayor present a bouquet of roses. Ladbrook had driven the Buick straight through from France and was also waiting. The Windsors thanked the mayor and the crowd, and the Buick started up the steep, twisting, spine-jolting road that led to the castle, perched on the shoulder of a high ridge.

The Duchess never forgot that wild climb: "Even by daylight the road was dangerous—terribly narrow, barely wider than the car, and straight up the side of the mountain. I was terrified! The Duke was nervous too, but for a different reason: he had chosen the castle after only one quick visit, and he wasn't sure I'd care for it."

True, the lodgings he was providing for his bride's third honeymoon were less impressive than those he could have provided as monarch, but they were still superior to the hotels where she had spent her first and second. This "honeymoon cottage" was a thirteenth-century castle of some forty rooms, walled, towered, and turreted, its huge bulk softened by the faint moonlight. A platoon of servants were drawn up in the cobblestoned courtyard to greet their new chatelaine: the butler and chef whom the Duke had found through the British Legation in Vienna, the several footmen and maids he had engaged locally, and the skeleton staff left behind by Count Münster. Morning would reveal

a breathtaking view of the mountains, but the Duchess did
not need this bonus. She said, "To come upon the castle
so—in the moonlight—was utterly enchanting. I fell in
love with it immediately."

Her enchantment did not last long. At that advanced
stage in her relationship with the Duke, there was little in
his personality likely to bring her a rapturous surprise, and
(what would prove decisive in their marriage) her mastery
of his spirit was already complete. Too, after their months
of exile on their separate islands of discontent, neither had
much desire for privacy. Their immediate concern was to
revive old friendships in suspense or default, and to salvage
what they could from the ruin of their lives. They did not
want to sit and gaze into each other's eyes while the spell
deepened. They wanted to be attended, surrounded, cos-
seted, and consoled.

Happily for their simpler social needs, the Austrian Tyrol, with its picture-book lakes and slopes, its charming
chalets and restaurants, was well sprinkled that summer
with English friends of theirs on holiday; and noble
Austrian families whom the Duke had known earlier had
houses and shooting lodges close by, overlooking the
Wörther See or the flowering valleys. So the honeymooners
did not lack company. Friends came and went. Aunt Bessie Merryman arrived early in July to spend ten days, and
wrote home, "I found a happy pair." A month later,
Gladys and Mike Scanlon flew in from London, bringing a
frisky young cairn, Detto, as a companion for Pookie. Wallis found the new puppy "most alluring, combining the
Scanlon charm with that of his own." The Windsors dined
out several times a week and had friends in on the other
evenings. Nor did they lack facilities for recreation. The
castle offered a tennis court, a heated swimming pool, and
a stable. There were stag and chamois on the hills for
stalking, and a nine-hole golf course in the neighborhood.
Sometimes Ladbrook took them touring until they found a
pleasant restaurant for lunch. When the mountains, the forest, the lakes, the simpler inns, and local society palled,
bride and groom made an excursion to Vienna or Venice,
or to Salzburg for the music festival. On specially fine
mornings, the bridegroom, decked in Alpine vest and scarf,

Lederhosen, stout boots, and white woolen stockings, climbed a steep trail behind the castle to work up the sweat he craved. The summit gained, he used a hand mirror to signal his safe ascent to his bride on the terrace far below.

His passion for exercise was a carry-over from his youth. At Oxford, his daily schedule had almost invariably begun with his rising at seven and running twice around "Adder's"—Addison's Walk. He exercised partly from his terror of the family tendency toward corpulence, and partly in rebellion against one of the occupational impositions on kings and princes: having to stand rigidly at salute or sit rigidly on a horse or a throne, or at a surfeiting, interminable dinner. As Prince and then as King, he had come to loathe inertia and to long for activity of any sort. Now, as Duke, since his intellectual interests were few and narrow, he found satisfaction in exercising until he dripped.

Outwardly, the Windsors gave the impression of lovers well launched on an idyllic union. The Duchess said, "We *adored* Austria! Oh, we were so very happy there! We could go about peacefully and not be bothered. Best of all was being together again."

Another secretary, Peggy Benton, who had been borrowed from the Legation in Vienna to deal with the sackfuls of mail that were arriving from all over the world, has drawn a sunny vignette of the Duke adapting himself to the role of man-about-the-house. Miss Benton's "office" was a small sitting room between the drawing room and the Windsors' bedrooms. During her first morning's work, a door opened behind her and a diminutive figure entered— sunburned, in bright shorts and an open sports shirt. "Pay no attention to me," the Duke commanded her cheerily. "The Duchess would like to dictate some letters. I'll take my typewriter into the garden." A little later, she saw the former King pecking away at his portable in the shade of a lime tree, the very picture of a contented man.

Yet, before Miss Benton finished her term at Wasserleonburg, she realized that the Windsors' contentment was not unalloyed. She perceived in the Duke a deepening loneliness, "a nagging homesickness" for England, "an inner conflict" which she did not attempt to identify; and in the Duchess, a restlessness and an unconcealed boredom with the rustic existence to which the marriage had brought her. The Duchess herself, in her autobiography, confessed that the honeymoon had been a difficult time for both of them, partly because of the arguments that enmeshed them over the events that brought on the Abdication. Her book did not specify the subjects of their arguments, but she could be brutally explicit when she wished to. The Duke needed never to have yielded the throne, she would lecture him. Ignoring her own primary role in promoting that unhappy proposition, she blamed him first for pressing the morganatic marriage plan on Baldwin, and then for failing to withdraw it before the Dominions had time to reject it. If he had pulled back while Baldwin hesitated, had submitted to being crowned alone, and had exercised patience—as Churchill, Beaverbrook, and Duff Cooper all had counseled—he would still be on the throne in the summer of 1937, a working and beloved King. He and she would still have each other; she would not have become the hated, reviled woman that the Abdication had made her; and there would still be a chance of marriage in the kingship.

That was how, in hindsight, Wallis Windsor came to view the whole ruinous sequence. A compulsion to rationalize the real reasons for their lost cause drove her to return to it again and again, until the Duke in his despair finally cried out, "If we keep this up, we're never going to agree! Let's drop it for good!" In the Duchess's book they vowed then and there never to bring up that part of their past again, and she implied that they never did. But she did, continually.

The sad truth is that the roots of their discontent went deeper than a lover's tiff over the blame for mistakes past mending. The Duchess's restlessness and boredom, and the frustrations that were roiling the Duke's spirit, all had the same source: his eagerness to satisfy her every desire, and his lost power to satisfy even the ones most important to her. She had begun to blame him and his lawyers for their failure to stipulate in the Abdication compact the title that was rightly hers by marriage. He desperately wanted it for her, not because he considered the lack degrading, but because he realized he would have no peace until he had exhausted every means of obtaining it. Also, she began

prodding him to find a job in England, for two reasons:
She longed to live there again, and she did not want an
idle, love-besotted ex-King underfoot throughout the working day. Her two former husbands had been active executives; mornings saw them briskly off to the flight line or the
office, leaving her free to pursue a woman's interests. The
Duke was no less eager for a job in England, though for
reasons of pride; but he realized that life there would be
unbearable for himself and his wife unless his family accepted her and she was received at Court in equal rank
with his brothers' wives.

These claims were not altogether unreasonable. There
was, after all, the understanding reached with his brother
at the end. Windsor himself was frank to admit, in later
years, that the question of his future service as the King's
principal deputy had been left vague, not because it was
touchy, but because it did not seem important at the time.
"One must remember," he said, "that my brother and I
parted not as rivals, but in affection. The most I ever had
in mind for myself when I returned was a modified reversal
of our pre-Abdication relationship. I would give Bertie a
hand, just as he had given me a hand when I was King. I
was quite unable to comprehend how other members of my
family—namely, my mother and my sisters-in-law, as I
learned later—could possibly suspect me of harboring a desire to return to the center ring through a side door, in
search of a starring role."

There was no Prince of Wales standing by in 1937, nor
could there be one for at least another generation. Princess
Elizabeth was only eleven years old. Kent was too flighty
and Gloucester too wooden to help the King much in the
more decorative, as well as the more subtle, subsidiary
business of the monarchy; so a vacancy existed below the
throne. Windsor's two-year, self-imposed exile would not
expire until December 1938. In these circumstances, he
readily persuaded himself that it would be to his brother's
advantage, no less than to his own, if he were to return to
England then and pick up some minor part of the task for
which his gifts and exceptional training had qualified him.

If it had not been for the passions which the Abdication
had released and, more importantly, for the revulsion
which Queen Mary, Queen Elizabeth, and indeed all the

women of the Royal Family felt for Wallis Windsor, such a coexistence might have worked, unprecedented though it would have been. When, therefore, the Duke, wincing under the Duchess's rowel, began to "pester" (Monckton's word) the King by telephone and letter for a favorable ruling on his new series of demands, he put his brother in a painful predicament. Bertie could not bring himself to tell David that Elizabeth did not want him back, and that their mother and she would not receive Wallis in any capacity. Queen Mary would never forgive her son's desertion in the face of a sacred duty; and Queen Elizabeth was both apprehensive about his charm and contemptuous of his wife. As Duchess of York, she had witnessed for herself the love, admiration, and trust that her husband felt for his elder brother. A decade earlier she had respected David for defending them all against a martinet father, in their feeble efforts to fit themselves into the twentieth century. But now, in 1937, the duty and responsibility having passed to Bertie and herself, her main concern was to shield her husband from his brother's overpowering personality.

Through that first year, the brothers consulted Monckton almost daily on their dissensions, and he soon perceived that the most stubborn, the wholly unyielding, obstacle to Windsor's ambition was his straitlaced senior sister-in-law.[1]

Monckton was loath to aggravate his friend Windsor's distress by pronouncing his petition hopeless. He tried to mollify him with assurances that the King and the Government were considering alternatives, and that he could afford to be patient, since the earliest possible date for his return to England was still more than a year away. But Windsor was not to be put off; his inability to get a forthright answer from the Palace maddened him. He became corroded by the suspicion that his family were drawing away from him, and his sense of grievance was further darkened by a discourtesy on the part of his sister-in-law Marina.

The Kents came to the Tyrol that summer, to visit friends not far from Wasserleonburg. Prince George was eager to see his brother, but Princess Marina refused to accompany him. Kent decided to go anyway and telephoned Windsor that he would be along; his wife, he said, unfortunately had a previous and unbreakable engagement with her parents. Windsor told him curtly, "Well, then, if you can't bring your wife, don't *you* come! Wait until she can come, too." The King, learning of the impasse, cautioned Kent about Windsor's extreme sensitivity to any affront to Wallis and directed him to take Marina along. Even then, she balked; and Kent, disregarding the caution, went to Wasserleonburg alone. Windsor said, "When he showed up without Marina, the Duchess properly refused to see him, and I gave him a brotherly lecture he wouldn't soon forget."

That Christmas, perhaps partly as balm, Kent sent Windsor a handsome gold box. Back it came at once, with this note: "The only box I have come to expect from my brothers is a box on the ear."

Monckton, in an effort to heal the wounds, had already interrupted his own August holiday to go to Wasserleonburg and review the situation with the Windsors. Their discussions were always long and uncomfortable, and at times tense. Clever as Monckton was in advocacy, he could not persuade Windsor to relax his pressure on the King, or the Duchess to let time erode the barriers raised against her. He was heartbroken to see the man who had so recently been his monarch reduced to self-pity in idleness and to quarreling over crumbs. It was not in Monckton's character to criticize a woman, but he was never in doubt about the source of Windsor's malaise. He wrote in private: "She wanted him to eat his cake and have it, too. She could not easily reconcile herself to the fact that by marrying her the Duke had become a less important person."

Monckton was sure that the King wanted to be generous, that he would rejoice at having his brother home and in harness alongside. He told the Duke as much, explaining that the King's reluctance to settle on a date for the return and to come forward with a job was not foot-dragging, but a prudent bending to political winds. He reminded the Windsors that the Abdication had left a residue of bitterness that would be slow to dissolve, and it was therefore in the interests of all parties—the Royal Family, the Court, the Government, even the Windsors themselves—to let the King make his delicate preparations unharassed.

However, as Frances Donaldson has noted,[2] Monckton

may have been mistaken about the King's real attitude. Only three months after Windsor gave up the throne, one of his staunch supporters, Lloyd George, had an audience at the Palace. He related the conversation to his wife, who recorded it in her diary: "H.M. is most anxious that the Duke should not return to this country, but D. told him that he did not take that view and thought H.M. would be wiser not to oppose it. 'She would never dare to come back here,' said H.M. 'There you are wrong,' replied D. 'She would have no friends,' said H.M. D. did not agree. 'But not you or me?' said the King anxiously." [3]

The Duchess of Windsor was convinced from the start that the opposition to her, while it centered in the King, was really organized by the women of the Royal Family. "The reign of George VI," she once said, "is a split-level matriarchy in pants. Queen Mary runs the King's wife, and the wife runs the King." Years later, discussing the rift that opened between the Duke and his family during the honeymoon, she added:

"He and I really had no firm plans beyond Austria, other than to take up temporary residence in a hotel in Paris. There was no law, no rule, to prevent our going back to England to live. After all, we were private citizens, free to return at any time. The only thing that restrained us was the question of how we'd be received. The Duke had no thought of forcing himself back into the limelight; he truly wanted to help his brother. Then we learned from our private sources that his family were determined to block it. They were more of a block to his having an official position than the Government was.

"Their big reason was that they didn't want *me* to have a position. They figured that the farther down they pushed me, the sooner I'd be destroyed. I'm convinced that they'd really have *liked* to see our marriage turn wretched and unhappy; then they'd have got him back all to themselves. A nasty game was being played. The object was to encourage the rest of the world to follow their example in being rude to me. They thought that eventually I'd be unable to go on taking the snubs. I would become cross and disagreeable with him, and he would throw in the sponge. Well, they miscalculated. Their little game only made me all the more determined not to be put down.

"A man's family has a right to disapprove of his marriage. If they won't accept his wife, or try to find out the kind of woman she really is, that's their privilege. I tried to make the Duke feel that I didn't mind what was being done to me, but I was sad about what they were doing to him because of me. It made me unhappy to see him unhappy on my account. One thing I was determined not to let happen, and that was to let the quarrel put me between him and his mother. That is something no wife should have on her conscience.

"The Duke and I had a long talk about how best to cope with the situation. Our decision was to make a life for ourselves as if his family didn't exist. The task I set myself was to give him what he had always wanted: a house of his own—not a palace, but a place where, as at the Fort, he would live the sort of life that his temperament needed."

Brave though these words are, they add up to an acknowledgment of private disaster. At Castle Wasserleonburg, the bitterness of defeat suffused the Duchess's whole being. She never purged it. Certainly on her side, the honeymoon put an early end to "the love affair of the century." The Duke had, in John Ray's strong metaphor, "tied a knot with his tongue that he could not untie with all his teeth." Providentially, he had no wish to, then or ever.

CHAPTER 5
The Visit to Hitler's Germany

*He poureth contempt upon princes and causeth them
to wander in the wilderness, where there is no way.*
—Psalm 107

"The Devil finds work for idle hands." Before Windsor's
honeymoon was half over, the Devil, in the plausible guise
of Charles Bedaux, had devised a sorry piece of work for
the brother whom George VI had unwisely left in idleness.

Not long after the bridal couple settled in at Wasserleonburg, Bedaux traveled to Germany, to test the ground for
the visit he had urged upon Windsor at Candé. Being host
for the wedding of the former King had vastly heightened
his prestige among the Nazi leaders, parvenus like himself.
In Berlin, he was received by Dr. Hjalmar Schacht, the
Nazis' financial genius, and in return for fifty thousand
dollars, most of which was an outright contribution to the
National Socialist Party, Dr. Schacht authorized him to resume his German operations, but under the supervision of
the Nazi Labor Front, headed by the notorious Dr. Robert
Ley. Whether it was now that Bedaux broached Windsor's
desire to visit Germany is not clear. Windsor himself remembered only that the Bedaux stopped in at Wasserleonburg sometime in July, either on their way back from Berlin or soon afterward. "My recollection," he said, "is that
Bedaux was enthusiastic about the splendid things I would
find in Germany. However, he had gone no farther than
hints to German friends that I would welcome an opportunity to see for myself how well the country was doing under National Socialism. He talked mostly about Dr.
Schacht's grasp of monetary theory, a subject which fascinated Bedaux. I remember his explaining to me a scheme
for having the 'Bedaux work-unit' adopted as an interna-

tional unit of value, as an alternative to gold. It was all over my head. He did advance a new thought, though, during this talk. It was that if our tour ever came off, I should broaden it to take in different segments of German industry, as well as the latest housing developments. Such an inspection would show me why German workers were more productive than the British and French, in their obsolete plants. Later, I came to understand what was probably in Bedaux's mind. With Dr. Ley the patron of his interests in Germany, he expected to curry favor with him by edging my trip under his auspices. I saw nothing wrong in having a look at the new factories, but it was the housing that really interested me. I was wholly ignorant of the politics and economics of labor. I did know something about housing."

If the implications of his German visit were vague to Windsor, they were not to the promoter. Bedaux was gambling that in his bid for preference in the Nazi industrial system, Windsor could be his high card. His appearance in Germany would be construed worldwide as approval of the Nazi regime. It would also spread embarrassment and confusion through Whitehall and the whole Empire, by suggesting that a substantial body of British opinion agreed with him that the Germans weren't all bad. Bedaux was additionally counting on an extra dividend for them both: If the trip started Windsor on a comeback, he would go on to acquire international influence in his own right; and Bedaux, as the mastermind in the salvage of a famous reputation, would benefit in proportion.

Windsor's enthusiasm for the German excursion was stimulated by Bedaux's own, all the more so because of the Palace's shilly-shallying about his job. Before Bedaux took his leave, he informed the now trusting Duke that he would return to Berlin presently, to draw up a dignified and not too demanding itinerary. By the end of August, he had in hand an official invitation for the Windsors to come to Germany as Ley's guests. More importantly, Bedaux appears to have drawn Windsor into an informal alliance under his private flag. He urged Windsor to follow up the German tour with another, even more elaborate: a tour of the United States. On this second one, as on the first, Windsor would present himself as a keen, well-grounded student of housing and labor. In the States, however, he would appear openly under Bedaux's sponsorship, and Bedaux's American enterprises would pay the expenses.

The proposal fell on fertile ground. The Duchess was eager for them to go to the States as soon as possible. She was confident that her countrymen would accord them the accolade which the Duke's former subjects had withheld— confident, too, that the Duke would have little trouble finding useful and profitable activity there. Windsor himself, fuming over his shrinking prospects in Britain, also was receptive to any promise of an escape from oblivion. In his vulnerability, he was tempted by a notion that, in collaboration with Bedaux, he would carve out a distinguished career as the promoter-sponsor of large-scale housing projects on both sides of the Atlantic.

"I was only half attracted to the idea," he said later. "Still, it wasn't a bad one, nor unworthy. But nothing was ever firmed up. A lot of public and private financing would have been necessary, and I doubted that I, as a member of the Royal Family and enjoying an annual remittance from the Privy Purse, could properly associate myself with an enterprise that involved risk for others."

However cloudy the understanding, the Duke summoned the aging Mr. Carter back to Castle Wasserleonburg and put him to work preparing for the two trips. On September 3, Carter issued this rather pretentious communiqué: "In accordance with the Duke of Windsor's message to the world press last June that he would release any information of interest regarding his plans or movements, His Royal Highness makes it known that he and the Duchess of Windsor are visiting Germany and the United States in the near future for the purpose of studying housing and working conditions in these two countries."

Bedaux returned to Berlin to tidy up the arrangements with Dr. Ley. Afterward he went to his hunting lodge at Borsodivanka in Hungary, where, in the second week of September, he and his wife entertained the Windsors, then traveling with Herman and Katharine Rogers. Bedaux gave them a detailed briefing of the tour being planned; it was to last two weeks and would take them from Berlin to Dresden, Nuremberg, Essen, Stuttgart, and Munich. They would be shown housing, hospitals, youth camps, factories, and other public works, and would have private meetings with senior Nazi officials. They were also assured that the Führer would almost certainly receive them; this would be the surprise grand finale, and no public announcement of the time and place would be made beforehand.

So far, so good; but presently Windsor was shocked to learn that Ley wanted to stage an enormous Nazi rally at every stop, in order to show "Germany's admiration for the King whom the British ruling classes had foolishly and ungenerously dismissed." Windsor protested that such demonstrations would embarrass him. He told Bedaux that "I can not and will not have any part in an anti-British display," and insisted that he immediately put Dr. Ley straight. Bedaux assured him that his wishes would be respected; he and the Duchess would be everywhere honored as private citizens.

If the Duke had any qualms about Bedaux's role in the arrangements, he did not express them. Nor was Herman Rogers troubled; his banker brother had never doubted Bedaux's motives. Years later, when the Duchess thought back to the hunting lodge, her clearest recollections were of the Bedaux's English butler—the one who had looked after them at Candé—now flanked by Hungarian footmen in garish scarlet-and-blue peasant dress; the baked potato-skins stuffed with caviar, served as a first course; and the huge, agile frog she found splashing in her bath. Her shrieks brought the Duke running, and he had the honor of capturing the creature between his hands. It would prove to be his principal triumph for some little while.

Late in that summer of 1937 the Windsors came to Paris and took a suite at the Meurice, overlooking the gardens of the Tuileries. They thought of renting a town house for a year, but deferred to the possibility of the King's permission for their early return to England. Besides, serious house-hunting had to be put aside until after the German trip, the preparations for which now absorbed their attention. Bedaux, back from Berlin, came by to assure them that Ley appreciated their desire to travel as private citizens. This assuaged whatever misgivings Windsor harbored, and it was agreed that he and his party would arrive in Berlin on October 11.

Doubtless because he was determined on a show of independence, Windsor never asked his brother's opinion about the wisdom of the German visit. Nor did he ask Winston Churchill or Walter Monckton or George Allen or Duff Cooper, all of whom would have advised against it. His friends knew he was going to Germany; he had publicly announced his intention to do so. But none was disposed to intervene unasked, perhaps for the same reason that Monckton gave in the aftermath: "None of us had ever heard anything bad about Bedaux. In fact, I never knew of his existence, until I met him at the wedding. I assumed the trip would be nothing more than what the Duke said it would be—a quiet look around various public works in Germany."

Lord Beaverbrook was the only friend of influence whom the Duke consulted. He did so indirectly, through one of the Beaver's executives, Capt. Michael Wardell, who had been a companion during the Prince of Wales's fox-hunting days. Windsor told Wardell that if Max happened to be in Paris soon, he would like to discuss his German visit. Beaverbrook's correspondents in Germany had already warned him of the intention to exploit Windsor's presence as a token "defection" from the anti-Nazi policy of the Chamberlain Government; alarmed, he flew to Paris, to see if he could derail the trip. He warned Windsor that his consorting with Hitler's bullies not only would offend all Britons, but would look like a deliberate flouting of British State policy. On observing that Windsor was unmoved, Beaverbrook offered to send his plane to fetch Churchill, who would back up his arguments. But Windsor's only comment was that since he and the Duchess would travel as private citizens, he could not understand how a simple tour of social and industrial works could embarrass his Government. Beaverbrook now realized that in this act of stubborn folly, as in the Abdication, Windsor had turned to him because he sought not a counselor, but a supporter of a project to which he was already committed. The sole purpose of the consultation was to enlist the favorable interest of Beaverbrook's newspapers and to hope that the rest of the popular press would follow after. Failing there, Windsor went ahead anyway.

Without his fully realizing it, the controlling circumstance at this stage of his life was that he was altogether on his own. Monckton, during the nearly two years of their crisis-laden association, had never had any decisive influence on his reasoning except where the factors were tactical or legal: Fruity Metcalfe could scold and expostulate, but to no avail. Windsor looked only to Wallis for direction, and she looked only to herself. Bedaux, having started Windsor on the way into the Third Reich, faded discreetly into the background. Windsor's fortunes were thereafter in the clever hands of the Nazi propagandists.

The train bringing the Windsors to Berlin arrived at Friedrichstrasse Station on October 11. Even as they set foot on the platform, the Duke was made to feel his Government's chill disapproval. Awaiting him was a large, formal Nazi delegation, headed by Dr. Ley. The British delegation consisted solely of the Embassy's young Third Secretary. The Ambassador himself, Sir Nevile Henderson, had quitted the city, under orders from the Foreign Office to take no official cognizance of the visit. Also conspicuously absent was the chargé d'affaires, Sir George Ogilvie-Forbes, an old friend of the Duke's. Sir George drew some of the sting by sending, by his junior, a warm, tactful note of apology and explanation; and not long after the Windsors had settled in at their hotel, he called upon them to pay to his former King and friend the respects he had been forbidden to pay in public. Windsor said, "He and I talked a bit. He told me some interesting and useful things about the Germans whom I was to meet. Even so, we were scarcely prepared to cope with the terrible Dr. Ley."

Through most of their travels in the Third Reich, their escort was not a dignified industrialist, as they had been led to expect, but Ley, a drunken, boastful, onetime street brawler, and a relentless practitioner of personal *Schrecklichkeit*. To take them sight-seeing, he provided a glittering black Mercedes-Benz, top down, half a block long, with two black-uniformed SS guards stiffly erect on the box. Ley squeezed his bulging body between his frail guests and raced them at *Autobahn* speeds along the main avenues, the wind clawing at their faces, and the sirens blaring.

Windsor said, "We were made to feel like trophies, on exhibition." After the first such hurricane spin, he and the Duchess returned to their hotel white and shaken, and next morning he told Ley that he would have to slow down: "The Duchess and I cannot take this speed! If your schedule is so tight that you have to travel at a hundred and fifty kilometers an hour to keep your appointments, then I'll start out well ahead of you in a separate motor, and we'll both be on time!"

Ley yielded, though with poor grace. The Windsors detested him and dreaded his morning arrival. The Duke judged him "very lewd, very coarse, fond of off-color jokes." The Duchess was even less flattering: "A drunkard, a fanatic, quarrelsome, a four-flusher." More than once Windsor found himself thinking that the shade of his "Uncle Willie"—Kaiser Wilhelm II—must be aghast at the spectacle of his cousin and former fellow-Emperor being whirled around his previously circumspect realm by such a ruffian.

The Duchess's judgments of the Nazi leaders were sharp. Dr. Goebbels, the Director of Propaganda, "a tiny, wispy gnome with an enormous skull," she marked as the cleverest of the lot; Rudolf Hess, the dilettante who was Hitler's closest political adviser, "charming of manner and good-looking," as the most civilized; Heinrich Himmler, the chief of the Gestapo, as the most deceptive, a "bespectacled meekness" giving him the misleading air of "a clerk caught up in politics"; and Field Marshal Hermann Göring as the most trustworthy. Her account of tea with the Görings at their forest lodge outside Berlin describes the array of weight-reducing gear in their gymnasium, the elaborate toy-train trackage for their children in an immense attic, and the unusually comfortable quarters for their large household staff. Hitler at once fascinated and repelled Wallis; she remembered his "pasty pallor," his "musician's hands," long and slim, and most of all his eyes—"burning with the same peculiar fire I had earlier seen in the eyes of Atatürk."

All the while, the Germans, in turn, were taking her measure. After the Windsors left Berchtesgaden, Hitler remarked to his interpreter, "She would have made a good Queen." [1] Frau Göring, too, thought that Wallis would have "cut a good figure on the Throne of England," although she was unable to comprehend how a woman could have lent herself to a marriage that required her husband to sacrifice his duty.[2]

The evidence strongly suggests that the Windsors' fortnight in the company of Hitler and his lieutenants—all of whom but Hess would be dead by the hangman's noose or by their own hands within ten years—was nothing more reprehensible than a sight-seeing trip, devoid of politics and ill-chosen in its timing and sponsorships. Indeed, Windsor insisted that politics was never discussed, at least on his side, not even during the meeting with Hitler. Paul Schmidt was present throughout it; his diary recorded, "In these conversations there was, so far as I could see, nothing whatever to indicate whether the Duke really sympathized with the ideology and practices of the Third Reich, as Hitler seemed to assume he did."

Ley's boorishness aside, Windsor enjoyed himself in Germany. He entered easily into conversation with his hosts, and gave little speeches and disquisitions in the second language of his childhood. The high standards of social welfare set by both the Nazi masters and private industry genuinely surprised him and aroused his admiration. But that did not make him pro-Nazi. Many highly placed Britons and most American tourists were equally impressed by Germany's surge of prosperity under Hitler. In 1936–37, France was being plagued by sit-down strikes and profound social unrest; Britain's slump and its embittered workers were the despair of its leaders; whereas Hitler's Germany was indubitably successful in bettering the lot of its working class and invigorating its industries. Windsor had toured a good many of the world's competing industrial systems and could not resist showing off his expertise, by comparing Germany's to the disadvantage of the others. Moreover, his German inheritance—or perhaps simply the intoxication of being among crowds who liked him—tempted him into a number of grosser indiscretions. At least twice he flung out his right arm with fingers stiff, in what looked to be a Nazi salute—once at a military parade, and again as he took leave of Hitler. Later, somewhat ashamed, he insisted that his gestures were in acknowledgment of salutes and were "a friendly wave," altogether casual. "I did salute Hitler," he admitted, "but it was a soldier's salute." Yet, twenty years after World War II, the Duke remarked to Lord Kinross, "I never thought Hitler was such a bad chap. . . ."

His most egregious blunder was in going to Germany at all, as the guest of a brutal dictatorship. His fast-dwindling legion of admirers were disturbed by his presence there; his critics were suspicious of his motives. Rumors had him belittling in private conversations the competence of British politicians, and even doubting their ability to resist a resolute German bid for the domination of Europe.

None of this went down well in Whitehall or in the Palace. It escaped becoming a scandal only because the British press minimized the trip from start to finish. Correspondents' reports were limited to the bare details of the Windsors' public appearances. The first sour notes were sounded in America, and loudest in the liberal journals, which had become aroused by Hitler's persecution of the Jews. A *New York Times* dispatch from Berlin on October 23 summed up the political impact of the Windsors' visit and concluded that the Duke "has lent himself, perhaps unconsciously, but easily, to National Socialist propaganda. There can be no doubt that his tour has strengthened the regime's hold on the working classes."

Strangely, both the Windsors and their lurking sponsor, Bedaux, were slow to sense the storm a-brewing. While the Windsors were still in Germany, Bedaux and his associates in the United States had embarked on a campaign to stir up public interest in the American extension of the tour, by then in preparation. The Duke had already booked their passage on the new, fast North German Lloyd liner *Bremen,* which would dock in New York on November 11, less than three weeks after his farewells to Germany. He had originally chosen the luxurious New French liner *Normandie* over the equally luxurious *Queen Mary* (which he as King had cheered on her maiden voyage the year before), because the *Queen*'s sailings from Cherbourg would have landed him in New York either too early or just too late for the schedule of engagements that he and Bedaux were putting together. Now he abruptly switched to the *Bremen,* on the excuse that the *Normandie* would call at a

British port, Southampton—an intrusion into his former realm which the compact with his brother forbade. The further fact that the Germans had offered his party free passage was hardly unattractive; nor was he loath just then to show his respect for German competence. Unfortunately, the change suggested, though surely unintentionally, a further renunciation, deliberate and petty, of his British loyalties.

The new tour promised to be triumphal. In five weeks, it would take the Windsors into a dozen or more of the principal cities and industrial areas of the eastern and midwestern United States. The British Ambassador, Sir Ronald Lindsay, invited them to be his guests during their stay in Washington. President and Mrs. Roosevelt asked them to tea at the White House. The mayor of Baltimore promised the Duchess a truly royal homecoming. Scores of other mayors, hungry for a share of the publicity, begged the Bedaux organization to bring the Windsors to their municipalities for receptions and parades.

To Bedaux, till then unknown outside certain managerial and labor circles, this was dizzying stuff. Ignoring the counsel of his associates, the puppet master came out from behind the scene and took his place before the audience, hand in hand with the Windsors, as their sponsor and impresario. From Janet Flanner's analysis,[3] it is clear that what started him toward disaster was his vanity and ambition. He was persuaded that the attraction which Windsor still had for Americans, despite their scattered criticism of the German episode, now presented him—Bedaux—with an opportunity to achieve world renown. Sharing the limelight with his illustrious protégé, he would be recognized as the man of parts he thought himself to be: industrial genius, patron of the arts, the international personage who was launching the former King of England on a second career.

Alas, before the Windsors had even finished their packing, Bedaux's cloud-capp'd towers had dissolved. So had his business career in the United States. Inevitably, the publicity exposed his trafficking with the Nazis and his backstage role in the Windsor's German excursion. Worse still, it brought all parties to the attention of two groups whose publicists were scanning the horizon for targets of opportunity in their separate appeals for support on certain highly charged issues.

One group was the Jews; justly appalled by the persecution of their kin in Germany, they determined—with the help of their liberal, leftist, antifascist sympathizers in the media and in public life—to shame those who lent respectability to the Nazi dictator. They chose to ignore the fact that when Windsor sought refuge in exile, it was with not merely a Jew, and not merely an Austrian Jew, but with the kind of Austrian Jew—a member of a powerful banking family—that the Nazis particularly hated. The other group was organized labor; its American tacticians had had no institutional interest in the Windsors until their connection with Bedaux came usefully to hand. Labor had always found Bedaux's incentive system offensive, but because he was small fry alongside the major industries which the unions were fighting to organize, it had not deemed him worth much ammunition. The disclosure of his link with Windsor's German tour now, in 1937, made him a profitable target.

Both the Congress of Industrial Organizations (C.I.O.) and the American Federation of Labor (A.F. of L.), competitors for leadership in the labor movement, were fiercely anti-Nazi and antifascist. They hated Hitler and Mussolini for smashing the labor unions in their countries and for intervening in the Spanish Civil War. The furor touched off in the press and radio had already exposed Bedaux's soiled credentials; and the Windsors' association with him, coupled with their behavior in Germany, was dismaying quarters which thitherto had sympathized with them as lovers heartlessly banished. By directing their fire on Bedaux, both as an exploiter of labor who was secretly doing business with Hitler and as a schemer who had promoted the Windsor tour of America in furtherance of his own nefarious interests, labor's propagandists were able with a single stroke to bring fascism into wider disrepute, to range themselves on the side of the political moralists by scolding the offenders, and incidentally to crush a minor nuisance, Bedaux himself.

The practical result of the attacks was to make the Windsors a shuttlecock in an ideological contest. New York longshoremen threatened to boycott their ship. In

Baltimore, the local unit of the A.F. of L. attacked Bedaux as the "archenemy" of labor and vowed that its members would ignore the receptions being arranged for the Windsors, "whether emissaries of a dictatorship or uninformed sentimentalists." Its president remarked acidly that when the former Wallis Warfield lived in Baltimore, he had never noted her concern for its working class, and urged the other local trade unions to ignore "slumming parties professing to study and help labor." At higher headquarters, the Bedaux "work-like-hell" system was damned as an "indirect, cumbersome mystifying" tax on the workingman's energies. The C.I.O. called it "the most completely exhausting, inhuman 'efficiency' system ever invented," and accused Bedaux himself of living "on workers' sweat."

So loud was the outcry that only three days after the Windsors returned to Paris from Germany, and barely a week before they were to leave on their new tour, the Duke felt obliged to call a press conference. The "misstatements" in the press about their visit to Germany and to America had, he complained, caused him and his Duchess "considerable concern and embarrassment." His reason for going to America was as innocent as the one which had taken him to Germany: to make "a study of the methods which have been adopted in the leading countries of the world in dealing with housing and industrial conditions."[4]

That same day, Bedaux sailed hastily for New York, in the forlorn hope of abating the criticism. He was too late; he found that his associates' anxiety and their disgust over the uproar in the press had already made them mutinous. Some resigned. His chief executive presented an ultimatum that demanded the dissolution of all the companies he had floated and their reorganization in a new grouping in which Bedaux would relinquish his name and all authority. Boxed in, stunned, and powerless, he sent off this cable to Windsor: "BECAUSE OF THE MISTAKEN ATTACK UPON ME HERE, I AM CONVINCED THAT YOUR PROPOSED TOUR WILL BE DIFFICULT UNDER MY AUSPICES. I RESPECTFULLY . . . IMPLORE YOU TO RELIEVE ME COMPLETELY OF ALL DUTIES IN CONNECTION WITH IT."[5]

The British Ambassador to Paris, Sir Eric Phipps, had given the Windsors a farewell luncheon. The American Ambassador, William C. Bullitt, had given them a farewell dinner and reception, attended by the Premier, Léon Blum; his Foreign Minister, Georges Bonnet, recently Ambassador in Washington; and assorted members of the British and French communities in Paris. Indeed, the Windsor luggage, numbered and ticketed, was waiting on the quay at Cherbourg,[6] when the Duke had a sudden change of heart. He canceled his passage, announced the abandonment of his tour, and in a tardy effort to cleanse himself of the malodor soaked up from both Bedaux and the Nazis, issued a Pilatian disclaimer: "The Duke emphatically repeats that there is no shadow of justification for any suggestion that he is allied to any industrial system, or that he is for or against any particular political and racial doctrine."

Bedaux was on the run by then. On November 10, having surrendered his American properties to the mutineers, he slipped out of the Plaza Hotel by a service door, eluding the reporters on watch in the lobby, and fled by train to Montreal, whence he sailed to France. On his arrival in Paris, one of the first messages he received was from the Duke, inviting him to call at the Meurice. If he had expected recriminations, he was pleasantly disappointed. The Duke never blamed him for the wreck of their splendid enterprise. Both agreed that they had been the victims of a slanderous attack by a cabal of Communists, radical unionists, and influential Jews.

"But for them," Windsor said pathetically, "the Duchess and I would have gone to America and we might well have settled there."

Why did Windsor let himself be gulled? Why did he choose Nazi Germany—of all nations!—for beginning his apprenticeship in mass housing and labor-management relations? Dudley Forwood, who went to Germany with him and who made the preparations for the American tour, was never in doubt of the Duke's real reasons: "He wanted to give his wife the experience of a Royal Progress. He wanted to prove to her that he had lost nothing by abdicating—that as a Duke, he was as important and influential as he had been as King." It was equally obvious to Forwood that the Duchess was pushing him. "The Duke liked that in her," Forwood said. "It showed her spirit."

The wife's autobiography makes no mention of her husband's project for taking her back to her native land in style. She dismissed the disaster as something too trifling to mention. But in their private recollections, she had no inhibition about placing the blame:

"The trouble came not so much because Charles Bedaux was a man of mystery, but rather because we knew absolutely nothing about him, other than what Herman Rogers told us. It may sound stupid, but I can honestly say that the Duke and I had never heard his name until he offered us the Château de Candé. The strange thing is that neither the Palace nor Whitehall ever flashed a warning to steer clear of him. British intelligence has always been very good at spotting people who can be dangerous or embarrassing to British interests. The Government knew—it *must* have known!—that the Duke would get into hot water if he went to Germany. They couldn't help being aware that Bedaux was a slippery fellow, and that his operations had come under fire in several countries.

"If they knew these things—and I'm *sure* they did!—then they should at least have sent a minor official over to France to explain the risks for the Duke. Since they didn't, they must have wanted to see him on the front page, and unfavorably. He and I must bear part of the blame. We were babes in the woods. I couldn't have been more inexperienced in coping with that sort of thing. As for the Duke, he'd been thrown out of his own country and beaten flat as a flounder. His father had been advised all his life by his Ministers about what he should or should not do, and the father had drilled the rules into the son. Shut off as he then was from all the accustomed do's and don'ts, he could hardly be expected to make wise decisions on his own, right off the bat, could he?" In her opinion, the guilty parties were the Royal Family and their lackeys in the Foreign Service.

There was no want of advice after the event. Herbert Morrison, the British Labour leader, was one source. In a stern homily published in the party journal, *Forward*, a few days after the collapse of the American trip (but written before it), he suggested that Windsor had best pursue his inquiry into social matters by quietly reading instructive books and seeking advice in private, rather than "put his foot into it," as he was all too plainly doing. In any case, Morrison noted, Windsor could make no practical use of what he observed, inasmuch as "he cannot be permitted to re-enter public life—in Britain, anyway." For Windsor, as for all ex-kings, the choice was "either to fade out of the public eye or to be a nuisance"—and Morrison's cold advice was for him to fade.[7]

The only salvage from the fiasco was negative: The Duke escaped the utter moral and political destruction toward which Bedaux was luring him. Credit must go to a benign Providence, rather than to a belated awakening on his own part. He never awoke to the danger that Bedaux presented, never closed his doors against this typhoid-carrier. On the contrary, their strange friendship flourished; they continued to meet for the next two years; and the Bedaux dined with the Windsors as late as November 1939, well after the beginning of World War II.

By then, Bedaux was already beginning to build a reputation as the Nazis' ranking industrialist collaborator. The breakaway of his American companies had not seriously compromised his European operations; and after the fall of France in 1940, he emerged as the Germans' favored instrument for a number of major jobs. When retribution finally overtook him, in November 1942, he was in Algiers, making ready to build them a 2,000-mile pipeline to bring peanut oil from the Niger, on the equatorial shoulder of Africa, across the Sahara to Europe. A 1,400-mile railroad, paralleling the pipeline, was to have been a companion project.

The American landings in North Africa put an end to both. Bedaux was arrested first by the Free French, then released because he carried an American passport, then arrested again, in December, at the request of the United States Army. He was held for a year in a military prison at El Biar, a suburb of Algiers, while a team from the Federal Bureau of Investigation untangled the skein of his enemy dealings. In December 1943, he was flown to Miami, then the clearinghouse for immigrants arriving from Europe by the South Atlantic air routes. There, in his jail cell, on the night of February 18, 1944, while a court was attempting to decide whether he should be tried for treason as an American citizen and possibly hanged, or sent back to

France to be shot, he took his own life with a handful of the sleeping pills which he had hoarded from his nightly ration of two.

The Windsors, who had been his guests at Candé seven years before, were at Nassau just then, two hundred miles away. They would make a kindly comment to the press about Mr. Jardine's death, but it seemed prudent for the Governor and his lady to say nothing about Charles Bedaux's.

✿ CHAPTER 6 ✿
Robinson Crusoe on the Riviera

Ask the travelled inhabitant of any nation, in what country on earth you would rather live? Certainly in my own. . . . Which would be your second choice? France.

—Writings, THOMAS JEFFERSON

So it all ended in a shambles: the abdicated monarch's well-intentioned spur-of-the-moment scheme for returning to public life, with his American consort by his side, in the dual role of peacemaker and urban sociologist. Thanks to his calamitous series of misjudgments and odious associations, the applause which had always attended his past excursions was not forthcoming this time; nor—even more painful—was the approval which he craved as a lover. The double disappointment might have crushed someone else, but Windsor never let it show. A lifelong tutelage in the royal discipline of hiding one's feelings armored him in adversity. It was not in his nature to admit error or be diverted by criticism.

Indeed, he continued to impersonate a man buoyant on a wave of private joy. The staff at the Meurice would remember him for his unfailing civility to them all; for his gallantry toward his wife—kissing her when they were alone in the lift, and helping her into and out of their car; and for his cheery, tuneless whistle as he set across the Rue de Rivoli with Pookie and Detto for a walk in the Tuileries. Their apartment, on the third floor, consisted of a living room between two bedroom suites. The tall windows faced south, toward the famous gardens and the Seine and the low winter sun. The cadre of what would become a large household was settled across the hall. Mrs. Bedford had set up her typewriter, files, and ledgers in a bedroom

renamed "the Secretariat"; the valet, the Duchess's Swiss
maid, and Chief Inspector Storrier were farther along the
corridor. To the Duke, it was a "bivouac," a temporary
camp on the road to a destination not yet in view, but
which he was sure would be a worthy one.

Christmas was soon upon them, their first together.
They spent it at Cannes, in Lou Viei, lent them by Herman
and Katharine Rogers, who had gone to America for the
holidays. The Meurice was too cramped, the Windsors decided on their return to Paris, so they looked for a furnished house to rent until a suitable permanent residence
came on the market. The Château de la Maye, in Versailles, was a happy compromise between what the Duke
sought and what the Duchess sought: He liked it because it
was "country," to the extent of having a pleasant garden
and spreading grounds; she, because it was "city," being
only twenty minutes from Paris and having a drawing
room and dining room large enough for entertaining.

They took a short lease; the staff assembled at Wasserleonburg was recalled from furlough, and the Windsors
moved from the Meurice in March. The Duchess remembered that winter as "gray and dreary," although it was
briefly brightened by the announcement of her election to
the list of "The World's Ten Best-Dressed Women," a distinction she would hold for nearly four decades. But a chill
deeper than that from Paris's steel-gray mists had gripped
their spirits. For all the Duke's outward joy, inwardly he
was tormented. Nothing had gone right for him since leaving Enzesfeld; and his immediate prospects, as he viewed
them, were anything but promising. The brief trip to
Cannes had not been altogether happy; they had been entertained by acquaintances, but the Duke was finding the
company of comparative strangers a strain. His long
months of desuetude were chafing his spirit. He wanted
damnably to return to England, to settle again in his beloved Fort, to gather his friends about him and his wife,
and in due course to take a job at the King's shoulder. He
was galled that his younger brother was still refusing to
give him so much as a hint of a job or to shorten the two
years' absence, which the elder had himself proposed. But
in truth neither petition, if granted, would have counted
for anything unless a third, unspoken need was fulfilled:

that his wife be received by his family and accorded her rightful status. Without that, the other two would have been impossible of fulfillment. It was this prideful and understandable conviction which kept them in permanent, self-imposed exile after the two years had lapsed, and indeed for the rest of their lives.

There was no way back for the Duke; and now, finding himself unable to budge his once docile brother, or to spur his high-placed friends into pressing his case, he succumbed to the panicky conviction that he had been thrown onto the dustheap. Long afterward, he would say of this interval, "It was a ghastly time for me, for both of us—much worse than I have ever cared to admit. I felt that I had been shipwrecked a second time. How was I to survive, with all backs turned to me?"

Walter Monckton sensed his friend's deepening sadness. By now he was the Duke's last open channel to the King and to 10 Downing Street. Not long after the Windsors' move to Versailles, he paid them a call, on the pretext that a legal question needed discussion. What he saw grieved him. The Duke had all too plainly lost confidence. The Duchess was pressing him to do something about their dilemma: either force his brother to clear their way home, or quit Europe for the United States. He wanted to linger in France no more than she did; neither was fluent in the language, or altogether at ease with the French. But he shunned America while the Bedaux mess was still reeking; and he argued that it would be wiser to remain in Europe until he had worked out his problems with his brother. The Duchess insisted that in the United States the Duke would enjoy all his usual honors. "Besides," she said, "anything would be better than this, huddled in a rented house like orphans in a storm."

The quarrel over what to do and where to live was tearing at the Duke's heart; and as Monckton listened to their woes, he noted with consternation the Duke's loss of poise, his indecisiveness, his childish terror of the Duchess's displeasure. His hands trembled when he lit a cigarette; he could not sit still or hold a thought for more than a moment. "This is his nadir," Monckton told himself, and he briefly harbored a fear that the Duke was on the verge of collapse.

The only counsel that Monckton could offer was a plea for patience. He reminded them that the King was aware of his brother's desires and needs, and he expressed his confidence that they would be gratified. The question of the title, he explained, was more delicate—extremely so. The King was himself uncomfortable about it; how best undo what had been unjustly done? Monckton proposed that he seek out a certain eminent constitutional authority and ask for a judgment on the legality of the action. The Duke approved.

The problem of where to live admitted an easier solution. Monckton had little trouble talking the Windsors out of settling in America. The tax laws there, he reminded them, were strict and egalitarian; only churches, schools, charities, and other nonprofit institutions escaped the tax collector's clutch. An exception had never been made for exiled monarchs or other royal personages, and it was altogether unlikely that the U.S. Treasury could be induced to exempt someone of the Duke's conspicuous means. Inasmuch as the Dominions had no appeal, and Paris was their choice among European capitals, he urged them to find a house there and become reconciled to what might be a long stay. Even though the French Government was controlled by the radical Front Populaire, Monckton was confident that it would be hospitable to the Duke in all matters befitting his station, including the remission of taxes, the granting of full diplomatic privileges, and the protection of the Sûreté. He had already sounded out the French Ambassador in London; and George Allen, having made tentative inquiries into the attitude of the French Treasury, further assured them that no difficulties were expected.

Monckton took his leave with mixed emotions. He felt that he had steadied the Duke, at least to the extent of grasping the practical advantages of making Paris his base, if only temporarily; but he was not sanguine about his success with the Duchess, who was patently the source of the Duke's discontent. She was galled by the ambiguity of their position. She blamed the Queen for heading the resistance to their return.[1] She was furious at being spurned by the Duke's resplendent family, in full view of the world. She was convinced that they and the Court were working to undermine her marriage by isolating the Duke, and to humble him by refusing him a proper role within the monarchy.

Monckton was not without sympathy for the lady. From the beginning, he had measured her less as a possible ally than as a likely adversary. During the early months of their association, he had taken care not to be drawn into her little court, thinking it prudent to keep his distance and thus preserve the impartiality of his counsel to the monarch. She both attracted him and repelled him. He had never known a woman like her—"a coquette," he called her, "chic rather than feminine, half artifice, half steel." She had deceived him about her divorce, but knowing what he did about such stratagems among the upper classes, he did not disrate her for it, and he would laughingly concede that her lie had made it easier for him to serve the King. But he had been left mistrustful of her integrity and, observing her influence on the King during the duel with Baldwin, he had decided that she was tone-deaf to political subtleties. He did not believe that she had lured the Duke into the association with Bedaux, nor did he blame her for his warmth toward Nazi Germany. What alarmed him was her near-paranoid hatred of things British, her thirst for acceptance, and her attraction to people on the make.

In common with most Britons of his station, Monckton considered another European war improbable. Nevertheless, Hitler's bombast, the resurgence of German militarism, and the brashness of Nazi intrigue were hardening Tory opinion. The alienation of the Windsors made the Duke vulnerable to the influence which Bedaux exercised; and Monckton took home a conviction that the most useful service he could render the Duke would be to pull him back into the mainstream of British thought at all possible speed. This, he decided, could best be accomplished by enlisting the Duke's most trusted friends—especially those in Parliament and the Government—to open a correspondence with him. The Duke had complained that his former ministers were ignoring him and leaving him in the dark about British policy; so, to hasten the bridge-building, Monckton made several visits to Whitehall. The ministers whom he knew, he urged to pay courtesy calls on the Duke when they visited Paris and give him the benefit of the Government's thinking. Monckton's excellent lines of communication had brought him assurance that the King would not object to his brother's receiving this official attention, and he was able to satisfy the more timid politicians that their standing at the Palace would not be impaired by these friendly conversations. Monckton's papers contain an eloquent explanation of his motives: "Kings not only live in glass houses, but have constant access to the best advice in every sphere. It was hard to convince people at home how much more difficult it was for the Duke, because of the position which he had held and the advice which had been available to him, to keep an even and temperate judgment when responsible Ministers never went near him, and instead he was surrounded by friends who, for one reason or another, lived abroad largely divorced from English society and interests. With someone so quick to take a point, and so impressionable as the Duke, this was a constant anxiety to me."[2]

Among the personages whom he persuaded to call were Prime Minister Chamberlain, who had succeeded Baldwin in May 1937; Lord Halifax, the Foreign Secretary, who succeeded Anthony Eden the following February; and the Duke's good friends, Duff Cooper, still Secretary of State for War (though not for much longer), and Winston Churchill, still out of power. Their attention flattered Windsor, and Monckton congratulated himself on having "improved the atmosphere."

One wonders. There is no evidence that Windsor's views on war and politics— in particular his conviction that Britain should make common cause with Germany against bolshevism—were affected even slightly by the dribble of information and advice. Nor did Monckton manage to advance the Duke's petitions. Yet in another and altogether constructive respect, so far as concerned the Duke's peace of mind, Monckton succeeded brilliantly, if indirectly. By force of his firm counsel, given over a series of visits to France during the spring and summer of 1938, he managed to turn the thoughts of his clients away from their preoccupation with their grievances, and to redirect them toward creating an existence appropriate to the Duke's exalted title, his changed circumstances, and, above all else, to his temperament.

* * *

The results were spectacular. Once the Duchess had swallowed the bitter truth that there was no penetrating the wall which the Palace had raised against her, she devoted all her energy and ingenuity to carrying out Monckton's recommendation. "The question," she said, "was whether we should conduct ourselves like fugitives, always on the run, or put on a show of our own. David was born to be a king; he *had been* a king. In marriage, the palaces were lost; so was the trained staff that smoothed out everything for him. But he still had the mind and character and, yes, the interests of a king; and my duty, as I saw it, was to evoke for him the nearest equivalent to a kingly life that I could produce without a kingdom."

Her Americanized equivalent of a kingly life became her masterpiece: a succession of increasingly beautiful houses, together with private entertainment on a scale and of a quality unsurpassed in its time; a spectacle of jewels, marvelous gowns, liveried servants, and other trappings of luxury and sumptuousness. And for the Duke, whose career was already at a dead end so far as having any serious purpose—though he had not yet accepted the fact—it all led, splendidly but pathetically, to an endeavor of a different sort: the pursuit of idleness disguised as motion, and the achievement of a level of conspicuous consumption that remains unsurpassed.

Paris was the perfect starting place for the Duchess's singular enterprise. Its ateliers were stocked with magnificent antique furniture, bric-a-brac, porcelains, and tapestries; and if an item in view fell short of what a setting needed, the clever decorators and *antiquaires* now emerging as personages in the world of wealth were sure to know a château where a superior substitute could be coaxed—for a price—from its impoverished owner. Although the franc was weak between the wars, and prices were cheap, the Duchess could never have achieved half so brilliant a success as a chatelaine without the Chippendale furniture, the Georgian silver, the portraits of the Duke's royal forebears, the lifetime hoard of trophies and gifts, not to mention more liquid assets, which he brought to their ménage. Still, it was the American woman who put it all together, as carefully as if she were making a setting for a play. And a

play of sorts it was—a play in which she acted Girl Friday
to the shipwrecked (so he described himself) monarch's
Robinson Crusoe, in making their island of exile an isle of
enchantment.

The truly great houses of Europe were grander than
those the Duchess would in time preside over, grander in
their furnishings accumulated over the generations, and in
their formal gardens, spreading lawns, and forested pre-
serves. What set the Windsors' houses apart was the cunning, always elegant combination of old and modern, of
brightness and soft shadows, of line and color. Everything
gleamed or glowed: the mahogany and rosewood, the silver, the candelabra, the mirrors placed to catch and reflect a spray of fresh flowers, a precious *objet d'art*, a
painting on the opposite wall, or the light of candles in
the dining room.

It was while she manipulated this splendid material that
Wallis Windsor, rising from personal defeat, finally found
her true calling. Luckily, her talents flowered at an ideal
time—a time when multimillionaires were impatient to display the Croesan wealth they newly commanded; when
professional guides to good taste were opening boutiques
and ateliers in Paris, London, and New York; and when
Vogue, Harper's Bazaar, and *The Tatler* were standing
double watches for fresh examples of "gracious living" and
"high style" with which to instruct their readers. As the
Duchess of Windsor's dinners became talked about, as the
beauty of her houses and her superb skills as a hostess began to attract attention and admiration, she supplied these
vendors, publicists, and their clients with standards to
which they could safely and proudly repair. The demure,
frugal innovator of Bryanston Court, now able to draw
with a prodigal hand on the funds of a royal duke, began
to emerge in the first two years of her marriage as a transatlantic symbol of social sophistication.

In the course of the marriage, she would put her stamp
on five houses. The first was the Château de la Croë, at
Cap d'Antibes, which Herman Rogers had recommended
as the setting for her wedding. She and the Duke had visited it while they were spending Christmas 1937 at Lou

Viei, nearby; it took their fancy at once, and they asked to make a thorough inspection.

What they found was a property of twelve acres, with a residence and dependencies. A high wall, interrupted by a single tall wrought-iron gate, enclosed it on three sides; the Mediterranean guarded the fourth. Additional privacy—an inducement precious to the Duke—was promised by the yews, palms, pines, eucalypti, and flowering shrubs that screened and shaded the grounds. The residence, which was only seven years old, was actually a villa, though its heavy stone construction, its boxy shape, and its huge size—three stories—could justify its promotion to "château," despite the classic pillars front and back, and the crowning skylight of varicolored glass. On its seaward side—south—a lawn sloped from a breezy, half-moon terrace down to a swimming pool and two bathing pavilions. On the north side were greenhouses, garages, servants' quarters, gardens, and a tennis court.

If not another tennis court, certainly a court for badminton could have been laid out indoors, in almost any of the residence's rooms; all were amply large, even to their twenty-five-foot ceilings. Some were painted with clouds. A later visitor would remark, "A waste of the artist's time and paint! The ceilings are quite high enough for clouds to form there naturally." A wide hall ran the full depth of the house, to doors opening onto the terrace. On the right of the hall was a dining room that could seat twenty-four; on the left, a drawing room and a paneled library. Many of the rooms had murals; the master bathroom boasted a stone tub, gilded, with a swan's neck at each end; there was a lift; finally, and most impressive of all—as plain proof that the owner, Sir Pomeroy Burton, an American-born Fleet Street executive, had opened his purse to his architect and contractor—there was that rare luxury in Riviera villas of the day, central heating. La Croë could thus provide not only a cool oasis when Paris steamed in summer, but a warm shelter when it shivered in winter. The Windsors, in their enthusiasm, signed a ten-year lease, at 100,000 francs a month—nearly three thousand dollars.

The magic which the Duchess would work in and about La Croë established her as something of a genius, considering that it was her maiden effort at nest-building on a ducal scale. Moreover, her scope was restricted; not only were the rooms partly furnished already, but the Duke insisted on using his heirlooms from the Fort and York House. They had been stored at Frogmore since the Abdication, in charge of his clerk, Mr. Carter, who was now asked to fetch his inventories to Paris for a decision on what would go to La Croë. Late in the spring of 1938, their lease at Versailles having run out, the Windsors returned to the Riviera and took an apartment at the Hôtel du Cap d'Antibes, close by. From here they supervised the repainting and alterations which they had commissioned, and made ready to receive the shipment from Frogmore.

The convoy of vans arrived late one afternoon, with Mr. Carter leading. One of the Windsors' servants looking on said that the scene was indescribable: every open patch of ground covered with boxes, crates, trunks, hampers, suitcases, chests of linen enough for a palace, chest upon chest of silver, dozens of cases of wine from the cellar at St. James's Palace, scores of pictures swathed in canvas, racks of clothes and bags of shoes beyond counting. The Duke charged about the cluttered lawn, shouting glad cries as he came upon a treasured belonging, and directing where things were to be put. The Duchess watched from a distance, doubtless amused to see the former monarch happily engaged in the role and authority of a baggage master. On the morrow, however, after the movers had departed, she was in charge; and before the onset of the mistral, La Croë was ready to be occupied. The Duchess refused to take full credit for its transformation. Only the blue-and-white motif, the colors of the surrounding sea and sky, was hers alone, she maintained. She had not been timid about seeking counsel as the work went forward. Her chief adviser had been the famous Lady Mendl, one of the earliest and most successful interior decorators. Born Dé Wolfe in 1865 and christened "Elsie," she counted decorating among her many accomplishments; she was equally renowned as a hostess and for standing on her head at her dinner parties when she was well past seventy. Her home in Versailles, Villa Trianon, was a showplace of her craft—a private museum of priceless pieces which she had brought together and disposed with taste and originality. Her urbane, charming husband, Sir Charles, was press attaché at the

British Embassy in Paris, where some tasks he had discharged for the Duke, during the Windsors' residence at the Château de la Maye, had led to a close friendship between the couples. They went to each other's dinners; the Duke talked politics with Sir Charles, while Lady Mendl, an experienced guide to French Society, briefed the Duchess on its mazes and pitfalls.

Thus, when the redecoration of La Croë began, Elsie Mendl stood ready to give advice when asked. She also put at the Duchess's disposal two specialists: Tony Montgomery, a former apprentice of hers and an authority on antique furniture; and her close friend Johnny McMullen, a writer for *Vogue* and an expert at teaching the new rich how to live riper lives than their backgrounds had prepared them for. Both men were welcomed into the Windsors' circle, and each made anonymous contributions to the Duchess's scheme for her villa.

The exterior remained unchanged; it still gave the impression of a noble white vessel afloat on a calm sea, a perfect house for summer living, "a dream-like place"—as one of the secretaries phrased it—"cool, serene, and aloof." But the interior was now altogether different. Now there were mirrors everywhere—over the fireplaces, on the doors of the reception rooms and bedrooms, and on the double doors of the dining room. The Duchess liked the illusion of light and spaciousness that they conveyed; her deployment of mirrors would become one of her trademarks. So would the elaborate gold-and-white moldings that she used on her ceilings and walls. The blue-and-white motif was sometimes brightened with yellow. The dining-room curtains were yellow and white; and yellow and light blue prevailed in the drawing room. There were also splashes of scarlet: Over the sideboard in the dining room hung the famous Munnings portrait, "The Prince of Wales on Forest Witch," with the brilliant "pink" of the hunting coat; and from the gallery above the foyer hung the great banner, massively embroidered in scarlet and gold, which had marked the Duke's Garter stall in St. George's Chapel since his seventeenth birthday. Its arms invalidated by his abdication, it had been removed from the chapel and replaced by one with modified arms. An ancient Dutch lac-

quered chest now stood under it, holding a leather book for
guests to sign; on either side were gold-backed chairs with
red leather seats. In the drawing room, two Chinese chests
in red, gold, and black lacquer stood on gilt consoles between the windows; and a mahogany desk with a tapestried
chair, both from the Fort, was placed against a far wall,
beyond a square of chairs and sofas. A portrait of Queen
Alexandra gazed across the library at the shelves of unread
books.

But for all the elegance and originality at La Croë, what
caught the eyes of the press was that gilded bathtub, with
the swans. As if this were not Sybaritic enough in itself, the
press transmuted the gilt to solid gold; and Miss Maxwell,
who should have known better, believed the absurd canard—or perhaps *cygne*—and solemnly printed it.

The Duke's and Duchess's bedrooms were on the first
floor, hers in soft pink and apricot, his in scarlet and beige.
A damask tapestry in black and gold, royally rich, hung
over his bed. Two items in the Duchess's bedroom bore
what was coming to be known as "the Wallis Windsor
touch." They were a dressing table and small chest decorated festively in the style called *trompe l'oeil*—that is,
with objects so cunningly painted as to appear real. Elsie
Mendl was fond of the conceit and popularized it among
her clientele. Her apt pupil, the Duchess, with the collaboration of a clever artist in Paris, memorialized in her boudoir some of the more affecting or amusing milestones in
the royal courtship. The top of the dressing table seemed
bestrewn with a jeweled handbag, a scarf, a lipstick, and
even a book, all so realistically executed as to appear to
have been laid there haphazardly, to be swept up by their
owner hurrying off for a rendezvous or an appointment
with her hairdresser. The symbolism of the chest was a bit
racier—a perfect rendering of the first crested invitation
from the Prince of Wales delivered at Bryanston Court;
fragments of a torn letter; a bouquet with an attached card
bearing the Prince of Wales's feathers; a pair of long white
evening gloves; and a pair of men's white golfing socks
connected, one may suppose, with an event that must have
been either hilarious or precious. A friend familiar with the

arrangements at La Croë remarked, "Whenever the Duke
was in that bedroom, he could hardly have lacked for reminders of how it all began."

There were two guest rooms on the first floor: a Rose
Room, done (Miss Hood writes) "in soft tea rose shades,"
and a Venetian Room, "in red and gold with two striking
antique beds and a bow-fronted Venetian chest." On the
floor above were four more guest rooms: the Direc-
toire, the Blue Room, the Wedgwood, and the Toile de
Jouy, each with a pair of antique beds, each with rugs,
curtains, coverlets, cushions, towels, and even breakfast
trays and stationery in matching colors. On every bedside
table was a printed list of the not-inconsiderable services
which could be commanded by bell or telephone: the
Duchess's hairdresser from Paris (he also doubled as barber), a manicurist, a secretary (two were on the premises
from the start, and a third was added), and of course a
footman. Fresh flowers came from the garden or green-
house every morning; every day the bed linen was replaced
or removed to be pressed; decanters of gin and Scotch were
kept brimful for guests who needed support through the
night or a drowsy day.

For the Duke's old friends, one of the most revealing
things about the house was his name, "Fort Belvedere," for
the modest jurisdiction that he reserved for himself. Atop
the villa was a penthouse which the original owner had
intended to use as an office; the Duke had it made over
into a combination of office, private sitting room, and a
fleet admiral's quarters. The roof terrace gave him an
unobstructed view of the sea to the south, east, and west,
and a telescope permitted closer inspection of the yachts
that passed. The flavor of the decor was nautical: deep-
blue curtains, chairs and a sofa with white slipcovers. A
ship's chronometer that had belonged to George V, a ship's
brass bell, and a barometer further sharpened the briny
tang of the premises. Golf and hunting trophies from his
princing days decorated the walls. Photographs of his father and mother stood on the desk; round about were half
a dozen snapshots of Wallis, taken by himself. A tiny lift
hoisted him to his "bridge" in the forenoon, for an hour or
so with the morning mail and perhaps some dictation; he
would return in the late afternoon, after golf, for another

erratic stab at letter-reading and telephoning; and later still, toward the hour of seven, for a drink with a guest or a visitor, before descending for his evening bath.

Walter Monckton was invited to La Croë while the renovation was still in full swing. The Duke showed him around and explained his and the Duchess's long-range intentions for the work still unfinished. What she had been able to manage in so short a time surprised Monckton; his praises of the changes she had made were sincere. For his own part, he was profoundly relieved that the remodeling was taking the Windsors' minds off the petty tribulations which had all but unhinged the union during the winter just past. Yet there was no diverting either of them for long from the sense of injustice and rejection brought on by the Palace's continued silence. In the notes which Monckton allowed to be published posthumously, he recorded how his formal business with the Duke at La Croë almost invariably ended with them retiring to the penthouse, where they would "draft the letters in which the Duke's grievances were conveyed to the Prime Minister, the King and his mother."[3]

Some months earlier, Monckton had kept his promise to ask one of Britain's foremost constitutional lawyers, Sir William Jowitt, if he would look into the legality of the Letters Patent of May 1937, which had deprived the Duke's wife of the title of Royal Highness by restricting it to himself alone. Jowitt was reputed to possess the finest legal mind in England. He agreed to take on the job and traveled to Paris in January 1938 for a talk with the Duke. Some time later he advised the Duke by letter that in his opinion the King's action in withholding the title was highly questionable and the matter "cried aloud" for clarification.[4] He contended that George VI had mistakenly and wrongfully repealed what Queen Victoria had decreed in Letters Patent of February 1864: "that besides the children of Sovereigns of these Realms, the children of the sons of any Sovereign of Great Britain and Ireland shall have and at all times hold and enjoy the title, style and attribute of 'Royal Highness,' with their titular dignity of Prince or Princess prefixed to their respective Christian names. . . ." Under this sweeping decree, Jowitt reasoned, the act of abdication had not put the Duke's princely rank in forfeit; the rank was his because he was the Sovereign's son, and by its nature was his to share with his wife.

He was by no means alone in this judgment. The editors of *Debrett's Peerage*, in the 1967 and 1973 editions, would also argue that George VI had acted illegally. A telling point in the Duke's favor was that when Bertie himself had married Lady Elizabeth Bowes-Lyon fourteen years earlier, the *London Gazette* reported matter-of-factly that "in accordance with the settled general rule that a wife takes the status of the husband" she would assume the styles, titles, and attributes of a royal duchess. It was further argued that the King, even as the Fountain of Honor, was powerless to narrow the boundaries of a title already his brother's by birth, and one which he had himself reaffirmed in the abdication process.

Windsor was greatly heartened by Jowitt's opinion and was all for pressing his case forthwith. But the fight went out of him when Monckton, who himself had judged the King's denial of the title "a mean and petty gesture," reminded him that the senior law officers of the Government would support the King in resisting any effort to reverse the original ruling. To challenge his prerogatives in a matter affecting the private sensibilities of the royal family would stir up a storm not only in Britain but throughout the Empire. The certain result, Monckton warned the Duke, would be to bare every unusual aspect of the Duchess's character and conduct that the press could uncover. The Duke grudgingly yielded. A decade later, after Jowitt had been raised to Lord Chancellor in the postwar Labour Government, Windsor reminded him of the earlier opinion and suggested that he now was in a position to right the wrong. The only recorded aspect of that meeting was a sour comment from the Duchess: "All that the Duke got from the Lord Chancellor was a fishy stare which he interpreted to be an unfavorable legal ruling."

What the Duke could not gain in fact, he created in make-believe. Within the realm of his own household, he reconstituted himself as Fountain of Honor and conferred upon his Duchess, for all within earshot to hear, the title and style so brutally withheld elsewhere. The Windsor servants were under stern instructions to address her directly as "Ma'am," and when referring to her—whether among themselves or to outsiders, guests, vendors, and callers alike—to speak of her as "Her Royal Highness." A note to her from a member of the staff began with the salutation "Madam," and ended with the flourish, "I am, Madam, Your Royal Highness's devoted and obedient servant." A curtsey was not obligatory, though some liked to make a quick bob; but all were required to remain standing in her presence. Where the Duke was concerned, the customs of royalty prevailed. With the servants, it was "Yes, Your Royal Highness," or "No, Your Royal Highness," or "His Royal Highness wants" this, or "His Royal Highness has just left for the golf course."

A *laissez-faire* attitude governed the degree of deference which their close friends were disposed at this delicate stage to render the Duchess. A small number of English-women who had known her as Wallis Simpson curtseyed to her after the marriage, not because they felt bound to do so, but because they knew it pleased the Duke. By con-trast, her American friends adopted the gesture for a differ-ent reason: A graceful curtsey let them display their ease with a fairly demanding civility which lay outside the expe-rience of their sisters. All this was innocent enough; it helped sustain the fantasy which increasingly regulated the Windsors' relationship with the rest of humankind—so much so that they fell into a strange, stilted manner of speaking of one another in the presence of others. When they were with their handful of very old friends, she would address him as "David," and he would call her "Wallis," although the terms most often on his lips were "Sweet-heart" or "Darling." But in other company, even in general conversations with people whom they knew well and had entertained, or been entertained by, she would bring her husband into the discussion through some such device as "The Duke doesn't agree with that view at all," or, "If you were to ask the Duke, I suspect you'd get a contrary opin-ion." Similarly, he always referred to her in these situations as "Her Royal Highness" or "the Duchess," much as junior officers use the third-person expression "the General" or "the Admiral." They never spoke of each other as "my husband" or "my wife." The artificiality of the form, and even more the Duke's pathetic resolve to ennoble the

Duchess, provided Harold Nicolson with a biting entry for his diary in August 1938, when he was staying with Somerset Maugham at Cap Ferrat, and the Windsors came for dinner:

> Willie Maugham had prepared us carefully. He said that the Duke gets cross if the Duchess is not treated with respect.
> She, I must say, looks very well for her age. . . . He entered with his swinging naval gait, plucking at his bow tie. . . . Cocktails were brought and we stood around the fireplace. There was a pause. "I am sorry we were a little late," said the Duke, "but Her Royal Highness couldn't drag herself away." He had said it. The three words fell into the circle like stones into a pool Her (gasp) Royal (shudder) Highness (and not one eye dared to meet another).

Pity was hardly a conspicuous element in Nicolson's character. He had witnessed his former monarch's fall with indignation and disgust and had come to have little respect for him. Yet as he observed Windsor's behavior that summer evening, he seems to have sorrowed at the evidence of the moral defeat of the man who had personified the British system which Nicolson venerated—the woeful loss of all significant purpose, the sudden vulnerability to which marriage had exposed him and the pitiful need to play a part in a situation doomed to lead nowhere. The diary continues:

> We went into dinner. . . . I sat next to the Duchess. He sat opposite. They called each other "darling" a great deal. I called him "Your Royal Highness" a great deal and "Sir" the whole time. I called her "Duchess." One cannot get away from his glamor and his charm and his sadness . . . but it is pathetic the way he is sensitive about her. It was quite clear to me from what she said that she hopes to go back to England. When I asked her why she did not get a house of her own somewhere, she said, "One never knows what may happen. I don't want to spend all my life in exile."[5]

Exile was to be her fate and her bitter choice. A premonition that she would never realize her desire to return to England on her own terms seems already to have possessed her. Earlier in the summer of 1938, while the remodeling of La Croë was in its final stages, she made several trips to Paris, principally with the object of finding a town house to rent through the winter months, now that their summer flank was secured. "We looked and we looked and we looked," she said, and finally they found a stopgap pied-à-terre at 24 Boulevard Suchet, in the fashionable Sixteenth Arrondissement. The Suchet was and remains one of the most heavily traveled thoroughfares in Paris. Fortunately, a tall, dense hedge screened the front of the house from the traffic, and thick walls deadened the thump and clatter of the trucks streaming past. Inside were vistas to stir the imagination of a homemaker for an uprooted monarch: a curved marble staircase, ascending from a pillared entrance hall; lofty drawing rooms and salons, *petit* and *grand*, giving one into the other and looking out over the Bois through tall windows; and everywhere halls, walls, recesses, mantels, fireplaces, and corners crying for a decorator's loving attention. It was a perfect house for entertaining. It may well have been this staircase that persuaded the Duchess to sign the lease. She could hardly have helped picturing herself at the top, gorgeously jeweled and gowned, watching—with the ex-King of England at her side—the *gratin* of Paris and the cream of London and New York mount the marbled heights to make their obeisances.

Before the summer was out the Windsors took a long lease on Number 24, to Walter Monckton's immense relief. When they wound up their summer holidays at Cap d'Antibes and returned to Paris in early September to temporarily reoccupy their former suite at the Meurice, their foremost concern was to have the house ready for them to move into directly after their gala Christmas and New Year's at La Croë.

It was just as well that the season found them so absorbed, for Walter Monckton had meanwhile run into another stone wall in his negotiations with the King. Windsor was continuing to prod Monckton to elicit from his brother a straight answer to the question of whether he was ready to honor their earlier bargain for his return to England in November. The King, loath to make the decision alone and in truth loath—as it would turn out—to make it at all, suggested that Monckton join him at Balmoral in late August, when Prime Minister Neville Chamberlain would be there, and the Duke's petition could be weighed in the interest of the Government as well as of the Royal Family.

Monckton had already judged, from his associations with Chamberlain's close advisers, that he was of two minds about having the Windsors back. He bore the Duke no ill will. Though himself of the opinion that England was well rid of him as its sovereign, he had no objection to his residing in Britain with his wife; that was his right, as a British citizen. All the same, being well aware of the unyielding opposition within the Royal Family, Chamberlain made it clear to his associates in Whitehall that he had no intention of taking sides in the little war. The invitation to the Duke, if one was to be issued, would have to come from the King himself.

Mr. Chamberlain arrived at Balmoral on August 31, for a four-day stay. Monckton went up from London a day or so later. The King informed them that he thought it best for the Queen to participate in the discussion, which went quite as Monckton had expected. Chamberlain offered his judgment that the Duke's early return to England would create no problems for the Government, as long as the public understood that his rank would be merely that of a younger brother. In fact, he suggested that the King might well find his own burdens lightened by having so practiced a hand to relieve him of certain ceremonial chores. But he took care not to urge the point; and the King, while seeming not to disagree with the Prime Minister, was forthright in stating that it would be best for everyone if the return were put off. The message which Monckton was obliged to transmit to his impatient principal in Paris was thus a deliberately muddied one: The King's bargain would be honored, but not right away.

Before leaving Balmoral, Monckton was given a bleak, yet affecting glimpse into the dark gulf which the Abdication and the character of Mrs. Simpson had opened in the family. After the King withdrew with the Prime Minister for a private talk about more serious affairs of State, the

Queen invited Walter to accompany her on a walk around the grounds. He never told Windsor of their conversation, but in the notes which he put down years later, he made bold to remark: "I think the Queen felt quite plainly that it was undesirable to give the Duke any effective sphere of work. I felt then, as always, that she naturally thought that she must be on her guard because the Duke of Windsor, to whom the other brothers had always looked up, was an attractive, vital creature who might be the rallying point for any one who might be critical of the new King who was less superficially endowed with the arts and graces that please."[6]

But, as Monckton was made to perceive, her fear of a humiliating, even dangerous, rivalry was only the ingenuous mask over a more profound emotional opposition to putting out a latchstring for the prodigal. What weighed with her more heavily by far was her hatred, and Queen Mary's, for "the woman" who had lured the mainstay of the family into shattering the monarchy and leaving his brother to pick up the pieces. The Duchess would never be received by her or her sisters-in-law; there was no place for her in British life. "After that talk," Monckton acknowledged to George Allen, "I realized that the Duke's case was lost for as far ahead as I care to look. He never will come back—he can't come back—if they won't have his Duchess among them as an equal."

Knowing only too well how taut the Duke's nerves already were, and not wishing to excite him into a fresh onslaught on the King, Monckton found it more comfortable to confine his report to the facts that the Prime Minister had shown himself hospitable to an early end of the exile, but that the King still considered so early a return premature. Monckton further soothed the Duke with the tidings that Chamberlain would call on him when next in Paris, which, considering the tense state of European politics, was certain to be soon.

At Balmoral, Monckton had been embarrassed to find himself pressing so petty an issue at a time when the King and his Prime Minister were deeply troubled by Hitler's vow to return the Sudeten Germans in Czechoslovakia to the Reich, by invasion if necessary. In such an event, France was bound by treaty to go to Czechoslovakia's aid.

The unspoken possibility that another general war was in the making hovered over the King's table. Only a fortnight later, the seventy-year-old Prime Minister was off to Berchtesgaden on the first of his three historic and unavailing meetings with the Führer. Hard pressed by life-and-death issues of statesmanship and wearied by travel and argument, he nevertheless made place on his burdened schedule in late November for a call on Windsor at the Meurice. Windsor would remember their talk as civil and unhurried, but baffling, so far as his own projects were concerned. The Prime Minister supplied him with a matter-of-fact account of his negotiations with Hitler, and the Duke congratulated him on what was still being praised as his "brilliant" stroke of diplomacy at Munich. "Appeasement was not then the dirty word it later became," Windsor asserted. "Chamberlain's views were hardly different from mine— that another war for mastery in Europe had to be avoided, that the French were unready and dispirited; and that Hitler's real targets probably lay in the East, in Soviet Russia." Only toward the end did Windsor introduce his personal predicament. The Prime Minister's answer was much the same as the one he had given Monckton at Balmoral; he would like to see the former monarch back in England, at the King's side; the Government itself had no objection to his return, but the matter was one where the King's desires were naturally paramount. "I couldn't get him to hold the hot potato," Windsor summed up, without bitterness. The truth is that Chamberlain, on his return to London, did speak up for the Duke, but inside his own party the opposition to the idea was so intense that he decided to abandon the enterprise. When he wrote to the Duke, it was to say, sadly, that the hour was inopportune and he could do no more.[7] His final judgment was expressed in a letter dated February 22, delivered by hand to the Windsors in Paris. He hoped that the Duke would agree with him that his return should be "completely successful," but because it was certain to provoke controversy, he was obliged to say that the time was not yet. And there the hot potato was left, never to be picked up in the Duke's lifetime.

Because of the barrier, Windsor chose not to go to London in September for the funeral of his cousin, Prince Arthur of Connaught; nor was he among the mourners for his

The Duke and Duchess of Windsor with Adolf Hitler, 1938

Château de la Croë, Cap d'Antibes

Government House, Nassau

24 Boulevard Suchet, Paris

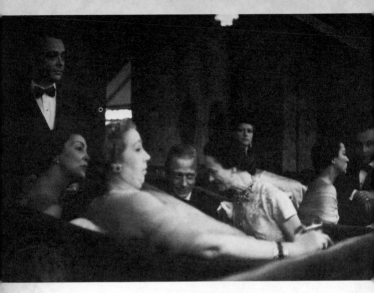

An evening with Jimmy Donahue

On the beach in Venice, 1956

The Duchess and Jimmy Donahue

Opening night at the Lido, Paris, 1962

Leaving the Ritz, Paris, 1969

Sir Winston Churchill and the Duke of Windsor

The Duke and Duchess with pugs

Planning the house in Marbella, 1963

New York, 1947

New York, 1947

Lausanne, 1958

Leaving Maxim's, Paris, 1971

Arriving at the Lido, Paris, with Maurice Chevalier, 1969

Arriving at the Ritz, Paris, 1968

The Duchess of Windsor receiving Prince Charles

Leaving the London Clinic, 1965

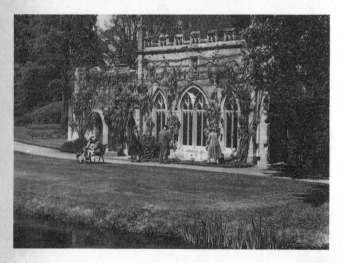

Frogmore

Queen Elizabeth and the Duchess of Windsor

The Duke of Windsor lying in state at the R.A.F. chapel, Benson, Oxfordshire, 1972

The Duchess leaving the hospital, 1979

aunt, Queen Maud of Norway, in November. One of the closest friends of his youth, Edward Stanley, died about the same time, and Windsor's absence from the services was marked again. The bitter penalties of the isolation imposed by his marriage were thus borne upon him in many ways. He sent the condolences expected of him and hid the hurt by throwing himself wholeheartedly—and at times rather childishly—into the myriad little chores and errands involved in furnishing and refurbishing the house on Boulevard Suchet—an enterprise in profligacy sweeping enough to stimulate a small boom in the community.

Although he could not bring himself to admit it, he was slowly, morosely fitting himself into the glittering made-to-order realm of exile which his Duchess was assembling, piece by piece, to make up for the splendid one which he had renounced for her. His early afternoons were, to be sure, reserved for golf at Saint-Cloud, but the rest of his day saw him traipsing around the antique shops in the Duchess's wake, or badgering, cajoling, and bargaining in his highly Anglicized French with the electricians, plumbers, painters, cabinet-makers, and other artisans who kept the new house filled with commotion. As his second year since the Abdication approached an end, his only direct connection with his family was a brief encounter with his brother Harry and his wife, Alice. The Gloucesters, having done a stint of "princing" in Kenya, stopped off in Paris on their way home and put up at the Meurice. The Windsors had little affection for Henry and none at all for Alice, but they had them for lunch in their suite, showed them the new house, took them to call on Eugène de Rothschild, and had them for dinner at Larue. Crowds collected to watch the royal comings and goings, and there was polite applause for the two British princes and their ladies. Although the reunion failed to reconcile the brothers completely, Windsor was overheard to remark to Wallis later, "Travel seems to have broadened dull old Harry."

A week or so before Christmas, Aunt Bessie Merryman arrived from Baltimore and accompanied the Windsors to La Croë for the holidays. With them on the *Train Bleu* went a maid and valet, two security agents, and Pookie and Detto. The rest of the staff had set out the morning before by car, laden with presents. When the party descended at the Antibes station, the mayor was on the platform, splendid in frock coat and top hat, to welcome them back and present the Duchess with a bouquet. The party gathered for Christmas was made up of Perry and Kitty Brownlow, Edward and Caroline Cust, Charles and Elsie Mendl, and Elsie's friend and protégé, John McMullen, who would oversee the decoration of the Christmas tree. The Duke's old friend and occasional aide-de-camp, Colin Davidson, came over from London to act as equerry during the festivities. The fortnight was passed in cards, gossip, leisurely rounds of golf at Cannes, dinners and dancing at restaurants in Monte Carlo and Cannes, and a bit of gambling at the casinos. Mike and Gladys Scanlon also came. Mike would say later that for the first time his heart ached for his friend's all-too-visible loss of grace and purpose. "The atmosphere," he said, "was artificial, even garish. One had the sense that the gaiety was forced and false, a play with the parts being managed by Wallis and that clever fellow McMullen." For Scanlon, an old-school military officer, the worst part came on New Year's Eve. Toward the end of the dinner at La Croë, the Duchess, finding the conversation dragging, suddenly jumped up from the table, exclaiming, "Let's go to the Casino!" The Duke and Davidson dutifully herded the party into two cars, and they saw the New Year in at Monte Carlo, surrounded by a sea of revelers, strangers all, and trying desperately to persuade one another they were having fun. "A wretched setting," Mike Scanlon wrote in his diary, "for a man who had been King Emperor only two years before."

A fading of serious purpose, the decline in dignity which a saddened Scanlon observed in Windsor, had indeed set in, never to be reversed. Not so much as a trace remained by then of the saving and sincere interest in urban housing and labor-management relations which had set him apart from the rest of the monarchical establishment. After his marriage, so far as his friends could observe, he never exhibited even passing curiosity in the revolutionary ideas and dramatic innovations that would agitate these highly charged fields through the rest of his lifetime. The vast literature which was already beginning to proliferate around these two activities went unrepresented by a single volume on the library shelves being stocked at La Croë and Boulevard Suchet. Without so much as a sign, he abandoned his interest in these dreary and insistent problems much as he put out of mind the Welsh miners whose misery had wrung from him the memorable exhortation, "Something must be done!" His horizon was already bounded by a woman's iron whims.

For the Duke, the whim was brass-bound and copper-riveted, but for strangers it could be star-bright. On their return to Paris early in January 1939, the Windsors moved directly into Number 24 and the Duchess set about making it ready for their first guests. The Charles Lindberghs dined there in March, and Mrs. Lindbergh was her usual observant self. Everything was "rather formal and French: lots of footmen in uniform." She was welcomed in "a little room paneled in gold and white, with yellow tulips and dusty black iris arranged beautifully." The dining room was "lovely," with "red and gold curtains and mirrors." After dinner, the ladies retired to "a tiny sitting room . . . enchanting . . . paneled in a pale blue-gray and white with gay chintz and white lilacs and white calla lilies in vases and a pale pink and pale blue spray of orchids on the mantel."[8]

The Duchess liked to say, "Fitting out a house is one of the most absorbing things a woman can have to do—but she needs money to do it properly." She had the money now. Ten years before, Ernest Simpson had given her hundreds of pounds for fitting out the flat in Bryanston Court; now the Duke was giving her tens of thousands. She thought nothing of spending 8,000 pounds for a single Meissen figure to adorn her drawing room, or 30,000 pounds for a pair of canary diamonds to adorn her person. These were her favorite stones. In later years, she would find it increasingly irksome to sustain her local primacy in the market, narrow though it was. When her friend Jayne Wrightsman, whose husband's wallet was considerably thicker than the Duke's, walked off with a specially brilliant canary that the Duchess had been dickering for, it put an end to their friendship. Charles Wrightsman is a former president of Standard Oil of Kansas. He once scoffed,

"Paul Getty? Why, he hasn't got a penny more than half a billion dollars to his name!" Another rival collector, though briefly, was the late Margaret Biddle. The daughter of William Boyce Thompson, who had made an enormous fortune as a mining expert for J. P. Morgan & Co., she married, first, a Mr. Schultz; and second, Anthony J. Drexel Biddle—"Tony"—of Philadelphia. Her gallery of Impressionists was magnificent; so were her jewels. The Duchess soon had to break off the competition. Sighing, she told a friend, "How can I match Margaret's millions? She can buy out Cartier and Van Cleef whenever the impulse strikes her, and as soon as they've replaced their stocks, she can buy them out again!" The Duchess was a hard bargainer and a shrewd one; the deal concluded, she paid cash; there were no records and no taxes.

Though she herself discovered many of her rarest and most beautiful furnishings in antique shops on the Left Bank, she bought many others, as well as her carpets and curtains, through Stephane Boudin, of Maison Jensen, on the Rue Royale. His clients also included the Chips Channons, for whom he designed a dining room in blue and silver, with an ocher-and-silver gallery, at a cost of more than 6,000 pounds. A pale, spare little man with a dapper moustache, M. Boudin combined immaculate taste with consummate tact and salesmanship. A friend said, "All the Duchess had to do was suggest a certain arrangement, and Boudin would clap his hands and cry, '*Votre Altesse Royale*, I believe that by great good fortune, I have *precisely* the piece to fill out your so *charming* scheme!' and always"—the friend added—"for a couple of million francs. The furniture was mostly Louis Quinze. I'm told that the Duchess's bedroom was done in white and royal blue, and featured an ermine rug—*real* ermine. Me, I'd have been afraid to step on it. . . . *Boudin* means 'blood pudding,' you know. Such a coarse name, I always thought, for such an elegant fellow!"

With all credit to M. Boudin's taste and the Duchess's, not even the most precious of her paintings and bibelots and Louis XV armchairs could outshine the Duke's own contributions to the setting: his heirlooms from York House and the Fort. What gave them their special aura, and imparted uniqueness and significance to the whole, was something no dealer or decorator could supply: their illustrious, historical associations with the Royal Family, *his* family. Few other hostesses could set their dinner table with—for example—four George II silver saltcellars and say of them, "These belonged to my husband's great-great-something-granduncle, the Duke of Cumberland, the one the Scots call the 'Butcher of Culloden.' *We* prefer to think of him as the sportsman who bred Eclipse, the greatest racehorse in the history of the turf. You know: 'Eclipse first, the rest nowhere.' "

While Boudin and his men polished up Number 24, the Duchess, in addition to directing the general operations, addressed herself to the equally demanding task of assembling a staff big and versatile enough to keep the two houses humming. The mere mechanics of managing in alternating cycles a large tropical villa and a spacious town mansion are understandably complicated, and for a careful account of how the former Mrs. Spencer Simpson did it, history is indebted to Dina Wells Hood, the British woman who served as Number Two personal secretary to the Duke during this period. Miss Hood had been hired the year before in London, where she ran a stenographic service operating in a half-dozen different languages, including, of course, English. Some seven years earlier, while working in Rio de Janeiro, she had been pressed into emergency service by the British Embassy there to provide secretarial help to the Duke, then on his famous Latin American tour as Prince of Wales. She dealt with his mail and took dictation for his little speeches. She made an excellent impression on him and he on her.

By Miss Hood's account, the permanent staff rose to sixteen after the acquisition of Number 24. The roster was made up of the English butler, Hale; the French chef, Dyot, and his assistant, also French; two English housemaids; a senior *lingère*; two scullery hands; the Duke's Austrian valet; the Duchess's Swiss maid; two chauffeurs—the Duchess's was English, the Duke's Austrian; three women secretaries, all English; and the head gardener at La Croë, Antoine, who was French. When the flow of entertainment was at flood, the kitchen staffs were reinforced by temporary recruits. Happily for the Duke's purse, the two security police, one provided by Scotland Yard and the other by the French Sûreté, were not on the household payroll. The faithful and worthy Storrier had retired the year before. His place was taken by another senior Scotland Yard officer, Philip Attfield, who worked in harness with his French colleague, a M. Magnin, a detective of quiet dignity and impeccable manners. Because the Duke was no longer a beneficiary of the Civil List he had to provide his own equerry and a.d.c., and the skilled and polished gentlemen who had performed that unique calling in the past, Colin Davidson and Dudley Forwood, came back into the Duke's service to spell each other in that demanding duty, the latter with the start of the entertaining at Number 24. So there were as many as a full score of men and women in constant attendance on the Windsors.

It was a taut ship, by any standard. Directly after breakfast and before she had pored over the morning newspapers, the Duchess would summon the chef to her room, to go over his menus for the luncheon and dinner of that day. He submitted two proposed lists from a book in which he kept a record of past meals. If she did not care for the choices, she would be ready with alternatives of her own. All of her chefs—and the line numbered more than half a dozen over the years—were agreed that no woman whom they had served knew food and its more exotic and eclectic arrangements as thoroughly as she did. Her instructions were precise and they testified to her improving command of French grammar. She also proved that access to an all but bottomless purse had not spoiled a thrifty, meticulous, even penny-pinching housekeeper. The butler, the chef, the head chauffeur, and the gardener were all required to submit detailed accounts of their expenditures, down to the smallest items. Sometimes with the Duke looking over her shoulder, she inspected and analyzed the various entries. A detailed record of the household accounts was kept in a big ledger: The monthly rise and fall in the levels were a cause for satisfaction (when the level was down) and for instantaneous screw-turning (when it was up). The Windsors knew what was being spent for everything—wine, food, petrol, clothes, telephone, the feeding of the servants, even the costs of the dogs.

Soon it all began to take on a strongly marked style, a

cachet, of its own. A handsome livery was invited for
the staff by the Duke in collaboration with his London tailor—scarlet coats with gold cuffs and collar and gold buttons for the footmen on formal occasions, black suits and
waistcoats striped with red for ordinary occasions, and
dress suits of dark-gray alpaca for the summer uniform
at La Croë. A coroneted monogram, "WE," from their en-
twined initials, began to decorate the linen, the stationery,
the menu cards, gifts of jewelry to friends, even the buttons
on the staff's livery. (The Duke's chauffeur wore on his
cap the famous flaring insignia of the Grenadier Guards,
the Duke's wartime regiment.) But the figurehead Sovereign
of this luxurious and insular principality, in the course of
adapting himself to his changed circumstances, began to
take on more and more a somewhat contrary character—
the fidgets and crotches of the ruler of a petty kingdom
in the misty past of his own Saxe-Coburg-Gotha line. The
secretiveness that had shadowed his character from youth
and crippled his friendships gripped him harder now that
he was on his own. He trusted no one except the Duchess.
All mail went to him first; he opened the letters himself,
save those addressed to the Duchess. The sensitive correspondence that passed between him and his brother,
Monckton, and other dignitaries was seldom entrusted to
the secretaries. He tapped out his private letters on a portable typewriter or penned them in a somewhat immature
hand, and kept the papers locked up in tin dispatch boxes,
for which he alone had the keys. He managed the fi-
nances well, adding up the accounts, making ledger entries, disbursing checks, and, in various other ways, concealing the important affairs from his own staff.

From the inside, it must have been a painful spectacle to
watch. For the lesser servants of the regime—not the butler or the chef, who were supreme in their own exalted
spheres, but the maids, footmen, and chauffeurs—life under the Windsors could be hazardous in the extreme. A
dropped plate, a careless intrusion, or a slip in attentive-
ness could be counted upon to bring a swift dressing down,
followed often by peremptory sacking. The hours were
long, praise was scanty. It is doubtful that any household
staff in all of Paris was driven as hard as the one that
served the Windsors. But the favored company that the

Windsors began to assemble around themselves in the months before the outbreak of the war, to dine at the magnificent black-and-gold table with two gleaming gold caskets heaped with flowers at the center and held aloft by seductive onyx blackamoors, could not help sensing the meticulous preparations, the precise schooling, and the untiring discipline that out of sight supported the dazzling show.

So the Windsors passed the second year of their marriage as Europe drifted into war. To an unkindly British eye, their achievements in marriage "demonstrated the iceberg principle in exact reverse. Everything was on the surface; underneath there was nothing."[9] Still, it can be rightly said of Windsor that he was not yet wholly devoid of serious purpose or that self-indulgence had altogether eroded his conscience. The false lull after Munich was shattered in March by Hitler's invasion of Czechoslovakia, and the specter of war returned to haunt Europe once more. Now with Hitler demanding the retrocession of Danzig and the erasure of the Polish Corridor, Poland was all too plainly moving up on the Nazi calendar. On March 31, Mr. Chamberlain announced in the House of Commons that Britain would come to Poland's assistance if Hitler attacked. A fortnight later the British guarantee was extended to Greece and Romania. Watching on, Windsor was inspired, quite on his own and outside any institutional or official auspices, to speak out against the waste and folly of war, and he did so from the best of motives and, alas for him, with the worst of results.

The locale he chose from which to make his plea for peace was the little town of Verdun, where a million men had fallen in World War I. Windsor knew the battlefield far better than most, from his service with the British Army. And for his vehicle, he chose the National Broadcasting Company because it offered him access to a huge American radio audience. The arrangements for the broadcast were made by his friend, Fred Bate, NBC's European manager and a former Bryanston Court "regular." In the furor that followed the event, Bate was suspected of having lured Windsor into an act of folly, to gain a scoop for himself, but Windsor laughed off the suspicion. "I needed no urging," he said. "The idea was mine. I was not without my own sources of intelligence at the time. The German, Italian and Spanish Ambassadors were all good friends of mine. So was Bill Bullitt, in the American Embassy. And I still had one or two lines into Whitehall, even though my own Ambassador was hardly forthcoming. From these and other sources, I became convinced that Europe was headed down the slippery slope to war. Only the Americans had the influence to arrest the slide. That was why I decided to aim my appeal at them."

Early in May, Bate and a crew of technicians arrived in France from London to prepare for the broadcast, which was scheduled for the eighth. A suite was engaged at the modest Hôtel Coq Hardi in Verdun, and a microphone was set up in the bedroom. The Windsors, accompanied by Bate, drove there from Paris the day before, to be greeted by the Mayor and other town dignitaries. That was the only fanfare. But, as matters turned out, the little enterprise could hardly have been more inopportune. Three days before the broadcast, King George VI and Queen Elizabeth sailed from England on the Canadian Pacific liner, *Empress of Australia*, on a goodwill trip to Canada and an overnight stay as President and Mrs. Roosevelt's guests at their Hyde Park estate on the Hudson. In the highly charged atmosphere then prevailing in British politics, the King's Atlantic crossing, though planned long before, inevitably took on a considerable diplomatic significance. When, therefore, the British learned tardily of the imminent broadcast in preparation at Verdun, the reaction at the Palace and in Whitehall was one of dismay: Windsor (some said) was moving to deaden the impact of his brother's arrival in North America.

So disturbed were some of his stoutest friends about the damage which his intrusion into international affairs might cause, even though the text of his broadcast was known only to himself, the Duchess, and Bate, that they tried to head him off with a personal appeal. Their telephone calls across the Channel went unanswered. Lord Beaverbrook, in an effort to deflect him at the last hour, ordered up an editorial that was published in the *Daily Express* on the morning of the broadcast, lecturing him on the impropriety of speaking up before the King had completed his mission to Canada and for a lack of tact in failing to understand that "any word spoken on America at present should come from him."

Windsor went ahead with the broadcast anyway, the Duchess at his side. The BBC refused to relay the talk. The British newspapers, however, carried fairly full accounts from their correspondents in the United States. In truth, his theme was a simple one, touched here and there with eloquence. He began by saying that in speaking from Verdun, he was sensible of "the presence of the great company of the dead"; that, representing only himself, his words were those of "a soldier of the last war whose earnest prayer is that such cruel and destructive madness shall never again overtake mankind." There was not much more to the statement than that—no precepts for statesmen, no calls for action. Only a forlorn hope that calamity might be avoided if the mass of people who would have to bear the sacrifice would look beyond the political slogans of the hour, and instead set about preserving the values of civilization. It all could have come without offense from a bishop, or, for that matter, from any number of British politicians and peers of the realm who shared his sentiments. But because the message came from him, at the time it did, and because its vague hint of appeasement aroused memories of his ridiculous post-honeymoon excursion to Germany less than two years before, he infuriated far many more people than he persuaded. Nearly four decades later, his biographer, Frances Lady Donaldson, dismissed the modest text as "completely banal" and scolded him for not perceiving that "war and peace are majestic themes that do not lend themselves to the tongues of private citizens"—a stricture which might properly apply to a recently abdicated monarch, but which exhibits a surprising lack of sympathy for a citizen's well-established rights and interests, where war and peace are concerned.

The sad fact is that Windsor failed again. "I got nowhere," as he himself put it. The roar of approval which he had hoped to elicit from the throats of millions of ex-servicemen on both sides of the Atlantic failed to find voice. But he was consoled by the flood of mail, most of it approving, that came from the United States, and from his former subjects in the British Dominions who heard the rebroadcast over shortwave wireless. His German professor at Oxford, Dr. Herman Fiedler, wrote that he had listened to him in Germany in the company of friends and they were all agreed that it was "a wonderful peace speech."

The occasion also had a humorous side. He liked to tell of Fred Bate's frantic efforts, just as they were about to go on the air, to shut out the ear-splitting noise of a loud-speaker blaring out the melody of an American Western folk song, "The Last Round-up," below the hotel windows as a country fair got off to a festive start in the village park.

To his credit, if not to his advantage in history, Windsor never backed off from his theme of reconciliation with the Germans. His correspondence swelled in the immediate aftermath of Verdun, and his answers brooded on the hope that "war, the irrevocable disaster, the final catastrophe for mankind, would by some means be averted."[10] Was he really as much out of step with British opinion as he was declared to be? Anthony Eden at the time of the reoccupation of the Rhineland had unashamedly described British policy as one of "appeasement." Windsor himself, in com-mon with his friend Duff Cooper, was an ardent proponent of an Anglo-German understanding, and not an admirer of Hitler. His father had remarked sadly to Samuel Hoare, at the height of the uproar over Mussolini's lunge into Ethio-pia, "I am an old man. I have been through one war. How can I go through another?"[11] To the degree that logic ruled the foreign policy of the Baldwin and Chamberlain governments, it was the idea that the German threat could best be neutralized by wooing the allies that Hitler had to have, notably Italy. That was an important item in Wind-sor's private foreign policy. True, Hitler had encouraged him to believe, in their conversation at Berchtesgaden two years before, that the Soviet Union was his real target, not Britain. "I thought," Windsor wrote afterward, "that the rest of us could be fence-sitters while the Nazis and the Reds slugged it out."[12] He was sadly mistaken, but he was hardly alone.

When the Windsors left for La Croë late in June, their enormous impedimenta included two white doves in cages—gifts from strangers who thereby saluted him as their "ambassador of peace." The doves were not with him long. As the crisis tightened, the Windsor staff felt the effects. First, Inspector Attfield was recalled by Scotland Yard for special security duties, then Dudley Forwood was ordered to report to his regiment, the Scots Guards. One of the French footmen was called up, and the Austrian valet was under orders to report home for military duty. There was another, perhaps more shattering, change. Head chef Dyot gave regretful notice; his former employer, the Duke of Alba, having been posted to London as the Ambassador of the victorious Franco government, had asked him to return to his service. The Windsors let him go, but before hanging up his apron, he recruited for them a replacement hardly less gifted than himself, a M. Pinaudier.

Despite these upheavals and the gathering storm, the Windsors were still at La Croë on September 1, 1939, when Hitler's troops invaded Poland.

CHAPTER 7

The Windsors' War—I:

An Uncertain Trumpet

There stood the Queen in front of them with her arms folded, frowning like a thunderstorm.

"A fine day, your Majesty!" the Duchess began in a low, weak voice.

"Now, I give you fair warning," shouted the Queen, stamping on the ground as she spoke; "either you or your head must be off, and that in about half no time! Take your choice!"

The Duchess took her choice and was gone in a moment.

> —Alice's Adventures in Wonderland,
> LEWIS CARROLL

Never did the Duke of Windsor have a brighter chance of escaping from the wasteland of his self-centered life, and recovering an honored, useful position, than was offered him by the outbreak of World War II. But through a succession of gaffes and myopic judgments, the chance was repeatedly thrown away, largely because of the Duchess's obsession with being accepted by the family in the same status as her sisters-in-law.

There is no question of the genuineness of his desire to serve Britain in the war. For all his loneliness in youth and the realization of his inadequacy at the Royal Naval College, he was grateful for his association with the Navy, and proud of it. And his long years of service with the fighting forces in France and Italy during the Great War, remote from the stifling discipline of his father's houses, and among men from all walks of life, had given him his first intoxicating draft of independence

Windsor as the War Prince had been a marvelously appealing figure. Everything that his father, the Government, and the High Command asked of him, he did well; and he longed to do much more than was ever allowed him. The Army matured him, undergirded a wavering self-confidence, and imparted to his public manner a sense of style that was classically British, a flashing charm, a hint of uncommon spirit, that formed the image which Britons of his own and older generations would always cherish.

He enjoyed being a soldier and putting on a uniform; he looked his best in one, particularly if it required breeches and boots; he had "a leg for a boot," and alone among the menfolk in his immediate family, he was not knock-kneed. To the day of his death, he kept all the uniforms he had ever worn. If George V had hung on long enough for the new bachelor King, again in uniform, to materialize dramatically at Churchill's side, his place in history would surely have been a nobler one. It was not to be, of course; yet the drift of time would have carried him into just such a heroic role; and the frustrations that sought fulfillment in a frivolous, middleaged woman might have dissolved in the purposeful duties that war lays upon a King of England.

The pity is that his return to England did not start well. The outbreak of war, on September 1, found the Windsors taking their ease at Château de la Croë, well out of the prostrating heat of Paris in August. Except for the faithful Fruity Metcalfe, they were alone. None of their friends, French, British, or American, had taken up invitations to join them, from fear of being marooned by hostilities. On the eve of Hitler's *Blitzkrieg* against Poland, Windsor had sent him a telegram, begging him not to plunge the world into war. Hitler replied that he had no wish for war with England and if it came, it would be England's fault. Windsor had always sympathized with Germany's desire for *Lebensraum*, so the *Blitzkrieg* did not overly distress him. The practical result, he reasoned, would bring superior German power face-to-face with Soviet power along Europe's easternmost marches, and the Germans would then in their own time finish off communism, to the general advantage.

On the morning of September 3, he listened to a French radio report that the collapse of Polish resistance was imminent. He finished his breakfast, scanned the mail, and tried in vain to put a call through to London, in the hope of getting a sound opinion on whether the war would spread. He, Wallis, and Fruity were on their way down to the swimming pool when a servant notified him that the British Ambassador in Paris was on the telephone. Britain had entered the war on Poland's side. The Duchess remembers his telling her, "I'm afraid this may open the way for world communism." He plunged into the pool.

His offhand remark was not unprescient. Appraising Soviet Russia as the ultimate threat to Europe, he remained convinced that for England and France to fight Germany—the "good Germany" of the "good Germans," as exemplified by his own family connections—was a monstrous blunder. A trip he had made there in the spring of 1913, when he was eighteen years old, had printed the land and its people on his memory forever; and subsequent images from the 1938 trip—images of swastikas and jackboots and the hoarse baying at helpless Jews—failed to darken the original sunny scenes. When he thought of Germany now, he still thought of watching a merry Easter-egg hunt in the palace garden at Darmstadt, with "Uncle Ernie and Aunt Honoré," the Grand Duke and Grand Duchess of Hesse; and of eating enormous, soporific meals with "Onkel Willie and Tante Charlotte," the King and Queen of Württemberg, and then driving out in their victoria, while they took the salutes of their affectionate subjects. Uncle Ernie—the Prince wrote in his diary—was "charming," and Onkel Willie was "the most comfortable, easy-going king I ever saw." Windsor never realized that the Germany of his personal vision had been hopelessly degraded by Hitler. He was loath to accept the difference, and his obtuseness would continue to bring frequent embarrassment both to himself and to the British Government.

Notwithstanding, he wanted to take his place among his countrymen in the struggle. Before the third was out, he got through to London, to Walter Monckton, who had remained his channel to the Palace, and instructed him to convey his wish to return to England and to serve in any post the King deemed suitable. Three days after receiving the Duke's message, Monckton came to La Croë, with considerable difficulty. His vehicle was a small R.A.F. Leopard Moth. Darkness forced them down at a grassy lit-

tle airdrome in southern France, and Monckton was congratulating himself on their safe landing, when he was arrested by the Mayor, who could not reconcile his civilian
clothes with the military plane. The news that he brought
Windsor was mixed. Some was good: The King wanted
him back at all possible speed. Even better, he was offering
a choice of jobs: Deputy Regional Commissioner to Sir
Wyndham Portal in Wales (i.e., Civil Defense), or an assignment as a liaison officer in the Number 1 Military Mission from the War Office to the French General Headquarters. The other news was less palatable: The Windsors
should not expect to be put up at Windsor Castle, or in
any other royal accommodations; nor should the Duchess
expect to be received.

Walter Monckton flew home, and the Windsors followed
by road next day: one car for their luggage, another for
themselves, Metcalfe, and Pookie, Preezie (from the
French *surprise*), and Detto. The drive to Cherbourg took
them a leisurely four days.

Meanwhile, Windsor's staunchest friend, Winston
Churchill, had been returned to his old and favorite post,
First Lord of the Admiralty. On September 5, the Palace
having asked him to arrange for bringing the Windsors
across the Channel, he sent for Capt. Lord Louis Mountbatten, R.N., and ordered him to pick up the ducal party
at Cherbourg.

"This will be a historic trip," Churchill said. "I want my
son, Randolph, to be along."

Mountbatten, the Royal Navy's youngest captain, had
just commissioned the destroyer leader *Kelly* and was
"working up" at Portland. They sailed from there soon
after sunrise on the twelfth and slipped into Cherbourg
Harbor just before noon. The Windsors had arrived the
previous afternoon and had spent the night as guests of the
admiral commandant of the port. Whenever travel was
ahead, the Duke liked to prove his handyman competence
by supervising the packing and stowing of their baggage.
He and the Duchess were out on the lawn next morning,
she remembered, gathering up suitcases and boxes and parcels when "in strode Dickie Mountbatten, complete with
everything possible—aiguillettes, everything he *could* have
had on—followed by Randolph Churchill in army uniform,

dragging a sword on the ground, sort of flopping. Dickie was very nice. . . ." Lord Mountbatten rejects the Duchess's recollection of this scene. He says, "I was in ordinary working uniform. Naturally I put on aiguillettes, because I'd been the Duke's personal a.d.c."

The Windsors welcomed him warmly, and the Duke had turned to greet young Churchill when something caught his eye and brought him up short. Churchill had come aboard the *Kelly* in battle dress, but on the run across the Channel had decided that its simplicity was inappropriate to the "historic trip," and had changed to the more impressive uniform of an officer of the 4th Hussars. Mountbatten, a horseman, had noticed at once that Churchill's spurs were on wrong, but mischievously had said nothing. Not so Windsor, who had both a horseman's eye for correct tack and royalty's for the minutiae of correct military dress.

"Randolph," he cried with delight, "your spurs are not only inside out, but upside down! Haven't you ever been on a horse?"

Churchill swallowed his chagrin until he was alone with Mountbatten. Then he demanded furiously, "Damn it, why didn't you tell me?"

Mountbatten laughed. "I wanted the Duke to have the pleasure. Don't take it to heart! It broke the ice."

Ice was there; Windsor resented Mountbatten's not having attended his wedding, and Mountbatten resented Windsor's not having invited him. Nearly thirty-three years would pass before the misunderstanding was cleared up and their old intimacy restored.

The *Kelly* cast off at 4 P.M. for the six-hour, high-speed run. The sea was calm, the dinner pleasant. After it, Windsor joined the captain on the bridge. Their cousinly talk soon turned to the choice that Windsor would have to face. Mountbatten advised him, "Forget the Civil Defense job! You won an M.C. for valor in the Great War. Get back into uniform!"

"As a field marshal! I kept the rank, remember."

"Forget that, too. Become a major general."

Portsmouth was completely blacked out, but the scene that presently burst on their view is still brilliantly clear in Mountbatten's memory: "We came alongside the Royal Jetty, went astern, and passed our lines. At that instant the

jetty lights flashed on, revealing a guard of honor and a red
carpet at the foot of the brow. As the Duke stepped ashore,
he turned to me and said, 'God bless you and keep you
safe!' The guard presented arms, and the Royal Marines
band broke into 'God Save the King.' He inspected the
guard and walked to the car, where the Duchess was waiting. The car door closed on them, the lights went out, and
silence reigned again. It all took only a few minutes, but
the drama and the unexpected pageantry of the scene I
shall never forget. Incidentally, the jetty where he landed
was the very one he had sailed from after the Abdication."

It was the last time the cousins would meet for eleven
years.

The Duchess assumed that the Duke's silence, as they
drove off, was because he was as stirred as herself. Not
altogether, it presently appeared. When he spoke at last, it
was enigmatically: "The short version, by God!"

"The short version of *what*, David?"

" 'God Save the King.' The monarch gets the full treatment, other royalty only the first six bars." He patted her
hand. "I'd become rather used to the full treatment."

The Marine band may have shortchanged him, but he
ended up ahead, with the three cairns. One of Britain's
most stringent laws bars dogs from the country before they
have undergone six months' quarantine. No one else would
have dared flout this law so openly; and not even Windsor
could quite get away with it. A few days later, the Duchess
took the dogs for a walk, and "Some Nosey Parker spied
them and complained to the Home Office, so we had to
put them into quarantine after all."

Because Fruity Metcalfe was with the Windsors, his wife
knew when and where they would be arriving; she had also
learned—to her astonishment—that no member or representative of the Royal Family would be meeting them, and
that no accommodations in Buckingham Palace or elsewhere were being offered. Accordingly, she sent word for
Fruity to invite them to South Hartfield House, their place
in Sussex; and to greet them on their return to England,
she and Walter Monckton drove down to Portsmouth in
one Metcalfe car while her chauffeur followed in a station
wagon for the luggage. The *Kelly* would dock too late for
the party to reach South Hartfield House that night, so

Lady Alexandra and Monckton stopped off at a hotel in Portsmouth and reserved for the Windsors "its best red-plush suite"; she liked to describe how she "bounced" on the beds, to make sure that they met the Duchess's high standard of comfort.

Churchill, too, had noticed—and with resentment—the plain intention to snub the Windsors; and he, too, had decided to take action. As First Lord of the Admiralty, he was able to provide the guard of honor, the band, and the red carpet; and finally, having waited until the last minute for a sign from the Palace, he ordered the admiral commanding the Portsmouth base to welcome them to Admiralty House. As a result, the Metcalfes took over the red-plush suite, and the Duchess—not for the first time in her life—slept on Navy-issue bedding.

Next morning, with the Palace's cold, inhospitable silence still unbroken, the Windsors prepared to move to South Hartfield House. Lady Alexandra had rented a house for them in Ashdown Forest, nearby, but they chose to stay with her and Fruity. The Duke, perhaps naïvely, had expected a car from the royal garage to be put at their disposal, but none appeared. The missing car was a portent of more to come—rather, *not* to come. The day passed without any offer of rooms at the Palace, or lodgings of any kind; or even a temporary office, or a secretary; nor—so thorough was the snub—did any member of the Royal Family communicate with the Windsors in any way, much less invite them to call. Still more surprisingly, though a few of their old friends came down to South Hartfield House for lunch, not one opened his house to them. The Windsors had become nonpeople, wraiths—except to the ever-loyal Metcalfes. They hastily made room for their otherwise homeless visitors in their country house; Lady Alexandra also had the dust covers stripped from her town house at 16 Wilton Place and turned it over to them as a London base; and almost every other day, for the fortnight they stayed in England, she herself drove them up to town—a forty-five-minute trip—and back.

The Duke lost no time in trying to establish his military position. As early as the fourteenth, the day after his arrival at the Metcalfes', he motored up to London to keep the appointment with his brother, which Walter Monckton had been able to arrange only on the King's stipulation that the Duchess not be present. Monckton escorted the Duke to the King's Room, then withdrew to the Equerries' Room to wait.

This, the brothers' first meeting in the three years since the Abdication, should have been an affectionate reunion. It was, instead, all but a confrontation. Windsor also called on his mother, but there is no record of what passed between them. The evening before, he and his Duchess had jointly decided that he would reject Mountbatten's advice and would plump for the Civil Defense post in Wales. They would offer La Croë as a convalescent home for officers, and themselves would settle in England, as they longed to do. When he returned to the Palace to announce his choice to the King, it was received with less than enthusiasm. The reason—he would presently discover—was that the King, too, had changed his mind. He no longer wanted the Windsors underfoot during a war that bade to be protracted. There would be far less chance of family friction and, worse still, of brotherly rivalry if Windsor were across the Channel, and on the back page, with the Military Mission. Naturally, the King did not share his reasoning with the Duke. By Windsor's recollection, the King merely noted in passing that the liaison job looked more exciting; and Windsor, in turn, agreed. As they separated, the King temporized by telling him, "There's no urgency about committing yourself. Tomorrow at four, I have arranged for you to see Hore-Belisha," the War Minister.

That ended the interview. When Windsor came to narrate it to the editor of his autobiography, the editor asked, "What was the King's attitude?" Windsor: "What he'd always been. He was—" Duchess (interrupting): "Agreeably weak." Windsor: "That's right." They walked to the Equerries' Room together, the King slightly in the lead. As they entered, he murmured to Monckton, "I think it went all right."

But Monckton sensed unease. No sooner had he and Windsor quitted the Palace than Windsor demanded to know what the King had murmured. Monckton told him. Windsor: " 'Went all right,' eh? It went all right because on your advice I kept off contentious subjects!"

* * *

Next day, as his conversation with Hore-Belisha developed, Windsor was puzzled to find that there was no further discussion of the choice of jobs. Hore-Belisha seemed to assume that the liaison post had already been accepted, and went directly to the questions of what rank Windsor would take, and whether he planned to spend any time with one of the Commands before returning to Paris. Unknown to Windsor, Hore-Belisha had that morning received a letter from the Palace, saying that the King's preference was for Windsor to take the liaison job, and that Windsor had consented. Windsor did not contest Hore-Belisha's assumption. He merely asked, rather wistfully, if he might keep his field marshal's baton. Hore-Belisha had to tell him that this would raise awkward problems of precedence. Windsor accepted this disappointment, too, and said merely that before leaving England he wished to visit as many of his old Commands as possible, and to take the Duchess with him. Hore-Belisha promised to see what he could do, although intuition told him at once that the Palace would balk. It did. The King sent for him next morning. "He was in a distressed state," Hore-Belisha's official diary records. "He thought that if the Duchess went to the Commands, she might have a hostile reception, particularly in Scotland." The Scots, prim, thin-skinned, and unforgiving, strongly disapproved of the Abdication and still resented her having caused Windsor to default the ceremony at Aberdeen in order to meet the train bringing her to Ballater. She was one Wallis they would never bleed with. The diary continued, "The King did not want the Duke to go to the Commands in England. He seemed very disturbed and walked up and down the room. He said the Duke had never had any discipline in his life. . . ."

Three hours after this emotional interview, Hore-Belisha was astonished to find himself again summoned to the Palace, this time with the Chief of the Imperial General Staff, General Sir Edmund Ironside. The King's resolution had stiffened in the luncheon interval. He now declared it best for his brother to leave for Paris at once; Ironside would issue the necessary orders. This second interview, though briefer than the first, ended even more emotionally. The King said that all his ancestors had succeeded to the throne after their predecessors had died, whereas "mine is not only alive, but very much so."

When Hore-Belisha returned to his office at three o'clock, the Duke was waiting, primed for visiting the Commands and circulating among the troops, as he had done well in the Great War. Hore-Belisha had the delicate task of quenching these ardent plans. He explained that it was customary for a soldier to take up a new appointment without delay, that the Duke's orders were even then being issued, and that the Chief of the Mission was impatient for him to report.

Windsor had failed to carry a single one of his major objectives, but before retiring from the field, he requested three minor concessions. First, might he have back his honorary colonelcy in the Welsh Guards? Answer: The King would have to decide this. Windsor, knowing that his brother had already assumed the honor, dropped the matter. Second, might he wear his decorations from the Great War? Yes. Third, might he have Fruity Metcalfe as his equerry? Yes.

Despite the crushing proofs that the Palace wanted nothing more to do with them, and despite nudges by Hore-Belisha and Ironside, Windsor delayed reporting—"I had no uniforms or anything. I think it took us at least ten days before we went back." Meanwhile, he and the Duchess made daily trips to London and passed pleasant, unhurried hours in lunching with friends, shopping, and revisiting old scenes. Their only "business"—one they never neglected—was a renewed campaign for the Duchess's title, although by now even their sympathizers were becoming bored with it.

One afternoon the Windsors made a sentimental journey to the Fort, only to find it shuttered, damp, and dark, the lawn shaggy, the garden gone to weed. The Duke had hoped that his brother would invite him to take up residence there for the duration of his wartime job, but the hope had decayed with the Fort itself. His affection for "Toyland" was deep and enduring. Some fifteen years after this sad last pilgrimage, he was driving from London to Southampton on a wintry day when he caught sight of a familiar turret through the leafless trees. "Look! Look!" he cried. "The *Fort*!" Then, a moment later, "I loved it. My happiest days were spent there. . . ." Its wings torn down, it was later occupied for a while by Princess Mary's second son, Gerald Lascelles. In 1976, the Sultan of Dubai, a United Arab Emirate, bought it for "an undisclosed sum."

Eventually, if reluctantly, the Duke had to hearken to the call of duty. He and the Duchess, Fruity Metcalfe, and the three cairns, now sprung from quarantine, reembarked for France in a Navy vessel on September 29, accompanied by numerous hampers of delicacies, including fine liquors retrieved from Edward VIII's cellars in the Palace, and by George Ladbrook, whose last service had been to drive the newly married Duke and Duchess to the station for the train to Venice. In grateful requital of the Metcalfes' two weeks of hospitality, the Windsors gave Lady Alexandra a pair of ice buckets.

Why the cold shoulder at the Palace? Why had the King reneged on his offer to let Windsor return to England and serve out the war there? He had himself opened the avenue voluntarily; what had led him to block it off? The earnest, plodding Bertie could hardly have helped being jealous of David's panache. That the Abdication had lessened it but little had become plain eight months before, when a Gallup poll asked Britons whether they would like the Windsors to come back and live, and 61 percent had voted "Yes" against 16 percent "No." Even in the two days since his return to London, crowds had been clustering around his car, cheering him and shouting, "Good old Ted! Good old Teddy! Glad to see you back!" At the same time, they were being deluged by hundreds of letters a day. The majority were friendly welcomes, but not all; some were obscene and abusive, cursing the Windsors for daring to return to England, or cursing the Metcalfes for receiving them.

Reports of the affectionate demonstrations had reached the Palace, and undoubtedly had detonated the King's unprecedented outburst of bitterness in the presence of Hore-Belisha and Ironside. But the determining factor, in the opinion of many who were close to the Royal Family, was Queen Mary's implacable opposition to having her renegade eldest son and his "adventuress" wife on the premises again. Not only was her face set against David's being readmitted to a position where he might outshine Bertie, but—in the opinion of a peeress in her circle—she was "apprehensive of his attempting to regain the throne."

Queen Mary's anxieties, especially those toward the Duchess of Windsor, pervaded the whole Royal Family. Though this was their first opportunity to welcome Wallis as David's wife, or even to receive her, the castle draw-bridge was never lowered. But unlike the Queen Mother, the Queen had fewer apprehensions of what the Duke might do than resentment of what the Duchess had already done. The Queen had been supremely happy in her quiet life with her quiet husband and their daughters, on the edge of "that fierce light which beats upon a throne," and she had had no wish to move stage center. Nonetheless, despite her retiring nature, she was "bloody-minded." She alone of the old King's three daughters-in-law had never feared him; she alone of the whole family was not keel-hauled for being a bit late to dinner, but excused, with "You are *not* late, my dear! We must have sat down two minutes too early"; she alone of the sisters-in-law had dared twit Wales as "You old empire-builder, you!" Wind-sor, in anger and in exile, sometimes spoke of her as "that fat Scotch cook"; and Wallis had never balked at referring to her as "the Dowdy Duchess" and "that fourteen-carat beauty" and even "the monster of Glamis"—the ancestral castle of the Bowes-Lyon family, which legend invests with a monster of indescribable hideousness.

Wallis's presence in England was utterly ignored. "My little cold war with the Palace" is how her memoirs refer to this interval. When she came to write them, her editor asked, "Was there no sign from the Palace during your visit? Nothing at all?" Duchess: "Oh, no! Heavens!" Editor: "They didn't send you flowers or anything?" Duchess: "My goodness! Really! It didn't make any difference to them, war or anything. An atomic bomb wouldn't change them."

And in accounting for her husband's relegation to the Siberia of the Military Mission, Vincennes, she offers this theory: that the family refused to bring him back out of fear that his "gift for dealing with troops—the gift of the common touch and understanding . . . might once more shine brightly, too brightly."

CHAPTER 8
The Windsors' War—II: French Leave

> Jim says, "Don't it s'prise you de way dem kings
> carries on, Huck?"
> "No," I says, "it don't."
> "Why don't it, Huck?"
> "Well, it don't because it's in the breed. I reckon
> they're all alike."
>
> —The Adventures of Huckleberry Finn,
> MARK TWAIN

The Number 1 Military Mission from the British War Office to Gen. Maurice-Gustave Gamelin, the French *Chef de la Défense Nationale et Commandant en Chef des Forces Terrestres*, was headed by Maj. Gen. Sir Richard G. H. Howard-Vyse. It consisted of a dozen officers and some thirty men, and was based in two villas side by side at Nogent-sur-Marne, five miles southeast of central Paris, and a mile and a half from General Gamelin's headquarters at the Château de Vincennes. The ground floor of one villa was the office; of the other, the officers' mess; the officers' bedrooms were on the upper floors.

They were a happy lot, officers and men alike, thanks in part to General Howard-Vyse's popularity—because of his service in Australia, the whole Army knew him affectionately as "Wombat"; even the French came to speak of him as *"notre cher Wombat"*—and in part to the excellent mess. Its president, the general's aide-de-camp, had been secretary of the Travellers Club, famous for its cellar and kitchen; and the mess's chief cook had been second chef at the equally famous Hôtel Crillon.

Duty was light. Every morning at ten, Howard-Vyse and his GSO-1 (Senior Operations Staff Officer) called on Gamelin to pick up his overnight report, which an officer-

messenger would then fly to London. Some officers who
served with Gamelin remember him as "a charming, im-
perturbable intellectual"; some as "a trench-warfare hold-
over from the Great War"; and a few as "the best general
the Germans had." *The Book of Lists* rates him among "10
of the worst generals in History."[1] He was so indifferent to
military security that he once left a sheaf of documents,
clearly stamped SECRET, in a public room at the Hyde Park
Hotel in London, where an Italian waiter found them.
Howard-Vyse's principal staff officer, Lt. Col. George M.
O. Davy, had still another reason for remembering Gamelin: "He had this *depressing* handshake! His hand simply
collapsed on contact"—not unlike (Davy might have
added later) the French defense. In those early, static days
of "the Phony War" or "the Great Bore War," the French
reports consisted of little more than "One patrol went out;
one man wounded; one prisoner taken"; so the meetings
seldom lasted longer than ten minutes; and once the morning's business was concluded, according to Davy, "Military
problems were salted down with the saltiest of stories."

On September 13, not long after the Mission had set up
shop, General Ironside called Howard-Vyse back to London. His Majesty, he was told, wished to know if he could
make room on his staff for the Duke of Windsor, perhaps
as some sort of "extra liaison officer." Before Howard-Vyse
could answer, Ironside suggested that he consult his staff.
Ironside well knew that the Abdication had divided the
loyalties of the services—that the Army resented their
Commander in Chief's having "chucked his job"; and that
the officers, particularly, had been appalled by the prospect
of having Wallis Simpson as Queen. Best make sure, Ironside suggested, that the Duke would be welcome.

Howard-Vyse put the question to his staff thus: "Would
you object if the Duke of Windsor were attached to us?"

The unanimous "No" was not exclusively a tribute to
the Duke. It was also recognition of a heaven-sent opportunity to accomplish a vital and hitherto impossible task: inspection of the Maginot Line—the elaborate network of
fortifications that stretched along the Franco-German frontier from Switzerland to Luxembourg. The French had
come to regard *la Ligne Maginot* as their palladium, not to
be overwhelmed. West—or left—of the Line was the

Luxembourgeois-Belgian frontier and the Meuse River, with access only by the treacherous roads of the Ardennes Forest, which the French believed impassable to tanks. Still farther west, a lesser Maginot extended to the Channel. The main Line featured *grands oeuvres*, which were especially strong fortresses constructed at intervals of a few miles. Aboveground were gun cupolas, pillboxes, and machine-gun turrets connected to one another by tunnels, and by shafts to the installations below: kitchens, barracks, magazines, and dressing stations. The western Maginot had no *grands oeuvres*.

The British Mission did not share French confidence in either the Meuse or the Ardennes; their tank experts rated both of them as of doubtful value. When the British reminded Gamelin that ten German divisions had poured through the Ardennes and across the Meuse in August 1914, his staff refused to believe it. The British were reserving their opinion about the Maginot until they could see it for themselves, and this the French refused to permit. Even when the *Illustrated London News* published photographs of the Line, reprinted from a German magazine, the secretive, mistrustful French still declared it off limits to their allies. But here, suddenly, was a chance to rectify this frustrating situation. French soldiers were notorious for their rabid royalism. Might it not extend to their offering the Duke, in homage, the freedom of the Maginot area? Howard-Vyse's inquiries at Gamelin's headquarters did not disclose his true purpose, and the French evidently did not suspect it; for before long he was able to assure the War Office, in a message classified VERY SECRET, that "General Gamelin has no objection to [the Duke's] going anywhere in the French zone."

Windsor's job was waiting; he had only to grasp it. When he and the Duchess returned from London, they decided not to open the Boulevard Suchet house for the moment. Instead they took a temporary apartment at the Trianon Palace Hotel in Versailles, and the Duke commuted from there to headquarters. Fruity Metcalfe put up at the Travellers Club. The Duke reported for duty on Monday morning, October 2, wearing the uniform of a major general, but with the jacket buttons spaced like the Welsh

Guards'; whether this departure was for private reasons, or to save the expense of new jackets with the buttons conventionally spaced, no one dared ask him. As he came in, everyone rose and gave him the "neck bow"—the deep nod that British men traditionally accord to royalty; otherwise, he received no special deference. Howard-Vyse presented his officers, took the Duke to "make his number" with Gamelin and his subordinate, General Georges, commanding the Armies of the North, and briefed him on his special function. A three-day visit to the French First Army was already scheduled to begin that Friday; Capt. Count John de Salis, once retired from the Coldstream Guards and now on active duty again, would accompany him as his interpreter, and Major Metcalfe as his equerry.

Windsor's delight in being back in uniform and in doing something useful was plain and pleasant to see. He took his job seriously and discussed it intelligently, "although"—a brother officer observed—"it sometimes had to compete with the Duchess for his attention." When he was mingling with the troops, he was at his informal best: interested, sympathetic, and joking in his wretched French. If he chanced across an officer he had met in the Great War, the old camaraderie was instantly rekindled. It was not unusual for him to recall the man's name. One of his aides saw him approach an old soldier with the ribbon of the Victoria Cross. "Are you Brown or Jones?" he asked. "I'm not sure which, but I remember that it's a very ordinary name."

The man smiled. "It's Smith, sir."

"Of course!" Windsor said. "Forgive me. And you won your V.C. at Gallipoli."

"Correct, sir!"

The aide complimented him on his extraordinary feat of memory. Windsor said, "Not so extraordinary as you think. During the first war, I memorized the careers of the living V.C.'s, all one hundred and thirty-seven of them, and studied their photographs. My father trained me, you know." He explained that when he was ten years old, he would be brought into a room where fifty people were having drinks before dinner, and introduced to everyone there; he would then be taken to another room and shown a sketch of where the guests were standing, and invited to repeat their names. "A few months' practice, and I could remember between thirty-five and forty of them."

His visits with the French troops "went down well," it was generally agreed, and helped lay the foundations for a happy relationship. According to former Air Commodore Roland Vintras, Windsor's flaccid grasp of the French language made a memorable contribution to their happiness: "At a distinguished luncheon at which he was the guest of the French Army, he had the tables in an uproar without even knowing why . . . by proclaiming that '*Après la guerre, il faut que nous fassions, tous ensemble, un paix formidable.*' Unfortunately, *paix, meaning* 'peace,' is feminine, whereas its masculine homonym, *pet*, means a 'fart.' Perhaps it was unwittingly a fair comment on the outcome of the war."[2]

De Salis drafted the official report on the tour. Howard-Vyse approved it and made one suggestion: Let it go forward to General Ironside over Windsor's signature. Windsor had become depressed on learning that he was forbidden to visit the British front, and Howard-Vyse felt that credit for the report would revive his morale. Ironside was generous with his praise; Howard-Vyse wrote him on the seventeenth, "I am glad you were pleased with the Duke of Windsor's report. He took a great deal of trouble over it."

The report had carried a cautionary endorsement: "It will be realized that to give the French any . . . inkling of the source of this information would probably compromise the value of any missions [General Howard-Vyse] may ask H.R.H. to undertake subsequently." No inkling seems to have been given, for the French did not hesitate to authorize another mission for early November. The first had been a trial run, a warm-up. This was the important one, the one where Windsor would furnish cover for an inspection of the Maginot Line. His five-day tour would begin at Verdun and would include most of the Strasbourg–Vosges front, the Line's northern sector. Metcalfe would again be Windsor's equerry, but De Salis would be replaced by Lieutenant Colonel Davy, a veteran of the Great War and an experienced career soldier.

The tour was a social success, as before. Davy, recalling it, said, "The Duke made an effort." The phrase brought back an evening when they were billeted in a little hotel with an officers' mess. Someone was banging on a tinny piano when they came in, and the rest were having a sing-song. The pianist, recognizing Windsor, broke off at once, and the crowded room fell silent.

Windsor begged them, "Please carry on!" and while the noise built up again, he made the rounds, shaking hands with everyone.

Later, Davy said to Metcalfe, "He looked as if he were enjoying himself."

Metcalfe said glumly, "He wasn't."

Davy also recalled another incident from that evening. During dinner, the Duke said to him, "I hear you were asking Fruity what the medal was that my brother [the King] gave to Gamelin's chauffeur. It would have been the Royal Victorian Order [bestowed for personal service to the sovereign], I'm sure." He smiled. "If you remember, for eleven months I had the distribution of those things."

Fruity's own chief recollection was of the next morning, and the first of a series of embarrassing scenes when the hotel bills had to be paid. "He was *frightful*," Fruity wrote home; again, a few days later, "He still fingers bills in res-taurants for *such* a long time, debating and deciding on the remuneration for waiters, etc."

Their luncheons were always with one or another of the French Army commanders, and though the food and wine were usually notable, Windsor ate little and drank nothing, not even coffee. Instead, when coffee was served, he would produce a small silver teapot, which he spoke of as "kettly," and a tin of his favorite tea, and ask permission to make himself a cup. According to Davy, the teapot "never failed to stimulate conversation." This traveling silver tea-pot had a predecessor with King George V. Just before Christmas 1912, Queen Mary wrote to her son David that his father had chosen "a small gold soup bowl for his travel kit" as the present he wished David to give him. She added, "It costs £150, but he is very anxious to have it." Years later, something recalled the bowl to Windsor's mind, and he remarked, laughing, "Imagine it: a *gold soup bowl* for his *travel kit*! I still don't know why he wanted the damn thing! I never dared ask him. But it would cer-tainly make a handsome piece of field equipment here." Another conversation piece was the series of scarves that

Windsor now began knitting for the French troops. Whenever he had a moment of leisure, out came his wool and needles, and the scarf in hand lengthened another inch or so. Queen Mary's skill at needlework had been communicated to her children; the mottoes they had embroidered so laboriously when they lived in York Cottage at Sandringham are still there: "Feed My Lambs" and "Dear Mama" and "Look Unto Jesus."

Meanwhile, behind the facade of bonhomie the work went forward. Davy watched and listened and took mental notes. Their gist was disquieting. The French had made almost no attempt to conceal their casements anywhere along the Line; their anti-infantry barbed wire was carelessly sited; their antitank traps were inadequate; and their efforts to remedy these defects were anything but dogged. Worst of all, the defenses back of the Line were dangerously shallow; nowhere were they deeper than five miles, and in some places only three. When the French commanders' attention was invited to these conditions, their replies reflected the "Maginot mentality": Why should we spend further time, money, and manpower on additional defenses back of the Line when the existing ones not only are impregnable, but probably will never be tested?

All this went into Davy's report. He showed it to Windsor, who read it, changed a "but" to "however"—nothing else—and turned it in to Howard-Vyse, who again invited him to sign it. Alas, the kindly Wombat's self-effacement was self-defeating. On his orders, Davy carried the report to the War Office, and put it into General Ironside's own hand, while Howard-Vyse himself delivered a copy to Gen. Viscount Sir John Gort, Commander in Chief of the British Expeditionary Force. Yet when, seven months later, the Germans began to exploit the very weaknesses that the report had pinpointed, the War Office expressed surprise, and Gort's staff were heard to complain, "Why didn't somebody warn us?" One possible explanation is that Ironside failed to pass the report up to the War Minister. Another is that though he did so, its importance was disguised by the Duke of Windsor's signature. In any case, it didn't matter very much. The German panzers outflanked the Line.

Alas, too, for the kindly Wombat himself! Windsor's verdict on him was unworthy of both judge and judged: "He was a very jealous man and he was very pleased with his position. He was never a friend of mine, but I think he was delighted to have the Duke of Windsor under him."

Windsor was sent on his third mission, a minor one, just before Christmas. Between times there was little for him to do. At the start, he had reported to his office at 11 A.M. daily, looked at the situation map, chatted with Howard-Vyse for half an hour, then knocked off for the afternoon. But presently he was dropping in only three times a week, then twice, then scarcely ever, except for an occasional luncheon with Gamelin. To his delight the ban against his visiting the British front was lifted in February. The three tours he made there always included calls at C-in-C, B.E.F.'s headquarters. The facts that Gort's chief liaison officer was the Duke of Gloucester, and that Gloucester was Windsor's senior in rank, caused a certain stiffness. The two had never been close; and though one of Gloucester's most conspicuous social qualities was his pleasantness, it had embraced Windsor less and less from the day that Windsor had—so to speak—embraced Mrs. Simpson. Now, when the brothers met, their greeting was formal; and when they were part of a group inspecting British troops they walked separately, Windsor with Gort, Gloucester with Howard-Vyse. Gloucester was furious when Windsor once took a salute meant for himself as the senior major general.

So passed Windsor's wartime winter of 1939–40, in long stretches of idleness relieved by an occasional front-line tour. An officer in the Mission said of him, "Everything he was asked to do, he did to the best of his ability. The trouble was, precious little was asked." Still, he might have survived on these scanty rations of activity if either the Palace or the War Office had supplemented them even once with a morsel of hope, or had even given a sign that he had not been forgotten. Neither morsel nor sign was forthcoming.

The Duchess, for her part, was convinced that the Royal Family were not only restricting the Duke's war service, but deliberately minimizing it. "They're jealous of him," she complained to Clare Boothe Luce, the journalist and playwright.

Mrs. Luce, who had come to France to report the war for her husband's magazine *Life*, was an old friend of the Windsor's. She asked, "Why doesn't he try to get permission to spend more time at the front, showing himself? His presence would have a tremendous impact."

"What!" cried the Duchess. "And get himself killed in this silly war?"

She had been too busy with her own concerns at first to notice the Duke's thickening discontent. On their return from London, she had at once joined the Colis de Trianon, an organization founded by Lady Mendl for distributing comfort kits—soap, socks, gloves, cigarettes, toilet articles—to the French troops. By late October, there was—in the words of a memorable communiqué from the Great War—"a slight touch of autumn in the air," and the troops were beginning to feel it. The Duchess and Lady Mendl appealed through the newspapers for warm clothing, and in a trice the Colis de Trianon's offices were buried under an avalanche of gifts. Here at last was a public action that Wallis Windsor could take justifiable pride in.

Hotel life soon began to pall; the war remaining as cold as the weather, she decided to open the house on Boulevard Suchet. "When I say 'open the house,'" she explained, "I mean we opened our bedrooms and the dining room and one sitting room, that's all. We left the rugs rolled up and the dust-covers on and the chandeliers lying in the middle of the floor—they were so big and heavy, we'd had them taken down for fear they might be bombed down." Colonel Davy remembers bringing a document to Windsor at Boulevard Suchet: "The Duchess walked through the room while he was reading it. She didn't even glance my way in passing. She never entertained the Duke's associates. She didn't look kindly on us British."

Major Gray Phillips of the Black Watch had now joined the Windsors as the Duke's Comptroller and lived in the house with them. When the air-raid sirens began to go, several times a week, they all trotted down to the *rez-de-chaussée* and sat on the floor until the "all clear" sounded. "We weren't *frightened*," the Duchess said. "We had a sense of uneasiness, as against a sense of alarm."

Now that she was in Paris, she also joined the local branch of the French Red Cross's *Section Sanitaire*, and

photographs of her in its crisp, chic uniform began to flood
the world press. Hers was no token job. It required her to
make three runs a week up to the Line in her station
wagon, with a load of plasma, bandages, and pajamas for
the hospitals. Her trips usually began before dawn, and she
and her driver, the Comtesse de Ganay—the Duchess
never learned to drive—had more than one close call
among the convoys of army lorries that hurtled, blacked
out, along the narrow roads near the front. The Red Cross
ladies made their deliveries to the hospitals, had lunch
there, and visited the wards to chat with the patients—
many of them Moroccans, the Duchess remembered. Once
she was invited to lunch in a *grand oeuvre*: "The food was
excellent, but it was spoiled for me because I kept telling
myself, 'The war's going to start *right now*, and I'll be
stuck in here for the duration!' "

After a run, they usually spent the night in the nurses'
quarters, but the Duchess once had to stay at a château
just behind the Line: "I remember a great big room with a
bed in the corner with a canopy over it. I was absolutely
too terrified to put out the light! The guns boomed all
night long. I didn't sleep at all! I don't say my life was ever
in danger during the war, but at least I got that near to the
fighting."

At Christmas, her group packed gift boxes of food and
candy and tobacco and took them forward. But soon, as
with the Duke, the glow of accomplishment began to fade.
Nothing fed it, from the Palace or elsewhere in London—
no recognition of any sort, much less gratitude and encour-
agement; she was still an alien. The depression and resentment that began to settle around her inevitably spread to
the Duke. Geoffrey Bocca described them at this low point
as "eager to help but with nothing to do, all dressed up
. . . but with nowhere to go."[3] They went slack.

With warmer weather and clearer skies, the Duke's attendance at his office became more and more perfunctory.
Sunny afternoons usually found him on the golf course at
Saint-Cloud or Saint-Germain or Mortefontaine. He and
the Duchess often allowed themselves long weekends at La
Croë or Biarritz. Their evenings in Paris were increasingly
beguiled by dinners at home or at some smart restaurant—
usually the Grand Véfour—given for visiting friends. En-

glish or American, the elder among them were agreed on one point: that this Second World War found the Duke of Windsor almost unrecognizably changed from the Great War's gallant, serious, dutiful Prince of Wales. Plainly, he had stopped fighting Hitler and had turned to face two other enemies: boredom and his family. His concern was no longer with the morale of the troops, but with that of the Duchess, now even more bitter than himself at the Palace's refusal to recognize their attempts to help England win the war.

As if the war had ended for them, the Duke, on the Duchess's prodding, started pulling strings in high places in both armies to have their chef, who had been called up by the French Army, demobilized and restored to their kitchen. He was so persistent that the French complained to British headquarters that he was "upsetting the whole bloody army" (Metcalfe's words); and Windsor was summoned to his own headquarters to explain his action. Even more scandalously, he and the Duchess were consorting freely with Charles Bedaux. As early as October 3, Metcalfe had written home: "I've had a few interesting talks with Mr. B. (of Wedding fame). He is like a will-o-wisp—he is never in the same place, town or *country* for more than six hours at a time. I can't make him out. He knows *too* much."⁴ And again on November 20, this note in his diary: "I dined at Suchet last night. The Bedaux were there."⁵ The continuing association showed how low the Windsors' standards had fallen.

The ruin of his purpose and the ferocity of her vengefulness were soon and tragically to be revealed. In May, the German armies lunged forward, broke the Allied hinge, and raced into France. There are at least three versions of the Windsors' behavior in this emergency. The most circumstantial is Clare Luce's:

One evening in Paris, she dined in a bistro with Fruity Metcalfe. The French and British armies were in retreat; Parisians were fleeing their city; Mrs. Luce and the major found themselves almost alone. Their privacy encouraged him to open his mind: "You have to help me, Clare! The Duke has ordered me to take those bloody cairns to La Croë. I was a *soldier*! When I resigned from my regiment in India to serve the Prince, it wasn't to be a valet to his

Goddamned dogs!" He hesitated a moment, then blurted out, "You're seeing the Windsors tomorrow. Tell the Duke he should release me!" Mrs. Luce promised.

When she joined the Windsors next evening, they were playing cards with Gray Phillips and a fourth. Fruity was present. Their radio was tuned to the BBC news. The *Luftwaffe* was strafing English coastal villages.

"That upset me," Mrs. Luce remembers. "I mentioned that I had driven through many of these same villages, and I hated to think of those decent, kindly people being so wantonly attacked. The Duchess glanced up from her cards: 'After what they did to me, I can't say I feel sorry for them—a whole nation against one lone woman!' "

In her indignation, Mrs. Luce declared that Fruity felt as she herself did, and was leaving to request combat duty.

The Duke stared at him. "Really? You didn't tell me. When did you decide this?"

Metcalfe, embarrassed, answered, "Only yesterday, sir. I was going to tell you this evening."

"When did you intend to leave?"

"First thing in the morning." His embarrassment was acute. He stood up. "If you'll excuse me, sir, I'll go and pick up my things now."

"Very well," said the Duke. Turning to the Duchess, he asked, "What's the score, darling?"

By a second account, the Duchess's, Metcalfe stayed on at his job. The Germans crossed the Meuse on May 13 and began their month-long advance on Paris—an ugly turn that naturally alarmed the Duke. His first thought, forgivably, was for his wife. He ordered her to pack at once; he would escort her to Biarritz, he said, leave her there, return to his post, and rejoin her as soon as the situation permitted.

Describing the incident some years later, the Duchess remembered that "Kitty de Rothschild dropped in one day just before this. She told me, 'It's none of my business, but I don't think you ought to stay here. Suppose the Germans take Paris and capture you?' There was that chance, of course, but I told the Duke, 'I'm with the Red Cross. It's not the thing for me to do, to leave the minute Paris is in danger. My job is to stay.' "

For once in his life, he dared oppose her. He said, "I'll give you two hours to pack, and not a minute more!"

The round trip, over roads choked with refugees, took him several days. When he returned to Boulevard Suchet, he began telephoning Biarritz every evening. The Duchess had become obsessed with the notion that he was risking capture, and begged him with almost hysterical fervor to leave Paris and join her. Presently he did. Toward the end of May, having been granted a short leave of absence to lock up La Croë and hide the silver and linen, his papers, and other valuables, he was issued orders attaching him to French headquarters facing the Italian frontier—an assignment that cloaked his tantamount desertion from the British Mission. Even so, he did not proceed to his post direct; he went via Biarritz. Fruity, meanwhile, the Duchess recalled, had been ordered home to England.

Not so, according to the third account, Lady Alexandra Metcalfe's:

One afternoon at the end of May—it was the twenty-seventh—the Duke and Fruity were astonished to learn from General Howard-Vyse that the Mission had been told to destroy its records and fall back to the nearest port. Fruity asked the Duke as they separated, "What are your orders for tomorrow, Sir?"

"I don't know yet," the Duke said. "Ring me at nine-thirty."

When Fruity rang, it was to learn from the concierge that soon after six o-clock, his Royal Highness had started for Biarritz with Ladbrook, after leaving instructions for Major Phillips to close the house and join him at La Croë. A Lovelace in reverse, he had fled—oblivious of honor—from war and arms to his Lucasta. "Plainly," said Lady Alexandra, "Wallis had told him, 'I'm leaving now. You follow!' "

Dumbfounded, Metcalfe asked, "Any instruction for me?"

"Nothing, sir."

Without orders, without headquarters, and without authority to commandeer transportation to help him find either, since his position had never been regularized (he was not even entitled to draw pay), Metcalfe, hurt and angry,

set out to hitchhike to Cherbourg through the chaos of col-
lapsing France. He got there safely, and eventually to England, where, loyal as always, he shouldered the blame: "I
must have made a mistake in the time."

When his wife heard his story, she said, "I don't want to
see the Windsors again, ever!" Later her comment was
milder: "It would seem that the Duke set little value on
friendship." Later still, she offered this theory: "That last
evening in Paris, if the Duke had told Fruity that he intended cutting and running, Fruity would have gone
through the roof. He'd have told the Duke, 'Sir, you damn
well *can't* do that!'"

When Lord Mountbatten heard it, he said, "David
would never have behaved like that in the old days. He
was brave to the point of rashness in the Great War, but
now something—I won't speculate *what*—but something
had drained away his courage. He was a totally different
man." Sir John Aird had made a similar observation at
Enzesfeld: Windsor had become "something quite different, something apart."

He and Fruity did not meet again until 1946. Windsor
was visiting his mother at Marlborough House; Walter
Monckton called on him there, and Windsor suddenly announced, "I want to see Fruity!" Fruity came. Windsor
took his arm affectionately: "Fruity, how *marvelous*!"—
and at once it was as if their long friendship had never
been interrupted. When Fruity told his wife about the reunion, she asked incredulously, "He didn't even *apologize*?"

A month after the German breakthrough and the Duke's
flight, the British press printed an inconspicuous paragraph: The Duke of Windsor had been away from his
"purely nominal job" for more than four weeks, and had
"relinquished his appointment as liaison officer between
the British and French armies." That was all.

The Duke did not say even that much. He ignored the
incident in his memoirs. He never apologized to Fruity,
never even attempted to communicate with him until after
the war. The harshest observation was General Howard-
Vyse's: "I wish never to be asked about that man again! I
intend never to discuss him." The report that Howard-Vyse

filed on July 6, "on the work of various officers . . . under my command," does not mention the Duke. The War Office seemed to share the general's opinion; it failed to award the Duke even the most minor of its decorations, although military custom showers gauds on royalty for merely making an appearance on the field. Lastly, History shares it; there are few laurels it can bestow on this heir of English kings who fought at Hastings, Agincourt, and Jerusalem; this descendant of a King who fought at Dettingen; this brother of a King who fought at Jutland; and this King himself who, as that "sword-and-buckler Prince of Wales," had once won the Military Cross for his presence on many battlefields.

CHAPTER 9

The Windsors' War—III:
Tug-of-War at Lisbon

To the wars, my boy, to the wars!
He wears his honor in a box unseen,
That hugs his kicky-wicky here at home.
　　　　　　　　　—All's Well That Ends Well,
　　　　　　　　　　　WILLIAM SHAKESPEARE

He lay conceal'd throughout the war,
　And so preserv'd his gore, O!
　　That unaffected,
　　Undetected,
　　Well-connected
　　Warrior,
　The Duke of Plaza-Toro!
　　　　　　　—The Gondoliers, W.S. GILBERT

The Second World War was to rage over Europe until early May 1945, but it was finished for the Duke of Windsor as of May 28, 1940, the day he abandoned his post in Paris and fled to Biarritz. There he scooped up his Duchess and dashed across southern France to La Croë. His superseding anxiety was for her safety; hers was for the safety of their silver, linen, and other chattels. Surrounded by them, and in their own villa, they had hoped to ride out the storm; but Italy's entrance into the war on June 10 and the German occupation of Paris on June 12–14, together with the desperate plight of the British Army at Dunkirk, put their situation in an alarming new light.

The French air base at Saint-Raphaël, a few miles to the west, was a standing invitation to an Italian bombing attack in which far "shorts" might possibly spatter La Croë, so the Duke and his gardeners dug a foxhole and put "a very nice chair in it" for the Duchess. "But I wouldn't use it. Whenever the sirens sounded, I went to the room in the basement where the iceboxes were, and shut myself up there. I thought it was safer, though if the house had fallen in, I could never have gotten out."

Presently, Gray Phillips turned up, happily and most unexpectedly, his pockets bulging with the precious George II saltcellars. He had made part of his way down from Paris by train, and had hitchhiked and walked the rest. He was exhausted, but undefeated. "I'm not going to run from any more damned Germans!" he gasped as he sank into a chair with a restoring drink. A British neighbor, George Wood, drove over that afternoon and warned the Windsors that the Germans were already at Lyons, only two hundred miles away. (Captain Wood lived nearby; Windsor had known him in Austria and would soon appoint him his aide.) The Duchess said, "If they overflowed the Riviera and caught us, people would say that we had deliberately given ourselves up. That was an important factor in our decision to head for Spain. Packing was like when a house catches fire: you simply grab the nearest things to hand, however odd and useless. For instance, we packed an enormous lump of cheese—" Still, their flight was not so panicky that the day of their departure, June 19, slipped past without the Duke's remembering that it was the Duchess's birthday, her forty-fourth, and giving her a bouquet of tuberoses.

They traveled in a three-car convoy. The leader was the Windsors' Buick, driven by Ladbrook, with the Duchess's maid beside him; and the Duke (in plain clothes), the Duchess, Major Phillips, and the three cairns in the rear seat. The second car was Captain Wood's Citroën; his passengers were his Viennese wife, Rosa, her maid, and a Sealyham; behind them yawed a trailer with their luggage. The Windsors' luggage needed a car to itself, a truck; it brought up the tail of the convoy and was driven by a hired hand.

For six days they inched along the congested roads, stopping to have their papers scrutinized and stamped, then inching forward again. Rosa Wood said later, "You get to know someone extremely well in the terrors and discomforts of such a trip. The Windsors were wonderful, both of them! Never a complaint, never a protest, nothing but courage and trying to help others." At last they reached Madrid, to find an urgent message from Churchill which said in effect: Come back to England immediately; two flying boats will be at Lisbon to pick up you and your party; the Duke of Westminster offers you his country house as a residence.

The Duke also found there that familiar Tory work-horse, Sir Samuel Hoare, who—having served as Foreign Secretary, First Lord of the Admiralty, and Home Secretary under Baldwin and Chamberlain—had been posted to Madrid in May as Ambassador, in the Cabinet shakeup that followed Churchill's rise to Prime Minister. They were friendly adversaries. Hoare had ranged himself on Baldwin's side during the Abdication crisis and had himself, at the interrupted shooting party at Sandringham, tried to talk the Duke out of marriage. Years earlier, a youthful, even impertinent, Prince of Wales had told him half in malice, "You are out of date. You know nothing of the modern world," causing the older man to reflect in his reminiscences, "If I thought too much of the past, he seemed to me to think too little of it."[1] Now in a foreign and nakedly hostile capital, Hoare found himself called upon to pull a middle-aged Duke, like himself on the slide, out of a dangerous present and back from a shameful future. Hoare was well aware of Windsor's German leanings, although he found nothing reprehensible in that. What did disquiet him was the Duchess's hatred of Britain, and her earlier, too open hospitality to the clever Italian and Spanish diplomats and Intelligence agents who found favor at Bryanston Court.

Hitler's *Wehrmacht* stood on the Pyrenees, and Madrid fairly crawled with German agents. Hoare had already measured the ranking German representatives, Baron and Baroness von Stohrer, as a formidable pair—both of them tall, commanding, and superb linguists, and the only members of the Diplomatic Corps with ready access to General and Señora Franco. Churchill, according to Lord Beaverbrook, on taking over at Number 10, was immediately dominated by two purposes: to save a port in the South of France for carrying the war back to Europe after Britain had been rearmed, and to whisk the Windsors off the Con-

tinent and out of Hitler's grasping hands. The impressionable and volatile Windsor was too tempting a prize to leave
unattended in the cockpit of Madrid, where the Von Stoh-
rers, ambitious Nazis both, wielded unparalleled influence
in the highest political and social circles, and where their
unique standing with Franco himself was additionally reinforced by their intimate relationship with the Foreign Minister, Colonel Beigbeder. More useful still, they had a
working relationship with the powerful Minister of the Interior, Ramon Serrano Suñer, Franco's brother-in-law, an
open Anglophobe whose secret security services had been
in close collaboration with the German clandestine services
since the Civil War. To leave the Windsors in the midst of
this company of plotters and schemers, while Britain tee-
tered on the last thin edge of survival, was to run the risk
of having the former King co-opted by the Germans with a
promise to restore him on the throne, if he would declare
himself for them before their invasion of England.

Alive to the dangers, Hoare drew upon his considerable
powers of persuasion to induce the Duke to accept
Churchill's offer and move on without further delay to neutral Portugal. *"But David tarried still."* For one thing, he
was exhausted after the wild run across France. For another, he was resettled in luxury among people he knew
well. One of his cousins by marriage, the Infante Alfonso,
married to one of Queen Victoria's granddaughters and
himself a general in the Spanish Air Force, had called on
him at once, to discourse on Britain's imminent collapse.
From the Duke of Alba's sister, Doña Sol, also well known
to him, he received the theatrical fascist salute. The Marqués de Estella, son of Miguel Primo de Rivera, the dictator and himself a leader of the fascist Falangists in Madrid,
also came to his hotel to court and flatter him. And the
dashing Spanish diplomat Javier Bermejillo, the "Tiger" of
the Bryanston Court regulars, having magically materialized out of nowhere to escort the Windsor party into Madrid from the frontier, had deftly attached himself to the
Duke as a volunteer liaison with the Spanish officialdom.

Hoare's reminiscences of his duel with German diplomacy in Madrid make no mention whatever of his even
more painful struggle for the soul of the Duke of Windsor.[2] Perhaps in a work published so soon after the war

(1947) he could not bring himself to bare the squalid details. The bitter fact is that he had the devil's own time persuading his former monarch to heed Churchill's call to hasten back to England, home, and duty. Two conditions had to be met, Windsor insisted, before he would consent to move on. First, he must know if Churchill had an important job in mind for him; and if so, what it was. Second, his wife had to be raised in status to the level of his royal brothers', and received—if but once—by the King and Queen. He refused to expose her and himself again to the cold shoulder that the Royal Family had shown them ten months before. Difficult as it is to believe that the former King of England would impose such a frivolous irrelevance on the Prime Minster at an hour when he was carrying, almost alone, the burden of Britain's fate, the melancholy truth is that Windsor did just this.

The subject of the Duchess's status had become an obsession with him, overshadowing the vast surrounding catastrophe of war and the perils of a reckless thirst for revenge. The Palace's inhospitality on their September trip to Britain—an inhospitality which the Duke harbored as a direct insult—had transformed the obsession into a monomania so powerful that it drove him to pepper Churchill for a whole long week with a fusillade of messages urging his tuppenny points. Partisans of the Duke may draw comfort from the fact that he was being goaded by his Duchess; her hunger for the styles and titles of "Royal Highness" was in truth far fiercer than his own, despite the belated, face-saving admission in her autobiography that it was "scarcely seemly" to stand on such trivialities in such momentous times. Hope deferred had made her heart sick, and his also.

The Duke's own explanation, as published in his New York *Daily News* series in December 1966, was somewhat different: "[Winston's] personal advice to me was not to quibble about terms, but come home and wait patiently while he 'worked things out.' But I could not in honor take this line. The year before, while we had been in England, the presence of the Duchess at my side had never been acknowledged, even perfunctorily. Before going back, I wanted assurance that simple courtesies would be forthcoming—"

The Duchess seems to have believed that the Duke's terms would be met instanter, because during their brief stopover in Madrid, she told the American Ambassador, Alexander W. Weddell, on June 30 that she was expecting to leave for Lisbon on the second and fly from there to England.[3] But, the Duke continues, "Winston could not manage this. From a distance, what I insisted on may look to be of small value. But the perspective of my life had changed, and the matter loomed mightily large for me."

Nothing in the melancholy tale of the Abdication and its aftermath is more difficult for an outsider to understand than this interminable, divisive bickering between the Royal Family and the former King over an augmented title for his wife. On one side was the husband who never bewailed the gauds and glories he had given up for his wife's sake. On the other was the wife, a woman who had spent her first forty years as a mere "Miss" or "Mrs." without noticeable discomfort, and who then found herself suddenly raised to the proud rank of duchess. And now, at an hour when her husband was struggling back toward usefulness, respectability, and honor, she was badgering him for further adornment of a title already—one would have thought—sufficiently exalted. But if she was foolish in her pride, and the Duke in abetting her, the Royal Family was hardly less so, in obdurately denying what her husband rightly gave her. Her elevation at that late hour would not have cheapened the monarchy; on the contrary, it would have voided the accusations of pettiness and vengefulness. More constructively, it would have ended the Duke's torment, restored his old, affectionate relationship with his family, even closed the sorry tale in reconciliation.

The Windsors and their retinue arrived in Lisbon early in July. As they drove into town, they saw the two flying boats at their moorings on the Tagus River. The British Ambassador, their friend Sir Walford Selby, formerly Minister to Austria, had engaged a villa for them, luxurious and fully staffed, at Estoril, fifteen miles from the capital. It belonged to a Portuguese banker and art collector, Dr. Ricardo de Espirito Santo e Silva, well known to the Duke's family. Here, in this palmy, flowery, drowsy scene, now resumed the splenetic haggling that had begun in Madrid.

It continued through two nights and a day, and was made even more wearisome by the need to encode or decode every message. At the end, Churchill was obliged to notify Windsor that while he and his Duchess would be welcome in England, no royal title awaited her. Windsor, exhausted, threw in his hand. He cabled that under the circumstances he could not return to Great Britain, but he was ready to serve the King anywhere else, in any capacity. He so informed Selby, who, in relief, could at last send the two impatient flying boats back to the starveling Coastal Command.

Walter Monckton would write of the Duke, "He was not an easy man to place"; where to put him, now that he had stood down, must have taxed Churchill's ingenuity. The offer he came up with was an appointment as Governor and Commander in Chief of the Bahamas. The Duke reported it to his wife: "Winston said he was sorry, but it's the best he could do. I shall keep my end of the bargain."

But first he had fresh requests to make, as trivial and irritating as before; and another series of messages began to blanket desks up and down Whitehall. He wished to visit the United States on the way to his new post; the Duchess, he said, had to go there for medical reasons. The Colonial Office fielded this one. It tried to make him realize that the presence of a royal visitor from a belligerent nation would embarrass President Roosevelt in an election year, but Windsor was not to be convinced. His increasingly fretful insistences met with increasingly blunt refusals, until he finally dropped the project. Then, it became "absolutely essential" for two of his former menservants, Fletcher and Webster, to be released from their Guards regiment and assigned to him as chauffeur and valet. This campaign began sometime prior to July 17, and it headed up so quickly that by the twentieth, Churchill himself had been recruited to help hold the line. His message to the Duke said, "Regret . . . no question of releasing men from the Army to act as servants. . . ." But by the twenty-fourth, the paramount consideration was to get the Windsors out of Europe and into the Bahamas at all possible speed, and the man Fletcher was promised them as a sop. It was the Duke's first and only victory in the long war.

To make sure that he understood exactly what his new

job would entail, and to hold him steady on the new course, Churchill sent Walter Monckton to Estoril. His arrival, with the rank of Minister—he had been made Director General of the Press and Censorship Bureau the preceding October—puzzled the Nazis on watch there, especially when he moved straight into the Windsors' villa. A Nazi agent's telegram to Berlin identified him as "Sir Walter Turner Monckstone," probably "a member of the personal police, or a bodyguard, of the reigning King."

Monckton found it difficult to orient himself. A few hours behind him was London, thunderous with guns and bombs, shrill with sirens, red with fires, and murky with smoke. And here was Estoril, with the Windsors' dinner guests in white jackets or smart long gowns, no fires wilder than the candles on the table, no noise louder than the string quartet under the palms in the patio; and in the center of it all, remote from the world at war, the former King. The incongruity haunted Monckton throughout the week of his visit and for the rest of his life.

He was too good a friend of the Duke's to pretend that the Bahamas were an important strategic area. They were nothing more than an archipelago of some 700 islands (thirty inhabited), plus 2,000 cays and rocks, with a total population of 200,000, of which 85 percent was Negro or mulatto; Nassau, the capital, was a city of 15,000. Nor did Monckton make any bones about the insignificance of the post—it was usually bestowed on a senior member of the Civil Service or an elderly general, retired, who deserved well of his country. Monckton might have added that Nassau, having no conscription, had become a haven for rich refugees whom explosions made nervous, as well as for healthy young Britons with a distaste for war duty. But knowing that Windsor would discover this soon enough for himself, Monckton passed on to a topic of livelier, more personal interest: British Intelligence had uncovered signs of a German plot to kidnap the Windsors and hold them hostage.

The Windsors, in their own later accounts, affected to find the notion hilarious. Yet a plot of sorts was certainly afoot, one in which they appear to have been, if not active accomplices, at least highly interested parties. Churchill's determination to hurry them off the Continent was now

matched by Hitler's, to lure them to a convenient quasi-
neutral country—preferably back to Spain—where the
Duke would be under German influence, and where his
smoldering fury against his King and Prime Minister could
be exploited to Germany's advantage. Windsor had given
his Spanish friends—and through them the Germans—a
clear impression that he did not consider himself committed to the post in the Bahamas; he even let it be known in
Lisbon that he was delaying his departure in the expectation of a better offer. Moreover, Spaniards who called on
him were soon informing Madrid that in addition to proclaiming his opposition to the war and his support of a
negotiated peace, he was saying that England could be
bombed into surrender; and that if he had remained King,
England would not have gone to war.

Although there is little doubt that Windsor's mood was
mutinous, and that he said things that no loyal Englishman
should, it must be borne in mind that the Nazi sympathizers who listened to him were eager to ingratiate themselves
with their masters, whether German or Spanish, and therefore were inclined to give their reports a slant and an exag-
geration favorable to German policy. The most fervent
Spanish advocate of an alliance with the Nazis was the
Minister of the Interior, soon to become Foreign Minister,
Ramón Serrano Suñer. Franco himself favored it, but he
wished to be paid to join, and the price he asked—
Gibraltar and all French Morocco, plus enough war supplies for staving off a British attack—was higher than Hitler would go. Hitler felt that he had already given Franco
enough, and had been given nothing in return. Still, the
negotiations stayed open, and Windsor now became a chip
on the table.

While Windsor dallied and dilly-dallied, the German
Foreign Minister, Von Ribbentrop, stealthily set in motion
a scheme to slip him from under the British diplomatic and
intelligence network in Lisbon, and spirit him back to
Spain, with the cooperation of Serrano Suñer. On July 11,
Von Ribbentrop outlined his scheme in a telegram to his
adroit Ambassador in Madrid, Von Stohrer:

Spanish friends of the Windsors were to invite them to
Spain for a fortnight or so, "on pretexts which would ap-

pear plausible to [the Duke], to the Portuguese, and to the British agents." Once across the frontier, however, "the Duke and his wife must be persuaded or *compelled* [italics added] to remain on Spanish territory." Were the Duke to have a change of heart, then, being still a British officer and still attached to the expeditionary force that had been defeated in France, he could be legally arrested by the Spanish authorities as "a military fugitive." As for the use that Germany had in mind for him, Von Ribbentrop said this: "At a suitable occasion in Spain, the Duke must be informed that Germany wants peace with the English people, that the Churchill clique stands in the way of it, and that it would be a good thing if the Duke would hold himself in readiness for further developments. Germany is determined to force England to peace by every means of power, and upon this happening would be prepared to accommodate any desire expressed by the Duke, especially with a view to the assumption of the English Throne by the Duke and the Duchess. If the Duke should have other plans, but be prepared to cooperate in the establishment of good relations between Germany and Britain, we would likewise be prepared to assure him and his wife of a subsistence which would permit him, either as a private citizen or in some other position, to lead a life suitable for a King."

Though evidence is lacking that Windsor was ever drawn to the German scheme, however briefly, or, for that matter, that it was ever broached directly to him, there is no doubt about the strong pull on him from Spain, or of his apathy toward the Bahamas post, or of his volubility about his private and official frustrations. The German Ambassador in Lisbon, Baron Oswald von Hoyningen-Huene, through his own access to the Windsor circle, was no less closely informed about Windsor's attitude than was Von Stohrer in Madrid. Windsor's host, Espirito Santo, seems to have been as liberal to the Germans as he was to the British, in supplying their intelligence agents with the substance of the Duke's opinions. Windsor himself, throughout his stay in Lisbon, kept open a private channel to Serrano Suñer, who several times sent emissaries to see him. On July 23, Von Stohrer advised Berlin of an astounding report brought back from Lisbon the day before by Serrano Suñer's man: "He had two long conversations with the Duke of Windsor; at the last conversation the Duchess was present also. The Duke expressed himself freely. In Portugal, he felt almost like a prisoner. He was surrounded by agents, etc. Politically he was more and more distant from the King and the present English Government. The Duke and Duchess have less fear of the King, who is quite foolish [*rechlich töricht*], than of the shrewd Queen, who is intriguing skillfully against the Duke and particularly against the Duchess." The report went on to say that the Duke was considering making a public statement in which he would disavow the current English policy and break with his brother.

British Intelligence was on to these exchanges at once. The Duchess's autobiographical account of the Duke's duel with Churchill mentions, almost in amusement, that at the height of the quarrel, Windsor decided to give the British Embassy a wide berth. He suspected that Churchill might have him arrested in British jurisdiction for refusing to obey the order to proceed to the Bahamas. Thereafter, communication between the Embassy and the villa was by courier. Windsor's own account, carried back by Serrano Suñer's emissary, stated that he had had oral warning (presumably from Ambassador Selby) that he would be court-martialed as a serving British officer if he did not follow orders and proceed at once. He complained that Churchill's letter conveying his appointment was "very cool and categorical." Furthermore, Selby apparently felt obliged at this juncture—perhaps on Churchill's instructions, perhaps because Windsor's intentions had become so murky—to sequester his passport, a strange footnote in royal annals.

On Windsor's arrival in Lisbon, he had left his passport at the Embassy with a request for French and Spanish visas, so that he could return to Paris to pick up his furniture, stopping off in Madrid on the way. Instead, Selby ignored the request and held the passport "for safekeeping." When word of this new impasse flashed from Lisbon to Madrid and on to Berlin, Von Ribbentrop seems to have decided that the time was ripe for German Intelligence to take over. Accordingly, a senior agent, the perky, self-confident Walter Schellenberg, was sent to Lisbon posit-haste to mount an operation for whisking the Windsors back across the border into Spain. Schellenberg was one of the handful of covert-action specialists in the stable of the notorious Reinhard Heydrich, Himmler's chief operator in the business of spying, counterintelligence, kidnapping, and other forms of political action, and, of course, liquidation as well.

At this point, late in July, with Windsor playing golf at Estoril and Churchill fuming in London, the German-Spanish scenario entered the realm of melodrama. The plot which Schellenberg devised was an elaboration of the one first proposed by Von Ribbentrop: Aristocratic Portuguese friends would invite the Windsors to spend a few days at a mountain lodge, convenient to the border. The Windsors would accept. A hunting expedition would take the party to "a precisely designated place at a particular time," where a Portuguese frontier captain would obligingly look the other way. A Spanish patrol would "happen" past, to offer instant protection; and Schellenberg's strong-arm squad, hovering near, would fend off any intervention by the Portuguese or British.

Von Stohrer laid out the plot in a MOST URGENT TOP SECRET telegram to Berlin on July 26. Schellenberg was then in Madrid, having arranged the Spanish role with Serrano Suñer's people. He notified them that his men would keep the Windsors under surveillance even after they were inside Spain; but that German participation must remain secret, on Von Ribbentrop's insistence, so that the propaganda value of the Duke's defection could be exploited to the utmost. His step must appear wholly voluntary, prompted by his revulsion from the war, and accomplished with the help of Spanish friends interested only in giving him sanctuary in a "free" political climate. Windsor may even have provided the germinal idea for the little enterprise by having asked Serrano Suñer, only three days earlier, to help him and the Duchess return to Spain. Later that same day, the twenty-sixth, Von Stohrer learned from the Spanish Foreign Office that Selby had just handed back Windsor's passport, with a Spanish visa. The German plot now seemed foolproof, and Von Stohrer advised Berlin that Schellenberg would go into action.

What happened next is not manifest in documents yet accessible. But *something* happened, for the plot collapsed—suddenly, and so thoroughly that only two days later, on the twenty-eighth, Von Hoyningen-Huene was informing Berlin that the Windsors were about to leave for the Bahamas after all!—they would sail on August 1.

Von Ribbentrop still refused to accept defeat. On the day before the sailing, he sent a MOST URGENT TOP SECRET telegram from his special train, urging Von Hoyningen-Huene to apply all possible pressure on Espirito Santo to induce Windsor to stay in Europe and, failing that, to arrange a contact through whom the Germans could reach him in the Bahamas.

As the quarry first hesitated, then wavered, Von Ribbentrop resorted to scare-tactics. A week or so after Windsor had accepted the job in the Bahamas, Von Ribbentrop had instructed Von Stohrer to inform the Spanish Foreign Office that its go-betweens should get word to him that the German Foreign Office had learned from a Swiss agent with "many years [of] close connections with the British Secret Service" that he was being sent to the Bahamas so that British agents could "do away with him." Now, at this late hour, in a final effort to persuade Windsor that his well-being lay on the Axis side, Serrano Suñer rushed the Marqués de Estella over to Lisbon on July 31, the day before the Windsors were to sail, to warn the Duke away from the Bahamas because of "a great danger which threatens [him] and his Duchess": Information had been received that the British Government intended having him killed there.

Windsor took the tale to Walter Monckton, who told Estella, in "a long and bizarre conversation in the garden of the villa," that if he could produce hard evidence of the plot, the Windsors would not sail. Estella demurred; the information was so sensitive that he dared produce it only on Spanish territory.

Not good enough, Monckton said.

Very well, said Estella at last; if Monckton could keep the Windsors in Lisbon for ten days more, Estella would manage to bring him the evidence there.

No, Monckton said again; they'd sail on schedule. But if Estella could bring him the evidence, and if it convinced him, he'd intercept them at Bermuda. There the affair rested.

The evidence was never forthcoming. No trace of the alleged Swiss agent and his information was ever found in the German files. It was all a desperate fabrication, yet it so gulled the Windsors that they were still discussing it with Estella the next morning, past their sailing time; their ship had to be held for them. More damning still, evidence was found in the captured files of the German Foreign Office to show that even after Windsor was safely delivered in Bermuda, he managed through a secret courier to stay in touch with Von Ribbentrop's agents in Lisbon, and to imply that his mind was still open to the earlier arrangements.[4]

What is one to make of Windsor's behavior? Was he serious about skipping back into Spain? Was he ever tempted by the delusion that he could be crowned at Westminster, as Britain's Quisling King, with his Duchess beside him, on the throne where his great-grandmother, his grandmother, his mother, and his brother's wife had all been crowned?

History is unlikely to find a clear answer. Windsor himself could never be drawn into a frank discussion of his understandings with his Spanish and Portuguese friends. The Duchess, for her part, maintained to the end that he kept these transactions to himself. The man who was with them throughout, Gray Phillips, was probably the only other person privy to the Duke's real intentions. If Phillips indeed knew them, he had not said a word one way or the other when he died in 1973.

This much, though, is self-evident: If Windsor was only playing a game with the object of forcing his Government's hand, it was brinkmanship of an appalling kind. In Churchill's secret little struggle for Windsor's soul in Estoril—as in his fiercer struggle for England's survival, that desperate summer of 1940—he was the towering figure, the leader who was summoning Englishmen everywhere to their duty. Although he had failed, a scant four years before, to keep Windsor as England's King, his tenacity certainly helped save him from going down in history as its worst, and as the war's most pitiful casualty.

* * *

Both of the Duke's negotiations—for an "H.R.H." for his wife and for a post of prestige for himself—having failed so dismally, the Duchess showed him how such affairs should be handled. Lisbon's beautiful suburban beaches reminded her that in the rush of her packing, she had left a favorite bathing costume behind at La Croë. Forthwith she notified the American Minister at Lisbon that she would be grateful if he would have his colleague, the American consul at Nice, retrieve it for her. Although that part of the Riviera was now occupied by the enemy, and La Croë was locked and shuttered, and the Duchess wasn't sure exactly where the costume could be found, she said that the consul would have no trouble recognizing it: It was Nile green. In the midst of war, Minister and consul did her bidding, and the costume was duly fetched. A junior Foreign Service officer, later Ambassador Eldridge Durbrow, who master-minded the transaction, code-named it "the Cleopatra Whim."

Another bathing costume also figured in the Portuguese episode. Those beautiful beaches had struck a chord in Major Phillips, too, and he had responded. Because he was thin to the point of cadaverousness, he had attracted a certain amount of attention when he appeared in his bathing trunks. This he had gloomily expected, but he had not expected to be accosted by the police and charged—he, a member of his Royal Highness's household—with *indecent exposure*! In vain he protested that trunks were considered ample for a French beach. The police said that that was as may be—French immodesty was notorious; but this was Portugal, and Portuguese beaches required a bathing shirt as well. It was the law, and Phillips had broken it. The poor man eventually managed to have the mortifying charge dismissed, but not before it had been blazoned in the Lisbon newspapers and picked up by the world press.

A move for the Windsors usually meant inconvenience for others. Their departure from Lisbon was no exception. Because they refused to fly, and because there was no direct steamer service from Lisbon to the Bahamas, Whitehall had had to arrange for the diversion of a Lisbon–New York steamship, already overcrowded with Americans, including five ambassadors, impatient to get home, and refugees impatient to get anywhere, so long as it was away from the war zone. The ship, the American Export Line's *Excalibur*, named for the king's sword that had been flung away, dropped down the Tagus an hour behind schedule because of the Windsors' tardy arrival; they were the last passengers aboard.

Their suite shared a private veranda with one of the ambassadors, "Tony" Biddle, and his wife, Margaret. The Biddles had brought along two potted palms from their Lisbon hotel and had positioned them on the veranda for the comfort and convenience of their harlequin Great Dane, Okay. Hospitably, they invited the Windsors' cairns to make free of the facility, so, despite the overcrowding among the passengers belowdecks, topside the dogs and their owners had space and freedom, and all in all this leg of the trip was a pleasant prelude to the new job. At Bermuda, the Windsors and their staff transferred to a Canadian liner which put them ashore at Nassau on August 17, 1940. The Duke had failed to meet his first challenge in the war. Now he faced his second.

✿ CHAPTER 10 ✿
The Bahamas: A Mixed Performance

*The Duke says, " 'Tis my fate to be always ground
into the mire under the iron heel of oppression. Misfortune has broken my once haughty spirit; I yield, I
submit; 'tis my fate. I am alone in the world—let me
suffer; I can bear it."*
> —The Adventures of Huckleberry Finn,
> MARK TWAIN

Scarcely had the Windsors unpacked when the Duke
learned that the Palace's strictures had preceded him, and
had lost none of their implacability en route: The Duchess
was to be addressed only as "Your Grace" and was not to
be accorded the curtsey corresponding to the bow her husband would receive. Though the honors that protocol still
allowed her were few, the Duke saw to it that "she damn
well got them," as he later told a friend—"every last one of
them!" His determination was never exhibited to better advantage, or more smoothly, than on the Windsors' first formal introduction to Nassau Society, at a dinner dance for
two hundred at the Emerald Beach Club, a stronghold of
the colonials who then owned and ran Nassau. An American banker seated at the Duke's table remembers a gratui-
tous affront to the Duchess that might have blown up into
a *cause célèbre* but for the Duke's adroitness:

"The president of the club, Sir Frederick Williams-
Taylor, was a very old, very rich Canadian. When he began his speech of welcome, he addressed it only to the
Duke and failed to mention the Duchess. The Duke was
supersensitive about Nassau's accepting the Duchess on the
same terms that they accepted him. Earlier in the dinner,
when the waiters, who were naturally agog at serving the

former King, brought the platters to him before anyone else, he told them vehemently, 'Serve the Duchess first!'

"As Sir Frederick's speech rambled on, still without mentioning her, the Duke became more and more agitated, and began tapping the table. I knew something was going to pop, and sure enough it did. When the Duke rose to reply, he began by saying that the speech we had just heard had been submitted to him before dinner. In the original, which he had approved, the welcome had included the Duchess. That she was not mentioned in the spoken version was doubtless due to the dim light at the speaker's table—Sir Frederick could not see the speech clearly enough to read it in full. The Duke was sure this would not happen again. Having made his point, he moved on and gave us a gay and charming talk."

When the House of Assembly convened in the December after the new Governor's arrival, he was ready with a program, drafted by the colonial bureaucrats, which proposed the establishment of a training school for native farmers and of a Civilian Conservation Corps to drain off the unemployed; he also requested funds to improve public utilities, preserve historic monuments, and beautify public gardens. The Assembly turned him down on every count, in part because many members were reluctant to take on additional expenses with the war budget still fluid. Politically—he was to learn—he would be allowed to function only as a figurehead, except in those frequent small ceremonies that rejoice the colonial heart; socially, he could be as active as he wished—rather, as the Duchess wished; and it had already become plain that she wished to be very active indeed, as soon as Government House could be made fit for entertaining.

Her first sight of its tall white columns reminded her pleasantly of the "old manse" architecture of Maryland and Virginia. She was further heartened by the *E R VIII* displayed in the tilework of the swimming pool, as evidence of recent construction. But the interior, with what the Duke dubbed its "rust and discomfort," was a sore disappointment to them both. Although the previous Governor had only just moved out, hastily and reluctantly, the

Windsors found the woodwork so riddled with termites and pervaded by dry rot that the house was—according to the Duke's petulant cable to the Minister for the Colonies—"impossible to occupy . . . in its present condition. . . . It will take at least two months to make it habitable." Moreover, it was dowdy—"an awful old barn," Wallis decribed it to an American friend; "the dining room looks like a ski hut in Norway." In the emergency, hospitable, well-to-do residents of Nassau moved out of their own houses and turned them over to the Windsors, while a decorator imported from New York helped the Duchess bring the dowdy old barn up to her high standards—which required the instant removal of portraits of King George IV and Queen Victoria. The refurbishment was an obligation, she explained to a reporter:

"I must make a home for him. That's why I'm doing this place over: so we can live in it with comfort as a home. All his life he has traveled, and a palace to come back to is not always a home. The only one he ever had he made for himself at Fort Belvedere, he had to leave it, you don't know what it meant to him. I must make him a home—"

This she did, at a cost of 21,000 dollars, including 1,500 dollars for a new dining-room table. The Assembly had authorized the expenditure of no more than 6,000 dollars in all, and there is some question whether the Government or the Windsors made up the difference. No matter; presently the 1,500-dollar table was shining under the Duchess's favorite ivory-colored candles and smiling with the ducal silver. The Duke's first cousin once removed, Princess Alice Countess of Athlone, visited Government House shortly after the war and admitted that it had been "much improved . . . by the Duchess of Windsor." As at the Fort and at La Croë, the climax and *pièce de résistance* of their dinner parties was often a bagpipe solo by the Duke, in kilts.

There is no record that their evenings' entertainments ever included any of the many calypsos composed in their honor, and already wafted on the sea breeze from Trinidad to Nassau—for instance:

It's love, it's love alone
That caused King Edward to leave the throne.

We know King Edward is noble and great,
But love caused him to abdicate. . . .

"If I can't get a boat to set me free,
I'll walk to Miss Simpson across the sea."
He said, "My robes and crown is upon my mind,
But I cannot leave Miss Simpson behind."

And this anonymous fragment:

What is love, Mister? I do not know,
But dat it's powerful was clearly shown,
When it made a monarch give up his throne.

And this one:

Mrs. Simpson, she no fool!
She make her aim the big Crown Jewel.[1]

The reporter to whom the Duchess had explained her
nest-building obligation was Adela Rogers St. Johns, one of
Hearst's stars. She had arrived in Nassau soon after the
Windsors themselves, to do a newspaper series about them,
having promised to write nothing that would embarrass either the Duke and Duchess or His Majesty's Government.
She kept her promise; but when she wrote her autobiography, *The Honeycomb*, in 1969, she felt free to speak her
mind, and did.

Frail, tiny, delicate, floating, graceful, dainty, she had
described the Duchess in her series; nearly three decades
later, she repeated the compliments and added, "My memory forces me to say that I saw her like that. . . . Yet my
deepest recording insists I always had the impression that
Wallis Warfield Simpson could play tackle for the Green
Bay Packers."[2]

What completed Mrs. St. Johns's disillusionment was the
lack of grace and sensitivity which the Duchess showed
during the Stateside visit she presently made with the
Duke—himself still unaware, apparently, of his responsibilities both as Governor of a British colony at war, and as a
representative of his brother, the sovereign of a nation with
its back to the wall.

When the Windsors told Mrs. St. Johns that the trip was being planned, they led her to believe that its purpose was to promote a closer rapport between the Bahamians and the Americans, in furtherance of the British war effort. Its real purpose was, of course, to let the Duchess escape the heat and tedium of Nassau and refresh her wardrobe, as well as her stock of ideas, in cosmopolitan New York. Mrs. St. Johns suspected as much. She felt, she wrote, "a cloud of dark foreboding" about the wisdom of trying to make the skeptical American public reconcile the obviously irresponsible Windsors with Britain's vaunted resolution to "see things through." Her foreboding drove her to consult with Capt. Vyvyan Drury, who would accompany the Duke as press officer; and together they drew up a list of suggestions for the Windsors' guidance:

DO [in black ink]

Land somewhere other than New York.

Go to Wakefield Manor, the Duchess's ancestral home, as the first stop.

Wait for the White House to move before making any social engagements.

Keep very strictly to all wartime regulations.

Bring as small a staff as is possible to do with and little luggage.

DON'T [in red ink]

Go to a big New York hotel.

Bring much luggage!!!!

Have too many servants.

Wear jewelry.

Attend parties in either Washington or New York unless guests are carefully checked.

Same about Wakefield Manor.

DO NOT GO to cafés or restaurants at first.

Nearly all this excellent advice was wasted. Mrs. St. Johns, on watch, would decide that the Duchess "did those things she ought not to have done, and left undone those things she ought to have done. . . . She went to the Waldorf, where they took an entire floor, brought more trunks than the harassed customs men could count, *all* her dogs, maids, a full staff AND all her jewels. . . .

"They did not go to Wakefield Manor. In New York they began almost at once to go about in what was then known as Café Society, and though the British Embassy did its best and His Royal Highness Prince Edward was received by the President, the Duke and Duchess of Windsor did not receive an invitation to the White House.

"Mrs. Roosevelt had been willing, but the Secretary of State and the President had vetoed it.

"The Duchess was neither color-blind nor stupid.

"Yet definitely, defiantly, she went against everything that was calm, discreet, patient, tactful, wise, and proper to win the approbation of her own countrymen and women to gain her the recognition at the White House that was essential to any chance the Duke had of a return to England for service like unto that of the time when he was the idolized Prince of Wales.

"As I think of it my heart sinks a little."

In justice to the Duchess, she had a valid excuse for leaving undone at least one of "those things she ought to have done": making a pilgrimage to Wakefield Manor. First, it was not her ancestral home; she never pretended that it was. The property had come by marriage to Mrs. Basil Gordon (Lelia Sinclair Montague), who had later married General Barnett, U.S.M.C. Lelia Barnett was a first cousin of Wallis's mother, and Alice and Wallis had visited Wakefield Manor summer after summer. Second, the advisers were probably not aware that Mrs. Barnett was Newbold Noyes's mother-in-law. The then Mrs. Noyes (now Mrs. Albert H. Lucas, the present chatelaine) has written, "My mother asked [the Windsors], but Newbold was bedridden and dying in the [manor] cottage, and although he wanted to encounter the Duke face to face, I knew it might be dangerous for him, so I persuaded my mother to 'uninvite' them." Noyes died a few months later.

The Bahamas remained a tranquil backwater during the Duke's first sixteen months *en poste*; his duties as Governor were few and undemanding. But on December 10, 1941, Japanese torpedo planes sank the new battleship

H.M.S. *Prince of Wales* and the battle cruiser H.M.S. *Repulse*, off the Malay coast. The loss of these two stalwart ships meant the collapse of Allied sea power in Southeast Asia, but the grievous news must have struck Windsor with a special, personal poignancy: The battleship was his namesake. Was there doom in his touch? The events of the past few years made it seem so. The *Prince of Wales* was originally to have been christened H.M.S. *King Edward VIII*, and although the Admiralty quietly made the change, the Fates were evidently not to be appeased. The Royal Navy had considered her an unlucky ship ever since the Abdication, and took wry satisfaction in pointing out that she sank almost on its fifth anniversary.

To be sure, the United States' entry into the war on December 7 was already so accelerating the pace and broadening the scope of the Windsors' activity that they were left little time for repining. The Duke found himself charged with supervising construction of an airfield, for the joint use of the R.A.F. Coastal Command and the U.S. Air Transport Command. The tough American work gangs struck sparks from the black Bahamian workers, who demanded equal pay. A riot broke out, and Windsor showed considerable skill—and not a little nerve—in suppressing it without bloodshed. He also obtained a raise of a shilling a day for the natives, plus a free meal at midday. The arrival of American airmen could have caused further friction if he had not seen to it that the mingling went easily.

At sea, meanwhile, German submarines were swooping down from the North Atlantic to prey upon the ore boats and tankers plying between South America and the East Coast ports of the United States. The Duchess, as president of the Bahamian Red Cross, had to prepare facilities for receiving and succoring the crews being brought in almost daily from the torpedoed ships; before long she would have between three and four thousand men on her hands. A letter of hers dated April 1942, to a friend in New York, broke off abruptly, with the explanation that she had to dash out and receive another boat-load of survivors.

The Red Cross building burned to the ground that August, a total loss, but two months later Wallis could report that she was converting an abandoned gambling casino into a canteen for British and American airmen. Lord Nuf-

field had given her the money for the alterations, and the
American construction company, Pleasantville Contractors,
was supplying the labor free of charge. To show an equal
friendliness, and her gratitude, Wallis began spending
much of her spare time at the site, chatting with the night
shift. Presently the survivors' hospital at the Victoria Hotel
was ready to be opened, and her load of work increased
still further. "Aren't I the busy bee?" she liked to ask. At
least once she went on, "But I wish it were somewhere
else. . . ."

On behalf of the survivors, she was in constant touch
with the British War Relief Society in New York. Her first
requests were for necessities—"100 suits (50 medium, 25
small and 25 large)"—but once these had been supplied,
she felt she could ask for recreational equipment. The Society responded nobly, with "pingpong bats & balls, 25 doz.
packs of playing cards, 6 card tables with linoleum tops
and detachable legs," not to mention "vegetable parers and
2 gross 'Windsor' stainless steel teaspoons." In addition to
these quasi-military concerns, and to the normal charities
of the wife of the Governor, she also found time for the
Dundas Community Center, which helped native young-
sters become self-supporting. She arranged for native wom-
en on the outlying islands to be brought to the Nassau
Hospital and taught the basics of hygiene, diet, and general nursing. For other native women, she promoted
courses in domestic service. For still others, she started a
class in needlepoint, with two evacuated Englishwomen as
instructors; on her trips to the mainland, she tried to persuade American and Canadian department stores to put
their work on sale, along with Bahamian jewelry and
weaving. And with her own funds, she started a pre- and
postnatal baby clinic that cared for ninety-eight infants
a day, five days a week. The grateful mothers insisted that
the clinic be named for her; a watercolor of its facade
hangs in her Paris library.

Two years of this "busy bee" life took its toll of her
health, and presently she wrote again to her friend in New
York: "I have been having a really bad time with my old
ulcer—just dragging myself around, half-doing too many
things. I don't seem able to find 3 weeks off to put myself
right once again. My canteen is very involving—you know

how they are—not to mention all the little rows among the 'ladies' that have to be smoothed out. . . . Everything gets more difficult every day in the way of supplies, etc.—but I have nothing to really complain of except my stomach and the fact that we are left here so long."

Her lot in "Elba," as the Duchess spoke of Nassau when she was in a mild mood, and "this lousy hole" when she wasn't—the land crabs that scuttled along the sidewalks were a special annoyance—was hardly all work and no play. She and the Duke often visited the States for "rest and rehabilitation"—to shop, see old friends and new shows, get medical checkups, and tend to business affairs. One trip took him as far afield as Calgary, Alberta, where he had begun to cherish hopes of striking oil on the acreage he had bought (1,600) and leased (2,400) there during his Canadian tour in 1919.

He first looked on the E. P. Ranch (for "Edward Prince") as another bolt-hole, like the Fort. That he came to look on it also as a potential source of income was suggested in 1930, when he applied for and was granted the mineral rights—a concession unique in the whole Dominion, where, since 1905, all such rights had been reserved to the Government. He had visited the E. P. in 1923, 1924, and 1927 and had stocked it with purebred cattle, ponies, and sheep, with the intention of raising pedigreed prize-winners. His agents had even recruited youths from cattle areas in Britain and sent them out as staff. The war renewed his interest in the E.P., but in another aspect than livestock; now the magic word was "oil."

The enemy had overrun the rich oil fields in the Balkans and Southeast Asia, and were harassing the tankers struggling up from South America and around the Cape of Good Hope. The Western Allies, desperately short of fuel and lubricants, were intensifying their search for fields in North America; and when the Duke received cuttings from the Calgary newspapers with such headlines as "Shell Oil Co. Planning Great Search for Oil," over reports that Shell had already leased 453,700 acres in the vicinity, his financial horizon was bathed in a rosy glow. He made a flying trip to Calgary in 1941, and presently sent in an American geophysicist, who reported that the prospects of oil were excellent. Standard Oil of New York was invited to share the expenses of exploration, but declined. The Duke was not discouraged; he pressed on, even when his project began meeting "considerable opposition" from the Government of Alberta, which took the narrow view that the property should not be exploited for private gain. A contour map of the E. P. made in August 1942 raised his expectations even higher. The Duchess wrote to an American friend that she wouldn't be surprised to find herself the wife of an oil magnate someday. The following April, the Duke was notifying one of his advisers, "I have had several offers of purchase." Another year, and he had formed a syndicate to participate in the drilling. Its name, Ecushwa Oils, Ltd., represented the principal officers and stockholders: *E* for Edward; *cush* for his friend and Palm Beach golfing companion, Charles G. Cushing, a New York investment broker; and *wa* for Elisha Walker, of the banking house of Kuhn, Loeb & Co.

The first golden promises were never fulfilled. The drillers found a small pocket of natural gas, but only traces of oil. Ecushwa melted into the mist that had swallowed the Windsor-Bedaux partnership. Even so, the Duke's hope of bringing in a gusher stayed warm until 1962, when he reluctantly sold out for a reported $190,000. He wanted to hold on, but the Duchess pressed him to let go. He used to say, "I'm *sure* the E.P. will make me rich!" It was the only real estate he ever owned, until he bought the Mill, near Paris, in 1952.

Wherever the Windsors appeared on the mainland—Miami, Washington, Baltimore, New York—the crowds in the streets gave noisy proof that their affection for the Duke embraced the Duchess, too. Baltimore could have been forgiven if its welcome had been less than exuberant. Wallis was not its first native daughter to marry a king; in 1803, Elizabeth Patterson had married Napoleon's younger brother, Jérôme, the future King of Westphalia. But when the Windsors' three-car special train arrived in Baltimore in October 1941, two hundred thousand people, all cheering, awaited it. The Duchess had only one surviving uncle: Henry M. Warfield, known as "the General" because he had twice been Adjutant General of Maryland. It was he who, when Wallis wrote him from London in

1936 for a copy of the Warfield family tree, had replied curtly, "If you behave like a lady, you won't need papers to prove that you are one." Yet here was the General at the railway station, greeting them, and sweeping them off to his country house, Salona Farm, in nearby Timonium. All was forgiven; when he died in 1947, he left her 15,000 dollars of his 850,000-dollar estate.

Back home in Britain, enthusiasm was rather more restrained. The frequency of these trips during the Duke's first year in office moved a Labourite M.P. to demand his recall, for neglect of duty. Pearl Harbor happened to be attacked just then, and though the awkward demand was shelved, unfavorable criticism continued—and the Windsors continued to offer it a foundation. In 1943, they made two trips to the mainland, one of seven weeks, and the other—which included jaunts to such fashionable resorts as Newport and the Hot Springs of Virginia—of nine. The following year, they made only one trip, but it lasted eighteen weeks, which allowed revisits to the resorts and time for the Duchess to have her appendix removed in New York. The hospital felt it necessary to deny a rumor that she had six nurses and a ten-room suite. In addition to these derelictions, there was an embarrassing series of minor gaffes and major strategic blunders:

The Duke sometimes attended a church service, but he never lent his presence to a local concert, art exhibit, or lecture; his explanation was that they bored him. (Nassau could have answered, "You are *paid* to be bored!") More damaging was his resolute policy of segregation. Although "coloreds" make up more than four-fifths of the islands' population, the Duke never hid his dislike and contempt for them. When they visited Government House, he required them to use the back door. (Anthony Trollope reported from Jamaica in 1858 that the only table where white men and black men dined together was the Governor's.) The Duchess's canteen for troops was segregated. One of the most prominent and powerful men in the islands, Étienne Dupuch (pronounced du-POOTCH), the editor and publisher of the Nassau *Tribune*, was colored—somewhat aggressively so. In his book *The Tribune Story*, he devotes a whole chapter to the Duke's exacerbating prejudice. Twice Dupuch quotes him as rejecting an applicant for a post with a blunt "We can't have a colored man for this job"—in Dupuch's presence. He seems even to have rejected an engineer, Scottish, noncolored, and highly qualified for an important assignment, simply because Dupuch had recommended him.

It was when the Duke tried to suppress legitimate news that Dupuch, a newspaperman first, let his resentment show—at the cost, he implies, of a knighthood or a decoration. (He received both of them after the Duke's departure.) The most conspicuous case in point was the memorial service held in Nassau's Christ Church Cathedral for the Duke of Kent, who was on active duty with the R.A.F. when he was killed in an air crash on August 25, 1942, leaving his widow and their three children—Prince Edward Duke of Kent, born in 1935; Princess Alexandra, born in 1936, now the Hon. Mrs. Angus Ogilvy; and Prince Michael, born in 1942. Of all Queen Mary's sons, he was most like her; she had a special affection for him, and his death was a shock from which she never completely recovered. With his death, and with David lost by defection, the family which she had raised at Sandringham was now without its two most attractive and joyous spirits, the brothers whom the British liked most. If Kent had lived, almost certainly he would have been appointed Governor General of Australia. In Nassau, the complete information about the service that had been originally supplied to the local press was abruptly withdrawn "for security reasons." An official told Dupuch, "You never know what the Germans might do if they knew the Duke was going to be in the Cathedral at a certain time. They might bomb the place!"

"How?" Dupuch asked. "From where?"

Windsor seems to have actually entertained the possibility of not merely a bombing raid, but worse, for Susan Mary Alsop quotes him in her *To Marietta from Paris, 1945–1960* as telling her that "if Dakar had been taken and the Bahamas invaded he would have sent the Duchess to Miami and fought it out to the last in Nassau."[3]

It may have been Dupuch's "impertinence" that jumbled Windsor's wits, or it may have been his still bitter remembrance of Princess Marina's refusal to call on him and his Duchess at Wasserleonburg; whatever the explanation, he never sent a message of condolence to the widow of the brother who had so long been his favorite. When she inventoried his personal possessions, she found the gold box that he had sent David as a Christmas present in 1937. Still in it was the curt note which David had put there when he sent it back.

The Duchess shares the Duke's blame for tactlessness. They had been in Nassau only a few months when one of her teeth became infected, and she announced that she was going to Miami for treatment. The local dentists took umbrage at her implied disparagement of their professional ability, but she offended a far wider audience when it was learned that she and the Duke would make the trip in Axel Wenner-Gren's yacht, *Southern Cross*. The news inspired a modest quip in Washington. Someone there having noticed that ships associated with the Windsors often bore appropriate names—*Enchantress, Fury, Excalibur*—now asked if she had considered requesting President Roosevelt to lend her the cruiser U.S.S. *Tuscaloosa*. Wenner-Gren was a millionaire Swedish industrialist. Tall and powerful, with white hair and cold blue eyes, he had founded the Electrolux Company, was the principal stockholder in Bofors—arms and armament—and owned some five million acres of timberland in Sweden. As a resident of Nassau, he had established a foundation for the benefit of Negroes, and himself defrayed its annual budget of 25,000 dollars; he had also built a fish cannery and had organized a real-estate development which together were providing steady employment for more than one thousand people. On the other hand, he was known to be a close friend of Hermann Göring's, and had been blacklisted by both the British and American governments for his Nazi connections. Roosevelt's adviser Harry Hopkins would report on his arrival in England in January 1941 that "H.R.H.'s recent yachting trip with a violently pro-Nazi Swede did not create a very good impression."

A political indiscretion of this sort was rare for the Duchess, though not for the Duke. Far more frequently she was criticized for her absorption in chic—hairdos, frocks, shoes, jewelry—to the neglect of other concerns which some critics considered more deserving in wartime. Elsa Maxwell once brought this charge against her in peacetime: "Why do you devote so much time and attention to clothes? It seems so frivolous!" The Duchess answered, "My husband gave up everything for me. I'm not a beautiful woman. I'm nothing to look at, so the only thing I can do is dress better than anyone else. If everyone looks at me when I enter a room, my husband can feel proud of me. That's my chief responsibility."[4] When she and the Duke traveled, the public could not help perceiving their insensitivity to the proprieties of self-restraint which the war had imposed on others. A tumulus of luggage always accompanied them, once as many as 146 pieces, according to a reporter's tally. Not only did they allow the unsavory Wenner-Gren to transport them; they entertained him in return, at Government House. Many Americans came home from the Windsors' dinners to report the Duke's contention that the war was a mistake, and that peace should be negotiated. One of their guests was a notoriously loose-mouthed woman from Colorado, who hurried home to spread the story: "My dear, did I tell you that I dined with the Windsors in Nassau last week? . . . Yes, *couldn't* have been cozier! But do you know what the Duke told me, he himself? He said that the war—"

Word of his indiscretions reached the British Ambassador in Washington, Lord Halifax, who had three sons in uniform, one of whom would be killed in the Desert War. Halifax was fearful that American isolationists, a powerful sect, might accept the Duke's fatuities as representing the real British position. Since it was only hearsay at first, the Embassy could do nothing about corking him, until he tossed off the same dangerous nonsense to a reporter in Miami, during a visit to the States in 1941. The wire services spread the story across America, and isolationists seized on it to reinforce their arguments. Halifax had been disturbed before; now he was appalled. The criticism generated by the Windsors' first trip to the mainland, when they had foolishly rejected the St. Johns-Drury guidelines, had only just begun to subside when the Duke's statements to the press, plus his chumminess with Wenner-Gren, aroused it anew. Halifax tried to contain the damage by issuing disclaimers, but he was loath to go to the source of the trouble and meet his monarch's brother head-on. Worse, the Duke had recently informed the Embassy that he was scheduling another such trip. If, during it, he were to compound his usual social and protocolary blunders with fresh brink-of-treason pronouncements, his continued presence in the Bahamas would be not only embarrassing to Britain, but a danger to the pro-British sentiment that Roosevelt was trying to cultivate.

Lord Halifax's staff at the Embassy included four especially clever and distinguished young men. John Foster, the First Secretary, was later an M.P., a Fellow of All Souls, a much-decorated brigadier, and the author of many articles on constitutional and private law. John Wheeler-Bennett, who would be commissioned to write the official biography of George VI, was a prime mover in the British Information Service, as was Aubrey Morgan, a wise, tough, charming Welshman who married the Dwight Morrows' eldest daughter, Elizabeth, and on her death, their youngest, Constance; he would become personal assistant to Sir Oliver Franks when he succeeded Halifax as Ambassador. The fourth member of the team was René McColl, of the Embassy's press section. Together they devised an ingenious stratagem for making the Duke and Duchess realize how very harmful had been both his statements and their public conduct.

According to Foster, "McColl was to fly to Nassau on the pretext of forearming the Duke with acceptable answers to certain questions which the American press was sure to fire at him. But the questions we contrived were loaded; actually, they were subtle criticism of the Windsors' behavior, as already reported. One question, I remember, was 'Why do you and the Duchess have to travel with a hundred and forty-six pieces of baggage?' Another was 'Do you really advocate a negotiated peace?' A third was 'Is it true that the Duchess had two dozen dresses flown to Nassau from New York, and a hairdresser, too?'

"McColl discharged his mission and reported that he doubted if the Duke had tumbled to our plot. In any event, when the Duke next met the American press, he was a credit to himself as the former King Emperor—at least to the extent that he now said he'd be content with nothing short of total victory for the Allies. However, he would never recant having endorsed a negotiated peace during 'the Phony War, before Hitler lost his head.' "

What, if anything, the Duke learned from McColl's little drill in international comportment seems to have been soon forgotten. On July 8, 1943, Sir Harry Oakes, one of the richest men (Canadian mines) in the Western Hemisphere and by far the most prominent ornament to the Bahamian community, was savagely beaten to death, and his body set afire in the master bedroom of Westbourne, his great house in Nassau—the Windsors had stayed there while waiting for Government House to be made "habitable." The police woke the Duke early next morning to apprise him of the murder and to admit that they had no definite clues to the murderer. Windsor rightly concluded that the case was too big for the local detectives; but instead of appealing to Scotland Yard, as was appropriate, he appealed to Miami, where he had come to admire a detective who had been his bodyguard on several visits there.

This officer, Captain Edward Melchen, raced over to Nassau with an assistant, and together they decided that the murderer was Oakes's son-in-law, Count Alfred de Marigny, a playboy with a shady reputation. De Marigny's young wife, Nancy, retaliated by summoning Raymond Schindler, a famous private detective in New York. By now the trail was cold and muddied, but Schindler was able to satisfy the jury that Melchen's evidence was of doubtful worth; and De Marigny was acquitted, but later forced to leave the colony. The fact that the murderer is still at large, if alive, many attribute to Windsor's blunder in bringing in the Miami detectives, when the Yard's long experience in working with colonial police might have led to a solution. The crime still hangs over the islands, just as the blunder still hangs over Windsor's record.

As the war receded from the western Atlantic, and tourists began supplanting the military in the again untroubled Bahamas, the Duke found more time on his hands than ever, and resumed his request for appointment to a more exalted post. Four months after the Windsors' arrival in Nassau, the British Ambassador to Washington, Lord Lothian, a Christian Scientist, had refused the simple medical treatment necessary to cure a minor ailment, and had died. Windsor had at once mounted an ill-disguised and footling campaign to be nominated as his successor; and

letters and telegrams in his support bombarded President
Roosevelt, Secretary of State Stettinius, and various American
editors. They availed nothing; the post was offered to
Lloyd George, who refused it; and after consideration of
other candidates, including Beaverbrook and Eden, it finally
went to Lord Halifax. As 1944 turned, and Halifax's
retirement approached, Windsor renewed his solicitations
for Washington or, failing that, for Ottawa. Again it was
useless. Washington was still out; so was Ottawa, though
for a different reason: strongly Catholic French-Canada
had not budged from its 1936 position on kings—and now
governors—with twice-divorced wives. When Lord
Tweedsmuir was Governor-General of Canada, he wrote
that it "is the most puritanical part of the Empire, and
cherishes very much the Victorian standards in private
life." The best that Churchill could offer the Windsors was
Bermuda, but the Duchess would have none of it: "We
aren't fond of islands." The Duke added, "Patience is a
great virtue when living on an island, but one becomes
buried in this backwater after a while."

He said that to a New York friend in June 1944. By
then he had realized how little the Assembly would support
his programs; everything he advocated, including a
better police force, was being voted down. Moreover, the
Duchess's health was becoming precarious. As early as
January 1942, she had complained that "Hell hath no fury
like Nassau's heat!" Government House was not air-
conditioned. By the end of '44, the heat and the work had
fined her down from a slender 110 pounds to a gaunt 95.
Although she liked to remark that " a woman can never be
too rich or too thin," so severe a loss, coupled with her
annoying ulcer, alarmed her and the Duke. Aunt Bessie
flew over from Miami—her first flight ever—to spend
Christmas with them. The Windsors had already decided
not to wait until his term expired in August, but to send in
his resignation at once, with a request that it become effective on March 15. Then, with the social Sahara of Nassau
behind them, they would refresh themselves at the oases of
Palm Beach, New York, and Newport before making their
leisurely way home to Paris.

Nassau was sincerely sorry to see them go. The organizations they had headed or sponsored showered them with

silver trays and boxes, farewell dinners, testimonial parchments, and other mementoes. The House of Assembly presented the Duke with an address of appreciation. A War Office inspector of the defenses of British possessions in the Atlantic reported that, among all the colonial governors he had visited, he had found the Duke of Windsor the most capable. Even Whitehall praised him; the new Labour Government's Secretary of State for the Colonies said that Windsor had given the Bahamas their best administration in recent times. An unidentified native woman went even further; the New York *Daily News* quoted her as lamenting, "Lawd save us, we've lost the best man we ever had!" But for the Duchess's contributions to the war effort and to Nassau, there was nothing from Whitehall nor, as usual, from the Palace, not even the minimal O.B.E.—thereby giving her something else in common with Freda Dudley Ward, who received no official recognition for her years of work in behalf of the Feathers Clubs.

The Windsors having signed a separate, early peace with the enemy, it may be interesting to glance at Ernest Simpson's war career. Just over a year after Wallis divorced him to marry the Other Man, Ernest married the Other Woman, Mary Raffray, a fortnight after her own divorce. The Simpsons returned to London at once, and there, on October 27, 1939, was born the son whom Mary reported as looking "just the teensiest bit like Mr. Pickwick without his glasses." They christened him, in the Guards Chapel, Ernest Henry Child Kirk; his first fond nickname was "Whistlebinkie," but Henry (for Mary's father) was the name he would be known by until he eventually scrapped the lot and adopted another set.

Somebody took the news of the baby's birth to Wallis and boldly asked her, "Why don't you and the Duke have one, too?"

"Because," she is said to have answered, "David isn't heir-conditioned."

Although Ernest Simpson was forty-one at the outbreak of World War II, he signed up for the Officers' Emergency Reserve and enrolled in the Home Guard, while Mary trained and qualified as a St. John's Ambulance First-Aider. The following July, they sent young Henry to safety in America. He was there when his mother died of cancer, a week before his third birthday. She loved England and is buried in Somerset. Ernest meanwhile had been commissioned second lieutenant in the Royal Army Ordnance Corps. Now that there was nothing to hold him at home, he volunteered for overseas duty, and within a month of Mary's death he was in India, where he spent the rest of the war, the last three years as a major. In 1948, he married for the fourth time, and for the fourth time a divorcee: Mrs. Avril Joy Leveson-Gower. She was at his bedside when he died in London, November 30, 1958. To the very end, he kept his silence about the Simpson Affair.

Henry Simpson stayed on in America, living in Sewickley, Pennsylvania, for more than six years with the Morgan Schillers, of the steel-scaffolding company for which Wallis had once considered becoming a saleswoman. When he reached maturity, he emigrated to Israel, where he changed his name to Aaron Solomon,[5] married a local girl, was divorced, and married another. He is believed to have enlisted in the army and to have seen action at the Golan Heights in the Arab-Israeli War, but his American relatives are not sure. He has not communicated with them for many years. If he is associated with his father and grandfather's old firm, Simpson, Spence & Young do not acknowledge it.

As for Win Spencer, a glimpse of him about the time of Wallis's marriage to the Duke is given by Gene Markey, then a film producer, and now a rear admiral, U.S.N.R. (Ret.): "I was writing and producing for 20th Century-Fox in those days. One film that we planned was about the sub-chasers in the First World War: *Splinter Fleet*, it was called, to be directed by the great John Ford. Both Jack and I were in the Naval Reserve, so we knew a good many Navy people, and when we were ready to hire a technical adviser, we passed the word to Coronado, which is the Happy Hunting Grounds for retired officers. Commander Spencer was the first to apply. That was forty years ago, but I remember him clearly, especially how his manner suggested that he was not so much applying for the job as considering whether he would *accept* it if it was thrust on him. Well, for various reasons, it wasn't thrust.

"He had been handsome once, you could see that. You could also see that he was middle-aged before his time. I found him likable, though I'm sure he didn't give a curse whether I—or anyone else—liked him or not. He had a sort of tired arrogance that armored him against the world's opinion. I got the impression that life may have disappointed him, but he was far from disappointed in himself."

Physical disability forced Spencer's retirement from the Navy in 1939, as a commander; and Pearl Harbor found him too old, at fifty-three, for recall to active duty. He died in 1950, in the presence of his fourth wife, as would his successor, Ernest Simpson.

❧ CHAPTER 11 ❧
"The Suitcase Years"

And now a curious process of disintegration set in. The peculiar and highly artificial society of London had acted as a preservative; it had kept him in being; it had concentrated him into one single gem. Now that the pressure was removed, the odds and ends, so trifling separately, so brilliant in combination, which had made up the being of the Beau, fell asunder and revealed what lay beneath.

—Beau Brummel, VIRGINIA WOOLF

No passage across the Atlantic being available to civilians until the end of the war in the Pacific, the Windsors spent the summer of 1945 in the United States. As soon as they returned to Paris, in September, one of the Duchess's first telephone calls was to "Wahwee" MacArthur, the wife of Douglas MacArthur II, an American Foreign Service officer and a nephew of the general. He had been on duty at Vichy in 1942 when the Germans interned him in a prison camp for diplomats, and there he stayed until the Liberation freed him to help reopen the Embassy. The MacArthurs were old friends of the Windsors, and the Duchess knew that they would have the latest news and gossip.

"We're here!" she told Wahwee; then, in the same breath, "Who's in town? . . . Not many, eh? Well, you and Douglas come for dinner and fill us in on what's going on. We have an apartment at the Ritz."

That evening she put them through a catechism: Was it true that A—— had collaborated? That B—— came out of the war with a fortune? That the Duke of C—— and the Countess of D—— were quite open about their liaison? Whose star was rising in the political world? In Society?

Whose was falling? Who was in trouble? Whose houses were open? The MacArthurs answered as best they could.

When the Duchess, once again *au courant,* moved toward reopening the house on Boulevard Suchet, she was dismayed to learn that it had been sold, though the bad news was somewhat sweetened by the purchaser's courteous offer to let the Windsors stay on while they looked for a suitable new residence. Moreover, their stored possessions were intact; the house had been sealed by the Swiss Legation and the American Embassy, and German guards had stood at the door throughout the Occupation. As for La Croë, they were surprised and delighted to find, a few weeks later, that except for the curtains and a few pieces of furniture, it, too, was intact, despite the fighting that had raged along the French Riviera. To be sure, there were still mines in the villa garden, a rusting radar on the roof, and massive pillboxes on the seawall. German prisoners were already digging up the mines, but not even a start on dismantling the radar and demolishing the pillboxes could be made, the Windsors were told, until the next spring. No matter: Their silver and linen, which had been hidden in a hill village, were safe and could be retrieved as soon as they were wanted.

Before the Duke committed himself to "putting down roots," he made yet another effort to obtain a useful and dignified post somewhere in the British Empire overseas. As he would write in the New York *Daily News* in 1966, "I'd thought that my performance as a colonial governor, and the spirit in which I had gone about my duties, would have persuaded the skeptics in Britain that my desire to stay on in my country's service was a genuine one, and that I had fairly earned my passage back. I was resolved, in any case, to make one more hard try at drumming up interest in the Palace and in Whitehall for putting me to work somewhere in the British Diplomatic Service, in the absence of any marked enthusiasm for making a place for me in Britain."

He had been encouraged to believe that he would have better luck with the Labour Government than he had had with the departed Tories. He hoped that his popularity with the British workingman was still untarnished, and that the Socialists still cherished his words of compassion for the Welsh miners on the eve of his Abdication (he had not been told that when the newsreels showed him being married in the luxury of Candé, the miners refused to rise for the National Anthem). In this sanguine mood, he flew over to England on October 5. He would stay with his mother at Marlborough House, so the Duchess did not come with him, in the face of Queen Mary's steadfast refusal to receive her. It also hurt him that his brother the King, whom he had not seen for six years, failed to meet him at the airport or even to send someone from his household; but when he reached London, the welcome he received in the streets was balm aplenty. It was "tumultuous," according to *The New York Times*: "A cheering throng broke through the police cordon and surged around him, with cries of 'Good old Edward!' and 'You must come back, Teddy! We want you back!' Several people were thrown to the ground and trampled on as the besieging mob milled around the automobile."

Heartened, he called on Ernest Bevin, the Foreign Secretary in Clement Attlee's Cabinet, and proposed that the post of ambassador-at-large to the United States be created for him. He assured Bevin that there would be no trespass on the established ambassador's conduct of diplomacy; the role he visualized for himself was that of "a front man." "I would concentrate on the public relations aspect," was the way he later explained it to the *Daily News*. "Such a job would require my bringing Americans and visiting Britons together, providing a good table and a comfortable library for informal talks, and helping along what Winston Churchill called 'the mixing-up process.' " He did not expect even to operate from Washington; he would rove the country, in his old princely role of promoting British trade. The novelty of the proposition interested Bevin, but only at first glance. The record of those ducal blunders soon came to mind: the hapless association with Bedaux, the deplorable fraternizing with the Nazis, the foolish omissions and commissions in the Bahamas. Bevin's memorandum of the interview went forward to the Prime Minister without recommendation. That finished Windsor's chances for the time being. Privately, Attlee still held him in contempt for giving up the throne.

The Duchess had her own explanation of why her husband, whose motto as Prince of Wales had been "*Ich Dien*" ("I Serve"), was no longer able to put it into action: "His family would never let him have any position. They would block it more than the Government would. The reason was, they didn't want *me* to have any."

Windsor would allow himself a harmless boast in his *Daily News* series: "Of all the world's unemployed, none can be more practiced in the art of weaving a tolerable existence from loose ends than a former King in a foreign land. I got to be rather good at it." Actually, he found that idle hours were painfully slow to pass. Early in December, two months after the Bevin brush-off, Susan Mary Alsop ran into him in Paris, and wrote another of her chatty letters to Marietta Tree:

> He is so pitiful. . . . I never saw a man so bored. He said to me, "How do you manage to remain so cheerful in this ghastly place? . . . You know what my day was today? . . . I got up late and then I went with the Duchess and watched her buy a hat, and then on the way home I had the car drop me off in the Bois to watch some of your [i.e., American] soldiers playing football and then I had planned to take a walk, but it was so cold that I could hardly bear it. In fact I was afraid that I would be struck with cold in the way people are struck with heat so I came straight home. . . . When I got home the Duchess was having her French lesson so I had no one to talk to. . . ." I thought this description of a day was pretty sad from a man who used to be Edward VIII by the Grace of God of Great Britain, Ireland and the British Dominions beyond the Seas, King, Defender of the Faith and Emperor of India.[1]

His boredom impressed Lady Diana Cooper, too. She remembered it and remarked on it in an interview in 1978: "He had such an awful life in Paris. He couldn't speak French, he didn't enjoy nightclubs and he had very few friends he could talk with. If only I had been Mrs. Simpson, I would have bought him the most lovely house in

Virginia. He was violently pro-American and he would have enjoyed it so much."[2] But France continued to offer them both something irresistible—no taxes.

About a year after the Bevin interview, Windsor returned to England—this time accompanied by the Duchess—to urge his brother to help him find useful employment. There was little other business to occupy him, so he had plenty of leisure for a visit to Ednam Lodge, the country house of his old friend Eric Dudley, next to the Sunningdale golf course. The Duchess had brought with her a jewel case so huge that when the party decided to go up to London for a night, the Dudleys' butler asked her to let him put it in the strong room. She refused. It would be quite safe, she said, under her maid's bed. The Duke had already begged her not to bring along Queen Alexandra's unset jewels, notably some superb rubies and emeralds, which he had given her during their courtship, because they were to be set in Paris, not London. She had refused this advice, too.

On Wednesday evening, October 16, the butler rang Lord Dudley in London to report that the house had been robbed, but that the burglars seemed to have touched nothing but the Duchess's jewel case, which they had stripped. Indeed, they had taken more than they could carry; some of the Duke's gold cigarette cases they had left on a windowsill; and some earrings—oddly, there was not a matching pair among them—eventually turned up in one of the sand traps on the Sunningdale links. The rest was a clean haul. The only survivors from the Duchess's collection were a sapphire-and-diamond brooch which she had worn up to London; an enormous sapphire which she had left behind in Paris for Van Cleef & Arpels to fashion into a bird-of-paradise, with jeweled wings; and some smaller, miscellaneous sapphires.

Scotland Yard was satisfied that the burglar or burglars had waited until the servants were gathered for six-o'clock dinner and then had thrown a grapple through Lady Dudley's daughter's window, which was open. They seemed to know exactly what they wanted and exactly where it was; they did not even enter Lady Dudley's room or any other; they finished their job in a few minutes and were gone, leaving not a single clue. The press pointed out that none of the dogs in the house, either the Windsors' or the Dudleys', had given the alarm; Sherlock Holmes had found a similar silence significant (cf. "Silver Blaze"), but the Yard did not. They preferred to suspect "a gang of international jewel thieves," and dropped dark hints about "a man in an American Army officer's uniform" and "a large black saloon car"; neither ever materialized. The case continued to flare up more and more feebly, at longer and longer intervals. At length the file was closed. No one was ever charged with the crime. Nothing was ever recovered.

A member of the Duke's staff remembers that the Duchess's collection had been insured for 1,600,00 dollars. This was rather less than its replacement value, not to mention the additional historical value residing in that part of it which had belonged to Queen Alexandra. The difference was so substantial, indeed, that it was not reconciled until the underwriters and the Duke's solicitors had wrangled long and bitterly. The Duke's fear that leakage of the true worth of his gifts to the former Mrs. Simpson would excite curiosity about his remittances from the Crown worried him almost as much as the prospect of being out of pocket. At the end, the underwriters were generous; they paid for copies to replace the lost pieces; and they reinsured the collection, restored and augmented, for 3,200,000 dollars (double the original appraisal), provided that at least half of it remain in a bank vault at all times.

In 1948, Windsor tried once more to wangle a job from the Socialists. This time he carried his appeal to Attlee himself, only to be refused as before. When Churchill returned to power in 1951, Windsor made his fourth and final solicitation, but Churchill affected not to hear, and Windsor did not press. The Duchess knew it would have been useless. She realized that the doors were closed, and that if—as was unlikely—they ever opened again, it would be only onto another dreary cul-de-sac like the governorship of the Bahamas, to her further ignominy. She accepted this final turndown with a shrug. She had gone to London with him, and they had stayed in a friend's house on Upper Brook Street in the West End. The instant he entered the drawing room in the late afternoon, after the call at Number 10, she knew from his drawn, pinched face that he had failed again. "Was it 'No'?" she asked. He made a grimace, raised his right hand, and then turned the thumb down. She walked to the tall window, to stare broodingly into the fog. "I hate this place," she said, oblivious to an American friend standing close by. "I shall hate it to my grave!"

For the Duke it meant only that he had arrived at the end of the road years before he ever realized that he was finished with large affairs and that the Bahamas had been offered to him not so much as a fresh route but as a convenient dumping ground. Never again did he try to do anything useful or constructive on a scale larger than his garden. No one needed or wanted him, except as an exhibit or for his fine table. It was much the same for her.

As such, they became lodestars for the café socialites whose seasonal migrations were being speeded by the expansion of the transatlantic airlines and by the great liners, now demobbed and returned to the Atlantic run. This was the new Society: restless, moneyed pilgrims in search of a Mecca. The Windsors' house would eventually provide it; but in the early postwar years the Duke and Duchess served only as a master clock by which the others set their watches: *tick*, to New York; *tock*, to Paris; *tick*, to Palm Beach; *tock*, to Cap d'Antibes; *tick*, to the Lido; *tock*, to Biarritz. On the weekend that Edward VIII abdicated, Westbrook Pegler predicted that "he will go from resort to resort, getting more tanned and more tired." Alistair Cooke wrote in his *Six Men,* "The governorship of the Bahamas was no more than the gift of a sun lamp between the twilight grandeur of his eleven-month reign and the long night of his banishment to the transatlantic social tour."[3] Elsa Maxwell said, "Wherever the Duke and Duchess go, the world goes"—the *fashionable* world, of course, the world of the "Beautiful People." The Windsors were its sun and moon, its center, its focus, its pivot. The Duke's old, aristocratic English friends took no part in the whirl, nor could they have done so if they had wished; currency restrictions kept them at home. So, into the vacuum left by the new poor surged the new rich, chiefly Americans.

In the winter of 1945–46, the Duke was fifty-one years old and the Duchess forty-nine. Fifty-one is the prime of life for anyone creative, anyone able to draw upon intellec-

tual and spiritual capital; for those who have none, it can
be merely barren existence. In such a desert the Duke
would wander for his remaining twenty-seven years. Job-
less, and with no field for exercising his one superb natural
talent—lending his romantic presence and princely show-
manship to state ceremonials—he had few moral or intellectual resources within himself for nurturing a spirit that
had lost its bearings. Literature, music, or art awoke no
response in him. He had no serious interests of any sort,
and but four enthusiasms: In ascending order, they were
gardening, money, golf, and the Duchess. Since she herself
shared only in the last, her geisha-like task of finding ways
to beguile his time, to keep him from brooding on what-
might-have-been, to engage and hold his flickering, grass-
hopper attention, all but exhausted her.

She once admitted, "I was frightened in his first years of
idleness after the war. I realized that I had to take the
place of the King's boxes—the red dispatch cases that used
to bring him his daily business of State from Whitehall." It
pleased him to hear her tell friends that she filled up his
day by taking the place of Canada, or New Zealand, the
Falkland Islands, or the Foreign Secretary, in the problems
and challenges with which she presented him. She worked
at being a consort, but years afterward she told an American friend almost wistfully, "You have no idea how hard it
is to live out a great romance!"

One of woman's natural roles is solacing men who have
been defeated in struggle, whatever the nature: restoring
their pride and will to fight and returning them to the
front. But Wallis Windsor's man was self-defeated, with no
chance of recovering not from what his foes had done to
him, but rather from what he had done to himself. Worse
still, to their common loss, Wallis's own temperament, ro-
bust enough in other respects, was but meagerly endowed
with the simple feminine tenderness which the kingly casualty in her care needed. It was her misfortunes, not his,
that more and more fed the furies latent in her nature. The
appalling truth which she had to live with was that, far
more even than he, she was an outcast: the woman against
whom a whole society had shut its doors; an item of curiosity to the world not because of merit, but because of the
mystery and speculation over the particularities of her

being which were powerful enough to induce a man to give up so much. To her credit, she tried hard in the beginning to breathe life into the sand castles under her hands; but inevitably her inventiveness flagged, her patience wore thin. The specter of boredom would emerge from the shadows and stand behind the Duke's chair, and in his eyes would appear the stricken look of a man beaten and lost. Since there was so little left for them to find in each other, the only recourse left was motion, to be on the move, lest they stay too long in one place and the death of their meaning to each other became overwhelmingly plain.

The late 1940's and early 1950's were the years when the Windsors, as parched for amusement and as windblown as the rest of the international set, would alight at Palm Beach or Newport or New York, either in rented apartments or as the guests of rich friends, and after a few gala weeks, would take wing again. Their American intimates included the Robert R. Youngs (president, the New York Central Railroad), the William S. Paleys (president, the Columbia Broadcasting System), the Charles Wrightsmans (president, Standard Oil of Kansas), the Arthur Gardners (tubing manufacturers and a future Ambassador to Cuba), and the Clinton Murchisons (Texas capitalist)—new money and big money, all. Older money (and not quite so big) was represented by the George F. Bakers (First National Bank of New York) and the Winston Guests (iron and steel). The Windsors also saw much of the Gilbert Millers (Broadway producer), the Richard Berlins (president, the Hearst Corporation), Diana Vreeland (*arbiter elegantiarum*; fashion editor of *Harper's Bazaar*, and later editor-in-chief of its rival, *Vogue*), the Henry J. Taylors (newspaper correspondent and future Ambassador to Switzerland), the Harold E. Talbots (tycoon, speculator, and briefly Secretary of the Air Force), the Charles Blackwells, Mrs. Polly Howe, and Charles Cushing (investment banker, playboy). Wallis remembered that time as "the Suitcase Years—always packing."

On one of the Windsors' visits to the Guests on Long Island, young Alexander Guest, aged ten, sauntered in while the Duke was taking his evening tub, perched on the rim, and chatted away, man to man, as if they were fellow clubmen in deep chairs. When the Duke mentioned it to his hostess, she was horrified. "Nonsense!" the Duke said. "I enjoyed it!" He added sadly, "I could never have done that with my father. . . ." Later that same evening, he and Alexander played pool, and the boy made a miscue and dug into the felt. "I did that once at Windsor," the Duke remarked. "My father wouldn't let me play again for a whole year."

A regular stop on the Windsors' American circuit was at Horseshoe, the George Bakers' shooting plantation near Tallahassee, Florida. A lady who was frequently there at the same time remembers that "they'd arrive with a valet, a maid, two pugs, and more luggage than you'd believe, including a fitted basket for the Duke's afternoon tea when he was out in the field—and all this for one week's stay! He loved shooting quail and everything that went with the sporting life. *She* was bored stiff."

The Windsors' American base, from which they sortied in winter, was an apartment in the Waldorf Towers; they had another apartment in Paris, the Ritz's largest—they moved there from Boulevard Suchet in April 1946; and their summer base was La Croë. During the few months of the year that they used the château, the Duchess saw to it that tides of their friends washed through it regularly, bringing the Duke tidbits of news and gossip. Many came to visit: the Dudleys, the Buists, the Metcalfes, the Airds; Winston Churchill; handsome and dashing young Gianni Agnelli, chairman of F.I.A.T.; Aunt Bessie Merryman; the Mike Scanlons; Kenneth de Courcy, who ran a private intelligence service; and the Aga Khan. Noel Barber tells of a British Embassy's answer to a hostess who had appealed for a ruling on whether the Aga Kahn took precedence over the Duke of Windsor: "His Highness the Aga Khan is regarded as God on earth by his many million followers. But an English duke of course takes precedence."[4] Many other friends lived in the vicinity: the Herman Rogerses, Maugham, Lady Norman; ex-king Leopold of the Belgians and his wife, the lovely Princesse de Réthy; Gen. Georges Catroux, former commander of the first regiment of the Foreign Legion and French Ambassador to the U.S.S.R., 1945–46, with his heroic wife, who had been gassed at the front in the Great War and wounded in the Second, and was a commander of the *Légion d'honneur*.

Not even all this gadding and entertaining with the accompanying golf, gossip, and drinking, gin rummy, canasta, and backgammon, could wholly occupy the Duke's thoughts. Inevitably there were times when they turned to the verdict that history had begun to render on his career. At home in England, the record was already being obliterated; the souvenirs readied for his Coronation—the commemorative mugs, plates, and ashtrays—had been dumped at remainder prices; his photographs and portraits had been banished to the attic and the dustbin; the coins that would have helped fade-proof his profile were never circulated. Those handsome features, recently so clear and sharp in the public memory, had begun to blur. Edward VIII was becoming as dim and unsubstantial as Edward II. To arrest this process, to restore the luster of his reputation, to assure that his side of his story was presented fairly, and to regain some measure of his self-respect, he decided to write an apologia, although it would be disguised as his autobiography.

> If ther's any literary ability in a feller, gettin' fired out of a good gover'ment job'll bring it out.
> —Kin Hubbard

His choice of a professional collaborator was surprising. Instead of picking one from the ranks of royal biographers generally available in England—a Phillip Magnus, a Harold Nicolson, or a Shane Leslie—he turned to an American, Charles J. V. Murphy, a *Time-Life* editor known to him only by chance sight of some articles on Winston Churchill which Murphy and a colleague had written for *Life*. Windsor feared that an English writer might not be sufficiently sympathetic with the case he was determined to make for himself; further, in line with his increasing Americanization, he wanted an American flavor in the writing. When it began, he would insist that they use American spellings: *flavor, honor, clamor*, etc.

He had made his first tentative approach to Murphy in 1945, on his way home from the Bahamas, but Murphy, who was not particularly attracted to the idea, was about to leave for the Pacific. Instead of returning for another talk with Windsor, he went to China and forgot about the invitation. The Duke sought him out again a year or so later on his return to the United States, and Murphy's editors at *Life* were all for the project. Work began in the summer of 1947, at La Croë. Murphy and his fellow editors at *Life*—who were lending him for the assignment in the hope that a publishable series of articles might be condensed from the book—had pictured it as occupying him for a year at the utmost. It took him three and a half, thanks in part to the Duke's capricious working habits; in part to his reluctance to contemplate any subject longer than momentarily; and in part to the Windsors' sudden decision in early 1949 to give up both the Ritz apartment and La Croë—the latter because, she said, "The riffraff have taken over the Riviera," and because, he said, "There's not one good golf course within motoring distance."

Vacating La Croë was not the chore it would have been normally. The preceding June, two men whom the Windsors admired for their perspicacity—Robert Young and Henry Taylor—persuaded them that Russia's blockade of Berlin might bring on another war at any minute. Forthwith the Windsors crated most of their household goods and shipped them to safety in New York; much of the rest they packed for instant departure, sparing only what they needed for day-to-day living. Wallis told an American friend, "Well, here we go again! Each time I hope it will be the last time, and that we will be able to settle somewhere soon." She added, "I've got the movies!" The crisis passed, but it left a shadow over the sunny villa, and the Windsors let its lease expire with few regrets.

Some visitors had felt a shadow there from the beginning. One couple remembers dining there in the summer before the war: "A tiny little white table for us four was set on the huge lawn. There were rows of footmen—anyhow, it *seemed* like rows. The night was furiously hot, but the Duke was in full Scottish regalia. I thought he was staging a production of some sort." Another couple remembers another evening, just after the war, when the Duchess insisted on carrying the party off to a gala in Monte Carlo: "She had on every jewel. He wore a kilt. It was like watching a couple in pantomime—the studied gestures, the automatic smiles."

The Duchess managed to keep the Duke amused at La

Croë, but it was at Charles Murphy's expense. Murphy became increasingly disheartened to see how much time the Duke devoted to idleness, and terror at being caught in another war, and how little he could find for his autobiography. It languished; worse was ahead. When the Windsors forsook La Croë for Paris and established their new French base in a rented house at 85 rue de la Faisanderie, work on the half-finished book was suspended altogether, not only because of the disorganization entailed by such a major move, but also because the large, handsome house encouraged the Duchess to entertain on a grander and more eclectic scale.

The center of her circle was still, of course, the *gratin* of Paris, as represented by the Gabriel de la Rochefoucaulds, the Duc de Gramont, the Melchior de Polignacs, the Eugène de Rothschilds—recently of Schloss Enzesfeld—and their cousins the Philippe de Rothschilds; the Cabrols, the Comtesse de Ganay (the Duchess's companion and chauffeur in her Red Cross days), the Talleyrands, and the Charles de Chambruns. But their frothy social chatter now had to compete for attention with the orotundities of statesmen and politicians.

Margaret Biddle—of whom it was said, "She collects celebrities like scalps"—had sponsored most of them. They included four French premiers, past and future: Paul Reynaud, 1940, who had spent three years as a prisoner in Germany; Georges Bidault, 1949–50; René Pelven, who served twice: for part of 1950–51 and part of 1951–52; and Antoine Pinay, for part of 1952. Henri Bonnet, the French Ambassador to the United States in 1945, was often there; so was Paul Morand, a member of the Academy and the sole ambassador from the realm of letters; and Douglas MacArthur II, the future U.S. Ambassador to Japan, Belgium, Austria, and Iran, and his wife, Wahwee. Sir Charles Mendl, from the British Embassy, came with his wife, the super-chic Elsie; and Reginald Fellowes with his wife, the super-chic Daisy.

The pace of the Duchess's entertaining slackened in the course of time, and work was resumed; but another obstacle now appeared: her jealousy of the Duke's absorption in a golden past which she had never known. It began to display itself in constant interruptions. One of the Windsors' secretaries, Miss Hood, has described them—the Duchess's summons and the Duke's instant response: "Sometimes she would call him from a distance—from the garden or from another part of the house. Then he would leave whatever he was doing and go to her, hurrying eagerly. You could hear his voice calling to her from afar: 'Coming darling!' 'Yes sweetheart!' I have seen him in the middle of a haircut in his dressing room get up and run to his wife, leaving his astonished hairdresser agape."[5] A dozen times a day she would telephone to the Duke in his workroom, reminding him of a dinner party that evening, or asking him to fetch her a letter from his files, or ordering him to attend at once to some trifling household detail ("Go tell the butler—" or "Go tell the gardener—"). With a "Yes, darling!" he would leap to his feet, glad of the excuse to break off, and would sprint away on her errand, flinging over his shoulder to Murphy, "Back in a minute!" On his better days, the "minute" would stretch into ten or fifteen; on normal days, into an hour; on bad days, overnight. The Duke's reluctance—or inability—to concentrate being abetted by his fear of crossing the Duchess, Murphy was helpless, with no ally and no appeal.

The Duchess's disservice to the enterprise went even further. Several nights a week she would drag the Duke out to a dinner and on to a nightclub, and keep him there past dawn, with the result that the next morning's work, which had been scheduled to begin at ten o'clock, would be pushed back to eleven or half-past, if not canceled altogether. The flow of the Duke's narrative never, even at best, invited comparison with the cataract of Lodore; his span of attention, by Murphy's measurement, was two and a half minutes maximum; and when the story of the preceding night was plainly written in his trembling hands and bloodshot eyes, Murphy knew that another workday would have to be scrubbed.

Although the deadline that *Life* had set was drawing ever nearer, the Duchess refused to recognize its importance and, rather than let the Duke finish his job in peace, insisted that he observe their seasonal social migrations as usual. This required the selection and dispatch of boxes of books, documents, and other reference material, plus a supply of the Duke's favorite red ink, his "India strings"—

short red cords with toggles at the ends, which had been introduced into the Palace in Queen Victoria's time and still survived there—and the memorandum pads with the royal arms in scarlet, which he believed essential to his inspiration. During these changes of venue, which occurred every few months, all work had to stop. Peter Paul Rubens once remarked sadly, "Long experience has taught me how slowly princes act when someone else's interest is involved." Murphy was learning the same lesson.

He was also learning that though he could usually cajole the Duke into working—at long intervals and for short stretches—he could not cope with the Duchess at all. Her disruptiveness grew by the week. Fewer and fewer words were reaching paper, as more and more she resented the Duke's daily immersion in the past, and she seemed determined to allow him less and less time there. Young David Metcalfe, Fruity's son and the Duke's godson and namesake, spent an evening at the Rue de la Faisanderie house. Going in to dinner, he and the Duke brought up the rear and paused in the doorway to finish a chat about old times at the Metcalfes' place, South Hartfield House. Suddenly the Duchess called from the table, "Come and sit down! *Stop talking about the past!*" One of the Windsor servants said, after his dismissal, "She could never stand anything *old*, anything in his life before her time."

In despair that the book would ever be finished, Murphy begged Henry Luce to let him withdraw. Luce refusing, Murphy returned to the chore and served out the two more years that it took him to wind up. Dragging the last few chapters from the Duke proved far more difficult than Murphy was braced for, by reason of an unforeseen development. The Duchess, too, was persuaded that the book would never be finished. Indeed, her behavior all along had strongly implied that she did not wish it to be, perhaps because she wanted to deny the Duke the satisfaction of finally carrying something—anything—through to completion. How nomadic the Windsors' life had become is shown in the calendar of their travels that she sent to Corinne Murray from the Waldorf Towers on March 5, 1950: They were just back from Texas and Mexico, she wrote, and were preparing to leave for Palm Beach and then Canada, returning to New York at the end of April, and crossing to "*filthy* France" (as she sometimes called it) at the end of May. She added that the Duke was working on some memoirs to be published in May, but was behind schedule. (A series of three articles, based on *A King's Story*, had begun to run in *Life* on December 8, 1947; the second series, of four articles, to which the Duchess refers here, began to run on May 22, 1950.)

Scant, obviously, as was the time she let the Duke devote to his task, she begrudged him even that. She protested that he was neglecting her; that he was becoming so preoccupied with the next day's work, he no longer kept up his end of the small talk at their dinners; that he was selfishly quitting parties early, on no more valid excuse than that he needed a fair night's sleep, leaving her without an escort. Before long, in the summer of 1950, she had acquired one, a steady one: Jimmy Donahue.

CHAPTER 12
The Donahue Affair

> 'Twas not
> Her husband's presence only, called that spot
> Of joy into the Duchess' cheek.
> —"My Last Duchess," ROBERT BROWNING

> As a jewel of gold in a swine's snout, so is
> a fair woman which is without discretion.
> —Proverbs 11:22

James Paul Donahue, Jr., known to the gossip columns as "Jimmy," was thirty-four when he first met the Windsors, in 1950. It was a red-letter year for him in another respect as well: He inherited 15,000,000 dollars from the estate of his grandfather, Frank W. Woolworth, who had died in 1919, leaving 78,000,000 dollars and some six hundred "five-and-dime" stores. Jimmy was the younger son of Woolworth's daughter Jessie, whose husband had committed suicide in 1931, but whose memory she kept green in the acronym of her 350,000-dollar private car, *Japauldon*. (Mrs. Donahue liked acronyms; her house at Southampton was Wooldon Manor.) Another Woolworth daughter was the mother of Barbara Hutton, who made seven marriages, none of them to an American.

Jimmy was blond and slender, with a merry Irish smile. He was friendly; he could fly a plane; he played the piano well; and was a wisecracker. His admirers liked to quote an illustration:

Jimmy, to his chauffeur: "Where are we?"
Chauffeur: "Lexington Avenue, Mr. James."
Jimmy: "Take me over to Fifth where I belong."

* * *

Knowing that he would never have to get a job, he had never prepared for one by carrying his education further than partway through a prep school, Choate. At eighteen, as "Jimmy Dugan," he had danced in the chorus of a musical comedy, *Hot and Bothered*, which opened in September 1933 at a theatre in Jackson Heights, about five miles from Broadway, and was unable to get any nearer before it closed, ten nights later. At twenty, he had flung open the window of his hotel in Venice and shouted *"Viva Ethiopia!"* at the young Fascists below, celebrating the 1935 invasion; for this, he was expelled from Italy, but was allowed to apologize and return. When the United States entered World War II, he applied for deferment on the grounds that he was already making a major contribution to the war effort by developing an airfield in Florida; further, he had been flying with the Civil Air Patrol for the past two years. His draft board seemed to accept his arguments, for he heard nothing more until November 1944, when he was stunned to learn that he had been classified 1-A and could expect immediate induction. His appeal was refused. At 8 A.M. on the tenth, he was sworn in at the Delmonico Hotel in New York and was marched down Park Avenue with a straggle of other inductees. Press photographers accompanied the disconsolate little parade. *The New York Times* remarked, "There were none of Mr. Donahue's café society friends in the crowd apparently. He said it was too early for them to be up."

Lilli Palmer wrote, "Jimmy Donahue was a cheerful playboy who never did a stroke of work, never had a thought in his head, but knew everyone, remembered the first names of the maîtres d'hôtel of all the best restaurants, [and] was good company."[1] This was true as far as it went, but it stopped short of Jimmy's most conspicuous characteristic. His addiction to frivolity had made him well known over the years, but he was more widely known for another addiction: homosexuality, with a strong infusion of exhibitionism. Clients of the notorious Bricktop's *boîte* in Paris looked up from their drinks one night in the early 1930's to see Jimmy at the top of the stairs, nude except for a *cache-sexe* improvised from a red-and-white checked napkin; he was then sixteen—the first of the "streakers." It was common gossip that he had dared dress in women's clothes to receive his mother's good friend Francis Cardinal Spellman at dinner. This was one of his milder escapades. It was also common gossip that his family kept a lawyer on twenty-four-hour call to buy him out of his more dangerous scrapes and off the front pages.

There was, for example, the April night in 1945 when a man was found semiconscious on a street in Long Island City, with an ugly wound in his scalp. He had no hat, coat, socks, or shoes, and his trousers were back-to-front. Eventually he was able to give the police his name, address, and occupation—salesman—and to recall that he had been on a party with several men. He had gone to sleep on the floor of someone's apartment; next thing he knew, he was being shoved from a moving automobile. The police asked who the other men were. Well, one was an Army private named Donahue—James P. Donahue. Two weeks later, the case came up for a hearing. Although the victim refused to press charges, the newspapers carried the squalid story.[2] Still, such was Donahue's generosity, his blithe nature, and his unquenchable merriment that he was quickly forgiven, and it continued to be said on all sides, "Everybody loves Jimmy!"

Until 1950, he had been a court jester in search of a court. Now he found it: the Windsors'. His mother had entertained them in Palm Beach, and Jimmy had met them there. The Duke loathed what he called "those fellers who fly in over the transom." He could not mention them without making little flapping gestures and declaring, "I won't have 'em in my house!" Whenever he became especially obstinate, the Duchess would ask, "Where am I going to find stray men in Paris? If you want to fill out the table, you've got to invite the pansies!" and he would subside, grumbling. Once she added, "Don't worry. They'll fly away. And you should listen to them, because they're much brighter than you are!"[3] The Duke had a long period of coolness toward Noel Coward; even Somerset Maugham was sometimes on his black list, despite the toing and froing that continued between La Croë and Maugham's Villa Mauresque at nearby Cap Ferrat.

But Jimmy Donahue was something special. He captivated the Duke as instantly and as thoroughly as he had the Duchess—so much so, indeed, that when the Windsors sailed back to France that spring, they invited him to come along. The Duke's about-face was no surprise to other men, even the most unimpeachably masculine, who had been exposed to Jimmy's charm. One such talks about first meeting him at a luncheon in Hollywood: "I knew a lot about him and I didn't like what I knew, so I walked in with my prejudices set on hair trigger. Two hours later I walked out, convinced that Jimmy Donahue was not only the best raconteur I'd ever heard—and I've heard Jimmy Cagney and Marc Connelly and David Niven—but the most attractive man I'd ever met." Oscar Wilde, of course, had the same gift for captivating the brawniest and most hostile audience, including even his lover's father, the Marquis of Queensberry.

The voyage to France was one long giggle. The three of them had such a good time together that the party spun on in Paris through June and July, and moved to Biarritz in August. Jimmy had made himself indispensable, at least to the Duchess. He had lifted from her shoulders the burden of being the entertainer; now it was she who was being entertained, and by an expert. Simultaneously, he lifted from the Duke the burden of paying for their dinners and drinks. Jimmy was a tireless, determined host, and he fielded the restaurant bills with the hands of a Briareus. The Duchess's unconcealed liking for his company—they were on display together from noon until dawn—did not go unnoticed, nor did her open enjoyment of his quips and pranks.

Friends also noticed that the Duke was beginning to drop out of the evening's fun earlier and earlier, and that the Duchess no longer protested. It was not that the Duke always wanted to drop out, but that his collaborator, Murphy, now had to remind him that his lawyers had committed him to a full-length book, the manuscript of *A King's Story* to be delivered that summer to G. P. Putnam's Sons for fall publication—Putnam's had, in fact, already embarked on an expensive promotion campaign. As early as the past February, 1950, it had again become plain to Murphy that the Duke's aversion to work would make them miss this deadline, too. The articles for *Life* had to start going to press in the spring, presumably to be ex-

cerpted from the full-length book, and if the book draft was
not in hand by then, Murphy would have to leave the project. Throughout the association, he had been on *Life*'s
payroll; *Life* had paid his salary and expenses, while providing two researchers as well. There was no contract between *Life* and the Duke; he had not wanted to be bound
to a schedule or even to a commitment to publish. As a
result, the work had put no strain on his purse, which no
doubt helped to account for his dilatoriness. But now, with
the approaching emergency, Murphy tried to harness him
to a schedule, however light; and the Duke, moved as
much by consideration of the handsome royalties at stake
as by his contractual obligations to Putnam's, attempted to
discipline himself and cut short his partying and nightclub-
bing. A side effect of his self-reform was to throw Jimmy
and the Duchess even more into each other's company. By
the time they returned to Paris that spring, they had developed an attachment as deep—it seemed to onlookers—as,
in the light of Jimmy's known proclivities, it was difficult
to explain (unless, in her case, it was simply an attack of
the twice-seven-year itch).

There were onlookers aplenty, especially in the fashionable *boîtes* that the pair of them favored: Monseigneur,
L'Eléphant Blanc, Schéhérezade. They danced together.
They sang duets of the sentimental song hits of the season:
"La Vie en Rose" and "Autumn Leaves," "If I Were a
Bell" and "C'est Si Bon." If they did not happen to be
seated side by side, they wrote notes to each other and
passed them behind the intervening chairs, and each's lan-
guishing glance seldom left the other's face.

One evening a guest at their table, a Spanish *marquesa*,
watched the pretty byplay and had a sudden realization—
so sudden and so startling that she blurted it aloud: "Why,
they're in *love*!" Appalled, she looked around her. No one
had heard, least of all Jimmy and Wallis, locked in their
trance. The Duke was aware that their constant association
in public could not fail to invite criticism. When he warned
the Duchess, in his mild way, she protested, laughing,
"*Really,* David! What could possibly be more harmless?
Everybody knows what Jimmy is. Why, his friends call me
the Queen of the Fairies!"

He did not press his point. Perhaps his anxieties were

assuaged. Or perhaps he had been cast so often as the dashing Other Man in these domestic-triangle dramas— with Freda and William Dudley Ward, with Thelma and Duke Furness, and with Wallis and Ernest Simpson—that he could not realize that this time, willy-nilly, he was playing the passive role of the Deceived Husband. He should not be blamed for his obtuseness. Donahue was a development that had not been foreseen even by Evangeline Adams and Cheiro, for all their greater gifts.

As the summer of 1950 wore on, it became clear that the Duke had fallen too far behind with his book ever to deliver the manuscript on time. The articles had meanwhile gone to press, and Murphy's editors, their obligations fulfilled, had ordered him to wind up his service in the royal cause and return to New York, where, in their judgment, more stimulating assignments awaited him. But Murphy, having led the Duke so far down the autobiographical road, was at this point reluctant to leave the book unfinished. On the Duke's urging, he asked for and was given a short leave of absence from *Life*, and agreed to stay on in France to help write the unfinished chapters. He was buoyed but not wholly persuaded by the Duke's promise that thereafter it would be all work and no play for him until the draft was completed, with the target now set for the late fall. The Windsors' schedule called for them to return to New York in November and to begin a two-month round of social engagements. The Duke suggested postponing the trip until he had finished his job, but the Duchess denounced the idea as a discourtesy to their friends, and refused even to consider it. He now faced a dilemma: Should he let the book slide, and return with her, as his heart dictated? Or should he stay in Paris, and work with Murphy, as his conscience dictated?—and as the Duchess strongly urged. It was his *duty*, she argued, just as hers was to "show the flag," lonely though she protested she would be. The argument extended into the fall. The diversions and the distractions continued; work lagged. As the time for sailing neared, the book still unfinished, he gave in, as he always did; and when she sailed on the *Queen Mary* in November, she sailed without him.

The Duke was sanguine that the work would now race forward. "There'll be no distractions," he said, rubbing his hands. "We should wind up the job in a month or six weeks." They didn't.

The *Queen Mary* usually took five days to cross the Atlantic. On the sixth day, the Duke telephoned their apartment in the Waldorf Towers. The Duchess was not in, so he left a request for her to call back. She failed to. The following afternoon, Paris time, he called again, expecting to catch her before she went out for lunch. Their private phone did not answer. It did not answer for four days. Now he began calling at five and six in the morning, between her return from dinner and her bedtime; he was still unable to reach her. The sleepy maid who sometimes came on the line was never able to tell him where her mistress was or when she would be home. When the Duke finally caught up with her, she said only that she had been with friends, and cut the conversation short.

Three weeks of her evasiveness brought him to the edge of a breakdown. The work had been slowing; now it came to a halt. Murphy, hopeful that a change of scene might stimulate a fresh effort, suggested that they try a weekend at Fontainebleau, where Margaret Biddle had put her house at their disposal. The Duke and he drove down on a Friday afternoon. That evening the Duke was abstracted, seemingly lost in some private anxiety; he had more to drink than usual and retired early, on the excuse that he wished to look over the draft chapters that Murphy had prepared. Instead, he was up half the night, vainly trying to reach the Duchess. He did not come downstairs next day until just before luncheon; then, complaining that he was too tired to work, he insisted on touring the famous palace and its gardens. He tried to call New York again that evening, again in vain, and again all day Sunday, except to take time out for a glum picnic in the Barbizon woods. He pulled himself together for a brief stint on Monday morning, but his thoughts were plainly elsewhere, and he suddenly abandoned his narrative in favor of the subject that was consuming him: "The Duchess is very proud, you know. Very independent," he said, and went on to list some of her other qualities and characteristics. As he talked, Murphy's secretary jotted them on her desk calen-

dar, until he ran down and stopped. He tried another stint
that afternoon, but soon broke that off, too, with the startling explanation that unforeseen developments in the Korean War, which had opened some weeks before, were
threatening certain of his investments.

He said, "My friends in the British and American embassies here have warned me that Russia is secretly preparing to enter the war, and may well strike in Europe. If this
happens, I intend to be with the Duchess, as I was in the
last war."

Murphy's specialty as a journalist was military affairs.
He, too, had friends high in the American military and
diplomatic missions in Europe, and none of them had
sounded this alarm. He and the Duke had often discussed
the Korean situation, but this was the first time that Murphy had ever heard him express more than perfunctory
concern, much less a fear that it would affect his personal
welfare.

At luncheon on Tuesday, the Duke announced abruptly,
"I must return to Paris this afternoon. Something has come
up that I must deal with." He did not state what it was. He
dropped Murphy off at his hotel and went home. They did
not meet next day or the day after, though the Duke telephoned several times to express his conviction that "the
danger of another World War, this time with the Russians
or the Chinese, has become very real. I am trying to work
out a contingency plan"—a term he relished—"with the
Duchess."

On Friday morning, December 1, at seven o'clock—an
unheard-of hour for him to be about—he telephoned to
Murphy again: "I've been up all night. I've decided to sail
for New York and join the Duchess. I'm taking the boat
train for the *Queen Elizabeth* this afternoon. . . . I'm
sorry. I've got to give up the book. I doubt that people
would have paid much attention to it anyway. But with the
risk of war what it is, I must in duty join her." His voice
broke. Murphy was left with the feeling that he had hung
up hurriedly, just as he burst into tears.

Windsor had good reason to weep, not only because of
the Duchess's coldness, but because he had run out on yet
another job—and knew it. His despair was so evident that
it frightened Murphy. Might it not deepen during his five

days alone at sea, until in his brooding he destroyed himself? Murphy called him back: "Sir, I'm going with you."

The Duke, in his panicky preparations for flight, had not troubled to advise his counselors that he was abandoning the book. It was Murphy who had to perform that unpleasant task. He telephoned the Duke's lawyers in London, George Allen and Walter Monckton, and notified them of the Duke's extreme distress and the end of the project. He also telephoned the Duke's lawyer in New York, Henry G. Walter, Jr., who had drawn up the contract with Putnam's. Walter himself was alarmed by the newspaper gossip linking the Duchess and Donahue and had telephoned Murphy in Paris to ask whether the Duke knew what was being said and to inquire whether the marriage was breaking up. Murphy also notified Putnam's editor, Kennett L. Rawson, a close friend, that the Duke had thrown in his hand and that whatever small chance might remain of saving the book would depend upon the character of his reunion with the Duchess in New York.

Murphy was familiar with what the gossip columnists were writing. Friends in New York had sent him press clippings. And he also learned from a member of the household staff before that painful morning was over, what was driving the Duke to New York. On his recent return to Paris from Fontainebleau, he had found in the accumulation of mail a packet of clippings which had arrived from the United States. They had been forwarded routinely by a clipping service, addressed to the Duchess, but someone else's name on an envelope had never fettered the Duke's curiosity. As he glanced through the sheaf, which were mostly from New York gossip columns, he was startled to find that they nearly all coupled the Duchess's name with Jimmy Donahue's and reported them together in one nightclub after another. A line of Walter Winchell's in the New York *Daily Mirror* was particularly disquieting: "The Duke and Duchess of Windsor are phfft!" Providentially, no columnist reported a prank of Jimmy's that was titillating his "set" at the time: He had borrowed his mother's apartment to give one of his little dinners, for the Duchess alone. When she arrived, she found the butler and footman nude.

The Duke, already distraught enough, was also spared

more of the back-fence chatter that was printed while he was on the high seas. On Sunday, December 3, for instance, "Cholly Knickerbocker" reported in the *New York Journal-American* that "The Duchess of Windsor 'closed up' Gogi's Larue the other night. She came in with Jimmy Donahue, Elsa Maxwell and Constantin Alajélov. . . . Everybody had a roaring good time." Winchell's Monday column was the widest read of the week. On Monday the fourth he opened it with "The Duke and Duchess thing is now a front." But when the *Queen Elizabeth* docked on the sixth, the Duchess was waiting on the pier. So was the lawyer, Walter. So were the ship-news reporters, alert for indications of the rift which her bold association with Jimmy Donahue had suggested. According to *The New York Times*, "The couple denied published reports that they were estranged . . . [and] embraced for the benefit of camera men."

Other accounts, rather less cynical, interpreted the occasion as a reunion of lovers. Kindly, sentimental Louis Sobol, writing in the *Journal-American*, said that "the Duke threw his arms around the Duchess, gave her a few affectionate, even fervent smacks—seven times they kissed—and kerflooie, there went flying all those juicy rumors that the famed lovebirds had finally drifted apart. [It was] a real kayo punch to the society and Broadway columnists who had visions of fatter and fatter paragraphs about the parted pair until finally Page One would take the play from them."

Sobol went on to mention the gossip that "linked her with an innocuous youth Jimmy Donahue, never noted in the past for any particular romantic fervor." He ended, "So the laugh is on all of us who doubted and hastened into print with our snide hints. The corny moral has something to do with the inevitable triumph of true love. It's nice to have it that way."

But the staff back in Paris that had witnessed the Duke's near disintegration—the secretary who had seen his face when he opened the envelope from the clipping service; the valet who had been up with him all night, packing for the voyage; the footman who had brought him the breakfast he barely touched—all were privy to the anguish consuming his pride; and reading about the "reunion of lovers" and the "triumph of true love," they must have wondered at the American press's capacity for self-deception.

The ferocious Winchell remained unappeased. His next column ended, "The Duchess certainly put on a swell act at the dock. Tch-tch, hmf." Two days later, he snapped at her again: "The Duke of Windsor explained his prolonged stay in France, where 'I had to read proofs on my memoirs.' No more air mail, you know. . . ." And a final nip: "The Duchess of Windsor's friends are the ones who are embarrassed. The Duke is a very sad person these days."

He tried to pick up his life as if nothing had happened. A day or two after his arrival, he telephoned Murphy and suggested that they pick up where they had left off. But he still could not concentrate. The year before, Murphy had roughed out the chapters about the Prince of Wales's service in the Great War and his world travels afterward, but had put the drafts aside for revision. These were the brightest, most useful years of his life—the years when responsibilities laid on him he had met, and met well on the whole, to the pride of Crown, Church, and Government—and he wanted to focus his full attention on this account, for the sake of his eventual reputation. But now that the rough drafts had been relayed from Paris and laid before him, he would not face them. His excuse was "I don't want to waste time on things that happened so long ago." As a result, Murphy had to finish the book with only fitful help from the Duke, and it went to press with these crucial chapters skimped. The publishers offered it in two editions: trade and (at a higher price) limited, autographed. When the Duke presented anyone with a copy, it was always the trade edition; and if he was asked to sign it, he wrote his name and the recipient's on a separate slip of paper which he pasted onto the title page, so as not to depreciate the value of the limited edition. Even the copy he gave to General Eisenhower was signed thus. *A King's Story* earned the Duke close to one million dollars. He began to preen himself on it; eventually it became "my book," and one on which he had lavished unremitting energies.

A transcript of the press launching, which took place at the Windsors' apartment in the Waldorf Towers on April 16, 1951, includes this exchange:

Reporter: When you actually started writing, how many hours a day did you put on it?

Duke: I worked an average of about eight hours a day.

Yet Lilli Palmer's "Garbo and the Duke" quotes the following scrap of dialogue:

Miss Palmer: . . . Just think of your book, *A King's Story*. That's a fascinating tale and very well written.

Duke: Didn't write it myself.[4]

The transcript also includes this:

Reporter: Do you plan to stay here?

Duke: Until the end of May. Then we are going to Europe.

Reporter: Are you going alone?

Duke: I certainly am not!

The waning of the Duke's attention could be blamed partly on the fact that Jimmy Donahue was still constantly on hand and underfoot. By now he had achieved almost official status as a courtier: both a lady-in-waiting for the Duchess and an aide-de-"camp" for the Duke. His principal duty was keeping the Duchess company—and amused. Almost nightly, the three of them went to El Morocco, New York's Monseigneur—where the Duke never failed to give the hatcheck girl a courtly kiss—and when midnight fatigue sent him home, Jimmy came into his own, wisecracking, mugging, camping, telling naughty stories, and gossiping about the other patrons, all for the Duchess's delight. Next morning, the haggard Duke would make his way to the Duchess's room to assure himself of her safe return, only to be brought up short by a scrawled warning taped to her door: KEEP OUT, or STAY OUT, or DON'T COME IN HERE.

As the most conspicuous figure in the Windsor retinue, Jimmy had accompanied them down to Palm Beach late that winter, back up to New York in the spring, and across to Paris again in June. An American woman remembers an evening, that June of 1951, at the Pré Catelan, a fashionable restaurant in the Bois de Boulogne, when Jessie Donahue gave a dinner for eight in honor of the Duke and Duchess. The woman said, "This was the season that the *haute couture* sponsored the *jeune fille* look, perhaps its cruelest infliction on aging beauties. Dior's interpretation was a strapless gown, ballerina-length, in palest pastel shades, worn with low-heeled slippers. Unfortunately, both the hostess and her guest of honor had chosen this model that evening: the Duchess, very dark, very thin, in pale blue; and Mrs. Donahue, golden blond, rosy-cheeked, and plumpish, in pale pink. The orchestra struck up, and Jimmy whirled the Duchess onto the floor while the Duke led out Mrs. Donahue. Again unfortunately, she had added to her costume a pink tulle scarf, yards and yards of it, and almost at once the diminutive Duke found himself swaddled and almost smothering. He stopped dancing and fought for his breath, only to swaddle himself worse. The whole room watched his exertions—everyone, that is, but Jimmy and the Duchess. They glided on, unnoticing, lost in the dance and in each other. One couldn't help wondering—"

Not long afterward, the Windsors gave a dinner for twelve at 85 rue de la Faisanderie. The Duke's back was troubling him; after dinner he tried to switch on a lamp near his chair, but could not quite manage it. The Duchess, whispering with Jimmy at the other end of the room, came over to help him. As she leaned across him to reach the lamp, he patted her, affectionately. She stiffened, threw him a freezing look, and marched back to Jimmy, to resume their whispering.

There are several variant accounts of the incident that follows, each sworn to by a different eyewitness—some say that it, too, happened at Number 85, others that it was at the Neuilly house—but the basic facts are the same. Those present included the Duff Coopers, the Eric Dudleys, Charles de Bestegui—himself a giver of spectacular parties—the Henry Fords, and others. Donahue joined them after dinner. Bestegui spilled his cocktail on a small table and was so elaborately distressed that the Duchess, to console him, gaily mopped it with her fan of white ostrich feathers. Lady Diana Cooper thought this "a bit odd" and even odder that instead of changing the sopping fan for another, she kept it all evening. The plan called for everyone to move along to Elsa Maxwell's "semi-fancy-dress" party. The Duchess wore a blue wig with her red dress and white fan, and Lady Diana Cooper was costumed as Raphael's *"La Belle Jardinière."* Miss Maxwell had provided a very special inducement for the Duke; she had managed to engage for the evening the famous platoon of violinists from his favorite nightclub, Monseigneur. He was overjoyed, and merriment—or a reasonable facsimile—reigned for the first few hours, but around four in the morning, the Duchess, as so often, became restless. The only place to enjoy Monseigneur's violins, she insisted, was at Monseigneur itself, so everybody must hurry over there, fly to Monseigneur, the platoon of violinists with the rest.

Here Donahue came into his prodigal own. On sale at the door were flagons of expensive perfumes and armloads of expensive flowers. No one remembers how many flagons he unloaded from his pockets when he arrived at the Windsors' "usual table," but he presented four dozen red roses to the Duchess, three dozen to Lady Diana, two dozen to Mrs. Ford, and a dozen apiece to the other ladies. The Duchess called for the largest vase on the premises. When she had filled it to her satisfaction, she part-opened her ostrich fan (still wet) and shoved the handle down into the vase.

"Look, everybody!" she squealed. "The Prince of Wales' plumes and Jimmy Donahue's roses!"

One of the ladies noticed that the Duke's eyes filled with tears.

In another incident, a journalist, calling at the Neuilly house to pick up a manuscript from the Duke, heard the Duchess rant at him for littering the dinner table with his papers: "I've got twenty guests dining here in two hours! Why didn't you make this mess somewhere else?"

His answer could well have been that he *had* nowhere else. Large as the house is, he had denied himself an office in order to give her an extra room of her own. Instead, he said pathetically—and the journalist never forgot his exact words—"Darling, are you going to send me to bed in tears again tonight?"

It was the cry of a forlorn battered child to its angry nurse. She had become like that other Duchess, the one whose savagery the White Rabbit feared if he kept her waiting. Yet "Darling" or "Sweetheart" was still the way he always addressed her, and no one hearing him could fail to believe that the words were not shopworn courtesy, but coins fresh from his heart's mint. As Chips Channon had said years before, "He worships her." Wallis's love for him seemed to be faltering, but his for her was as steadfast as ever.

Jimmy was becoming bolder now. The few shackles that his behavior had worn were falling away. The Duchess, on her side, was increasingly careless of opinion; she even defied it. When they went to the Paris *boîtes*, they became oblivious to their audience, as the night wore on and the champagne took hold—oblivious even to whatever chaperoning couples the Duchess was always careful to bring with them. One of these chaperones remembers an evening at Monseigneur when the Duke left early, after buying the Duchess a gardenia from the flower girl's tray. Jimmy had bought her one, too. As soon as the Duke had gone, the Duchess snatched his flower from her corsage, flung it into the champagne bucket, and tamped it down in the ice with the bottle. Jimmy's flower she then tucked into its place. Unmanned by her tenderness, he took her hand, and they wept.

What the public surmised, the staff knew. When they came down in the morning, they would find little souvenirs of Jimmy's late snacks with the Duchess. He liked to dip his fingers in the frosting on a cake and scrawl cheerful compliments on the kitchen mirror: "DEAR CHEF WE LOVE YOU." The staff were not only shocked but astonished; they had never known the Duchess to enter the kitchen before. (The days of her personal supervision had ended at Bryanston Court.) The impudence and familiarities that Jimmy had been confining to the nightclubs, he now was bringing into the Duke's very home. His greatest impudence he was to save until they returned to New York, where he concocted a cunning scheme for persuading the Duchess to become converted to the Roman Catholic faith. His mother was one of the principal supporters of the Archdiocese of New York; and Jimmy, like his whole family, was on intimate terms with Monsignor Fulton Sheen as well as with Cardinal Spellman. Sheen, of the burning eyes and eloquent tongue, was the Church's most successful proselytizer. Among his converts were Clare Boothe Luce, whose father-in-law had been an ornament of the Presbyterian Church as a scholar-missionary in China; Heywood Broun and Gretta Palmer, journalists; Louis Budenz, a disaffected Communist; and Irvin S. Cobb's daughter, "Buffy." What would have been Sheen's most lustrous trophy, Jimmy Donahue now brought within reach: the Duchess of Windsor, whose husband as King of England had been Defender of the Faith of the Anglican Church. Jimmy introduced her to Spellman and Sheen; a desultory series of discussions began in 1951 and continued for several years. Sheen said that although he tried to interest her in a deeper love of God, she expressed no desire for conversion. Her response was tepid, but it was not negative. In short, she seems to have at least contemplated this sensational act—sensational and unprecedented, because the one explicit restraint that the British Constitution puts upon the King is that he must not marry a Roman Catholic. The former Edward VIII could not have forgotten this, yet he himself attended some of the discussions, and it had been noted that both he and the Duchess had worn a gold cross on a gold chain necklace since before their marriage.

What prompted Donahue to lay such a trap? Nothing in his character or record encourages a belief that he had in mind either the greater glory of his Church or the spiritual welfare of the Duchess. It could have been only his irrepressible mischief, a desire to cap his jester's career with this supreme iconoclasm. Finally, what induced the Duchess to take the first step down such a slippery slope? It could have been only her desire to punish the Duke for his ineffectiveness, for the boredom that pervaded her days, and for being in the way when she tried to escape it with Jimmy. Further, in punishing the Duke, she would be taking a ringing slap at the royal family. The friends who saw the Windsors in this period were aghast at the vengefulness which still was feeding on her. Still foremost

in her mind and speech was the title *manqué*. A modern
Medea, she raged at her fate, and all but destroyed her
marriage. . . .

> Marcus was the only man in the empire who
> seemed ignorant or insensible of the irregularities of
> Faustina; which, according to the prejudices of every
> age, reflected some disgrace on the injured husband.
> —*The Decline and Fall of the Roman Empire,*
> Gibbon

The Donahue Affair was now so overt that it was being
discussed in Mayfair. To the insistently circulating question, "What *can* be holding them together?" the Duchess's
partisans could offer only this weak answer: "Well, she's
an attractive woman, and he's an amusing man." The true
explanation could have come only from the principals, and
they were in New York, absorbed in frivolity and in each
other.

An example of their frivolity was the Duchess of Windsor Ball early in 1953, promoted by Elsa Maxwell and
sponsored by the Duchess herself, in aid of wounded ex-
servicemen. It was held at the Waldorf; Cecil Beaton did
the decor; and the climax came when the band struck up
"The Windsor Waltz," which had been composed especially for the occasion and included this inflammatory quatrain:

> If you wish for love warm and shining,
>   The one who's just for you,
> Surrender your hearts when the Windsor waltz starts
>   And make your wish come true,

and the Duchess entered on the arm of Prince Serge Obol-
ensky, leading a parade of Society fashion models. Although every New York newspaper would report next day
that she was wearing "a $1200 dress of white taffeta
beaded with coral," and that she had changed it twice during the evening, fewer eyes followed the lovely dresses, or
even the lovely Duchess, than were on the Duke's table,
where, grimacing and twittering, sat her *cavalier servente,*
Jimmy.

Mary Van Rensselaer Thayer, writing in the *Washington Post,* said that although Elsa Maxwell was once "a bosom pal of the Duchess's," they came to an "acrimonious parting of the ways." However, Miss Maxwell "was shrewd enough to keep telegrams and such despatched by her erstwhile friend. Among the many thus preserved for posterity, are messages requesting Miss Maxwell to invite 'the third man' to such and such a party. The third man being, of course, ten-cent-store heir Jimmy Donahue."[5]

A group of the Duke's oldest and closest friends, worried about the disgrace that threatened him, deputized one of their number to convey their alarm. He did so: "Sir, people are talking about the Duchess and young Donahue—"

They were indeed, most of all young Donahue himself, who was blabbing the spiciest details of the affair to anyone who would listen. In 1936, the Duke had summarily dismissed both Admiral Halsey and Brigadier Trotter for venturing to bring gossip to his attention; but by the 1950's his fiber had become so flaccid that his only comment to the deputy was a resigned "Anything that makes Wallis happy is okay with me." He spoke almost as if he would have raised no objection to *anything* she wanted to do. Just as absolute power corrupts absolutely, so utter infatuation seems to stultify utterly.

The Duchess, too, illustrated the truism. It was folly enough for her to have so intimate an association at all, but to have one with a braggart homosexual was reckless insanity. He robbed her not only of her reputation, but of the last shreds of her judgment. To some looking on, her recklessness seemed a raffish taunt at the Royal Family for their hostility to her. Certainly time in its passage was producing no softening on their side. When, on February 6, 1952, while the Windsors were wintering in Florida, George VI died in his sleep of coronary thrombosis, aged fifty-six, the preparations inside the family for the vast state funeral in London and Windsor pointedly excluded her. The Duke, to his distress, was obliged to sail for England alone except for an aide. It was in the company of his mother, Queen Mary, that the abdicated monarch went to Westminster to pay his respects to the brother who despairingly had taken his place on the throne. In the uniform of an Admiral of the Fleet, he walked beside his last surviving

brother, Gloucester, and the other two Royal Dukes, Edinburgh, now the Consort of the Queen, and his nephew,
Kent, behind the casket of Sandringham oak in the great
processions. He stood with them in St. George's Chapel at
Windsor when the brother who loved and had looked up to
him was laid to rest. Although his gentleness toward his
mother was marked, so too was his anguish; his demeanor
toward his other kin was reserved. He did not linger
among them but sailed for New York as soon as the ceremonies were concluded.

The sense of banishment was made even more acute to
Wallis Windsor barely a year later, in March 1953. Queen
Mary became ill. The Windsors were back in the United
States. The family was advised by the doctors to gather without delay. Once again the Palace made it clear to the Duke
that his wife would not be welcome in the family circle.
So, leaving her behind in New York, he once again crossed
the Atlantic alone, arriving in London on March 11. He
was at hand when his mother died, on the twenty-fourth,
two months short of her eighty-sixth birthday. *The New
York Times* telephoned the news to the Duchess and requested a comment. Her secretary reported that she was
"very deeply distressed. There is nothing more that one
can say on such occasions." Perhaps not. But by the day of
the funeral, enough of her distress had been dispelled to
let her join Jimmy at a nightclub. A friend saw her there
and remarked, *"That* finished *me!"* Felipe Espil should
have been present, to warn her once again. *"Ça ne se fait
pas!"*

The Windsors rejoined in Paris soon afterward, and
presently the Duke's thoughts were occupied by the approaching Coronation of his niece Elizabeth. He had ignored her father's, in 1937, perhaps from bitterness, perhaps because it would have been painful, perhaps from
simple indolence; when it took place, he was at Candé,
preparing for his wedding. But the announcement that
Elizabeth II would be crowned on June 2, 1953, caused his
emotions to oscillate widely. First he was elated; he admired Lilibet and loved her and looked forward eagerly to
being present on this grandest occasion in her life. Then he
was dejected; word reached him that his invitation to the

Abbey would not include the Duchess, and of course he would not go without her. Then he was elated again, though more mildly; Margaret Biddle was giving a Coronation party at her house on the Rue Las Cases, where she had an exceptionally fine television set, and she wanted him to come and comment on the ceremony as it unfolded. Not only that, but the United Press was offering him a fat fee for the exclusive right to photograph him in action. He accepted.

Mrs. Biddle's other guests—diplomats, ministers, and high socialites—agreed that the Duke gave the UP its money's worth. From his gilt chair in the front row, with his Duchess beside him, he identified the dignitaries as they moved across the screen. The sight of old friends drew from him a glad cry. Sometimes he muttered, "There's So-and-so! An idiot!" He joined in the hymns. When the Bahamian Guards marched past, he remarked, "They've not improved. They never learned to drill." Hervé Alphand, then the French Ambassador to NATO, and soon to be Ambassador to Washington, was triply impressed: by the Duke's evident affection for the lovely young Queen, by his familiarity with "all the details of the ceremony and all the protocol," and by how fluently and clearly he explained each stage of the long, complex ritual. He seemed disappointed when it came to an end, and the spell was broken by the entrance of footmen with trays of rattling glasses.

The embers of the Duchess's unnatural liaison with Jimmy Donahue were beginning to cool now, and a year later they would finally expire, quenched by—it was said—two circumstances. One was his mother's threat to cut him out of her will if the Duchess forsook her husband for him. The other was Jimmy's insolence, his presumption and outrageousness, which had swollen to an extent where even the forbearant Duke could no longer tolerate it. The breaking point came one evening when the three of them were having supper in the Windsors' rooms in a hotel at Baden-Baden. Something the Duchess said piqued Jimmy into a burst of temper; he kicked at her under the table. She yelped with pain and jumped up. Her stocking was torn, and her shin bled. The Duke called for the maid to fetch towels and Mercurochrome and helped the Duchess to a sofa, where he wiped away the blood and dressed the scrape. Only then did he turn to Donahue. The acid responses, pungent and searing, that the slightest lese majesty had once generated in the Prince and the King had become so diluted on his marriage that, even under this extreme provocation, all he said was, "We've had enough of you, Jimmy. Get out!"

In a few minutes, the phone rang. It was Jimmy: "Sorry, sir. I'm trying to leave on the early plane, but I can't find my valet to pack for me. He's off somewhere with yours."

This was a plight that the Duke could sympathize with. He once confessed, "I'm so ashamed of myself that I am dependent on a valet. It's terrible to have been brought up that way!"

He told Jimmy, "Very well. Good-bye."

They never saw each other again. Some months later, a friend of the Windsors met Jimmy on Fifth Avenue, back once more where he thought he belonged, strolling with a willowy youth. He had lost none of his flippant vulgarity. "Let me introduce you," he said, "to the boy who took the boy who took the girl who took the boy off the throne of Merry Old England." The word around New York was that the whole fairy queendom was preening itself on Jimmy's triumph.

A year after the final rift, the Duke broke out with a severe case of shingles. The wonder is that it had held off for so long.

In 1960, Jimmy gave 100,000 dollars to the new Metropolitan Opera in Lincoln Center, to install an orchestra lift as a memorial to his grandfather Woolworth. This was his next-to-last appearance in the press. His last was on December 7, 1966; the morning before, his mother had found him dead in his bed in her Fifth Avenue apartment. He was fifty-one. The medical examiner reported the cause of death as "acute alcoholic and barbiturate intoxication," adding, "I don't think this was a suicide."

Even then gossip would not let Jimmy rest. It was said that he left the Duchess 300,000 dollars in his will.

🏵 CHAPTER 13 🏵
The Locust Years

A life of pleasure requires an aristocratic setting to make it interesting or really conceivable.
— The Life of Reason, GEORGE SANTAYANA

Although the Rue de la Faisanderie mansion had been the Windsors' main residence since 1949, they were never quite easy in it. For one thing, it was not theirs. Its owner, Paul-Louis Weiller, a millionaire Alsatian industrialist, refused to sell, preferring to ask—and get—an extremely high rent. For another, it became too cramped, as the years passed, for the Windsors' scale of entertaining; the drawing room was large, though rather crowded with furniture, but the dining room seated a scant twenty-four, and there was no guest room at all. For a third, the Duke never liked the house; its windows were few and narrow, and the rooms were cold as well as dark; his office opened onto the garden, which made him feel on view; and he objected to the huge organ in the foyer, even though it was disguised as a bookshelf. Despite all its faults, Number 85 served them until 1953, when they finally found, in the Bois de Boulogne, near Neuilly, a house where they felt they could settle for good.

This was 4 Route du Champ d'Entraînement, a small château in its own two-acre park, complete with garages, a pair of greenhouses, a curving graveled drive, and a gatekeeper's lodge, all surrounded by a high spiked fence and screened by a hedge of rhododendrons. Number 4 is owned by the City of Paris, which leased it to the Windsors at a token rent of fifty dollars a year. General de Gaulle had lived there in 1944–45, but any traces of his austerity quickly disappeared, as a procession of vans arrived to disgorge the goods and chattels from Rue de la Faisanderie and from La Croë. An assistant decorator whom the Duchess had engaged to help her deploy them to their best advantage said, as the crates were being opened, "I could have been a rich Baghdad merchant, watching his men unload a caravan from Samarkand." When the last royal portrait was hung, and the last Louis XVI chaise sited, the last Aubusson unrolled and laid, and the last bibelot assigned its plotted position on one of the tables, the result was something between a house and a museum, more sumptuous than the former, warmer than the latter. *The Sunday Times* wrote, "The style is extremely ornate, extremely grand and in good taste." The Windsors' friend Margaret Biddle had been appointed European editor of *Woman's Home Companion* in 1952; presently she was regaling her readers with the Duchess's favorite recipes and "household hints," including this one: "She sets the ornament in place, outlines it with chalk, then removes the piece and melts candle wax around the outline. The ornament, replaced while the wax is still soft, is then secured against accidental jostling."

A first-time visitor to Number 4—once its gates had been unlocked, and he had been cleared for admission— was almost immediately given a hint of what to expect inside. There, a few yards along the driveway, stood a tall black lamppost topped by a gilded crown. Its message was clear: "This is royal property." Frequent reminders lay just ahead.

The front door opened onto a marble hall dominated by a sedan chair on the left and, on the right, a globe of the earth that seemed to just miss being life-size. Next to the globe was a broad marble console with two jets of white flowers leaping from silver vases, and between them a red box; during the final frenzy of the Abdication, it had somehow escaped being turned in. The royal arms, carved in wood, hung above the console, flanked by sconces and wooden swags. A Chinese screen loomed in the background. Near it was a pair of octagonal mirrors, five feet high. A taboret held a Creille plate with a design of scattered playing cards, the hearts and diamonds echoing the bright red of the dispatch box.

A marble stairway climbed along the left wall. Halfway up hung another splash of color: a painting by Lorjou of

peonies in a green vase. Farther up, from a staff fixed to
the balcony, hung the Garter banner that had been the
Duke's when he was King. Its silk stirred in the lightest
draft; seeing it, the visitor would have had a heart of stone
for it, too, not to have stirred. Straight through the entrance hall was the drawing room, its French windows
looking southward across the terrace and the lawn. The
ceiling was high, with a magnificent chandelier. The decor,
again by little M. Boudin, was pale French blue and silver:
boiserie, curtains, upholstery, all. A grand piano, also blue
and silver, stood in the far left corner. Above it were a
Degas landscape and a cluster of roses by Fantin-Latour.
Two full-length portraits, somewhat smaller than life, faced
the windows: Queen Mary, by William Llewellyn, and the
Duke as Prince of Wales in his Garter robes, by James
Gunn, after the original by Sir Arthur Cope. The other
paintings in the drawing room included a Utrillo, a Fou-
jita, and a Boudin view of Antibes. On one of the tables
was a miniature of George IV, after Lawrence. Three other
miniatures—of Queen Victoria, Queen Alexandra, and
Queen Mary—stood on other tables.

Small, low tables were everywhere: marble tables, lacquer tables, marquetry tables. Some were for cigarettes,
ashtrays, flowers. Others, larger, held the gold and silver
caskets, the swords of honor, the Maori greenstone war
clubs, and the silver-lidded rock-crystal inkwells that had
been bestowed on the Prince of Wales during his Empire
tours. Heirloom treasures from the Fort and York House
gleamed among them: heavy gold snuffboxes and gold
seals, all bearing the royal arms and cipher. Still other tables were reserved for the Duchess's collections of china
and porcelain; thirty-one Meissen pugs had a stage to
themselves. On an end table handy to her favorite seat in
the corner of a settee stood a miniature unicorn, gilded; it
had been given to her by Elsie Mendl, and she liked to
fondle it while she talked. The settees and chairs were deep
and comfortable, and bright with varicolored cushions;
one, in needlepoint, displayed the Prince of Wales's three
feathers and his motto, *"Ich Dien."* The visitor's impression was one of wealth and splendor under cool, firm control.

The east end of the drawing room opened into the dining room, which featured a tiny "musicians' gallery" high on one wall. The west end opened into the library; its fireplace faced the door, and from the chimney breast, overwhelming the room, glared Gerald Brockhurst's portrait of the Duchess, so square-faced and square-jawed as almost to be Cubist. Sir Cecil Beaton expressed the general opinion: "It looks *nothing* like her." A more agreeable portrait was above the settee on the right: "Assheton, 1st Viscount Curzon, with his mare Maria, by Stubbs, 1806." The Stubbs was happily bracketed by individual portraits of six Windsor pugs, arranged in two tiers of three. Recessed shelves on either side of the mantel held the Duke's books. Some dozens of them were the various translations of *A King's Story* and *The Heart Has Its Reasons*, richly and uniformly bound. Others were first editions of contemporary English authors, presentation copies, respectfully inscribed by humble servants of His Royal Highness "in the hope that—" The hopes were vain; most of the volumes were mint, unopened; "bookish he never was." Wallis Warfield's school, Oldfields, will try to "recreate" this library at its Wallis Duchess of Windsor Museum and Fine Arts Center, "so that visitors can sense first-hand the style, superb taste and life-style of the Duke and Duchess."

Upstairs were the Duchess's suite and the Duke's, with a parlor in pale tangerine overlooking the lawn. At the foot of the Duchess's bed was a chaise longue, where she had her afternoon massages; betweentimes it served as a grandstand for her kennel of stuffed toy pugs. A sofa was nearby, heaped with cushions embroidered with mottoes: "Take It Easy," "Don't Worry—It May Never Happen," "My Romance," and "British Reserve." Presumably each of them had private significance for the Windsors; they were a far cry from the childish sentiments at York Cottage—"Feed My Lambs"—and even further from the illuminated text in a room at the E. P. Ranch, "As for Me and My House, We Will Serve the Lord." Everywhere in her bedroom, on every shelf and table, were snapshots and formal photographs of herself and the Duke. The only photograph on her bed table was—almost unbelievably—one of Queen Mary. The bedroom led into a dressing room, with her costumes row on row, and some two hundred pairs of shoes. The front of the bureau was painted *trompe l'oeil*, to suggest that a chemise and a pair of stockings were hanging from the part-opened drawers.

The Duke's suite was smaller and Spartan; all it had in common with hers was dozens and dozens of photographs, and a sofa heaped with more of those mottoed cushions. One was the most enigmatic of the lot: "A Night in Cherbourg." His gallery of photographs included twenty-three of the Duchess alone, and seven of their cairns and pugs. Scattered around were miniatures of his parents and grandparents; of "Uncle Nicky," the last Czar of Russia; and of his adored "Aunt Augusta"—Princess Augusta Caroline of Cambridge, the Dowager Grand Duchess of Mecklenburg-Strelitz, who was Queen Mary's mother's elder sister and lived to be, at ninety-four (1822–1916), the last survivor among George III's grandchildren. Also in his bedroom was his desk, which his valet kept stocked with sharp pencils and crested memorandum pads, his stapler, paper clips, and his old-fashioned India strings. Behind these lesser accessories were his cigarettes and pipes. More photographs stood in the rearmost rank in military row, the file closers being his jars of tobacco and pipe cleaners and fountain pens—half a dozen of them, each with ink of a different color. The Duke often remarked that he "liked things orderly"; it upset him to find on his desk a pencil left unsharpened.

Two guest rooms and a bath were on the top floor, but they were seldom used; the Duchess's excuse for not inviting friends to stay was that "there simply aren't enough guest bathrooms." One peeress, thus turned away, reflected, "When I was a girl in Scotland, there was a single bathroom for the twelve of us."

The Neuilly house was the Duchess's domain, and she ruled it absolutely. The Duke's was The Mill. Ever since surrendering Fort Belvedere, he had wanted a country place where he could garden and spend his weekends. Almost his sole stipulation was that it be close enough to Paris for him to drive there after his daily golf, to putter around with spade and trowel, and to be back in town in time to change for dinner. His financial adviser estimates that he himself traveled 2,500 miles through the environs of Paris before he found what the Duke had in mind. The

Mill was le Moulin de la Tuilerie, a property of twenty-six acres, part arable and part woodland, about fifteen miles southwest of Neuilly, near the village of Gif-sur-Yvette, in Seine-et-Oise. The millhouse had been built in the seventeenth century; it had long been idle, but the millstream still ran past. The Duke loved it on sight, but before offering to buy it, he prudently asked to rent it for a year. The owner, Étienne Drian, the fashion artist and stage designer, was willing. Long before the year was out, the Duke made up his mind, and in July 1952 Drian accepted a price of about eighty thousand dollars.

The next step was to engage a pair of architects, one French, the other American, to do the remodeling. The goal the Duke assigned them was to reproduce in the French countryside an approximation of an English country house. His private goal was to recapture the happy years at the Fort and some measure of the peacefulness and freedom he had felt there, along with the satisfaction of making something with his own hands. The complex consisted of the mill, a barn, and several dependencies. The stone walls of the mill were two feet thick, and the hand-hewn beams were nearly so. Little more than the walls, the beams, and the old gray roof-tiles, furred with moss, were left when the architects had finished their preliminary gutting. When they finished the reconstruction, three and a half years later, they had spent 100,000 dollars more. Although the result could never have been mistaken for an English country house, or by any stretch of the imagination for the Fort, it was a joy to the Duke's heart, and he liked to tell his guests that the stairs, some of the furniture, the andirons, and many of the doorknobs and hinges had been in the Fort originally. He wanted to bring over its flagstones as well, but they proved too difficult to dislodge and transport.

The millhouse he shared with the Duchess. Her bedroom was there, all white except for the great beams waxed to a dull gold, and her vast four-poster bed, mountainous with pillows and canopied with lawn. His bedroom, across the corridor and on a different level, held only a barracks cot and a few built-in shelves for his linen. The Duchess said, "He always lived in the simplest way. I mean, he always took the worst room in the house." In addition to his favorite photographs of her, the only decoration was a collection of framed prints of the Grenadier Guards' uniforms from 1660 on.

The Duchess also "did" the downstairs rooms, assisted by a series of decorators. The entrance hall, with its floor of old, worn tombstones and its *trompe l'oeil* paintings of fruit and vegetables in mock-tortoiseshell frames, was especially effective, even though Sir Cecil Beaton found everything "overdone and *chichi*. Medallions on the walls, gimmicky poufs, bamboo chairs. Simply not good enough!" Mrs. Gilbert Miller agreed: "There was too much stuff everywhere—such a clutter in my bedroom, I couldn't find a place to put my handbag." The guest bedrooms were in a connecting wing, known as *"la Célibataire."* Any irritation caused by the clutter was soon soothed away by the cooing of the white doves on the roof, and the murmur of the millstream under the windows.

It was in the former barn that the Duke's tastes were allowed full—or almost full—expression. Its main room, more than forty feet long, he made into a sort of clubroom. Over the stone fireplace he hung a huge Mercator's projection of the earth, its seas and continents painted in, and crisscrossed with the routes of his travels as Prince of Wales. Showing it to a visitor, he would often smile and admit, "I've always been crazy over maps!" Opposite the fireplace stood the desk from which he had made his Abdication broadcast. A bass drum from the Grenadiers regimental band supplied the pedestal for a coffee table. Scattered about were small trophies and souvenirs: photographs of his family and friends, and silver cups won in hurdle races and point-to-points. The feature of the room was Munnings's striking portrait, "The Prince of Wales on Forest Witch."

The Duke's Englishness, which he had been consciously or unconsciously suppressing, now began to find its happiest outlet in The Mill's gardens. Over several years, he built two: one formal, with geometrical beds; and on a hillside across the millstream, a rock garden, casual and apparently natrual, through which he led a cheery trickle of water. With the Duchess engrossed in decorating, and with his gardens growing under his hands, the Duke felt fulfilled for the first time in years. For him, this "corner of a foreign field" would be, in the recesses of his homesick soul, "forever England."

That The Mill had a somewhat feebler hold on the Duchess's affections is suggested by a cynicism which she had had lettered on a wall there: "I'm not the miller's daughter, but I've been through the mill." True, an article that appeared in *Woman's Home Companion* for October 1954, over her signature and under the title "Our First Real Home," strikes a gentle, Darby-and-Joan note: "After living in rented houses with other people's things for so long, we've gathered together in this enchanted spot all our most cherished possessions. Like the garden we've planted here, we've put down roots." But Joan was speaking for Darby, not for herself. The Duchess found few charms in rural life. She tolerated The Mill for only two reasons: It was useful for weekend entertaining and it kept the Duke from underfoot during the forenoons and afternoons. "Roots" and all, she offered it for sale immediately after his death and was delighted when it was snapped up. In a display of sentiment rare for her, she stipulated, before signing, that the new owner promise perpetual care for the little cemetery where are buried so many of the Windsors' dogs.

As chatelaine of two large houses, the Duchess finally had a stage worthy of the entertainments she had been impatient to produce—entertainments fit for a king, or at least an ex-king. Moreover, she had carefully put together a staff of servants entirely capable of carrying out whatever orders she gave them. The butler, Ernest Willemotte, was English, as all good butlers are; but the cornerstone of the household was the chef, a Frenchman, as all good chefs are. René Legros, who was said to be one of the four greatest chefs in the world, had come to the Windsors from the Spanish Embassy in London, whence every other embassy and every great family had longed to recruit him. Legros had four helpers: an assistant chef, a pastry chef, and two kitchen boys. Under his headmastership, the Duchess's kitchen became a famous chef-school; one of his graduates went to Douglas Dillon, U.S. Ambassador to France, 1953–57, another to the British Embassy in Paris, a third to the Shah of Persia, and a fourth took over Legros's post

when he retired. The butler also had a second man: Sidney
Johnson, a Bahamian Negro whom the Windsors had
brought with them from Nassau.

The housekeeper—the *lingère*—Anna, had been with
the Duchess since before the war. Anna also had her staff:
four housemaids, in addition to the two personal maids
who took care of the Duchess's clothes, drew her bath, and
turned down her bed. The Duchess never failed to inspect
the table before lunch and dinner, and the guest-room
beds. Before they were made, and even after a nap, the fine
linen sheets had to be pressed flat, without crease or wrin-
kle. The rest of the inside staff included the comptroller; a
private secretary for the Duke and one for the Duchess—
hers was Denise Hivet, a former Air France stewardess—
and the Duke's valet, Campbell. Total, eighteen.

Campbell's duties also entailed putting the three pugs—
Disraeli, Davy Crockett, and Impy (short for "Imperial")
—out for their nightly relief; and, if the Duke himself
was not at home, leaving a report, such as "Dizzy 1, Davy
2, Impy 1." If the Duke, returning, read that any dog's
performance had been unsatisfactory, he or a footman
would take him out again. Despite the Duchess's fastidi-
ousness, the dogs were never completely housebroken.

It may have been the recurring memory of little Slipper's
tragic death at Candé that persuaded the Windsors to give
up cairns in favor of pugs, or perhaps a love of pugs was in
the Duke's blood. Queen Victoria had one named Bully,
and Queen Alexandra wrote to thank someone for giving
her "that *darling* puggy . . . simply *adorable* . . . a
black-faced angel." The Windsors made the changeover
gradually, by way of a Scottish terrier named Thomas.
Their Christmas card for 1952 carried sketches of Thomas
and Disraeli; with Trooper and Minoru, "Dizzy" was one
of the first pugs they owned. Palm Beach society paid a
touching tribute to Minoru: The day he died, a dinner for
the Windsors was canceled out of sympathy. All their pugs
were males. They once considered buying a bitch, but decided that her presence might "upset the old gentlemen."
There was a time when they had four of them, all dressed
in collars made like wing collars, with bow ties. Pugs became a Windsor "logo," like FDR's cigarette holder and

Churchill's cigar. At the Duke's death, his favorite, Black Diamond, was by his bed.

The two chauffeurs, Ronald Marchant and David Boyer, both Army veterans, had charge of the four motorcars: a Humber sedan, a Buick sedan, a big Buick station wagon (with THE DUKE OF WINDSOR in metal letters on both front doors), and a Cadillac limousine which had been modified to the Duke's specifications—a sliding pane behind the chauffeur, smaller windows for privacy, and a roomier rear compartment—without charge, compliments of Alfred P. Sloan, Jr., then chairman of the board of General Motors. Boyer's French wife, Germaine, was gatekeeper at the Neuilly house and doubled at the switchboard. The outside staff at Neuilly also included four gardeners, who tended the lawn and the greenhouses. Five more gardeners stayed at The Mill, along with another gatekeeper. Total, thirteen servants; grand total, thirty-one.

King George V once said, "To get things properly done, one ought to provide a man and a half for every job." His eldest son accepted his counsel in this regard at least.

The inside staff were called by their first names, the outside by their last. Early one morning, as Boyer was driving the Windsors home from a nightclub, the Duchess asked, "What are you having for breakfast, David?"

Lack of sleep had fuzzed Boyer's wits. He answered, "Quite frankly, ma'am, I never take breakfast."

The Duchess snapped, "I wasn't speaking to *you!*"

Again, one afternoon at the Saint-Cloud golf club, the Duke was sitting on the tailgate of his station wagon, changing his shoes, when he heard someone behind him call impatiently, *"Viens ici, David! Tu as fini ton pipi!"* Astonished, the Duke turned, and was relieved to find that a small dog was being summoned by its owner.

The larger the organization, the larger the rear echelon in logistic support. The Windsors' vast staff consumed vast supplies, plus the time to fetch them and to serve one another, and to keep the household machine humming. The Duke constantly complained about the backstairs over-head: the "staggering" bills for their electricity, petrol, food—"We feed them far too well! *Far* too well!"—and even for their soap and toilet paper. When the Windsors were in residence at the Waldorf Towers, the secretary,

butler, valet, and maids who accompanied them were allowed $2.50 a day apiece for their meals—barely enough
to buy coffee and a sandwich. The secretary indignantly
supplemented their pittances from her own pocket, although she could ill afford it. The comptroller said, "The
Windsors never grudged how much they spent on themselves, but the household costs brought out their fear and
fury—fear that they might be going broke, and fury at the
staff's 'extravagance.'" Wages included, the cost of running the establishment varied from 125,000 to 150,000
pounds annually. The figure would have been considerably
larger but for two reasons:

First, the wages the Duke paid were some 20 percent
below the scale prevailing in Paris. English servants drew
top pay, French next, then Spanish, with Italians at the
bottom. The butler, for instance, received 50 pounds a
month (about 140 dollars), the chef, 60 pounds; the valet,
between 50 and 60 pounds; the French secretary, 50
pounds. To be sure, the butler's pay was tripled and even
quadrupled by his commissions from the wine merchant;
and the chef's by commissions from the butcher, the fish-
monger, and the greengrocer. When the great Legros took
over the kitchen, his wages went up to 100 pounds, and his
commissions to 300 and even 400 pounds, depending on
the extent of the Windsors' entertaining. The valet and the
secretary had no access to commissions. At Christmas,
members of the staff received an extra month's pay, under
French law. Each of the men was given, in addition, a bill-
fold or a pair of cuff links with the royal cipher; and each
of the women, a cashmere sweater or some nylon stockings, which were then in short supply.

The comptroller who did the hiring was instructed to
justify his offer of substandard wages on the grounds that
the honor of serving the Windsors was a compensation in
itself, and that the training received under their roof was
tantamount to a guarantee of higher wages elsewhere later.
Another placebo was the Duke's promise, often repeated to
the senior servants, that those who stayed on would be
handsomely rewarded in his will. Several times during his
last years he called in Sidney, Boyer, Anna, and Marchant
to assure them that the promise still stood. Indeed, he and
the Duchess were given to dropping frequent—and appar-

ently casual—remarks that *all* their money would be the
staff's. The intoxicating prospect was lent additional po-
tency by the obvious absence of heirs on either the spear or
distaff side; and annual visits by the London solicitors to
review the wills were construed belowstairs as further evidence of the testators' benevolent intentions.

The staff's glittering future did not wholly blind them to
the drabness of their present—the exhausting hours and
heavy demands of their working day. Tongue-lashings,
harsh and overt, were routine; holidays were ignored, as
was overtime; nothing earned praise or seemed to give satisfaction. As one result, the turnover was high, though res-
ignations—far less dismissals—received only the meagerest
severance pay, if any. When a resignation threatened, the
comptroller always urged against it and warned, "Remember, you may be sacrificing your place in the will!" A kid-
ney disorder brought on by long vigils outside Paris nightclubs forced Marchant to resign after more than twenty
years' service. He received no pension, and his parting present was a mere few thousand francs. The other chauffeur,
Boyer, stuck it out for twenty-seven years, only to be
sacked on less than a week's notice, along with his wife.
Both brought suit in 1979 for "wrongful dismissal."

The second reason that the Duke was able to economize
on his household expenses was that, thanks to Walter
Monckton's early negotiations, he continued to enjoy diplomatic status and its many attendant privileges and envi-
able fringe benefits. War, occupation, and the rise of the new
Republic had left his "perks" undisturbed. He bought his
whiskey, gin, tobacco, numerous household staples, and
petrol through the British Embassy and military commis-
sary, duty-free, along with his toilet staples. His television
set, the electric mixers, and vacuum cleaners also came in
duty-free, as did his fleet of motorcars.

Still, these privileges, being subject to review by the
French Government of the hour, were by no means immutable. They could be curtailed or even withdrawn entirely, as Windsor learned to his dismay in 1954, when
Mendès-France rose to power. By then the number of for-
eigners sheltering under the Tricolor, and paying no taxes,
was becoming a national scandal. Among them were ex-
Emperor Bao Dai of Indo-China, the Aga Khan (who

never paid taxes anywhere), ex-King Michael of Romania, assorted Russian grand dukes, and, of course, the ex-King of England. Single-handed, Michael might have halved the tally of ex-monarchs if the fast car he was driving had not narrowly missed a crash with the Windsors' Humber one afternoon on the Riveria. The Duke remarked sourly, "Too damn many ex-kings around here!"

More than any other French party, Mendès-France's Socialists, being socialist, resented the fact that the stream of taxes which these titled freeloaders should have been pouring into the French treasury was actually no more than a trickle. They decided to take action. Presently word flew among the group that *agents fiscals* were sniffing at their bank accounts. Windsor was more vulnerable than the others; he was probably richer and certainly more conspicuous, and he had been indiscreet in boasting about his profits on the New York and Canadian stock exchanges. He was also acquiring his francs through what he called "the free market," others called "the black market," and the French "*le marché parallèle.*" Suspicion could hardly help falling upon him; but happily his French lawyers were able to allay it, without publicity, and the good life at the Neuilly house and The Mill continued unabated.

True, the Duke did exhibit a certain caution in his black-market dealings. Instead of going in person to keep the weekly rendezvous with the Swiss bagman, usually in some backwater bistro, he prudently sent one of his staff. Here, the Duke's checks for dollars having been deposited in a Zurich bank, the agent would receive in return dozens of packets of fresh French bank notes, wrapped in a newspaper. These would then be used to redress the Windsor balances at the Morgan Bank, to the increasing alarm of its officers, who begged the agent to have the Duke at least make some substantial dollar deposits to help them account for the continuing heavy inflow of francs. The Duke dismissed their suggestion; he saw no reason why he should be penalized by the French Government's "ridiculous" inflationary policies; and he continued his unofficial dealings in "the free market" until 1959, when De Gaulle's return to power stabilized the franc and ended the game. The agent, now long retired, sometimes looks back on the days of his Paris operations with a sense of glory lost. "They told me," he once remarked proudly, "that I was the biggest operator the free market had, although Margaret Biddle was a close second."

It would border on lese majesty to accuse the Duke of chicanery. As Prince and King, he had always done what he wanted. No tiresome nonsense about exchange rates had been allowed to intrude on him then; why should it now? Moreover, he was impelled toward these "parallel market operations," as he called them, in order to spare himself more of the "little belt-tightenings," into which he was being forced by the Duchess's headlong extravagance. With her it was not a matter of mere soap and toilet paper, but of silks and sapphires and Ming. This was something the Duke could not understand. As a youth, he had been ridden on a tight financial rein; when his father finally slacked it, he was thoroughly broken; he had no temptation to squander—the reverse, indeed. For all his dapperness, even in his last years his wardrobe was stocked with made-over hand-me-downs from his father and grandfather; the materials were so durable that fashion wore them out first. The Duchess, too, had known a tight rein in her youth, but with this difference; her rider had been not discipline, but necessity. And when her rein was slacked, she bolted—straight to Cartier, Van Cleef, Mainbocher, and Jansen. All are famous houses, but none is famous for its bargain basement. Their accounts with the Duchess totaled half a million dollars or so a year.

The Duke was not wealthy by Onassis-Niarchos standards, and even less by those of the Texas "big rich" who were beginning to invade his life; but neither was he poor by any standard. The fortune he had brought from England was still almost intact, since he had made no major property purchases except The Mill and the Duchess's jewels. Indeed, thanks to judicious investments, it had increased to something between 3,000,000 and 4,000,000 pounds—sums which should have yielded him, on a conservative basis, an annual 150,000 to 200,000 pounds. Against this, the Windsors' total annual outlays were running about double. It was the Duke's horror of "dipping into capital" that drove him to such compensatory economies as his cheese-paring with the staff and his dealings under the financial table.

He saw nothing petty in the first and nothing unbecoming in the second. To be sure, his royal faith that rank has its privileges was not his alone in the household. The valet, Campbell, shared it. One of his duties was to put a bottle of Scotch in the Duke's dressing room before the evening bath, so that his master and mistress could nip at it while they were dressing. Just before the Duke went downstairs, he would pencil an inconspicuous mark on the label at the level of the contents. When he was safely at dinner, Campbell would return upstairs to put away the clothes and lay out the pajamas. This done, he would reward himself with a dollop from the Duke's bottle, erase the mark, and make a fresh one, identical, at a new and considerably lower level. Boyer, the chauffeur, said in admiration, "It was beautifully organized!"

It was *all* beautifully organized, and no part better so than the Duchess herself. Only her maid ever saw her before ten-thirty in the morning, when her breakfast came in, with the newspapers. She would merely glance through the ones in English, knowing that the Duke would catch anything of importance or special interest; she gave more time to those in French, knowing that he would not read them at all. When she was done, she would have skimmed off enough information on enough topics to let her hold her own at luncheon and dinner. "I've always been a great skimmer," she said; it was a habit she had acquired during her early years in London, to beguile her loneliness.

Sharp at eleven-thirty, the Duke was admitted for her morning levee. Usually he had some comments on the news, but they had to be kept brief, because of her impatience to give him his orders for the day, along with those for passing on to his side of the staff: Boyer to take the chef to market (the chef was now Lucien Maisy, a graduate from Legros's school); Marchant to pick up a package at Dior; there'll be twenty for dinner tomorrow, so tell Georges (the butler, who had replaced Ernest) about the wines. Who ran the house was no more in doubt than that she ran it with a brisk, executive efficiency.

Often, of course, the Windsors dined at a friend's or at a restaurant. The Duke did not care for Maxim's and the Tour d'Argent; they were the most celebrated tables in town, but also the most expensive. He preferred Laurent, the Grand Véfour, Fabien, and Paul Chêne, where the charges were slightly more moderate, though only slightly. His favorites, especially if he was the host, were two bistros: the Petit Montmorenci and the Coquille.

As soon as the Duchess had dismissed the Duke from her command post, she turned her attention to Lucien. She would ring him on the house phone, to remind him how many they would be that evening, discuss his suggestions for the menu, and make sure that their final selections were harmonious, even in the finical respect of color.

"Chefs are curiously color-blind," she once wrote. "Leave them to their own devices, and you may end up with an all-rose dinner—Crème Portugaise, Saumon Poché with Sauce Cardinal, Jambon with Sauce Hongroise, and Bombe Marie-Louise."[1]

Whatever else might appear on the menu, it was not soup. One of her firmest rules was "Don't start a dinner with soup! It's an uninteresting liquid that gets you nowhere."

These conferences with Lucien never included a compliment on the dinner he had prepared the evening before, or any other evening; or for any of the staff for any service; or even any thanks, ever. This was the staff's most enduring grievance. A woman who had served the Windsors for ten years said this: "It was impossible for either of them to express gratitude. Their servants were made to feel that they were anything but indispensable—the Duke and Duchess were doing them an honor by having them around."

By one o'clock, she would be up and dressed, and the Cadillac would be waiting to take her to her luncheon engagement at some chic restaurant like l'Espadon at the Ritz, or to some friend's. She rarely lunched at home with the Duke; she is quoted as having said, "I married David for better or for worse, but not for lunch." She ate lightly, as always. Luncheon at a friend's would often be followed by cards—bridge, gin rummy, or canasta—though the gambling game she most enjoyed was craps. "What a pity," she once sighed, "that the French are too stiff and hidebound to get down on the floor and 'roll dem bones'!"

If a dress collection were being shown, especially by one of her favorite couturiers—Dior, Balmain, Rochas, Mainbocher, or Givenchy—she would drop in, sure of a front-row seat—and of a discount of at least 25 percent on everything she bought. She was also sure of being on the annual list of the Ten Best-Dressed Women. She never set a style, unlike her friend Elsie Mendl, who sponsored the "little white gloves"; and unlike the Duke, who sponsored the Windsor knot, the backless evening waistcoat, and the double-breasted dinner jacket. The Duchess's specialty was an elegance so simple, so subdued, so neat, that it could have been achieved only after expert tutelage and at great expense. Her chief tutor was Mainbocher; when he had brought her taste and judgment to maturity, she began venturing to request minor modifications—a collar narrowed, a button removed, a belt raised—even in a design by one of the masters. Dior once complimented her on a linen dress she was wearing. He said, "I don't often admire clothes from other *ateliers*, but this is something special!"

The Duchess corrected him: "It's not from another *atelier*. It's from yours—only you made it for me in velvet, and I had it copied in linen. Simpler, more informal."

No one but an innocent, to be sure, would give weight to *taste* as a qualification for the Ten Best-Dressed. No suburban matron, assisted only by her *taste*, however fault-less, and her own little sewing machine, ever won election to those exalted ranks. The fact is, it is not a matter of election at all, but of *appointment*—by the *grands couturiers*, in appreciation of the sums spent among them by their more prodigal clients. The Duchess was one. Professionals trained to make such appraisals estimate that her wardrobe cost her not less than 100,000 dollars a year, including her furs, which came from Maximilian, of New York. Moreover, the share of the 100,000 dollars that went to Dior, say, was only a fraction of the total that she brought him, for she had only to appear in a chic, attractive Dior dress for the house to receive orders for perhaps six hundred just like it. Other *maisons de grand luxe* —say, Porthault—also benefited from the stimulus of her patronage.

That 100,000 dollars was the *net* cost of her wardrobe, it must be realized. The gross cost was considerably more; but she had arranged for a small private agency associated with Dior to resell such of her clothes as had gone out of style or lost her favor. Still, 100,000 dollars a year for one woman's clothes! Possibly there are wives who would consider this outlay extravagant. The Duchess did not; she was living up to the role that the Duke wished her to play—the most admired woman on view. Most women dress for other women; the Duchess dressed for the whole public— to be looked at, admired, and envied on all sides. The severe simplicity of her costumes was an artful background for the eye-catching magnificence of her jewels. "When people looked at me and stared, I rather liked it," she said, "and it pleased the Duke."

She did not enjoy the public stare from the start. She once said, "When we were first married, if I went to a shop to buy a yard of pink ribbon, I was likely to come out with three yards of red ribbon. The people who crowded around to look got me so flustered, I couldn't remember what I wanted and I just took anything to get out. The Duke, now, *he'd* go into a shop, and no matter what he wanted to buy, he'd take hours buying it and he wouldn't care if five thousand people were watching him."

Dudley Forwood remembers escorting her to call on various English residents in Paris when the Windsors first moved there: "She was beautifully dressed, as always, but she was blazing with rings, earrings, brooches, bracelets, and necklaces, and almost stooping under their weight. I said, 'Ma'am, I wonder if you aren't wearing a few too many jewels?' She said, 'You forget that I am the Duchess of Windsor! I shall never let the Duke down.'" As Kin Hubbard wrote, "I don't know of nuthin' better'n a woman if you want to spend money where it'll show."

If she happened to have one of her almost daily appointments with her hairdresser, chiropodist, and masseur, she would be back home at half-past five. Before going upstairs she would inspect the vases of flowers in the reception rooms and the dining room, brought in from the greenhouses for that evening's party. She knew flowers—her favorites were lilies—and how to arrange them; it was another art she had learned in China. Cecil Beaton remembers being in her house when a large basket arrived from Paris's best florist. "It didn't suit her," Beaton said, "so she pulled it apart right there and put the flowers together again, differently and marvelously improved."

The hairdresser she went to was the famous Alexandre, of the Rue du Faubourg Saint-Honoré, who owned much of his réclame to her early sponsorship; the one who came to her was his former assistant, Édouard. As a girl at boarding school, she had begun parting her hair in the middle, Madonna-style, and had never changed. (Thelma Furness was another who favored this coiffure; Windsor seems to have had a special fancy for twice-married American women with Madonna coiffures, and with their current husbands in the shipping business.) Many considered that the Duchess's best feature, second to her eyes, was her high, wide, square forehead; this coiffure set it off to good advantage, and helped convey an instant impression of poise and intelligence.

At seven in the evening, she faced probably the most taxing decision of her day: Which of her seventy to eighty evening gowns would she wear? and which pieces of jewelry with it? Once the gown was chosen, choosing among her two hundred pairs of shoes became comparatively simple. Dressing, speeded with the help of the two maids, but slowed by the Duke's chatty little interruptions, took an hour or more. The final result showed it. When she went downstairs to await her guests—and to look over her dinner table before they arrived—she was perfection in the "exquisite propriety" of her appearance.

"Her style of dress," Daphne Fielding wrote, "was based on classical simplicity of line and, with her trim figure, clear complexion and spick-and-span American grooming, she was capable of eclipsing more beautiful but less *soignées* English roses, who in her presence looked like croquet mallets beside a polished arrow."[2]

CHAPTER 14
Life in Limbo

It don't make any difference how rich ye get
   to be,
How much yer chairs and tables cost, how
   great yer luxury . . .
Home ain't a place that gold can buy or git
   up in a minute;
Afore it's home there's got t' be a heap o'
   livin' in it.

—"Home," Edgar A. Guest

People usually enjoy doing what they do conspicuously well. The Duchess of Windsor entertained well and beautifully, and she enjoyed it. "I *like* giving parties," she said. "I *like* dressing up." She once told Jack Aird at a ball, "I spent four hours getting ready for this, and David insists on being home by midnight! Let's push on to a nightclub!"

A guest going to his first dinner at the Neuilly house could hardly help being awed as—punctually at the specified eight forty-five—he was admitted to the entrance hall, dimly lit by candelabra and heavy with incense. The marble console on the right now held a visitors' book, open, and the butler stood by with a pen, to make sure that everyone signed it. The chairs and settees in the drawing room were clustered for conversational groups. One would already be forming around the Duke, more often than not in his evening kilts or in tartan trews, and black velvet slippers embroidered with gold crowns on the toes; and another around the slim, trim Duchess, who might be wearing purple velvet, square-cut at the neck and tiny in the waist, with a magnificent choker of amethysts and turquoises, and matching earrings.

Windsor parties were notable for their mixture of personalities: nobles and aristocrats with painters, statesmen, writers, and self-made multimillionaires. The reason for the mixture, and for the frequency of the dinners, was that the Duke could not bear to be alone; he had to have a variety of people around him as bodyguards against boredom. The Duchess's article in *Vogue* paid this tribute to a friend of hers: "For bringing together all kinds of people in a gay, airy but flawless setting . . . I have never known anyone to equal Lady Mendl. She mixes people like a cocktail—and the result is sheer genius."[1] Lady Mendl could have returned the compliment with equal sincerity and truth.

On this evening in the middle 1950's, the company might include the British Ambassador and Ambassadress to the Quai d'Orsay; Prince and Princess Dmitri Romanoff (the former Lady Milbanke) and his cousin Prince Yussupoff, who had conspired in the assassination of Rasputin (and was married to Czar Nicholas II's niece, Princess Irina); Cyrus Sulzberger, of *The New York Times,* and his Greek wife, Marina; Count and Countess Czernin, of the Austrian aristocracy; Margaret Biddle, who had begun maneuvering for an appointment to the American Embassy; the Philippe de Rothschilds; the Supreme Allied Commander in Europe, Gen. Alfred M. Gruenther, U.S.A., and his wife (and later their successors, Gen. and Mrs. Lauris Norstad, U.S.A.F.); Jacques Prouvost, publisher of *Paris Match*; Pierre Lazareff, publisher of *France-Soir* and *Le Journal de Dimanche,* and his wife, Hélène, editor and publisher of *Elle*; and Count von Bismarck, and his beautiful, much-married Countess (originally Mona Strader of Louisville, Kentucky, she was successively Mrs. Henry Schlesinger of Chicago, Mrs. James Bush of New York, Mrs. Harrison Williams of New York and Long Island, Countess von Bismarck of Paris and Capri, and Countess de Martini of Rome). Maurice Schumann might be there; as a young journalist, he had covered the Windsors' wedding and was now on the verge of a brilliant career as Foreign Minister, a Senator, and a member of the French Academy. Another Frenchman often present was Gaston Palewski, a man of such brilliance and charm that the ladies pouted to see him, knowing that after dinner the Duke would surely monopolize him for a private chat. M. Palewski directed General de Gaulle's staff in 1942–46, and helped found the Gaullist Party in 1947; since 1974, he has been editor of *Revue des Deux Mondes*.

John F. Kennedy dined at Neuilly once, when he was a Congressman and before his marriage. The Windsors had never liked his father, who, as Ambassador in London, had consistently disparaged Britain's prospects during the war; but they liked the son. The Duchess said, "Out of a litter of nine, there's almost bound to be one good pup."

An occasional guest was Sir Oswald Mosley, the former British Black Shirt leader, and now an exile in Paris like the Duke himself. The Windsors admired the Mosleys; the Duke often said, "Tom would have made a first-rate Prime Minister." And the Mosleys admired the Windsors; Sir Oswald's autobiography ridicules "the stiff absurdity of the English ruling class [at the time of King Edward VIII], when they rejected any form of [his] marriage with an American of beauty, intelligence, charm and character."[2] But having the Mosleys to dinner meant that no one from the Embassy could be invited at the same time. Indeed, when Sir Gladwyn Jebb, later Lord Gladwyn, was Ambassador (1954–60), he ruled that if a member of his staff found himself at a table with Mosley, he had to make an excuse and leave. At one dinner, the Duchess suddenly turned to Christopher Phillpotts, then Counselor of the Embassy, and asked, "What would you have done if you had found Sir Oswald here?"

Phillpotts told her, "You are clearly familiar with the instructions in the Embassy circular. You know very well what I'd have done."

The Duchess laughed. "I give you high marks for your candor!"

Generally, the Windsors rubbed along smoothly with their Embassy, especially when Duff Cooper had it; and most of the ambassadors were scrupulous about accepting and returning their invitations. Still, there was always that awkwardness about "His Royal Highness" and "Her —er, Highness," as prescribed by the Foreign Office. The American ambassadors usually followed suit, for fear of offending their British colleagues; but at least one, Wallis's old friend from Bryanston Court days, Bill Bullitt, who had the Embassy when they first set up house in Paris in 1937, refused to withhold her "Royal" either in address or on her place card. Anne Lindbergh saw the Windsors at a dinner of Bullitt's in February 1938, and wrote of the Duchess, "Although she is not beautiful, she was easily the most distinguished-looking woman [of the thirteen] in the room, but most formal, stiffened by dignity." The Duke struck Mrs. Lindbergh as "a bit peaked and bored." The Duchess, she went on, told Colonel Lindbergh that they had moved to Paris because "so many of the Duke's friends had to go so far to see him [in the South of France]. . . . (C. [Charles Lindbergh] said he immediately thought maybe nobody *was* coming to see them!)"[3]

Footmen in scarlet livery circulated with trays of highballs, martinis, sherry, and champagne; they were offered twice, no more. The Duchess said firmly and often, "Forty-five minutes of drinking before dinner is *quite* enough!" After that, the butler bowed to her and announced, "Your Royal Highness, dinner is served!" She never liked to seat more than ten at one table, so this evening there were two, she presiding at one, the Duke at the other. The settings were identical: flat silver with Meissen handles, crested linen and crystal—always four glasses at least—and towering silver candelabra with her ivory-colored candles, the flames multiplied by the mirrors. At every place was an antique silver snuffbox, holding cigarettes. The food and wine deserved the elegance of the table; the Duchess and the chef had seen to the one, the Duke and the butler to the other. Lady Diana Mosley has written that the Windsors' dinners were "the perfection of perfection"; Douglas MacArthur II agreed: "They were probably the best on the entire postwar Continent." The Duchess preferred serving Bordeaux ("the best wine for conversation") to Burgundy ("deadly to the liver"); her own favorite was a Traminer. The Duke drank wine chiefly to be companionable. He had no real palate for it; besides, he was waiting for the brandy. Both of them ate sparingly; to the ends of their lives, they made a fetish of keeping thin.

The Duchess did not need Bordeaux or any other stimulant for her conversation. Her talent for light talk and for kindling it, for drawing out even the shyest guest, for bringing a table to life—as brilliantly practiced by Elsie Mendl, Emerald Cunard, and Elsa Maxwell—was what had awakened the Duke's interest when he first went to the Simpsons' flat in Bryanston Court. He once said, "Wallis taught me that life could be fun." One of her tricks for keeping the talk going was to switch her conversational partner with each course, thereby forcing the whole table to switch.

"But one mustn't be too obvious about it," she warned. "It's disconcerting to find a grimacing countenance suddenly turning in your direction, its robot-like action saying, in effect, 'Here's the fish, and here am I!' "

If the party was small enough for her and the Duke to be at the same table, she would maneuver the conversation toward the fields of contention where his opinions lay cocked in friendly ambush, for he liked to "drop little bombs," usually political. As Prince and King, he had been barred for so many years from expressing any political opinions whatever that as Duke he jumped at every chance to let people know exactly where he stood.

He could chatter away breezily and, for the most part, sensibly on a variety of topics, excluding arts and letters, yet he knew almost nothing about the royal genealogy much beyond Queen Victoria. She could trace a minor German dukedom back into its dim past; so could Queen Mary. But when Princess Dmitri, sitting next to Windsor at dinner, remarked to him, "Your Stuart ancestors—" he interrupted angrily, "I haven't got a drop of Stuart blood in my veins!"

Surprised, she made bold to inform him exactly how much of it he had and exactly where it came from: He was James I's nine-times-great-grandson.

Again, when Lord Beaverbrook persuaded him, for a handsome fee, to lend his name to a book about George III and the Hanoverians, and the ghostwriter, J. Bryan III, brought him the manuscript for approval, he listened to the chronicles of the four Georges and their connections with mounting surprise and horror.

"I had no *idea* they were like that!" he cried. "Why, they were dreadful people! *Dreadful!* I can't possibly sign it!"

It was useless for the hapless Bryan to protest that the reality was far worse, that he had palliated or ignored many of the Georges' more heinous crimes, cruelties, adulteries, and follies; Windsor only repeated plaintively, "I had no *idea!*" Yet he remembered clearly his great-grandmother Queen Victoria—"Gangan"; and *she* remembered sitting on her uncle George IV's knee, and kissing him at his request, and it was "too disgusting because his face was covered with grease paint."

The eighteen guests at this dinner might represent half a dozen nationalities. If one of the Duke's partners was German or Spanish, or if she was fluent in either language, he would rattle along with her through the whole meal, ignoring his other partner. He preferred speaking German to English and prided himself on his mastery of the soft, "cozy" Viennese accent. But if his partner was French, he made little effort to use her language. He considered German and Spanish masculine languages, and French feminine. Behind his disinclination may also have lain a confession that his father once made to him: "I was brought up to be a sailor, so I never learned anything more than schoolboy French. Maybe that's why I always feel *ashamed* when I have to speak the damn stuff!" Windsor's French was far better than "schoolboy." He had a firm grasp of the grammar, and his vocabulary was rich enough to support him even in a political argument, but his accent was atrocious—perhaps deliberately so, to keep the French at arm's length. He liked to quote an exchange with one of his gardeners:

The Duke: *"Qui est-ce qui vous êtes?"*
The gardener: *"Je travaille pour le Duc de Windsor."*
The Duke: *"Mais c'est moi, le Duc de Windsor."*
The gardener: *"Pardon, monsieur, mais je ne parle pas anglais."*

The Duke chose an Alsatian to be his head gardener at The Mill, so that they could discuss their plans without hobbles, in German.

His favorite brandy was a Forge de Sazerac, more than seventy-five years old when it was bottled. It gave him an almost voluptuous pleasure to cup the *ballon* in his hands and swirl the brandy while it warmed. With it went an Upmann cigar the shape and approximate size of a torpedo. When the United States broke off relations with

Cuba in January 1961, the Duke had a modest supply of Upmanns stored in his Waldorf apartment and at the New York Dunhill's; but the supply being unreplenishable, he resorted to an economy which he enjoyed revealing to his close friends. Charles Murphy, who had called to pay his respects, was thereby given a cherished memory. It happened in New York. The Duchess being elsewhere for the evening, the Duke had invited him to the Waldorf Towers apartment for a quiet dinner alone. When it was over, the footman, Sidney, brought in a handsome mahogany humidor of Upmanns, virgin in their aluminum tubes. Murphy refused, explaining that he had recently stopped smoking.

"Ah," said the Duke, "in that case, Sidney, take away Box A and bring me Box B."

Now Sidney brought in another humidor, no less handsome except in its contents: a ragged collection of part-smoked butts. As the Duke rummaged among them, Murphy could only conclude that after each had expired, it had been thriftily salvaged and the smoked end snipped off for a subsequent relighting. The Duke, seeing his astonishment, wrinkled his nose and whinnied with pleasure. "These are desperate times," he said, "and desperate times demand desperate measures."

As he tugged first at the cigar, then at the brandy, his seamed face would begin to smooth out, and his tired eyes to sparkle. His chair became a throne; he would settle back in it, legs crossed, and discourse with increasing confidence on the affairs of the day. He was King again, for this mellow hour. Only an impatient summons from the drawing room would bring it to an end.

If the Windsors were having dancing after dinner, as they usually did in the 1950's, the drawing room would have been cleared, an orchestra would be tuning up and additional guests arriving. As soon as the music began, the Duke began waving his arms to the beat and "conducting" with an imaginary baton; sometimes he imitated the motions of a violinist or a cellist. He liked to dance and hum along, but he preferred taking a turn at the drums. The Duchess loved to dance; she was graceful and light on her feet, and she enjoyed wriggling through the Twist and swooping through a tango. Between dances, footmen of-

fered champagne and highballs. Smaller parties would be
entertained by a nightclub star—a singer or a pianist. The
Duke made a point of keeping up-to-date on the latest romantic song hits. His favorites were those from *South Pacific, Oklahoma!*, and *Annie Get Your Gun*; he played the
recordings over and over, and when he had the lyrics by
heart, he sang them in his light baritone. If the party was
both small and intimate, he might persuade the Duchess to
join him in singing their favorite Viennese waltz—the one
about the small hotel "where the night is so short, and the
day comes so quickly."

Noel Coward's biographer, Cole Lesley, has written this
about a dinner at the Windsors' in 1959:

> The Duke was in a party mood and sang to us in
> German and then in Spanish . . . then made some of
> us cluster near the piano and sing "Alouette," and
> "Frère Jacques" as it should be sung, as a round.
> When the music changed, the Duke unexpectedly
> went into a solo Charleston and called out, "Come
> on, Noel!" Noel faced him and the two of them
> danced the Charleston of their youth in the 'twenties,
> each egging the other on as they remembered all the
> variations. The Duke's face became boyish again with
> his enthusiasm, his still slim figure youthful, the
> whole picture clearly recalling at moments the days
> when he had been the idol of the Empire. Next, of
> all things, he suggested a sailor's hornpipe, which
> they danced merrily enough, again remembering the
> different movements of the dance one after the
> other.[4]

Windsor's lifelong antipathy toward homosexuals had led
him, as Prince of Wales, to cut Coward in public, and
Coward nursed his grievance for nearly twenty years. He
had been heard to remark that the Prince had "the charm
of the world, with nothing whatever to back it up";[5] and
when, just before the Abdication, Winston Churchill asked
a luncheon table why the King shouldn't be allowed to
marry his "cutie," as Churchill and Beaverbrook referred to
Mrs. Simpson, Coward snapped, "Because England doesn't

wish for a Queen Cutie."[6] But the old rancor had blown away by the late 1940's, and thereafter Coward dined with the Windsors often.

Anyone was welcome to sing or play the piano or do card tricks. Maurice Chevalier, a frequent guest, could always be counted on for a song or two. Those who failed to volunteer were sometimes dragged onstage. One elderly gentleman remembers his surprise at finding himself leading a conga line, which he did "with all the grace of a Pullman porter setting up a deck chair." He added, "There was never anything stuffy about the Windsor parties!" Both the Duke and the Duchess enjoyed parlor games, especially the more elementary quizzes. He liked to match his knowledge of American data against that of his American friends. He had the sequence of presidents complete and correct and he could rattle off all the states and their capitals. The Duchess's only "stunt" was an impersonation of the Duke—his accent, his gestures, his way of inhaling a cigarette; she was perfect in the role. Host and hostess were quite willing to keep things going until the last diehard was ready to leave; neither wished to be alone. Often the Duchess herself was the diehard, and would insist on transferring the remnants of the party to a nightclub. One of the Duke's favorites was Ciro's on the Rue Daunou, but he was happy in any of them where the orchestra would grant his request for German songs—even inconsiderately soon after the war—and let him troll along. The *patron* of Lucas-Carton, on the Place de la Madeleine, had been an active member of the Resistance and was less than pleased, one evening in 1945, to hear the Duke, who was dining there, loudly talking in German. Around three in the morning, his head would be nodding with fatigue, his pale eyes bleary and blinking, his dinner jacket strewn with cigar ash, and the Duchess would allow him to take her home. It was small wonder that the household was almost never put in gear again before ten o'clock in the morning, when the Duke rang for his breakfast.

For all the care and thought that the Duchess devoted to her parties, in her attempts to surround the Duke with the dignity and splendor of the Court affairs that he would never see again, she could not quite bring it off. One reason was, the only court she really knew was Bryanston

Court, where, as here, entertainment was a pastime and nothing more. It had no deeper purpose and substance, unlike the Court of St. James where the dinners, the levees, the balls, all had for their end the recognition of achievement, the bulwarking of tradition, and the exercise of venerable ceremonials. Any participant in a Court affair took away a lasting memory of having witnessed—even shared in—something majestic and authentic, centered around the meaning of the monarchy. This the Windsors' little court at Neuilly could not hope to match. The golden hours spent there were fairy gold, fleeting; and little memory of them, except the look of things, survived the morrow.

The Duchess was doomed to fail also because her court centered not around a monarch, but the shell of one. The Duke was quite incapable of occupying himself with anything useful, or even with anything at all. His "workday"—a term he adopted after he started on his book—began with the newspapers that came up with his breakfast tray. He took the London *Times,* the *Telegraph,* and the *Express* for British political news; the Paris *Herald Tribune* for American news and the New York stock-market quotations; and *Figaro* for French news. By the time he had finished them, Campbell would have drawn his bath and laid out his clothes. He dressed slowly, wandering from bedroom to bath to dressing room, stopping to fiddle with the trinkets on his bureau and desk, and to straighten one of his photographs of the Duchess. His toilet was usually completed by eleven, and although he hated to resume his "workday," the mail awaited his attention. Reading the letters usually took fifteen minutes; answering them took rather less. A holograph letter of his is a rarity. When he was a youth, his parents had required him to write to each of them once a week. There were also other occasional "Duty letters"—to his sister and brothers, to his numerous aunts and uncles, to cousins near and far, together with thank-you letters at Christmas and on his birthday, all by hand in full. The result of this labored correspondence was that in his maturity he had to drive himself to handwrite even the shortest note.

The mail done, it was time for him to report to the Duchess's bedroom, to get his orders for the day and to learn her schedule. His own schedule seldom included anything more than an engagement to play golf or to have his hair cut. The Duchess was almost always out for lunch, the Duke almost never. Among the pleasures of an active man's working day is lunch with a friend or an associate, to talk business, to exchange ideas, or merely to chat, and so to break routine. The Duke, with no business and with few friends whose company he enjoyed, lunched alone, on a slice of cold meat and a salad. On golfing days, he had only the salad, and sometimes not even that. The Bruce Lockhart diaries record a golfing lunch when the Prince "ate some prunes and drank water."

In Paris, one of his golfing companions was Ambassador Malik of India, a bearded and turbaned Sikh popularly known as "H.S." At Palm Beach, his usual foursome included Christopher Dunphy, Charles Cushing, and "Doc" Holden. He was never quite at ease on a Palm Beach course, until Dunphy arranged an honorary membership for him at the Seminole Club. Previously he had been known to refuse an invitation with "No, no, no! I couldn't afford it! It costs ten dollars a round there." The fee would prey on his mind all through the match, and compete for his attention with *head-down* and *stiff-left-arm*. For the same reason, he never played for more than two dollars Nassau, and preferred to play for one dollar. Seminole became one of his four favorite American courses; the others were on Long Island: Piping Rock, The Links, and The National. In Paris, he liked to play Saint-Cloud on weekdays and Saint-Germain-en-Laye on Sundays.

Many courses confronted him with hazards that did not trouble ordinary players. Often, when he had driven, a souvenir-hunter would pop from behind a bush and make off with his ball. Similarly, his laundry seldom came back intact.

His stance and grip were normal; his swing was smooth, except for a tiny hitch at the top, and his follow-through was thorough. His basic trouble was that he had neither the leverage nor the strength to hit a "big" ball; the longest drive he could manage was about 150 yards. Despite the thousands of pounds he had paid Archie Compston and other professionals for instruction, and the thousands of hours he had devoted to practice and play, and the thousands of divots he dug out of the lawn at Neuilly, and despite his handicap of 18 in America and only 14 in Europe, his average score stayed in the high 90's. Sometimes he succeeded in breaking 90; and, rarely, 85. In 1928, he shot an 81 against James Braid, five times British Open champion; and on one red-letter afternoon at Biarritz in 1962, when he dodged every hazard and sank every putt, he shot a glorious, never-to-be-forgotten 75. Chris Dunphy, who was playing with him, says that "He went back to the Hôtel du Palais that evening singing!"

The Princess de Réthy, ex-King Leopold's wife, told Cyrus Sulzberger that the Duke's game was "pathetically bad," but that he was always eager to win, and tended "to forget his score."[7] Leopold added unkindly, and probably unjustly, "Once I saw David take three shots in a trap, then give himself a five." No one else ever brought such a charge against him.

One of his golfing friends said, "No question, he was *mad* about the game! He loved it less than he loved the Duchess, but—this is a considered opinion—more than money. If you wanted to give him a present he'd really value, give him his putt. He preferred teeing off at two-thirty, but he was quite willing to play at any time, in any weather." Bruce Lockhart also records a game when "it came on to rain cats and dogs, but [the Prince] insisted on finishing the round." He was pleasant to play with, all agree. When his partner or an opponent made a good shot, he was quick to praise it; when he himself made one, he merely grinned. His bad shots he ignored; he never excused them or cursed them, and he disliked hearing another player curse.

His idol was Ben Hogan, who won the British Open once, the P.G.A. twice, the Masters twice, and the U.S. Open four times. Not only did the Duke, along with a multitude of other golfers, consider him the greatest player in the history of the game, but the short, slight Hogan was an inspiration, living proof that one didn't have to be a Hercules to become a champion. Proud as the Duke was of that 75 at Biarritz, he was even prouder of having scored three holes-in-one over the years, whereas, he liked to point out, the otherwise incomparable Hogan had scored only one. The three balls he had used, he mounted on little pedestals and kept in his bedroom at Neuilly. They

were Ben Hogan balls, of course, and his clubs were Ben
Hogan clubs. After his death, his putter, a Ben Hogan
"Sinker," and a pair of his golf shoes were sent to the
World Golf Hall of Fame at Pinehurst, North Carolina,
for permanent display in its "Heads of State Gallery."

The act of loosening his muscles on a golf course failed
to have a sympathetic effect on his purse strings. The caddies at many French courses are women, often elderly. To
ease a caddy's load, a player may rent her a pull-along
trolley for a few francs. Not the Duke, one of his foursome
remembers; his caddy had to shoulder the bag and trudge.
When the match was over, the same player, an Englishman, saw her flip the tip the Duke had given her—one
franc, then about a shilling—and heard her mumble, *"Il
n'est pas très généreux, votre ancien monarque!"* The
player, embarrassed, was about to give her a few coins
from his own pocket when it occurred to him that if the
other caddies saw him, all those whom the Duke had
short-tipped after previous matches might "storm me,
clamoring for *their* supplement, to my bankruptcy."

Although Windsor scrupulously obeyed the rules of golf
(Leopold to the contrary), he tended to ignore the rules of
the course, at least to the extent of sometimes bringing
along one of his dogs. An American friend remembers a
hot afternoon at The Links when the Duke suddenly noticed that the pug lurching down the fairway behind him
seemed about to collapse. He broke off the game at once
and rushed the dog to the hopsital. Other members of The
Links were divided between the dog-lovers and the stick-
lers for the rule barring dogs from the premises.

For years his standard golfing costume was a Fair Isle
pullover and plus fours: after World War II he changed to
a turtleneck sweater and slacks. He also changed to nine-
hole matches; not only were they less exhausting, but they
allowed him, when he was in Paris, to finish his tea, which
he always brought with him, and still have time for some
gardening at The Mill before dark. On cold or rainy afternoons, when there was neither golf nor gardening, he
would telephone to his banker in Zurich or to his investment counselors at the Morgan Guaranty Bank in New
York. His judgment of the state of Western civilization was
colored by the behavior of the stock market. If it was

buoyant, so were his spirits, and all was right with the world. But if it was depressed, so was he. He liked to chart each stock in his considerable portfolio from one trading day to the next. He bought a set of ledgers and a small adding machine, and at the end of a trading day, he could usually be found "in his countinghouse, counting up his money." His bankers and brokers, with their computers, could have supplied the figures out of hand, but the Duke preferred to make his personal calculations. As the years passed, investments became his favorite topic. After dinner, he would steer the talk toward Wall Street. If the guests included corporate executives or—better still—bankers, he would sound out their opinion on the market's prospects, and fish for a good tip. Oils and mining stocks, especially gold, had a strong attraction for him. The growth of his fortune to somewhere between twelve million and fifteen million dollars at his death argues that he was a shrewd investor.

One of his most respected advisers was Charles Allen, of Allen & Co., a prominent New York financial house (no connection with the Charles Allen who was Wallis's second stepfather). Allen said, "The Duke was very alert about finance and day-to-day affairs—very up on them. We briefed him on several of our companies. For instance, he became an early investor in Syntex [pharmaceuticals] and did well in it." Another adviser was Robert Young, of the New York Central, whom the Windsors first met at Newport and through whom they first went to Palm Beach. These friendships—perhaps "understandings" would be more nearly accurate—worked to mutual advantage: One hand washed the other. In return for a financier's promising tip, Windsor would play golf with him, dine with him, even stay at his house, to the elevation of his family's social status.

Thus, when Clint Murchison, the Dallas capitalist, came to Palm Beach, and Young introduced him to Windsor, the appreciative Murchison put them both into Canadian Delhi (oil and natural gas), from which Windsor made more than half a million pounds. The three of them then set up a trip to Mexico, where Young hoped to sell rolling stock to the national railroads, and Murchison to acquire the mineral rights to certain offshore properties. The former King of England served as such impressive window dressing in the negotiations that Murchison, who was in the process of organizing a Canadian corporation, would have appointed him chairman of the board, if the Toronto moneymen had not jibbed at accepting so patent a figurehead. But Murchison in turn jibbed at Windsor's proposal that he drill for oil on the E. P. Ranch.

Considering the violence that Windsor did to monarchical traditions—the gadding about, the ephemeral enthusiasms, the want of serious purpose—he was surprisingly fixed in certain of his habits and tastes. The high point of his day was his seven o'clock appointment with himself—one which he never broke. It was unalterable; nothing was allowed to cancel it or intrude on it, advance it or retard it. As the minute hand rounded six-thirty, his attention wandered; he became restless, drummed on the table, leapt up to roam about the room, his ear alert for the rumble and squeak of the butler's serving cart, and the tinkle and clink of its cargo. The Duke was no braggart, but there was one boast that he made again and again: "I never take a drink until seven o'clock, *never!*"

Sharp at five to seven the serving cart was wheeled in, and from that moment on it was touch-and-go whether the Duke would jump the gun and breach his rule. He never did; but when seven struck at interminable last, he would sprint over, snatch up his bottle of St. James's Scotch whisky, and, hiding his glass behind the cart, pour himself a drink that was appropriately king-size. A guest would be offered a drink, too, of course, but some were favored, unknown to them, with a less expensive brand. A quarter-hour later, it was time for a second round. And at half-past seven, now jocund and refreshed, he went up to dress for dinner, and further refreshment from the bottle in the dressing room.

He had his sports clothes made in Rome and some of his "business" suits in New York; but since boyhood, all his evening clothes and most of his suits had come from Davies, of Hanover Square. His father wore his trousers creased down the sides, long after the Edwardian style had become outmoded, and he insisted that his son's be worn the same way. Davies remembers how shame drove the young Prince to order extra trousers with each suit, creased fore and aft, to wear when he was beyond his father's purview. He did this until the "new" fashion finally won acceptance at the Palace. To be sure, the Prince had sartorial idiosyncrasies of his own, including "horse-blanket" tweeds so bold that—someone remarked—"he'd have to wear two pairs of trousers to get the whole pattern in." His haberdashers, Hawes & Curtis of Burlington Gardens, grieve to recall that his evening shirts—the stiff ones—had to be made with soft French cuffs, and his neckties lined so as to produce a "knot like a pudding," in their disapproving phrase. On the other hand, they also recall, and happily, his orders for "three or four dozen shirts at a crack," before leaving on one of his Empire tours.

Dunhill supplied his cigarettes, small and short and specially blended, and also his tobacco, "Yacht Club," packed in little cartridges of yellow-brown paper, of caliber to fit his pipes. He enjoyed the elaborate ritual of swabbing out the pipestem, reaming the bowl, tamping in the fresh charge, and getting it to draw smoothly. Nervousness made him smoke too much; he had acquired the habit at Oxford, and the Great War confirmed him in it. When his mother and father reproached him, he explained, "It calms me." The Duchess also tried to make him stop. A nonsmoker herself, she used to challenge him, "Why must you always have something hot in your mouth?" She doubled her efforts when he developed a chronic cough, but it was too late then, both for him to swear off and for arresting the throat cancer that would kill him.

He was fussy about trifles like the "pudding" knot of his tie and the set of the flower in his buttonhole. He would tug at the knot again and again, until the Duchess burst out, "There's nothing wrong with your tie! For heaven's sake, let it alone!" Her own nervous habits were "teasing" her back hair, repeatedly pursing her lips, pressing her cheeks upward between her palms, and fondling the little gilded unicorn.

He was gallant with women, quick to compliment them, to pull up a chair for them, to snap his lighter for their cigarettes. His hip gave him constant pain during his later years, so he used to carry a shooting stick to rest on between golf shots. One of his golfing partners remembers

him offering it to a woman waiting on a tee at the Deep-
dale Club, on Long Island, despite the discomfort he would
have to endure. He attached great importance to respect
and good manners; any infringement of his dignity or the
Duchess's, any presumption of intimacy made him distant.
At the same time, he resented and often rebuked even a
hint of obsequiousness. Another of his golf partners remembers him telling an overly attentive waiter at Saint-
Cloud, *"Vous êtes trop fidèle!"*

He was rarely profane and never obscene; he never told
an off-color story and he expected the same restraint from
others. If anyone except an old friend spoke of "Wallis," he
became visibly cool; and hearing her called "Wally" froze
him; he himself referred to her only as "the Duchess" or
"Her Royal Highness." Although his signature to even an
informal note was always "Edward P," with the bottom
line of the *E* slashed under the whole name, he was not
"the Prince" to himself, but "the Dook." When he rang up
a friend, he always began, "Oh, it's the Dook—" At the
end of his life there were left fewer than a dozen of his
relatives and friends who were privileged to address him as
"David": the Queen Mother, the Gloucesters, Dickie
Mountbatten, Olaf of Norway (his first cousin), Leopold
of Belgium, and of course Freda de Casa Maury and the
Duchess.

❧ CHAPTER 15 ❧
Her Book

The Windsors always had a bad press. The newspapers
were determined to emphasize the emptiness of his life
in order to point the obvious moral.
> —A Life of Contrasts, DIANA MOSLEY[1]

A scandalous story began to circulate in the Windsors'
world in late 1951. Its details varied from tattler to tattler,
but the basic facts were always the same:

Barry Bingham, the publisher of the *Louisville Times*
and the *Courier-Journal*, learned that the Duke and Duchess of Windsor were coming to the Kentucky Derby, and
invited them to the dinner party that he and Mrs. Bingham
were giving afterward. The Windsors replied, through a
secretary, that they would accept on two conditions: first,
the list of other guests must be submitted for their approval; second, no one might arrive at the dinner after
them or leave before them. The Binghams agreed, the party
came off—and a fortnight later, the Windsors sent their
host a bill for one thousand dollars, as their fee for being
present. In some accounts, the fee was five thousand dollars. In some, the Windsors had demanded the right to approve the menu, too. But this is the essential story that was
whispered from Newport to Palm Beach, and in the course
of time from Mayfair to the Lido.

It is a lie, of course—a whole-cloth fabrication, utterly
false in every respect, except that the Windsors had indeed
gone to the 1951 Kentucky Derby, and had indeed dined
that evening with their old friends the Binghams. Mary
Bingham was a cousin of the Duchess's on the Montague
side, and Barry's father, Robert Worth Bingham, had been
American Ambassador to the Court of St. James's in
1933–37.

A companion canard says that the Windsors paid their bills with painful slowness, if ever; yet one of the Duke's tailors has testified, "His bills were paid promptly, practically on receipt of invoice. If there had been any question about his credit, I would have known." Another item from the slander file had him in the receiving line at a Baltimore charity ball, smoking a cigar. Still another had him always insisting, when dining at someone's house, that the Duchess be seated on his right. (But it is true that if the flowers and candles on the table screened her from him, he would ask to have them moved.)

How did these ugly stories get started? And why did they start? The explanation is obvious. Whereas Edward Prince of Wales had been the most admired and adored young man of his time, with the possible exception of Charles Lindbergh, Edward Duke of Windsor had become a rather ridiculous, mildly contemptible, and half-forgotten figure. The chambermaids' press still tried to preserve the illusion that the affair which had cost him his throne was "the greatest love story since Antony and Cleopatra," but people wouldn't buy it; they remained interested, even fascinated, but disapproving. Windsor's inglorious career in World War II, his and his Duchess's coddled, sterile lives, and their unabashed egocentricity did nothing to redeem their reputations. The Donahue affair added to the general shabbiness. Though few were aware how close the Duchess's folly had carried her to irretrievable disaster, few would have rejected almost any gossip about her and the Duke, however far-fetched and derogatory—the Bingham dinner, for example—so tarnished now were their names.

The Duke forgave her for Jimmy, of course; he would always forgive her everything. But he had to prove to the world that the bargain he had made in London and sealed at Candé was worth it. As he once told an American friend, "There are millions of people who want us to have made a mistake." When he surveyed his possible courses for regaining public favor, he must have seen that the most obvious would be to abandon some of his conspicuous extravagances and devote the savings to a worthy purpose. Instant second thought persuaded him that his straits were not so desperate as to require measures so extreme. The third thought was the Duchess's: Why not consult Henry and Clare Luce? They were highly intelligent, and were not only their friends, but their neighbors in the Waldorf Towers. So Mrs. Luce was invited to tea, and the Duchess stated her problem. "Our publicity has been *frightful!*" she said. "The Duke is worried sick! What can we do?"

Mrs. Luce promised to think about it, and left. She was back within minutes. "I have it! Why don't you adopt a British war orphan, a boy? You might even name him 'David Windsor.'"

The Duke nodded approval. "But, of course," he said, "the boy wouldn't inherit any of my titles. My brother has seen to that!"

Mrs. Luce said, "That's not important. The important thing is that the adoption would remind the English people of your love for England."

He asked the Duchess, "How do you like the idea, darling?"

"It's silly!" she declared. "Who knows how an orphan will turn out? He might turn out as stupid as Harry Gloucester. In any case," she added, "the Palace would fix it for Prince Charles to get all the attention."

So much—it proved—for Operation Orphan.

The next idea was the Duke's: Let them present themselves as patrons of the arts. Forthwith, in September 1956, they announced from New York the establishment of Windsor Awards, Inc., to "make it financially possible for young artists to enjoy the stimulating experience of travel, and to exchange with contemporaries abroad their ideas, theories and techniques."

The first awards would go to a French and an American artist to be selected by a jury, but the program would eventually be broadened to include other countries. The American artist was duly selected and handed fifteen hundred dollars for a year's study in Paris. He was never heard of again. Nor was Windsor Awards; like Operation Orphan, it sank without a trace.

Now it was once more the Duchess's turn, and this time she came up with a plan which was carried to successful, if painful, completion: It was to supplement the Duke's autobiography with her own, making sure that her life and her role in the Abdication were presented as favorably as possible. For her collaborator, she chose—at the urging of her husband and their lawyers—the same Charles Murphy who had helped the Duke. Murphy had meanwhile returned to *Fortune*'s board of editors after a tour of duty in the office of the Chief of Staff of the U.S. Air Force. Understandably, he was less than enthusiastic about subjecting his work habits afresh to the Windsors' demoralizing regime; moreover, he doubted the Duchess's readiness to apply herself seriously. Before accepting the contract, he made three conditions: first, that her account of her divorce from Ernest Simpson would be straightforward; second, that the Duke's dealings with the Nazis would not be glossed over; and third, that she would not use the book as a rostrum from which to berate or ridicule the Royal Family. The Duchess agreed, and contracts were signed—with a newspaper, the London *Daily Express*; an American magazine, *McCall's*; and a book publisher, David McKay, of New York—for guarantees totaling 700,000 dollars. Murphy took a year's leave of absence from *Fortune* and joined the Windsors in Paris in November 1954.

All went smoothly at first. The Duchess's "workday" began at eleven, later than the Duke's, but it suffered fewer interruptions. The Duke sat in on most of the interviews and discussed and even "edited" the pages as they were being drafted. Murphy had decided to postpone the childhood chapters until the last, reasoning that the book would be judged primarily by how honest and complete were the Duchess's accounts of her two previous marriages, of the Prince's courtship, and of her conduct during his brief reign and the Abdication. By May 1955, thanks largely to her unexpected candor and the easy flow of reminiscence, the first draft was two-thirds done, and Murphy had hopes of meeting their October deadline. But then a strain developed—two of them. The tone of the draft was more serious than the Duchess wished; she had changed her mind about her proper place in her times; the new picture of herself that she had resolved to project was that of the charming leader—eternally youthful, eternally gay—of what would soon be called "the jet set." She saw herself as the ingenue star of a perpetual light opera. Indeed, one of her favorite tunes was Rodgers and Hammerstein's "Younger than Springtime"; she and the Duke hummed it constantly; for a while it was their theme song. A secretary said, "The Duchess liked to be with young people, as if their youth could rub off on her. She couldn't grow old gracefully. She couldn't slow down. She kept pressing."

The second strain was less of a surprise. She began hinting that, after all, the book was an ideal opportunity—and one not to be missed—for exposing the Royal Family in what she insisted were their true colors. Murphy, certain of the Duke's support in this decision at least, irritated the Duchess by ignoring her hints and by expressing skepticism at some of her more improbable "recollections." As she told the story to Clare Luce, he had fallen into the irksome habit of interrupting her from time to time with "Oh, come, *come*, Duchess!" Murphy does not recall these particular offenses but he does recall a rejoinder, quickly regretted, to her accusation that he had "an old mind":

"But Duchess," he protested, "this is a case of sixty calling fifty antique," which was the difference in their ages.

Whether for his seeming indifference or for something else, she fired him, though not until she had engaged a substitute writer, one not only a happy chronicler of the jet set, but eager to promote her to its leadership. He took over the draft, and work resumed—or so the prospective publishers thought, as did the Duchess, who presently sent a gay cable to Corinne Murray, signed "Authoress." But when another four months had passed, and the publishers asked to see a sample of the new collaboration, they were dismayed to learn that little progress had been made, and that the little was mostly an unsatisfactory account of her Baltimore background. In their consternation—the deadline was looming—they sent a delegate to Paris, charged with warning the Duchess that unless Murphy were brought back, the contracts would go down the drain, and with them the 700,000 dollars.

The Duke now faced the embarrassment of telephoning Murphy, who had returned to his desk at *Fortune*, and asking him to take up again. Reluctantly, Murphy did so. He had to complete the draft at a breakneck pace that permitted little reflection or revision, but the deadline was met; *The Heart Has Its Reasons* was published in the spring of 1956, and the 700,000 dollars saved, although—

as Earl Wilson of the *New York Post* quoted from "a prominent figure" at the Duchess's "champagne-and-caviar book-launching" at the Waldorf—"This babe didn't do it because she needed scratch."

Considering the malice in her mind, her book was surprisingly mild in effect. There was no mockery of the Royal Family, no upbraiding, no bitterness. Not the least of her revelations was the gently phrased letter that she had sent to Queen Mary from Nassau, in the hope of persuading that obdurate old lady to end the estrangement from her eldest son, for his peace of mind. It drew no answer. The suppression of the Duchess's ill will had no visible effect on the Palace. If anyone there ever read her book, no sign was given. Their interest could hardly have been fanned to white heat by the London *Times*'s review, which said only, *"The Heart Has Its Reasons* carries the memoirs of the Duchess of Windsor from her childhood in Baltimore to the present day" [2]—twenty-two words, of which five were the book's title. By then, of course, nothing that she said or did mattered to the Palace greatly. King George VI had died five years before; Queen Mary's death would follow in a year; and young Queen Elizabeth II, much as she admired her famous uncle and deplored the gulf between them, had no intention of bridging it— certainly not while her implacable mother was alive.

Yet, candid as the book was in most respects, it was not altogether so in three. The Duchess followed the Duke's lead in ignoring old flames; she failed to give Jimmy Donahue even a footnote, despite the five years when he was the focus of her most ardent thoughts. Again, she was evasive about just when she and the Prince of Wales had decided to marry, and how they had broached their intentions to Ernest Simpson. And she was less than honest in steadfastly maintaining that the title "Her Royal Highness" meant nothing to her. The truth is, it meant everything. Without it, she would always feel half-clad and cold in the presence of her warmly wrapped sisters-in-law. It was a fox in her vitals, gnawing at her pride. She had been brought up to believe that the Warfields and the Montagues were as wellborn as any families in America, so denial of the title was an insult she could never forget. To the very end she refused to accept that it was withheld not because of her American birth, but because of her two divorces and the fact that the Royal Family considered her—as Queen Mary had indeed branded her—an adventuress.

The hollowness of her disclaimers was again revealed soon after she had put them on paper. Walter Monckton and George Allen had come to Paris with their wives and were dining with the Windsors. Lady Monckton described the imbroglio that presently occurred:

"It was the only time I ever saw Walter really angry. Halfway through dinner, I caught him glaring at me with such a face of thunder that I wondered if I'd said something tactless. The moment we rose from the table, he told me, 'We're leaving!' and we left at once. What had happened was, the Duchess—he was sitting next to her—had wheeled on him and lashed out with 'You got yourself a title, but you didn't get *me* one!' [He had been created First Viscount Monckton of Brenchley in 1957.] Walter growled at me, 'This from *her,* after all I've done for the Windsors!—selling Sandringham and Balmoral, and getting the money out of England for them, and persuading the French government to let them live here without paying taxes!' Oh, he was *furious!*"

The Duchess did not often let her temper slip, except toward her husband, but a second instance occurred at another dinner in Paris, this one given by the Duke of Verdura in honor of former King Umberto of Italy. According to Chips Channon, "It appears [Umberto] arrived 45 minutes late, and omitted to apologize to the Windsors who by that time were hungry and cross. The Duchess was stung into saying half-jokingly, 'At least we weren't kicked out—we went of our own accord!' King Beppo was not amused."

The continuing quarrel over the lesser title, after the Duke had given up his own—the most refulgent in all royalty—discloses perhaps more than anything else how distorted their sense of values had become. The Duke's inability to carry the point with his younger brother was further proof to her of his growing ineffectuality. She no longer bothered to conceal her exasperation, as in this exchange overheard at Neuilly:

Duchess: "David, come here a moment."

Duke: "Just a second, darling! I have something on my mind."

Duchess: "On your *what*?"

Duke (apologetically): "I know, darling. I haven't much of a mind."

On the occasions when her exasperation approached open contempt, it wounded him; his ineffectuality deepened; he wept in front of her. That it was harder and harder for him to make a decision, and harder yet to act on one, became pitifully clear to his friends when Fruity Metcalfe died, on November 18, 1957, age seventy.

For nearly forty years, he had been Jonathan to Windsor's David. As his widow said, "Whatever happened, Fruity went on loving him." Her "whatever" covered a great deal: the King's failure to make Fruity a member of his household when he came to the throne, or to give him any honor at all; his failure to arrange for Fruity to draw pay as his equerry; and—most notably—the abandonment in Paris in 1940. Now Fruity was dead. His son David telephoned the news to Paris: "Sir, my father died today."

"That's terrible!" the Duke said. "Terrible! I must tell the Duchess, tell the Duchess." He seemed rattled. "When is the funeral?"

"Sir, it will be held shortly, with a memorial service in a week or so."

"I must attend, of course. I must attend. But I won't be coming to London for a month—"

When David Metcalfe reported this to his mother, she said only, "Your father would want the Duke to be there. We'll have to postpone the memorial service until he can come."

He found he could come on December 3. By permission of the Queen, the service was held in the Chapel Royal, where Lady Alexandra had been christened and married. The Duke turned up in a costume which David Metcalfe remembers in detail. Instead of the formal morning coat which the other men were wearing, he had chosen an overcoat of outlandish pattern and ancient cut, several sizes too large, frogged, and with an astrakhan collar. No one knew what was underneath it, since he never took it off. The top hat he carried was also too large; it would have smothered him if he had put it on. The surmise was that although he had almost certainly borrowed the hat from Eric Dudley, who had met him at Victoria Station and brought him to the service, the coat was probably an inheritance from his father or even his grandfather.

Recalling the extraordinary spectacle, Lady Alexandra said, "I couldn't help thinking that Fruity would have burst out laughing."

For those in the Chapel Royal who had known the Duke as Prince and King, it must have been as difficult to recognize the quondam fashion plate in this caricature, as it was to believe that one so punctilious about correct dress could have become so disrespectful to Fruity's memory. It could mean only that the final decline had set in, and that he was giving up on himself and on the remaining simple standards he had lived by.

The death of Fruity Metcalfe touched the Duke's heart as had no other—outside of the Royal Family and a few pets—since Hugh Lloyd Thomas had been killed in 1938. Fruity's followed closely on one that had affected the Duchess as profoundly as anything could: Four weeks earlier, her old and loyal friend Herman Rogers had died. True, she had not seen him in four years—she had deliberately allowed the friendship to cool—but there had been a time in the latter 1940's, after the Windsors settled in at La Croë, when the association which Wallis had shared with the Rogerses in Peking was happily restored, though now with the former waif as the benefactress. In a society where the Duchess knew few people at all, and where the Duke knew too many whose company he did not enjoy, the Windsors and the Rogerses formed a foursome. They went to each other's villa for dinner two or three times a week, or to one or another of the famous restaurants close to Cannes. They played golf together and backgammon. Presently the ranking hostesses of the Côte d'Azur seldom invited the Windsors for dinner without the Rogerses. Only one other couple was made equally welcome at the little courts at La Croë and Lou Viei: Air Commodore Archibald Wann, a retired Royal Air Force officer, and his wife, Lucy, an attractive young Alsatian.

Archie Wann had begun his military career in the Royal Navy, in the same term at Dartmouth as Prince Bertie, but had transferred to Naval Airships in 1915. In 1921, he was commanding the dirigible R-38 when she broke in two, caught fire, exploded, and fell into the Humber. Of the forty-nine men aboard (fifteen were Americans—the ship was on order to the U.S. Navy), only five survived, among them Flight Lieutenant Wann. He was terribly burned, but recovered, and commanded the air defenses at Malta for a time during World War II. In 1946, he retired to the benign climate of the French Riviera, where he renewed his acquaintanceship with the Duke, who often welcomed him and Lucy at La Croë. The Wanns met the Rogerses there, and the Windsor-Rogers foursome was being expanded to a sixsome when three unexpected disruptions occurred: Archie Wann died, in October 1948; Katharine Rogers died the following May; and the widower fell in love with the widow.

When Herman wrote the news to Wallis in the late spring of 1950, he added that the wedding would be held at Lou Viei on August 6 and expressed his hope and Lucy's that the Windsors would be their witnesses. Wallis telegraphed back that she and the Duke were already booked for the sixth, but if the ceremony could be advanced a few days, they would of course be present. Her telegram ended, "Wait for your guardian angel!"

Was she being equivocal? Lucy Rogers would eventually decide that she was. In the course of her life with Herman, she came to know much—and to surmise more—about his relationship with Wallis that no one before her may have even suspected, except perhaps Katharine Rogers and a few close friends from the Peking interval. There is no doubt that ever since then Wallis had been in love with him off and on; nor did Herman ever disguise his affection for her, or his disapproval of her conduct.

Having himself married, in Katharine, a strong-willed, rather masculine woman, he thoroughly understood Wallis's influence over the Duke, and as thoroughly disliked seeing her exercise it. When she took refuge at Lou Viei in December 1936, Herman lent his calm support to Perry Brownlow, who was entreating her to give up her plans for marriage, rather than have the King give up his throne.

Herman's private opinion was that the Abdication was an act of folly; that the King's infatuation had reached the point of scandal, and that Wallis's acquiescence in the role of all-but-proclaimed mistress was degrading her. Sensitive and introspective, he had never been altogether comfortable on the yachting parties or the weekends at the Fort. He lent himself to the charade partly out of friendship for Wallis and partly because Katharine was intoxicated by the intimacy with royalty.

If Herman and Wallis had ever been lovers in Peking, he did not drop the faintest hint of it. But when Lucy Wann first became acquainted with the Windsors and Rogerses, she sensed that the Duchess, bored with the Duke, regarded Herman as *her* property, on continuing loan to Katharine. Indeed, Wallis's air of proprietorship had become unmistakable when Herman stunned her with the news of his engagement.

"Lucy was in trouble from the start," a friend remembers. "She did not realize how strongly Wallis had come to look on Herman as a form of reserve capital which Katharine's death now promised to make available for the first time. For the prize to fall so swiftly and easily to a comparative stranger wounded Wallis deeply, and the wound was plain to see. Her boredom in her own marriage had become acute, and she was no longer as discreet as before, when it came to hiding her feelings. The flashy Donahue, now the main string to her bow, would distract attention from solid, comfortable Herman in the background, and perhaps this made Wallis careless."

Her first reaction was to chide Herman for his impetuousness. Her next was to seed his mind, in various and less than subtle ways, with the idea that once again he was marrying beneath himself. The main reason why he had chosen to become an expatriate is said to have been his family's coolness toward Katharine. Wallis's request that the wedding date be advanced had already miffed Lucy, but this was only the opening gun in a fusillade of snubs and provocations which Lucy could not help interpreting as a deliberate attempt to hurt and belittle her. Next, a light, studied insult accompanied the Windsors' wedding present—a handsome antique sterling salver, bearing their monogram of interlaced W's and an inscription which caused Lucy to recoil. The date was wrong, and Lucy's participation in the marriage was ignored. It said:

To
Herman Livingston Rogers
on the occasion of his marriage
August 9th [*sic*] 1950
from
Edward and Wallis

Wallis's jealous hostility flared up again at Lou Viei on the wedding morning, just before the party was to start for the *mairie*. Without asking leave, she began tugging at the collar of Lucy's wedding dress: "We can't have you looking like this *today*! It doesn't fit! Let me just—" She pulled and twisted the satin until it was shapeless and ruined. "There!" she said, patting it. "That's better!"

Some weeks later, Mrs. Rogers took the dress to Worth and showed it to them. She said, "They were shocked. They cried, 'But it was beautiful when we sent it to you! What on earth happened?' I told them, and they said, 'Ah, yes! Of course. . . .'"

Herman gave the wedding breakfast at La Belle Auberge, near Antibes, and then they separated to rest for the reception, which would be held at Lou Viei from six to eight. Many of the guests were coming as much to see the celebrated Duke and Duchess as to congratulate the bride and groom, and when the Windsors had not shown up by eight-fifteen, they began to drift away, disappointed. All were gone when Wallis and the Duke finally arrived, at eight forty-five. Mrs. Rogers remembers Wallis's explanation: "She said, 'I'm dreadfully sorry, but the [So-and-So's] picked this of all afternoons to stop in. They talked on and on, and we simply couldn't get rid of them.'"

"I told her, 'Wallis, the [So-and-So's] were here at our reception.'"

They went on to dine together at a restaurant in Cannes, as they had planned, but despite Herman's efforts and the Duke's to make the evening run smoothly, Wallis was to be neither appeased nor diverted. She addressed her entire conversation to Herman alone—the Duke was innocently delighted; he always enjoyed practicing his German, and Lucy's was fluent—and her parting shot was to bustle the Duke into their car immediately after dinner and drive off, leaving the bride and groom to find a taxi.

The honeymoon began next morning. Herman Rogers had chartered a yacht, and again the Windsors squared off the party. Lucy retains three vivid impressions of their cruise. The first was of Wallis changing her costume several times a day. The second was of a dinner at the Hôtel de Paris, in Monte Carlo. Lucy said, "I was wearing a gold and diamond ring which Wallis noticed at once and remarked on. I explained that Herman had given it to me as a wedding present, much against my wishes—I already had all the jewelry I wanted, and I was going to send it back. Wallis became more and more agitated, until she jumped up from the table and beckoned me out to the ladies' room, where she urged me, 'Don't send it back! Don't be a fool! It's *money*!'" Lucy's third impression was of the morning when they moored next to a yacht which the Duchess recognized as Jimmy Donahue's. Her romance with him was just beginning: The pull was powerful; she insisted that everyone join Jimmy for lunch. Herman had never met Donahue, but did not like his reputation. He told the Windsors, "You two go, if you wish. Lucy and I will stay here."

Lucy Rogers, looking back, says now that they should have realized that the antagonism between her and Wallis could never be reconciled. The couples exchanged a few insipid letters at longer and longer intervals, until their once flourishing friendship had faded into indifference.

Herman Rogers sold Lou Viei in 1956 and built another villa not far away. "Crumwold," he named it, after his family's estate in New York. He had been born there, at Crumwold-on-Hudson, and at Crumwold-super-Cannes he died, in 1957, aged sixty-five. He had buried Katharine Rogers in the Cannes cemetery; now Lucy Rogers buried him beside her.

How he occupied himself in those last years is unclear. The stream of his life changed its volume as often as its course. He was an enthusiast without direction or perseverance. After Yale, he had planned to study farming at Cornell, but had switched to civil engineering at the Massachusetts Institute of Technology. The Great War made him look for a higher purpose, and an ample income let him postpone work and prolong his honeymoon. In Peking, Wallis thought he was writing a book about "somebody in mythology—Perseus, or somebody like that," but nothing more was heard of it. His youthful promise somehow evaporated. He became a gentleman-dilettante, speaking five languages, well read in history and the philosophies of religion, and at home everywhere but in his native land. Dedicated only to living fastidiously and well, he retained his style and charm to the end, and to the end Wallis was more or less in love with him.

The slow diminuendo of his life recalls Dick Diver's, in *Tender Is the Night*: "He bicycled a lot, and was much admired by the ladies, and always had a big stack of papers on his desk that was known to be an important treatise on some medical subject, almost in process of completion. He was considered to have fine manners . . . and Nicole [his ex-wife] . . . liked to think that his career was biding its time. . . ." [3]

Nor had Wallis seen much in recent years of another former intimate, one whom she had known even longer and more affectionately: Aunt Bessie Merryman. The comfortable income given her by appreciative friends had allowed her to answer Wallis's more urgent calls for help, beginning with their trip to Europe in 1927. Then came the holiday at Biarritz in August 1934, the desperate summons to stand in as chaperone during the last terrible days at the Fort in December 1936, the trip to Cannes to join Wallis soon afterward, to Candé for her wedding that June, and to Wasserleonburg during her honeymoon. Mrs. Merryman spent the Christmas holidays of 1938 with the Windsors at La Croë, and those of 1944 with them at Nassau. Whenever and wherever Wallis needed her, Aunt Bessie went, wise, soothing, urbane, discreet.

It is hard to say how much of this unselfish devotion Wallis returned, but an American woman who knew the Simpsons well in London remembers a frantic telephone call from Wallis a few minutes before her flight with Lord

Brownlow, begging a "promise to see Aunt Bessie every single day!" Inevitably, the relationship had moments of friction. The Duchess of Windsor sometimes forgot that she had once been plain young Bessiewallis Warfield to her aunt, and—perhaps because she had become openly critical of the Duke's sometimes primitive table manners—once chided her for using the "wrong" fork. Aunt Bessie told her sharply, "I am ninety years old. I know all that there is to know about flat silver. If I choose one fork over another, it is because I know exactly what I want the fork for!"

She had turned ninety in 1954. The vigor of her body was now impaired, but her mind would remain strong for several years more. She resented having to forgo her regular Atlantic crossings and restrict herself to short motor trips into Virginia and Maryland. On her announcement that she was planning a visit to her native Baltimore, someone asked, "To look up your old friends?"

"No," said Mrs. Merryman. "I'd have to *dig* them up!"

Her one-hundredth birthday fell on August 19, 1964. Weeks ahead, her cousin Lelia Noyes—who became Mrs. Albert H. Lucas in 1970 and was widowed again in 1973—had begun organizing the family celebration that would be held at Wakefield Manor. Wallis sent regrets. She said she would love to be there, but the trip would be too exhausting, as she did not travel by air. (This was not quite accurate. She had flown from Miami to Nassau in 1940, and would fly from Houston to New York within five months, and from Paris to Lisbon for the big Patiño party in 1968, and to London and back for the Duke's funeral in 1972, and there again the year following. In all, she flew at least half a dozen times, and perhaps as many as a dozen.) Besides—Wallis told Lelia—she and the Duke were saving themselves for the funeral, which could not be far in the future. But Lelia was to order champagne and a birthday cake, and send her the bill. The total was thirty-two dollars; the Duke paid. Mrs. Noyes had the cake baked in the shape of a daisy, so that the petals could accommodate all those candles. When it was brought in, blazing, and the company had admired it, and Aunt Bessie had blown out the candles, with a little help, Corinne Murray proposed a toast:

> We know a great lady named Bess
> Who has lived to one hundred; we guess
> She *is* a bit fragile
> But still very agile,
> So everyone thinks she is less.

Mrs. Noyes read out the birthday messages, including a jocular cable from the Windsors, and then proposed another toast: "To my Cousin Bessie—'Aunt Bessie' to the world—a great lady whom the King of England called 'a wise and gentle woman.' She liked to tease us Montagues by referring to us as 'the Montageese,' but she was one 'Montagoose'—according to my mother—who never said a silly thing in her life. We all know she never said an unkind one. Now that she has so grandly accomplished her first hundred years, let's all drink to her next hundred!"

They drank and cheered, and Mrs. Merryman responded:

"Thank you for putting up with me all these years. I can't say more—I'm close to tears."

She died just over three months later, on November 28. Wallis wrote Lelia Noyes from New York that she could not come to the funeral; she was confined by a recent operation on her foot. The Duke came. The British Embassy lent him a Rolls-Royce; he picked up Mrs. Noyes and Mrs. Murray in Washington, and together they led the cortege to Cockeysville, Maryland, where Aunt Bessie was buried in the Merryman family plot at the Episcopal church.

The grief of her family and friends was shared by all prospective biographers of the Windsors and all historians of the Abdication, when they considered what a unique hoard of anecdotes went with her to her grave. She never gave an interview; she kept no diary; she destroyed all letters, and—discretion's self to the end—left no memoirs or notes. If the Warfield-Windsor coffer of her recollections—or of Herman Rogers's—could ever have been unlocked, it might have been like unlocking a combination of Solomon's treasury and Pandora's box. More important, of all the leading actors in the drama of the Windsors, Mrs. Merryman is the only one whose character and behavior were immaculate throughout.

* * *

Ten days after her funeral, the Duke and Duchess took a train from New York to Houston, for him to have an aneurysm removed from his abdominal aorta. It had been enlarging slowly since its first appearance four years before, and his medical advisers were agreed that it was time he saw the famous heart surgeon Dr. Michael E. DeBakey, of the Houston Methodist Hospital. The operation was a specialty of Dr. DeBakey's; he was said to perform a thousand of them a year, sometimes six a day.

A squadron of motorcycle policemen met the Windsors at the station and escorted them to the hospital. A suite of six rooms was waiting: one each for the Duke and Duchess, one each for their valet and maid, and two for entertaining. These two were bright with flowers: Princess Mary had sent some; so had the Queen, with a request for daily reports on her uncle's progress. Other sympathizers, many of them strangers, had sent him get-well cards with their warm good wishes. Several local housewives were offering to roast his Christmas turkey.

The operation was scheduled for December 16, two days after his arrival, and the Duke would have to remain in the hospital over the twenty-fifth.

A reporter asked him, "What does Christmas mean to you?"

"Presents," said the Duchess.

"Paying for them," the Duke said.

Early on the morning of the sixteenth, Dr. DeBakey snipped out the aneurysm—"the size of a small canteloupe or a large grapefruit," he said—and replaced it with four inches of Dacron tubing (thereby inspiring Mrs. Nicholas du Pont to send the patient a cheery telegram: "Now we can claim there is a little du Pont in you"). The operation, which usually takes about ninety minutes, took only sixty-seven. Dr. DeBakey announced, "A complete recovery is expected," and successive bulletins reported, "Smiling, talking, doing fine. . . . Rapid progress. . . . Brief walk. . . . Solid food," and on New Year's Eve, "Discharged."

The Windsors rested for a week in a Houston hotel before flying back to New York with their staff and their personal doctor. They sailed for France at the end of January, and within another fortnight, the seventy-year-old

Duke was in hospital again, for two more operations. Fortunately for his stamina, both were minor—to repair a detached retina; and fortunately for his composure, they would be performed in the homier atmosphere of London, at the London Clinic. Lady Monckton arranged for word to reach the Queen that a visit to her uncle would cheer him and invigorate him. She went to see him twice, once at the Clinic and again when he moved to Claridge's, and invited him to come and walk in the Palace gardens if he wanted privacy. The Duchess was present—she and the Queen met at the bedside—and the press made much of the fact that this was the first time the Queen had called on her. Other members of the Royal Family—Princess Marina, Princess Alexandra, Princess Mary—were quick to follow her lead. The Duke was deeply moved by his sister's sympathy; he had always held her in special affection, mixed with pity. One of the rare coolnesses between him and their mother developed because he felt that she was repressing her daughter, just as Queen Alexandra had repressed Princess Victoria Louisa, and Queen Charlotte had repressed all her six. Brother and sister met just in time; Mary died on March 28, aged sixty-eight.

Dickie Mountbatten came. Since September 1939, when he had ferried the Windsors from Cherbourg to Portsmouth, they had met only once, in 1951, and then briefly. Duty had kept him far from home during much of those sixteen years. He had begun World War II as a captain, R.N., had served throughout it with the utmost gallantry, and had ended it as Supreme Allied Commander of all Southeast Asia. His peacetime career was no less distinguished; he became India's last Viceroy in March 1947, and a few months later the first Governor-General it had ever chosen. In 1953, he had been promoted to the topmost rank in the Royal Navy, Admiral of the Fleet; and in 1959, to the topmost in the combined military services, Chief of the Defense Staff. Along the way he had acquired a title, Earl Mountbatten of Burma, and enough other honors and awards to fill nearly two columns in *Who's Who*. Because of his dash and courage and his zest for reckless operations, he had acquired a nickname: "Betty Mountlouis"; and through the marriage of his nephew Prince

Philip of Greece, he had also acquired a niece, who had become Her Majesty Queen Elizabeth II.

Windsor, now seeing Mountbatten again after fourteen years, must have felt a twinge, even a pang. Mountbatten was tall, and still handsome and athletic. Windsor was short; his "boyish good looks" had long since withered away; his face was wrinkled, the skin hanging in loose folds as if the bones beneath were shrinking; his hair was gray and thinning; his body frail. Mountbatten's career had gone from strength to strength, Windsor's from failure to futility. In short, Mountbatten was the model of noble looks and conduct which Windsor should have been. Though the contrast must have been awkwardly obvious to them both, Windsor might have accepted it without rancor if the Duchess had not been seizing every opportunity to express her dislike of Mountbatten, and had thereby infected the ever suggestible Duke. Her dislike had three sources: She was jealous of Mountbatten's achievements and appearance; she had never got over his failure to remember their first meeting, at San Diego in 1920; and she resented his having been an integral part of Windsor's past before she came onstage. She had discouraged Windsor's association with Eric Dudley because she could not bear to hear them reminisce; for the same reason, she was discouraging any renewal of the old attachment to Dickie Mountbatten.

He had no suspicion of the Windsors' hostility. To the end, he thought—and often spoke—of himself as "David's closest friend." So he had been, until the alienating arrival of Wallis Simpson. To be sure, it is all but impossible for two youths to establish a firm friendship across the chasm of six years' difference in age (*exactly* six years, but for two days); the firmest friendships are founded on mutual interests, and these cousins had little in common besides their kinship, their youthful affection for the Navy, and a sporadic association that included two Empire tours together. Betweenwhiles, their different natures, skills, and aspirations had taken them apart. Both were horsemen, polo players, but Windsor had come to prefer fox hunting and steeplechasing, while Mountbatten, whom he had taught to swing a mallet, had stayed loyal to polo. He once

632   CHARLES J. V. MURPHY AND J. BRYAN III

achieved a handicap of five goals; he designed a new mallet head; and, under the facetious pseudonym "Marco," he wrote *An Introduction to Polo,* which was translated into several languages and, in 1979, was in its sixth printing. His friend Winston Guest, the former ten-goal international star, posed for some of the photographs that illustrated correct play.

Windsor's passions were golf and gardening; Mountbatten's hobbies were shooting and spearfishing. They were no less unlike in temperament. Windsor was an arrested adolescent, the heir apparent who never found the path to moral sovereignty over himself, let alone the Commonwealth-Empire awaiting his accession. Freda Dudley Ward had said of him, "He bloomed late and he never came to full bloom. He stayed a little naïve, a little childish, to the end." Mountbatten, on the other hand, matured quickly; he was intelligent, ambitious, self-disciplined, and, above all else, dutiful—which was why, although he had frequently visited the Fort, he had never really belonged to the frivolous "Fort set," especially after Wallis Simpson took over the chair of the membership committee.

Still, here he was now, at cocktail time, unaware that his old friend David's opinions had become merely a reflection of Wallis's. Mountbatten remained for three-quarters of an hour, and a lady who came in just as he was leaving remembers the Windsors' unkind account of his visit:

"I thought he'd *never* go!" the Duchess told her. *"Too* boring! He talked of absolutely *nothing* but himself the whole time."

The Duke said, "He was always like that. And those calls from Whitehall every few minutes—!" (Lord Mountbatten was still C.D.S.)

In 1960, Lady Mountbatten, as superintendent-in-chief of the St. John Ambulance Brigade and chairman of the Red Cross Service Hospitals Welfare Department, was making her annual tour of the Far East and had reached North Borneo when she died in her sleep, February 20–21. Her coffin was flown home and carried aboard a frigate at Portsmouth. Four miles at sea, it was committed to the deep, at her special request.

The Windsors attended the memorial service for Prin-

cess Mary in London on April 1. By June the Duke was
strong enough to frolic at the big Bestegui bash in Paris—
being seen there was obligatory for the Duchess—and
when he went back to Houston in October for a checkup,
Dr. DeBakey sent him away with congratulations and only
the mildest restrictions. So did his ophthalmologist. The
Windsors returned to Paris early in November. The following June, 1966, the Duke was in London again, and again
for his mother's sake, to witness the unveiling of a memorial tablet set in the wall of Marlborough House, where she
had lived for so many years. The occasion was extra-note-
worthy. Not only would he be there at Queen Elizabeth's
personal behest, but his Duchess would be with him, for
still another "first": her first official appearance at a public
ceremony with other members of the Royal Family.

She once said, "I think the Duke's mother was devoted
to him and I did everything in my power to make him
keep in contact with her. His Christmas and birthday telegrams to her and to the whole family, well, I wrote them
for him and saw to it they were sent."

Soon after the date for the unveiling was set—June 7,
twelve days after the centennial of Queen Mary's birth—
Queen Elizabeth had told Lord Mountbatten, "I'm asking
Uncle David to come. Of course, he must bring his wife."

When Windsor accepted, and notified her that they
would be arriving at Southampton on the *United States,*
she assigned Mountbatten to meet them as her official representative and give them an official welcome. The Windsors liked to sail on the *United States* less because she held
the blue ribbon for the Atlantic crossing (3 days, 10 hours,
40 minutes) than because she was the flagship of the
United States Lines, whose president, Gen. John M.
Franklin, was a nephew of Aunt Bessie Merryman's and
therefore could be expected to oblige the Duke with special
accommodations at specially reduced rates. Not so the
Waldorf Towers, which held him to the public rate of
1,280 dollars a month for his apartment, a bargain at today's prices. When the Windsors traveled, their comptroller did the tipping. The Duke sometimes instructed
him to give "a little something special" to the staff of a
liner. The Duchess, never. The comptroller said, "She felt
that the world owed her the service." (A duplicate of the

Duke's usual place setting on the *United States* recently went on display in the Smithsonian's Hall of American Maritime Enterprise, along with some of the aluminum paneling, goldpainted, from his favorite suite.)

The Court rustled and murmured at this fresh "first": the first time a member of the Royal Family had been sent to welcome the Duke of Windsor since his Abdication. Mountbatten went aboard, greeted his cousins, and accompanied them the few miles from the dockside to Broadlands, his estate at Romsey, where Princess Elizabeth and Prince Philip had spent the first part of their honeymoon. There he had arranged for the Duke and Duchess each to plant a tree in celebration of their visit, and for the local photographer, who doubled as mayor of Romsey, to take pictures of the planting and then deliver an address of welcome.

The Mayor asked, "What do I call them?"

"The Duke is 'Your Royal Highness,'" Mountbatten told him, "and the Duchess is 'Your Grace.'"

The salutation to the Duke was letter-perfect: "Your Royal Highness—" But when the mayor turned to the Duchess, he blew his lines: "—and Your Royal Highness— I *beg* your pardon! Your Grace—"

If the Duchess noticed, she gave no sign. But when her turn came in the protocol, she squared things. Some onlookers were surprised that the Duchess did not curtsey to the Queen Mother as well as to the Queen. They might as logically have expected the Archbishop of Canterbury to break into a voodoo chant, for in the Duchess's private demonology, the Queen Mother was Grand Diabolarch and would remain so.

The feeling was reciprocated. When the storm winds of 1936 began to reach gale force, the Duchess of York had said, "None of this would have happened if Wallis hadn't blown in from Baltimore!" Yet Elizabeth, as Queen and then Queen Mother, was a beneficiary of the change. She became famous; she won respect, even popularity; she became the matriarchal eminence of the court—Clarence House is hers; so is a splendid Grace and Favour house at Windsor. All this she has Wallis to thank for, although the queenship was the last thing she wanted at the time, knowing as she did the price it would exact from her husband.

The strangest aspect of her animosity is that she has always been—with this sole exception—a person of intellectual and emotional balance, the most sensible, most sensitive, and most imaginative of the whole Royal Family. She is also the least Philistine since George IV, being well informed on such diverse subjects as music, horses, painting. She enjoys people and talks with them easily. Yet long, long after the Abdication had passed into history, she kept her vindictiveness on the boil, as, of course, did the Windsors. A forgiving hand extended to the prodigals could hardly have marred so admirable and exemplary a character. Had she and Queen Mary been moved to do so when the Windsors returned to England at the start of the war, the annals of the reign might well have been the more lustrous for it.

✿ CHAPTER 16 ✿
The Millionaire Miser

Some dukes have been curiously mean to family and friends. For this I can find no explanation.
——The Dukes, BRIAN MASTERS

The restless, gadabout Windsors began to slow down as the century reached the middle 1960's and they their seventies. It was no longer like the frenetic 1950's—like the summer of '57, for instance, when they flitted about the Mediterranean, first on a Guinness yacht, then on one of Niarchos's. They still kept to their seasonal circuit—Paris, New York, Palm Beach, the Riviera—but their last major excursion was to Lisbon for the big Patiño bash in 1968. After that, their travels were shorter, mostly side trips and stopovers.

One such was in Washington, where the Nixons gave them a white-tie, White House dinner in April 1970. The 107 guests included at least one of the Duke's old friends, Fred Astaire, and one of his new heroes, Arnold Palmer. They also included—Wallis was surprised to find—two of her second cousins: Vice Adm. Lloyd Montague Mustin, U.S.N., and his wife; and Frances Montague Dyer and her husband, Brig. Gen. E. Colston Dyer, U.S.M.C. She was surprised because she had not asked for them to be invited; Mrs. Nixon's press secretary had done it on her own initiative. Since Wallis's marriage to the Duke, she had had little communication with her family, excepting Aunt Bessie Merryman; and since Aunt Bessie's death, she had had almost none. Still, her greeting was "warm and delightful," Admiral Mustin remembers. He was Rinny Murray's son by her first marriage, and Rinny was Wallis's favorite cousin. Wallis told him, "You were always a good little boy, Lloyd, and now I see"—pointing to his rows of ribbons—"that you're a good big boy, too!" Neither the Mustins nor the Dyers ever saw her again, or ever heard from her.

Many who came to know the Windsors in their last years were mystified by how very slightly they had allowed themselves to be absorbed into the French community. In the thirty years that they lived in France, mostly in Paris, they made almost no close friends among the French. They would exchange occasional dinner invitations with the Guy de Rothschilds and his cousin Philippe; and they made a point of attending Baron Guy's famous annual ball at his estate, Ferriére, forty miles from town. They went on shooting parties at other great estates; and Margaret Biddle had introduced them to the French politicians and diplomats of the day, and the proprietors of important publications. But the Windsors encouraged none of these acquaintanceships to mature. They made no effort to understand the French. Indeed, they did not like them.

An American woman arrived at the Neuilly house one summer evening in the midst of a thunderstorm. The Duke met her at the door. She showed him her white satin slippers, soiled with mud, and exclaimed, "What a storm! This country of yours—!"

"This is *not* my country!" he snapped, with a sharpness that startled her. Wondering about it later, she asked herself—as so many have done—Why, then, did he settle there? A fellow expatriate, also resident in Paris, offered this cynical explanation: "France is the only country where one can live comfortably without being in contact with the natives." Windsor's dislike for the French, which he never bothered to conceal, had roots deep in his childhood. A French governess, Mlle. Bricka, and a French tutor, M. Hua, had dragged him through the elements of France's language and history; and a later tutor, M. Escoffier, had taken him on a four-month tour of France beginning in April 1912; but its beauties and splendors had been spoiled for him, and forever, by his parents' insistence that he send them a weekly report in French on everything he had seen. The reports do not survive, but his diary does; and the seventeen-year-old boy's Francophobia is clear and strong:

The Eiffel Tower was huge and hideous.

The French were gluttons.

His companion at a horse show, Baron D——, was a worse bore than the show itself.

A certain French painting of a British naval review was frightful.

The curator of a museum in the Marais was a senile idiot.

Gèrard M—— came to dinner and proved to be a bounder.

A celebrated photographer talked nonsense.

The Jardin d'Acclimatation was a wretched sort of zoo. . . .

And so on, for the rest of the tour. The aversion thus acquired was intensified during the Great War, when he absorbed something of the English Tommy's immemorial mistrust of his ancient enemy, the poilu. The *entente cordiale* which the Francophile Edward VII had promulgated in the hope of dispelling this mistrust did not enlist his grandson's sympathy. Both the Windsors complained that the French aristocracy was cold, inhospitable, and boring, and that "You have to invite them at least three weeks ahead, and then send them a card of reminder."

At the same time, although the Duchess spoke of "*filthy France*," she granted that "the French had always been marvelous about letting us lead our lives. They are so civilized about that. They give you more freedom. You are a human being, allowed to make your mistakes and live with them quietly."

There were four reasons why the Duke stayed on, in the face of these lively dislikes. The first and, regrettably, strongest was his cupidity. To the end of his life, a sympathetic French Government offered Windsor such hospitality as he could have found nowhere else in contemporary society, with the possible exception of some remote Polynesian chiefdom: diplomatic status, modest property taxes, no income tax at all, and a security guard around the clock and around the calendar. Whenever the Windsors left their house, they were followed by two plainclothesmen in an unobtrusive black Citroën.

The second reason was that France, especially Paris, was a place where they could indulge their luxurious tastes, and one not only attractive to their English and American friends, but convenient for their visits. The third reason was that in the egalitarian Republic of France, royalty was still treated royally; wherever the Windsors went, it was _"Majesté"_ this and _"Altesse Royale"_ that until even the Duchess must have been surfeited by the echo. The final reason was that the Duke loved the French countryside; its only fault, he once said, was that it was "populated with Frenchmen." When an American asked him if he knew why the country air in France was so fresh and sparkling, and answered himself, "Because the natives sleep with their windows shut," the Duke laughed until he nearly strangled.

France might easily and understandably have countered the Windsors' disaffection with disaffection on its own part, but it continued to harbor them and to give them much. They gave little in return: a few hundred francs a year to the _Société pour la Défense et Protection des Animaux_ (the French equivalent of the SPCA) and a few hundred more for tickets to the annual ball in behalf of the American Hospital at Neuilly. Nothing else, at least so far as any public record shows, or any member of their staff recalls.

Why they gave so little was only in part their dislike of the French; mostly it was the Duke's natural stinginess. The trait was so strong that one is tempted to assume that it had been bred into him, like the Bourbon randiness and the Hapsburg lip. But who bequeathed the gene of parsimony? The Hanoverians, with very few exceptions, were notorious for their squandering, not for their thrift. By the time that the future George IV was twenty-seven, he had run up a bill of 16,744 pounds with his tailor alone. His brothers were hardly less debt-ridden, through their gross extravagance. Queen Victoria was neither a spendthrift nor a pinchpenny, but Edward VII seldom hesitated to indulge his every appetite. Did the gene come from Queen Mary's side? James Pope-Hennessy wrote that her mother, Princess Mary Adelaide, was given to "keeping used paper for parcels, hoarding pieces of string in her bureau drawers . . . and scrupulously snipping off any blank sheet at the end of a letter," but these were merely economies, imposed by the Tecks' chronic neediness—their long residence "in short street," as Queen Mary put it.

No, her son's parsimoniousness seems to have been spontaneous, parthenogenetic. It also seems to have waxed with the passing years. In his twenties, he had written Freda Dudley Ward a check for "several" thousand pounds "without a question or a murmur," to discharge her friend's gambling debts; but this is almost a unique example of openhandedness on his part. In his forties, one of the first acts of his reign was to order an immediate 10 percent wage cut for every employee in the royal service, prefiguring the 20 percent lower wages he would pay his Paris household. His friends quickly became aware of the development, discussing it freely and with alarm. When, in 1938, Windsor yielded to an unwonted impulse and presented the Metcalfes' young son with a five-pound note, the guileless lad cried, "Sir, thank you! Mummy will be *so* surprised!" Most likely the gift was less a spasm of generosity than evidence of the awkwardness that Windsor always showed in the presence of his friends' children, presumably because they made him feel old. Before that, he had embarrassed even Fruity by his reluctance to tip the servants at Enzesfeld, and later, during the war, by his haggling over hotel and restaurant bills on their tours of the front. Fruity was not his only critic. Bruce Lockhart's diary for January 9, 1949, records a luncheon with the Duke's former equerry Sir Piers Legh, who said that "though he liked the Duke, he could not defend his conduct. His greatest vice . . . was meanness about money. The worst two cases . . . were 'Angy' [*sic*] Ward (now Laycock), who was his god-daughter [she was not]. . . . He never went to her wedding or sent her a present. He did nothing for his favorite private detective [Chief Inspector Storrier] who died in his service and left a widow."

The next stage was acute: When Windsor gave a dinner at a restaurant, he would often try to evade his obligations as a host by pointedly ignoring the *addition* put beside his plate, as though it were some guest's dentures, retrieved from the floor and vulgarly exposed to public view. His dillydally tactics included staring into the middle distance, whistling a light tune, and drumming his fingers on the table, until one of the guests finally picked up the bill and paid it, as his only hope of getting home before dawn.

The Henry Luces were caught in such an ambush in Venice, when Mrs. Luce was American Ambassador to Italy (1953-57). The Windsors had invited them to luncheon. When it was finished, the waiter laid the bill precisely between the two men. The Luces waited and waited for the Duke to pay it and release them, but he made no motion to do so. At last Harry Luce stood up: "Clare and I must be getting back. There are some cables from Washington she must attend to. Thank you!"

"We understand," Windsor said. He, too, rose, bowed to Mrs. Luce, and left with the Duchess—and left the check, too.

Luce told his wife angrily, "I don't mind being stuck for the lunch, but to be stuck *so blatantly!*—and by a man who was once King of England!—and *he* had invited *us*, damn it!"

The Windsors once had a young English businessman to dinner at a Paris restaurant. The moment of truth arrived: The *addition* lay there, and long minutes dragged by while the Duke desperately sought an excuse for lobbing it across the table. A possibility suddenly occurred to him, and his face brightened: "Are you by any chance on an expense account?" he asked. Alas, the young man was not.

There were rare occasions when a guest, finally realizing that his choice lay between exhaustion of his person and exhaustion of his purse, clenched his teeth and resolved to outsit the Duke—whatever the cost in chair sores—only to have the Duchess come to his rescue with an impatient *"David, pay that bill!"* But he was rash indeed who counted on her merciful intercession. All too often, she not only failed to protest when the Duke began his bamboozlement, but acted as his confederate. A penurious American writer whom she had led to the slaughter could not help admiring the deftness with which the job was done. He had completed some ghost-writing for the Duke in Paris—a job of perhaps a week—and he and his wife were packing to fly home to Washington next morning when their telephone rang: "Oh, it's the Dook! Will you come to a farewell dinner with the Duchess and I tonight? [His English grammar was faultless except for this ingrained solecism.] . . . Splendid! I've booked a booth at the Berkeley, and we'll pick you up at eight."

The Berkeley, then at the corner of the Avenue Franklin D. Roosevelt and the Rue de Ponthieu, but now gone, was one of the most expensive restaurants in Paris. A guidebook wrote of it, "The ever-escalating price of its oysters would be justified only if there were a pearl in each." Its other dishes accorded. The American couple loved fine food and wine, but the Berkeley's tariff had kept them away. Tonight the bars were down. As soon as the party was seated, the Duke took charge and made it clear that he was playing a no-limit game:

"We'll start with iced vodka, I think—vodka and caviar. The caviar here is excellent, *excellent*! Or perhaps some of you would prefer smoked salmon? Two hands. Good. Waiter, two caviar, two smoked salmon. I recommend a melon next. Those delicious little Charenton melons are in season, aren't they, waiter? Splendid! Melons all round, then. Now let's move straight along to the entrée. I recommend a double mutton chop, with soufflé potatoes and fresh asparagus. Oh, no meat for you, Darling? Very well. Rare for me, waiter, and how about you two? One rare and one medium. Green salads, of course. Got all that, waiter? We'll see about a sweet later. Thank you."

Visions of these sugarplums began dancing in the Americans' heads. "Picture us," the wife said long afterward, when her wounds had healed, "little us, with the former King of England and his famous Duchess, in a chic Paris restaurant, about to be served a marvelous dinner, and—"

"—and *snap*!" her husband interrupted. "The former King of England's famous Duchess sprang the trap. She turned to me and asked, 'Now, then: Isn't it time you ordered the wine?'

"There was no doubting the meaning. The *sommelier* was already pressing the wine card into my palsied hands —palsied by my sudden realization that it was a trailbreaker for a murderous tab. I felt like that poor devil in *Treasure Island*—Ben or Bill or whatever his name was— 'old Flint's first mate'—when Blind Pew tipped him the black spot at the Admiral Benbow Inn, and he knew he was marked for death. In fact, I felt *exactly* like him, because if you remember what was written on the other side of the black spot, it was 'You have till ten tonight.'

"I thought of the crumpled bank notes in my pocket, pitifully few and pitifully small, and I prayed that my wife would have enough with her to make up the deficit. By

God's grace, she did. We scraped through, just barely. The last ten-franc note went to the doorman. And, you know, in time I came to value the experience. It was all so smoothly done. The timing was perfect, especially the invitation to assume the honor of choosing the wine. A charming piece of footwork! I was never able to bring myself to believe that practice accounted for its perfection."

The Duke never stinted his hospitality at home. As one superb course succeeded another, the cups overflowed with memorable wines, and at the end rose the pale lavender smoke from vintage cigars, to hang above the table like a benison. No one could have faulted the quality of the Windsors' meals, though the Duke's old friends were increasingly distressed by the quality of the people who came to eat them.

Sir Cecil Beaton said, "The Bryanston Court group were not out of the top drawer. They were fairly respectable upper-middle class—ordinary, boring people. But the café society the Duchess took up with in Paris was downright *trashy*!" Cyrus Sulzberger described the guests at a 1951 dinner as "a weird collection of social derelicts."[1] An English friend of the Duke's said, "He was a snob. He and his Duchess had two all-purpose words for people they disliked: 'horrible' and 'ghastly.' They used them more and more often in their later years, and with reason. Their circle of associates kept changing, but seldom for the better. As friends from their London days died off or dropped out, climbers and self-made men whom the Duke would never have let *approach* his table at the Fort or in the Palace now not only sat at it, but—if the truth were told—sometimes slid under it. I remember an appalling American boor—the Duchess didn't know him, but one of her Palm Beach friends had asked to bring him along—well, he was half-drunk when he arrived, and partway through dinner he chuted the chutes, and the butler and footman had to drag him out, face down. Imagine! . . . I shall never forget the way his toes rucked up the carpet."

Another English guest, a peeress, had an experience at the Neuilly house which she described as "horrifying." Her neighbor at the table, a South American, emptied his larg-

est wineglass and concealed it in his lap, under the tablecloth. She was mystified until, a moment later, he put it
back beside his other glasses, full.

Some of the Duke's old friends, perhaps fearful of repris-
als from the Palace, dropped him after his Abdication—
Hugh Sefton was one. But the loyalists continued to call:
"Lady Monckton, Lord Hardwicke, the Eric Dudleys,
Lady Alexandra Metcalfe, Colin Buist, Robin Beare (the
Duchess's plastic surgeon), Count and Countess Czernin,
Max Aitken, the Winston Guests, Prince Dimitri, the Mosleys, and others, though they were being leavened by the
Alexander Farkases (Alexander's department stores, New
York), the Charles Engelhards (precious metals), the Nathan Cummingses (Consolidated Foods), and other Americans of large affairs. (Mr. Cummings and Mrs. Guest are
on the advisory committee of the Duchess of Windsor Museum at Oldfields School.) A secretary of the Duke's in his
last years said of him, "He had enormous admiration—a
kind of open, adolescent hero worship, really—for men of
vast wealth, especially for those who hadn't inherited it,
but had accumulated it. You know: tycoons. His friendships with Bob Young, Cling Murchison, Farkas, and the
rest were rooted in his awe of their moneymaking prowess.
The fact that they commanded such vast assets simply en-
tranced him."

In this respect he resembled his grandfather King Edward VII, of whom John Pearson has written, "Bertie possessed the true rake's attitude toward wealth. He was a
great materialist and would have agreed with Byron when
he wrote—'Money is power and pleasure and I like it
vastly.' Unlike Byron he also liked people who possessed it,
frankly regarding great wealth as proof positive of social
worth. Money was power, and Bertie would always relish
the company of those fortunate enough to exercise it."[2]

On Windsor's seventieth birthday, in 1964, Cummings
chartered a *bateau mouche* and gave a dinner dance for
about two hundred, while cruising on the Seine. As a climax, a second *bateau mouche* steamed up with a birthday
cake which one of the guests remembers as "at least ten
feet tall." The friendship between the Duchess and Fran-
cine Farkas, a vice-president of Alexander's and its fashion

director, progressed fast and far enough for Mrs. Farkas to offer—and for the Duchess to accept—the loan of her villa, La Roseraie, at Cap Ferrat for three weeks in the late spring of 1973. The Duchess always loved the French Riviera and always regretted the Duke's decision not to buy La Croë when it was offered to him for 75,000 dollars—according to the Duchess's lawyers; according to the Duke's former comptroller, the figure was 100,000 dollars. The property would have been a bargain at a far higher price. When the widowed Lady Burton sold it in 1954 to a corporation formed by Stavros Niarchos, it was for 600,000 dollars; and Niarchos is now said to be asking ten times that.

Strangely, in the twenty-odd years that he has owned La Croë, he has spent only a few nights in the guesthouse and none at all in the château proper. No one has, except spiders and mice. By the summer of 1978, the estate had come to look as if its owner were not a multimillionaire, but Edgar Allan Poe's mad Usher twins. Vandals have torn down the PRIVATE sign from the great wrought-iron gates at the entrance, and have carted off the marble head of Neptune which once spouted into the swimming pool. Creepers are strangling the yews and oleanders; weeds infest the graveled driveways; lichens blemish the stone pillars. Indoors, the vast rooms are vaster for their emptiness. The library is littered with packing cases, but no other room in the whole house holds so much as a chair or a picture or a lamp—nothing but dust and broken glass—vandals have been inside, too. Even the lighting fixtures have been removed, leaving the naked black wires, like dead nerves, sticking from the bare walls. Dampness and decay have established squatters' rights and have treated the house as squatters do. The paint is peeling, the plaster cracking, the ironwork rusting, the murals flaking. The marble mantels are streaked with grime, and some of the mirrored doors in the Duchess's bathroom are shattered. The famous swan bathtub has molted its gorgeous gilt feathers and has become an ugly duck. No trace remains today of the elegance and luxury that the Windsors had brought. Indeed, the only indication that they were ever there at all is a small stone tablet. On the far side of the tennis court is a wooden pergola, and behind the pergola is a wall arrased with wild vines. Part them, and the tablet can be seen:

PREEZIE
A FAITHFUL LITTLE FRIEND
EDWARD AND WALLIS
DUKE AND DUCHESS OF WINDSOR
1938–1949

The Duke found losing La Croë painful enough, in retrospect, but soon he felt obliged to take sad leave of a property ever dearer to him: The Mill. The operations on his aorta and his eyes led off a period when he would seldom be free from worry about his health, and from discomfort, even pain. A hip began giving trouble; he took to walking with the help of a stick; soon he could no longer stoop and kneel, and with his garden off limits, he lost interest in The Mill itself and put it up for sale. A few more rounds of slow-paced golf were still ahead of him, but as his strength waned, so waned his passion for the game. Just before he gave it up forever, there occurred a trivial but illuminating incident. The Duchess's private secretary, John Utter, a retired U.S. Foreign Service officer, remembers it clearly: "This was in December nineteen sixty-eight. I was cutting myself in two to find something for the Duke for Christmas. It was the old problem: What do you give a man who has everything twice over? Finally the butler suggested a small bag for carrying his golf shoes out to the course. I bought one and gave it to him. He thanked me and then said—or rather, stammered—'I'm sorry, John, but until The Mill has been sold, I'm afraid we can't afford a present for you.'"

✿ CHAPTER 17 ✿
"Good Night, Sweet Prince!"

*Time hath his revolutions. There must be a period
and an end of all temporal things, finis rerum, an
end of names and dignities and whatsoever is terrene;
and why not of De Vere? For where is Bohun; where
is Mowbray, where is Mortimer; nay, which is more
and most of all, where is Plantagenet? They are en-
tombed in the arms and sepulchres of mortality.*
  —LORD CHIEF JUSTICE CREWE

*For a king, death is better than dethronement and
exile.*

  —EMPRESS THEODORA

In the late summer of 1971, when the Duke's voice sank
to a hoarse whisper, his doctors found a small tumor in his
throat. A biopsy was taken on November 17; the tumor
proved not only malignant but inoperable. Deep therapy
was prescribed: forty-one days of daily cobalt treatments.
The Duke began them on the thirtieth; they rapidly enfeebled him; and when the series ended on January 12, the
doctors decided not to renew it—all too clearly it had
failed in its purpose—and sent him home.

There, early in February, he read that Dickie Mountbatten had arrived in Paris to dub the French version of a
twelve-part television program based on his career; later he
would dub the German version as well. Windsor telephoned him at once: "Dine with me tonight, will you,
Dickie?" Almost as a casual afterthought, he added, "Wallis is away, having a minor operation in Switzerland."

"Delighted!" Mountbatten told him. He was eager for a
too-long-deferred evening of unhampered man-talk about
their youth, and "Wallis was never one for reminiscences

of the days before she came on the scene." *Any* reminiscence, indeed, was likely to bring from her a curt "Nobody wants to hear about *that*!" In preparation for such an evening, she liked to put on her table a small bell in the shape of a turtle; touch its tail, and it rang. When the Duke and his cronies, reminiscing, were unable to recall a name or a date at first attempt, but finally and laboriously succeeded, the Duchess rang her bell in mock congratulations.

They sat down at eight. Conversation was strained at the start; the Duke was carrying a secret burden of resentment, but presently he brought it into the open: "I was deeply hurt when you didn't turn up at my wedding, Dickie. You were my greatest friend and you let me down."

Mountbatten protested, "Surely *I'm* the one to be hurt! You didn't invite me! Not only that," Mountbatten went on, "but you refused my offer to be your best man."

The Duke shook his head as if he could hardly believe what he was hearing. From there on, Mountbatten said, "The years rolled back," and the two cousins wandered through happy old times, laughing, until Mountbatten feared for damage to the Duke's throat, and rose to leave. It was midnight, but the Duke held him for a final observation: "There's something I'll bet you don't realize. If I hadn't abdicated, I'd have completed thirty-six years of my reign by now—longer than either my father or my grandfather." It was the nearest he ever came to admitting that he sometimes contemplated what might have been. Then, "Thanks, Dickie! I haven't had such a good time in I don't know how long!"

(Although Windsor seems to suggest that he would have enjoyed reigning for thirty-six years, he once observed to another friend, "Too bad that Parliament never worked out a sovereigns' retirement plan, like those the military services and certain corporations have. Twenty-five years—a quarter-century—is long enough for a reign. After that, the heir apparent should take over, while he's still in his prime. My grandfather was fifty-nine when he acceded. He was too old. He'd been kept waiting too long." Another innovation he strongly favored was one he had encountered in Nepal in 1921: "There, when the Crown Prince becomes mature, he takes over the administration of the practical side of government, as a sort of Prime Minister, and the old King restricts himself to dealing with the priests, the nobles, charitable organizations, and so on. It worked in Nepal. It might work in England.")

Mountbatten flew off next morning, taking with him the happy impression that the Duke had been trying to weld a broken link with the past. The impression nourished a hope which he had been entertaining for the past few years: that the Duke was also trying to break his wife's terrible grip and to reassert his independence. His hope gained further strength ten days later, on his return to Paris. The Duke telephoned again, with another invitation: "Will you come to tea this afternoon at five?"

Mountbatten answered cautiously, "Won't Wallis be at home?"

"Yes, but she rests at five. That's why I want you to come then."

He accepted. Later he said, "Now that we had refound our old friendship, we had an even better time." It was fortunate; they never met again. Nor did even the most sanguine among the Duke's other friends ever find grounds for cultivating Mountbatten's hope of his emancipation.

A fortnight later, the Duke underwent an operation for double hernia, again at the American Hospital. It was successful, but his cancer remained unchecked and past arresting. His convalescence was far from complete when he insisted on being taken home. "I want to die in my own bed," he said. That this was only an excuse to escape from the hospital was obvious to the doctors, the nurses, and its president, Perry H. Culley, a retired American diplomat and a friend and golfing companion of the Duke's. His real reason was his chivalrous wish to spare the Duchess the chore of a daily visit to his bedside. In the three months of life that remained to him, *he* made the visits to the hospital, to continue the therapy, although his expressed wish to die in his own bed suggests that he knew it was useless.

His surgeon, Dr. Jean Thin, had not told him so; French medical ethics forbid such disclosures. But the rapidity of the Duke's decline—his face was wizened, his hands shook, and his tiny body had shrunk to less than one hundred pounds—roused pity and apprehension among the few friends whom he asked to call.

One was David Bruce, the American diplomat. They had been chatting about merry evenings long ago in London, when the Duke abruptly changed the subject: "I envy you, David. You knew Wallis when she was a girl. I wish I'd known her then! I've spent the best part of my life with her, and I can tell you that nothing I gave up for her equals what she has given me: happiness, of course, but also *meaning*. I have found her to be utterly without faults, the perfect woman"—his pet epithet for her again. He enlarged his tribute in a conversation with Mrs. Winston Guest: "The Duchess gave me everything that I lacked from my family. She gave me comfort and love and kindness."

Alongside what his life had been meant to be, the life he actually led, with its days of make-work, may seem to dispassionate observers tedious and sterile, but since it was alongside *her*, it seemed to *him* a continuous enchantment. Never for an instant did he display any regret for his marriage. He loved Wallis deeply and her alone. And she—in her undemonstrative way, and intermittently—seems to have loved him. Fruity Metcalfe testified to it. The Duke had made a short trip away from Paris in January 1940, and when he returned home to his Duchess, Fruity wrote, "It was really delightful to see how pleased he and W. were to get together again. It is *very true* & deep stuff."[1]

Another visitor from London was Walter Monckton's widow, Biddy. She was shocked by the Duke's deterioration in the few months since she had seen him last. It had been announced in November, she remembered, that the Queen would travel to Paris in mid-May, in connection with her Government's decision to bring the United Kingdom into the Common Market. If her uncle and former monarch were to die beforehand, the visit would have to be postponed, along with the elaborate arrangements that attended it; and if he were to die during it or soon afterward, a pall would be cast over the new alliance. On Lady Monckton's return to London, she hurried to call on the Queen's private secretary, Sir Martin Charteris, and warned him that if the Queen wished to see her uncle still alive, it might be necessary to advance her visit. The Palace telephoned to the British Ambassador to France, Sir Christopher Soames, and requested him to ask Dr. Thin if the

Duke was likely to survive through May. Thin felt free, even duty-bound to tell Soames what he could not tell anyone else: It was too early for a reliable forecast, but "the timing would be close." So it proved—desperately close.

"Uncle David" had always spoken of "Lilibet" as "a marvelous girl," and she had always wanted to be close to him. The bond between them was strong enough to withstand the strains of the Abdication and of her mother and grandmother's hostility toward the Duchess. Now the Queen sent word that she would like to call on her uncle during her coming visit. The appointment was set for four o'clock on the afternoon of Thursday, May 18, three days after her arrival in Paris. As the time drew nearer, and her itinerary took her about France, the tension at the Embassy tautened; it requested Dr. Thin to step up his daily bulletins to twice a day. He could report nothing more definite than "a slow, steady weakening" until almost the eve of the visit, when he was able to give assurance that the Duke's chances of "making it" were good.

A few days earlier, he had become unable to swallow, and had to be fed by glucose dripped into his veins. But on the morning of the eighteenth, he declared firmly if indistinctly that he would not let Lilibet remember him as a bedridden invalid in rumpled pajamas and "bristling" (his own word) with needles and tubes. He did not even wish her to know that he had cancer—"the damn rigging will have to come out!" Thin consented: What could it matter now? One needle would remain, but he promised it would be out of sight.

Thin and Nurse Una Shanley started making him ready at noon. The task took almost four hours. But when the Queen was shown into his upstairs sitting room, she found him in his favorite armchair, wearing a jaunty blue blazer. He could not rise to welcome her; indeed, he could hardly speak; but he managed a smile and to bow over her hand. She chatted brightly with the dying old man for half an hour, then bade him good-bye, choking back her tears, and joined Prince Philip and Prince Charles in the library, where they were having tea with the Duchess.

Culley said, "The Duke put on an incredibly courageous performance!" Thin added, "So did the Queen. Between them, they carried it off in the best tradition of the stiff upper lip."

For fear of a possible crisis, Thin had stayed in the sitting room, but inconspicuously. As soon as the Queen went downstairs, he came forward to help prepare the Duke for bed. The Duke had forgotten that he was there and was "furious with himself," Thin said, for not having presented him.

Only a few days were left now: nine, eight, seven . . . and finally one, Saturday, May 27. As it dragged by, the Duke roused himself to ask Nurse Shanley, "Am I dying?"

She told him briskly, "You're quite intelligent enough to decide that for yourself!"

He had relapsed into a coma when Thin paid his regular visit that evening. The Duke's favorite pug, Black Diamond, usually lay at the foot of the bed and usually growled when Thin approached. This time he was on the rug, his head turned away. Thin whispered to Nurse Shanley, "See? The dog knows what's happening!"

A little past midnight, the Duke came out of his coma and asked for the Duchess. Nurse Shanley brought her. It would have been curiously fitting if he had happened to echo George IV's last words, to the doctor, Sir Wathen Waller, who was holding his hand: "Wally, what is this? It is death!" But the Duke said nothing. He died in his wife's arms at one twenty-three on Sunday morning, four weeks short of his seventy-eighth birthday. The man whom Churchill had called "a cherished and unique personality" was gone. The Duchess was too stunned to sob, to move, even to speak. When she finally let herself be led to her own room, Sidney, the Negro footman, took over the vigil in the death chamber and spent the rest of the night there, weeping.

Not long afterward, Sidney's wife, a French girl, also died, leaving him with three small children. The Duchess usually kept him on hand until late, but now he had to feed the children and put them to bed. He tried to engage a nurse or housekeeper; none being available, he was forced to ask the Duchess if he might begin going home at five. Although he had served the Windsors for nearly thirty years, she told him, "If you go at five, don't come back." He left and did not come back.

The Royal Air Force sent a jet to Le Bourget on the Wednesday, to pick up the body in its coffin of English oak and fly it to the air station at Benson, Oxfordshire. An air marshal and three air vice marshals in full ceremonial dress came to escort it. The Duchess had wanted to go, too, but she collapsed that morning, and her physician, Dr. Arthur J. Antenucci, who had just flown over from New York, would not permit her.

A strong, cold wind, unusual for Paris at the end of May, blew across the airfield; the French guard of honor had difficulty holding their line. The British Ambassador, the British Defence Attaché, the French Deputy Head of Protocol, the Prefect of the District, and the Duchess's secretary, John Utter, watched the plane into the air. Once the exile was on his way home, they did not linger; the wind was cruel. Utter remembered what the Duchess had told him when she engaged him ten years earlier: "One of your duties will be to bury us." He remained with her until 1975, when he resigned, with no severance pay and no promise of a pension.

Another guard of honor met the plane at Benson, along with the Duke and Duchess of Kent, members of the Government, and the French Ambassador. A band played the first six bars of the National Anthem ("I'd become rather used to the full treatment"). The coffin rested in the station chapel that night, and early next mornig was taken to Windsor Castle, where the Duke would lie in state in St. George's Chapel. As the hearse drove through the Henry VIII Gate, bringing Windsor back to Windsor, the Union Jack on the great Round Tower was hauled down to half-staff. The lying-in-state would not begin until the next day, Friday, but the town was already preparing for the crowd. Television vans had arrived and were being camouflaged, so as not to intrude on the solemnity; one of them seemed to be an outcropping from the Castle wall. Souvenir hawkers were warming up; their most popular item was reprints of the *Daily Mirror*'s front page for December 12, 1936, with the headline: "ABDICATION! King Edward VIII Will Broadcast Tonight!" Flowers by the vanload were being spread over the lawns of the Castle's Lower Ward, in which the Chapel stands. There were modest nosegays "From a devoted subject" and elaborate sprays "In re-

spectful memory" and small, untidy bunches "For our beloved King." There were formal arrangements from institutions of which the Duke had been patron, from clubs
and hunts to which he had belonged, and from the three
military services. There were wreaths with gilt-lettered ribbons from various royal families. There was a white ensign
of carnations and cornflowers "From the surviving officers
of the 1st Exmouth Term, Royal Naval College, Osborne,
1907." By evening the scent of the flowers was heavy on
the warm air.

When the public was admitted to St. George's Chapel at
eleven o'clock on Friday morning, some had been in the
queue for thirteen hours. Among them was a woman who
declined to give her name; "I didn't come for the publicity,"
she said, "I came to render homage." They saw that the
huge Chapel had been stripped almost bare, to concentrate
attention on the catafalque, which was centered on a dais
carpeted in the pale blue of the Garter sash and was itself
draped in the darker blue of the Garter mantle. The casket
was covered with the Duke's personal banner: the royal
standard with "a label of three point-argent, the center
point charged with an Imperial Crown proper." His Garter
banner had been taken down from above his stall in the
choir, and was laid by the high altar. On top of all was a
single wreath of Easter lilies from the royal Windsor gardens, sent by the Duchess. A cross stood at one end of the
dais; also on it, at the same level, were six tall candle-
sticks—the ones that had been used at Churchill's funeral
—with mourning candles of orange wax, unbleached. On
the tier below, officers of the House-hold Cavalry and the
Brigade of Guards, four at a time, kept twenty-minute
vigils.

That morning, Friday, Dr. Antenucci decided that the
Duchess had recovered enough strength to face the double
ordeal of the Royal Family and the obsequies. A plane
from the Queen's Flight came over in the forenoon to pick
them up: the Duchess; her close friend, the Countess of
Dudley; the Ambassador's wife, Lady Soames; and Dr. Antenucci and John Utter. Lord Mountbatten met them at
Heathrow Airport—the Duchess was offended that it was
not Prince Charles or some other member of the Royal

Family—and whisked them to Buckingham Palace, non-stop. Considerately, the Queen had ordered cross-traffic along the whole route blocked off until the Duchess's cavalcade had passed, to save her from being stared at while her car was held up at intersections. It was the first time that the Duchess had entered the Palace since the State Ball on May 14, 1935, in honor of King George V's Silver Jubilee—the ball where she thought she "felt the King's eyes rest searchingly" upon her. Her apartment on the first floor, the State Suite, looked straight down the Mall. "It was comfortable," she reported later, "but like a *morgue*— and oh, that *dreadful* damask!" Grace Dudley was close by, as were Utter and Antenucci. They felt that she was "still numb, in shock." She was pale when she went to luncheon, and her black dress emphasized her look of exhaustion.

The Queen's welcome was warm. To help keep things friendly and informal, she had brought the children in, "because they get through." Princess Anne was present at luncheon, and Prince Charles at dinner. The Duchess said later, "They were polite to me, polite and kind, especially the Queen. Royalty is always polite and kind. But they were cold. David always said they were cold." This was her only comment; a newspaper photograph of her anguished face, framed in a Palace window, told the rest.

All day Friday and Saturday, grieving crowds shuffled past the catafalque, two thousand of them an hour. At one time, the queue was a mile and half long. Some wept, some took snapshots; a number of elderly men were carrying copies of *Edward VIII—Our King,* an illustrated biography which had been published in 1936. More than sixty thousand of the Duke's admirers had paid their respects when the last few were turned away on Saturday evening.

Saturday, June 3, was the Queen's official birthday in 1972. Her actual birthday is April 21, but because it is thought desirable to announce a Birthday Honors List six months after the New Year's Honors List, her official birthday is now scheduled for early June—on a Saturday in recent years, so that commercial traffic will suffer a minimum of disruption by the crowds come to see the Trooping. Always a spectacular feature of the public celebration, that year it was more spectacular than ever.

When the Queen rode out to take the salute, the massed pipe bands of the Scots Guards and the Irish Guards formed up opposite her—something they had never done before—and played a lament, as a special Act of Remembrance for their late Commander in Chief.

The Duchess spent the day in her apartment. She had been invited to the ceremony, but she preferred to watch it on television with a few friends. She had been notified that a lament would be played; she knew how heartrending it could be, and she did not trust her composure in public, even though Dr. Antenucci had numbed her with sedatives. They were strong ones. Prince Charles, her favorite in the Royal Family, presently came in to say that he would meet her at St. George's Chapel that evening; and he had scarcely left when she confessed piteously, "I can't remember what he's just told me—where I'm to go and what I'm to do! Isn't it terrible?"

She had not planned to see the lying-in-state, but Lady Monckton told her, "It is most impressive. You *must* go!" Lord Mountbatten, again, escorted her from the Palace to Windsor. Prince Charles was waiting. The splendor and dignity of he Chapel, the officers at their vigils, the scarlet of their uniforms, darker in the dimness—all this moved her deeply. "I was proud and stirred," she said. She crossed to the catafalque and stood for two minutes at each of its four corners. "Thirty-five years! . . . [June 3 was the Windsors' thirty-fifth wedding anniversary.] I always prayed that I would die before him. Why should *I* be the one to survive? I can't bear to think of life without him!"

She was whispering to herself, but Prince Charles heard her, and tears rose to his eyes.

Lord Mountbatten, meanwhile, went to an inconspicuous alcove where the B.B.C. had set up a microphone, and broadcast a final tribute to his cousin, friend, and former sovereign:

> When I married fifty years ago, he was my best man. . . . More than my best man, he was my best friend all my life. . . . An attractive American woman, Wallis Simpson . . . changed the course of his life. Indeed it changed the course of history. They

were very much in love. . . . I remember the dreadful day of the Abdication—

His voice broke; presently he went on:

> His brothers and myself . . . were trying to dissuade
> him. I was bitterly opposed. . . . He knows [*sic*] it,
> but it made no difference to our friendship. What a
> great debt the people of this country, and indeed the
> whole Commonwealth, owe him for all he did for us
> when he was Prince of Wales! Nobody who knew him
> then can ever forget him. We shall miss him. But nobody more than myself.

On Sunday, when St. George's Chapel was closed, the coffin was removed to the Albert Memorial Chapel, adjoining, where the body was transferred to a simpler coffin for burial. Meanwhile the grave was being dug. The Duke had decided long before not to rest in the Chapel vault—alongside his brother King George VI; his father, King George V; his grandfather King Edward VII; and many, many other kings of England—but in the lawn at Frogmore, half a mile away, behind the mausoleum which his great-grandmother Queen Victoria had built for herself and Prince Albert. It was not that the Duke had held her in special reverence or affection. On the contrary, he once confessed that his dominant recollection of her was having to take her hand, when he was a child of six, and "how horribly *boneless* it felt!" He chose Frogmore because in time his beloved Duchess would join him there, which would never be allowed her in St. George's Chapel. Here in this lawn, screened by azaleas, rhododendrons, and cypresses, already lay the Duke's favorite brother, Prince George Duke of Kent, with Princess Marina; and another of his favorites, his great-uncle Prince Arthur Duke of Connaught; Princess Victoria—"Aunt Toria"—is there, and a dozen more of the family.

In 1955, during one of the Duchess's recurrent fits of pique with the British, she told the Duke that she refused to be buried in England, and urged him to buy them a plot in Green Mount Cemetery in Baltimore, where many of her Warfield and Montague relations lie. Obligingly, the

Duke sent his comptroller to choose the plot, and in 1957 he bought it: one large enough for six graves (to permit suitable landscaping). A few years later, the Queen let it be known that the Duchess would be welcome at Frogmore, and the plot was reassigned to Green Mount.

On the morning of the funeral, the Duchess left the Palace soon after ten, with Lady Dudley and Douglas Greenacre, a former equerry of the Duke's. They reached the Castle a few minutes before eleven and went to the Dean's Room in St. George's Chapel, where the Royal Family were gathering. Sedatives had helped the Duchess through the long night, and many observers thought that their effect had not yet worn off. She was trim and immaculate as always—"like a Tanagra figurine," someone said—but she seemed dazed, even frightened, almost as if she did not know where she was or with whom.

She had asked Mountbatten nervously, "How will I recognize them all?" and he had soothed her: "I'll help you." Now he introduced them: "This is Eddie Kent and his wife, Katharine. And Alice Gloucester." Her husband, Harry, the Duke's only surviving brother, was too ill to come. Windsor had once said sadly, "It looks as if I shall be—and perhaps by a small margin—the last survivor of a large family." He was nearly right. John, George, Bertie, and Mary died before himself and Harry, but Harry lived until June 10, 1974. Mountbatten went on: "The Ogilvys, Alexandra and Angus. And Margaret and Tony Snowdon. And Anne and Charles, of course." Princess Anne and Prince Charles greeted her as "Aunt Wallis." The younger women stood back, respectfully, but the elder came forward and kissed her. Her old archenemy, the Queen Mother, was a few minutes late arriving; she went up to the Duchess at once and murmured her sympathy.

Windsor Castle's two-ton curfew bell, which rings only for the birth of a prince or a royal marriage or a Garter service or the death of a sovereign, had been tolling for the past hour. At eleven-fifteen, it fell silent, and the toll was taken up by Westminster Abbey. The mourners went to their seats in the choir; next to the Queen was the Duchess. Dr. Antenucci was placed where he could watch her, and reach her side at once if needed. Thickly veiled, she leaned forward with her head bowed and did not lift it as the cortege entered from the Albert Memorial Chapel.

The Constable-Governor of Windsor Castle, in full-dress uniform, came first; next, the Military Knights of Windsor, elderly men, with plumed hats under their arms; then the choir and the clergy. The Archbishop of Canterbury, the successor to Windsor's adversary, Cosmo Lang, wore a white miter and a black-and-gold cape. The Duke's insignia were carried in on three blue velvet cushions: his Garter in the center, his field marshal's baton on one side, and on the other, his decorations of gold and silver, jeweled and enameled in scarlet and blue and purple, like fragments of the Chapel's great, glowing west window.

A bearer party from the Prince of Wales's Company, 1st Battalion, Welsh Guards, their boots squeaking and scraping in the hush, brought in the coffin. Behind it marched the Duke of Edinburgh and King Olaf of Norway. The young princes and dukes of the royal family followed. Last of all were Earl Mountbatten of Burma and the Duke of Beaufort, present not as the Master of the Horse, but as the husband of Queen Mary's niece, the daughter of the Duke of Cambridge.

After the hymns and prayers, the Garter King-of-Arms stepped forward in his gorgeous heraldic costume and proclaimed the styles and titles of the late Duke: "Knight of the most excellent order of the Garter, Knight of the Thistle, Knight of St. Patrick, Knight Grand Commander of the Bath, Knight Grand Commander of the Star of India, Knight Grand Cross of St. Michael and St. George . . . Military Cross . . . Admiral of the Fleet, Field Marshal of the Army, Marshal of the Royal Air Force . . . and sometime the most high, most mighty, and most excellent monarch, King Edward the Eighth, Emperor of India, Defender of the Faith, and uncle of the most high, most mighty, and most excellent monarch, Queen Elizabeth the Second!" The Archbishop of Canterbury gave the blessing. Four trumpeters of the Household Cavalry sounded "Last Post" and "Reveille." It was over.

If there was grief anywhere in the Chapel, it was not seen or heard. Even allowing for British reserve, and for the self-control instinctive with the Royal Family, the

mood seemed less one of sorrow for a lost leader than of
relief at reaching the end of an uncomfortable chapter. To
some, the insincerity of those worshipful phrases—"most
high, most mighty, and most excellent monarch, King Edward the Eighth"—suggested that these were cinema obsequies, with jewels of paste and with the other properties of
plastic and cardboard, like the mourners' emotions; and
with a cast and crew impatient for the scene to end and let
them be off.

The Queen had invited the male members of the Windsors' staff to his funeral at her expense, but their flight was
delayed at Orly, and they did not arrive until the trumpet
notes were dying away and the mourners were leaving.
Each of the Royal Family paused to bow to the casket.
The Duke of Edinburgh supported the widow out of the
Chapel and up to the Castle for luncheon. While cocktails
and sherry were being served, the Queen Mother drew the
Duchess to a settee and chatted with her. The Duchess did
not remember it; the trance was still upon her; she remembered only that "We exchanged a few words, nothing
more." Then, in an uncontrollable upwelling of bitterness,
"*She* is the one who kept the King from giving me the title
that David wanted for me!"

Some forty sat down, at five tables, the Duchess on
Prince Philip's right, with Lord Mountbatten on her own
right. Afterward came the last part of the last ordeal. Two
motorcades followed the hearse to the Frogmore lawn,
where the coffin was lowered into the grave, under a wide-
spreading plane tree. Still distraught and overwrought, the
"bedlam brain-sick Duchess" drifted from person to person, asking, "Where's the Duke?" and "Are you having a
good time?" and "Why isn't the Duke here?" until the
Queen Mother, pitying her, came forward again and took
her unresisting arm, gently, as if she were a lost child.

"I know how you feel," she said. "I've been through it
myself."

A simple ledger of cream-colored Portland marble now
marks the grave:

H.R.H. The Prince Edward
Albert Christian George

Andrew Patrick David
        Duke of Windsor
Born 23rd June 1894
Died 28th May 1972
King Edward VIII
20 January–11 December 1936

Everyone returned to the Castle for refreshment and a rest. The Duchess stayed only briefly; she was impatient to get home. The whole Royal Family came to the door to see her off to Heathrow with her retinue, Dr. Antenucci, Lady Dudley, and Utter. The Queen sent the highest official in her household, the Lord Chamberlain, Lord Maclean, to accompany her. He was new in office; the public did not recognize him, nor did the press; and a newspaper photograph showing the Duchess entering the plane apparently alone, fostered a report that the Queen had callously turned her out, to make her way to Heathrow as best she could. It is possible that she herself was unaware of the Lord Chamberlain's presence; Dr. Antenucci's sedatives still held her in thrall, and would not release her for some hours yet. When the pilot had delivered her to Paris, she told him, "You must come out and see us, next time you're here. The Duke would so enjoy meeting you!"

Then she drove to her empty house. But most of her heart was still under the plane tree, and the years ahead loomed as empty as the house.

Even as the service in St. George's Chapel was moving to its stately close, Labour members in the House of Commons were denouncing it as so much "nauseating cant." But one of them, Willie Hamilton, a notorious Scottish "monarch-basher," paid an unexpected tribute to the Duchess: "No woman could have behaved with more dignity and grace in the torrent of humiliation and indignity from various governments and from Commons over thirty-six years." He said that he was planning a Commons motion condemning "the hypocrisy and humbug of the current Establishment, including the Royal Family, over the treatment meted out to the Windsors. I hope," he ended, "that Prince Charles will marry a divorced hippy!"

The Duchess did not share Mr. Hamilton's ignoble hope. An interview she gave in May 1974 quotes her as saying, "I think the Prince will marry an English girl. But if he does marry an American, let's just hope it's not a divorced one."

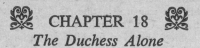

CHAPTER 18
The Duchess Alone

Let not poor Nelly starve.
—KING CHARLES II

When the Duke of Windsor's will was read, his widow learned that the man who had given up so much for her sake—position, the world's respect, and much of its affection ("Never before," it has been said, "did any man give up so much for so little")—now gave her all that remained to him. Only his French attorneys and his Swiss bankers know the tally of his fortune. Still, a former comptroller once let slip that when he last saw the Duke's portfolio, in the early 1960's, the liquid assets amounted to 3,000,000 pounds, then about 8,500,000 dollars. The total was almost certainly higher at his death, since he had cultivated knowledgeable men of money, sought their financial advice, and profitably followed it.

Over the years, he had given the Duchess jewels estimated to be worth more than 6,000,000 dollars. He had inherited most of them from Queen Alexandra, so although they were his personal property, they are also—in a sense—Crown jewels. A press syndicate has reported that "The British Royal Family is starting negotiations with the Duchess to ensure that after her death [the jewels] come to Prince Charles. . . . One expert says, 'If they don't go to Charles, you can expect fireworks.' " In addition to the jewels and to stocks and bonds, the Duke left her another fortune in real estate (The Mill was sold in June 1973 for a reputed 640,000 dollars); and a third fortune in chattels which ranged from those portraits by Stubbs, Llewellyn, Gunn, and Munnings, to coffers of gold and silver, and jeweled trinkets: cuff links by the score, pearl studs, cigarette cases, and lighters. Add the jeweled orders and decorations. Add the rich caskets and plate presented by grateful guilds and committees. Add the furniture, the other paintings, the dinner services, the inscribed first editions. Add such historic treasures as the Abdication desk and the Garter standard. Add the unique set of crystal beakers, mugs, and goblets engraved for his Coronation. Even these were now hers.

Windsor had bequeathed not a penny to charity or the Church, nor even a single memento, however trivial and valueless, to a relative or a godchild—among them David Metcalfe, David Earl of Westmoreland, and David Marquess of Milford-Haven. The sole exception was one of Mountbatten's daughters, Lady Patricia Brabourne, to whom he left an inscribed copy of a Royal Family tree which her father had had privately printed and had given him. Nor was anything left to a friend, an associate, or—despite his promises annually renewed—a servant. Everything he possessed went to his Duchess—as no one knew better than herself. Before illness drove her to her bed, she was seen to make a gesture embracing the four walls of her living room, and was heard to exclaim, "Everything here—everything in this house—everything connected with me and the Duke is *mine*! *Everything*!"

Not long after the Duke's funeral, his widow telephoned Lord Mountbatten in London and asked him to come over and advise her. He flew to Paris at once.

She said, "Thank God you're here! Look at all these things of David's—" She gestured toward the silver and gold bric-a-brac that loaded the tables. "What on. earth shall I do with them? He left no instructions, none!"

"If I were you," Mountbatten told her, "I'd begin by handing his uniforms, robes, orders, and decorations over to the Queen—not as your niece, but as the Sovereign. That would be the dignified thing to do." The Duchess agreed. In course of time, the uniforms and robes (some two dozen, including his Garter robe and his uniforms as Field Marshal, Admiral of the Fleet, Marshal of the Royal Air Force, and honorary colonel of various regiments) and the orders and decorations (well over a score) all were sent to England, for display first at Windsor Castle and later in the National Army Museum. Mountbatten added,

"The Queen should have his papers, too—especially his papers." These were also sent.

The Duchess asked, "What about his red box?"

"Why not give it to some relative of yours?"

"I have no one," she said firmly, "no one that he'd approve my leaving it to. There are no more Montagues—they are all gone, wiped out—and no more Warfields." True, there are none closer than second cousins, but she had at least nine second cousins at that time.

"Then tell your executors it must go to a member of the Royal Family. . . . Have you decided what you're going to do with your money?"

"I don't know how much I've got. I don't think it's enough for me to stay here. Besides, the French Government might not let me."

Mountbatten laughed. "The French Government built up so much goodwill by its hospitality to David, it's certainly not going to sacrifice any of it by expelling his widow!"

He was right. The French Foreign Minister presently called in person to express his Government's sorrow at the Duke's death, and to assure the Duchess that there would be no death duties to pay, and that she was welcome to stay on in her house as long as she wished.

"As for your money," Mountbatten continued, "you can't have less than two million pounds, and possibly as much as several million."

She was amazed. A friend of hers once remarked, "Wallis thinks she's the poorest woman in Europe." The Duke shared his wife's misconception. Both of them were haunted throughout their lives together by the utterly groundless fear of sudden penury. His Swiss banker once told him, "If you and the Duchess started spending your capital with both hands right now, you couldn't exhaust it in your lifetimes!" The Duke refused to be comforted. Again, his solicitor, Sir Godfrey Morley, who had succeeded George Allen as senior partner in Allen & Overy, found him distraught and moaning, "Our expenses have gone *wild*! I don't know how I can meet my bills! We shall have to dismiss the staff and move into smaller quarters!" His panic had been triggered by the window cleaners' request for a modest raise in pay.

Mountbatten's assurance of her liquidity allayed one of the Duchess's worries only to rouse another: "What shall I do with so much money?" She added, "The Duke always took charge of our financial affairs. The last time—the *only* time—I ever managed the purse was when I was a Navy officer's wife, and there was mighty little to manage." She smiled, then went on: "What I'd really like to do is something to perpetuate David's memory—a foundation of some sort, perhaps the Windsor, or Duke of Windsor, Foundation. . . . Do you think Charles would become involved with it?"

"I'm certain he'd be delighted," Mountbatten said. "You could staff the board with David's surviving friends—Colin Buist would be one—and make Charles chairman. All you'd have to do then is nominate the beneficiaries—the individuals or organizations you think David would have liked to support—and the trustees would apply the income accordingly, in his memory."

She clapped her hands. "It's a *wonderful* idea. I'll get Godfrey Morley to redraw my will at once, then we'll clear it with my French lawyer."

This was Maître Suzanne Blum, whose shrewdness had much impressed the Duchess and on whose judgment she had come to rely. Said to be a distant relation of the late Premier Léon Blum, Maître Blum went to the United States before the German occupation of France and studied law at Columbia University. Later she worked for the French Consulate in New York and, on her return home, for the Free French. In 1958, she represented Rita Hayworth in her divorce from Aly Khan; her other Hollywood clients have included Charlie Chaplin, Jack Warner, and Darryl Zanuck. Her first husband, also a lawyer, had long been Allen & Overy's Paris correspondent; it was he who brought her to the Windsors' attention. On his death in 1960, she took over his part of the firm. Her present husband, Gen. Georges Spillmann, is an Arabic scholar, a veteran of Morocco, and a Grand Officer of the *Légion d'honneur*; she is an officer. A woman of about the Duchess's age, her reputation as a trial lawyer is "quick, cool, clever, tough."

But far from Morley's being instructed to provide for the Duke of Windsor Foundation in the Duchess's will, the next word he had from her, the following January, was a letter stating: 1) that the Foundation had been abandoned; 2) that she no longer required his services; and 3) that Maître Blum would be her sole legal adviser thenceforth, in complete control. Morley never learned what had brought about his abrupt dismissal or why the Foundation had been abandoned, though there was talk that Maître Blum had alarmed the Duchess by speculating that if such a foundation were established, and the income spent in England, the French Government might tax the Duke's estate, despite the Foreign Minister's promise. Morley said only, "I had the feeling that she wanted to end the British connection—*any* connection with Britain." Twenty years before, Windsor Awards, Inc., had briefly flared, then fizzled; "Operation Orphan" never got past the stage of discussion; nor, now, did the Duke of Windsor Foundation.

When Lord Mountbatten heard the news, he was outraged. "Damn it!" he said. "The money was *his*, not hers!"

Late in 1972, it became the Duchess's turn to suffer physical misfortunes. They began in her drawing room; she was walking with a cane when a small rug skidded under it and she fell, breaking her hip. In Biarritz the following summer, she fell again and cracked five ribs. A sympathetic friend said, "Her bones are becoming like glass." Forced inaction was more galling for her than for most invalids, since, like the Duke, she had no inner resources, no hobbies, no pastimes, no interests except clothes, no talents except for wearing them, and for arranging flowers, running a house, and entertaining—hardly a rich enough variety of material to fill one's life.

For her, music fell on deaf ears, literature was a closed book. The scene in the television series *Edward and Mrs. Simpson,* which showed "Wallis" reading *Wuthering Heights,* somewhat discredited the authenticity of the production among those who knew her, none of whom had ever seen the original reading anything weightier than *Vogue,* the daily newspapers, and detective stories. Perhaps she had been frightened away from books by one, *Ida,* which Gertrude Stein had written and sent her, with a message saying that it was about her and the Duke. The Duchess dutifully sat down to it. On page 25, she met this passage: "Ida went to buy some shoes. She liked to look at yellow shoes when she was going to buy red ones. She liked to look at black shoes when she was not going to buy any shoes at all." Still, the Duchess plowed on to the end, which was this: "She dresses in another hat and she dresses in another dress and Andrew is in, and they go in and that is where they are. They are there. Thank them. Yes."[1]

The Duchess thanked Miss Stein, but admitted privately and understandably, "I am no wiser than when I started Chapter One."

The Windsors had devoted their lives to looking after each other and to giving and attending parties. They had measured out their lives with coffee spoons. One of their intimates said, "They were the most egocentric pair that ever lived!" They were quite alone in a disapproving world, and now the Duchess realized it. Long ago, she had faced down the temptation to absorb herself in any charity. She was on the board of the American Hospital and of the Animal Society, but their demands on her time and purse were negligible. Before her health failed, John Utter repeatedly tried to persuade her to visit the charity patients in some hospital for a few hours every week, in order to "redeem her image. It would have cost her no effort," he said, "but she refused." She rarely went to the theatre or the cinema. When she appeared in public, it was not to see but to be seen. She said, "Now all that I once was is finished, done for, gone. I'm out of the newspapers. People have forgotten me—I imagine they think I'm dead. That doesn't bother me. I don't want any more publicity." Yet she gave at least four interviews in the next three years. They were published in *Time*, November 19, 1973; *Women's Wear Daily*, May 3, 1974; *People*, August 12, 1974; and the London *Times*, April 15, 1975. She insisted that all press photographs of her show one of the Duke on a table at her side.

During her convalescence, she turned to the newspapers, television—especially for football and hockey—and detective stories—"mostly a lot of trash." In her last years, an increasing preference for mere entertainment caused her to reject the harsh realities of the news. "It's a bombshell world," she often said, "full of violence and horror. I no longer like it or understand it. China baffles me but fascinates me." When friends came to call, they noticed that many of her sentences began, "The Duke used to—" and that sooner or later she turned the conversation to something about him: how she first met him; his consideration for others; his straightforwardness ("He knew what he liked and didn't like; he was quick to form an opinion—it was often a prejudice—and very, very slow to change it"); his obstinacy; his patience; the sweetness of his disposition ("He never directed a cross word at me"—a pretty echo of Freda Dudley Ward's "We never exchanged ugly words"); and finally, how grievously she missed him. She might have added two more to her list of his fine qualities: his resilience and his inexhaustible forgiveness.

A friend asked, "Isn't it hard to run a house without a man?"

"Yes," the Duchess said. "My ship is without a captain."

Plainly, the Duke had been given a posthumous promotion.

Friends also noticed that she now raised and dwelt on a subject that had long been closed: her two previous husbands. "Win" and "Ernest" rose to her lips again and again, particularly the former, always against the background of Pensacola and the tensions of a naval aviator's wife. She talked of both men freely and kindly—but never of Jimmy Donahue.

She also liked to talk about her hopes to travel, when her recovery would be complete—"Not back to Maryland. It has no pull for me anymore. When I was a girl, I used to divide my summers between Uncle Henry Warfield's place and Uncle Emory's, both just outside of Baltimore, but now I am the last. They are all gone. I'd like to see new countries—South Africa, for instance—countries where I've never been. . . ."

She never went. One of her few trips was to Frogmore, the year after the Duke's death, on his birthday, June 23. The Queen sent her plane, and Lord Mountbatten and the Duke of Kent met her at the airport; no one else was notified. She put flowers on the grave, had tea with the Queen, and flew back to Paris. It was probably ill health that forbade her to make the pilgrimage again, though she found strength to go to America twice, both times by the Italian Line, from Cannes. Nor did she move to a hotel, though she sometimes talked of that, too. True, she exchanged their old apartment in the Waldorf Towers, 28-A, for one smaller and less expensive, 40-F. Their new friend Nate Cummings thought it depressingly bleak for her, so he lent her a Sisley and a Renoir. Mr. Cummings was the prime mover in trying to have a "suitable memorial" to the Duke erected at a site on Park Avenue opposite the Waldorf; but, he says, "Due to a combination of factors, the idea had to be abandoned."

She decided against making any hotel her principal residence. What persuaded her was her natural timidity and her desire to continue having her familiar, cherished *objets d'art* around her. "I like to be with my own things," she said. "Besides, the Duke wanted me to keep on this way." She was also reluctant to disband the staff of seventeen who had served her so long and so faithfully. Finally, there were the pugs, Black Diamond and Gin-Seng (Tibetan for "long life"); she said, "They're far happier on our lawn than they'd ever be in a hotel. The two of them insist on sleeping with me." She added archly, "It is flattering to know that there are creatures who still want to share my bed. . . . Yes, we're all happier here in Neuilly, happier and safer."

She used to make fun of her fears: "I've always been something of a scaredy-cat. Thunderstorms frighten me. I never traveled in planes if I could avoid it." When she traveled by train, it was always in a locked compartment. There was also the problem of transporting the retinue—the doctor, the secretary, the maid, and, importantly, the two dogs—that would have had to accompany her on a trip of any length, such as to South Africa. A voyage would have meant exile, not only from her house with its familiar furnishings, but from the small, personal items, especially the intimate mementos of the Duke. His suits still hang in his dressing-room closet. His shirts are stacked in their drawers, his toilet articles spread in his bathroom, his desk ready for instant use, with supplies of pipe cleaners and assorted stationery, all as during his lifetime. His favorite photographs of the Duchess still stand on his bedroom mantel and on his bookcases, all exactly as he left them. In the morbid tradition established by Queen Victoria and continued by King Edward VII, nothing has been changed; the bedroom has not even been disinfected, nor the mattress turned. Every night she goes to his rooms before retiring to her own. She makes sure that the lights are on and that everything is in place, then says aloud, "Good night, David!" Her final inspection is to see that his pistol—the one he had carried in the Great War—is on her bed table.

The possibility of attack is never far from her mind. She has been threatened so often that her apprehensions are excusable. Beginning with that day late in 1936 when the King's determination to marry her became known, public resentment had exploded in a fury of abusive letters, bomb warnings, anonymous telephone calls, chalked epithets, and even a brick through her window. The expression abated, but the resentment remained. No other woman in modern times has been so disliked, and no one knew better than the Duke that though he had hoped to make her Queen of England, he had succeeded only in making her notorious and vulnerable. What should have been the serenity of his last hours was disturbed by his awareness that all too soon he would no longer be present to shield her. Philemon begged Jupiter to let "one and the same hour" take him and his beloved wife, Baucis, "that I may not live to see her grave, nor be laid in mine by her." And George Eliot's husband wrote to Thomas Adolphus Trollope, "When people love each other and have lived together any time they ought to die together." They might have been speaking for the Duke. Right to the end, he was constantly concerned for Wallis's happiness, comfort, and safety—mainly her safety.

So is she. The Neuilly house has become a fortress. The heavy gates are always locked and guarded, though she looked on this, before illness confined her to her room, not as added protection, but as a potential source of danger; she dreaded having to wait in her car while the gates were being unlocked and swung open; she thought it offered a kidnapper or assassin an ideal opportunity to spring at her from the shrubbery. An electronic alarm system supplements the bars at every window. A former French paratrooper, a veteran of Indo-China and Algiers, patrols the grounds with a big guard dog, Pompidou. The Duchess has her own "hot line" to the police station at the corner—she tests it from time to time—and special security agents were on call to accompany her when she went out after dark. Although she sleeps lightly and irregularly, she never takes a sedative or uses earplugs, because "I want to be alert." Often at night she used to leave her bed and peer through the window, to assure herself that the watchman was duly making his rounds.

But no watchman, no spiked fence, no barred windows or bolted doors could keep at bay her oldest enemy: boredom. She tried hard. As soon as she had sufficiently recovered from her two falls, she resumed entertaining. She once observed, "I miss American friends, the kind you can call up in the middle of the night and you know they'll respond. The French aren't really your friends, even when you've known them for twenty years. If and when you need them, they think about it for a week." One theory why she disliked the French is that she couldn't wisecrack in their language and was jealous of those who could. Her attitude sweetened in the early phases of her illness; she said merrily, "I see more of my French friends now. I like having French people around me. They make me feel young. The Duke was never too comfortable with them because he didn't like to speak French. I love having people in—three or four, half a dozen. Two tables of ten is a gala for me! We used to have music. The Duke loved to dance and to take a turn at the drums. But I don't dance anymore. Nor do my friends. We're too old. I've got used to that."

Presently she found that more than the dancing had gone out of her parties. Her guests no longer seemed as amusing as in the old days, nor did she seem so to them. It was she who had changed. Her spells of forgetfulness at the Duke's obsequies had been charitably blamed on the interaction of exhaustion and sedation. But graver agents had been at work for some time. Their first foreshadowings had disquieted the Duke as early as 1969, when he had begun telephoning to friends late of an occasional afternoon: "Our secretary has gone home, and the Duchess can't seem to recall just where we are dining tonight. By any chance, do you happen to know?" A year later, he sadly admitted to the Winston Guests, "I'm afraid the Duchess is losing her mind. . . ."

* * *

At about the time when the Duke died, Lucy Rogers sold Crumwold and moved to the sunny apartment in Monte Carlo where she still lives, kept company by mementos of Herman: his cuff links; the fraternity pins and symbolic watch charms awarded him at Yale; the lacquer cabinets he had collected in China; the gold-and-sapphire cigarette case from the Windsor wedding and the silver salver from his own—locked away now, with its exacerbating inscriptions out of sight. But the news of the Duke's death purged her old bitterness; she broke her more than twenty years' silence and wrote Wallis a gentle note of sympathy, ending, "I shall always remain your friend, in memory of Herman and the Duke." Wallis's only reply was an engraved card. It offended Lucy; it suggested that she had been enrolled on the long roster of those whom Wallis had once cherished, and then rejected: Thelma Furness, Mary Kirk, Newbold Noyes, and the many others. This is possible, but fairness to Wallis requires that another possibility be mentioned: the arteriosclerosis that soon would riddle her memory may have been giving advance notice of its onset. The name "Lucy Rogers" may have fallen into a just-opened crevice. Perhaps rudeness and coldness were not to blame for the slight, but illness.

Its effects were mild and intermittent at first, and she enjoyed long periods when, for all that her close friends could tell, she was in full possession of her faculties. Lady Sefton remembers a dinner at the Neuilly house in November 1973 when the Duchess introduced nearly a score of other guests without a fumble. Yet by the following spring, such a feat had become too much for her, and it was clear that her mind was not only enfeebled and disordered, but subject to sudden, total collapses. One of the most dangerous occurred when she was convalescing from her broken hip. In the course of a normal conversation with her nurse, she asked, "Can you do the Charleston?"

"No, ma'am. I never learned."

"You should," the Duchess told her. "It's easy and it's fun. Watch!" She swung out of bed, wriggled away from the nurse's terror-sticken clutch, and managed to take a few wild steps before her hip broke again.

These collapses sometimes alternated with hallucinations. Lady Monckton was visiting her that summer when the Duchess suddenly cried, "I'm frightened! They've been here again! They've moved my things!"

After a moment she said more calmly, "It's the second time they've hijacked me." Lady Monckton knew that nothing in the room had been disturbed for years.

It was also noticed that her remarks were often taking on a sharp edge. One guest remembers a dinner in 1974 when she abruptly demanded of the table, "What do you think of Kissinger? Everybody say what he thinks!" She pointed to Count X, an old friend of the Windsors': "You!"

X said, "I don't think he's proven himself yet, Duchess. I think he—"

"How *dare* you say that!" she broke in. "What have you ever done to prove *your*self?"

Her outbursts of aggressiveness could be shrugged off, but her lapses of memory were often difficult to deal with. At another dinner in 1974, she leaned toward Mr. Y on her left and whispered, "Who's that man across from me? Who brought him?"

Since, unmistakably, she was indicating her secretary, Y whispered back in bewilderment, "You don't mean Mr. Utter, do you?"

"Utter? Who's he?" she said loudly and clearly. "I never saw him before in my life!"

A similar lapse, but more awkward, occurred at dinner at the British Embassy in Paris. Ambassador Sir Edward Tomkins, a person of some portliness, had seated the Duchess on his right and could not help overhearing her piercing query to her other neighbor: "Who's this fat man on my left?"

Again, Mr. Z was having tea with her tête-à-tête one afternoon when she sighed and murmured, "What a pity about Z! He used to be *so* nice before he lost his head over that woman in his office. Threw his dear wife out of the house, you know, and then dropped from sight. How can anyone be such a fool, to give up so much?"

Z was on the point of suggesting hotly that the late Duke had been better qualified than himself to answer her question, when—he said—"She came back from her little trip to nowhere" and picked up the conversation, calling him "Z" as always before. A few moments later his discomfort was renewed, when an anecdote of his drew from her, "How *very* amusing! I must remember to tell the Duke."

"She drifts in and out," he explained. "The trouble is, sometimes you're not absolutely sure whether she's out or in."

Her friends, resentful of her bellicosity and embarrassed by her forgetfulness, began finding excuses for declining her invitations. Some of her former "regulars" died off. Others suggested by their unexplained absences that they had been attracted by the late former King, rather than by his Queen *manquée*. Still others were gentlefolk reluctant to accept hospitality which the towering cost of living would not let them return; they could no longer afford to buy the food and wine which they would have been embarrassed not to offer her in their homes, and far less in a Paris restaurant.

To be sure, a comforting number of old friends remained loyal and attentive: the Czernins, the Patiños, Princess Ghislaine de Polignac, several Rothschilds, and the Duke's cousin Prince Dimitri. The English included Lord Warwick, Lady Dudley, Lady Sefton, kindly, charming Lady Mosley, and the handsome Lady Monckton of Brenchley. Among the Americans were Mrs. Wolcott Blair, the Nate Cummingses, the Farkases, the Winston Guests, and, until her death in 1977, Mrs George F. Baker. But on too many evenings, despite the "desperate loneliness" that the Duchess admitted, places at her table were laid for only three: herself and her two secretaries, Utter, until his departure in 1975, and a Swiss girl, Mlle. Johanna Schütz, until hers in April 1978. The Duchess could as well have stayed in her drawing room, with the silver mug of iced vodka which had supplanted Scotch whiskey as her favorite tipple. She ate less and less, although her doctors told her that it was vital to build up her strength. She pled, "I *try* to eat, but I can't make myself do it."

The result was an extreme loss of weight (to eighty-seven pounds), and a gastric ulcer which perforated and hemorrhaged in late November 1975. She was rushed to the American Hospital "to be treated for physical exhaustion and long spells of weakness" (according to the official bulletin), and began receiving a series of blood transfusions. Six months passed before she could safely be discharged. The Royal Family had not invited her to Princess Anne's wedding in November 1973, but they sent flowers to the sickroom. Back home again, weakness kept her quietly indoors until a sunny morning in May encouraged her to have her chaise longue carried onto the lawn. Two photographers with telephoto lenses were lurking in the shrubbery; they snapped her as she was being lifted by a nurse in uniform, and their cruel picture of her fleshless face and haunted eyes appeared both in *France-Soir* and on the state television. She sued for "wrongful intrusion on her privacy" and was awarded damages of sixteen thousand dollars from each defendant.

The few friends who were allowed to see her reported that she was still piteously emaciated, but that her chestnut hair was as glossy as ever, and her skin as smooth and flawless. But her mind, they said, wandered further and more often. Once it wandered all the way back to Vienna, in February 1935, and—like a long-silent music box that, untouched, suddenly begins to tinkle— she suddenly began to murmur, *"Ich weiss auf der Weiden ein kleines Hotel"*—the sentimental waltz that once had meant so much to her and the Duke. Perhaps it reminded her of "The Windsor Waltz," with Jimmy Donahue mopping and mowing at her table, and behind Jimmy a shadowy file of her other old loves: Ernest Simpson, Felipe Espil, Hugh Spilman, Gerry Green, Win Spencer.

Lady Monckton, whom the Duchess trusted more than perhaps anyone else, visited her in the stifling summer of 1976 and found her surprisingly lucid, but surprisingly morbid. Her thoughts were fixed on death. Immortal longings were in her. She begged "Biddy's" promise to escort her body to Frogmore. Lady Monckton gave it; then, before moving along to a cheerier subject, she boldly told the Duchess, "Princess Alexandra and the Duchess of Kent are loyal, hardworking girls, both of them, and they haven't many jewels. Unless you've made other plans, you might remember them." The Duchess dodged the suggestion; she said only that her gravestone had already been ordered; it would match the Duke's and would rest beside it, under the plane tree. But she later told another friend, "Everything is going to Prince Charles—everything! He wrote me a *beautiful* letter after the Duke's funeral."

That October, Lord Mountbatten telephoned the Neuilly house to say that he was in Paris and would like to call. Mlle. Schütz, presumably after conferring with the Duchess, instructed him to come next afternoon, promptly at five. If this struck Mountbatten as peremptory, next morning's message from Mlle. Schütz struck him as demented: The Duchess, she said, wanted him to know that she was angry at his daring to bring with him her own doctor, Thin, when he called. Mountbatten protested that far from proposing to bring along Dr. Thin, he had never met the man or ever had any communication with him. "Give me his telephone number," he said. "We'll straighten this out!"

He rang Thin and explained the situation. Thin said that he was scheduled to pay the Duchess a professional visit and would assure her that she was mistaken. A day later Thin called back. "She is suffering from hallucinations," he said hesitantly. "I suggest that you not try to see her. It would be a—an unpleasant experience." Mountbatten never saw her again.

Nor did any of her close friends, except Lady Mosley, who was permitted to call once a month. Others were told that she was unavailable. David Pryce-Jones, writing in *The New York Times Magazine* for March 18, 1979, quotes a friend of the late Duke's: "I promised [him] I'd look after Wallis, and I'd like nothing better. But I can't get near her." The gates were locked, and Maître Blum was the sole keeper of the keys. Toward the end, the poor invalid Duchess's circle had shrunk to include only her doctors and nurses, two or three servants, and—to be sure—Maître Blum. One by one of the veterans on the staff had been dismissed until none were left except Georges, the butler, and his wife.

Maître Blum may have turned the Neuilly house into an isolation ward out of kindness to the disintegrating Duchess, who could no longer talk coherently. Before long, even being carried downstairs became impossibly exhausting. Her movements were restricted to a slow, painful shuffle between her bed and her sofa. Eventually, she could not manage even this; she was bedridden. The fairy tale had long since dimmed. Now the legend is taking root—a strange and bitter tale groping for an explanation of the pulls and drives that caused a King, once of boundless promise, to become besotted with a well-born, but impoverished middle-aged woman, twice married and with both husbands alive. He abandoned Empire, duty, and his own unique meaning to be with her. What was certain is that she will one day be "buried by her Antony." The inscription on her gravestone is to be—simply—

WALLIS DUCHESS OF WINDSOR
1896–19—

Winston Churchill is reported to have made a prediction about her: "One day a grateful Commonwealth will erect her statue." Until that unlikely dawn, this truthful epitaph might serve as her memorial:

WHATEVER ELSE SHE DID,
SHE MADE HER LAST HUSBAND HAPPY

Or, mindful of the value that he himself put upon her, this one, in the nobler words of Sir Thomas Malory (Lancelot is bidding his last farewell to Queen Guinevere):

LADY, I TAKE RECORD OF GOD,
IN THEE I HAVE HAD MINE EARTHLY JOY

Irony rules at the end. The Royal Family rejected Wallis Warfield Spencer Simpson Windsor in life; in death she will be among them forever.

Reference Notes

BOOK I

Chapter 1

1. Edwina H. Wilson, *Her Name Was Wallis Warfield* (New York: E. P. Dutton & Co., Inc., 1936), pp. 51, 53.

Chapter 2

1. The Duchess of Windsor, *The Heart Has Its Reasons* (New York: David McKay Company, Inc., 1956).
2. Lilli Palmer, "Garbo and the Duke," *Esquire*, Vol. 84, No. 3 (September 1975), p. 103.

Chapter 3

1. Anne Kirk Cooke and [her daughter] Elizabeth Lightfoot, *The Other Mrs. Simpson: Postscript to the Love Story of the Century* (New York: Vantage Press, Inc., 1977), p. 46.
2. *Ibid.*, pp. 17-18.
3. Sir Henry Channon, *Chips: The Diaries of Sir Henry Channon*, Robert Rhodes James, ed. (London: Weidenfeld and Nicolson, 1967).

Chapter 4

1. Margot Asquith, *More Memories* (London: Cassell and Co., Ltd., 1933), pp. 239-40.
2. Viktoria Luise, Princess of Prussia, *The Kaiser's Daughter* (New York: Prentice-Hall, Inc., 1977), p. 48.

3. Frances Donaldson, *Edward VIII* (London: Weidenfeld and Nicolson, 1974), p. 59.
4. James Pope-Hennessy, *Queen Mary* (London: George Allen and Unwin, 1959), p. 514.
5. Alden Hatch, *The Mountbattens* (New York: Random House, Inc., 1965), p. 124.
6. Hector Bolitho, *A Century of British Monarchy* (London: Longmans, Green and Co., Ltd., 1951), p. 205.
7. Mabell, Countess of Airlie, *Thatched with Gold* (London: Hutchinson & Co. [Publishers] Ltd., 1962), p. 146.
8. Palmer, *op. cit.*

Chapter 5

1. Evelyn Waugh, *Diaries*, Michael Davis, ed. (London: Weidenfeld and Nicolson, 1976), p. 630.
2. Robert Bruce Lockhart, *Diaries, 1915-1938*, Kenneth Young, ed. (London: Macmillan and Co. Ltd., 1973), p. 185.
3. *Cheiro's World Predictions* (The London Publishing Co., n.d.), pp. 69-70, 72.
4. Gloria Vanderbilt and Thelma, Lady Furness, *Double Exposure* (New York: David McKay Company, Inc., 1958), pp. 287-8.
5. *Ibid.*, p. 288.
6. The Duke of Windsor, *A King's Story* (New York: G. P. Putnam's Sons, 1951), p. 257.
7. The Duchess of Windsor, *op. cit.*, p. 166 *passim.*

Chapter 6

1. Diana Cooper, *The Light of Common Day* (London: Rupert Hart-Davis, 1959), pp. 161-2.
2. *Ibid.*, pp. 162-3.
3. Robert Bruce Lockhart, unpublished diary entry for August 30, 1926, Kenneth Young, ed.
4. Vanderbilt, *op. cit.*, p. 306.

Chapter 7

1. Leonard Slater, *Aly* (New York: Random House, Inc., 1964), p. 138.

2. *Ibid.*, pp. 86-7.
3. Vanderbilt, *op. cit.*, p. 312.
4. The Duchess of Windsor, *op. cit.*, p. 194.
5. Dina Wells Hood, *Working for the Windsors* (London: Allan A. Wingate, 1957), pp. 36-7.
6. Vanderbilt, *op. cit.*, p. 313.
7. *Cheiro's World Predictions, op. cit.*, p. 73.
8. Harold Nicolson, *Diaries and Letters,* Volume I (London: William Collins Sons & Co., Ltd., 1966), p. 255.

Chapter 8

1. Airlie, *op. cit.*, p. 113.
2. C. L. Sulzberger, *An Age of Mediocrity: Memoirs and Diaries, 1963-72* (New York: The Macmillan Company, 1973), p. 96.
3. On October 27, 1974.
4. On November 1, 1974.
5. Ronald Tree, *When the Moon Was High: Memoirs of Peace and War, 1897-1942* (London: Macmillan and Co., Ltd., 1975), p. 65.
6. Donaldson, *op. cit.*, p. 163.
7. Nicolson, *op. cit.*, p. 238.

Chapter 9

1. Sir Walford Selby, *Diplomatic Twilight* (London: John Murray [Publishers] Ltd., 1953), pp. 42-3.
2. The Duchess of Windsor, *op. cit.*, p. 216.
3. Channon, *op. cit.*, p. 46.
4. Anne Morrow Lindbergh, *The Flower and the Nettle* (New York: Harcourt Brace Jovanovich, Inc., 1976), p. 565.
5. Adela Rogers St. Johns, *The Honeycomb* (New York: Doubleday & Company, Inc., 1969), p. 524.
6. Airlie, *op. cit.*, p. 196.
7. John Betjeman, *Collected Poems* (London: John Murray [Publishers] Ltd., 1958), p. 43.
8. Andrew Sinclair, *The Last of the Best* (New York: The Macmillan Company, 1969), p. 30.

BOOK II

Chapter 1

1. John Wheeler-Bennett, *King George VI* (London: Macmillan and Co., Ltd., 1958), p. 266.
2. Keith Middlemas and John Barnes, *Baldwin* (London: Weidenfeld and Nicolson, 1969), p. 830 n.
3. Lord Birkenhead, *Walter Monckton* (London: Weidenfeld and Nicolson, 1969), p. 127.
4. J. G. Lockhart, *Cosmo Gordon Lang* (New York: The Macmillan Company, 1949), p. 408.

Chapter 2

1. Lord Birkenhead, *op. cit.*, p. 129.
2. Anita Leslie, *Edwardians in Love* (London: Hutchinson & Co. [Publishers], Ltd., 1973), p. 171.
3. John Pearson, *Edward the Rake, an Unwholesome Biography* (New York: Harcourt Brace Jovanovich, Inc., 1975), p. 158.
4. Nigel Nicolson, *Portrait of a Marriage* (London: Weidenfeld and Nicolson, 1973), p. 23.
5. Sonia Keppel, *Edwardian Daughter* (London: Hamish Hamilton, 1958).

Chapter 3

1. F. J. Corbett, *Fit for a King* (London: Odhams Press, 1956).
2. Geoffrey Bocca, *The Woman Who Would Be Queen* (New York: Rinehart and Co., 1954), p. 88.
3. Kenneth Clark, *Another Part of the Wood* (New York: Harper & Row, Publishers, Inc., 1975), pp. 51-2.
4. Robert Lacey, *Majesty* (London: Hutchinson & Co. [Publishers] Ltd., 1977), p. 87.
5. Clark, *op. cit.*, p. 270.
6. Sir Oswald Mosley, *My Life* (London: Thomas Nelson and Sons, 1968), p. 174.

Chapter 4

1. The Duchess of Windsor, *op. cit.*, p. 225.
2. Christopher Sykes, *Nancy: The Life of Lady Astor* (London: William Collins Sons & Co., Ltd., 1972), pp. 375-6.

Chapter 5

1. Diana Cooper, *op. cit.*, p. 178 *passim.*
2. *San Diego Union*, August 4, 1946.
3. Elsa Maxwell, *R.S.V.P.* (Boston: Little, Brown and Company, 1954), pp. 295-6.

Chapter 6

1. Cecil Beaton, *The Wandering Years* (Boston: Little, Brown and Company, 1962), p. 314.
2. H. Montgomery Hyde, *Baldwin: The Unexpected Prime Minister* (London: Hart-Davis, McGibbon, 1973).

Chapter 7

1. Airlie, *op. cit.*, p. 201.
2. *Ibid.*, p. 146.

Chapter 8

1. Duff Cooper (Viscount Norwich), *Old Men Forget* (London: Rupert Hart-Davis, 1954), p. 201.
2. Winston Churchill, *The Gathering Storm* (London: Cassell and Company, Ltd., 1954), p. 218.
3. Cooke, *op. cit.*, p. 40.
4. Nicolson, *op. cit.*, p. 280.

Chapter 9

1. Thomas Jones, *A Diary with Letters, 1931–1950* (London: Oxford University Press, 1954), p. 286.
2. W. M. A. Beaverbrook, *The Abdication of King Edward VIII* (New York: Atheneum Publishers, 1966).

3. G. M. Young, *Stanley Baldwin* (London: Rupert Hart-Davis, 1952), pp. 239-40.
4. Nicolson, *op. cit.,* p. 281.

Chapter 10

1. Young, *op. cit.,* p. 242.

Chapter 11

1. Brian Inglis, *Abdication* (London: Hodder and Stoughton, 1966), p. 55.
2. On December 21, 1936.
3. Upton Sinclair, *The Cup of Fury* (Great Neck, New York: Channel Press, 1956), p. 137.

Chapter 12

1. Baroness Ravensdale, *In Many Rhythms* (London: Weidenfeld and Nicolson, 1953), p. 201.
2. Arthur Bryant, "The Constitutional Crisis," *Illustrated London News* (December 19, 1936).
3. John Gunther, *Inside Europe* (New York: Harper & Brothers, 1940), p. 305.

Chapter 13

1. Attributed to, and much later acknowledged by, Gerald Bullett (1903–58).

BOOK III

Chapter 1

1. Lindberg, *op. cit.,* p. 564.
2. Bocca, *op. cit.,* p. 90.

Chapter 2

1. Maxwell, *op. cit.,* p. 310.
2. Ravensdale, *op. cit.,* p. 202.
3. Maxwell, *op. cit.,* p. 301.

4. Cooke, *op. cit.,* p. 48-9.
5. Janet Flanner, "Annals of Collaboration," *The New Yorker,* Vol. XXI (September 22, October 6, and October 13, 1945), pp. 28-47, 32-45, 32-48, respectively.

Chapter 3

1. Airlie, *op. cit.,* p. 203.
2. Donald Blythe, *The Age of Illusion* (Boston: Houghton Mifflin Company, 1964), p. 207.

Chapter 4

1. Monckton papers, cited by Donaldson, *op. cit.,* p. 341.
2. Ibid.
3. Frances Stevenson, *Lloyd George: A Diary,* A. J. P. Taylor, ed. (London: Hutchinson & Co. [Publishers], Ltd., 1971), p. 327.

Chapter 5

1. Paul Schmidt, *Hitler's Interpreter* (London: William Heinemann, Ltd., 1951), p. 75.
2. Emmy Göring, *My Life with Göring* (London: Bruce & Watson, 1972), pp. 88-9.
3. Flanner, *op. cit.*
4. In the *New York Herald Tribune* (October 28, 1937).
5. Bocca, *op. cit.,* p. 232.
6. Hood, *op. cit.,* p. 27.
7. Herbert Morrison, in *Forward* (November 13, 1937).

Chapter 6

1. Birkenhead, *op. cit.,* p. 168.
2. Ibid.
3. Ibid., p. 169.
4. Bocca, *op. cit.,* p. 216.
5. Nicolson, *op. cit.,* pp. 351-2.
6. Birkenhead, *op. cit.,* p. 166.
7. Bocca, *op. cit.,* pp. 222-3.
8. Lindbergh, *op. cit.,* pp. 564-6.
9. Bocca, *op. cit.,* pp. 235-6.

10. Hood, *op. cit.,* p. 88.
11. Samuel Hoare, *Nine Troubled Years* (Toronto: Collins, 1954), p. 223.
12. The Duke of Windsor, in the New York *Daily News* (December 13, 1966).

Chapter 8

1. David Wallechinsky et al., *The Book of Lists* (New York: William Morrow & Company, Inc., 1977), p. 79.
2. Roland Vintras, *The Portuguese Connection* (London: Bachman & Turner, 1974), p. 26.
3. Bocca, *op. cit.,* p. 242.
4. Donaldson, *op. cit.,* p. 352.
5. Ibid., p. 356.

Chapter 9

1. Hoare, *op. cit.,* p. 223.
2. Samuel Hoare, *The Complacent Dictator* (New York: Alfred A. Knopf, Inc., 1947).
3. Alexander W. Weddell, ALS in the Weddell papers, at the Virginia Historical Society.
4. Donaldson, *op. cit.,* pp. 275-7.

Chapter 10

1. From Joanna C. Colcord's collection, *Songs of American Sailormen* (New York: W. W. Norton & Co., Inc., 1938).
2. St. Johns, *op. cit.,* p. 527.
3. Susan, Mary Alsop, *To Marietta from Paris, 1945–1960* (New York: Doubleday & Company, Inc., 1975).
4. Maxwell, *op. cit.,* p. 301.
5. Cf. p. 45.

Chapter 11

1. Alsop, *op. cit.,* p. 55.
2. Patrick McCarthy, "An Original: Lady Diana Cooper,"

W (December 8–15, 1978), pp. 22-3.
3. Alistair Cooke, *Six Men* (New York: Alfred A. Knopf, Inc., 1977), p. 77.
4. Noel Barber, *The Natives Were Friendly . . . So We Stayed the Night* (London: Macmillan and Co., Ltd., 1977).
5. Hood, *op. cit.,* p. 36.

Chapter 12

1. Palmer, *op. cit.*
2. E.g., *The New York Times* (April 20, 1945).
3. Sulzberger, *op. cit.,* p. 581.
4. Palmer, *op. cit.*
5. Mary Van Rensselaer Thayer, in the *Washington Post* (March 2, 1956).

Chapter 13

1. The Duchess of Windsor, "When I Entertain," *Vogue,* Vol. 114, No. 9 (November 15, 1949), pp. 108-9, 162, 167.
2. Daphne Fielding, *Those Remarkable Cunards* (New York: Atheneum Publishers, 1968), p. 118.

Chapter 14

1. The Duchess of Windsor, "When I Entertain," *op. cit.*
2. Sir Oswald Mosley, *My Life* (London: Thomas Nelson & Sons, 1968), p. 374.
3. Lindbergh, *op. cit.,* p. 568.
4. Cole Lesley, *Remembered Laughter: The Life of Noel Coward* (New York: Alfred A. Knopf, Inc., 1976), p. 386.
5. *Ibid.,* p. 188.
6. *Ibid.,* p. 187.
7. Cyrus Sulzberger, *A Long Row of Candles: Memoirs and Diaries* [*1934–54*] (New York: The Macmillan Company, 1969), p. 443.

Chapter 15

1. Diana Mosley, *A Life of Contrasts* (London: Hamish Hamilton, 1977), p. 160.
2. September 27, 1956.
3. F. Scott Fitzgerald, *Tender Is the Night* (New York: Charles Scribner's Sons, 1934), p. 334.

Chapter 16

1. Sulzberger, *A Long Row of Candles, op. cit.,* p. 690.
2. Pearson, *op. cit.,* p. 125.

Chapter 17

1. Donaldson, *op. cit.,* p. 336.

Chapter 18

1. Gertrude Stein, *Ida* (New York: Random House, Inc., 1941), pp. 25, 154.

Bibliography

AIRLIE, MABELL COUNTESS OF, *Thatched with Gold*, Jennifer Ellis, ed. London: Hutchinson & Co. (Publishers) Ltd., 1962.

ALICE, H.R.H. PRINCESS, COUNTESS OF ATHLONE, *For My Grandchildren*. London: Evans Brothers, 1966.

ALSOP, SUSAN MARY, *To Marietta from Paris, 1945–1960*. New York: Doubleday & Company, Inc., 1975.

ASQUITH, MARGOT, *More Memories*. London: Cassell and Company, Ltd., 1933.

ATTLEE, C. R., *As It Happened*. London: William Heinemann, Ltd., 1954.

BARBER, NOEL, *The Natives Were Friendly . . . So We Stayed the Night*. London: Macmillan and Co., Ltd., 1977.

BEATON, CECIL, *The Wandering Years*. Boston: Little, Brown and Company, 1962.

BEAVERBROOK, LORD, *The Abdication of Edward VIII*. London: Hamilton, 1966.

BETJEMAN, JOHN, *Collected Poems*. London: John Murray (Publishers), Ltd., 1958.

BIRKENHEAD, LORD, *Walter Monckton*. London: Weidenfeld and Nicolson, 1969.

BLYTHE, DONALD, *The Age of Illusion*. Boston: Houghton Mifflin Company, 1964.

BOCCA, GEOFFREY, *The Woman Who Would Be Queen*. New York: Rinehart, 1954.

BOLITHO, HECTOR, *A Century of British Monarchy*. London: Longmans, Green and Co., Ltd., 1951.

BRIDIE, JAMES, *Storm in a Teacup*. A play, adapted from Bruno Frank's original *Sturm in Wasserglas*.

British Information Service, *The Monarchy in Britain*. H.M. Stationery Office, 1963.

BRODY, ILES, *Gone with the Windsors*. Philadelphia: Winston Publishers, 1953.

BROOK-SHEPHERD, GORDON, *Uncle of Europe: The Social and Diplomatic Life of Edward VII*. London: William Collins Sons & Co., Ltd., 1975.

BRUCE LOCKHART, SIR ROBERT, *Diaries, 1915–1938*, Kenneth Young, ed. London: Macmillan and Co., Ltd., 1973.

BRYANT, ARTHUR, "The Constitutional Crisis," *Illustrated London News* (December 19, 1936).

CHANNON, SIR HENRY, *Chips: The Diaries of Sir Henry Channon*, Robert Rhodes James, ed. London: Weidenfeld and Nicolson, 1967.

Cheiro's World Predictions. The London Publishing Co., n.d.

CHURCHILL, WINSTON, *The Gathering Storm*. London: Cassell and Company, Ltd., 1948.

CLARK, KENNETH, *Another Part of the Wood*. New York: Harper & Row, 1975.

COLCORD, JOANNA C., *Songs of American Sailormen*. New York: W. W. Norton & Company, Inc., 1938.

COLEMAN, TERRY, *The Queen*. Harmondsworth: Penguin Books, 1977.

COOKE, ALISTAIR, "Edward VIII, the Golden Boy," in *Six Men*. New York: Alfred A. Knopf, 1977.

COOKE, ANNE KIRK, and ELIZABETH LIGHTFOOT, *The Other Mrs. Simpson: Postscript to the Love Story of the Century*. New York: Vantage Press, 1977.

COOPER, DIANA, *The Light of Common Day*. London: Rupert Hart-Davis, 1959.

——*The Rainbow Comes and Goes*. London: Rupert Hart-Davis, 1958.

——*Trumpets from the Steep*. London: Rupert Hart-Davis, 1960.

COOPER, DUFF (VISCOUNT NORWICH), *Old Men Forget*. London: Rupert Hart-Davis, 1954.

CORBETT, F. J., *Fit for a King*. London: Odhams Press, 1956.

Daisy Princess of Pless, by herself, Maj. Desmond Chapman-Huston, ed. New York: E. P. Dutton & Co., Inc., 1923, 1929.

DIESBACH, GHISLAIN DE, *Secrets of the Gotha.* London: Chapman & Hall, Ltd., 1967.

DONALDSON, FRANCES, *Edward VIII.* London: Weidenfeld and Nicolson, 1974.

DUPUCH, ÉTIENNE, *The Tribune Story.* London: Ernest Benn, Ltd., 1967.

FIELDING, DAPHNE, *Those Remarkable Cunards.* New York: Atheneum Publishers, 1968.

FITZGERALD, F. SCOTT, *Tender Is the Night.* New York: Charles Scribner's Sons, 1934.

FLANNER, JANET, "Annals of Collaboration." *The New Yorker,* Vol. XXI (September 22, October 6, and October 13, 1945), pp. 28-47, 32-45, 32-48, respectively.

——"Letter from London." *The New Yorker* (November 4, 1936).

——*London Was Yesterday,* Irving Drutman, ed. New York: Viking Press, 1975.

——*Paris Was Yesterday,* Irving Drutman, ed. New York: Viking Press, 1972.

FURNESS, THELMA, LADY (see VANDERBILT, GLORIA).

GÖRING, EMMY, *My Life with Göring.* London: Bruce & Watson, 1972.

GUNTHER, JOHN, *Inside Europe.* New York: Harper & Brothers, 1940.

HALSTEAD, CHARLES R., "Diligent Diplomat: Alexander W. Weddell as American Ambassador to Spain, 1939–1942," *Magazine of the Virginia Historical Society* (January 1974).

HARE, AUGUSTUS J. C., *The Story of My Life.* New York: Dodd, Mead & Company, 1896.

HATCH, ALDEN, *The Mountbattens.* New York: Random House, 1965.

HOARE, SAMUEL JOHN TEMPLEWOOD GURNEY, *Nine Troubled Years.* Toronto: Collins, 1954.

——*The Complacent Dictator.* New York: Alfred A. Knopf, Inc., 1947.

HOOD, DINA WELLS, *Working for the Windsors.* London: Allan A. Wingate, 1957.

Hore-Belisha, The Private Papers of, R. J. Minney, ed. London: William Collins Sons & Co., Ltd., 1960.

HYDE, H. MONTGOMERY, *Baldwin: The Unexpected Prime Minister.* London: Hart-Davis, McGibbon, 1973.

INGLIS, BRIAN, *Abdication*. London: Hodder and Stoughton, 1966.

JONES, THOMAS, *A Diary with Letters, 1931–1950*. London: Oxford University Press, 1954.

KEPPEL, SONIA, *Edwardian Daughter*. London: Hamish Hamilton, 1958.

KINROSS, JOHN PATRICK DOUGLAS BALFOUR, *Atatürk*. New York: William Morrow & Co., Inc., 1965.

——*The Windsor Years*. New York: The Viking Press, Inc., 1967.

LACEY, ROBERT, *Majesty*. London: Hutchinson & Co. (Publishers) Ltd., 1977.

LESLEY COLE, *Remembered Laughter: The Life of Noel Coward*. New York: Alfred A. Knopf, Inc., 1976.

LESLIE, ANITA, *Edwardians in Love*. London: Hutchinson & Co. (Publishers) Ltd., 1972.

LINDBERGH, ANNE MORROW, *The Flower and the Nettle*. New York: Harcourt Brace Jovanovich, 1976.

LOCKHART, J. G., *Cosmo Gordon Lang*. New York: The Macmillan Company, 1949.

LONGFORD, ELIZABETH, "Personal Styles in Twentieth-Century Monarchy," *The Queen*. London: Penguin Books, 1977.

——*The Royal House of Windsor*. London: Weidenfeld and Nicolson, 1974.

MANGUS, PHILIP, *King Edward the Seventh*. London: John Murray (Publishers), Ltd., 1941.

MASTERS, BRIAN, *The Dukes*. London: Blond & Briggs, 1975.

MAXWELL, ELSA, *R.S.V.P.* Boston: Little, Brown and Company, 1954.

MCCARTHY, PATRICK, "An Original: Lady Diana Cooper," *W* (December 8–15, 1978), pp. 22-3.

MIDDLEMAS, KEITH and JOHN BARNES, *Baldwin*. London: Weidenfeld & Nicolson, 1969.

MINNEY, R. J., *The Edwardian Age*. London: Cassell and Company, Ltd., 1964.

MORRISON, HERBERT, in *Forward* (November 13, 1937).

MOSLEY, DIANA, *A Life of Contrasts*. London: Hamish Hamilton, 1977.

MOSLEY, SIR OSWALD, *My Life*. London: Thomas Nelson & Sons, 1968.

MUGGERIDGE, MALCOLM, *The Thirties*. London: Hamish Hamilton, 1940.

NICOLSON, HAROLD, *Diaries and Letters, 1930–1963*, 3 vols., Nigel Nicolson, ed. London: Collins, 1966.

——*King George V, His Life and Reign*. London: Constable, 1952.

NICOLSON, NIGEL, *Portrait of a Marriage*. London: Weidenfeld & Nicolson, 1973.

PALMER, LILLI, "Garbo and the Duke," *Esquire*, Vol. 84, No. 3 (September 1975), p. 103.

PEARSON, JOHN, *Edward the Rake, an Unwholesome Biography*. New York: Harcourt Brace Jovanovich, 1975.

PONSONBY, SIR F., *The Grenadier Guards in the Great War 1914–1918*. New York: The Macmillan Company, 1920.

POPE-HENNESSY, JAMES, *Queen Mary*. London: George Allen and Unwin, 1957.

RAVENSDALE, BARONESS, *In Many Rhythms*. London: Weidenfeld and Nicolson, 1952.

ST. JOHNS, ADELA ROGERS, *The Honeycomb*. New York: Doubleday & Company, Inc., 1969.

SCHMIDT, PAUL, *Hitler's Interpreter*. London: William Heinemann, Ltd., 1951.

SELBY, SIR WALFORD, *Diplomatic Twilight*. London: John Murray (Publishers), Ltd., 1953.

SINCLAIR, ANDREW, *The Last of the Best*. New York: The Macmillan Company, 1969.

SINCLAIR, UPTON, *The Cup of Fury*. Great Neck, New York: Channel Press, 1956.

SITWELL, OSBERT, "Rat Week." Unpublished.

SLATER, LEONARD, *Aly*. New York: Random House, Inc., 1964.

STEIN, GERTRUDE, *Ida*. New York: Random House, Inc., 1941.

STEVENSON, FRANCES, *Lloyd George: A Diary*, A. J. P. Taylor, ed. London: Hutchinson & Co. (Publishers), Ltd., 1971.

SULZBERGER, C. L., *An Age of Mediocrity: Memoirs and Diaries, 1963–72*. New York: The Macmillan Company, 1973.

——*A Long Row of Candles: Memoirs and Diaries [1934–1954]*. New York: The Macmillan Company, 1969.

SYKES, CHRISTOPHER, *Nancy: The Life of Lady Astor.* London: William Collins Sons & Co., Ltd., 1972.

THAYER, MARY VAN RENSSELAER, in the *Washington Post* (March 2, 1956).

TREE, RONALD, *When the Moon Was High: Memoirs of Peace and War, 1897–1942.* London: Macmillan and Co., Ltd., 1975.

VANDERBILT, GLORIA, AND THELMA, LADY FURNESS, *Double Exposure: A Twin Autobiography.* New York: David McKay, 1958.

VIKTORIA LUISE, PRINCESS OF PRUSSIA, *The Kaiser's Daughter.* New York: Prentice-Hall, 1977.

VINTRAS, ROLAND, *The Portuguese Connection.* London: Bachman & Turner, 1974.

WALLECHINSKY, DAVID, IRVING WALLACE, AND AMY WALLACE, *The Book of Lists.* New York: William Morrow & Company, Inc., 1977.

WATSON, FRANCIS, *Dawson of Penn.* London: Chatto and Windus, 1950.

WAUGH, EVELYN, *Diaries,* Michael Davis, ed. London: Weidenfeld & Nicolson, 1976.

WEDDELL, ALEXANDER W., ALS in the Weddell papers, at the Virginia Historical Society.

WHEELER-BENNETT, JOHN, *King George VI.* London: Macmillan and Co., Ltd., 1958.

WILSON, EDWINA H., *Her Name Was Wallis Warfield.* New York: E. P. Dutton & Co., Inc., 1936.

WINDSOR, THE DUCHESS OF, *The Heart Has Its Reasons.* New York: David McKay, 1956.

——"When I Entertain," *Vogue,* Vol. 114, No. 9 (November 15, 1949), pp. 108-9, 162, 167.

WINDSOR, THE DUKE OF, *A King's Story.* New York: G. P. Putnam's Sons, 1947.

——Series of six articles. New York *Daily News* (December 15–20, 1966).

YOUNG, G. M., *Stanley Baldwin.* London: Rupert Hart-Davis, 1952.

Acknowledgments

The list of our sources and other benefactors follows. We are profoundly grateful to them all.

Lord Adeane, London; the late Col. Sir John Aird, Bt., Berks.; Mr. Charles Allen, New York City; Sir George Allen, London; the late Monsieur Hervé Alphand, Paris; Mrs. Benjamin Alsop, Charles City, Va.; the American-British Numismatic Society (Mr. Richard J. Trowbridge, President), Glendale, Cal.; Dr. Arthur J. Antenucci, New York City; the Argentine Embassy in Washington, D.C. (H. E. Ambassador Alejandro Orfila and the Cultural Office); the Australian Embassy in Washington, D.C. (Mr. Douglas Cole, First Secretary, Information).

Mr. John Barratt, Romsey, Hants.; Maj. W. M. F. Bayliss, Sabot, Va.; Mr. Robin Beare, London; Sir Cecil Beaton, Salisbury, Wilts.; the Belgian Embassy in Washington, D.C. (Ms. Lucie de Myttenaere, Cultural Counselor); Prof. Thomas J. Bergin, Madison, Conn.; Mr. Barry Bingham, Louisville, Ky.; Maître Suzanne Blum, Paris; Mr. David Boyer, Paris; the British Embassy in Washington, D.C. (Mr. David de Boinville, Head of Reference Section); Mrs. John Nicholas Brown, Providence, R.I.; the late Lord Brownlow, Belton, Lincs.; the late Hon. David K. E. Bruce, Brookneal, Va.; Mr. Courtlandt D. B. Bryan, Guilford, Conn.; Mary Duchess of Buccleuch, Kettering, Northants.; Cdr. Colin Buist, R.N. (Ret.); Dr. James Burnham, Kent, Conn.

The Canadian Embassy in Washington, D.C. (Mr. S. J. Hennessy, Assistant Librarian); Brig. Ereld Cardiff, Ludlow, Salop; Mr. George G. Carey, Glyndon, Md.; the Earl of Carnarvon, Newbury, Hants.; Mr. Eugene Carusi,

Washington, D.C.; the Marquesa de Casa Maury, London; the Choate School (Mr. Edward B. Ayres), Wallingford, Conn.; the Hon. Robert Coe, Cannes; Mrs. Charles Cooke, Cooperstown, N.Y.; Lady Diana Cooper, London; the late Mr. Harry H. Cooper, Randolph, Va.; Mrs. John Sherman Cooper, Washington, D.C.; Mr. W. Sheffield Cowles, Farmington, Conn.; Lt. Col. Rex Cowley, London; Mrs. John Cronly, Richmond, Va.; Mr. Perry H. Culley, Washington, D.C.; Mr. Nathan Cummings, New York City; the Cunard Line (Mr. Clifford J. McLain), New York City; Count Hans Czernin, Paris.

Messrs. Davies & Son, London; the late Dr. John Staige Davis, New York City; Brig. C. M. O. Davy, Jordanstone, Perthshire; Dr. Michael E. DeBakey, Houston, Tex.; Brig. Gen. James P. S. Devereux, U.S.M.C. (Ret.), Glyndon, Md.; Lady Frances Donaldson, Kingsbridge, Bucks.; the Duchy of Cornwall Office (Mr. Michael Ruffer, Assistant Secretary), London; Messrs. Dunhill, London; the late Mr. Christopher Dunphy, Palm Beach, Fla.; the late Brig. Gen. E. Colston Dyer, U.S.M.C. (Ret.), New Canaan, Conn.

Mr. C. M. Eldridge, Richmond, Va.; the Ethel Walker School (Mrs. James S. Gregory), Simsbury, Conn.

Mr. Douglas Fairbanks, Jr., New York City; Mr. Finis Farr, Portland, Me.; Mr. Johnny Farrell, Delray Beach, Fla.; the Federal Reserve Bank of Richmond (Mrs. Ruth M. E. Cannon, Research Librarian); Mr. Hugh Fenwick, Aiken, S.C.; Dr. Henry Field, Coconut Grove, Fla.; Mr. Ben Finney, New York City; Mr. Alastair Forbes, London; the late Mr. J. Russell Forgan, New York City; Sir Dudley Forwood, Bt., Salisbury, Wilts.; Sir John Foster, London; Mrs. Frederick Frelinghuysen, New York City; the French Embassy in Washington, D.C. (Ms. Danièle Manier, Press Attaché); the French Embassy, Service de Presse (Mr. André Baeyens), New York City; the French Government Tourist Office (Mr. George L. Hern), New York City.

The late Mrs. Arthur Gardner, Washington, D.C.; the late Dr. R. Finley Gayle, III, Richmond, Va.; the Glenbow-Alberta Institute (Ms. Sheilagh S. Jameson, Chief Archivist), Calgary, Alberta; the late Count Charles de Gramont, Paris; the late Mrs. Lester Grant, New York City; Green Mount Cemetery (Mr. John D. Mayhew),

Baltimore; the Hon. Raymond R. Guest, King George, Va.; Mr. Raymond R. Guest, Jr., Front Royal, Va.; Mrs. Winston F. C. Guest, New York City.

Dr. Charles R. Halstead, Washington College, Chestertown, Md.; the late Earl of Hardwicke, London; the Harvard Club of New York (the Librarian); the Harvard University Alumni Bureau, Cambridge, Mass.; Messrs. Hawes & Curtis, London; Dr. William H. Higgins, Jr., Richmond, Va.; the Hill School Alumni Bureau, Pottstown, Pa.; Mlle. Denise Hivet, Paris; the late Mr. Eppa Hunton, IV, Richmond, Va.

The Imperial War Museum, London; the Italian Embassy in Washington, D.C. (Messrs. Fabio Pigliapoco, First Secretary, and L. Amaduzzi, Counselor).

Messrs. Jansen (M. Pierre Deshays, President), Paris; Dr. George W. Jeffers, Farmville, Va.; Mr. Sidney Johnson, Paris; Mr. Geoffrey M. T. Jones, New York City.

Mrs. R. Keith Kane, Charlottesville, Va.; Mr. John A. C. Keith, Warrenton, Va.; the late Lord Kinross, London; Mr. Herbert Kinsolving, Annapolis, Md.; Mr. Emil Klein, New York City.

Mrs. Nancy Lancaster, London; Mrs. S. Kent Legare, Washington, D.C.; Messrs. Richard Lobel & Co., London; the Countess of Longford, London; Mrs. William G. Lord, East Hampton, N.Y.; the Countess de Lubersac, Paris; Mrs. Albert H. Lucas, Huntly, Va.; the Hon. Clare Boothe Luce, New York City.

Madame Tussaud's (Miss Juliet Simpkins), London; Mr. William L. Marbury, Baltimore; the late Mr. Ronald Marchant, Paris; Rear Adm. Gene Markey, U.S.N.R. (Ret.), Miami Beach, Fla.; the Mayflower Hotel (Ms. Suzanne Ives), Washington, D.C.; Mrs. Peter McBean, Hillsborough, Cal.; Mr. James McCargar, Washington, D.C.; Mrs. Robert M. McKinney, Middleburg, Va.; the late Mrs. S. Buchanan Merryman, Washington, D.C.; Lady Alexandra Metcalfe, London; Mr. David Metcalfe, London; Monsieur L. Michotte, Monte Carlo; Mrs. Clarence L. Miles, Queenstown, Md.; Mrs. Gilbert Miller, New York City; the late Viscount Monckton of Brenchley, London; the Dowager Viscountess Monckton of Brenchley, London; the late Brig. Gen. R. Latané Montague,

U.S.M.C. (Ret.), Urbana, Va.; Rev. Msgr. Joseph N. Moody, Brighton, Mass.; Mrs. Charles Beatty Moore, Gloucester, Va.; Admiral of the Fleet the late Earl Mountbatten of Burma, Romsey, Hants.; Vice Adm. Lloyd Montague Mustin, U.S.N. (Ret.), Alexandria, Va.

The Names Society (Mr. Leslie Dunkling, President), Thames Ditton, Surrey; *The New Yorker* (Mr. Fred Keefe, Librarian), New York City; Mrs. Mark Norman, Much Hadham, Herts.

The Office Généalogique et Héraldique de Belgique (Monsieur Hervé Douxchamps, Secretary General), Brussels; the Office de Tourisme de Nice.

The Park Avenue Association (Ms. Marion L. Damroth), New York City; Mr. Frederick B. Payne, New York City; Lady Penn, London; Mr. Christopher Philpotts, Paris; the late Mr. James Pope-Hennessy, London; the Public Record Office (Mr. Nicholas Cox, Search Department), London.

Mr. Carroll Rasin, Jr., Brooklandville, Md.; Mr. Kennett L. Rawson, New York City; the Richmond (Virginia) Public Library (Ms. Elizabeth Engle Askew, Mr. William S. Simpson, Jr., Mr. Harry Wyland); the late Mr. Bernard Rickatson-Hatt, London; the late Mr. Herman L. Rogers, Cannes; the late Mrs. Katharine Rogers, Cannes; Mrs. Lucy Rogers, Monte Carlo; the Royal Library (Sir Robin Mackworth-Young, Librarian), Windsor Castle.

Dr. Herman Salinger, Duke University, Durham, N.C.; Mr. Herbert C. Sanford, New York City; Mr. John H. Saumarez Smith, London; the late Brig. Gen. Martin F. Scanlon, U.S.A.F. (Ret.), Washington, D.C.; Mr. Stuart Scheftel, New York City; Mrs. Morgan B. Schiller, Easton, Md.; the Scottish Tartans Society (Capt. T. S. Davidson), Comrie, Perthshire; the Seaboard Coastline System (Mr. Raymond L. Bullard), Richmond, Va.; the Countess of Sefton, London; H. E. Archbishop Fulton J. Sheen, New York City; Dr. James Asa Shield, Sr., Richmond, Va.; Mr. Levin G. Shreve, Baltimore; Mr. William M. Spackman, Princeton, N.J.; the late Mr. Hugh Spilman, Warrenton, Va.; Mr. Albert Stagg, Scottsdale, Ariz.; Mr. Chauncey D. Stillman, New York City; the late Mr. Whitney Straight, Southall, Middlesex; Mr. Christopher Sykes, Swyre, Dorset; the Hon. W. Stuart Symington, Washington, D.C.

Dr. Jean Thin, Paris; the late Mr. Cuthbert R. Train, Washington, D.C.; Trinity Church (Ms. Helen Rose Cline, Parish Recorder), New York City.

The U.S. Consulate, Istanbul (Mr. W. Kenneth Thompson, Consul); the U.S. Department of State (Mr. M. S. Lorraine, Ms. Lorraine P. Anderson), Washington D.C.; the U.S. Naval Historical Center (Mr. D. C. Allard), Washington, D.C.; the U.S. Navy Department (Office of Information), Washington, D.C.; the University of Texas Humanities Research Center (Mr. John R. Payne), Austin; Mr. John Utter, Paris.

The Virginia Historical Society (Mr. John Melville Jennings, Director), Richmond, Va.; the Virginia State Library (Mrs. Katherine M. Smith), Richmond, Va.; Mrs. Diana Vreeland, New York City.

Mr. Joseph Wechsberg, Vienna; the late Sir John Wheeler-Bennett, Oxford; Mr. J. Harvie Wilkinson, Jr., Richmond, Va.; Mr. and Mrs. Anthony Wilson, Washington, D.C.; the Hon. Reginald and Mrs. Winn, London; Miss Ellen Wright Wise, Richmond, Va.; the World Golf Hall of Fame (Mr. John Derr), Pinehurst, N.C.; Mr. Charles Wrightsman, New York City.

The Hon. Theodore Xanthaky, Lisbon.

Mr. Jerome Zerbe, New York City.

The following publications and journalists have also been helpful:

The Atlanta *Journal* (Mr. Jack Spalding); the Baltimore *Sun* and *Evening Sun* (Mr. Dave Woods and the late Mr. Price Day); the Beaverbrook Press (Sir Maxwell Aitken, Messrs. A. J. P. Taylor and Kenneth Young, and the late Lord Beaverbrook); the Hearst Newspapers (Mr. Joseph Kingsbury-Smith); the London *Evening News* (Messrs. Felix Barker, D. H. Boddie, Robin Esser, and John Leese); the London *Sunday Times* (Mr. Raymond Mortimer); the *Los Angeles Times* (Mr. Richard W. Smith); *The New York Times* (Mr. Cyrus Sulzberger); the Philadelphia *Evening Bulletin* and *Sunday Bulletin* (Mr. George R. Packard, III); the San Diego (Cal.) *Union* (Miss Eileen Jackson and Mr. Kenneth D. Zumwalt); *Time* (Mr. William Rademaekers); United Press International (Mr.

Kenneth Downs); the *Washington Post* (Mrs. Mary Van Rensselaer Thayer).

The manuscript was typed by these three skilled and patient ladies:

Miss Liz Noll, London, and Miss Barbara Smith and Mrs. Jennifer Nicol, Richmond, Virginia.

J. Bryan III
Charles J. V. Murphy

Index

PICTURE CREDITS

Dell Bestsellers